BESTSELLING
BOOK SERIES
FROM IDG

Taxe$ For Dummie$, 1999 Ed...
by Eric Tyson, MBA, and
David J. Silverman, EA

Quick Reference Card

1998 Federal Income Tax Brackets and Rates

Singles Taxable Income	Married-Filing-Jointly Taxable Income	Federal Tax Rate (Bracket)
Less than $25,350	Less than $42,350	15%
$25,350 – $61,400	$42,350 – $102,300	28%
$61,400 – $128,100	$102,300 – $155,950	31%
$128,100 – $278,450	$155,950 – $278,450	36%
Over $278,450	Over $278,450	39.6%

Your marginal tax rate is the rate of tax that you pay on your last or so-called highest dollars of income. For example, a single person with taxable income of $35,000 has a federal marginal tax rate of 28 percent. In other words, this single taxpayer pays 15 percent on the first $25,350 of income and 28 percent on the income above $25,350.

Your Tax Dollars at Work: Help from the IRS

You have more ways than ever to get the forms and information you need from the IRS:

- You can call the IRS's toll-free number to get tax forms or publications: 800-829-3676 (that's 800-TAX-FORM if you're alphabetically inclined).

- To ask questions, call 800-829-1040, or better yet, call your local IRS office (_____-_____).

- If you're cybersavvy, you can download tax forms and publications from the IRS Web site: www.irs.ustreas.gov.

Of course, you can always visit your local IRS office or obtain tax forms from your library or various government offices.

> Remember to sign and date your tax return!

Ten Last-Minute Tax Tips

Use these tips to make the most of your tax return.

1. **Double-check your return for mistakes that cost money, time, and audits.**

   Put your name and Social Security number on every page, check arithmetic, attach W-2s and any 1099s where federal tax was withheld, and sign and date the return. Verify that you've transferred over from last year's return items you need for this year's return.

2. **Scavenge for overlooked deductions, especially if you're self-employed.**

   Determine whether you can save money by electing the filing status of married filing separately or head of household.

3. **Check to see that correct data is on forms sent to you by financial institutions and your employer(s) that you use in preparing your return.**

4. **If you're self-employed, consider contributing to a tax-deductible SEP-IRA retirement account.**

   If you work for an employer that does not offer a retirement plan, consider contributing to an IRA.

5. **File extension(s) (Forms 4868, 2688), if necessary, to allow yourself more time to do the forms correctly and ensure that you're taking the deductions to which you're legally entitled.**

   Don't make the mistake of not filing until you have the money to pay. The penalty for doing so can be as much as 25 percent of the tax you still owe. Ouch!

6. **Organize and complete as much of your return as you can.**

   If you get stuck and are uncomfortable with part of the return, get a second opinion from a tax advisor or check out one of the tax preparation software packages we recommend.

7. **Keep copies of everything that you file with the IRS and your state, and obtain a mailing receipt if you file at the last minute and a lot of money (or a big issue) is at stake.**

8. **After all the time, trouble, and expense you put into completing your tax return, use the information that's tabulated on it to plan for the year ahead.**

   If you received a large refund or owed a large amount, review and, as necessary, change your tax withholding payments so you won't have the same problem next year.

9. **For the year ahead, make sure you take advantage of directing your employment earnings into retirement accounts (see Chapter 21).**

10. **Regardless of your income, assets, and goals, educate yourself about the tax system and the tax ramifications of financial decisions you make.**

    The place to start is Part V of this book!

...For Dummies: Bestselling Book Series for Beginners

Taxe$ For Dummie$, 1999 Edition
by Eric Tyson, MBA, and
David J. Silverman, EA

Quick Reference Card

Strategies for Tax-Wise Living

$ Take control of your taxes. Know enough about the tax laws so that you can prepare your own return or intelligently review your return prepared by someone else. You are the person best qualified to look after your financial interests.

$ Use tax preparers only when you need them. If your situation hasn't changed since last year, you're probably wasting your hard-earned dollars paying a tax preparer to plug your new numbers into this year's return. Unless your finances are complicated or the tax laws have dramatically changed in an area that affects you, try preparing your own return. If you get stuck or want another opinion, you can always take it to a preparer at that point.

$ Get and stay organized. Try to keep your tax and financial documents organized year-round. This practice saves many hours when preparing your tax return and making important financial decisions.

$ Use tax laws to reduce your taxes. If you educate yourself about the tax laws and incentives, you can dramatically and permanently reduce the taxes you'll pay over the course of your lifetime.

$ Remember that the IRS is not always right. Whether providing advice over the phone or challenging taxpayers' returns, the IRS has made more than its fair share of mistakes, so don't panic if you get a call from Uncle Sam. If you haven't knowingly cheated and defrauded the IRS, you have little to fear from audit notices or other IRS letters. Calmly organize your supporting documents to prove your case.

$ Learn from your return. After you've gone to all the time and trouble of preparing your tax return, don't let that effort go to waste. Use the information to identify areas for better financial management for the coming year.

$ Spend less! Save more! Remember: The more you consume, the more you'll pay in taxes. As you earn income and spend it, you not only must pay income tax on your earnings, but you also incur sales tax and other taxes on your purchases. Moreover, many of the best tax breaks available for people at all income levels are accessible only if you are able to save money to invest.

$ Invest tax-wisely. Don't overlook tax implications when investing your money. Remember, it's not what you make but what you get to keep that matters. The best way for people at all income levels to reduce their income taxes is to use retirement accounts. You reduce your taxes by contributing to these accounts now, and after the money is inside the account, it compounds without taxation.

$ Don't buy real estate only for tax purposes. Owning your own home and other real estate can be an investment that helps to reduce your taxes. But don't purchase real estate because of the tax benefits — these benefits are already reflected in the price you pay for a property.

$ Know when estate planning matters. Read up on this issue so that you know when and what you should do to arrange your financial affairs.

$ Be happy with success. Taxes are the inevitable result of making money. The more you make, the more you'll pay. If you pay a lot, be happy that you're earning a lot in the first place. Although it's tempting and easy to be cynical about the government and taxes, remember that without taxes, we wouldn't have public libraries, roads, bridges, national parks, museums, defense, and a whole lot of other things that make our lives better.

$ Keep taxes in perspective. There's more to life than working and making money. If you do such a good job reducing your taxes that you gain great wealth, don't forget to enjoy and share it with others.

IDG BOOKS WORLDWIDE

...For Dummies: Bestselling Book Series for Beginners

Praise for Taxe$ For Dummie$

"... the book does a terrific job of explaining the tax code. The tax advice ... is on target and has depth."
— Gannett News Service

"Among tax advice books is far and away the best. *Taxe$ For Dummie$* is fun to read and teaches about the tax system itself. The book also provides excellent advice about dealing with mistakes — created by you or the Internal Revenue Service. And it talks about fitting taxes into your daily financial planning. In other words, it's a book you can use after April 15, as well as before.
— Kathy M. Kristof, *Los Angeles Times*

"A witty, irreverant reference. ... And since laughter is good medicine, it most definitely is what it claims. But its focus on humor does not undermine its merit as a research tool. While the guide could be used just to answer individual questions, its friendly format is such fun that you may end up reading Eric Tyson and David Silverman's book from cover to cover. No kidding."
— The Times-Picayune

"The best of these books for tax novices. Substitutes simple English for tax-code complexities. Notable for its attitude (feisty but agreeable) and helpful icons."
— *Worth* magazine

"User-friendly income-tax preparation and sound financial advice you can use throughout the year."
— *The Seattle Times*

"This book is the most accessible and creative. It's also the best organized of the lot, presenting information in the order you need it to complete your tax forms."
— *USA Today*

"*Taxes For Dummies* will make tax preparation less traumatic. ... It is a book that answers — in plain English, and sometimes with humor — many puzzling questions that arise on the most commonly used tax forms."
— Stanley Angrist, *The Wall Street Journal*

"This is a lot of book for the money, filled with good examples ... and level headed advice. It follows the line-by-line format but also has year-round reference value for taxpayers who plan ahead ... A human heart beats in this highly intelligent tax tome."
— Michael Pellecchia, syndicated columnist

"There are plenty of books out there that do the job, but if you're looking for one which explains the tax laws using plain English, with a dash of humor, then *Taxe$ For Dummie$* is highly recommended. ... *Taxe$ For Dummie$* is the ideal guide for getting you through the Ides of April."
— Bill Peschel, *The Herald*

"Not only explains the intricacies of the tax code in plain English but also gives adivce on how to make tax time easier by planning throughout the year."
— Kim Mikus and Steve Warmbir, *Daily Herald*

"$$$$ — Highest rated among the annual tax guides ... superb writing and friendly organization."
— *Publisher's Weekly*

Praise for Eric Tyson's Other Bestsellers

Praise for David J. Silverman

Critical acclaim for David J. Silverman's book, *Battling the IRS:*

"The IRS loves to send out notices. Each year it mails out good news in the form of 26.6 million penalty notices, 3.5 million notices informing taxpayers they didn't report all their income, 3 million notices to taxpayers stating they failed to file a tax return and tens of millions of notices — the exact number is not knowable — stating that taxpayers failed to pay what they owed or made a mistake in preparing their tax return. Fortunately, Mr. Silverman's book provides replies to nearly every type of communication the IRS dispatches. It also tells you when you should seek professional assistance and when you can take the agency on alone."
— *The Wall Street Journal*

"David J. Silverman's book should help take the terror out of audits. It is a guide to notices and assessment from the Internal Revenue Service, and includes letters taxpayers can copy to deal with a variety of grievances, as well as a thorough explanation of taxpayer's rights."
— *The New York Times*

"Should the IRS come after you, defend yourself with David J. Silverman's excellent book."
— *Money* magazine

"This volume is the most definitive and informative compendium for dealing with the IRS that we have ever seen."
— *The New England Review of Books*

"Written in easy-to-understand language . . . A valuable source for the general consumer."
— *The National Public Accountant*

"A comprehensive self-help manual for IRS problems. It addresses every situation methodically in a 'how-to' fashion. . . .The average taxpayer will find it extremely helpful . . . a great survival manual."
— National Taxpayers Union

...FOR DUMMIES ™

BESTSELLING BOOK SERIES FROM IDG

References for the Rest of Us!™

Do you find that traditional reference books are overloaded with technical details and advice you'll never use? Do you postpone important life decisions because you just don't want to deal with them? Then our *...For Dummies®* business and general reference book series is for you.

...For Dummies business and general reference books are written for those frustrated and hard-working souls who know they aren't dumb, but find that the myriad of personal and business issues and the accompanying horror stories make them feel helpless. *...For Dummies* books use a lighthearted approach, a down-to-earth style, and even cartoons and humorous icons to diffuse fears and build confidence. Lighthearted but not lightweight, these books are perfect survival guides to solve your everyday personal and business problems.

> *"More than a publishing phenomenon, 'Dummies' is a sign of the times."*
>
> — The New York Times

> *"A world of detailed and authoritative information is packed into them..."*
>
> — U.S. News and World Report

> *"...you won't go wrong buying them."*
>
> — Walter Mossberg, Wall Street Journal, on IDG Books' ...For Dummies books

Already, millions of satisfied readers agree. They have made *...For Dummies* the #1 introductory level computer book series and a best-selling business book series. They have written asking for more. So, if you're looking for the best and easiest way to learn about business and other general reference topics, look to *...For Dummies* to give you a helping hand.

IDG BOOKS WORLDWIDE ™

9/98

TAXE$ FOR DUMMIE$®

1999 EDITION

by Eric Tyson, MBA
and David J. Silverman, EA

Technical Review by
CCH INCORPORATED
the leading provider of tax law information and software

IDG Books Worldwide, Inc.
An International Data Group Company

Foster City, CA ♦ Chicago, IL ♦ Indianapolis, IN ♦ New York, NY

Taxe$ For Dummie$® 1999 Edition

Published by
IDG Books Worldwide, Inc.
An International Data Group Company
919 E. Hillsdale Blvd.
Suite 400
Foster City, CA 94404
www.idgbooks.com (IDG Books Worldwide Web site)
www.dummies.com (Dummies Press Web site)

Library of Congress Catalog Card No.: 98-88385

ISBN: 0-7645-5125-6

Printed in the United States of America

10 9 8 7 6 5 4 3 2 1

1B/SU/RR/ZY/IN

Distributed in the United States by IDG Books Worldwide, Inc.

Distributed by Macmillan Canada for Canada; by Transworld Publishers Limited in the United Kingdom; by IDG Norge Books for Norway; by IDG Sweden Books for Sweden; by Woodslane Pty. Ltd. for Australia; by Woodslane (NZ) Ltd. for New Zealand; by Addison Wesley Longman Singapore Pte Ltd. for Singapore, Malaysia, Thailand, and Indonesia; by Norma Comunicaciones S.A. for Colombia; by Intersoft for South Africa; by International Thomson Publishing for Germany, Austria and Switzerland; by Distribuidora Cuspide for Argentina; by Livraria Cultura for Brazil; by Ediciencia S.A. for Ecuador; by Ediciones ZETA S.C.R. Ltda. for Peru; by WS Computer Publishing Corporation, Inc., for the Philippines; by Contemporanea de Ediciones for Venezuela; by Express Computer Distributors for the Caribbean and West Indies; by Micronesia Media Distributor, Inc. for Micronesia; by Grupo Editorial Norma S.A. for Guatemala; by Chips Computadoras S.A. de C.V. for Mexico; by Editorial Norma de Panama S.A. for Panama; by Wouters Import for Belgium; by American Bookshops for Finland. Authorized Sales Agent: Anthony Rudkin Associates for the Middle East and North Africa.

For general information on IDG Books Worldwide's books in the U.S., please call our Consumer Customer Service department at 800-762-2974. For reseller information, including discounts and premium sales, please call our Reseller Customer Service department at 800-434-3422.

For information on where to purchase IDG Books Worldwide's books outside the U.S., please contact our International Sales department at 317-596-5530 or fax 317-596-5692.

For information on foreign language translations, please contact our Foreign & Subsidiary Rights department at 650-655-3021 or fax 650-655-3281.

For sales inquiries and special prices for bulk quantities, please contact our Sales department at 650-655-3200 or write to the address above.

For information on using IDG Books Worldwide's books in the classroom or for ordering examination copies, please contact our Educational Sales department at 800-434-2086 or fax 317-596-5499.

For press review copies, author interviews, or other publicity information, please contact our Public Relations department at 650-655-3000 or fax 650-655-3299.

For authorization to photocopy items for corporate, personal, or educational use, please contact Copyright Clearance Center, 222 Rosewood Drive, Danvers, MA 01923, or fax 978-750-4470.

is a trademark under exclusive
license to IDG Books Worldwide, Inc.,
from International Data Group, Inc.

IDG
BOOKS
WORLDWIDE

About the Authors

Eric Tyson

Eric Tyson, MBA, is a financial counselor, best-selling author, syndicated personal financial writer, and lecturer. He works with and teaches people from a myriad of income levels and backgrounds, so he knows the financial and tax questions and concerns of real folks just like you.

After toiling away for too many years as a management consultant to behemoth financial-service firms, Eric decided to take his knowledge of the industry and commit himself to making personal financial management accessible to all of us. Despite being handicapped by a joint B.S. in Economics and Biology from Yale and an MBA from Stanford, Eric remains a master at "keeping it simple."

An accomplished freelance personal finance writer, Eric is the author of four other ...*For Dummies* national bestsellers on Personal Finance, Mutual Funds, Investing, and Home Buying (co-author) and is a syndicated columnist. His work has been critically acclaimed in hundreds of publications and programs, including *Newsweek, Los Angeles Times, Chicago Tribune, Kiplinger's Personal Finance Magazine, The Wall Street Journal,* NBC's *Today Show,* ABC, CNBC, PBS's *Nightly Business Report,* CNN, FOX-TV, CBS national radio, Bloomberg Business Radio, and Business Radio Network. He also was a featured speaker at a White House conference on aging and retirement. You can e-mail Eric at eric@erictyson.com or write to him in care of IDG Books Worldwide, Inc., at 919 E. Hillsdale Blvd., Suite 400, Foster City, CA, 94404.

David J. Silverman

David J. Silverman, EA, is an enrolled agent, which means that he can represent clients before the Internal Revenue Service. He has served on the Advisory Group to the Commissioner of Internal Revenue. David has a Certificate in Taxation from New York University and has been in private practice in Manhattan for over 25 years.

He regularly testifies on tax issues before both the Senate Finance Committee and the House of Representatives Committee on Ways and Means. As the result of his suggestions regarding penalty reform that he made while testifying before these committees, legislation was enacted that reduced the amount of penalties that may be assessed in a number of key areas.

David is the author of *Battling the IRS,* which has received critical acclaim in *The New York Times, Money, The Wall Street Journal,* and numerous other publications, and has been a contributing editor and writer of a monthly column for *SmartMoney* magazine. David is frequently interviewed on national TV and radio as an expert on tax issues. You can reach him through his Web site: www.naea.org/ea/002677.htm.

ABOUT IDG BOOKS WORLDWIDE

Welcome to the world of IDG Books Worldwide.

IDG Books Worldwide, Inc., is a subsidiary of International Data Group, the world's largest publisher of computer-related information and the leading global provider of information services on information technology. IDG was founded more than 30 years ago by Patrick J. McGovern and now employs more than 9,000 people worldwide. IDG publishes more than 290 computer publications in over 75 countries. More than 90 million people read one or more IDG publications each month.

Launched in 1990, IDG Books Worldwide is today the #1 publisher of best-selling computer books in the United States. We are proud to have received eight awards from the Computer Press Association in recognition of editorial excellence and three from Computer Currents' First Annual Readers' Choice Awards. Our best-selling *...For Dummies*® series has more than 50 million copies in print with translations in 31 languages. IDG Books Worldwide, through a joint venture with IDG's Hi-Tech Beijing, became the first U.S. publisher to publish a computer book in the People's Republic of China. In record time, IDG Books Worldwide has become the first choice for millions of readers around the world who want to learn how to better manage their businesses.

Our mission is simple: Every one of our books is designed to bring extra value and skill-building instructions to the reader. Our books are written by experts who understand and care about our readers. The knowledge base of our editorial staff comes from years of experience in publishing, education, and journalism — experience we use to produce books to carry us into the new millennium. In short, we care about books, so we attract the best people. We devote special attention to details such as audience, interior design, use of icons, and illustrations. And because we use an efficient process of authoring, editing, and desktop publishing our books electronically, we can spend more time ensuring superior content and less time on the technicalities of making books.

You can count on our commitment to deliver high-quality books at competitive prices on topics you want to read about. At IDG Books Worldwide, we continue in the IDG tradition of delivering quality for more than 30 years. You'll find no better book on a subject than one from IDG Books Worldwide.

John J. Kilcullen
John Kilcullen
Chairman and CEO
IDG Books Worldwide, Inc.

Steven Berkowitz
Steven Berkowitz
President and Publisher
IDG Books Worldwide, Inc.

VIII
WINNER

*Eighth Annual
Computer Press
Awards ≥1992*

IX
WINNER

*Ninth Annual
Computer Press
Awards ≥1993*

COMPUTER CURRENTS 1995
READERS CHOICE

X
WINNER

*Tenth Annual
Computer Press
Awards ≥ 1994*

XI
WINNER

*Eleventh Annual
Computer Press
Awards ≥1995*

IDG is the world's leading IT media, research and exposition company. Founded, in 1964, IDG had 1997 revenues of $2.05 billion and has more than 9,000 employees worldwide. IDG offers the widest range of media options that reach IT buyers in 75 countries representing 95% of worldwide IT spending. IDG's diverse product and services portfolio spans six key areas including print publishing, online publishing, expositions and conferences, market research, education and training, and global marketing services. More than 90 million people read one or more of IDG's 290 magazines and newspapers, including IDG's leading global brands — Computerworld, PC World, Network World, Macworld and the Channel World family of publications. IDG Books Worldwide is one of the fastest-growing computer book publishers in the world, with more than 700 titles in 36 languages. The "...For Dummies®" series alone has more than 50 million copies in print. IDG offers online users the largest network of technology-specific Web sites around the world through IDG.net (http://www.idg.net), which comprises more than 225 targeted Web sites in 55 countries worldwide. International Data Corporation (IDC) is the world's largest provider of information technology data, analysis and consulting, with research centers in over 41 countries and more than 400 research analysts worldwide. IDG World Expo is a leading producer of more than 168 globally branded conferences and expositions in 35 countries including E3 (Electronic Entertainment Expo), Macworld Expo, ComNet, Windows World Expo, ICE (Internet Commerce Expo), Agenda, DEMO, and Spotlight. IDG's training subsidiary, ExecuTrain, is the world's largest computer training company, with more than 230 locations worldwide and 785 training courses. IDG Marketing Services helps industry-leading IT companies build international brand recognition by developing global integrated marketing programs via IDG's print, online and exposition products worldwide. Further information about the company can be found at www.idg.com.
10/8/98

Dedications

My deepest and sincerest thanks to my family, friends, clients, and students for their enthusiastic support and encouragement. My wife Judy, as always, gets special mention for inspiring my love of books and writing.

— *Eric Tyson*

To my wife Betsy, who provided the inspiration; my late father Louis, whose writing skills I hope I inherited; and my daughters Joanna and Lisa, who assisted with the essential research and editing.

— *David J. Silverman*

Authors' Acknowledgments

Many extraordinary people contributed to this year's edition of *Taxe$ for Dummie$* and what came before it. First, I'd like to thank our counseling clients, students, and readers who have helped us to learn what issues and questions people at all income levels have. I would also like to thank the journalists and other leaders in their fields for citing, complimenting, and critiquing our previous writing.

My sincere thanks to Mary Dale Walters and her staff at **CCH** INCORPORATED for their expert assistance in reviewing this book. I would especially like to thank the many people who provided the technical review: David I. Altman, Raymond A. Brown, III, Janet P. Cadogan, Susan M. Jacksack, David C. Heires, and Lawrence Griffith. Every chapter in this book was improved by their knowledge, insights, and experience.

And finally, I'd like to thank all the good people at IDG Books. Special recognition goes to Kathy Cox, who, as project editor, guided the book to its successful completion . . . and Kathy Welton and John Kilcullen for their enduring vision and leadership at IDG Books.

— *Eric Tyson*

My sincere thanks to Mary Dale Walters of **CCH** INCORPORATED and her staff for their expert assistance in helping with my research in a number of key areas. Their contribution was invaluable in helping me bring clarity to an overly complex, confusing, and often contradictory tax system.

The reader-friendly nature of this book wouldn't be possible were it not for my editor, Kathy Cox, and the team at IDG Books, including Wendy Hatch and Kim Darosett, my copy editors. Just like my fourth grade teacher whose patience and understanding I constantly tested, Kathy brought more to this project than her ability to correct an author's punctuation. Kathy was instrumental in overseeing that a book on an extremely complex subject was both understandable and witty. When a reader looks up, with ease, a topic that saves them a bundle, Kathy, Wendy, and Kim deserve the applause.

— *David J. Silverman*

Publisher's Acknowledgments

We're proud of this book; please register your comments through our IDG Books Worldwide Online Registration Form located at http://my2cents.dummies.com.

Some of the people who helped bring this book to market include the following:

Acquisitions and Editorial

Project Editors: Kathleen M. Cox, Andy Cummings, Mike Kelly

Senior Acquisitions Editor: Mark Butler

Copy Editors: Wendy Hatch, Kim Darosett

Technical Editors: CCH INCORPORATED: David I. Altman, J.D.; Raymond A. Brown III, J.D., LL.M; Janet P. Cadogan, J.D.; Lawrence Griffith, J.D.; David C. Heires, J.D.; Susan M. Jacksack, J.D.

Editorial Manager: Rev Mengle

Editorial Coordinator: Maureen F. Kelly

Acquisitions Coordinator: Jonathan Malysiak

Editorial Assistants: Paul E. Kuzmic, Donna Love, Darren Meiss, Jamila Pree

Production

Project Coordinator: Karen York

Layout and Graphics: Steve Arany, Lou Boudreau, J. Tyler Connor, Maridee V. Ennis, Angela F. Hunckler, Anna Rohrer, Brent Savage, Janet Seib, Kate Snell

Proofreaders: Christine Berman, Kelli Botta, Michelle Croninger, Rachel Garvey, Betty Kish, Nancy L. Reinhardt, Rebecca Senninger, Janet M. Withers

Indexer: Ty Koontz

Special Help

R. Blaine Baker, J.D., LL.M; Leslie Bonacum; Mary Dale Walters; all of **CCH** INCORPORATED

General and Administrative

IDG Books Worldwide, Inc.: John Kilcullen, CEO; Steven Berkowitz, President and Publisher

IDG Books Technology Publishing: Brenda McLaughlin, Senior Vice President and Group Publisher

Dummies Technology Press and Dummies Editorial: Diane Graves Steele, Vice President and Associate Publisher; Mary Bednarek, Director of Acquisitions and Product Development; Kristin A. Cocks, Editorial Director

Dummies Trade Press: Kathleen A. Welton, Vice President and Publisher; Kevin Thornton, Acquisitions Manager

IDG Books Production for Dummies Press: Michael R. Britton, Vice President of Production and Creative Services; Cindy L. Phipps, Manager of Project Coordination, Production Proofreading, and Indexing; Kathie S. Schutte, Supervisor of Page Layout; Shelley Lea, Supervisor of Graphics and Design; Debbie J. Gates, Production Systems Specialist; Robert Springer, Supervisor of Proofreading; Debbie Stailey, Special Projects Coordinator; Tony Augsburger, Supervisor of Reprints and Bluelines

Dummies Packaging and Book Design: Robin Seaman, Creative Director; Kavish + Kavish, Cover Design

◆

The publisher would like to give special thanks to Patrick J. McGovern, without whom this book would not have been possible.

◆

Contents at a Glance

Cartoons at a Glance

By Rich Tennant

Table of Contents

- -

Introduction

••

Welcome to the 1999 edition of *Taxe$ For Dummie$* — the no-nonsense update of our annual best-selling book that answers both your tax-preparation and tax-planning questions in plain English with a touch of humor. And, if the Internal Revenue Service (that dreaded government division responsible for collecting taxes) audits you, this book can also help you get out and stay out of trouble.

As you may know, in 1997, Congress passed a major tax bill that changed the rules of the game. Although much hoopla surrounded the passage of those new laws, most of them didn't kick in until tax year 1998, which means that as you prepare your 1998 tax return, you should take the time to understand the changes. In addition, the budget bill signed into law in November 1998 added new wrinkles to the laws.

This book can help you make sense of the new tax laws, relieve your pain and misery, reduce your taxes, and help you get through your tax return with a minimum of discomfort. This book can also help you keep your mind on your taxes while planning your finances for the upcoming year. In addition to understanding how to deal with federal taxes, we also explain how to handle and reduce some of those pesky and not-so-insignificant taxes slapped on by states and other tax-collecting bodies.

Finally, *Taxe$ For Dummie$* shows you how to avoid breaking laws. Many honest and well-intentioned people unknowingly break tax laws, especially because Congress keeps changing the laws, as it did in a major way with the 1997 tax bill.

We show you how to jump, obediently and merrily, through all the proper hoops to keep the taxing authorities from sending threatening notices and bills. If you *do* get a nasty letter from the tax patrol, we even tell you how to deal with that frightful situation in a calm, levelheaded manner so that you get the IRS off your case.

Most people's tax concerns fall into three categories: filling out their forms properly, keeping as much of their money as possible out of the government coffers, and avoiding any penalties. *Taxe$ For Dummie$* addresses these concerns — and helps prevent the pulling out of hair and the gnashing of teeth.

At their worst, other annual tax-preparation books are as dreadful as the IRS instruction booklets themselves — bulky, bureaucratic, and jargon-filled. In some cases, preparation books simply reproduce dozens of pages of IRS instructions! At their best, these books tell you information you won't find in the IRS instructions — but the golden nuggets are buried in massive piles of granite. *Taxe$ For Dummie$* lays out those golden nuggets in nice, clean display cases so you won't miss a single one. There's still plenty of granite, but we promise not to use it to bury you *or* the key insights.

Between the two of us, we have nearly five decades of combined experience providing personal financial and tax advice to real, live people just like you. We understand the tax and financial concerns you may have and know how to solve your quandaries!

How to Use This Book

This book has many possible uses! We aren't talking about using it as a door stop or as fuel for your fireplace, although you could use last year's edition for those purposes! Here are the various practical ways you can use this book:

✔ **As a reference.** Maybe you know a fair amount about your taxes, but you don't know where and how to report the dividends you received from some of your investments. Simply use the table of contents or index to find the right spot in the book to find the answer your questions. On the other hand, if you lack investments — in part, because you pay so much in taxes — this book also explains legal strategies for slashing your taxes and boosting your savings. Use this book before and after April 15th.

✔ **As a trusted advisor.** Maybe you're self-employed, and you know that you should be salting some money away so that you can someday cut back on those 12-hour days. No problem. You can turn to Chapter 21 and find out about the different types of retirement accounts and which one may be right for you, how it can slash your taxes, and even where to set it up.

✔ **As a textbook.** Maybe you just want to know everything. If you have the time, desire, and discipline, by all means, go for it and read the whole shebang. And please be sure to drop us a note or visit the Dummies Web site at www.dummies.com and let us know of your achievement!

The Road Map

If you've already peeked at the table of contents, you know this book is divided into parts. Here's a brief description of what you can find in each of the six major parts:

Part I: Getting Ready to File

This part helps you understand how and why taxes work in the way that they do in the United States of America. You can explore how to fit taxes into your personal financial life. Here, you can also master time-tested and tax-advisor-approved ways to get organized and ready to file your tax return(s). We also help you figure out what taxes you may have to pay and what other tedious tax forms you may be required to complete at other times of the year.

Part II: Tackling the 1040

In this part, we walk you through the process of completing various versions of Form 1040 that contain the typical challenges that taxpayers face. We promise not to reprint pages from the incomprehensible IRS manuals, and we try to make the process of filling out the Form 1040 as painless as possible.

Part III: Filling Out Schedules and Forms

Schedules A, B, and C. No, this isn't an elementary school class! In this part, we show you, line-by-line, how to complete the common Form 1040 schedules — such as those for itemized deductions, interest and dividend income, profit and loss from a business, capital gains and losses, and so on. You'll also be happy to know that we give you a brief primer on other useful forms, such as those that self-employed and retired people must complete to make estimated tax payments throughout the year.

Part IV: Audits and Errors: Dealing with the IRS

No matter how hard you try to ward off nasty letters from the IRS, sooner or later you may receive that dreaded thin envelope from the friendly tax folks with a message challenging your return. The operative word here is *challenge*. As long as you think of this situation as an opportunity to play show and tell, you'll do fine.

So you'll be tickled to know that *Taxe$ For Dummie$* goes beyond dealing with the annual ritual of filing your tax return by offering tips, counsel, and a shoulder to cry on. You find out how to sweep the IRS off your doorstep swiftly, deftly, and without breaking a sweat. And you can keep those pesky IRS agents out of your bank account while you keep yourself (and your loved ones) out of jail.

Part V: Year-Round Tax Planning

Because taxes are a year-round obligation and an important piece of your personal finance puzzle, this part provides tons of practical planning advice that you can use in July, in September, and during the rest of year — as well as in April. We show you how to accomplish common financial goals such as purchasing a home, or squirreling away enough loot so you don't have to work into your 80s and 90s — all in a tax-wise manner.

You may be tempted to skip this section after you've made it past April 15. Don't make this mistake. Part V can pay off in tens of thousands of dollars someday, saving you headaches and heartaches when you file returns each and every year.

Part VI: The Part of Tens

These top-ten lists often cover big-picture issues that cry out for top billing in their very own section. You may also enjoy plowing through these short, but highly useful, chapters in record time. (For a quick look at what new tax laws will affect your 1998 return, be sure to peek at Chapter 27.)

Appendixes

Appendixes usually include horrible little technical details that are best avoided by normal readers. In this book, however, you can find a treasure trove of goodies back here, such as a list of IRS publications, addresses, phone numbers, an extension form in case you miss important dates, and a glossary.

You can also find the most-used tax forms and schedules that you can tear out, cut out, or photocopy (yes, the IRS lets you use photocopies of most forms to do your tax return) and use for filing.

Icons Used in This Book

This target marks recommendations for making the most of your taxes and money (for example, paying off your non-tax-deductible credit-card debt with your lottery winnings).

This friendly sign will be of great interest to folks who want to discover ways to reduce their taxes — hey, this stuff is all legal. Really.

This is a friendly reminder of stuff discussed elsewhere in the book or points we really want you to remember.

This alert denotes common costly mistakes people make with their taxes.

Don't become shark bait. This icon alerts you to scoundrels, bad advice, and scams that prey on the unsuspecting.

This nerdy guy appears beside discussions that aren't critical if you just want to know the basic concepts and get answers to your tax questions. However, reading these gems will deepen and enhance your tax knowledge. And you never know when you'll be invited to go to a town meeting and talk tax reform with a bunch of politicians!

Just to keep you off-balance, Congress enacted a host of new tax law provisions that take effect in 1998. This icon alerts you to a change you need to know.

'98

This highlights tax code provisions passed in 1997 that went into effect in 1998.

Part I
Getting Ready to File

The 5th Wave   By Rich Tennant

"I put an extension on my tax return like you suggested, but I still don't think it's going to get there on time."

In this part . . .

Are you in a bad mood because of all the forms you must complete and the taxes you have to pay? We can't eliminate all those forms and taxes, but we can help you to think about your taxes in the context of your overall financial situation and what our great politicians do with all the money you send them. Although it isn't as much fun as complaining about government waste, you also find out how to get organized — and stay organized — throughout the year. And we explain how to find competent tax help, should you be at your wit's end.

"In this world nothing can be said to be certain, except death and taxes."

— Benjamin Franklin

"While taxes may be certain, they can certainly be legally reduced."

— Eric Tyson & David Silverman

Chapter 1

Our Tax System and Rates

*W*henever money passes through your hands, it seems that you pay some kind of tax. Consider the following:

✔ When you work and get paid, you pay all sorts of taxes: federal, state, and local taxes (on top of having to deal with the migraines your bosses and difficult customers give you).

✔ After paying taxes on your earnings and then spending money on things you need and want (and paying more taxes in the process), you may have some money left over for saving. Guess what? Your reward for being a saver is that you also pay tax on the interest that you earn on your savings.

Most of us — including your humble authors — find taxes to be a pain. First, we face the chore of gathering all sorts of complicated looking documents to complete the annual ritual of IRS Form 1040. If your past financial year wasn't exactly like the preceding one, you may have to get acquainted with some forms that are new to you. Even if your financial life is stagnant, tax law changes in the past year may require some new forms or calculations.

Your financial life may have changed. Perhaps you have to figure out how to submit a quarterly tax payment if you no longer work for a company and now have self-employment income from independent contracting work. Maybe you sold some investments (such as stocks, mutual funds, or real estate) at a profit, and you must calculate how much tax you owe.

Unfortunately, too many people think of taxes only in spring, when it comes time to file that annual return. Throughout this book, you can find all sorts of warnings, tips, and other suggestions that help you discover the important role that your taxes play in your entire personal financial situation year-round. In fact, we devote a major part of the book (Part V) to showing you how to accomplish important financial goals while legally reducing your taxes.

Understanding Our Tax System

If you've ever tried to read (and make sense of) the tax laws, you know that you're probably more likely to win your state's lottery than you are to figure out the tax code. That's one of the reasons that tax attorneys and accountants are paid so much — to compensate them for the intense and prolonged agony of deciphering the tax code, day after day after day!

The good news is that you don't need to read the dreadful tax laws. Most tax advisors don't read them themselves. Instead, they rely upon summaries prepared by organizations and people who have more of a knack for explaining things clearly and concisely. We hope that you include this book as a comprehensible resource you can count on.

You CAN reduce your taxes

You should be able to keep a lot more of your money by applying the tax-reducing strategies we present in this book.

✔ You may be able to tax-shelter your earnings from employment in various retirement accounts. This strategy slashes your current taxes, enables your money to compound tax-free, and helps you work toward the goal of retirement.

✔ The less you buy, the less sales tax you pay. You can buy a less expensive, more fuel-efficient car, for example.

✔ When you invest, you can invest in a way that fits your tax situation. This strategy can make you happier and wealthier come tax time. For example, you can choose tax-friendly investments that reduce your tax bill and also increase your after-tax investment returns.

If you're like most people we know, you work hard for what you have and feel that you pay a lot in taxes. If you don't understand the tax system, you *will* pay more in taxes than necessary.

If *Taxe$ For Dummie$,* 1999 Edition, helps you discover how the tax system works and how to legally make the system work *for you,* our efforts won't be in vain. Quite possibly, this book may show you some things about the tax system that don't seem very fair. Maybe these things will bother you. But even if you don't agree with the whole tax system, you still have to play by the rules. Getting angry and having the veins in your neck bulge definitely won't help your situation or health. (We don't want to help you increase your *medical* deductions!) Your newfound insights can help improve your political vision at election time, or they may inspire you to call your travel agent for a one-way ticket to a low-tax tropical island.

The tax system, like other public policy, is built around incentives to encourage *desirable* behavior and activity. Home ownership, for example, is considered desirable because it encourages people to take more responsibility for maintaining properties and neighborhoods. Clean, orderly neighborhoods are supposed to be one result of home ownership. Therefore, the government offers all sorts of tax benefits *(allowable deductions)* to encourage people to own homes (see Chapter 24). But if you don't understand these tax benefits, you probably won't know how to take advantage of them, either.

If you're like most people, though, making sense of the tax jungle is more daunting than hacking your way out of a triple-canopy rain forest with a dinner knife. Even if you're an honest, earnest, well-intentioned, and law-abiding citizen, odds are that you don't completely understand the tax system. This ignorance wreaks havoc with your personal finances, because you end up paying more in taxes than you need to.

To add insult to injury, you may step on a tax land mine. Like millions of taxpayers who have come before you, you may unwittingly be in noncompliance with the myriad of ever-changing tax laws at the federal, state, and local levels. Your tax ignorance can cause mistakes that may be costly if the IRS and your state government catch your errors. With the proliferation of computerized information and data tracking, discovering gaffes has never been easier for the tax cops at the IRS. And when they discover your boo-boos, you have to pay the tax you originally owed *and* interest *and,* possibly, penalties. Ouch!

So don't feel dumb when it comes to understanding our tax system. You're not the problem — it's the complexity of our income tax system. Throughout this book, we help you to understand the tax system, and we promise not to make you read any of the actual tax laws.

Beyond April 15: What you don't know can hurt your personal finances

Every spring, more than 100 million tax returns (and several million extension requests) are filed with the IRS. The by-product of this effort is guaranteed employment for our nation's more than 1 million accountants and auditors, and 2 million bookkeeping and accounting clerks (not to mention more than a few tax-book authors and their editors). Accounting firms rake in about $30 billion annually helping bewildered and desperately confused taxpayers figure out all those tax laws. So that you can feel okay about this situation, keep in mind that at least some of the money you pay in income taxes actually winds up in the government coffers for some useful purposes!

Given all the hours that you work during the year just to pay your taxes as well as the time you spend actually completing the dreaded return, we're sure that you feel more than justified in forgetting, until the same time next year, about your income taxes after your return is filed. This avoidance is a costly mistake.

The brief history of U.S. income taxes

Federal income taxes have not always been a certainty. Earlier in this century, people could live without being bothered by the federal income tax — or by televisions, microwaves, computers, voice mail, and all those other complications. Beginning in 1913, Congress set up a system of graduated tax rates, starting with a rate of just 1 percent and going up to 7 percent.

This tax system was enacted through the 16th Amendment to the Constitution, which was suggested by President Teddy Roosevelt (a Republican), and pushed through by his successor, President William H. Taft (another Republican), and ultimately ratified by two-thirds of the states. (Sorry, Mr. Gingrich, Mr. Forbes, and Mr. Limbaugh — not all Republicans have been anti-tax-and-spend! Note that we, your good authors, are independents, which means that we happily take swipes at both political parties throughout our book.)

We should note that the 1913 federal income tax was not the first U.S. income tax. President Abraham Lincoln signed a Civil War income tax in 1861, which was abandoned a decade later.

Prior to 1913, the vast majority of tax dollars collected by the federal government came from taxes levied on goods, such as liquor, tobacco, and imports. Today, personal income taxes, including Social Security taxes, account for about 85 percent of federal government revenue.

In 1913, the forms, instructions, and clarifications for the whole federal tax system would have filled just one small, three-ring binder! (And we're not even sure that three-ring binders existed back then.) Those were indeed the "good old days." Since then, thanks to endless revisions, enhancements, and "simplifications," the federal tax laws — along with all the IRS and court "clarifications" of those laws — can (and should) fill several dump trucks. In just the five decades since World War II, the girth of the federal tax code has swelled by more than 400 percent! And according to the Tax Foundation, a nonprofit, nonpartisan policy research organization based in Washington D.C., complying with our tax laws costs us about $200 billion annually.

During the tax year, you can take many simple actions to ensure not only that you're in compliance with the ever-changing tax laws but also that you're minimizing your tax burden. If your income — like that of nearly everyone we know — is limited, you need to understand the tax code in order to make it work for you and help you accomplish your financial goals. The following case studies demonstrate the importance of keeping in mind the tax implications of your financial decisions throughout the year.

The perils and tax costs of procrastination

Consider the case of Sheila and Peter, the proud owners of a successful and rapidly growing manufacturing business. They became so busy running the business and taking care of their children that they hardly had time to call a tax advisor. In fact, not only did they fail to file for an extension by April 15, but they also didn't pay any federal or state income tax.

By the following August, Peter and Sheila finally had time to focus on the prior year's income taxes, but by then they had gotten themselves into some problems and incurred these costs:

- Penalty for failure to file, which is 5 percent per month of the amount due, up to a maximum of 25 percent (or five months).

- Interest on the amount due, which at that time was running about 9 percent per year.

- A larger tax bill (also caused by lack of planning), which turned out to be far more expensive than the first two expenses. Because they had incorporated their business, Peter and Sheila were on the payroll for salary during the year. Despite the high level of profitability of their business, they had set their pay at too low a level.

  A low salary wouldn't seem to be a problem for the owner and only employee of a company. The worst that you'd think could happen to Peter and Sheila is that they might have to eat more peanut butter and jelly sandwiches during the year. But because they received small salaries, they could only make contributions to tax-deductible retirement accounts based on a percentage of their *small* salaries.

  The rest of the business profits, however, had to be taken by Sheila and Peter as taxable income because they had their company set up as an *S Corporation.* (You find out about the different types of corporations and their tax consequences in Chapter 22.) This gaffe caused Sheila and Peter to pay thousands in additional taxes, which they could have legally — and easily — avoided.

- Loss of future investment earnings, which means that Sheila and Peter actually over time will lose *more* than the additional taxes. Not only could Peter and Sheila not reduce their additional taxes by making larger deductible contributions to their tax-sheltered retirement accounts, they also lost the chance for the money to compound (tax-deferred) over time.

The tax consequences of biased, wrong-headed advice

Getting bad advice from those with a vested interest in our decisions is another leading cause of tax mistakes. Consider the case of George, who wanted advice about investing and other financial matters. When he got a solicitation from a "financial advisor" at a well-known firm, he was game to give it a whirl. The polished, well-dressed advisor, who was actually a *broker* (someone who earns commissions from the financial products he or she peddles), prepared a voluminous report, complete with scads of projections for George's retirement planning.

Part of the "advice" in this report was for George to purchase some cash value life insurance and various investments from the broker. The broker pitched the insurance as a great way to save, invest, and reduce George's tax burden.

Through his employer, George could invest in a retirement account on a tax-deductible basis. However, the broker conveniently overlooked this avenue — after all, the broker couldn't earn fat commissions by telling people like George to fund their employers' retirement accounts. As a result, George paid tons more in taxes than he needed to. Funding the life insurance policy was a terrible decision for George, in large part because doing so offered no up-front tax breaks. (Check out Chapter 23 for the other reasons why life insurance generally shouldn't be used as an investment.)

When you contribute money to tax-deductible retirement accounts, such as 401(k) plans, you get to keep and invest over the years the money that you normally would have owed in federal and state income taxes. See Chapter 21 to find out more about retirement accounts.

My Taxes Are How High?

If you're like most working or retired people, you pay a great deal of money in taxes — probably more than you realize or care to. Most people remember only whether they got tax refunds or owed money on their tax returns. But you should care how much you pay in taxes, and you should understand the *total* and the *marginal* taxes you pay so you can make financial decisions that lessen your tax load.

When you file your income tax return, all you do is balance your tax checkbook, so to speak, against the federal and state governments' versions of your tax checkbook. You settle up with tax authorities regarding the amount of taxes you paid during the past year versus the total tax that you actually should have paid based on your income and deductions.

Some people feel happy or fortunate when they get refunds. You shouldn't feel so good, though — all a refund really indicates is that you overpaid your taxes during the prior year. Last year, the IRS issued about $100 billion in individual income tax refunds. If you figure that even a relatively low-yielding money market account pays at least 5 percent interest, taxpayers threw away about $5 billion in interest on money that they could have invested.

Total taxes

The only way to find out the total amount of income taxes that you pay is to get out your federal and state tax returns. On each of those returns is a line that shows the *total tax* (line 56 on federal 1040 returns). Add the totals from your federal and state tax returns, and you see one of the single largest expenses of your financial life (unless you have an expensive home or a huge gambling habit).

You should make note of the fact that your taxable income is different from the amount of money you earned during the tax year from employment and any investments. *Taxable income* is defined as the amount of income on which you actually pay taxes. You don't pay taxes on your total income for the following two reasons. First, not all income is taxable. For example, you pay federal income tax on the interest that you earn on a bank savings account but not on the interest from municipal bonds (which are essentially loans that you as a bond buyer make to state and local governments).

A second reason that you don't pay taxes on all your income is that you get to subtract deductions from your income. Some deductions are available just for being a living, breathing human being. In 1998, single people receive an automatic $4,250 standard deduction, and married couples filing jointly get $7,100. (People older than 65 and those who are blind get slightly higher deductions.) Other expenses, such as mortgage interest and property taxes, are deductible to the extent that your total deductions exceed the standard deductions.

Taxes are such a major portion of most people's expenditures that any personal budget or spending plan that doesn't address, contain, and reduce your taxes may be doomed to failure. That's why throughout this book we highlight strategies for reducing your taxable income and income taxes right now, as well as in the future. Doing so is vital to your ability to save and invest money to accomplish important financial and personal goals.

Your marginal income tax rate

"What's marginal about my taxes?" we hear you asking. "They're huge! They aren't marginal at all!" *Marginal* is a word that people often use when they mean small or barely acceptable. Sort of like getting a C– on a school report card (or an A– if you're from an over-achieving family).

But when we're talking about taxes, marginal has a different and very specific meaning. Your *marginal* tax rate is the rate you pay on the last dollars you earn because the government charges you different rates for different parts of your annual income. You generally pay less tax on your *first* dollars of earnings and more tax on your *last* dollars of earnings. Former President Ronald Reagan, who was arguably a better president than he was a historian, said of this system, "The entire graduated income tax system was created by Karl Marx." Actually, graduated tax brackets have been around a long time — recorded as far back as 2,400 B.C. in Greece.

Table 1-1 gives the federal tax rates for singles and for marrieds filing jointly.

Table 1-1	1998 Federal Income Tax Brackets and Rates	
Singles Taxable Income	*Married-Filing-Jointly Taxable Income*	*Federal Tax Rate (Bracket)*
Not over $25,350	Not over $42,350	15%
Over $25,350 – $61,400	Over $42,350 – $102,300	28%
Over $61,400 – $128,100	Over $102,300 – $155,950	31%
Over $128,100 – $278,450	Over $155,950 – $278,450	36%
Over $278,450	Over $278,450	39.6%

Your *marginal tax rate* is the rate of tax that you pay on your *last* or so-called *highest* dollars of income. For example, if you're single and your taxable income totaled $32,000 during 1998, you pay federal tax at the rate of 15 percent on the first $25,350 of taxable income and 28 percent on income from $25,350 up to $32,000, for a marginal tax rate of 28 percent. In other words, she effectively pays 28 percent federal tax on her last dollars of income — those dollars in excess of $25,350.

The fact that *not all income is treated equally* under the current tax system is not self-evident. If you work for an employer and have a constant salary during the course of a year, a stable amount of federal and state taxes is deducted from your paycheck. Therefore, you may have the impression that all your earned income is being taxed equally.

After you understand the powerful concept of marginal tax rates, you begin to see the value of the many financial strategies that affect the amount of taxes you pay. Because you pay taxes on your employment income as well as on the earnings from your investments held outside retirement accounts, many of your personal finance decisions should be made with your marginal tax rate in mind.

TECHNICAL STUFF

Are your income tax rates fair? You be the judge

With the possible exceptions of abortion and gun control, the issue of whether the tax system is fair inspires some of the most emotionally charged dialogue (and preachy monologues from radio talk show commentators). By "fair" we mean how much total tax you are asked to pay and how that total compares with that of your neighbors, your coworkers, and the guy in Brooklyn, New York.

If you're like most Americans, you probably feel that you pay too much in taxes. It may not be much comfort to you, but the average total taxes U.S. citizens pay are low in comparison to those of citizens of other industrialized countries in Europe and Asia. However, low- and moderate-income earners in the U.S. pay higher income taxes than do our overseas friends, while high income earners generally pay less.

A tremendous debate and gnashing of teeth exist over how much high-income earners and the wealthy (relative to other taxpayers) should pay in taxes. Folks such as failed 1996 presidential candidate Malcolm S. Forbes, Jr., and political commentator Rush Limbaugh argue that it's unfair and economically harmful to burden — with oppressive taxes — those who "work hard and generate jobs" (that is, the high-income earners). At the other end of the spectrum, you hear the likes of Jesse Jackson and Ted Kennedy pleading that the well-heeled don't pay their fair share and should face higher taxes to help pay for "deserving programs for the poor and disadvantaged."

As with many disagreements, those at the polar extremes feel that they are right (intellectually, not politically speaking) and that the other side is wrong. The politically liberal have a tendency to idealize how well government solves problems, and therefore advocate more taxes for more programs. On the other hand, the politically conservative have a tendency to idealize how well the private sector meets the needs of society at large, in the absence of government oversight and programs.

Although we can agree that easy access to tax revenue encourages some wasteful government spending and pork-laden programs, we also know that taxes must come from somewhere. The questions are *how much* and *from whom?* Equity, fairness, and stimulation of economic growth are concerns in the design of a tax system. You'll rarely hear blustery commentators or news programs thoughtfully discuss these issues.

Our advice is to keep an open mind, listen to all sides, and remember the big picture. Back in the 1950s (an economic boom time), for example, the highest federal income tax rate was a whopping 90 percent, more than double its current level. And whereas during most of this century the highest-income earners paid a marginal rate that was double to triple the rate paid by moderate-income earners of the time, that gap was greatly reduced during the 1980s. The highest-income earners continue to pay the lion's share of taxes, however — in fact, the top 1 percent of all income earners pay 25 percent of all income taxes. The top 25 percent pay more than three-quarters of total income taxes collected.

Your marginal tax rate enables you to quickly calculate additional taxes that you would pay on additional income. For example, you have the opportunity to work overtime or moonlight and earn some extra money. How much of that extra compensation you get to keep depends on your marginal tax rate.

Conversely, you can delight in quantifying the amount of taxes that you save by reducing your taxable income, either by decreasing your income — for example, with pretax contributions to your employer's retirement account — or by increasing your deductions.

Actually, there can even be more to your marginal taxes, especially if you're a high-income earner! Later in this chapter, we discuss the *Alternative Minimum Tax,* which annoys some taxpayers, mainly higher-income earners who have lots of deductions. And as discussed elsewhere in this book, some of the tax breaks are reduced when your income exceeds a particular level:

✔ Itemized deductions, which you find out about in Chapter 9 and record on Schedule A, are reduced for tax year 1998 when your adjusted gross income (total income before subtracting deductions) exceeds $124,500.

✔ Personal exemptions are a freebie — they're a write-off of $2,700 in tax year 1998 just for being a living, breathing, human being. However, this freebie is whittled away for single-income earners with adjusted gross incomes above $124,500 and above $186,800 for married people filing jointly.

✔ If you own rental real estate, you may normally take up to a $25,000 annual loss if your expenses exceed your rental income. Your ability to deduct this loss begins to be limited when your adjusted gross income exceeds $100,000.

✔ Your eligibility to fully contribute to the new Roth Individual Retirement Accounts (see Chapter 21) depends on your adjusted gross income being less than or equal to $95,000 if you're a single taxpayer or $150,000 if you're married. Beyond these amounts, allowable contributions are phased out.

Your marginal tax rate — the rate of tax you pay on your last dollars of income — should be higher than your average tax rate — the rate you pay, on average, on all your earnings. *The reason your marginal tax rate is more important is that it tells you the value of legally reducing your taxable income.*

State taxes

You should note that your *total marginal rate* includes your federal *and* state tax rates. As you may already be painfully aware, you don't pay just federal income taxes. You also get hit with state income taxes — that is, unless you live in Alaska, Florida, Nevada, South Dakota, Texas, Washington, or Wyoming. Those states have *no* state income taxes. As with federal income taxes, state income taxes have been around since the early 1900s.

You can look up your state tax rate by getting out your most recent year's state income tax preparation booklet. Alternatively, we've been crazy — but kind — enough to prepare a helpful little (okay, not so little) table that should give you a rough idea of your state tax rates (see Table 1-2).

Table 1-2	State Marginal Tax Rates			
State	**Filing Status**	**Taxable Income**		
		$25,000+	**$50,000+**	**$100,000+**	**$250,000+**
Alabama	all	5%	5%	5%	5%
Alaska	(no personal income tax)				
Arizona	singles	3.9%	4.8%	4.8%	5.17%
	marrieds	3.3%	3.9%	4.8%	5.17%
Arkansas	all	7%	7%	7%	7%
California	singles	8%	9.3%	9.3%	9.3%
	marrieds	4%	6%	9.3%	9.3%
Colorado	all	5%	5%	5%	5%
Connecticut	all	4.5%	4.5%	4.5%	4.5%
Delaware	all	6.45%	6.9%	6.9%	6.9%
District of Columbia	all	9.5%	9.5%	9.5%	9.5%
Florida	(no personal income tax)				
Georgia	all	6%	6%	6%	6%
Hawaii	singles	10%	10%	10%	10%
	marrieds	8.75%	10%	10%	10%
Idaho	all	8.2%	8.2%	8.2%	8.2%
Illinois	all	3%	3%	3%	3%

State	Filing Status	Taxable Income			
		$25,000+	$50,000+	$100,000+	$250,000+
Indiana	all	3.4%	3.4%	3.4%	3.4%
Iowa	all	7.55%	9.98%	9.98%	9.98%
Kansas	singles	7.5%	7.75%	7.75%	7.75%
	marrieds	3.5%	6.25%	6.45%	6.45%
Kentucky	all	6%	6%	6%	6%
Louisiana	all	4%	4%	6%	6%
Maine	singles	8.5%	8.5%	8.5%	8.5%
	marrieds	7%	8.5%	8.5%	8.5%
Maryland	all	5%	5%	5%	5%
Massachusetts[1]	Part A	12%	12%	12%	12%
	Part B	5.95%	5.95%	5.95%	5.95%
Michigan	all	4.4%	4.4%	4.4%	4.4%
Minnesota	singles	8%	8%	8.5%	8.5%
	marrieds	8%	8%	8.5%	8.5%
Mississippi	all	5%	5%	5%	5%
Missouri	all	6%	6%	6%	6%
Montana	all	8%	10%	11%	11%
Nebraska	singles	5.01%	6.68%	6.68%	6.68%
	marrieds	3.49%	6.68%	6.68%	6.68%
Nevada	(no broad-based income tax)				
New Hampshire[2]	all	none	none	none	none
New Jersey	singles	1.75%	5.525%	6.37%	6.37%
	marrieds	1.75%	1.75%	5.5%	6.37%
New Mexico	singles	6%	7.9%	8.5%	8.5%
	marrieds	6%	7.1%	8.5%	8.5%
New York	singles	6.85%	6.85%	6.85%	6.85%
	marrieds	5.25%	6.85%	6.85%	6.85%
North Carolina	all	7%	7%	7.75%	7.75%
North Dakota	all	9.33%	12%	12%	12%
Ohio	all	4.162%	4.857%	6.444%	7.004%
Oklahoma	all	7%	7%	7%	7%
Oregon	all	9%	9%	9%	9%
Pennsylvania	all	2.8%	2.8%	2.8%	2.8%
Rhode Island	all	Flat rate of 27.5% of federal income tax liability			
South Carolina	all	7%	7%	7%	7%
South Dakota	all	none	none	none	none
Tennessee[3]	all	none	none	none	none
Texas	all	none	none	none	none
Utah	all	7%	7%	7%	7%

(continued)

Table 1-2 *(continued)*

State	Filing Status	Taxable Income			
		$25,000+	$50,000+	$100,000+	$250,000+
Vermont	all	Flat rate of 25% of federal tax liability			
Virginia	all	5.75%	5.75%	5.75%	5.75%
Washington	all	none	none	none	none
West Virginia	all	4.5%	6%	6.5%	6.5%
Wisconsin	all	6.93%	6.93%	6.93%	6.93%
Wyoming	all	none	none	none	none

[1]Massachusetts taxes non-bank interest, dividends, and capital gains at the rate of 12%.
[2]New Hampshire taxes interest and dividends from bonds and other debts at 5%.
[3]Tennessee taxes interest and dividends from stocks and bonds at 6%.

The second tax system: Alternative Minimum Tax

You may find this hard to believe, but (as if the tax system weren't already complicated enough) there's actually a *second* federal tax system. This second system may raise your taxes higher than they would have been otherwise. Let us explain.

Over the years, as the government has grown hungrier for revenue, taxpayers who slash their taxes by claiming lots of deductions have come under greater scrutiny. So the government created a second tax system — the *Alternative Minimum Tax* (AMT) — to ensure that those with high deductions pay at least a minimum amount of taxes on their incomes.

If you have a lot of deductions from state income taxes, real estate taxes, certain types of mortgage interest, or passive investments (such as limited partnerships or rental real estate), you may fall prey to the AMT. The AMT is a classic case of the increasing complexity of our tax code. As incentives were placed in the tax code, people took advantage of them. Then the government said, "Whoa, Nelly! We can't have people taking that many write-offs." Thus was born the AMT.

At the federal level lurk two AMT tax brackets: 26 percent for AMT income up to $175,000 and 28 percent for everything over that amount, except capital gains. The AMT restricts you from claiming certain deductions and requires you to increase your taxable income. So, you have to figure your tax under the AMT system *and* under the other system and pay whichever amount is *higher* (ouch!). Unfortunately, the only way to know for certain whether you're ensnared by this second tax system is to complete — you guessed it — another tax form (see Chapter 8).

Chapter 2

Preparation Options: You, Software, and Hired Help

In This Chapter
▶ Preparing your own tax return
▶ Poring over IRS publications and seeking phone assistance
▶ Considering the pros and cons of using tax-preparation software
▶ Finding hired help: Preparers, EAs, CPAs, and tax attorneys
▶ Asking the right questions before hiring a tax advisor

*B*y the time you actually file your return, it's usually too late to take advantage of many tax-reduction strategies. And what could be more aggravating than, late in the evening on April 14, finding a golden nugget of tax advice that works great — if you had only known about it last December?

So *after* you complete the annual chore of filing your tax return, be sure to review Part V, which covers the important tax-planning issues that you should take advantage of in future years.

If you're now faced with the daunting task of preparing your return, you're probably trying to decide how to get it done with a minimum of pain and taxes owed. You have some basic options for how to complete your return. The choice that makes sense for you depends on how complex your tax situation is, how much you know about taxes, and how much you enjoy a challenge.

Taking Charge Yourself

You already do many things for yourself. You probably dress yourself every morning. Maybe you cook for yourself, do home repairs, or even change the oil in your car. You may do these chores because you enjoy them, because you save money by doing them yourself, or because you want to develop a particular skill.

Preparing your own tax return is the cheapest way to get it done — as long as you don't figure in the value of your lost leisure time, of course. Doing your own return is an especially good option if your financial situation doesn't change much from year to year. You can just pull out last year's return, fill in the new numbers for this year, do the required mathematical operations, make a copy of your completed return (you should always keep a copy of your tax return for your files), and put it in the mail.

Can I do my return without a preparer?

This isn't a simple question to answer. Odds are that you can. Most people's returns don't vary that much from year to year. So you have a head start and can hit the ground running if you get out last year's return — which, of course, you copied and saved in a well-marked place!

Preparing your own return may not work as well if your situation has changed in some way — if you bought or sold a house, started your own business, or retired, for example. In one of those cases, start by focusing on the sections of this book in Parts II and III that deal with those preparation issues. If you want more planning background, check out the relevant chapters in Part V.

Don't give up and hire a preparer because you can't bear to open your tax-preparation booklet and get your background data organized. Even if you hire a tax preparer, you need to get your stuff organized before a consultation.

As hard and as painful as it is, confront preparing your return as far in advance of April 15 as you can. That way, if you don't feel comfortable with your level of knowledge, you have enough time to seek help. The more organizing you can do before hiring a preparer, the less it should cost you to have someone else prepare your return. Avoid waiting until the 11th hour to hire an advisor — you won't do as thorough a job selecting a competent person, and you'll probably pay more for the rush job. If you get stuck preparing the return, you can get a second opinion from another preparation resource, such as a tax advice book or a good software package.

You may need to do a little reading to keep up with the small number of changes in the tax system and laws that affect your situation. Given the constant changes to various parts of the tax laws, you simply can't assume that the tax laws that apply to your situation are the same just because your situation is the same.

One potential drawback to preparing your own tax return(s) is that you may keep on doing the same old thing with your taxes — year after year. This means that you may be missing some legal ways to pay less in taxes.

You bought this book, so you must feel somewhat confused. If that feeling continues, you probably shouldn't try to do your return yourself. Give our advice a try before you throw in the towel and pay hundreds of dollars in tax-preparation fees. And if you stay alert while preparing your return, reading the list of deductions that *don't* apply to you may motivate you to make changes in your personal and financial habits so that you can qualify to take some of those deductions next year.

IRS "assistance"

If you have a simple, straightforward tax return, completing it on your own using only the IRS instructions may be fine. This approach is as cheap as you can get. The only costs are your time, patience, photocopying expenses, and postage to mail the completed tax return.

Working with IRS assistance has a lot in common with an Easter egg hunt. If you've ever hunted for Easter eggs, you know that the prizes are well hidden (from a child's perspective, anyway) and require some real searching to find. In our own egg-hunting experience, we don't recall seeing any large, flashing neon signs reading DON'T MISS THIS ONE! pointing to hidden eggs.

Likewise, IRS publications don't, in general, have helpful icons like this book has. For example, here's something you don't see in an IRS publication:

> **STOP! One of the most commonly overlooked deductions is a tax-deductible retirement account contribution. You still have time to start a retirement plan and whack off hundreds — maybe thousands — of dollars from your tax bill! HURRY!**

Another danger of relying on the IRS for assistance is that the IRS has been known to give wrong information on a more-than-infrequent basis. If you call the IRS with a question, be sure to take notes about your phone conversation to protect yourself in the event of an audit. Date your notes and include the name of the IRS employee with whom you talked, what you asked, and the employee's responses. File your notes in a folder with a copy of your completed return.

In addition to the standard instructions that come with your tax return, the IRS offers some pamphlets that you can request by phone:

- ✔ Publication 17 *(Your Federal Income Tax)* is designed for individual tax-return preparation.
- ✔ Publication 334 *(Tax Guide for Small Businesses)* is for (you guessed it) small-business tax-return preparation.

These guides provide more detail than the basic IRS publications. Call 800-TAX-FORM (800-829-3676 for those who hate searching for letters on phone key pads) to request these free guides. (Actually, nothing is free. You've already paid for IRS guides with your tax dollars!)

The IRS also offers more in-depth booklets focusing on specific tax issues. We list these booklets in Appendix A (for those gluttons-for-punishment who can't wait to read this kind of stuff). However, if your tax situation is so complex that this book (and Publications 17 and 334) can't address it, you should think long and hard about getting help from a tax advisor or from one of the other sources recommended in the "Hired Help" section, later in this chapter.

IRS publications are like law books. They have to give you the facts, but they don't have to make it easy for you to find the facts and advice you really need. The best way to use IRS publications is for you to *confirm facts* that you already think you know, or to check the little details. Never expect IRS guides to teach you how to cut your tax bill.

Preparation and advice guides

Tax-preparation and advice books are invaluable if they highlight tax reduction strategies and possible pitfalls — in clear, simple English. We hope that you agree with the reader and reviewer comments in the front of this guide that *Taxe$ For Dummie$* is top of the line in this category.

These books help you complete your return correctly while saving you as much money as possible. The amount of money invested in a book or two is significantly smaller than the annual cost of a tax expert! And books like this one come with commonly needed tax forms, saving you time and hassle.

Taxe$ For Dummie$ covers the important tax-preparation and planning issues that affect the vast majority of taxpayers. A minority of taxpayers may run into some nit-picky tax issues caused by unusual events in their lives or because of extraordinary changes in their incomes or assets. For these folks, this book may not be enough. In such cases, you should consider hiring a tax advisor, which we explain how to do later in this chapter.

Tax preparers in a box: Software

If you don't want to slog through dozens of pages of tedious IRS instructions or pay a tax preparer hundreds of dollars to complete your annual return, you may be interested in computer software that can help you finish off your IRS Form 1040 and supplemental schedules. If you have access to a computer and printer, tax-preparation software can be a helpful tool. Think of it as having a squadron of tax advisors living on your desktop. Plus, you don't have to race to the library to get all the forms for your particular return — only to discover that the library is out of them. And you don't have to call the IRS and wait for weeks for your forms to arrive in the mail. Your software has all the forms you're likely to need!

Tax-preparation software also gives you the advantage of automatically recalculating all the appropriate numbers on your return if one number changes — no more painting out math errors with a little white brush or recalculating a whole page of figures because your dog was sleeping on some of the receipts.

The best tax-preparation software is easy to install and use on your computer, provides help if you get stuck, and highlights deductions you may overlook. Some software packages let you import data you've been collecting throughout the year from other software, including checkbook packages such as Quicken, Microsoft Money, and others.

If you get a headache trying to figure out how to do something with the software, the best packages have accessible and helpful technical support people you can call in your time of need. Remember, though, that these people are software techies, not tax techies. Don't expect to get an explanation of whether you can deduct your last trip to Hawaii as a business expense.

Like a good tax advisor, the best programs clearly explain the rules, warn of items that may trigger an audit, and highlight commonly overlooked tax reduction opportunities.

Kiplinger TaxCut and TurboTax are the leading programs, and they all do a reasonable job of helping you through the federal tax forms. We like TurboTax best because it has the most comprehensive and comprehensible instructions and definitions and is loaded with helpful deduction reminders. And if you also want a state tax software program, TurboTax has a version for all states that levy an income tax. Users of the best-selling Quicken program also find they can transfer their Quicken spending data directly into TurboTax. (The other programs, by contrast, require an extra step of converting your checkbook program data to a "TXF" export file and then importing it.)

If you're undecided about which tax software package to buy, one way to break a tie between good software options is to consider price — you may be able to get a better deal on one software package (for example, TurboTax tends to be more expensive in most stores because it carries a higher suggested retail price). Procrastinating also offers some benefits, because the longer you wait to buy the software, the cheaper it gets — especially if you buy it after filing for an extension. Also, be sure to check whether the tax software you buy can import the data from the checkbook software you may have been using to track your tax-deductible expenses throughout the year.

Before you plunk down your hard earned cash for some tax-preparation software, know that it is not without its potential drawbacks. Here are the big ones:

- **Garbage in, garbage out.** A tax return prepared by a software program is only as good as the quality of the data you enter into it. Of course, this drawback exists no matter who actually fills out the forms; some human tax preparers don't probe and clarify to make sure that you've given all the right stuff, either. Tax software programs also may contain glitches that can lead to incorrect calculating or reporting of some aspect of your tax return.

✔ **Where's the beef?** Some tax software packages give little in the way of background help, advice, and warnings. This lack of assistance can lull you into a false sense of security about the completeness and accuracy of the return you prepare.

✔ **Think, computer, think!** Computers are good at helping you access and process information. They don't exercise judgment or think for you (although someday they may do more if the artificial intelligence gurus realize their dreams). In the meantime, remember that your computer is great at crunching numbers but has a far lower IQ than you have!

No matter which program you buy, don't waste your money on *electronic filing,* which all the programs push, unless you're champing at the bit to receive a large refund (electronic filing gets a refund to you a few weeks earlier than normal filing). Filing your tax return online enriches the software companies and saves the IRS on data entry (they should pay us to file electronically) but doesn't save you any hassles; you still must mail in your W-2 and yet another IRS form (**Form 8453-OL**).

Online and Internet tax information

In addition to software and guide books, the Internet offers some helpful resources that may save you some time, headaches, and perhaps even some tax dollars. Unfortunately, the better online tax resources are geared more to tax practitioners and tax-savvy taxpayers. But in your battle to legally minimize your taxes, you may want all the help you can get. Don't make the mistake of solely relying on IRS publications — remember that the U.S. Treasury Department has no incentive to explain clearly how you can reduce your taxes.

In addition to using your computer to prepare your tax return, you can do an increasing number of other tax activities via the Internet. But if you don't own a computer or know how to access online services and the Internet, we wouldn't recommend buying a computer or spending money on monthly usage fees for Internet service providers just for the online tax stuff. You aren't missing much tax information that you can't find through other, often more convenient, means.

Difficult as it is to believe, the IRS Web site, The IRS Digital Daily (www.irs.ustreas.gov/prod/cover.html), demonstrates its online mission to fight its humorless and stodgy reputation. With a home page formatted to look like a tabloid magazine, the IRS site offers fun graphics, some humorous writing, and access to all the IRS forms and instructions.

You have a choice of formats for downloading forms: PDF, PCL, or PostScript. In order to read and print the forms, you need a program such as Adobe Acrobat Reader, which you can download for free from the IRS site, or you can call Adobe at 800-272-3623 or visit the Adobe Web site at www.adobe.com. To download forms from the IRS site, start browsing at www.irs.ustreas.gov or the file transfer site at ftp.fedworld.gov. The IRS site even features a place for you to post comments on proposed tax regulations, with a promise that the "comments are fully considered." Is this the IRS we know and love?

The major online services, such as America Online, CompuServe, and Prodigy, also enable you to download tax forms and have financial forums where you can post messages and discuss issues.

We do not recommend that you depend on the accuracy of the answers to tax questions that you ask in online forums. The problem: You can't be sure of the background, expertise, or identity in some cases of the person with whom you are trading messages.

After you learn how to hop on and navigate the Internet, use it for what it's best at — possibly saving you time tracking down factual information or other stuff.

More Internet tax sites for the tax curious

As a reference for all things tax related on the Web, don't miss Dennis Schmidt's Tax and Accounting Sites Directory (www.taxsites.com). Organized into 20 categories, such as tax forms, software, and law, this site is the most comprehensive compendium of tax Web sites. There are no frills, graphics, advertising, reviews, or even commentary. If you want more guidance and commentary on sites, check out TaxResources (www.best.com/~ftmexpat/html/taxsites.html), although this site isn't as well organized as Schmidt's Tax and Accounting Sites Directory.

For true tax junkies, the U.S. Tax Code On-Line (www.fourmilab.ch/ustax/ustax.html) is a search engine that allows you to peruse the complete text of the Internal Revenue Code. Hyperlinks in the text let you cross-reference between sections with a mouse click.

Most tax software providers offer Web sites with technical support and some tax-saving advice. Among the popular software programs, both Kiplinger TaxCut (www.taxcut.com) and Intuit's TurboTax (www.intuit.com/turbotax) have solid sites. Intuit's site is more comprehensive and possibly of interest even to non-TurboTax users. It includes statistical data so you can see how your tax return compares to the national averages, recent tax law changes, and a tax calendar that lists important tax dates for the

coming year. One drawback: Loads of advertising results in slow navigation.

Although not yet a threat to the big tax software companies, the recently launched SecureTax (www.securetax.com) is a virtual tax preparation software program that lets you prepare a return at the Web site. You enter your data on forms provided at the Web site, and SecureTax handles the calculations. Although using the Web site to perform your calculations is free of charge, SecureTax charges you $9.95 if you want to print your filled-out IRS forms on your printer (requires using Adobe Acrobat Reader). Compared with the best off-the-shelf tax preparation software, this service has drawbacks. Most importantly, help and advice are spotty at best. And, because the program is coming in over your phone line, navigating it can be painfully slow compared to a software program on your hard drive. Still, this site is probably a sign of things to come.

On the Internet, a number of newsgroups, such as misc.taxes, offer information and discussion of tax issues. Again, take advice and counsel from other Net users at your peril. If you want to liven up your life — and taxes make you mad — a number of political forums allow you to converse and butt heads with others. You can complain about recent tax hikes or explain why you think that the wealthy still don't pay enough taxes!

Hiring Help

Because they lack the time, interest, energy, or skill to do it themselves, some people hire a contractor to handle a home-remodeling project. And most people who hire a contractor also do so because they think that they can afford hiring a contractor. (Although sometimes this last part isn't true, and they wind up with more debt than they can afford!) For the same reasons, some people choose to hire a tax advisor.

Competent tax preparers and advisors can save you money — sometimes more than enough to pay their fees — by identifying tax-reduction strategies you may overlook. They may also reduce the likelihood of an audit, which can be triggered by blunders you may make. Like some building contractors, however, some tax folks take longer, charging you more and not delivering the high quality work you expect.

Tax practitioners come with various backgrounds, training, and credentials. One type of professional is not necessarily better than another. Think of them as different types of specialists who are appropriate for different circumstances. The four main types of tax practitioners are preparers, enrolled agents, certified public accountants, and tax attorneys.

Preparers

Among all the tax practitioners, preparers *generally* have the least amount of training, and a greater proportion of them work part-time. H&R Block is the largest and most well-known tax-preparation firm in the country. In addition to H&R Block and other national firms, such as Jackson Hewitt and Triple Check, lots of mom-and-pop shops are in the tax-preparation business.

The appeal of preparers is that they're relatively inexpensive — they can do basic returns for $100 or less. The drawback is that you may hire a preparer who doesn't know much more than you do! As with financial planners, no national regulations apply to preparers, and no licensing is required. In most states, almost anybody can hang out a tax-preparation shingle and start preparing. Most preparers, however, complete some sort of training program before working with clients.

Preparers make the most sense for folks who don't have complicated financial lives, who are budget-minded, and who hate doing their own taxes. If you aren't good about hanging onto receipts or don't want to keep your own files with background details about your taxes, you should definitely shop around for a tax preparer who's going to be around for a few years. You may need all that paperwork stuff someday for an audit, and many tax preparers keep and organize their clients' documentation rather than return everything each year. (Can you blame them for keeping your records after they go through the tedious task of sorting them all out of the shopping bags?) Also, it may be safer to go with a firm that's open year-round in case tax questions or problems arise (some small shops are open only during tax season).

Enrolled agents (EAs)

A person must pass IRS scrutiny in order to be called an *enrolled agent.* This license allows the agent to represent you before the IRS in the event of an audit.

The training to become an EA is generally longer and more sophisticated than that of a typical preparer. Continuing education is also required; in fact, EAs must complete at least 24 hours of continuing education each year to maintain their licenses.

Enrolled agents' prices tend to fall between those of a preparer and a CPA. Tax returns with a few of the more common schedules (such as Schedule A for deductions and Schedule B for interest and dividends) shouldn't cost more than a couple hundred dollars to prepare. If you live in an area with a relatively high cost of living, expect to pay more.

The main difference between enrolled agents and CPAs and attorneys is that EAs work exclusively in the field of taxation, which makes them more likely to stay attuned to the latest tax developments. Not all CPAs and attorneys do. In addition to preparing your return (including simple to complex forms), good EAs can help with tax planning, represent you at audits, and get the IRS off your back. You can get names and telephone numbers of EAs in your area by contacting the National Association of Enrolled Agents (800-424-4339).

Certified public accountants (CPAs)

Certified public accountants go through significant training and examination to receive the CPA credential. In order to maintain this designation, a CPA must also complete continuing education classes — at least 40 hours worth every year.

CPA fees vary tremendously. Most charge around $100 per hour, but CPAs at large accounting firms and in high cost-of-living areas tend to charge somewhat more. Some CPAs charge $300+ per hour.

Who's best qualified? EA, CPA, or preparer?

Who is best qualified to prepare your return? That really depends on the individual you want to hire. The CPA credential is just that, a credential. Some people who have the credential will try to persuade you not to hire someone without it, but don't always believe this advice.

Some tax-preparation books perpetuate the myth that only a CPA can do your taxes. In one such book, in a chapter about choosing a tax preparer, misleadingly entitled "How to Prepare for Your Accountant," the authors say that "choosing an accountant is not something that should be done casually. There are over 300,000 certified public accountants." These authors then recommend that you ask a potential preparer, "Are you a certified public accountant?" (As you may have guessed, the firm producing the book is a large CPA company.)

What about all the non-CPAs, such as enrolled agents, who do a terrific job helping their clients prepare their returns and plan for their taxes throughout the year?

If you can afford to and want to pay hundreds of dollars per hour, hiring a large CPA firm can make sense. But for the vast majority of taxpayers, it's unnecessary and wasteful to spend this kind of money. And many enrolled agents and other tax preparers are out there who do super work for far less.

Competent CPAs are of greatest value to people completing some of the more unusual and less user-friendly schedules, such as K-1 for partnerships, Schedule C for self-employed folks, or Form 8829 for home office deductions. CPAs are also helpful for people who had a major or first-time tax event during the year, such as the sale of a home or child care tax-credit determination. (Good EAs and other preparers can handle these issues as well.)

If your return is uncomplicated and your financial situation is stable, hiring a high-priced CPA year after year to fill in the blanks is a waste of money. A CPA once bragged that he was effectively making about $500 per hour from some of his clients' returns, which required only 20 minutes of an assistant's time to complete.

Paying for the additional cost of a CPA on an ongoing basis makes sense if you can afford it and if your financial situation is reasonably complex or dynamic. If you are self-employed and/or file lots of other schedules, it may be worth hiring a CPA. But you needn't do so year after year. If your situation grows complex one year and then stabilizes, consider getting help for the perplexing year and then using preparation guides, software, or a lower-cost preparer or enrolled agent in the future.

You can obtain the names and phone numbers of CPAs in your local area by checking your local Yellow Pages under "Accountants — Certified Public." If you're considering hiring a CPA, be sure to ask how much of his or her time is spent preparing individual income tax returns and returns like yours.

Tax attorneys

Unless you're a super high-income earner with a complex financial life, it's prohibitively expensive to hire a tax attorney to prepare your annual return. In fact, many tax attorneys don't prepare returns as a normal practice. Because of their level of specialization and training, tax attorneys tend to have the highest hourly billing rates — $200 to $300 per hour is not unusual.

Tax attorneys sometimes get involved in court cases dealing with tax problems, disagreements, or other complicated matters, such as the purchase or sale of a business. Other good tax advisors can help with these issues as well.

The more training and specialization a tax practitioner has (and the more affluent the clients), the higher the hourly fee. Select the one that best meets your needs. Fees and competence at all levels of the profession vary significantly. If you aren't sure of the quality of work performed and the soundness of the advice, get a second opinion.

Finding tax preparers and advisors

The best tax advisors don't usually cold-call you at home, trying to get your business. The challenge for you is to locate a tax advisor who does terrific work, charges reasonable fees, and thus is too busy to bother calling to solicit you! Here are some resources to find those publicity-shy, competent, and affordable tax advisors:

- ✓ **Friends.** Some of your friends probably use tax advisors and can steer you to a decent one or two for an interview. In the sections that follow this one, we list questions that we suggest you ask potential tax preparers in advance.
- ✓ **Coworkers.** Ask people in your field which tax advisors they use. This strategy can be especially useful if you're self-employed.
- ✓ **Other advisors.** Financial and legal advisors can be helpful as well, but don't assume that they know more about the competence of a tax person than you do. Beware of a common problem: Financial or legal advisors may simply refer you to tax preparers who send them clients.
- ✓ **Associations.** Both enrolled agents (EAs) and certified public accountants (CPAs) maintain professional associations that can refer you to members in your local area. You can find more information on how to contact a tax professional in the following sections.

Ten interview questions for tax advisors

If you think that your tax situation requires outside help, make sure that you ask the right questions to find a competent tax practitioner whose skills match your tax needs. We recommend that you start with the questions discussed in the following sections.

What tax services do you offer?

Most tax advisors prepare tax returns. We use the term tax *advisors* because most tax folks do more than simply prepare returns. Many advisors can help you plan and file other important tax documents throughout the year. Some firms can also assist your small business with bookkeeping and other financial reporting, such as income statements and balance sheets. These services can be helpful if your business is in the market for a loan, or if you need to give clients or investors detailed information about your business.

Ask any potential tax advisors to explain how they work with clients. You're hiring the tax advisor because you lack knowledge of the tax system. If your tax advisor doesn't prod and explore your situation, you may be walking into a situation where "the blind are leading the blind." A good tax advisor can help you make sure that you aren't overlooking deductions or making other costly mistakes that may lead to an audit, penalties, and interest. Beware of tax preparers who view their jobs as simply plugging into tax forms the information that you bring them.

Do you have areas that you focus on?

This question is important. For example, if a tax preparer works mainly with people who receive regular paychecks from an employer, that tax preparer probably has little expertise in helping small-business owners best complete the blizzard of paperwork that the IRS requires.

Find out what expertise the tax advisor has in handling whatever unusual financial events you're dealing with this year — or whatever events you expect in future years. For example, if you need help completing an estate tax return for a deceased relative, ask how many of these types of returns the tax preparer has completed in the past year. Nearly one out of every seven estate tax returns is audited, so you don't want a novice preparing one for you.

What other services do you offer?

Ideally, you want to work with a professional who is 100 percent focused on taxes. We know that it's difficult to imagine that some people eat, sleep, and breathe this stuff, but they do — and lucky for you!

A multitude of problems and conflicts of interest crop up when a person tries to prepare tax returns, sell investments, and appraise real estate — all at the same time. That advisor may not be fully competent or current in any of these areas.

By virtue of their background and training, some tax preparers also offer consulting and financial planning services for business owners and other individuals. Because he or she already knows a great deal about your personal and tax situation, a competent tax professional may be able to help in these areas. Just make sure that this help is charged on an hourly consulting basis. Avoid tax advisors who sell financial products that pay them a commission — this situation inevitably creates conflicts of interest.

Who will prepare my return?

If you're talking to a solo practitioner, the answer to this question should be simple — the person you're talking to should prepare your return. But if your tax advisor has assistants and other employees, make sure that you know what level of involvement these different people will have in the preparation of your return.

It isn't necessarily bad if a junior-level person does the preliminary tax return preparation that your tax advisor will review and complete. In fact, this procedure can save you money in tax-preparation fees if the firm bills you at a lower hourly rate for a junior-level person. Be wary of firms that charge you a high hourly rate for a senior tax advisor who then delegates most of the work to a junior-level person.

How aggressive or conservative are you regarding the tax law?

Some tax preparers, unfortunately, view their role as enforcement agents for the IRS. This attitude is often a consequence of one too many seminars put on by local IRS folks, who admonish (and sometimes intimidate) preparers with threats of audits.

On the other hand, some preparers are too aggressive and try tax maneuvers that put their clients on thin ice — subjecting them to additional taxes, penalties, interest, and audits.

Assessing how aggressive a tax preparer is can be difficult. Start by asking what percentage of the tax preparer's clients get audited (see the next question). You can also ask the tax advisor for references from clients for whom the advisor helped unearth those overlooked opportunities to reduce tax bills.

What's your experience with audits?

As a benchmark, you should know that about 1 percent of all taxpayer returns get audited. If the tax advisor works with a more affluent client base or small-business owners, expect a higher audit rate — somewhere in the neighborhood of 2 to 4 percent.

If the tax preparer proudly claims no audited clients, be wary. Among the possible explanations, any of which should cause you to be uncomfortable in hiring such a preparer: He isn't telling you the truth, has prepared few returns, or is ultraconservative (so you probably will overpay your taxes because he's afraid of taking some legal deductions).

A tax preparer who has been in business at least a couple of years will have gone through audits. Ask the preparer to explain his last two audits, what happened and why. This explanation can shed light not only on a preparer's work with clients, but also on a preparer's ability to communicate in plain English.

How does your fee structure work?

Tax advisor fees, like attorney and financial planner fees, vary all over the map — from $50 to $300 or more per hour. Many preparers simply quote you a total fee for preparation of your tax return.

Ultimately, the tax advisor charges you for time, so you should ask what the hourly billing rate is. If the advisor balks at answering this question, try asking what her fee is for a one-hour consultation. You may want a tax advisor to work on this basis if you've prepared your return yourself and want it reviewed as a quality-control check. You also may seek an hourly fee if you're on top of your tax preparation in general but have some very specific questions about an unusual or one-time event, such as the sale of your business.

Clarify whether the preparer's set fee includes follow-up questions that you may have during the year, or if this fee covers IRS audits on the return. Some accountants include these functions in their set fee, but others charge for everything on an as-needed basis. The advantage of the all-inclusive fee is that it removes the psychological obstacle of your feeling that the *meter's running* every time you call with a question. The drawback can be that you pay for additional services (time) that you may not need or use.

What qualifies you to be a tax advisor?

Tax advisors come with a variety of backgrounds. The more tax and business experience they have, the better. But don't be overly impressed with credentials. As discussed earlier in this chapter, tax advisors can earn certifications such as CPAs and EAs. Although gaining credentials takes time and work, these certifications are no guarantee that you get high-quality tax assistance or that you won't be overcharged.

Generally speaking, more years of experience are better than less, but don't rule out a newer advisor who lacks gray hair or a logbook full of hours spent slogging through thousands of returns. Intelligence and training can easily make up for less experience.

Newer advisors also may charge less in order to build up their practices. Be sure, though, that you don't just focus on each preparer's hourly rate. Also ask each practitioner you interview how much total time he or she expects your tax return to take. Someone with a lower hourly fee could end up costing you more if he or she is slower than a more experienced and efficient preparer who has a higher hourly rate.

Warning signs that you hired an incompetent tax preparer

- He got kicked out of a major accounting firm for not filing his tax return.

- He's rarely in his office when you call because his client's returns are always being audited.

- You find a trail of your tax receipts leading from his car to his office.

- He scoffs at people who organize their tax records as "anal retentive."

- He's the co-author of *The Leona Helmsley Guide to Tax Reduction.*

- He wants to complete your tax return on a postcard even though the Flat Tax is still just an idea.

- He encourages you to deduct the cost of your trips to visit your in-laws and to write off "laughing at their jokes" as a charitable contribution.

- He thinks Quicken is a chocolate drink.

(Of course, the "he" could be a "she." All sorts of folks are tax preparers, and there's no gender-hold on incompetence.)

Do you carry liability insurance?

If a tax advisor makes a major mistake or gives poor advice, you could lose thousands of dollars. The greater your income, assets, and the importance of your financial decisions, the more financial harm can be done. We know that you aren't a litigious person, but your tax advisor should carry goof-up insurance, sometimes known as *errors and omissions,* or *liability* insurance. You could, of course, simply sue an uninsured advisor and hope the advisor has enough personal assets to cover a loss, but don't count on it. Besides, you'll have a much more difficult time getting your due compensation that way!

You may also ask the advisor whether he or she has ever been sued and the result. It doesn't occur to most people to ask this type of question, so make sure that you tell your tax advisor that you're *not* out to strike it rich on a lawsuit! You may discover that a tax advisor has gotten into hot water by checking with the appropriate professional organization to which that preparer may belong. You can also check whether any complaints have been filed with your local Better Business Bureau.

Can you provide references of clients similar to me?

You need to know that the tax advisor has handled cases and problems like yours. For example, if you're a small-business owner, ask to speak with other small-business owners. But, don't be overly impressed by tax advisors who claim that they work mainly with one occupational group, such as physicians. Although there is value in understanding the nuances of a profession, tax advisors are ultimately generalists — as are the tax laws.

When all is said and done, make sure that you feel comfortable with the tax advisor. We're not suggesting that you evaluate an advisor the way you would a potential friend or spouse! But if you're feeling uneasy and can't understand what your tax advisor says to you in the early stages of your relationship, trust your instincts and continue your search. Remember that you can be your own best tax advisor — finding out the basics will pay you a lifetime of dividends and can save you tens of thousands of dollars in taxes and tax advisor fees!

Chapter 3
Getting and Staying Organized

Do you want to make your tax preparation easier? Keep good records.

Do you want to make sure you can claim every deduction you're entitled to? Keep good records.

Do you want to survive an IRS audit and not pay additional tax, interest, and penalties? Keep good records.

Do you want to save money by not paying tax preparers $50 to $200 an hour to organize your stuff? Keep good records.

If you're like most people, you probably aren't a very good bookkeeper. But without good records, you could be in trouble, especially if you're ever audited. Furthermore, some tax preparers and accountants love to see people walk into their offices with shoeboxes full of receipts. They charge you a hefty hourly fee and then turn around and pay someone else $20 an hour to organize your receipts.

You may realize when you sit down to complete your tax return that you're going to have to rummage through a box of paper scraps containing not only your important tax records, but also cool things like your homework assignments from seventh grade and your 1986 holiday shopping list.

Or this may be the year you know you can itemize deductions on Schedule A and save those big bucks — if only you could remember where you stashed your medical bills and the receipts from your favorite charity.

Finally, perhaps you can easily imagine yourself the night before an IRS audit wondering how you're going to support your claim for all those business entertainment costs. Do you know what happens if you're audited and can't document your claims? First, you'll owe additional tax and interest. Then come the penalties, and the IRS has a lengthy list of them.

But enough horror stories! You know that you must take some steps now to avoid the misery associated with not keeping good records. It may be too late for you this time around, but it's never too late to establish good habits for next time. In this chapter, you discover a few tried and proven ways to keep track of everything you need to survive not only this tax preparation season, but future tax situations as well.

To deal effectively with the IRS, you need documentation because the tax laws place the burden of proof primarily on the taxpayer. (Do you think this policy means that you're guilty until proven innocent? Unfortunately, the answer is *yes*.) But don't let that depress you. Remember, documentation is required only if you are audited. Even if you're not being audited, you should still organize your records now; but if you are audited and lack the tax records you need to support your case, don't throw in the towel. This chapter also shows you how to overcome such a problem — just in case you failed Recordkeeping 101.

As a result of the IRS horror stories broadcast on TV, Congress shifted the burden of proof when taxpayers and the IRS end up in court. But don't get too excited over this provision. The fine print is murder. You still have to present credible evidence and be cooperative (Boy Scouts to the head of the line), and the provision only applies to tax audits that began after July 22, 1998. Remember, too, that few cases go to court. The Taxpayer Bill of Rights in Chapter 19 explains the fine print.

Keeping Good Records

Tax records pose a problem for many people because the IRS doesn't require any particular form of recordkeeping. In fact, the IRS recommends, in general terms, only that you keep records in order to file a "complete and accurate" return. Need a bit more detail? Read on.

Ensuring a complete and accurate tax return

"Hey, my return *is* complete and accurate," you say. "All the numbers are within the lines and neatly written without any math errors." In case you don't feel like flipping through countless pages of government instructions on what constitutes a "complete and accurate" return, we thought you'd like to see at a glance several common problem areas and the types of records normally required.

- ✓ **Charitable contributions:** No longer will a canceled check alone be sufficient to support this deduction. If your donation is valued at $250 or more, you now need a written receipt from the charity indicating the amount of money you gave or a description of the property you donated. Technically, you have to have those receipts by the time you file your return. (See "Lines 15–18: Gifts to Charity" in Chapter 9 for more information.)

- ✓ **Dependent care expenses:** If you plan to claim someone as a dependent, you need to be able to prove, if you're audited, that you provided more than 50 percent of that person's total support. This case applies especially to college students and children of divorced parents. The length of time you provide the support doesn't mean anything — it's the total cost that matters. So be ready to show how much you paid for your dependent's lodging, food, clothes, health care, transportation, and any other essential support stuff. (See Chapter 4 for the rules for claiming dependents.)

- ✓ **Car expenses:** If, for the business use of your car, you choose to deduct the actual expenses instead of the standard mileage rate (which is 32.5 cents per mile for 1998), you need to be able to show the cost of the car and when you started using the car for business. You also must record your business miles, your total miles, and your expenses, such as insurance, gas, and maintenance — you'll need a combination of a log and written receipts, of course! (See "Line 10: Car and truck expenses" in Chapter 11.)

- ✓ **Home expenses:** Besides the records of your purchase price and purchase expenses, save all the receipts and records of improvements and additions that affect the value of your residence (see Chapter 24). House sales are also discussed in Chapter 6.

✔ **Business expenses:** The IRS is especially watchful in this area, so be sure to provide detailed proof of any expenses that you claim. This proof can consist of many items, such as receipts of income, expense account statements, and so on. Remember that canceled checks alone won't always be accepted as substantiation, so make sure that you hang on to the bill or receipt for every expense you incur (see Chapter 11 if you're self-employed, and "Lines 20–26: Job Expenses and Most Other Miscellaneous Deductions" in Chapter 9 if you're an employee).

Setting up a record-keeping system

The tax year is a long time to keep track of what records you'll need (and where you put them) when the filing season arrives. So here are some easy things you can do to make your tax-preparation burden a little lighter:

✔ Invest in an accordion file. You can buy one with slots that are already labeled by month, by category, or by letters of the alphabet, or you can make your own filing system with the extra labels — all this can be yours for less than $10.

✔ If $10 is too much, you can purchase a dozen or so of those manila file folders for about $3 (or less). Decide on the organization that best fits your needs, and get into the habit of saving all bills, receipts, and records that you think you can use someday for your tax purposes, as well as things that affect your overall financial planning. This basic advice is good for any taxpayer, whether you file a simple tax return on Form 1040EZ or a complicated Form 1040 with lots of supplemental schedules. Remember that this is only a minimal plan, but it's much better than the shoebox approach to recordkeeping.

✔ If your financial life is uncomplicated, then each new year, set up one file folder that has the year on it (so in January 1999 you establish your "1999" file). During the year, as you receive documentation that you think you'll use in preparing your return, stash it in the folder. In January 2000, when you receive your dreaded Form 1040 booklet, toss that in the file, too. Come springtime 2000, when you finally force yourself to sit down and work on your return, you should have everything you need in this one bulging file.

✔ If you're a 1040 user and a real perfectionist, you can arrange your records in a file according to the schedules and forms on which they'll be reported. For example, you can set up folders such as these:

   • **Schedule A:** Deductible items (such as mortgage interest, property taxes, charitable contributions, and job-related expenses)

   • **Schedule B:** Interest and dividend income stuff

   • **Schedule D:** Documents related to buying, selling, and improving your home, and the sale and purchase of investments such as stocks and bonds

You 1040 filers have so many options that you really should take the time to learn about your return — we'll help you there — so that you can anticipate your future tax needs.

Tracking tax information on your computer

A number of financial software packages may be able to help you with tracking your spending for tax purposes. Just don't expect to get the benefits without a fair amount of up-front and continuing work. You need to learn how to use the software, and you need to enter a great deal of data in order for it to be useful to you come tax time.

If you're interested in software, consider personal finance packages such as Quicken (from Intuit) or Microsoft Money. With these packages, you can keep track of your stock portfolio, pay your bills, balance your checking account, and best of all, get help with tabulating your tax information. Just remember that the package tabulates only what you enter. So if you use the software to write your monthly checks but neglect to enter data for things you pay for with cash, for example, you won't have the whole picture.

Deciding when to stash and when to trash

One of the most frequently asked questions is how long a taxpayer should keep tax records. The answer is easy — a minimum of three years. That's because there's a three-year statute of limitations on tax audits and assessments. If the IRS doesn't adjust or audit your 1995 tax return by April 15, 1999, it has missed its chance. On April 16, 1999, you can start disposing of your 1995 records if you want — and celebrate because you've gone another year without an audit! (If you filed an extension, you must wait until three years after the extension due date rather than the tax date of April 15. Same thing if you filed late — the three-year period doesn't start until you file your return.)

We should add one point to the general three-year rule, however: Save all the records for those assets you continue to own. These records could include purchase slips for stocks and bonds, automobiles, the purchase of your home (along with its improvements), and expensive personal property, such as jewelry, video cameras, or computers. Keep these records in a safe-deposit box in case you suffer a deductible casualty loss, such as a fire. You don't want these records going up in smoke! Some taxpayers have taken the practical measure of videotaping their home and its contents (make sure to keep that record outside your home as well). You can save money on safe-deposit box fees by leaving your video with relatives who may enjoy watching the video because they don't see you often enough. (Of course, your relatives may also suffer a fire or an earthquake.)

In situations where the IRS suspects that income was not reported, IRS agents can go back as far as six years. And if possible tax fraud is involved, forget all time restraints!

Reconstructing Missing Tax Records

The inscription above the entrance to the national office of the Internal Revenue Service reads:

> *Taxes are what we pay for civilized society.*

But any taxpayer who has ever had a tax return examined would probably enjoy a little less civilization.

Our experience has shown that the number-one reason taxpayers must cough up additional tax when they get audited is lousy recordkeeping. They don't get themselves into this situation by fabricating deductions. Rather, because most taxpayers aren't very good bookkeepers, they fail to produce the records that properly substantiate the deductions they claim.

When taxpayers misplace tax records or simply don't save the tax records they need in order to claim the deductions allowed under the law, all is not lost. Other ways exist to get the evidence that will establish what was actually spent — but obtaining the necessary evidence may prove time consuming. However, when you consider the other option — paying additional tax, interest, and penalties on disallowed deductions from an audit where you couldn't prove what you spent — your time and energy expended will be amply rewarded. What follows are some ways to reconstruct lost or forgotten records. (You may also want to look at Chapters 16 and 17, which tell you how to fight back against an IRS audit when it comes to tax records.)

WARNING!

Watch out for state differences

Although the IRS requires only that you keep your records for three years, your state may have a longer statute of limitations with regard to state income tax audits. Some of your tax-related records may also be important to keep for other reasons. For example, suppose that you throw out your receipts after three years. Then the fellow who built your garage four years ago sues you, asserting that you didn't fully pay the bill. You may be out of luck in court if you don't have the canceled check showing that you paid.

The moral is to hang onto records that may be important (such as home improvement receipts) for longer than three years — especially if a dispute is possible. Check with a legal advisor if you have a concern, because statutes of limitations vary from state to state.

Property received by inheritance or gift

The starting point for determining whether you made or lost money on a sale of a property is the property's *tax basis*. (Remember, to the IRS, property is more than just real estate; it also includes items such as stocks, bonds, cars, boats, and computers.) Tax basis is an IRS term for cost. Your basis is usually what you paid for something.

However, the rule for determining tax basis for property you inherited or received as a gift is different. Because you don't know the cost of the inheritance or gift, the tax basis for determining the taxable gain or loss of property you inherited is the fair market value of the property on the date of the title holder's death. For property received by gift, the tax basis is the donor's cost. But in some instances, the tax basis could also be the fair market value on the date you received the gift. For example, if your father left you 100 shares of General Motors that were worth $10,000 when he died, the $10,000 is your cost for tax purposes. If he gave you the shares before he died, however, and the shares cost him $5,000, then $5,000 is your tax basis. (See Chapter 12 for more about determining tax basis in order to figure out if you have a taxable profit or deductible loss.)

A rather simple rule exists — at least in theory. IRS instructions state that when a taxpayer sells a property received by inheritance or gift, the taxpayer should use the values as stated in the decedent's **Form 706, Estate Tax Return,** or in the donor's **Form 709, Gift Tax Return** — if you're required to use the gift's value on the date of the gift; usually, it's the value on the date the donor acquired it. The only problem is that these tax returns may no longer be available or may no longer exist when you need them, especially when someone sells an asset that they inherited many years earlier.

TIP

When you inherit something, don't automatically assume that its fair market value as reported on the estate tax return is correct. This is especially true of real estate and art. The IRS constantly challenges the value placed on an item for estate tax purposes and so can you.

Establishing the value of real estate (farm or residence) received by inheritance, when original tax records aren't available, is not as formidable a task as it may first appear. Taxpayers can use four methods to compute their tax basis. These methods include the use of newspaper ads, local real estate board and broker records, the assessed value of the property, and the Consumer Price Index (CPI). You know what they mean by CPI: What cost $10 last month costs $50 this month. Seriously, it probably costs $10.02, and the CPI is an official government measure that tells how much prices increase over time.

Researching newspaper ads

If the property value you're trying to determine is for property acquired by gift, the deed tells you when the donor acquired the property. If the property was inherited, it's the date-of-death value that you have to determine. With this plan in hand, you're ready to proceed.

Start at your local library or your local newspaper to obtain a copy of the newspaper printed on the date for which you're trying to establish the value. The classified ads in the real estate section should reveal the price of similar property offered at the time. Back issues often are kept on microfilm, so it shouldn't be too difficult to go back or forward six months or so, in case you come up blank for a particular date.

If a piece of real estate exactly like yours wasn't offered for sale at that time, you may have to find an ad for one as close as possible in description and just estimate the price. For example, suppose that you are trying to figure out how much Uncle Jesse's farm was worth when he left it to you in 1970. You now want to sell the 100-acre farm and are searching for its 1970 value. You check out some 1970 ads from *The Daily Bugle* and find the following information:

- ✔ An ad showing a house and 50 acres for $75,000
- ✔ An ad showing a house and 60 acres for $85,000

Because the farm with ten more acres was selling for $10,000 more, assume that an acre was worth around $1,000. The IRS will find your assumption reasonable. Therefore, Uncle Jesse's farm has 40 more acres than the one selling for $85,000, so you can figure that the value of the farm in 1970 was $125,000 ($85,000 + $40,000).

The IRS won't simply accept your statement that you looked up this information. Remember, all IRS agents act as if they come from Missouri (the "Show Me" state — in case you were absent from school the day your fifth grade teacher lectured on state mottoes). If you go to all the trouble to visit the library, make sure you come away with a photocopy of the paper's real estate section. The IRS requires documentation, especially if you're using an alternative method to establish what something is worth.

Consulting local real estate board and broker records

If your trip to the library or local newspaper office comes up short, try the local real estate board or a real estate broker (one may owe you a favor or want to hustle for your business). Individual brokers or local real estate boards usually keep historical data on property sold in their area. Again, you may have to estimate selling prices if you don't find a property exactly like yours.

Obtaining assessed values

The assessed-value method may uncover the most accurate estimate of a property's value. Because property taxes are collected on the basis of assessed values, try to obtain the assessed value on the date you're interested in. With this information, along with the percentage of the fair market value that the tax assessor used in determining assessed values, divide that percentage into the assessed value to come up with the market value.

You can obtain assessed values for property (and the percentage of the fair market value of property assessed in its vicinity) from the office of the receiver or collector of property taxes, usually found in the courthouse of the county where the property is located. Don't forget to get a copy of this information. For example, if the assessed value was $2,700 and the percentage of the fair market value at which the property was assessed was 30 percent, the fair market value would have been $9,000 ($2,700 ÷ 30 percent).

Using the Consumer Price Index

It's not three strikes and you're out. When all else fails, use the Consumer Price Index (CPI) method. Because you already know the amount for which you sold the property, another trip or call to the library will enable you to determine the increase in the

Consumer Price Index between the acquisition date and the sale date. For example, say you sold a tract of land for $300,000. If the CPI went up three times since you inherited it, your tax basis would be $100,000.

Determining the property's acquisition date depends on *how* you acquired it. If you inherited the property, the acquisition date is the date of the previous owner's death. If the property was a gift, the acquisition date is the date the property was originally purchased by the person who gave you the gift.

If your local library doesn't have the CPI data you need, you can obtain it by writing to the U.S. Department of Labor, 200 Constitution Avenue, N.W., Washington, D.C. 20210. This information is also available on the Internet at the Consumer Price Index home page (stats.bls.gov/cpihome.htm).

Securities received by inheritance or gift

Establishing the price of a stock or a bond on a particular date is much easier than coming up with the value of other property, especially if the stock or bond is traded on a major securities exchange.

When you receive a stock or bond by inheritance, your tax basis is usually the value of the stock or bond on the deceased's date of death. Sometimes an estate — to save taxes — uses a valuation date that is six months after the date of death. If you receive the security as a gift, you often have the added task of establishing the date when the donor acquired the security, because you normally must use the value on that date (including any commission expense). Not to confuse you, but sometimes you have to use the value on the date you received the gift. All this is explained in Chapter 12. You can write to the transfer agent in order to find out this information. The *transfer agent* is the company that keeps track of the shares of stock that a company issues. Your stockbroker can tell you how to locate the transfer agent, or you can consult the *Value Line Investment Survey* in your local library.

After you determine the acquisition date, either the back issue of a newspaper or a securities pricing service can provide the value on any particular day for a certain security. A back issue of a newspaper doesn't reveal, however, if any stock dividends or splits (which affect the share price) have occurred since the acquisition date. A good pricing service can provide this information.

One service that we recommend in order to obtain the value of stocks and bonds (plus any stock splits or stock dividends) is Prudential-American Securities, Inc., 921 East Green Street, Pasadena, CA 91106 (818-795-5831). This company charges a small fee, typically a couple of bucks for a stock quote.

Also, consider checking with the investment firm where the securities were (or are still) held — the firm may be able to research this information as well, maybe even for free.

Improvements to a residence

How many homeowners save any of the records regarding improvements that they make, even if those expenditures are substantial? Not nearly enough. Why? Because improvements to a home quite often are made over a 30- to 40-year span, and it's a lot to ask people to save records for that many years. For example, landscaping expenditures — one tree or bush at a time — can really add up.

For married couples filing jointly, a profit of up to $500,000 on the sale of a principal residence after May 6, 1997, is completely exempt from tax. For singles, it's $250,000. (See Chapter 12 for details.)

Although the 1997 law eliminated the fiendish recordkeeping requirements for sales of $500,000 or less if married and $250,000 for singles, for sales above these amounts you still need records to prove, for example, that you didn't make more than $500,000. And if you buy a house today, say for $350,000, you don't know what the sales price will be in 10, 20, 30, or more years when you finally sell. Here's hoping it's $1 million. So, tax records are still important.

Before you estimate how much you spent on residential improvements, you first have to determine what improvements you spent the money on. This step is necessary because if you can't document the amount spent, you at least can establish that an improvement was made. Your family photo album (which may contain before and after pictures) is probably the best source for obtaining such information.

Obtaining a Certificate of Occupancy

If you can't get a receipt from the contractor who made the improvement to your home, hike down to the county clerk's office to obtain a copy of the Certificate of Occupancy (the house's birth certificate, so to speak), which shows what your house consisted of when it was built. Records at the county clerk's office also reveal any changes in the house's assessed value as the result of improvements that you made, along with building permits that were issued. Any of these documents will clearly establish whether improvements were made (assuming, of course, that you *did* obtain the proper permits for these improvements).

Getting an estimate

When original invoices, duplicate invoices, or canceled checks aren't available, obtain an estimate of what the improvement would cost now, and then back out the increase in the Consumer Price Index (as explained earlier in this chapter). This procedure may establish a reasonable estimate of what the improvement originally cost.

Casualty losses

A casualty loss is probably the most difficult deduction to establish. Few people consistently save receipts on the purchase of personal items, such as jewelry, clothing, furniture, and so on. If the casualty loss occurred because of a fire or hurricane, any receipts that you may have had were probably destroyed along with your property. Although a police, fire, or insurance company report establishes that a casualty loss was sustained, how do you establish the cost of what was stolen or destroyed? The answer: with a little bit of luck and hard work.

For example, the value of an expensive necklace that was stolen was once established by using a photograph that showed the taxpayer wearing the necklace. The taxpayer then obtained an appraisal from a jeweler of the cost of a similar necklace. Because jewelry is a popular gift, receipts sometimes don't exist.

Although you can prove to the IRS that you have enough money to afford the lost or stolen item, the IRS also needs proof that you had the item in your possession. For example, suppose that your $10,000 Rolex watch is stolen (we feel for you). In order to make the IRS folks happy, you have to prove two things:

- That you could afford the Rolex; your total income from your tax return will prove that.

- That you had the Rolex; a statement from a friend, a relative, or an acquaintance establishes that you actually owned the item. If the Rolex was a gift, a statement from the giver also would help.

Effective August 5, 1997, an appraisal used to obtain a disaster loan from the Federal Emergency Management Agency (FEMA) can be used as evidence for tax purposes to claim a casualty loss.

Business records

If business records have been lost or destroyed, you can often obtain duplicate bills from major vendors. You shouldn't have a great deal of trouble getting copies of the original telephone, utility, rent, credit card, oil company, and other bills. A reasonable determination of business use of an automobile can be made by reconstructing a typical month of automobile use. If that month's use approximates an average month's business use of an auto, the IRS usually accepts such reconstructed records as adequate substantiation.

Using duplicate bank statements

If all your business income was deposited in a checking or savings account, income can be reconstructed from duplicate bank statements. Although banks usually don't charge for copies of bank statements, they do charge for copies of canceled checks. These charges can be quite expensive — about four to five dollars per check — so do some legwork before ordering copies of all checks. For example, you should obtain a copy of a lease and a statement from the landlord saying that all rent was paid on time before you request duplicate copies of rent checks.

Ordering copies of past returns

By ordering copies of past returns with **Form 4506, Request for Copy or Transcript of Tax Form,** you can have a point of reference for determining whether you have accounted for typical business expenses. Past returns reveal not only gross profit percentages or margins of profit, but also the amounts of recurring expenses.

Requesting Copies of Lost Tax Returns

Last year's tax return is the starting point for filling out this year's tax return. It serves as a guide to make sure you don't forget anything. But what if you lost the return from 1997? Or suppose that you need a return from a previous year but can't find it?

You can request a copy of your previous returns and all attachments (including Form W-2) by using **Form 4506.** Send the completed Form 4506 to the Internal Revenue Service Center where you filed the return. You must pay a $23 charge when you file the form, but there is no charge for asking for a copy of Form W-2 or a transcript of your tax account.

Returns filed six or more years ago may or may not be available for making copies, but tax account information generally is still available for those years.

You also can use Form 4506 to request a tax return transcript that will show most lines from your original return, including the accompanying forms and schedules. A transcript tells you the amount of penalties, interest, and payments made subsequent to the filing; it also tells you if an amended return was filed.

You also can order a transcript by calling the IRS at 800-829-1040. Press selection 2 for "personal tax information." Your tax account transcript for the year in question will arrive in three to five business days.

Understanding the Cohan Rule

Before we end this discussion about undocumented claims, we must tell you about the case of George M. Cohan and the resulting *Cohan Rule*. It's the story of one person's victory over the IRS, and it may inspire you to defend your own rights as a taxpayer. Even if some of the rights that taxpayers earned because of his victory have been eroded over the past years, Cohan's battle for the right to estimate deductions still has repercussions today.

In 1921 and 1922, George M. Cohan deducted $55,000 in business-related entertainment expenses. The IRS refused to allow him any part of these entertainment deductions on the grounds that it was impossible to tell how much Mr. Cohan spent because he didn't have any receipts to support the deductions he claimed.

Later, Mr. Cohan appealed to the Second Circuit Court of Appeals, and the court established the rule of *approximation*. The court instructed the IRS to "make as close an approximation as it can, bearing heavily, if it chooses, upon the taxpayer whose inexactitude is of his own making." (Isn't "inexactitude" a lovely way of saying "no records"?)

For over 30 years, the *Cohan Rule* allowed taxpayers to deduct travel and entertainment expenses without having to substantiate what they spent. Taxpayers only had to establish that it was reasonable for them to have incurred travel and entertainment expenses in the amount that they claimed they spent.

Congress changed the law regarding travel and entertainment expenses in the early 1960s. Since this change, taxpayers no longer can deduct travel or entertainment expenses without adequate substantiation.

The *Cohan Rule* still applies, however, to other expenses whose records are not available. Under the *Cohan Rule,* the Tax Court routinely allows deductions based on estimates for the following deductions:

- ✔ Petty cash and office expenses
- ✔ Delivery and freight charges
- ✔ Tips and business gifts
- ✔ Cleaning and maintenance expenses
- ✔ Small tools and supplies
- ✔ Taxi fares
- ✔ Casualty losses (fire, flood, and theft losses)

For some expenses, it is impractical, if not downright impossible, to obtain receipts for what you spend. Petty cash and tips are just two examples of such expenses.

The *Cohan Rule* doesn't mean that you can stop keeping receipts and simply use estimates. You must have a valid reason for relying on the *Cohan Rule,* such as impracticability or lost or destroyed records. In fact, taxpayers have had penalties assessed against them for not attempting to obtain duplicate records that were lost when they moved, and for periodically destroying all business records immediately upon the filing of their tax returns. One court held that the unexplained loss of corporate records carries a strong presumption that the records would have prejudiced the taxpayer's position.

Chapter 4

No Form Fits All (Or, What Kind of Taxpayer Are You?)

In This Chapter
▶ Understanding the differences between the tax forms
▶ Deciding on a filing status
▶ Walking through joint return issues
▶ Understanding the Innocent Spouse Rule
▶ Calculating personal and dependent exemptions
▶ Getting Social Security numbers for dependents
▶ Filing returns for dependents
▶ Answering the where, when, why, and how filing questions

*Y*ou have to make some key decisions before grabbing those good ol' tax forms and marking them up. Even though you're anxious to begin, read the relevant portions of this chapter first. We explain some important issues you must resolve each tax year before you knuckle down to complete your return.

What Rendition of 1040 Shall We Play?

If you could get across town by taking one bus rather than having to transfer and take two, you'd do it, right? That is, unless you enjoy riding city buses, sightseeing, or wasting time and money by transferring.

Like your transportation options, you have a few choices of tax forms — three to be exact. In order from mind-challenging (read *simplest* in IRS jargon) to mind-numbing (read *complex*), they are Form 1040EZ, Form 1040A, and Form 1040.

The simpler forms are easier to finish because they have fewer lines to complete and far fewer instructions to read. Having to read additional IRS instructions is like having to diagram sentence structures from a Faulkner novel.

The simpler forms save you time and maybe a headache or two, but — and this is an important b-u-t — the simpler forms offer you far fewer opportunities and options to take deductions to which you may be entitled. Thus, in a rush to save yourself a little work and time, you could cost yourself hundreds, maybe thousands, in additional tax dollars.

Form 1040EZ

Here's the low-down on this *EZ-est* of tax forms. (They actually test-marketed this form before they started using it — very much like Procter & Gamble does before they try something new, like purple-colored Crest. Unfortunately, the IRS has a bit of an advantage over Procter & Gamble — if you don't like the forms, you can't switch to Brand X.)

The easiest form to fill out and file is the 1040EZ. All you need to do is insert your name, address, occupation, Social Security number, wages, unemployment compensation, and taxable interest. Your refund can be deposited directly in your bank account. To find out whether you should use this form, see "Who Can File a 1040EZ?" in Chapter 5. Form 1040EZ is a breeze. You don't have to make any computations if you don't want to. Just plug in the numbers and skip the math, if you'd like. If you owe, the IRS bills you. And if you're due a refund, the IRS sends you a check. How EZ! (Just don't forget to attach your W-2s.)

Form 1040A

For those of you who are several rungs up the economic ladder, congratulations! You have just graduated from Form 1040EZ. Your reward is Form 1040A. But there's something you need to know: The best way to be certain that you should use Form 1040A is to review Form 1040 before you reach for Form 1040A. Check to make sure there isn't any deduction or tax credit you could use on Form 1040. To find out whether you qualify for Form 1040A, see "Who Can File a 1040A?" in Chapter 5.

Form 1040 (the long form)

Because Forms 1040A and 1040EZ are easier to complete than Form 1040, you should use one of them unless Form 1040 allows you to pay less tax. But if you don't qualify for filing Form 1040A or 1040EZ, you must use Form 1040.

This is the form that everybody loves to hate. *The Wall Street Journal* believes that the form was invented by tax professionals — the newspaper's editors even refer to our tax laws as the "Accountants and Lawyers Full Employment Act." We think that complicated tax laws should be called the "IRS Guaranteed Lifetime Employment Act."

If you itemize your deductions, claim a host of tax credits, own rental property, are self-employed, or sell a stock or bond, you're stuck — welcome to the world of the 1040.

If you have the option of using or not using the 1040, a quick review of Schedule A (see Chapter 9) will help you find out whether it's worth your while to itemize.

If you're depressed because you have to use the simpler forms for your 1998 return and you want to be able to deduct more and have more favorable adjustments to your income in the future, all is not lost. At a minimum, you can make things better for 1999 by planning ahead. (Be sure to read Part V.) You may be able to do some last-minute maneuvering before you file your 1998 return. We direct you to these maneuvers as we walk you through the line-by-line completion of your return.

Can I itemize? Should I itemize? And what the heck are itemized deductions?

Deductions are just that: You subtract them from your income before you calculate the tax you owe. (Deductions are good things!) To make things more complicated, the IRS gives you two methods for determining the total of your deductions: itemized and standardized deductions. The good news is that you get to pick the method that leads to the best solution for you — whichever way offers greater deductions. If you can itemize, you should, because it saves you tax dollars. The bad news is that if you choose to itemize your deductions, you must use Form 1040.

The first method — taking the standard deduction — requires no thinking or calculations. If you have a relatively uncomplicated financial life, taking the standard deduction is generally the better option. Symptoms of a simple tax life are: not earning a high income, renting your house or apartment, and lacking unusually large expenses, such as medical bills or loss due to theft or catastrophe. Single folks qualify for a $4,250 standard deduction, and married couples filing jointly get a $7,100 standard deduction in 1998. If you're age 65 or older or blind, your standard deduction is increased by $1,050 if single, and by $850 if married.

Some deductions — moving expenses, the penalty for early withdrawal from savings, and so on — are available even if you don't itemize your deductions. The bad news: You have to file Form 1040 to claim them.

The other method of determining the total of your allowable deductions is itemizing them on your tax return. This method is definitely more of a hassle, but if you can tally up more than the standard deduction amounts, itemizing saves you money. Use Schedule A of IRS Form 1040 to total your itemized deductions.

See Chapter 9 for more about using Schedule A to itemize deductions.

Choosing a Filing Status

When filing your return, you must choose the appropriate filing status from the five filing statuses available for 1040A and 1040 users. (Users of Form 1040EZ must file as *single* or as *married filing jointly,* with no dependents.) You select a status by checking the appropriate box directly below your name on page 1 of Form 1040:

- ✔ Single
- ✔ Married filing jointly
- ✔ Married filing separately
- ✔ Head of household
- ✔ Qualifying widow(er) with dependent child

Each filing status has its own tax rates. As a general rule, you pay the lowest tax by filing jointly or as a qualifying widow(er), and then comes head of household and single. Those who are married filing separately pay tax at the highest rate. However, like every rule, a few circumstances exist in which married filing separately saves couples money, as explained later in this section.

Single

Most people who aren't married file as *single.* The IRS doesn't recognize couples living together, regardless of sexual orientation, as being married for filing purposes.

However, if you were widowed, divorced, or legally separated by the end of the tax year (December 31, 1998) and provided support to dependents, such as children or an elderly parent, you may be able to save yourself some tax dollars by filing as *head of household* or as a *qualifying widow(er)*. You can find out more in the upcoming section, "Head of household."

Married filing jointly

If you're married, you probably share many things with your spouse. One of the more treasured tasks you get to share is the preparation of your annual tax return. In fact, this may be the one time during the year that you jointly examine and combine your financial information. Let the fireworks begin!

For your 1998 return, you're considered married if you got married by or were still married as of the end of the tax year — December 31, 1998. In some rare instances, married folks can save money by filing their taxes as *married filing separately.* This somewhat oddball status can be useful for couples who have large differences between their two incomes and can claim more itemizable deductions by filing separately. See the section "Married filing separately," later in this chapter, to determine whether you can save money by filing separately.

If you file a joint return for 1998, you may not, after the due date for filing, amend that return to change to a married filing separately filing status. You're "jointly" stuck!

You can file jointly if you meet any of the following criteria:

- You were married as of December 31, 1998, even if you did not live with your spouse at the end of the year.
- Your spouse died in 1998, and you did not remarry in 1998.

  If your spouse died during the year, you're considered married for the entire year, providing you didn't remarry. You report all your income for the year and your spouse's income up to the date of his or her death.
- Your spouse died in 1999 before you filed a 1998 return.

You and your spouse may file jointly even if only one of you had income or if you didn't live together all year. However, you both must sign the return, and you're both responsible for seeing that all taxes are paid. This means that if your spouse doesn't pay the tax due, you may have to.

The Innocent Spouse Rule (explained later in this chapter) can, in some instances, relieve a spouse who was unaware of his or her spouse's shenanigans from sharing joint responsibility for what is owed.

A couple legally separated under a divorce decree may not file jointly. On the other hand, if one spouse lived away from the home during the entire last six months of the tax year (July 1, 1998, through December 31, 1998), the remaining spouse, if taking care of dependents, may be able to file under the more favorable head of household status (see "Head of household," later in this chapter).

Although this suggestion is decidedly unromantic, if you're considering a late-in-the-year wedding, especially in December, you may want to consider the tax impact of tying the knot so soon. A considerable number of couples pay higher total taxes when they are married versus when they were single.

Spouses who are nonresident aliens or dual status aliens

If one spouse is a nonresident alien and does not pay U.S. income taxes on all his or her income, regardless of what country or countries in which it is earned, then the couple may not take the married filing jointly tax status.

The same is true if your spouse is a dual status alien — that is, if during the year, your spouse is a nonresident as well as a resident.

You may file jointly if:

✔ You were married as of December 31, 1998, even if you did not live with your spouse at the end of 1998.

✔ If your spouse is a nonresident alien, or if either of you are dual status aliens, you can make a special election to file jointly. IRS Publication 519 *(U.S. Tax Guide For Aliens)* explains how to make this election.

Some couples have been known to postpone their weddings until January and use the tax savings to pay for the cost of their honeymoons! Others choose not to marry, and they cohabitate instead. Although we don't want to criticize or condone such decisions, it is unfortunate that such a high tax cost to getting married exists for a sizable minority of couples (see "The marriage penalty" sidebar, later in this chapter).

Married filing separately

The vast majority of married couples would pay more taxes if they chose to file separate returns. The IRS won't stand in your way of doing this. However, by filing separately, you may be able to avoid the marriage penalty and save on your combined tax bill. To determine whether filing separately is to your benefit, you should figure your tax both ways (married filing jointly and married filing separately).

Besides saving money, another reason you may choose to file separately is to avoid being responsible for your spouse's share of the joint tax bill if you suspect some kind of monkey business (for example, your spouse is underreporting taxable income or inflating deductions).

If you file separately, be aware that the following restrictions may apply:

✔ You can't take the standard deduction if your spouse itemizes deductions. Both spouses must itemize their deductions, or both must claim the standard deduction.

✔ You can't claim the credit for child and dependent care expenses in most cases.

✔ You can't claim a credit for qualified adoption expenses.

✔ You can't take the earned income credit.

✔ You can't exclude from your taxable income the interest you earned from series EE U.S. savings bonds issued after 1989, even if you paid higher education expenses in 1998.

✔ You can't take the credit for being elderly or disabled unless you lived apart from your spouse for all of 1998.

✔ You may have to include up to 50 or 85 percent of any Social Security benefits you received in 1998 as income.

✔ You usually report only your own income, exemptions, deductions, and credits. Different rules apply to people who live in community property states (see "Filing separately in community property states," later in this chapter).

✔ If you actively own and manage real estate, you can't claim the passive loss exception (see "The $25,000 exemption" section in Chapter 13).

✔ You can't claim the new (for 1998) Hope Scholarship and Lifetime Learning credits.

Instead of filing separately, you may be able to file as a head of household if you had a child living with you and you lived apart from your spouse during the last six months of 1998. See the "Head of household" section later in this chapter for more information.

Marriage is a tax issue that can be confounding. Most of the time, you pay lower taxes if you're married, but because of certain vagaries of the tax law and the way our society is shifting toward more two-income families, you can end up paying more tax than two unmarried persons with the same income would.

To see whether you need to escape the marriage penalty, you have to prepare three returns — two separate and one joint. We know it's a time sink, so you may want to spend $50 and spring for a computerized tax program that can do the number crunching for you. (See Chapter 2 for our software recommendations.)

TECHNICAL STUFF

The marriage penalty

Some couples' first year of marriage brings surprises. Others find that the song remains the same. But of all the many things that newlyweds discover about being married, one of the most annoying is the marriage penalty, a tax-law inequity that forces millions of married couples to pay more tax than they would if they were single and living together.

It's a fact of life for millions of married couples: As single taxpayers, their combined taxes are less than when they're married. The tax law changes enacted in 1993 made the marriage penalty even worse because the tax rates were raised for higher-income earners. And many of the tax benefits enacted in 1997 are phased out for higher-income couples.

Couples most likely to be hit with the marriage penalty are two-income-earning households, especially spouses who have similar individual incomes and/or are higher-income earners. Why? Because U.S. tax brackets are graduated, which simply means that you pay a higher tax rate at higher-income levels (see the discussion in Chapter 1). When two people get married, the second person's income is effectively added on top of the first person's income, which can push the couple into higher tax brackets. Not only that, but the couple may also lose some itemized deductions and personal exemptions with a higher combined income level.

Can you do anything about it? In a small number of cases, married couples can cut their tax bills simply by filing separately.

Some people opt for another approach — not marrying, or getting a divorce. By living together as unmarrieds, you and your significant other each pay taxes at the individual rate. We're not advising this course, but it's simply what we hear and see. You should also know that you can't divorce in December just to save on your taxes and then remarry the next year. Taxpayers who have tried this scam in the past have been slapped with penalties in addition to the extra taxes they would have owed if they had stayed away from divorce court.

If you decide not to stay married for the long haul just to save on income taxes, be warned that unmarried couples aren't eligible for any of the significant survivor's Social Security benefits if one partner passes away or splits. A person who doesn't work is particularly vulnerable; if he's married and his spouse passes away or divorces him, the nonworking spouse qualifies for Social Security benefits based on the working partner's income history and Social Security taxes paid. If you aren't married and you don't work, you aren't entitled to Social Security benefits if your partner leaves you.

You should also know that not all couples pay higher taxes. In fact, some couples find that their joint tax bill is less. This situation usually occurs with couples in which one person doesn't earn any income or has a very low income.

Write your Congressperson with your thoughts on this situation. Several bills are on the horizon to eliminate the marriage tax.

Married couples most likely to save tax dollars filing separately are those who meet both of the following criteria:

✔ Couples who have two incomes

✔ Couples who have hefty deductions for medical expenses, miscellaneous itemized deductions, or casualty losses

If you fall under this umbrella, by all means complete the three tax returns to determine which filing status works best for you.

Here's an example to show how those deductions come into play. To figure out your medical deduction, take your medical expenses and subtract 7.5 percent of your adjusted gross income (AGI). For example, if your AGI is $100,000 and you have medical expenses of $10,000, you perform the following calculation: Multiply $100,000 by 7.5 percent ($7,500); then subtract this amount from your $10,000 of medical bills. This leaves you with a $2,500 medical deduction. For miscellaneous deductions, you subtract 2 percent of your income instead of 7.5 percent. And for personal casualty losses, subtract 10 percent of your income.

As Table 4-1 shows, these deductions may be a lot more valuable if you file separately. Say your spouse had a $9,000 casualty loss. If your income is $60,000 and your spouse's is $40,000, none of that $9,000 casualty loss is deductible. The math: $9,000 minus $10,000 ($100,000 × .10) equals –$1,000, which means that you're not entitled to a casualty deduction. But by filing separately, your spouse gets to deduct $5,000, because 10 percent of your spouse's income amounts to only $4,000. For the purpose of this illustration, the $100 nondeductible portion of casualty loss isn't being considered.

Table 4-1	Filing Jointly versus Separately: A Sample Couple		
	Jointly	**Husband**	**Wife**
Gross income	$130,000	$70,000	$60,000
Casualty loss	$10,000	$0	$10,000
Less 10 percent of income	($13,000)	($0)	($6,000)
Deductible casualty loss	$0	$0	$4,000
Medical expenses	$6,500	$500	$6,000
Less 7.5 percent of income	($9,750)	($5,250)	($4,500)
Deductible medical	$0	$0	$1,500
Miscellaneous deductions	$3,000	$1,300	$1,700
Less 2 percent of income	($2,600)	($1,400)	($1,200)
Deductible miscellaneous	$400	$0	$500
Taxes	$5,000	$3,000	$2,000
Mortgage interest	$9,500	$9,500	$0
*3 percent itemized deduction phaseout	($165)	($233)	$0
Total itemized deductions	$14,735	$12,267	$8,000
Personal exemptions	$5,400	$2,700	$2,700
Taxable income	$109,865	$55,033	$49,300
Tax	$25,484	$12,773	$11,051

* *When your income exceeds $124,500 filing jointly, or $62,250 filing separately, your itemized deductions get reduced by 3 percent of the difference between your income and these two amounts ($130,000 – $124,500 = $5,500 x .03 = $165).*

Filing separately in community property states

Community property states are Arizona, California, Idaho, Louisiana, Nevada, New Mexico, Texas, Washington, and Wisconsin. If you and your spouse live in one of these states, you have to follow your state's law in determining what is community income and what is separate income if you want to file separately.

In a community property state, each spouse, as a general rule, must report one-half of the joint income. However, this step isn't necessary if you and your spouse lived apart for the entire year and don't file a joint return. To qualify, at least one of you must have salary, wages, or business income — none of which was transferred between you and your spouse. Child support is not considered a transfer. This is an area where you should either read IRS Publication 555 *(Federal Tax Information on Community Property)* or consult a tax advisor.

Amounts may vary slightly depending on whether you use the tax tables or the rate schedules.

The potential for savings doesn't stop there. If your combined income is $186,800 or more, congratulations! But as a reward for your financial success, a portion of your personal exemptions starts getting whittled away. (Personal exemptions are those $2,700 deductions you get for yourself and each of your dependents.) When one spouse's income is less than half that amount, you may be better off filing separately and piling the personal exemptions onto that person's return, if that spouse is otherwise entitled to the dependency exemption.

It's worth doing the numbers. For example, in Table 4-1, the sample couple saves a total of $1,660 by filing separately. Their combined separate tax bill comes to only $23,824 instead of $25,484.

If you think you could have saved money in a previous year by filing separately, sorry. There's nothing you can do about it now. After you file a joint return, you can't turn back the clock and change it to separate returns. On the other hand, if you and your spouse filed separately, you can (within three years from the due date of your return or two years from the date the tax was paid) file an amended return and switch to filing jointly. You may want to do this if, on audit, some of the deductions you and your spouse claimed were disallowed or if you get an insurance recovery greater than you expected, reducing the amount of the casualty loss. If you're making estimated tax payments during the year, it doesn't matter whether you make joint or separate payments. You can still file your actual return however you wish.

Head of household

You may file as *head of household* if you maintain a home under one of the following conditions:

✔ You paid more than half the cost of keeping up a home (see Table 4-2 to compute that figure) that was the main home during 1998 for a parent whom you can claim as a dependent. Your parent did not have to live with you in your home.

✔ You paid more than half the cost of keeping up a home in which you lived and in which one of the following also lived for more than half of the year (temporary absences, such as for school, vacation, or medical care, count as time lived in your home):

• Your *unmarried* child, adopted child, grandchild, great-grandchild, or stepchild. This child does not have to be your dependent. But you still enter the child's name in the space provided on line 4 of Form 1040A or Form 1040.

- Your *married* child, adopted child, grandchild, great-grandchild, or stepchild. This child must be your dependent. But if the married child's other parent claims him or her as a dependent under the IRS rules for children of divorced or separated parents, this child does not have to be your dependent. Enter this child's name on line 4 of Form 1040A or Form 1040.

- Your *foster* child, who must be your dependent.

- Any of the following relatives that you can claim as a dependent: parents, grandparents, siblings, step-relatives, in-laws, and, if related by blood, your uncle, aunt, nephew, or niece.

  You are related by blood to an uncle or aunt if he or she is the brother or sister of your father or mother. You are related by blood to a nephew or niece if he or she is the child of your brother or sister. If you are just living with someone, that won't cut it.

- One parent may claim head of household if more than 50 percent of the cost of maintaining a house is paid by that parent and the child lives with that parent for more than six months.

✔ You *cannot* file as head of household if your child, parent, or relative described in the preceding list is your dependent under a multiple support agreement.

✔ You are married but you did not live with your spouse. Even if you were not divorced or legally separated in 1998, you may be able to file as head of household if you fulfill all these requirements:

- You have lived apart from your spouse for the last six months of 1998, and you're filing a separate return.

- You paid more than half the cost of keeping up your home in 1998, and your home was the main residence of your child, adopted child, stepchild, or foster child for more than half of the year. Temporary absences, such as for school, vacation, or medical care, are counted as time lived in your home.

- You must claim this child as your dependent (or the other parent claims the child under the rules of children of divorced or separated parents). If this child is not your dependent, be sure to enter the child's name on line 4 of Form 1040A or Form 1040.

If all the preceding factors apply, you may also be able to take the credit for child and dependent care expenses, the earned income credit, and the $400 per child tax credit. You can take the standard deduction even if your spouse itemizes deductions. More details are in Chapters 5 and 6.

In the case of a birth or death of a dependent, you are considered to have provided more than half his or her support, even for someone who was born on December 31 or died on January 1.

Table 4-2	How to Compute the Cost of Maintaining a Household	
	Amount You Paid	**Total Cost**
Property taxes	$_____	$_____
Mortgage interest expense	$_____	$_____
Rent	$_____	$_____
Utility charges	$_____	$_____
Upkeep and repairs	$_____	$_____
Property insurance	$_____	$_____

(continued)

Table 4-2 (continued)

	Amount You Paid	Total Cost
Food consumed on the premises	$_____	$_____
Other household expenses	$_____	$_____
Totals	$(a)_____	(b)_____
(Subtract Total (a) from Total (b) and enter here)		($_____)

Note: If you paid more than half of the total cost, you qualify for head of household status.

Qualifying widow(er) with dependent child

If you meet *all* five of the following tests, you can use the tax table for married filing jointly.

- ✔ Your spouse died in 1996 or 1997, and you did not remarry in 1998.

- ✔ You have a child, stepchild, adopted child, or foster child whom you can claim as a dependent.

- ✔ This child lived in your home for all of 1998. Temporary absences, such as for vacation or school, count as time lived in your home.

- ✔ You paid more than half the cost of keeping up your home for this child.

- ✔ You could have filed a joint return with your spouse the year he or she died, even if you didn't actually do so. (But you can't claim an exemption for your deceased spouse.)

If your spouse died in 1998, you may not file as a qualifying widow(er) with dependent child. But see whether you qualify for filing jointly.

And if you can't file as a qualifying widow(er) with dependent child, see whether you can qualify as a head of household. If you don't meet the rules for a qualifying widow(er) with dependent child, married filing a joint return, or head of household, you must file as a single.

For example, suppose that a mother with children died in 1996 and the husband has not remarried. In 1997 and 1998, he kept up a home for himself and his dependent children. For 1996, he was entitled to file a joint return for himself and his deceased wife. For 1997 and 1998, he may file as a qualifying widow(er) with dependent children. After 1998, he may file as head of household, if he qualifies.

Protecting Yourself with the Innocent Spouse Rule

Many taxpayers not experiencing marital bliss or those in the throes of divorce proceedings continue to file jointly, if doing so cuts their current tax bill. This decision may be short-sighted because of the ramifications of one spouse not paying his or her share of the tax bill. Here's why:

When you file jointly, you are separately and jointly liable for any unpaid tax. Forget the legalese for a second. This means that if your spouse is a deadbeat and doesn't pay any tax owed, you may end up paying more than your fair share of the tax, or maybe all of it.

Under certain circumstances — if you didn't know about any omission of income or inflated deductions, for example — the *innocent spouse rule* may protect you, as we discuss later in this chapter. (Don't count on the innocent spouse rule, though. The IRS may not be so charitable in defining your case.)

Consider the real-life example of a couple who filed a joint tax return in the year they sold their residence. The following year, they divorced. The wife invested her share of the proceeds of the sale in a new home, thereby deferring the tax on her share of the gain, as allowed by law. But her ex-husband squandered his share. Because the proceeds of the sale weren't reinvested in a new home, the couple owed a bundle of tax. Guess who got stuck for it? Need a hint? Let's just say *she* didn't need the extra expense. The new rules regarding the sale of a principal residence greatly reduce the chances of getting stuck like this.

Filing separately, however, isn't entirely a one-way street. Certain tax breaks, such as deductions for losses on real estate that you actively manage, can't be claimed on a separate return if you and your spouse live together. Nor can you take an IRA deduction for a nonworking spouse if you file separately. When filing separately, you can't take the earned income credit or claim a deduction for dependent care unless you and your spouse lived apart for the last six months of the tax year. In addition, you can't claim the new (for 1998) Hope Scholarship or Lifetime Learning credits if you file separately.

There's another drawback to filing separately: You can't use one spouse's losses to offset the other's capital gains. For example, if you have a $6,000 capital gain and your spouse has a $9,000 capital loss, on a joint return you can net the two and claim a $3,000 loss. On separate returns, you are required to report your $6,000 gain, while your spouse can only deduct $1,500 of his or her $9,000 loss. Also keep in mind that by filing separately, half or maybe more of any Social Security payments automatically become taxable. When you file jointly or as a single person, the tax bill on your Social Security is almost always smaller.

To determine each spouse's share of a joint refund, see "You Haven't Received Your Refund" in Chapter 18. This knowledge can really help if things get sticky (maybe even nasty) in a divorce.

Getting innocent spouse relief under the new rules

Under the old rules it was next to impossible to claim *innocent spouse relief*. Although far from perfect, the new law is a vast improvement. Here's how it works: If you filed a joint return and didn't know — and had no reason to know — that your spouse was playing fast and loose with the deductions on your return or wasn't reporting all his or her income, you aren't responsible for any additional interest or penalties when the IRS discovers this.

Although you're responsible for any unpaid tax on the original return, the "didn't know or had no reason to know" rule can get you off the hook for the unpaid tax if you didn't know that the money intended to pay the tax was used for other purposes. The law also allows the IRS to grant innocent spouse relief if it would be inequitable to hold a taxpayer liable for part or all of the correct but unpaid tax. Don't count on the IRS's benevolence in cases like these, however.

Under what circumstances might the IRS say you aren't responsible for all or part of any unpaid tax? Your spouse runs off in the middle of the night with all your dough and jewelry. While this is extreme behavior, here is what the new law is intended to address. Suppose that the IRS discovers an additional $20,000 of income, $5,000 of which the IRS proves you had knowledge of. You and your spouse are responsible for the tax on the $5,000 you knew about. Your spouse is solely responsible for the tax on the remaining $15,000.

Electing separate tax liability

Innocent spouse relief is available even if the IRS claims you "should have known" that your spouse was using creative accounting in filing your joint return. You can elect to limit your liability for any additional tax owed to what you would owe if you filed a separate return.

Here's how the separate tax liability election works: Jack and Jill, who are now separated, filed jointly. They reported $150,000 of salary income. Jack earned $60,000, and Jill earned $90,000. The IRS audited their return and discovered that Jack failed to report $15,000 of interest he earned on assets held in his name only. The IRS assesses a $4,500 tax deficiency. Jill knew about a bank account in Jack's name that generated $5,000 of interest. Jill can only be held liable for one-third of the deficiency, or $1,500, if Jack doesn't pay the entire tax assessment ($4,500 × $5,000 ÷ $15,000). That's because Jill knew about one-third of the unreported interest income. Had she not known about the bank account, Jill wouldn't be liable for any portion of the $4,500 in extra tax.

To elect separate liability, you have to be divorced, legally separated, or not living with your ex for 12 months prior to making the election. In addition, you must have had no knowledge about the concealed income or phony deductions. This "actual knowledge" is a lower standard than the "knew or should have known" standard required for regular innocent spouse relief. "Knew or should have known" can be inferred; "actual knowledge" can't be inferred based on indications that the electing spouse had reason to know. Sounds like a distinction without a difference, doesn't it? The IRS can claim you should have known. The IRS can't claim that you had knowledge if you didn't. Even if you can't meet the rules for separate liability (for example, if you aren't divorced, separated, or living apart), the IRS has the authority to grant separate liability relief if it feels it would be inequitable not to do so. This also includes those situations where the tax shown on the return is correct but you can't pay because of your ex-spouse's shenanigans. But it's worth remembering that the folks at the IRS aren't overly charitable.

Transferring assets between spouses so that one spouse ends up owing all the tax but has no assets that the IRS can seize won't work.

Whether you elect innocent spouse relief under the regular or the separate tax liability method, the election must be made on an IRS form. The current **Form 8857, Request for Innocent Spouse Relief,** will probably be revised to incorporate the new rules.

You have to elect innocent spouse relief within two years from the day the IRS begins to enforce collection. A demand or notice addressed to both spouses isn't considered "collection activities." A garnishment or notice of levy is.

Relief is available under this provision for all taxes, no matter how old, if applied for by July 23, 2000. You can apply for relief even if you were denied innocent spouse relief under the old law.

No collection activity may be undertaken while your application for relief is pending. And if relief is denied, you can appeal to the U.S. Tax Court. You have 90 days after the notice of denial to make your appeal.

Now for the bad news: The IRS must notify your ex and give him or her the opportunity to object to what you are doing.

When a married couple separates, the IRS should be informed of each spouse's new address so that all notices received by one spouse are received by the other. You can take care of this by filing **Form 8822, Change of Address.**

The Taxpayer Bill of Rights enacted in 1996 allows you to ask what the IRS is doing to get your ex-spouse to pay and how much the spouse has paid. Because of possible hostility towards an ex-spouse, the IRS won't reveal the spouse's home or business address.

Figuring Personal and Dependent Exemptions

You 1040A and 1040 filers have another hurdle to jump: Lines 6a-d of these forms ask you to figure your total number of exemptions. (You 1040EZ filers have line 5 to contend with, but this line is a breeze. We explain it in Chapter 5 in the section "How to Fill Out a 1040EZ.")

Each exemption that you're entitled to claim reduces your taxable income by $2,700, so exemptions are a *good* thing, right? There are two kinds of exemptions: personal exemptions and dependent exemptions. They're discussed in the following two sections.

Personal exemptions

You can take one personal exemption for yourself and one for your spouse. Here are the details.

✔ **Your own:** You may take one exemption for yourself unless you can be claimed as a dependent by someone else. For example, if your parents can claim you as a dependent but they choose not to, you still can't claim an exemption for yourself. This situation usually applies to teenagers with part-time jobs. If this is the case, check the Yes box on line 5 of Form 1040EZ; don't check box 6a on Form 1040 or 1040A.

✔ **Your spouse:** If filing jointly, you can take one exemption for your spouse, provided that your spouse can't be claimed on someone else's return.

If you file a separate return, you can claim your spouse as a dependent only if your spouse is not filing a return, had no income, and can't be claimed as a dependent on another person's return.

If, by the end of the year, you obtain a final decree of divorce or separate maintenance, you can't take an exemption for your former spouse even if you provided all of his or her support.

If your spouse died and you didn't remarry, you can claim an exemption for your spouse only if you file jointly. For example, Mr. Jones died on August 1. Because the Joneses were married as of the date of Mr. Jones's death, Mrs. Jones can file a joint return and claim an exemption for her husband. Mrs. Jones reports all of her income for 1998 and all of Mr. Jones's income up to August 1.

On a separate return, you can take an exemption for your deceased spouse only if this person had no income and couldn't be claimed as someone else's dependent.

Dependent exemptions

You can claim an exemption for a dependent if you provide more than half of his or her support and this person passes the five dependency tests. (Don't forget that if you claim someone, that person can't claim a personal exemption for his or her own tax return.)

Okay, you may open your booklets and begin the tests now. Any person who meets **all five** of the following tests qualifies as your dependent:

Test 1: Member of your household or relative

Your dependent must live with you the entire year as a member of your household. But a person related to you by blood or marriage does not have to live with you for the entire year as a member of your household to meet this test. (But a cousin meets this test only if he or she lived with you as a member of your household for the entire year.)

Personal and dependency exemption phaseout

Depending on your filing status, each $2,700 exemption to which you are entitled is whittled away in $54 increments ($108 for married filing separately) as your income rises above these limits:

Married filing separately	$93,400
Single	$124,500
Head of household	$155,650
Married filing jointly or qualifying widow(er)	$186,800

Here's how it works: For every $2,500 or part of $2,500 of income above these amounts, you have to reduce every $2,700 exemption by 2 percent. For example, if your income is $131,900 and you're single, your personal exemption is reduced to $2,538.

Here's the math:

Your exemption	$2,700
Your income	$131,900
Phaseout amount	$124,500
Difference	$7,400
$7,400 ÷ $2,500	3
	(2.96 rounded up to 3)
3 x .02	6%
$2,700 x .06	$162
Exemption allowed ($2,700 − $162)	$2,538

We suggest that you pick up the wonderful (and free) IRS Publication 17 *(Your Federal Income Tax)* and use the official worksheet. Call 800-TAX-FORM to order the publication. (You can also find the worksheet in the 1040 instruction booklet.)

If you file a joint return, you don't need to show that a dependent is related to both you and your spouse.

Temporary absences are ignored. If a person is placed in a nursing home for constant medical care, the absence is also considered temporary.

Here are some more details you may need to consider:

✔ **Death or birth:** A person who died during the year but was a member of your household until death meets the *member of your household test*. The same is true for a child who was born during the year and was a member of your household for the rest of the year. A child who was born and died in the same year qualifies, but a stillborn child doesn't. The child must have been born alive — even if for just a moment — in order to qualify as an exemption.

✔ **Violation of local law:** A person doesn't meet the member of your household test if your relationship violates local law.

✔ **Adoption:** Before the adoption is legal, a child is considered to be your child if he or she was placed with you for adoption by an authorized adoption agency (and the child must have been a member of your household). Otherwise, the child must be a member of your household for the entire tax year in order to satisfy this test.

✔ **Foster care:** A foster child or adult must live with you as a member of your household for the entire year to qualify as your dependent. However, if a government agency makes payments to you as a foster parent, you may not list the child as your dependent.

Test 2: Married person

If your dependent is married and files a joint return, you can't take this person as an exemption. However, if the person and the person's spouse file a joint return in order to get a refund of all tax withheld, you may be able to claim this person if the other four tests are met.

Test 3: Citizen or resident

The dependent must be one of the following:

✔ A U.S. citizen or U.S. resident alien

✔ A resident of Canada or Mexico

✔ Your adopted child who is not a U.S. citizen but who lived with you all year in a foreign country

A child who isn't a U.S. citizen or resident and lives abroad (in a country other than Canada or Mexico) can't be claimed as a dependent.

Test 4: Income

The dependent's gross income must be less than $2,700. Gross income does not include nontaxable income, such as welfare benefits or nontaxable Social Security benefits. Income earned by a permanently and totally disabled person for services performed at a sheltered workshop school is generally not included for purposes of the income test.

Of course, there are exceptions. Your child can have a gross income of $2,700 or more under one of the following conditions:

✔ He or she was under the age of 19 at the end of 1998.

✔ He or she was under the age of 24 at the end of 1998 and was also a student.

Your child is considered a student if he or she is enrolled as a full-time student at a school during any five months of 1998. A school includes technical, trade, and mechanical schools. It does not include on-the-job training courses or correspondence schools.

Test 5: Support

You provided over half the dependent's total support in 1998. If you file a joint return, support can come from either spouse. If you remarried, the support provided by your new spouse is treated as support coming from you. For exceptions to the support test, see the sidebar "Children of divorced or separated parents and persons supported by two or more taxpayers," later in this chapter. (You can't miss it with a title like that!)

Support includes food, a place to live, clothing, medical and dental care, and education. It also includes items such as a car and furniture, but only if they are for the dependent's own use or benefit. In figuring total support, use the actual cost of these items, but figure the cost of a place to live at its fair rental value. Include money the person used for his or her own support, even if this money wasn't taxable. Examples are gifts, savings, Social Security and welfare benefits, and other public assistance payments. This support is treated as *not* coming from you.

Total support doesn't include items such as income tax and Social Security taxes, life insurance premiums, or funeral expenses. A person's own funds aren't considered support unless they're actually spent for support.

Children of divorced or separated parents and persons supported by two or more taxpayers

The parent who had custody of the child for most of the year is the one entitled to claim the child as a dependent — provided that both parents together paid over half of the child's support.

A noncustodial parent can claim the child if any of the following apply:

✔ The custodial parent gives up the right to claim the child as a dependent by signing **Form 8332, Release of Claim to Exemption for Child of Divorced or Separated Parents.** The form allows for the release of an exemption for a single year, a number of years, or all future years. The noncustodial parent must attach this form to the return.

✔ A decree or separation agreement signed after 1984 provides that the noncustodial parent is unconditionally entitled to the exemption and the custodial parent is not. You must list the child's name, Social Security number, and the number of months the child lived in your home. You also must attach a copy of the cover page of the decree or agreement with the custodial parent's Social Security number written next to his or her name, along with the page that unconditionally states that you can claim the child as a dependent. Don't forget to attach a copy of the signature page of the decree or agreement.

✔ A decree or separation agreement signed before 1985 provides that the noncustodial parent is entitled to the exemption, and that this parent provided $600 or more toward the child's support.

✔ In the extreme right column on line 6 of your 1040 where you list your total exemptions, you must list the number of dependents who didn't live with you separately from the number who did.

Even if you did not pay over half of a dependent's support, you may still be able to claim this person as a dependent if all five of the following apply:

✔ You and one or more eligible person(s) paid over half of the dependent's support. An eligible person is someone who could have claimed the dependent but didn't pay over half of the dependent's support.

✔ You paid more than 10 percent of the dependent's support.

✔ No individual paid over half of the dependent's support.

✔ Dependency tests 1 through 4 are met.

✔ Each eligible person who paid over 10 percent of support completes **Form 2120, Multiple Support Declaration,** and you attach this form to your return. The form states that only you will claim the person as a dependent for 1998.

Even if you can't claim a child because your spouse is claiming the child, you can still claim the child's medical expenses, and you are entitled to the child care credit. When the child reaches his or her majority, the custodial parent rules no longer apply. The parent who provides more than 50 percent of the child's support is entitled to the exemption. The education credits that kick in under the new law in 1998 may be a trap for the unsuspecting. These credits are available only to the parent who pays for the education expenses and who is allowed to claim the student as a dependent. So, where one parent pays the tuition and the other claims the kid as a dependent, jointly, they can both kiss these tax credits goodbye.

Securing Social Security Numbers for Dependents

You must list a Social Security number on line 6c column (2), Form 1040 and 1040A, for every dependent. If your dependent was born and died in 1998 and didn't have a Social Security number, write Died in column (2). No Social Security number, no deduction, and no right to claim head of household status. To obtain a Social Security number, call the Social Security Administration at 800-772-1213. You will be sent a one-page form called an SS-5. Based on your zip code, you will be directed to the nearest Social Security office. Take your driver's license, your child's original birth certificate (no duplicates), and another form of ID for your child, such as a birth announcement or a doctor's bill, together with the SS-5. It takes about two weeks to get a number.

If you are in the process of adopting a child who is a U.S. citizen or resident and cannot get a Social Security number until the adoption is final, you can apply for an *adoption taxpayer number* that can be used instead of a Social Security number. To get one, file **Form W-7A, Application for Taxpayer Identification Number for Pending U.S. Adoptions.**

Filing for Children and Other Dependents

If you as the parent can claim a child (or someone else) as a dependent on your return, the dependent must file a return under both of the following circumstances:

- ✔ The dependent had unearned income (interest, dividends, capital gains, and so on), and the total of that income plus earned income exceeds $700.
- ✔ The dependent had no unearned income but had earned income that exceeds $4,250.

For example, suppose that your teenager has interest income of $200 and salary from a summer job of $450. This dependent doesn't need to file because the total income was less than $700. If your teenager had no unearned income but gained $2,000 from a summer job, this dependent wouldn't have to file either because the earned income was under $4,250.

But here's an important point: The dependent must file to *get back* the tax that was withheld from the paychecks. This situation can be avoided, however, if a dependent who starts to work claims an exemption from having tax withheld by filing Form W-4 with the employer. That way, the dependent won't have to file a return to get back the tax that was withheld. When he or she reaches $4,250 in income, withholding will have to start.

A child under the age of 14 with more than $1,400 in investment income is subject to the *Kiddie Tax*. This income is considered earned by the child's parents at the parents' tax rate (see "Line 40: Tax" in Chapter 8 for more details on this wonderful tax law nuance).

Must I File?

Yes, you must file a tax return when your income exceeds the amounts for your age and filing status shown in Table 4-3.

Table 4-3	When You Must File		
Marital Status	*Filing Status*	*Age**	*Gross Income*
Single, divorced, legally separated	Single	Under 65	$6,950
		65 or older	$8,000
	Head of household	Under 65	$8,950
		65 or older	$10,000
Married with a child and living apart from spouse during last 6 months of 1998	Head of household	Under 65, 65 or older	$8,950 $10,000

(continued)

Table 4-3 (continued)

Marital Status	Filing Status	Age*	Gross Income
Married and living with spouse at end of 1998 (or on date of spouse's death)	Married (joint return)	Under 65 (both spouses)	$12,500
		65 or older (one spouse),	$13,350
		65 or older (both spouses),	$14,200
	Married (separate return)	Any age	$ 2,700
Married and not living with spouse at end of 1998 (or on date of spouse's death)	Married (joint or separate return)	Any age	$ 2,700
Widowed before 1998 and not remarried in 1998	Single	Under 65 65 or older	$ 6,950 $ 8,000
	Head of household	Under 65, 65 or older	$ 8,950 $10,000
	Qualifying widow(er) with dependent child	Under 65	$ 9,800
		65 or older	$10,650

* If you turn 65 on January 1, 1999, you are considered to be age 65 at the end of 1998.

When to file

If you don't file by **April 15, 1999,** you will have to pay penalties and interest. If you live or work outside the United States, you have an automatic extension of time to file until June 15, 1999.

If you know that you can't file by April 15, you can get an automatic four-month extension of time to file — until August 16, 1999 (usually, you have until August 15, but August 15 falls on a Sunday in 1999) — by filing **Form 4868, Application for Automatic Extension of Time to File U.S. Individual Income Tax Return.** Keep in mind that this form must be filed by April 15, 1998.

Form 4868 does not extend the time to pay. You will be charged interest and a late payment penalty of 0.5 percent a month if you don't pay at least 90 percent of your tax by April 15, 1999. (*Note:* You will be charged interest on outstanding tax owed.) If you still can't file by August 16, 1999, you can obtain an additional two-month extension of time to file until October 15, 1999, by filing **Form 2688, Application for Additional Extension of Time to File U.S. Individual Income Tax Return.** This form must be filed by August 16. You can't get an extension beyond October 15.

If you don't file

You could end up crushing rocks. But it's more likely that you'll be assessed penalties that make crushing rocks seem like a stroll in the park. Annually, the IRS prosecutes only 5,000 individuals (you can't call them taxpayers) for tax evasion. Some 80 percent are members of organized crime or drug dealers, and the balance is made up of high-profile individuals and others. You don't want to be one of the *others*.

If you don't file, based on the information reported to the IRS by your employers, the IRS will either prepare a substitute return and assess a late filing penalty of 25 percent, a late payment penalty of 0.5 percent a month to a maximum of 25 percent plus interest (and possibly a 75 percent fraud penalty) — or issue a summons for you to appear with your tax records so that the IRS can use those records to prepare a more accurate return. Interest and penalties are charged whichever way the IRS decides to proceed.

Where to file

We wouldn't want to leave you with any excuses not to get those tax forms in (sorry), so we list all the locations to which you can send your crinkled and tear-stained forms in Appendix A under "Where to File Your Federal Return."

How to file

Okay, so this whole book is supposed to be about this subject. But what we mean here is that you have several ways to get the forms — and the check, if necessary — to IRS Central. The most popular way to file is through the U.S. Postal Service. This is the preferred and the simplest way to file. But there are other ways to get it done, such as filing electronically, filing by phone in states that allow you to do so, and using computer-generated forms like the 1040PC.

Electronic filing

We should define this one. Your return is filed over telephone lines by a company that offers this service. A computer-generated tax return that you mail in is *not* electronic filing.

Generally, what you do is take your return to a firm like H&R Block that offers electronic filing. A number of tax-preparation software programs can submit returns electronically if you have a modem. What happens is that you use the software to send the return to the telephone number of an electronic filing service, and the service sends it on to the IRS.

The advantage of electronic filing is that you get your hands on your hard-earned dough two to three weeks faster. Also, you can have your refund deposited directly into your bank account. Some firms will not only file your return, they will also loan you money based on the projected amount of the refund. These clever loans are called *refund anticipation loans.*

The IRS Web site — www.IRS.ustreas.gov — offers links to companies that offer electronic filing for a fee. By going to these companies' Web sites, you can download the software necessary for their electronic filing services. They charge for this. Thirty-four states allow you to file your state return with your federal. The state then retrieves the information from the IRS. One transmission does it all.

Electronic filing may be one of the worst ideas to come down the pike in a long time. Our principal objection is that it's too pricey. According to the IRS, the average refund check for electronic filers is $1,300. By filing electronically, you can get your refund around 25 days earlier. But depending on where you live, you'll pay between $25 to $40 for this service. Suppose that you pay someone $35 to have your return filed electronically. The fee is the equivalent of paying a near 40-percent rate of interest just to get your refund 25 days earlier. If you're thinking about a refund anticipation loan, you can expect to pay a $20 fee for the service — that amounts to a 37.4-percent rate of interest!

Filing by phone

A single taxpayer who qualifies to use Form 1040EZ can file his or her return by means of a touch-tone telephone. The instructions for how to file by phone are included in the 1040EZ tax package you receive. However, if the IRS doesn't mail you a 1040EZ tax package, you can't file by phone. If the IRS does mail you a 1040EZ package, but you lose it, you can't file by phone. Finally, if you're married or you have unemployment compensation to report as income, you can't file by phone. The Telefile worksheet in your 1040EZ package guides you through the process.

Only the IRS would include more rules when trying to make things easier!

1040PC

Stay clear of this form. It's intended for accountants. This nifty one-page tax return that you prepare on a computer only has line numbers and amounts without any description as to what each amount represents. To the untrained eye, the return appears to be nothing more than a column of numbers. The IRS likes this return because it can be read by a scanner — a data processing clerk does not have to input everything manually.

A Final Bit of Advice

Here's an old saying from a wise man — the father of one of us. He said, "Son, there are two kinds of payments in the world you should avoid: too early and too late." That kind of advice also applies to filing your taxes. Filing taxes late leads to IRS interest and penalties; paying your taxes too early, or withholding too much, is simply an interest-free loan to the federal government. Thanks for the advice, Dad.

Part II
Tackling the 1040

The 5th Wave   By Rich Tennant

"...and this will calculate your earned average income, corporate tax rate, and allowable charitable contributions."

In this part . . .

Rituals make the world go 'round. And what ritual is quite so enjoyable as completing one's tax return? Visiting your local department of motor vehicles to renew your driver's license? Waiting in line at the post office to buy some stamps? Cleaning up an overflowing toilet?

It all starts with Form 1040 in its three guises: 1040EZ, 1040-A, and plain old 1040. After you get the form right, you have the challenge of finding the tax documentation needed to plug answers into those small lines. And just when you're ready to start (after pulling out your hair), you find yourself wading knee-deep through those dreadful IRS instructions.

Thanks to our plain English "...*For Dummies*" tax jargon translation, you get the information you need to know to get an A+ on tax return preparation. And we show you some tricks along the way to make it easier on yourself next time around. (By the way, did you know you can purchase stamps through the mail and eliminate those trips to the post office?)

"The nation should have a tax system which looks like someone designed it on purpose."

— William E. Simon, former U.S. Secretary of the Treasury

Chapter 5
Easy Filing: 1040EZ and 1040A

• •

In This Chapter

▶ Living the really EZ life: Using the 1040EZ

▶ Living the semi-easy life: Using the 1040A

▶ Letting the IRS do the math for you

• •

It's best to begin a challenging part of the book with something EZ. Trust us, things get much more complicated in a hurry (although if you can file a simplified tax form, you'll be able to bypass much of what's in the rest of Part II of this book). For now, take a look at the easier forms (1040EZ and 1040A). They're easier because you don't have as many lines to fill out, as many schedules to complete and attach, or as many receipts and records to dig out.

The most difficult decision to make is whether to choose the 1040EZ or the 1040A (the infamous Short Form). From then on, it's downhill. In fact, the forms are so simple that the IRS computes the tax for you.

Who Can File a 1040EZ?

With the 1040EZ (see Figure 5-1), all you have to do is fill in the numbers — a snap with this short form. The IRS likes this form, by the way, because it can be processed by optical scanner. You'll like this form, too, because you don't have to do the math. The nice folks at the IRS do it for you (see the sidebar "Let the IRS figure your tax" later in this chapter). You may use the 1040EZ if you meet all of the following criteria:

✔ You are single or are married filing jointly and don't claim any dependents.

✔ You (and your spouse, if married filing jointly) are under age 65 and *are not* blind.

✔ You have income only from wages, salaries, tips, taxable scholarships, unemployment compensation, and fellowship grants — and not more than $400 of taxable interest income.

✔ Your taxable income is less than $50,000.

✔ You aren't receiving any advance earned income credit (EIC) payments. You can find out whether you received any advance EIC payments by referring to box 9 of your W-2. (See "Box 9" in Chapter 6 for more on advance EICs.)

✔ You aren't itemizing deductions (on Schedule A) or claiming any adjustments to income or tax credits (such as childcare expenses).

If you can't file Form 1040EZ, all is not lost. You may be able to use another simplified form: 1040A (see "Who Can File a 1040A?" later in this chapter).

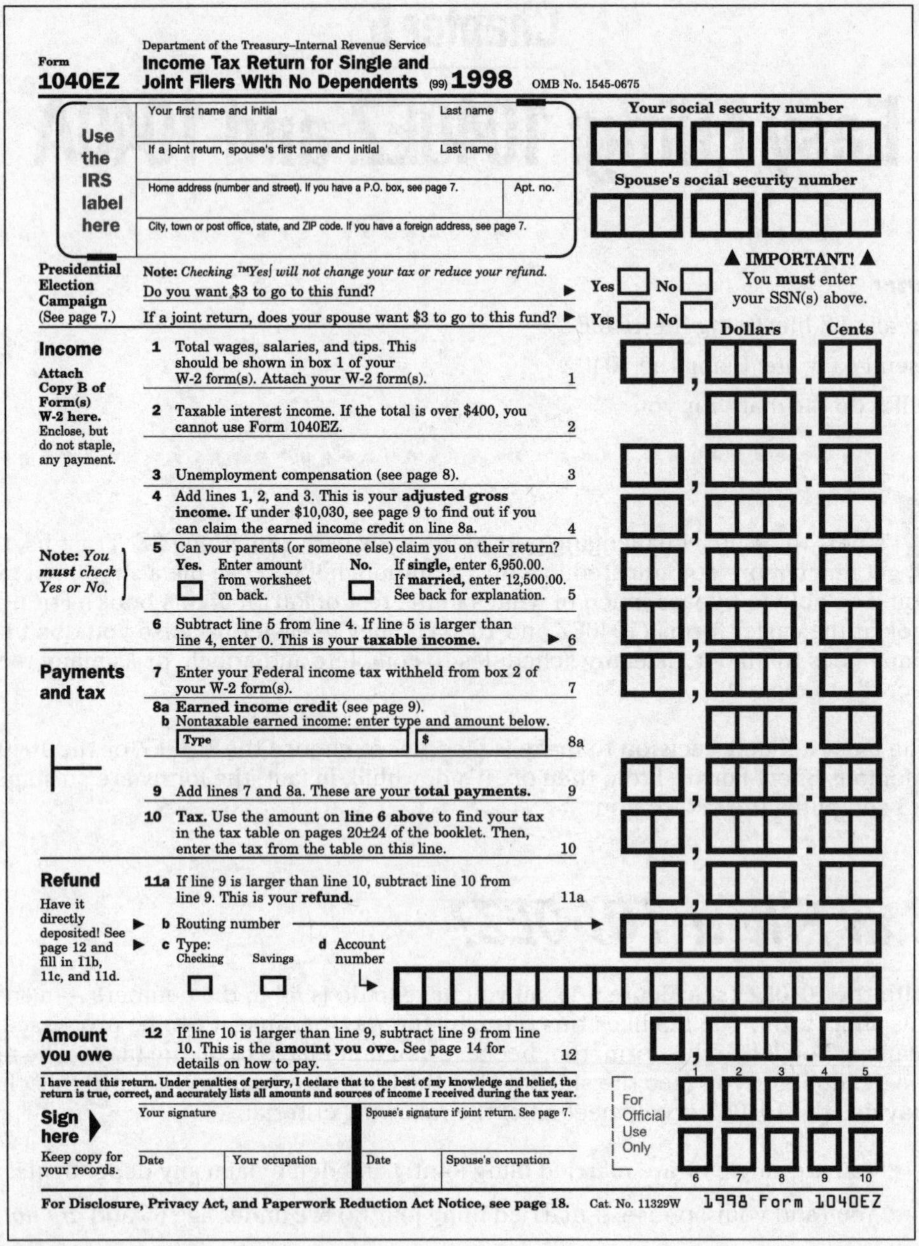
Form 1040EZ

Department of the Treasury–Internal Revenue Service

Income Tax Return for Single and Joint Filers With No Dependents (99) 1998

OMB No. 1545-0675

Use the IRS label here

Your first name and initial | Last name

If a joint return, spouse's first name and initial | Last name

Home address (number and street). If you have a P.O. box, see page 7. | Apt. no.

City, town or post office, state, and ZIP code. If you have a foreign address, see page 7.

Your social security number

Spouse's social security number

▲ IMPORTANT! ▲ You **must** enter your SSN(s) above.

Presidential Election Campaign (See page 7.)

Note: *Checking "Yes" will not change your tax or reduce your refund.*

Do you want $3 to go to this fund? ▶ Yes ☐ No ☐

If a joint return, does your spouse want $3 to go to this fund? ▶ Yes ☐ No ☐

Dollars | Cents

Income

Attach Copy B of Form(s) W-2 here. Enclose, but do not staple, any payment.

1 Total wages, salaries, and tips. This should be shown in box 1 of your W-2 form(s). Attach your W-2 form(s). 1

2 Taxable interest income. If the total is over $400, you cannot use Form 1040EZ. 2

3 Unemployment compensation (see page 8). 3

4 Add lines 1, 2, and 3. This is your **adjusted gross income.** If under $10,030, see page 9 to find out if you can claim the earned income credit on line 8a. 4

Note: *You must check Yes or No.*

5 Can your parents (or someone else) claim you on their return? Yes. Enter amount from worksheet on back. ☐ No. If **single,** enter 6,950.00. If **married,** enter 12,500.00. See back for explanation. ☐ 5

6 Subtract line 5 from line 4. If line 5 is larger than line 4, enter 0. This is your **taxable income.** ▶ 6

Payments and tax

7 Enter your Federal income tax withheld from box 2 of your W-2 form(s). 7

8a **Earned income credit** (see page 9).

b Nontaxable earned income: enter type and amount below. Type | $ 8a

9 Add lines 7 and 8a. These are your **total payments.** 9

10 **Tax.** Use the amount on **line 6 above** to find your tax in the tax table on pages 20±24 of the booklet. Then, enter the tax from the table on this line. 10

Refund

Have it directly deposited! See page 12 and fill in 11b, 11c, and 11d.

11a If line 9 is larger than line 10, subtract line 10 from line 9. This is your **refund.** 11a

▶ b Routing number

▶ c Type: Checking ☐ Savings ☐ d Account number

Amount you owe

12 If line 10 is larger than line 9, subtract line 9 from line 10. This is the **amount you owe.** See page 14 for details on how to pay. 12

I have read this return. Under penalties of perjury, I declare that to the best of my knowledge and belief, the return is true, correct, and accurately lists all amounts and sources of income I received during the tax year.

Sign here ▶ Your signature | Spouse's signature if joint return. See page 7.

Keep copy for your records. Date | Your occupation | Date | Spouse's occupation

For Official Use Only 1 2 3 4 5 6 7 8 9 10

For Disclosure, Privacy Act, and Paperwork Reduction Act Notice, see page 18. Cat. No. 11329W 1998 Form 1040EZ

Figure 5-1: Form 1040EZ, page 1.

Filling Out a 1040EZ

The IRS has provided nice little boxes where you can put your numbers (but please leave off the dollar signs). What a considerate organization!

Line 1: Total wages, salaries, and tips

Enter your wages (from box 1 of your W-2 form). If your employer hasn't provided you with this form, go squawk at your payroll and benefits department.

Rounding off dollars

No pennies please, even though the form has a column for cents. You're allowed to round to the nearest dollar. Drop amounts under 50 cents and increase amounts from 50 to 99 cents to the next dollar. If you have one W-2 for $5,000.55 and another for $18,500.73, enter $23,501 ($5,000.55 + $18,500.73 = $23,501.28) not $23,502 ($5,001 + $18,501).

Line 2: Taxable interest income of $400 or less

Enter your interest income on line 2. You can locate this amount in boxes 1 and 3 of your 1099-INTs, which your bank and other investment companies should provide. If this amount is over $400, you can't use the 1040EZ. Sorry!

If you keep lots of money in bank accounts, you may be missing out on free opportunities to earn a higher interest rate. Chapter 23 explains money market funds, a higher yielding alternative to bank accounts.

Also, if you're in a higher tax bracket, you may be able to gain a higher return with your savings by choosing tax-free investments. (This applies to you if you're in the 28 percent federal income tax bracket that begins at $25,350 in taxable income — line 6 on the 1040EZ — as a single filer or $42,350 as a married couple filing jointly.) See Chapter 23 to find out how to keep more of your investment income.

Line 3: Unemployment compensation

Once upon a time, this income wasn't taxable. But that was before "tax reform." To report your unemployment compensation received during the tax year, enter on line 3 the amount from box 1 of **Form 1099-G** that your state sends you.

Although you can elect to have tax withheld at the rate of 15 percent on your unemployment so you won't be caught short next April 15, this is one offer most people are likely to refuse.

Line 4: Adjusted gross income

Add the amounts of lines 1, 2, and 3 together and enter the total here. This is your *adjusted gross income* (AGI).

Line 5: Deductions and exemptions

From your AGI, you have to subtract your standard deduction and personal exemption. The amount you can deduct is indicated to the left of the boxes, but you first have to take the IRS "yes or no" test. Read the question on line 5: "Can your parents (or someone else) claim you on their return?" Mark your answer. (Aren't you glad that this isn't an essay test?)

If you checked "yes," you have to use the worksheet on the back of the form to figure your standard deduction. If your parents are entitled to claim you as a dependent, you aren't entitled to a personal exemption for yourself. As an example, pretend that you're preparing the return of a teenage dependent who earned $3,300 last summer. Because we know that at first glance this worksheet (on page 2 of the form) looks intimidating, we help you wade through it.

Line A.	Enter the amount of her wages		$3,300
	Additional amount allowed by law		$250
		Total	A. $3,550
Line B.	Minimum Standard deduction		B. $700
Line C.	The larger of A or B		C. $3,550
Line D.	Maximum Standard deduction if single		D. $4,250
Line E.	The smaller of C or D		E. $3,550
Line F.	Exemption amount (because you claim her, enter 0)		F. 0
Line G.	Add lines E & F and enter that amount on Line 5 on Form 1040EZ		G. $3,550

If no one else can claim you on his or her return, your life is just that much simpler now. Enter in the boxes the amount for single ($6,950) or married ($12,500), whichever applies. You should feel good about this number that you're deducting from your taxable income. The IRS is effectively saying that this amount of income is tax-free to you.

Line 6: Taxable income

Subtract the amount you entered on line 5 from line 4, and enter the remainder here. Line 6 is your taxable income.

Line 7: Federal income tax withheld

Enter your federal tax withheld (shown in box 2 of your W-2) here. Your federal income tax withheld is the amount of tax that you already paid during the tax year. Your employer withholds this money from your paycheck and sends it to the IRS.

Line 8a: Earned income credit

If your adjusted gross income (from line 4) is less than $10,030, you may be eligible for the earned income credit (see "Line 59a: Earned income credit" in Chapter 8 for more details on this credit). The credit can be as high as $341 and is subtracted from your tax. If you don't owe tax, the credit is refunded to you. You don't have to compute the credit. Just look up the credit for your income in your instruction booklet and enter the credit here.

Starting in 1997, Congress lowered the boom on people who claim this credit when they have no right to. In addition to all the penalties the IRS can impose, anyone who fraudulently claims this credit is ineligible to claim it for ten years. For those who are merely careless or unintentionally disregard the rules, the penalty is two years.

Line 8b: Nontaxable earned income and type

Although this affects only a few people, we explain what the IRS is up to on "Line 59b" in Chapter 8.

Line 9: Total payments

Add the amounts on lines 7 and 8, and put the sum here.

Line 10: Tax

To figure your total federal income tax for the year, look up the amount on line 6 in the tax tables located at the end of this book for your income bracket and filing status. For example, if you're single and your taxable income (on line 6) is $32,100, find the row for $32,100 to $32,150 and read across to the Single column. In this example, your tax is $5,700.

When you've found the appropriate row and column for your taxable income and filing status — and while you have your finger in the right place — enter the amount here on line 10.

Line 11: Refund time!

The last computation that you have to make is quite simple. Look at lines 9 and 10. If the amount on line 9 is larger than that on line 10, you're going to get a refund. Just subtract line 10 from line 9 and enter the amount on line 11a. The amount on 11a is your refund!

You can have your refund deposited directly in your bank account. This should speed up your refund by about ten days to two weeks. However, a number of people we know are reluctant to take the IRS up on this offer. Their reason: "The IRS knows too much about me already."

If we haven't scared you away, the sample check in Figure 5-2 shows you how to get the information that the IRS needs to wire the money to your account from your check. Your routing number referred to on line 11b is the 9-digit number marked RTN in Figure 5-2. On line 11c, check the type of account and then enter your account number (marked DAN in Figure 5-2) on line 11d.

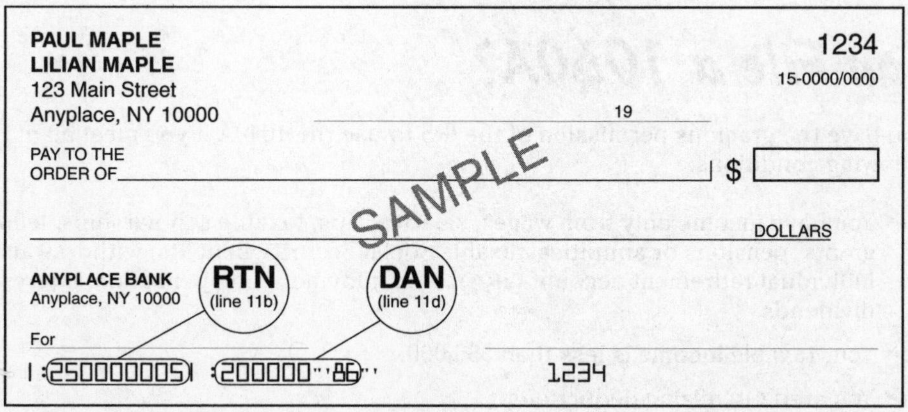

Figure 5-2:
A sample check. The RTN and DAN may appear in different places on your own check.

PAUL MAPLE
LILIAN MAPLE
123 Main Street
Anyplace, NY 10000

1234

15-0000/0000

19

PAY TO THE
ORDER OF_____ $

SAMPLE

_____ DOLLARS

ANYPLACE BANK
Anyplace, NY 10000

RTN (line 11b)

DAN (line 11d)

For _____

⑈250000005⑈ ⑈200000⑈86⑈   1234

Line 12: Payment due

Yes, you guessed it. If the amount on line 10 is larger than that on line 9, you still owe because not enough tax was withheld from your paycheck or paid by you during the year. Subtract line 9 from line 10 and enter the amount on line 12. 'Fess up and pay up.

Plastic anyone? Whether you file your return electronically, by mail, or by IRS Telefile, you'll be able to charge the balance due with a toll-free call. US Audiotex, of San Ramon, California (800-487-4567), expects to accept most major credit cards. For folks using TurboTax or MacInTax, Novus Services of Riverwoods, Illinois (800-347-2683) will allow them to charge what they owe on a Discover or Private Issue card.

There are four reasons why paying this way isn't especially attractive:

- ✔ The IRS doesn't charge 21 percent interest like many credit card companies do.

- ✔ Resolving billing disputes could prove to be a nightmare.

- ✔ Credit card companies may potentially release confidential information when they sell the mailing list of their customers, which most of them do.

- ✔ Credit card holders will pay a "convenience fee" (usually 2 to 3 percent) on top of their interest charges because the IRS doesn't pay the fee that credit card companies normally collect from merchants.

We can think of better ways to earn frequent flyer miles.

Finishing up

Don't forget to attach your W-2s to your return. Staples are just great! (And staples are preferable to tape and paper clips. You don't want your W-2s going one way at IRS Central while your tax return goes another way.) If you owe money, make sure you write your Social Security number in the lower-left corner of the front of your check, along with the notation 1998 FORM 1040EZ INCOME TAX — just in case the folks at the IRS think you're trying to make a payment on your new boat but sent them the check by mistake.

Spell out INTERNAL REVENUE SERVICE on the check. If your check goes astray, *IRS* is just too darned easy to alter (such as changing the IRS to MRS, and anyone can fill in her name — Mrs. Robinson, for example). Sign your return and mail it to the IRS Service Center for your area. Normally, an addressed envelope is provided with your tax form. If you don't have the address, see the addresses provided in the back of this book.

Who Can File a 1040A?

You have the gracious permission of the IRS to use the 1040A if you meet all of the following conditions:

- ✔ You have income only from wages, salaries, tips, taxable scholarships, fellowship grants, pensions or annuities, taxable Social Security benefits, withdrawals from your individual retirement account (IRA), unemployment compensation, interest, and dividends.

- ✔ Your taxable income is less than $50,000.

- ✔ You aren't itemizing deductions.

If you meet all the criteria for filing Form 1040A, be sure to check the section "Who Can File a 1040EZ?," earlier in this chapter, to determine whether you can file the even easier Form 1040EZ.

You can also use Form 1040A (see Figure 5-3) to claim the earned income credit, the deduction for contributions to an IRA, nondeductible contributions to an IRA, the credit for child and dependent care expenses, the credit for the elderly or the disabled, child tax credits, education credits, an adoption credit, or the student loan interest deduction. You may use the 1040A even if you made estimated tax payments for 1998, or if you can take the exclusion of interest from series EE U.S. savings bonds issued after 1989.

Form 1040A
U.S. Individual Income Tax Return 1998
Department of the Treasury—Internal Revenue Service
IRS Use Only—Do not write or staple in this space.
OMB No. 1545-0085

Label (See page 18.)
Use the IRS label. Otherwise, please print or type.

Filing status (Check only one box.)
1 ☐ Single
2 ☐ Married filing joint return (even if only one had income)
3 ☐ Married filing separate return.
4 ☐ Head of household (with qualifying person).
5 ☐ Qualifying widow(er) with dependent child

Exemptions
6a ☐ Yourself.
b ☐ Spouse
c Dependents:
d Total number of exemptions claimed.

Income
7 Wages, salaries, tips, etc. Attach Form(s) W-2.
8a Taxable interest. Attach Schedule 1 if required.
b Tax-exempt interest.
9 Ordinary dividends.
10a Total IRA distributions. 10b Taxable amount
11a Total pensions and annuities. 11b Taxable amount
12 Unemployment compensation.
13a Social security benefits. 13b Taxable amount
14 Add lines 7 through 13b. This is your **total income.**

Adjusted gross income
15 IRA deduction
16 Student loan interest deduction
17 Add lines 15 and 16. These are your **total adjustments.**
18 Subtract line 17 from line 14. This is your **adjusted gross income.**

For Disclosure, Privacy Act, and Paperwork Reduction Act Notice, see page 49. Cat. No. 11327A 1998 Form 1040A

Figure 5-3: Form 1040A, page 1.

Completing Form 1040A

We hope you've already figured out your filing status and exemptions. If you need help, see Chapter 4. You can round off to the nearest dollar so you don't have to fiddle with pennies. See the sidebar "Rounding off dollars" earlier in this chapter.

Line 6: Exemptions

Make sure you provide Social Security numbers for the youngsters (see Chapters 4 and 25 to find out how to obtain Social Security numbers for your children). Every dependent needs a Social Security number — even someone born on December 31. The IRS will disallow all exemptions without a Social Security number and will also kick you out of head of household status and penalize you $50 for every missing number. You can claim an exemption for yourself, your spouse, and your kids and other dependents on line 6. Enter the information for items a through d. Each exemption is worth a $2,700 tax deduction.

Lines 6a and 6b: Exemptions for you and your spouse

This is where you claim an exemption for you and your spouse. Living together doesn't count.

If someone else can claim you as a dependent, you can't check the box on 6a and claim an exemption for yourself. Not being able to claim yourself as an exemption also impacts the amount of the standard deduction you're entitled to on line 21. Just keep this bit of news in the back of your mind — we explain it all when you get to that line.

Line 6c: Dependents

This line is as easy as pie. List each dependent's name, Social Security number, and relationship to you, and indicate whether your child qualifies for the new Child Tax Credit (column 4). The following tax tip explains what this new credit is about.

Subject to the income limitations, each kid under 17 on December 31 can cut your tax bill by $400. So check the box if this applies to you, and don't forget to claim this new Child Tax Credit on line 28. If you have three or more kids, the credit may be refundable if it exceeds your tax. The refundable portion is claimed on line 38. This is known as the Additional Credit. Although this normally won't apply to most people, we explain it and something called the Supplemental Child Credit — a second variation of the Child Tax Credit — later in this chapter under "Line 28."

Tally all the exemptions you claimed on lines 6a through 6c.

If you're eligible for the Child Tax Credit and want to take immediate advantage of the reduction for 1999, you can do so by submitting a new **Form W-4, Withholding Allowance Certificate,** to your employer. For example, if you're entitled to a $1,500 child credit (three kids) and get paid monthly, your monthly take-home pay will increase by $125. We explain how to complete Form W-4 in Chapter 15. In case you're wondering, the credit jumps to $500 per child in 1999.

Don't confuse the new Child Tax Credit with the credit for child and dependent care expenses. See "Line 41" in Chapter 8 for the rules on claiming this credit.

Line 7: Wages, salaries, and tips

Enter your wages from box 1 of your W-2s (which your employer(s) should provide) here.

Line 8a: Taxable interest income

Enter your interest income on line 8a (you can find this amount on your 1099-INT: box 1 from banks and S&Ls, and box 3 from U.S. savings bonds). If you're rolling in interest dough (at least over $400), you have to fill out and attach **Schedule 1 (Interest and Dividend Income).** Just think of it as homework that you must hand in — unless you want the IRS to keep you after school. To complete Schedule 1, just put down the name of the payer and the amount in the amount column. If you need help with any part of it, call us (only kidding!). Actually, cruise ahead to Chapter 10, which walks you through completion of the nearly identical Schedule B, the schedule that taxpayers use to tally interest and dividend income for the cumbersome 1040. For example, if you need help determining what kind of interest income is taxable, the section "Line 1: Taxable interest" in Chapter 10 should help.

TIP

Let the IRS figure your tax

Instead of struggling with all the math, subtracting this from that, and looking up the tax for your tax bracket, the IRS will figure the tax for you. For 1040EZ and 1040A filers who don't want the hassle of doing the math, letting the IRS compute your tax after you enter your basic information on the forms is headache-free. If you're entitled to a refund, the IRS will send you a check. If you owe money, the IRS will bill you. And if you're entitled to the earned income credit or credit for the elderly or disabled, you don't have to spend hours filling out the forms.

Be careful, though: Even the IRS makes mistakes (no kidding!). If you're entitled to one of the credits, check the IRS computation (the credits will be itemized on it) when you receive your bill or refund check.

Here's how 1040EZ filers do it: On lines 1 through 8, fill in the lines that apply to you. If your income is under $10,030, you could be entitled to the earned income credit. So print EIC in the blank space to the right of the word "below" on line 8b. By doing this, you alert the IRS that you're entitled to the earned income credit.

Attach your W-2s. Sign your return and send it to the IRS Service Center for your area. Ignore all the "subtract this line from that and enter it here" on Form 1040EZ. The IRS does all that fun stuff.

For 1040A filers, fill in any of lines 1 through 16 that apply. If you're entitled to a credit for child and dependent care

expenses, you must complete Schedule 2 (the child and dependent care form) and attach it to your return. Enter the amount of credit on line 26.

If you're entitled to claim a credit for the elderly or the disabled, attach Schedule 3, and, on lines 1 through 9 of Schedule 3, check the box for your filing status (single, married, and so on). In the space to the left of line 27, print CFE. You won't have to tackle this nightmarish form. The IRS will prepare it for you.

If you're entitled to the earned income credit, the IRS will fill in the credit for you. Print EIC in the space to the right of line 37a. Fill in page 1 of Schedule EIC and attach it to your 1040A.

Fill in lines 28,29,30, and 37b if they apply.

Sign your return. Attach your W-2s and make sure that your Schedule 2 or 3 is attached if you're claiming any child care or elderly and disabled credits. Mail your return to the IRS Service Center (see Appendix B) for your area.

Here's a warning, however: Although this method sounds EZ, it may lead to a false sense of security because you may overlook something like an important deduction that could work to your tax advantage. Also, the IRS is not infallible and may make an error.

If you keep lots of your money in bank accounts, you may be missing out on free opportunities to earn a higher interest rate. Chapter 23 explains money market funds, a higher yielding alternative to bank accounts.

Also, if you're in a higher tax bracket, you may be able to make a higher return with your savings by choosing tax-free investments. (This means you if you're in the 28 percent federal income tax bracket beginning at $25,350 in taxable income as a single filer — line 24 on the 1040A — or $42,350 as married filing jointly.) See Chapter 23 to see how to keep more of your investment income.

Line 8b: Tax-exempt interest

If you received any tax-exempt interest (such as from a municipal bond or a tax-free money market fund), enter this amount on line 8b. This amount doesn't increase your taxable income unless you're receiving Social Security. If you collect Social Security benefits, tax-exempt interest is used to figure out how much of your Social Security is subject to tax. That's why this tax trap is here. Line 8b is not a harmless little line to some folks.

Line 9: Dividends

Enter on line 9 any dividend income (from box 1a of your **1099-DIV**). Once again, if this amount is over $400, you have homework to do on Schedule 1 (see Chapter 10 if you get stuck). As mentioned earlier in this chapter, if you're in a higher income tax bracket, it may be to your benefit to reduce taxable dividend income and instead focus on tax-friendlier investments (see Chapter 23).

Lines 10a and 10b: Total IRA distributions

The custodian of your IRA, bank, or investment company should send you a **1099-R** by January 31 for the prior tax year if you withdrew money from your IRA. The amount in box 1 of this form is entered on line 10a, and the amount in box 2a is entered on line 10b. Because this is an IRA, the amounts in boxes 1 and 2a are usually the same.

But if you made nondeductible contributions to your IRA, not all the money you withdraw is taxable. To compute what's taxable in such instances, you're going to have to fill out **Form 8606** (see "Lines 15a and b: Total IRA distributions" in Chapter 6 for the low-down on IRAs). If you elected to have tax withheld on your IRA payments, don't forget to enter the tax withheld (from box 4 of your 1099) on line 35 together with the tax withheld from your paychecks as reported on your Form W-2.

Lines 11a and 11b: Total pensions and annuities

If you received income from a pension or an annuity during 1998, the payer will provide you with a 1099-R showing the amount you received in box 1 and the taxable amount in box 2a. (See "Line 16a and b: Total pensions and annuities" in Chapter 6 to find out whether the pension plan computed the correct amount.) Enter the amount from box 1 on line 11a and the amount from box 2a on line 11b. If income tax was withheld, enter the amount from box 4 on line 35, along with the tax withheld from your salary as indicated on your W-2.

Line 12: Unemployment insurance

Believe it or not, unemployment benefits are taxable. Enter on line 12 the amount from box 1 of **Form 1099-G,** which your state will send you (see "Line 19: Unemployment compensation" in Chapter 6 to learn more about this issue).

You can now elect to have tax withheld at the rate of 15 percent on your unemployment so you won't be caught short next April 15.

Lines 13a and 13b: Social Security benefits

Yes, you have to pay tax on your Social Security benefits if your income is over the income levels indicated on the worksheets in "Lines 20a and 20b: Social Security benefits" in Chapter 6.

Basically, if you're single and your income — lines 7 through 12 plus one-half of your Social Security, less your IRA deduction on line 15 and your student loan interest deduction on line 16 — exceeds $25,000 ($32,000 if married), then up to 50 percent of your Social Security could be taxed. And it gets worse. If you're single and the preceding computation exceeds $34,000 ($44,000 if married), as much as 85 percent of your Social Security could be added to your taxable income.

Enter on line 13a the amount from box 5 of **Form SSA-1099** (which reports the amount of Social Security you received). Also, don't forget to add the amount from your spouse's SSA-1099. These forms should be sent by the Social Security Administration by January 31, 1999. (If you've moved or haven't received mail for some other reason, you may need to contact the Social Security Administration at 800-772-1213 to find out where your Form SSA-1099 is.) To determine the taxable amount of your Social Security, you have to complete the Social Security worksheet provided in Chapter 6.

To make paying your taxes easier, Congress passed a law that allows you to have tax withheld on your Social Security at rates of 7, 15, 21, or 28 percent so that you won't owe a bundle next April 15. Unfortunately, Congress forgot to change the Social Security law's ban on tampering with benefits, and that includes voluntary requests to have tax withheld. Stay tuned — there's a bill pending to correct this. It seems our government's right hand doesn't know what its left hand is doing. Maybe that's not such a bad thing.

Line 14: Total income

Here you put the total of lines 7 through 13b. All those numbers to add!

Line 15: Your (and your spouse's) IRA deduction

You're entitled to deduct up to $2,000 for contributions to IRAs. Do it if you can! However, if you're covered by a retirement plan at work, this deduction may be reduced or eliminated. See Chapters 7 and 21 for more than you care to know about this issue. You have to make this computation based on the IRS rules and enter the amount on this line.

In 1998, both tax-deductible and nondeductible IRAs became a somewhat more flexible savings vehicle, with more people eligible to contribute to them. See Chapter 21 for details.

The rules on line 15 also apply to your spouse's IRA. And even if your spouse isn't employed, you can also deduct $2,000 for him or her for a total deduction of $4,000 (see Chapter 7 again). Prior to 1997, the most that could be put away for a nonworking spouse was $250. You have to do the math and enter the amount here.

Line 16: Student Loan Interest Deduction

You can deduct up to $1,000 of interest on a loan used to pay higher education (what comes after high school) and certain vocational school expenses. Ask the vocational school if it qualifies for this deduction if you have to borrow to pay the tab. The deduction gets increased to $1,500 in 1999, to $2,000 in 2000, and to $2,500 thereafter.

A host of rules must be met before this deduction can be nailed down, the main one being that if you're single, the deduction quickly gets pared down once your income hits $40,000 and disappears altogether at $55,000. For joint filers, it starts to shrink at $60,000 of income, with the deduction getting wiped out at $75,000. In Chapter 7, we explain who's entitled to the deduction, for how many years it can be claimed, and what loans and education expenses qualify.

The beauty of the Student Loan Interest Deduction is that you don't have to itemize your deductions in order to claim it. You can claim the standard deduction (see line 21) and this deduction as well. This should be of great benefit to recent graduates.

Line 17: Total adjustments

Add lines 15 and 16. What could be easier?

Line 18: Adjusted gross income

Now you get to subtract the total of your IRA and student loan interest deduction (line 17) from your total income (line 14) and enter that amount here.

Don't forget that you may be entitled to an earned income credit if your adjusted gross income is less than $26,473 and one child lived with you (the cutoff is $30,095 if two children lived with you, and $10,030 if you don't have kids). See "Line 59a: Earned income credit" in Chapter 8 for more details. Your tax is figured on page 2 of the form, so turn the page over.

Line 19: Successful transcription of adjusted gross income to back of Form 1040A

You enter your adjusted gross income on line 19 (which you already totaled on line 18). Be careful; don't transpose numbers!

Lines 20a and 20b: Exemption amount

Check the appropriate box(es). If you or your spouse is 65 or older or blind, you're entitled to an increased standard deduction. To figure the increased amount, refer to the standard deduction chart for people 65 or older in Chapter 9. Enter that amount on line 21.

If your parent or someone else can claim you as a dependent, use the standard deduction worksheet for dependents in Chapter 9 to compute your standard deduction. Enter that amount (instead of the standard deduction that all others are entitled to) from the worksheet on line 21.

If you're married filing separately and your spouse itemizes deductions, check box 20b and enter 0 on line 19. You aren't entitled to any standard deduction because both you and your spouse must use the same method.

Line 21: Standard deduction

So many choices! Find your filing status and enter the number here.

- Single: $4,250
- Head of household: $6,250
- Married filing jointly or qualifying widow(er): $7,100
- Married filing separately: $3,550

If you checked any box on line 20a, you're entitled to increase your standard deduction by $850 if married, and by $1,050 if single. If you checked box 20b, enter 0 on this line. If you're single and both blind and over 65, the standard deduction gets increased by $2,100. If you and your spouse are over 65, your standard deduction of $7,100 gets increased by $1,700 for a total of $8,800. If you and your spouse checked both boxes (over 65 and blind), the increase in the standard deduction is $3,400, for a total of $10,500.

If you think that you can get a higher deduction by itemizing your deductions on Schedule A, you can't file with Form 1040A. The standard deduction versus itemized deduction option is only available when filing with Form 1040.

Line 22: IRS subtraction quiz

Go ahead and subtract the amount you have on line 21 from your adjusted gross income on line 19. Put the result of this mathematical computation here. If you ended up with a larger number on line 21 than on line 19 (and you started to wonder how you could subtract a larger number from a smaller number), you have to start over from the beginning. No! Just kidding! If line 21 is larger than line 19, you place 0 on line 22.

Line 23: Total number of exemptions times $2,700

Multiply the number of exemptions you claimed on line 6d by $2,700 and enter the total here.

Line 24: Taxable income

Now subtract the amount on line 23 from line 22, and carefully place that number here. Well done! You've arrived at your taxable income.

Line 25: Find your tax

Use the tax tables in the back of this book to find your tax. With the tax tables, you don't have to make a mathematical computation to figure your tax. For example, if you're single and your taxable income is $43,610, look up the bracket between $43,600 and $43,650 and read across to the single column. The appropriate tax is $8,920.

Line 26: Credit for child and dependent care expenses

Use Schedule 2 to figure this amount. See "Line 41: Credit for child and dependent care expenses" in Chapter 8 for more details.

Line 27: Credit for the elderly or the disabled

Use Schedule 3 to compute this credit. See "Line 42: Credit for the elderly or the disabled" in Chapter 8 for further explanation.

Line 28: Child Tax Credit

Every child under age 17 on December 31 that you can claim as a dependent can cut your tax bill by $400 if your income is under $75,000 ($110,000 for joint returns; $55,000 for married persons filing separately). The child also must be a U.S. citizen or resident. In 1999, the credit jumps to $500.

In order for you to claim the credit, your dependent must be one of the following:

✔ Your son, daughter, adopted child, stepchild, or foster child

✔ Your grandchild, great-grandchild, or even your great-great grandchild

A child placed with you by an authorized placement agency for adoption is considered an adopted child even if the adoption isn't final. A foster child has to live with you for the entire year. A child who was born and then died in that year qualifies.

Although part of your Child Tax Credit starts getting whittled away when your income exceeds $110,000 and you're filing jointly ($75,000 if you are single), Form 1040A filers can ignore these limits because you can't use Form 1040A if your taxable income exceeds $50,000.

To compute the Child Tax Credit, the IRS directs you to a worksheet on page 33 of your instruction booklet.

Line 1: Based on the number of kids qualifying for the credit, enter the credit you are entitled to (one kid $400, two kids $800, and so on).

Lines 2 through 6: You can skip these lines. Because you are a 1040A filer, your taxable income has to be under $50,000; therefore, these lines only apply in unusual circumstances.

If by chance your income, line 19, is more than $75,000 if single, $110,000 if married filing jointly, or $55,000 if married and filing separately, you can still file using Form 1040A because your taxable income is less than $50,000. We explain how to fill out lines 2 through 6 in Chapter 8, line 43. Our aim is to spare you from as many unnecessary rules as possible, so jump to line 7,

Line 7: Enter the amount from line 1.

Line 8: Enter the amount of your tax from line 25, Form 1040A.

Line 9: If line 1 does not exceed $800, check the No box and enter the total of the following lines

Child and dependent care expenses – line 26

Credit for elderly – line 27

Education Credit – line 29

If line 1 is more than $800, then check the Yes box and complete the worksheet on page 34 of your instruction booklet. The worksheet on page 34 is an eight-line schedule that is used to determine how much of your Child Tax Credit you are entitled to because you're claiming other tax credits.

Line 10: Subtract line 9 from 8.

Line 11: Enter the smaller of line 7 or line 10 on Form 1040A, line 28. This is your Child Tax Credit.

This new credit comes in three varieties:

- ✔ **The Child Tax Credit:** Most people who are eligible to claim this credit will find it easy to compute. With the preceding line-by-line instructions as a guide, compute the credit on the Child Tax Credit worksheet in the Appendix. Enter the credit you are entitled to per line 11 of the worksheet on line 28.

- ✔ **The Additional Child Tax Credit:** This one comes into play when you have three or more kids and the regular Child Tax Credit exceeds your tax. With the preceding line-by-line instructions as a guide, use the Child Tax Credit worksheet in the appendix to compute the regular credit to which you are entitled. Enter the amount from line 11 of the worksheet on line 28; then fill out Form 8812, Additional Child Tax Credit. Enter the amount from line 11 of Form 8812 on line 38.

- ✔ **The Supplemental Child Tax Credit:** You may be eligible for this credit if you can't use the regular Child Tax Credit because you can claim the Earned Income or Adoption Credit, for example. (And you don't need to have three or more kids to take advantage of this one, by the way.) With the preceding line-by-line instructions as a guide, use the Child Tax Worksheet to compute the regular credit to which you are entitled. Enter the amount from line 11 of the worksheet on line 28 and then fill out Form 8812. Enter the amount from line 11 of Form 8812 on line 38.

In case you're scratching your head, why three variations of the same credit?

Normally, the regular Child Tax Credit isn't refundable if the credit exceeds your tax. For example, if your tax is $700 and you're entitled to a $800 credit (2 kids × $400), sorry, no refund. But notice that we said *normally.* By filling out **Form 8812, Additional Child Tax Credit,** you may discover that you're entitled to the $100 difference in the above example. There's one Child Tax Credit worksheet for 1040A filers and another for the 1040 long form folks.

Line 29: Education credits

"The more you learn, the more you earn." The government likes it when you further your education because it can collect more tax.

In 1998, two new credits kick in: the *Hope Scholarship Credit* and the *Lifetime Learning Credit.* Remember, credits reduce your tax dollar for dollar. Both credits are claimed on **Form 8863, Education Credits (Hope and Lifetime Learning Credits),** though you can't take both credits in the same year. Even though we explain how to fill out the form and the requirements that must be met, the next two sections explain how the two credits work.

The Hope Scholarship Credit

This credit allows a credit of $1,500 per student per year for the first two years of college. The credit is equal to 100 percent of the first $1,000 of tuition expenses (but not room, board, or books) and 50 percent of the next $1,000 of tuition paid. The credit can be claimed for you, your spouse, and your dependents. But if you earn too much, you won't be eligible to claim the credit. For married taxpayers, the credit starts to phase out at $80,000 of income and is completely lost at $100,000. And if you're married, you have to file jointly to be entitled to the credit. For single taxpayers, the phaseout starts at $40,000 and is wiped out when their incomes reach $50,000.

The credit isn't available for anyone convicted of possession or distribution of a controlled substance. A student must carry at least one half the normal course load.

The Lifetime Learning Credit

Starting June 30, 1998, you may be eligible for the Lifetime Learning Credit, a 20 percent credit on up to $5,000 of tuition expenses (but not room, board, or books) paid after that date. This $1,000 credit is per family and not per student like the Hope Credit. If the $1,000 credit isn't used in one year, the balance can be taken in another year. The same income limits and stipulations about who can claim the credit that apply to the Hope Credit also apply to this credit. Unlike the Hope Credit, however, the student doesn't have to carry at least one-half the normal course load.

The IRS can check to see whether you're entitled to the credit because educational institutions are now required to issue **Form 1098-T** listing a student's name, Social Security number, whether the student was enrolled for at least half the full-time work load, whether the courses lead to a graduate level degree, and the amount of tuition paid.

Line 30: Adoption credit (Form 8839)

You may claim a tax credit of up to $5,000 for qualified adoption expenses. For a child with special needs, the credit is $6,000. If your employer pays or reimburses you for the adoption expenses, you don't get to claim the credit, nor do you have to pay tax on the first $5,000 that you receive. Both the credit and exemption are computed on **Form 8839, Qualified Adoption Expenses.** The amount of the credit you're entitled to per line 10 of the form gets entered on line 30. If your employer reimbursed your adoption expenses or paid them directly, the amount reimbursed that escapes tax is computed on page 2 of Form 8839. See "Line 45" in Chapter 8 to find out what expenses qualify and to determine when the credit starts to evaporate when your income gets too high.

Line 31: Total credits

Compute your total credits; add the amounts from lines 26 through 30 and enter them here.

Line 32: Another IRS subtraction problem

Gee whiz, it never ends, does it? Now subtract your total credits (line 31) from the amount on line 25. Enter that remainder here. However, if your total credits are more than the amount on line 25, you get the easy way out and enter zero (0).

Line 33: Advance earned income payments

This amount is in box 9 of your W-2s, which your employer provides for you.

This is a smart move. By filing **Form W-5, EIC Advance Payment Certificate** with your employer, you don't have to wait until you file your return to claim this credit. Sixty percent of the credit can be added to your paycheck throughout the year.

Line 34: Total tax

Add lines 32 and 33 to arrive at your total tax.

Line 35: Total federal income tax withheld

Get this amount from box 2 of your W-2s or box 2 of your W-2G. And don't forget to add in any tax withheld and listed in box 4 of **1099-INTs** and **1099-Rs,** or box 2 of **1099-DIVs.** These forms report the amount of federal income tax you already paid during the tax year — you want to make sure that you get credit for the total tax withheld from your income. Otherwise, you'll double-pay!

Line 36: 1998 estimated tax payments and amount applied from 1997 return

If you made quarterly tax payments, enter the amount here. You could be penalized for not paying at least 90 percent of your tax by means of withholding and quarterly tax payments. The IRS doesn't like to wait until April 15 to collect most of the tax you owe. For more on estimated tax penalties, see Chapter 19.

If you have income such as interest, dividends, pension, and IRA withdrawals, and the tax you owe for 1999 after what was withheld will be more than $1,000, you have to make quarterly estimated payments on **Form 1040ES.** If you don't meet one of the exceptions to this rule, you will be penalized (see "Line 69" in Chapter 8).

Line 37a: Earned income credit

You may be entitled to an earned income credit if your AGI is less than $30,095 and two children lived with you, or $26,473 if one child lived with you (less than $10,030 if no child lived with you). See "Line 59a: Earned income credit" in Chapter 8 for more details. If you qualify for the credit and have a qualifying child, you must fill out **Schedule EIC** (earned income credit) and attach it to your return.

Anyone who fraudulently claims the credit is ineligible to claim it for ten years. For those who are reckless or unintentionally disregard the rules, the penalty is two years.

Line 37b: Nontaxable earned income and type

If this sounds like the IRS is trying to put something over on you, guess what? You're right. Although this doesn't apply to many people, we explain it all in "Line 59b" in Chapter 8.

Line 38: Additional Child Tax Credit

This is the refundable portion of the Child Tax Credit we explain on line 28. To get part of the credit refunded, you have to file **Form 8812, Additional Child Tax Credit.** Flip back to line 28 for a quick refresher.

Line 39: Total payments

Now you get to add. Find the sum of lines 35, 36, 37a, and 38 — but don't include your nontaxable earned income from line 37b.

Line 40: We smell refund!

Subtract your total tax (line 34) from your total payments (line 39) — if line 34 is smaller than line 39. Here's your refund! Don't spend it all in one place.

Although refunds are fun, large ones are a sign that you made the IRS an interest-free loan. Contact your employer's payroll department (or call the IRS at 800-TAX-FORM) and request Form W-4 to adjust the amount of tax being withheld. See "Form W-4" in Chapter 15 for a quick guide through this form.

Lines 41a and 42: What to do with your refund

If you have a refund but think you're going to owe tax in 1999 and can't trust yourself to hang on to the cash, you may want to apply some or all of the refund toward next year's tax (do this on line 42).

Applying the refund to next year's tax is an excellent option for people who have to make quarterly estimated payments, eliminating the need to make a larger-than-necessary first-quarter payment on April 15 for your 1999 return and then wait for a refund based on your 1998 return. Once you make this choice, you can't change your mind and ask for it back. It can only be claimed as an additional payment on your 1999 return.

Lines 41b–d: Direct deposit of your refund

You can speed up the receipt of your refund by ten days to two weeks and minimize the chances of its loss or theft by requesting that it be deposited directly to your account. *Note:* Consider whether you want to share this type of confidential and personal information. See the instructions under "How to Fill Out a 1040EZ," earlier in this chapter. If you want your refund extra pronto (up to two weeks sooner), jot down the routing number from your checks on line 41b. (That's the nine-digit RTN number shown in Figure 5-2.) On line 41c, check the type of account. Your account number is the DAN number shown in Figure 5-2; enter it on line 41d.

Line 43: Amount you owe

Those are three of the most dreaded words in the English language. If the amount on line 34 is greater than that on line 39, subtract line 39 from line 34. Put your Social Security number on the check and write 1998 FORM 1040A on the line at the bottom left of your check. Make out the check to the Internal Revenue Service. (IRS is too easy to alter to Mrs. Jones if the check goes astray.)

If you want to charge what you owe on a credit card, go back to line 12 of the 1040EZ for the ins and outs of how to do this. (Before you whip out your Visa, though, read our cautions at the end of "Line 12: Payment due" in the "How to Fill Out a 1040EZ" section, earlier in this chapter.)

Line 44: Estimated tax penalty

If you owe $1,000 or more in tax, and the sum of the estimated tax payments you made in 1998 plus your withholding doesn't equal 90 percent of your tax, you'll be assessed a penalty. You can escape this penalty in a number of ways. Turn to "Line 69" in Chapter 8 to see if there's hope for you. **Form 2210, Underpayment of Estimated Tax,** is used to both compute and escape the penalty. Chapter 19 has valid excuses that should work.

Final Instructions

Put your John or Jane Hancock(s) on your form. (That means sign it, okay? Don't get funny and write in *John Hancock;* the IRS doesn't have our sense of humor.) Attach your W-2s and any 1099s where tax was withheld, as well as your check or money order (if required) to the form and mail it to the IRS Service Center for your area. See Appendix A for the correct address if you're missing the pre-addressed envelope that comes with your Form 1040A instruction booklet.

Chapter 6

Form 1040: Income Stuff

....

In This Chapter

▶ Your W-2

▶ Where to report different income on your 1040

▶ Your 1099-R

▶ Other income stuff

....

You surely remember the old war slogan "Divide and Conquer" (we think Alexander the Great or some other real famous warrior said it). Well, that's our strategy here. We break down each section and each line of Form 1040, and pound each one into submission.

Note: You're going to be jumping into a deeper section of the pool here. If you're unsure about which Form 1040 to use (EZ, A, or the "long" version), you need to take one step back to Chapter 5. Likewise, if you're unsure of your filing status (single, married filing separately, married filing jointly, head of household), take two steps back to Chapter 4.

Now for Chapter 6, which is the guts of the return, the income section (see Figure 6-1). Each heading has the specific line references of Form 1040 listed first. After you go through a segment, plug the correct number in the line of the 1040 and move on.

Figure 6-1:
The Income section of Form 1040 lists how much you made in 1998.

Income	7 Wages, salaries, tips, etc. Attach Form(s) W-2	7
	8a **Taxable** interest. Attach Schedule B if required	8a
Attach	b Tax-exempt interest. DO NOT include on line 8a . . . [8b]	
Copy B of your Forms W-2, W-2G, and 1099-R here.	9 Ordinary dividends. Attach Schedule B if required	9
	10 Taxable refunds, credits, or offsets of state and local income taxes (see page 15) . .	10
	11 Alimony received	11
If you did not get a W-2, see page 14.	12 Business income or (loss). Attach Schedule C or C-EZ	12
	13 Capital gain or (loss). Attach Schedule D	13
	14 Other gains or (losses). Attach Form 4797	14
Enclose but do not attach any payment. Also, please use Form 1040-V.	15a Total IRA distributions . [15a] b Taxable amount (see page 16)	15b
	16a Total pensions and annuities [16a] b Taxable amount (see page 16)	16b
	17 Rental real estate, royalties, partnerships, S corporations, trusts, etc. Attach Schedule E	17
	18 Farm income or (loss). Attach Schedule F	18
	19 Unemployment compensation	19
	20a Social security benefits . [20a] b Taxable amount (see page 18)	20b
	21 Other income. List type and amount—see page 18	21
	22 Add the amounts in the far right column for lines 7 through 21. This is your **total income** ▶	22

Lines 6a–6d: Exemptions

We don't like to repeat ourselves, so go back to these lines in Chapter 5 on Form 1040EZ to find out how to complete lines 6a through 6d. You can round off to the nearest dollar so you don't have to fiddle with pennies. It only takes a minute or two; we promise.

Lines 7–22: Income

Income is, in brief, money or something else of value that you receive whether you work for it or not.

Most of us know that wages earned from toiling away at jobs are income. But *income* also includes things such as alimony, certain interest, dividends and profits on your investments, and even your lottery winnings or prizes won on *Wheel of Fortune.*

All people who work for an employer are likely to receive the famous **Form W-2, Wage and Tax Statement,** which your employer issues at tax-year's end. That form helps you find out what you earned during the year, as well as what was taken away from you.

In this chapter, you discover the meaning of all those various boxes on your W-2 (your regular income stuff). We show you how to use this and other information to complete all those other line numbers in the big section of Form 1040 called "Income," lines 7 through 22. Don't worry, we go into more detail for the various schedules that some line numbers ask for.

We must warn you that you may become dejected to see your other nonemployment income (which you report in the lines ahead) as taxable income. We'll make sure that we highlight foolproof ways to keep this tragedy from happening again next year.

Line 7: Wages, salaries, tips

In order to fill in the blank on line 7, scrounge around for your W-2 (see Figure 6-2). You should receive your W-2 from your employer by January 31, 1999. It's a three-part form. Why three parts? Copy B gets nailed to the federal return; copy C is filed with your neat and organized records; and copy A is affixed to your state return. If you look at the lower-left corner of your W-2s, you see what to do with each copy.

Figure 6-2:
Form W-2 shows you how much dough you earned and how much you "donated" to the government.

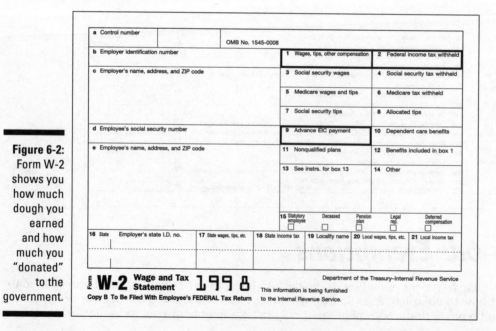

If you're self-employed and you don't receive a W-2, you get to skip this line, but you're going to end up doing tons more work completing Schedule C in order to fill in line 12 of the 1040. For farmers, it's schedule F. Retirees can skip 'em both — one of the many perks of retirement!

If your W-2 is wrong, contact your employer to have it corrected as soon as possible. Otherwise, you'll pay too much tax or too little — and you wouldn't want to do that. If you didn't receive your W-2, call your employer. If that doesn't work, file **Form 4852, Employees' Substitute Wage and Tax Statement,** which is a substitute for missing W-2s (as well as missing 1099-Rs). The magnanimous IRS allows you to estimate your salary and the amount of tax withheld on this form. You then attach Form 4852 to your tax return. You can get that form or any other form by calling the IRS toll-free (800-829-3676).

What those W-2 boxes mean

Each of the numbered boxes on your W-2 contains either welcome information (like your gross income, which momentarily makes you feel rich) or the type of information that will surely have you shaking your head in disbelief (like the total amount of different types of taxes that you paid throughout the year, which effectively makes you feel poor again). If you notice in the discussion ahead that we're skipping over some of those silly little boxes, rest assured that we explain them when we need to in the chapters ahead.

Box 1: Wages, tips, other compensation

Your taxable wages, tips, other compensation, and taxable fringe benefits are listed here. This is a biggie. Everything but the kitchen sink was thrown into box 1. Common examples are your salary, your tips, and the taxable portion of any fringe benefits like the personal-use part of your company car. Other stuff that your employer tossed into box 1 includes back pay, bonuses, commissions, severance or dismissal pay, and vacation pay. That whopping $7 per day that you were paid for jury duty isn't reported on your W-2. It gets reported on line 21 of your 1040.

Because box 1 is a catchall, the figure in it may be larger than your actual cash salary. Get it over with — fill in the amount on line 7. If you have one or more W-2s, add 'em up and put in the total.

Box 8: Allocated tips

If you worked in a restaurant and didn't report all your tip income, box 8 includes the difference between your share of at least 8 percent of the restaurant's income and what you reported. This income is **not** reported in box 1. Therefore, you must add this to the amount on Form 1040 (line 7). You must also enter this amount on **Form 4137, Social Security and Medicare Tax on Unreported Tip Income.** You get an earful about this form in the section "Line 52: Social Security and Medicare tax on unreported tip income" in Chapter 8.

Box 9: Advance EIC (Earned Income Credit) payment

If your income is less than $30,095 with two or more qualifying dependents or less than $26,473 for one dependent, you may be entitled to the earned income credit (see the stuff under "Line 59a: Earned income credit" in Chapter 8 for more information). If you're entitled to an EIC, you can file **Form W-5, EIC Advance Payment Certificate,** with your employer instead of waiting until you file your return to have this credit refunded. By filing a W-5, up to 60 percent of the credit that you're entitled to can be added to your paycheck. You can obtain this form from your employer or from the IRS at 800-829-3676.

The purpose of the EIC is to refund a portion of the Social Security and Medicare tax to low-income workers for working if their income is below the appropriate threshold, discussed in the preceding paragraph.

Box 10: Dependent care benefits

If your employer has a day-care plan or provides day-care services, this box includes the reimbursement from your employer for day-care costs or the value of the day-care services that your employer provides. The amount in box 10 above $5,000 is taxable and is also included in box 1. Don't report it again!

To determine whether any portion of the amount below $5,000 is taxable, you have to complete Part III of **Form 2441, Child and Dependent Care Expenses.** If any part of that amount is taxable, include it with the amount that you enter on line 7 of Form 1040. Next to it write DCB (which stands for dependent care benefits). The reason that you're being directed to Form 2441 is that the portion of the tax-free child care benefits that you received reduces the amount of your child care and dependent care expenses eligible for the child care credit.

Box 13: See Instrs. for Box 13

This cryptic message is meant to direct you to the instructions on the reverse side of your W-2 to find out what the symbols in this box mean. This box includes your 401(k) contributions, the premium on group life insurance over $50,000 (that amount is also included in box 1), nontaxable sick pay, employer contributions to your medical savings account, and uncollected Social Security and Medicare taxes on tips that you reported to your employer (and that your employer wasn't able to collect from you — the letter *A* will be next to the amount). Uncollected Social Security tax is added to your final tax bill and is reported on Form 1040 (line 52). Next to it, write UNCOLLECTED TAX.

Box 15: Statutory employee

Full-time life insurance salespeople, agents, commission drivers, traveling salespeople, and certain home-workers can file as self-employed instead of as employees. This status allows them to deduct their business expenses on Form 1040, Schedule C (Profit or Loss From Business) or on Schedule C-EZ.

Don't report the amount of your W-2's box 1 on line 7 of your Form 1040 if you want to deduct your business expenses. Report it on Schedule C or C-EZ. By doing it this way, you may be able to deduct all your travel, entertainment, auto, and other business-related expenses instead of having to claim them as itemized deductions. (See Chapter 11 for loads of Schedule C stuff.)

Business expenses taken as itemized deductions are reduced by 2 percent of your *adjusted gross income* (AGI) and then shaved a second time if your income is too high. So reporting business expenses on Schedule C is clearly to your advantage. Additionally, deducting these expenses on Schedule C lowers your AGI, which means that you pay less tax. You can do this stuff only if the statutory employee box is checked.

Line 8a: Taxable interest income

If your interest income (from boxes 1 and 3 of all your 1099-INTs) is $400 or less, enter the amount on this line. If this amount is over $400, you must complete a Schedule B. No biggie! Schedule B is easy to complete. For more information, you have permission to cruise to Chapter 10 to dive further into that schedule. When you get the total, come back and fill it in. With the exception of municipal bonds, all the interest that you earn is taxable. If you need examples, the IRS publications have pages of them. But don't report the interest that you earn on your IRA or retirement account; that interest is taxed only when you withdraw the funds.

If you keep lots of your money in bank accounts, you may be missing out on free opportunities to earn higher interest rates. Chapter 23 discusses money market funds, a higher yielding alternative to bank accounts.

Also, if you're in a higher tax bracket, you may be able to earn a higher return with your savings by choosing tax-free investments instead of keeping money in bank accounts. (You're in the 28-percent federal income tax bracket beginning at $25,350 in taxable income — line 39 on the 1040 — as a single filer or $42,350 as a married couple filing jointly.) See Chapter 23 to learn how to keep more of your investment income.

Line 8b: Tax-exempt interest

Because municipal bond interest is not taxable, you're not going to receive a 1099. Your year-end statement from your stockbroker has this information. The IRS wants you to fill in the interest that you received on tax-exempt bonds. Plug it in. Just so you know, although this interest isn't taxable, the number is used to compute how much of your Social Security benefits may be subject to tax.

Surprisingly, some people who invest money in tax-exempt bonds shouldn't. These people often are not in a high enough income tax bracket to benefit. If your taxable income isn't at least $25,350 if you're filing as a single (or $42,350 if married filing jointly), you shouldn't be so heavily into tax-exempt bonds. You'd be better off moving at least some of your money into taxable bonds or stocks (where gains can be taxed at the new 10- and 20-percent rates). See Chapter 11 so that you don't overpay. See Chapter 23 for more information about investments that are subject to more favorable tax rates.

Line 9: Dividend income

Dividends are income that you receive from stocks and mutual funds that you own. They're reported on **Form 1099-DIV.** Dividends come in three flavors: *ordinary* (which can be taxed at rates as high as 39.6 percent), *capital gains* (which can be taxed at one of two rates: either 10 or 20 percent, depending on your tax bracket; see Chapter 12 so that you don't overpay), and *nontaxable.* If your dividend income is under $400, enter the amount from box 1b on line 9. If you have more than $400 in dividend income, you have to fill out Schedule B. Again, we send you to Chapter 10 to find out how to complete Schedule B.

Be careful, though: You don't have to own a $100,000 nest egg to fill in this line; you may own one or two mutual funds and need to put some information here. Capital gain dividends are entered on line 13 of Schedule D. We explain all of this in Chapter 12.

If you're in a higher income tax bracket, you may benefit from reducing your taxable dividend income and instead focusing on tax-friendlier investments (see Chapter 23).

Line 10: Taxable refunds, credits, or offsets of state and local income taxes

As a general rule, state and local income tax refunds are taxable because you deducted your state tax payments on last year's federal income tax return.

State and local tax refunds that you receive are reported on **Form 1099-G,** a form that your state department of revenue sends to you. If you chose to apply part or all of your 1997 state tax overpayment to your 1998 estimated state or local tax payments that you have to make (instead of having it refunded), the overpayment is still considered a refund even though a check wasn't sent to you.

Different definitions of what you earned

Many of the boxes on your W-2 include wage information that you don't need to include on your Form 1040. Think of them as FYI boxes. They simply show you the different ways that the IRS computes income for assessing different taxes. For example, box 3, "Social Security wages," reports the amount of your wages for the tax year that is subject to Social Security taxation. (Not the benefits that the Social Security Administration is paying you!) Your Social Security wages may differ from your wages as reported in box 1 because some types of income are exempt from income tax but *are not* exempt from Social Security tax. For example, if you put $3,000 in a 401(k) retirement plan in 1998, box 3 is going to be $3,000 higher than box 1.

Box 5, "Medicare wages and tips," reports the amount of your wages that is subject to Medicare tax. For most people, their wages that are subject to Medicare equal their total wages that are reported in box 1, thanks to the tax law changes enacted in 1993. Although the amount of your wages that is subject to Social Security tax is 6.2 percent up to $68,400, there is no maximum on wages subject to the 1.45 percent Medicare tax.

Box 7, "Social Security tips," is the amount of tips that you received and reported to your employer. This amount is included in box 1, so don't count it again!

Box 11, "Nonqualified plans," pertains to retirement plans in which you can't defer the tax. If a portion of a Section 457 (State and Local Government Deferred Compensation Plan) over the deferred limits was contributed to the retirement plan, the taxable portion is included in box 11 and box 1.

Box 12, "Benefits," refers to taxable fringe benefits, such as your personal use of a company car, the cost of group life insurance in excess of $50,000 paid for by your employer, and education assistance exceeding $5,250. Benefits in this box are also included in box 1.

Under the new law, the tax-free portion of up to $5,250 of employer-paid educational assistance that expired on December 31, 1994, was extended retroactively through July 1, 1997, and again for another three years through May 31, 2000. If you paid tax on the tuition that your employer paid in 1995, you can get it back by filing an amended return, Form 1040X — see Chapter 19 for details. A new wrinkle in the law is that after June 30, 1996, you aren't entitled to the exclusion for graduate-level courses. Aren't you glad you went back to school so that you can understand all this stuff? Up to $175 per month of employee-provided parking and $65 per month for qualified commuter expenses are considered tax-free fringe benefits — if you opt for the cash, they're taxable.

But, like just about every tax rule, there is an exception. For example, your refund isn't taxable if you claimed the standard deduction in a prior year instead of itemizing your deductions.

Even though you may itemize your deductions, only the part of your refund representing the amount of your itemized deductions in excess of the standard deduction is taxable. But in order to make this computation, you have to do some number crunching. The following worksheet (see Table 6-1) gives you the answer. Suppose that your 1997 state refund was $700, you filed jointly, and your itemized deductions were $7,150.

Table 6-1	State and Local Income Tax Refund Worksheet	
	Example	*Your Computation*
1. Enter the income tax refund from Form(s) 1099-G (or similar statement).	1. $700	1.
2. Enter your total allowable itemized deductions from your 1997 Schedule A (line 28).	2. $7,150	2.

	Example	*Your Computation*
3. Enter on line 3 the amount shown below for the filing status claimed on your 1997 Form 1040: Single — $4,150 Married filing jointly or Qualifying widow(er) — $6,900 Married filing separately — $3,450 Head of household — $6,050	3. $6,900	3.
4. If you didn't complete line 34a on your 1997 Form 1040, enter -0-. Otherwise, multiply the number on your 1997 Form 1040, line 34a, by $800 ($1,000 if your 1997 filing status was single or head of household) and enter the result.	4. $0	4.
5. Add lines 3 and 4.	5. $6,900	5.
6. Subtract line 5 from line 2. If zero or less, enter -0-.	6. $250	6.
7. Taxable part of your refund. Enter the smaller of line 1 or line 6 here and on Form 1040, line 10.	7. $250	7.

Line 11: Alimony received (by you)

Because the person who pays the alimony can deduct these payments from his or her taxable income (on line 31a), the spouse who receives these payments must include alimony as taxable income. You report alimony received on line 11. You'll know the figure to enter by consulting the divorce decree or separation agreement.

You need to know what alimony is before you can report it as income or deduct it as an expense. The alimony rules aren't simple — Why should they be? Why simplify divorce? — but we've tried our best to clear them up. We offer a more detailed explanation of alimony in the section "Line 31a: Alimony paid" in Chapter 7.

Here's an important tip about alimony and IRAs. You can set up and make deductible contributions to an IRA if you receive taxable alimony and separate maintenance payments. Basically, if you receive taxable alimony, you can set up an IRA and deduct what you contribute to it — 100 percent of your alimony up to $2,000 is deductible. However, your deduction may be reduced or eliminated if you're covered by a retirement plan through your work. See Chapter 21 for more on how to set up IRAs. Chapters 7 and 21 give the lowdown on both deductible IRAs and the new Roth IRA.

Line 12: Business income (or loss)

If you're self-employed, you must complete a Schedule C to report your business income and expenses. If you just receive an occasional fee and don't have any business expenses, you can report that fee on line 21 as other income. And remember, if you're a statutory employee (a life insurance salesperson, agent, commission driver, traveling salesperson), you have a choice of reporting your income on line 7 or Schedule C.

As a general rule, you're better off reporting your self-employment income on Schedule C. Although slightly more complicated than entering your income on line 21, you can deduct business-related expenses against your income on Schedule C that will lower your income and the tax that you have to pay.

The amount that you enter on line 12 is the result of the figuring and jumbling that you do on Schedule C or C-EZ. Check out Chapter 11 to dive into that material.

Line 13: Capital gain or (loss)

You don't have to be Bill Gates to have a capital gain or loss. (We bet that Bill has mostly gains. How about you?) You have a capital gain or loss when you sell stock or bonds or investment property. When you sell an asset like your house for a profit, you have a taxable gain, but you have a nondeductible loss if you lose money on the sale of your house. Losses on other investments — such as stocks, bonds, and mutual funds — made outside retirement accounts are generally deductible. Chapter 12 gives you the scoop on this heady concept as well as the right amount to enter here.

Line 14: Other gains or (losses)

You guessed it, grab another form — **Form 4797, Sales of Business Property.** Fill out that form and enter the final figure on line 14. Form 4797 is used when you sell property that you've been depreciating (such as a two-family house that you've been renting out). This form is explained in Chapter 12.

Lines 15a and 15b: Total IRA distributions

One of the benefits from all those years of hard work and diligent savings is that someday, hopefully, you'll be able to enjoy and live off the fruits of your labor. Although this line number is for reporting money that you've withdrawn from an Individual Retirement Account (IRA), we must share with you some important information if you haven't yet started withdrawals and are getting to the age where you should.

You must start taking out a minimum amount from your IRA by April 1 of the year after you turn 70$\frac{1}{2}$ (see the sidebar "Don't forget these decisions," later in this chapter). If you don't, you're assessed a 50-percent penalty on the amount that you should have taken out. Suppose that you should have taken out $4,000, but you didn't. You'll have to pay a $2,000 penalty. You can request that the penalty be excused if your failure to make a minimum distribution was due to a reasonable error or if you're taking steps to remedy the error. Illness, a computational error, or incorrect advice are three examples of a reasonable error. You compute the 50-percent penalty on **Form 5329.** Chapter 21 gives you the lowdown on how much you have to take out.

If you just discovered that you should have been taking out money, start taking your distribution immediately. Then try to see if one of the preceding reasonable causes will help you avoid the penalty. Part IV, line 19, of Form 5329 will help you plead your case; write and attach a statement explaining why you didn't make the required distribution. A math error or illness are some of the valid reasons to have the penalty excused. In the statement, say that you corrected the error and are taking out what the law requires you to withdraw every year. Also, state that you don't feel that you should be penalized because it's the only time that it has happened, and you took immediate measures to correct the mistake.

Line 15a is for reporting money that you withdrew from your IRA during the tax year. If you receive a distribution from an IRA, the payer — your bank or broker — sends you **Form 1099-R** (see Figure 6-3).

CORRECTED (if checked) ☐			
PAYER'S name, street address, city, state, and ZIP code	**1** Gross distribution $	OMB No. 1545-0119 19**98** Form **1099-R**	Distributions From Pensions, Annuities, Retirement or Profit-Sharing Plans, IRAs, Insurance Contracts, etc.
	2a Taxable amount $		
	2b Taxable amount not determined ☐	Total distribution ☐	**Copy B**
PAYER'S Federal identification number	RECIPIENT'S identification number	**3** Capital gain (included in box 2a) $	**4** Federal income tax withheld $	Report this income on your Federal tax return. If this
RECIPIENT'S name		**5** Employee contributions or insurance premiums $	**6** Net unrealized appreciation in employer's securities $	form shows Federal income tax withheld in box 4, attach this copy to your return.
Street address (including apt. no.)		**7** Distribution code	IRA/ SEP/ SIMPLE ☐	**8** Other $ %	This information is being furnished to the Internal
City, state, and ZIP code		**9a** Your percentage of total distribution %	**9b** Total employee contributions $	Revenue Service.
Account number (optional)		**10** State tax withheld $ $	**11** State/Payer's state no.	**12** State distribution $ $
		13 Local tax withheld $ $	**14** Name of locality $	**15** Local distribution $

Form **1099-R**   Department of the Treasury - Internal Revenue Service

Figure 6-3: Form 1099-R tells you how you did on your IRA and other retirement plans in 1998.

As a general rule, distributions made from an IRA are fully taxable unless you made nondeductible contributions to the IRA, which we explain in the upcoming instructions for box 2a of the 1099-R. Here's a rundown of the important boxes that you need to read on your 1099-R in order to report an IRA distribution on Form 1040.

Effective January 1, 1998, you can benefit from two additional IRAs: an education IRA and a Roth IRA. See Chapters 7 and 21 for more on these new investment vehicles.

Box 1: Gross distribution (Form 8606)

This box represents the amount of money that you withdrew from your IRA and that was reported to the IRS. Make sure that it's correct by checking to see whether the figure matches the amount withdrawn from your IRA account statement. If you made a nondeductible contribution to an IRA — that's an IRA contribution for which you didn't take a tax deduction and thus filed **Form 8606, Nondeductible IRA Contributions, Distributions and Basis** — write the number from box 1 on line 15a of your Form 1040. However, if your IRA distribution is fully taxable (see the next section), don't make an entry on line 15a; write the number on line 15b instead. See Chapter 15 for information about how to fill out the form.

Box 2a: Taxable amount

This box contains the taxable amount of your IRA distribution. However, the payer of an IRA distribution doesn't have enough information to compute whether or not your entire IRA distribution is taxable. Therefore, if you simply enter the amount reported in box 1 on Form 1040 (line 15b) as being fully taxable, you'll overpay your tax if you made non-deductible contributions to your IRA. If you made nondeductible contributions, you must compute the nontaxable portion of your distribution on Form 8606. And you must attach Form 8606 to your return.

Box 7: Distribution code

A number code is entered in this box if one of the exceptions to the 10-percent penalty for distributions before age $59^1/_2$ applies.

       ✔ Code 2 — annuity exception

       ✔ Code 3 — disability exception

       ✔ Code 4 — beneficiary exception

Distributions before 59¹/₂

If you withdraw money from your IRA before you're 59¹/₂, not only do you have to include the amount in your income, but you also owe a 10-percent penalty on the amount that you withdraw. The penalty is computed on **Form 5329, Return for Additional Taxes Attributable to Qualified Retirement Plans.** Attach the form to your return and carry over the penalty to Form 1040 (line 53). The penalty doesn't apply to IRA distributions that are paid due to death or disability, paid over your life expectancy, or rolled over to another IRA.

The 10-percent penalty no longer applies to money withdrawals from an IRA that are used to pay medical expenses in excess of 7¹/₂ percent of your income. Additionally, anyone receiving unemployment for 12 consecutive weeks can withdraw money to pay health insurance premiums without paying the penalty. Self-employed people out of work for 12 weeks can also make penalty-free withdrawals to pay their health insurance premiums.

The 10-percent penalty doesn't apply to distributions paid over your lifetime or the joint lives of you and your beneficiary. You can switch out of this method after you reach 59¹/₂ and after you've used it for five years — for example, you're 56 years old and need some dough. After receiving distributions based on your life expectancy for at least five years, you can switch out of this method. At age 61, you can withdraw the remaining balance or any part of it, if you want. You don't have to elect the annuity method for all your IRAs. You can use it with the IRA that has the largest or smallest balance.

Starting in 1998, penalty-free (but taxable) withdrawals will be allowed for the purchase of a first home and to pay college expenses. This exception to the penalty includes the first home of you and your spouse, child, or grandchild. Penalty-free withdrawals for higher education also apply to you, your spouse, child, or grandchild. Withdrawals for graduate school are also penalty-free. A first home doesn't mean your first ever — it simply means that you didn't own one within two years of the withdrawal. For example, you sold your home, lived in a rented apartment for three years, and then purchased a new home — this purchase qualifies for the $10,000 penalty-free withdrawal. The home-buyer's exception has a limit of $10,000, but you can stretch the withdrawals over several years. For example, if you withdraw $3,000 now, you can withdraw $7,000 later. You must use the funds within 120 days of withdrawal to buy, build, or rebuild a "first home." There is no limit on the amount that you withdraw for college expenses. What expenses qualify? Tuition fees, books, and room and board (as long as the student is enrolled for at least a half-time basis).

Transfers pursuant to divorce

The transfer of an IRA account as a result of a divorce or maintenance decree isn't taxable to you or your former spouse. Nor is it subject to the 10-percent penalty. Here's how you deal with the reality of dividing an IRA in a divorce. If your divorce decree requires that you transfer all or part of your IRA to your former spouse, the transfer is *not* taxable, nor is it subject to the 10-percent early distribution penalty if you're under 59¹/₂.

To make sure that you don't run afoul of the 10-percent penalty, the spouse receiving the money should set up his or her own IRA account. Have the money transferred directly to that account.

Don't forget these decisions

If you're self-employed or retired from a company, on April 1 of the year following the year that you turn 70¹/₂, you have to make some important decisions about how the money will come out of your IRA. Your first choice: whether you receive yearly distributions based on your life expectancy or based on the joint life expectancies of you and your beneficiary. If your aim is to take out as little as possible, use a joint life expectancy; that stretches out your distributions over a longer period.

Next, you have to decide how you want your life expectancy to be calculated. With the method known as *term-certain,* you pick the current IRS estimate of your life expectancy and then reduce it by one year every year. So if this year the IRS figures that you'll live 23.1 years, next year you divide the balance of the account by 22.1, and so on. See IRS Publication 590 on the wonderful subject of how to calculate your life expectancy.

With the second method, known as *recalculation,* you go back to the IRS tables in Publication 590 and look up your new life expectancy each year. Over time, this method has you taking out a little less money per year than with the term-certain approach. (According to the IRS tables, your life expectancy doesn't decrease by a full year every 12 months.) But the recalculation method has some serious drawbacks. Namely, if one spouse dies, only the survivor's life expectancy is used. When you both die, the entire balance must be paid out by the end of the next year to whoever is next in line for the money. That could mean a big tax bill for whoever is getting the balance of your account — presumably an heir. If you use the term-certain approach, the heir can keep taking money out in dribs and drabs, just as you had been doing. To us, the term-certain method is the clear winner.

Inherited IRAs: Surviving spouse

If you're the beneficiary of your deceased spouse's IRA, you can choose to roll that IRA over into your own IRA. It can be a new IRA account (which we suggest) or an existing one. The advantage to rolling over your deceased spouse's IRA into yours is that if you're under 70¹/₂, you can delay making withdrawals until you reach that age. The money in the account continues to grow tax-free. Another advantage, even if you're over 70¹/₂ when your spouse dies, is that by treating your deceased spouse's IRA as your own and naming your own beneficiary, the minimum distributions that you have to take out at 70¹/₂ will be smaller than if you didn't treat the IRA as your own and instead took distributions from the account as a beneficiary.

Here are two other options. You can roll over part of your deceased spouse's IRA and withdraw part. You have to pay tax on the part that isn't rolled over. If you're under 59¹/₂, you're not subject to a 10-percent early withdrawal penalty, and you don't have to pay a penalty if you choose to receive distributions as a beneficiary of the account.

Because you may be dealing with large sums of money, you may want to seek professional advice or immerse yourself in IRS Publication 590, *(Individual Retirement Accounts).*

Inherited IRAs: Beneficiary other than a surviving spouse

Only surviving spouses can treat inherited IRAs as their own. Other beneficiaries have to start receiving distributions from the IRAs. If you're under 59¹/₂, the 10-percent early withdrawal penalty doesn't apply.

Here is where the rules get hairy. If an IRA owner dies after the required starting date for taking distributions (which is 70¹/₂), you must take withdrawals as rapidly as the owner was taking them. However, if the owner was using the recalculation method (see the sidebar "Don't forget these decisions"), you must withdraw the entire amount no later than the year after the year the owner died.

If the owner dies before the magical required starting date (70½), you can choose to receive the funds over your life expectancy or over the five-year period following the owner's death, or take out all the dough by the end of the fifth year and take a well-earned vacation.

Make sure that you read the terms of the plan so that you know all your withdrawal options.

Withdrawal of nondeductible contributions

If you made nondeductible contributions to your IRA, use **Form 8606** to compute the taxable portion of your withdrawal. You don't have to pay tax on nondeductible contributions that you withdraw. The total of your IRA distributions is entered on line 7 of Form 8606; enter that total on line 15a of Form 1040 as well. The figure from line 13 of Form 8606 is carried over to line 15b of the 1040. That's the taxable portion.

Lines 16a and 16b: Total pensions and annuities

Here's where you report your retirement benefits from your pension, profit-sharing, 401(k), SEP, or Keogh plan. How these plans are taxed depends on whether you receive them in the form of an annuity (paid over your lifetime) or in a lump sum.

The amount that you fill in on lines 16a and 16b is reported on a **1099-R** that you receive from your employer or another custodian of your plan. If the amount that you receive is fully taxable, only complete line 16b and leave line 16a blank.

Tax on excess withdrawals

If you're lucky enough to be receiving $155,000 per year or had more than $775,000 in your account in 1996, you just got luckier. Even though these thresholds have been adjusted for inflation every year, the 15-percent penalty tax on distributions and accumulations in excess of these amounts has been repealed. The nickname for this penalty was the "success tax."

Pensions and annuities

If you didn't pay or contribute to your pension or annuity — or if your employer didn't withhold part of the cost from your pay while you worked — then the amount that you receive each year is fully taxable. The amount that you contributed for which you received a deduction — such as contributions to a 401(k), SEP, IRA, or Keogh — isn't considered part of your cost.

If you paid part of the cost (that is, if you made nondeductible contributions or contributions that were then added to your taxable income on your W-2), you aren't taxed on the part that you contributed because it represents a tax-free return of your investment. The rest of the amount that you receive is taxable. To compute this amount, you can use either the *Simplified General Rule* or the *General Rule*.

Simplified General Rule

You can use this method for figuring out the taxable amount of your pension only under the following conditions:

- Your annuity starting payout date is after July 1, 1986.

- The annuity payments are either for your life or for your life *and* that of your beneficiary.

✔ You were 75 or under, or your payments were guaranteed for fewer than five years at the time the payments began.

✔ The pension or annuity payments are from a qualified employee plan, a qualified employee annuity, or a qualified tax shelter annuity. The word *qualified* is tax jargon for a retirement plan approved by the IRS.

Under the Simplified General Rule, the IRS allows you to declare as nontaxable part of the money that you receive from a certain number of payments made to you or to your beneficiary, based on your age when the benefits start. Divide the amount of your contribution to the pension by the number of payments that the IRS allows, using Table 6-2 to arrive at the nontaxable amount of each payment if your pension is based on one life or if it is based on two life expectancies and the pension starting date was before January 1, 1998.

Table 6-2	Simplified General Rule — One Life	
Combined Age at Annuity Starting Date	*Divide By*	*After 11-18-96*
55 and under	300 payments	360 payments
More than 55 and under 60	260 payments	310 payments
More than 60 and under 65	240 payments	260 payments
More than 65 and under 70	170 payments	210 payments
More than 70	120 payments	160 payments

For reasons that we can't explain, Congress won't make it simple and pick the beginning of a year as the date for making a change. If you started receiving payments after November 18, 1996, you have to use the payment schedule in the right-hand column.

You must use a separate table for pensions and annuities starting in 1998 that are based on the life expectancies of two or more retirees — for example, the life expectancies of you and your spouse (see Table 6-3). What's your life expectancy? The IRS determines everything, so send for IRS Publication 575, *(Pension and Annuity Income)*.

Table 6-3	Simplified General Rule — Two Lives
Combined Age at Annuity Starting Date	*Divide By*
110 and under	410 payments
More than 110 and under 120	360 payments
More than 120 and under 130	310 payments
More than 130 and under 140	260 payments
More than 140	210 payments

Suppose that you retired at age 65 and began receiving $1,000 per month under a joint and survivor annuity with your spouse (that is, an annuity that pays a benefit to you or your spouse as long as one of you is still living). Your spouse is 60 and you contributed $31,000 to the pension. Divide the $31,000 by 310 (the amount for your combined age of 125). The resulting $100 is the monthly amount that you receive tax-free. If you live to collect more than the 310 payments, you'll have to pay tax on the full amount of your pension that you receive beyond that point. Your contribution includes amounts withheld from your paycheck as well as any contributions made by your employer that were reported as additional income.

If you die before you receive 310 payments, your spouse continues to exclude $100 from each payment until the number of payments received, when added to yours, totals 310. If your spouse dies before the 310 payments are made, a miscellaneous itemized deduction on your spouse's final tax return is allowed for the balance of the 310 payments remaining to be paid multiplied by $100. This deduction isn't subject to the 2-percent adjusted gross income limit. If your spouse dies with 40 payments yet to be made, a $4,000 deduction would be allowed (40 × $100).

If your annuity starting date was after July 1, 1986, but before January 1, 1987, you can take the exclusion as long as you're receiving payments. You don't need to stop at the total number of payments you determined in Table 6-2.

General Rule

You must use the General Rule to figure the taxability of your pension or annuity if your annuity starting date is after July 1, 1986, and you do not qualify for — or you do not choose — the Simplified General Rule.

Under the General Rule, a part of each payment is nontaxable because it is considered a return of your cost. The remainder of each payment (including the full amount of any later cost-of-living increases) is taxable. Finding the nontaxable part is very complex and requires you to use actuarial tables. For a full explanation and the tables you need, get IRS Publication 939 *(Pension General Rule — Nonsimplified Method)* or consult a tax advisor.

The nontaxable amount remains the same under the General Rule even if the monthly payment increases. If your annuity starting date was before 1987, you continue to exclude the same nontaxable amount from each annuity payment for as long as you receive your annuity. If your annuity starting date is after 1986, your total exclusion over the years cannot be more than your cost of the contract reduced by the value of any refund feature.

If your annuity starting date is after July 1, 1986, and you (or a survivor annuitant) die before the cost is recovered, a miscellaneous itemized deduction is allowed for the unrecovered cost on your (or your survivor's) final income tax return. The deduction is not subject to the 2-percent AGI limit.

Lump-sum distributions

To qualify as a *lump-sum* distribution, the lump sum must be your entire balance in all your employer's pension plans and it must be paid within a single tax year. The distribution must be paid because of one of the following reasons:

- You die.
- You reach age 59¹/₂.
- You leave the firm.
- You become totally and permanently disabled (if self-employed and under the age of 59¹/₂).

A lump-sum distribution from your employer's pension plan can be rolled over to an IRA or to your new employer's retirement plan. If you don't need to make use of the money, a rollover probably is your best bet, because it allows you to defer taxation on the money. (It's also best to let your employer transfer the money on your behalf.) You don't have to roll over the entire amount. The part you don't roll over is subject to tax and possibly a 10-percent penalty. Voluntary after-tax contributions that you made to the plan can't be rolled over. They are tax-free to you when received and aren't subject to the 20 percent withholding tax that lump-sum distributions are subject to. See "Tax on early distributions," later in this chapter, for information on how to escape the penalty. Or this distribution can be given capital gain or special averaging treatment if the participant was in the plan for at least five years. These options are what we talk about next.

If you have your employer make a direct rollover from the retirement plan to your IRA, tax doesn't have to be withheld. If you receive the lump sum payment directly, however, tax must be withheld. ***Remember:*** You have 60 days from the receipt of the money to roll it over. Because you will be receiving only 80 percent if you receive the lump-sum directly, you will have to pay tax on the 20 percent withheld unless you make up the difference with your own dough.

A single tax year means exactly that. If, for example, you received $10,000 in 1997 and the balance in 1998, you're out of luck.

If your former employer's retirement plan includes the company's stock (say you work for GE, for example), you may want to transfer it to your taxable brokerage account instead of rolling it over into an IRA rollover account. Why? When you take the stock, you pay taxes on only the value at the time you purchased it and not at the value when you left the company. For example, you bought shares through your company's retirement account that cost $10,000; they're now worth $100,000. You pay tax on $10,000 and not on the current value. And if you're under 55, the 10-percent penalty is also computed on the $10,000 value. Only when you sell the shares are you taxed on the appreciation in value, and then you are taxed at the new 20-percent capital gain rate, or possibly the lower 10-percent rate if you're in the 15-percent tax bracket.

Capital gains treatment

If you reached the age of 50 before 1986, you can choose to treat a portion of the taxable part of the lump-sum distribution as a capital gain that is taxable at a 20-percent rate. This treatment applies to the portion you receive for your participation in the plan before 1974. You can select this treatment only once, and you use **Form 4972, Tax on Lump-Sum Distributions,** to make this choice.

The tax on the balance of the lump-sum distribution can be figured under the averaging method described in the next section. For most people, a tidy sum can be saved between the capital gain and averaging methods. Box 3 of Form 1099-R contains the capital gain amount.

Special averaging method

If you reached age 50 before 1986 (you were probably born before 1936, right?), you can elect either the special five- or ten-year averaging method of the ordinary income portion of your lump-sum distribution. (This procedure also includes the capital gain portion of the distribution if you don't choose capital gain treatment for it.) To qualify, you must elect to use special averaging on all lump-sum distributions received in the tax year. If you were born after 1935, you can use only the five-year averaging method.

To use special averaging, you must have been a participant in the plan for at least five full tax years. You can make only one lifetime election to use this method. If you choose the special averaging method, use Form 4972 and figure your tax as if you received the distributions over five or ten years, depending on the method selected.

When you treat the distribution as though you received it over ten years, you must use 1986 tax rates. Form 4972 is also used to compute your tax using the five-year method. The instructions accompanying Form 4972 contain a 1986 tax-rate schedule. Five- or ten-year averaging can save you a bundle. Although you can use the ten-year method only if you were born before 1936, you can use the five-year method if you're at least 59$^1/_2$.

After December 31, 1999, five-year averaging will no longer be available.

Which method is best? Unfortunately, only crunching the numbers both ways will tell. Here's where a good tax software program will prove to be invaluable. But, as a general rule, for amounts up to $400,000, ten-year averaging will produce a bigger savings; above $400,000, the five-year method offers bigger savings.

You pay the tax on the lump sum in the year that you receive it, even though the distribution is computed as if you received it over five or ten years. After you pay the tax, the balance is yours, free and clear.

Form 1099-R

If you receive a total distribution from a retirement plan, you will receive a Form 1099-R. If the distribution qualifies as a lump-sum distribution, box 3 shows the capital gain amount, and box 2a minus box 3 shows the ordinary income amount. Code A is entered in box 7 if the lump sum qualifies for special averaging. If you do not get a Form 1099-R, or if you have questions about it, contact your plan administrator.

Tax on early distributions

Distributions that you receive from your employer's retirement plan before the age of $59\frac{1}{2}$ are subject to a 10-percent penalty as well as being fully taxable. But here are some of the exceptions to the 10-percent penalty on employer retirement plans, which are more liberal than the exceptions to the 10-percent penalty for taking money out of an IRA before age $59\frac{1}{2}$ and vice versa:

- ✔ Death

- ✔ Total and permanent disability

- ✔ Distributions (after separation from service) paid over your lifetime or the joint lives of you and your beneficiary

- ✔ Distributions made after you stopped working (retirement or termination) during or after the calendar year you reach age 55

- ✔ Distributions made under a qualified Domestic Relations Court order

- ✔ Distributions made to you (to the extent you have deductible medical expenses in excess of 7.5 percent of your adjusted gross income)

Pension distributions on Form 1099-R

Pension distributions are reported on Form 1099-R, which is the same one used to report IRA distributions. The difference between how the information on an IRA distribution is reported to you and the distribution from your pension is as follows:

Box 3: If the distribution is a lump sum and you were a participant in the plan before 1974, this amount qualifies for capital gain treatment.

Box 5: Your after-tax contribution that you made is entered here.

Box 6: Securities in your employer's company that you received are listed here. The appreciation in value isn't taxed until the securities are sold. Only the actual cost of the shares are taxed when they're received. See the section "Lump-sum distributions."

Box 7: If you're under $59\frac{1}{2}$ and your employer knows that you qualify for one of the exceptions to the 10-percent penalty, the employer enters:

Code 2 —	separation from service after 55
Code 3 —	disability
Code 4 —	death
Code A —	qualifies for lump-sum treatment
Code G —	direct rollover to an IRA
Code H —	direct rollover to another retirement plan

If you are under $59\frac{1}{2}$ and your employer knows that no exception to the 10 percent penalty applies, a Code 1 (one) will be entered in Box 7.

Box 8: If you have an entry here, seek tax advice.

Box 9: Your share of a distribution if there are several beneficiaries.

You report the penalty you have to pay on **Form 5329, Additional Taxes Attributable to Qualified Retirement Plans,** if none of the exceptions apply. Attach the form to your return and carry over the 10 percent to Form 1040 (line 50).

The penalty-free (but taxable) withdrawals allowed for first-time home buyers and for paying college tuition that start in 1998 don't apply to your employer's pension plan, Keoghs, SEPs, or 401(k)s — only to IRAs.

Minimum distributions

The same rule that applies to IRAs also applies to pension plans for failing to take a minimum distribution by April 1 of the year following the year you turned 70$\frac{1}{2}$. See the sidebar "Don't forget these decisions" earlier in the chapter.

The 70$\frac{1}{2}$ rule doesn't apply if you are still employed. You can delay making withdrawals until you retire. This rule doesn't apply to IRAs or to someone who owns 5 percent or more of a business.

Disability income

If you retire on disability, your pension is usually taxable. If you are 65 or older (or if you are under 65 and are retired because your disability is total and permanent and you receive disability income), you may be able to claim a credit for the elderly or the disabled. You compute the credit on Schedule R (see "Line 42: Credit for the elderly or the disabled" in Chapter 8). However, payments made because of the permanent loss or use of part of the body, or for permanent disfigurement, are exempt from tax.

If you contributed to a plan that paid a disability pension, the part of the pension that you receive that is attributable to your payments isn't subject to tax. You report all your taxable disability on line 7 of your 1040, until you reach the minimum retirement age — that is, the age stated in your plan when you are entitled to a regular retirement annuity — and then on line 16a or b. You must use the Simplified General Rule or the General Rule to compute the part of a disability pension that isn't taxable due to your contribution. VA disability benefits are tax-free.

Here is a quick reference list on sickness and injury benefits:

- ✔ **Workers' compensation:** Not taxable if paid under a workers' compensation policy due to a work-related injury or illness.

- ✔ **Federal Employees' Compensation Act (FECA):** Not taxable if paid because of personal injury or sickness. However, payments received as continuation of pay for up to 45 days while a claim is being decided and pay received for sick leave while a claim is being processed are taxable.

- ✔ **Compensatory damages:** Not taxable if received for injury or sickness.

- ✔ **Accident or health insurance:** Not taxable if you paid the insurance premiums.

- ✔ **Disability benefits:** Not taxable if received for loss of income or earning capacity due to an injury covered by a *no-fault* automobile policy.

- ✔ **Compensation for permanent loss or loss of use of a part or function of your body, or for permanent disfigurement:** Not taxable if paid due to the injury. The payment must be figured without regard to any period of absence from work.

- ✔ **Reimbursements for medical care:** Not taxable; the reimbursement may reduce your medical expense deduction.

Effective August 21, 1996, damages received for age discrimination and injury to your reputation as well as emotional distress not related to physical injuries or sickness are not tax-exempt. Prior to this change, courts had reached differing results on this issue.

Line 17: Rental real estate, royalties, partnerships, S Corporations, trusts

This line is an important one for all you self-starters who are landlords, business owners, authors, and taxpayers collecting royalties (like us!), and those people lucky enough to have someone set up a trust fund for them. Jump to Chapter 13 to find out more about this and good old Schedule E — the necessary form to wrestle with for this line.

Line 18: Farm income or (loss)

What comes after E? You got it. If you have farm income or losses, seek ye olde Schedule F (see Chapter 14), fill it out, and fill in the final number on line 18. It's similar to Schedule C.

Line 19: Unemployment compensation

Losing your job was bad enough. And now you receive another nasty surprise — the news that the unemployment compensation you received is taxable. The government should have sent you a **Form 1099-G** (see Figure 6-4) to summarize these taxable benefits that you received. Unemployment compensation is fully taxable, and you enter it on line 19.

Figure 6-4:
Form
1099-G
shows the
unemployment
compensation
— and the
state tax
refund! —
you
received in
1998.

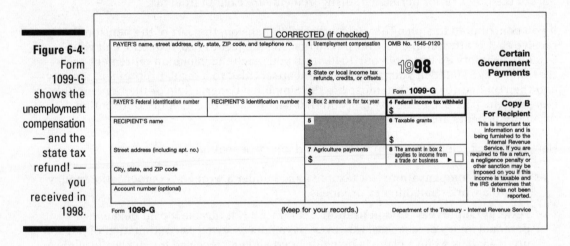

You can elect to have tax withheld at the rate of 15 percent on your unemployment so you won't be caught short next April 15. This is one offer most people are likely to refuse.

If you repaid some or all of the unemployment compensation benefits you received in 1998, you subtract the amount you repaid from the total amount you received and enter the difference on line 19.

Why would you have to give back some of your benefits? Because when you are collecting unemployment insurance, you have to be looking for a job. And if you aren't, the folks at the unemployment office may determine that you weren't entitled to all the benefits you received and you owe some money back. If you gave back the benefits in the same year that you received them, no problem; just subtract what you returned from the total you received and enter that amount on line 19.

But if you returned money in 1998 that you paid tax on in 1997, things aren't as easy. Suppose that in 1997 you received and paid tax on $10,000 of unemployment benefits. Then during 1998 you had to pay $2,500, as determined by the unemployment office. The $2,500 you paid back is deductible on Schedule A (see Chapter 8).

You should also enter REPAID and the amount that you repaid on the dotted line next to the difference on line 19. If you repaid unemployment compensation (that was less than $3,000) in 1998 that you included in gross income in an earlier year, you may deduct the amount repaid with Form 1040, Schedule A (line 22).

If the amount you repaid was more than $3,000, either you can take a deduction for the amount repaid as an itemized deduction, or you can take a credit against your tax for the amount of tax you originally paid by including this amount in your income in a prior year.

For example, suppose that in 1998 you repaid $4,000 of unemployment compensation that you received and paid tax on in 1997. Compute your 1997 tax without the $4,000 being included in your income. If your original tax was $10,000 and your tax without the $4,000 of unemployment was $8,416, you can claim the difference ($1,584) as a credit against your 1998 tax. If this credit is more than what you would save by deducting the $4,000 as an itemized deduction, enter the $1,584 on Form 1040 (line 63), and to the left of the $1,584 credit write IRC 1341. The credit to which you are entitled is considered an additional tax payment made. The term IRC 1341 comes from Section 1341 of the Internal Revenue Code of 1986. This is known as a *claim of right*.

Lines 20a and 20b: Social Security benefits

Politicians don't want to do away with Social Security; they just want to tax more of it. As a result, they have made retirement more complicated. Here's how to figure out what to plug in.

Don't forget that if you are married and file a joint return for 1998, you and your spouse must combine your incomes and your benefits when figuring if any of your combined benefits are taxable. Even if your spouse did not receive any benefits, you must add your spouse's income to yours when figuring whether any of your benefits are taxable.

Form SSA-1099

Every person who receives Social Security benefits will receive a **Form SSA-1099,** even if the benefit is combined with another person's in a single check. If you receive benefits on more than one Social Security record, you may get more than one Form SSA-1099. Your gross benefits are shown in box 3 of Form SSA-1099, and your repayments are shown in box 4. The amount in box 5 shows your net benefits for 1998 (box 3 minus box 4). This is the amount you will use to figure whether any of your benefits are taxable.

How much is taxable?

The starting point for determining the taxable portion of your Social Security is your base income, which is your adjusted gross income with a few adjustments. The base income worksheet we give you shows you how to compute this amount. It's an easy computation to make unless you're covered by a pension and decide to make a deductible contribution to an IRA because your income was under $60,000 (for joint filers) or $40,000 (for others).

Here's a suggestion. Unless you want to drive yourself crazy, stay away from making deductible contributions to an IRA if you're covered by a pension and are also receiving Social Security. But in case you want to do the math in this more complicated case, we show you how to do the calculations here.

Base Income Worksheet

Example: You're married filing jointly and have interest and dividend income of $10,000, a $20,000 pension, and you received $16,000 from Social Security.

1. AGI (1040, line 33) before addition of taxable Social Security	$ 30,000
2. Social Security (box 5, SSA-1099)	$ 16,000
3. 50 percent of line 2	$ 8,000
4. Tax-exempt interest income	$ 0
5. Foreign earned income exclusion	$ 0
6. Total of lines 3, 4, 5	$ 8,000
7. Base income (add lines 1 and 6)	$ 38,000

Now use one of the following worksheets to figure the taxable portion of your Social Security benefits: If line 7 is more than $44,000 (if you are married and filing jointly) or $34,000 (if unmarried) you have to use Worksheet II.

Worksheet I

1. Base income	$ 38,000
2. Enter the appropriate amount below.	
Married filing jointly — $32,000	
Married filing separately and living with spouse at any time during year — 0	
All others — $25,000	$ 32,000
3. Subtract line 2 from line 1.	$ 6,000
4. 50 percent of line 3	$ 3,000
5. Social Security (box 5, SSA-1099)	$ 16,000
6. 50 percent of line 5	$ 8,000
7. Taxable Social Security — smaller of lines 4 and 6	$ 3,000

Enter the amount on line 5 ($16,000) on line 20a, Form 1040 and the amount on line 7 ($3,000) on line 20b, Form 1040.

Worksheet II

Example: Assume the same facts in the example on Worksheet I, except that your AGI is $36,000, your Social Security is $16,000, and you had $6,000 in tax-exempt interest.

1. AGI	$ 36,000
2. Tax exempt interest	$ 6,000
3. 50 percent of Social Security	$ 8,000
4. Base income (add lines 1 through 3)	$ 50,000

Tier one adjustment

5. Enter the appropriate amount below.

   Married filing jointly — $32,000

   Married filing separately and living with spouse at any time during year — 0

   All others — $25,000 $ 32,000

6. Subtract line 5 from line 4. $ 18,000

7. 50 percent of line 6 $ 9,000

8. Enter the appropriate amount below.

   Married filing jointly — $6,000

   Married filing separately and living with spouse at any time during year — 0

   All others — $4,500 $ 6,000

9. The smaller of lines 3, 7, and 8 $ 6,000

Tier two adjustment

10. Enter the appropriate amount below.

    Married filing jointly — $44,000

    Married filing separately and living with spouse at any time during year — 0

    All others — $34,000 $ 44,000

11. Subtract line 10 from line 4. $ 6,000

12. 85 percent of line 11 $ 5,100

TAXABLE PORTION

13. Add lines 9 and 12. $ 11,100

14. 85 percent of box 5, SSA-1099 ($16,000) $ 13,600

15. Taxable Social Security (smaller of lines 13 and 14) $ 11,100

You would enter the amount in box 5, SSA-1099, ($16,000) on line 20a of Form 1040 and $11,100 from 15 on line 20b, Form 1040. On Form 1040A, it's $16,000 on line 13a and $11,100 on line 13b.

Repayment of benefits

In some cases, your Form SSA-1099 will show that the total benefits you repaid (box 4) are more than the gross benefits you received (box 3). If this situation occurs, your net benefits in box 5 will be a negative figure, and none of your benefits will be taxable. If you receive more than one form, a negative figure in box 5 of one form is used to offset a positive figure in box 5 of another form. If you have any questions about this negative figure, contact your local Social Security Administration office.

If you and your spouse file a joint return and your SSA-1099s show that your repayments are more than your gross benefits, but your spouse's are not, subtract the amount in box 5 of your form from the amount in box 5 of your spouse's form to get your net benefits when figuring whether your combined benefits are taxable.

Retirees, watch your step

People who retire but continue working part-time to supplement their Social Security income may be in for a nasty surprise when they sit down to complete their tax return.

If you are between the ages of 62 and 65, you lose out on $1 of Social Security benefits for every $2 you earn above $9,120 for 1998. (Remember, this is earned income only; unearned income, such as from investments or a pension, doesn't penalize your benefits.)

Between the ages of 65 and 69, you lose $1 of Social Security for every $3 earned above $14,500 for 1998. This is known as the Social Security *giveback,* though it seems like a *takeback* to us. (At age 70, you can earn as much as you like without forfeiting any of your benefits.)

Not only do you have this giveback to contend with, but more of your Social Security is subject to tax. Married couples with incomes above $44,000 and singles who make more than $34,000 will pay tax on 85 percent of their Social Security income.

The long and short of all of this is that if you're not careful, working a little extra to add to your income from Social Security income could cost you money. Suppose that you earned $2,000 above that $9,120 threshold and, bad luck, it pushed you from the 15- to the 28-percent tax bracket. First, you pay 7.65 percent Social Security tax on the extra $2,000 of income, which works out to $153. Next you have to pay an extra $1,036 of income tax because you're in a higher bracket now and more of your Social Security is taxable. Then you would have to give back $1,000 of your Social Security benefit. Your cost of making that extra two grand: $2,189!

Our advice to retirees under the age of 70: Once you reach either the $9,600 (if between 62 and 65) or the $15,500 (if between 65 and 69), which are the 1999 maximum earning levels, take a vacation until December 31.

Repayment of benefits received in an earlier year

If the sum of the amount shown in box 5 of each of your SSA-1099s is a negative figure and all or part of this negative figure is for benefits you included in gross income in an earlier year, you can take an itemized deduction on Schedule A for the amount of the negative figure — or you can claim credit for the tax that was paid on this in a prior year because you included it in your income. We explain how to make the computation for this *claim of right* in our previous discussion of unemployment insurance on line 19.

Line 21: Other income

Line 21 of Form 1040 is a catchall for reporting income that doesn't fit the income categories listed on page one of Form 1040. Hey, even if you *find* some money, the IRS treats it as income! Just report all this miscellaneous income here. Don't forget to write a description of these earnings on the dotted line next to the amount.

Here are some examples of stuff that goes on line 21.

Bartering

Bartering is the trading of your services for goods or other services. You usually must declare the fair market value of goods you receive. If you participate in a barter exchange, you may get a **1099-B** — and the IRS gets a copy, too. For example, suppose that you're a carpenter with a child who needs braces; you agree to make cabinets in a dentist's office in exchange for your child's braces and treatment. Although no cash changed hands, you have to pay tax on what the dentist would normally charge because that is your income from making the cabinets. The dentist makes out better. Because the cabinets are used in his business, he is entitled to a business deduction equal to the income he has to report. Even poor Jack of Beanstalk fame had taxable income when he traded his cow for those beans.

Lump-sum payment

If you receive a lump-sum payment of Social Security benefits in 1998 that includes benefits for prior years, you have two choices. You can consider the entire payment as the amount of Social Security received in 1998 and compute the taxable portion by using Worksheet I or II. Or you can allocate the amount that you received for a prior year as being received in that year.

It makes sense to do it this last way because prior to 1994 the maximum amount of Social Security that could be taxed was 50 percent — and if your income was lower in a prior year, even less than 50 percent may be taxable.

If you elect the second way of treating a lump sum that covers more than one year, you don't file an amended return for that year. Here's what you do. You compute the amount of the lump sum that would have been taxable had it been received in the prior year. You then add that amount to your income for the current year.

For example, suppose that you receive a lump-sum payment of $20,000 covering benefits for 1994 and 1995. If you report the whole amount in 1998, 85 percent, or $17,000, is taxable. But because $10,000 was for 1994 and $10,000 was for 1995, you have to report only $13,500 as taxable in 1998. That's because the $10,000 attributable to 1994 only increases your income by $5,000, and the $10,000 attributable to 1995 increases your income by $8,500.

Canceled debt

A canceled debt, or a debt paid for you by another person, is generally income to you and must be reported. For example, a discount offered by a financial institution for the prepaying of your mortgage is income from the cancellation of the debt. However, you have no income from the cancellation of a debt if the cancellation is a gift. For example, suppose that you borrow $10,000 from a relative who tells you that you don't have to repay it. It's a gift! (And be sure to invite *that* relative to Thanksgiving dinner every year.) If you received a sweetheart deal on a loan, make sure that you read the rules on below-market interest rates for loans in Chapter 10.

If your debt is canceled as the result of bankruptcy or because you are insolvent, the cancellation of the debt negates your having to pay tax on the income. And you do not have to report it as income if your student loan is canceled because you agreed to certain conditions to obtain the loan — and then performed the required services.

Under the old law, only student loans from governmental or educational organizations qualified for this exclusion from income rule when professional services were rendered in exchange for the forgiveness of the loan. After August 5, 1997, loans from tax-exempt charities also qualify.

Other stuff

Here are some more examples of things to be included on line 21:

✔ **Fees that you snare:** Maybe you're a corporate director, or a notary public, and you made some extra cash. Good job!

If these payments are $600 or more, you will receive **Form 1099-MISC.** If you receive a fee or commission from an activity you're not regularly engaged in for business, you report it instead on line 21. Fees are considered self-employment income, which means that you may owe Social Security tax on them. You compute the Social Security tax you owe on **Schedule SE (Self-Employment Tax).** The amount of Social Security tax owed is then reported on line 50 of Form 1040, and you get a deduction for half of the tax on line 27.

✔ **Free tour:** The free tour you received from a travel agency or the group organizer is taxable at its fair market value. Bon voyage.

✔ **Gambling winnings:** Gambling winnings are taxable. But you can also deduct your gambling losses — as long as they don't exceed your winnings — as an itemized deduction on line 27 of Schedule A.

✔ **Prizes and awards:** If you get lucky and hit the lottery or win a prize in a contest, the winnings are taxable. Sorry!

However, some employee achievement awards may be nontaxable. These are non-cash awards, such as a watch, golf clubs, or a TV, given in recognition for length of service or safety achievement. The tax-free limit is $400 if given from a non-qualified employer plan and $1,600 from a qualified plan. Check with your Human Resource department.

✔ **Jury duty:** The whopping $7 a day (more or less) that you got for jury duty goes here. If you must repay this amount to your employer because your employer continued to pay your salary while you served on the jury, you can deduct the repayment. The repayment gets deducted on line 31a of Form 1040. Write `Jury Pay` on the dotted line next to line 31a.

Deductions

You also use line 21 to claim two types of deductions: a net-operating loss and the foreign earned income and housing exclusion.

Net operating loss (NOL)

This deduction to your income occurs when your business expenses in a prior year exceed your income for that year. Unless you elect otherwise by attaching a statement to your return that says you want to carry the loss forward, you must first carry back the loss to the three prior tax years as a deduction and then forward for the next 15 years — until the total loss is used up. Chapter 19 deals with filing amended returns and how NOLs are carried back and forward. When you carry an NOL forward from a previous year, you enter it as a negative number (for example, <$10,000> on line 21).

Losses incurred after January 1, 1998, can only be carried back two years, but can be carried forward for 20 years instead of 15. However, the three-year carryback will still apply to the NOL of small businesses ($5 million or less of income for the past three years) attributable to losses in a presidentially declared disaster area. Farmers are allowed a special break; losses incurred after 1997 can be carried back 5 years and forward 20 years.

Foreign earned income and housing exclusion

U.S. citizens and residents working abroad are entitled to exclude up to $72,000 of their foreign salary or their self-employed income. (If you've ever considered working abroad, this exclusion may help you make up your mind.) The portion of their foreign housing costs above an annual threshold ($9,643 for 1998) can also be deducted. The exclusion isn't automatic. You have to file **Form 2555, Foreign Earned Income,** to claim the exclusion and the housing deduction, and attach it to your return. There is also a Form 2555-EZ.

Every year the exclusion increases in annual increments of $2,000 (for example, $74,000 for 1999) until it reaches $80,000. To qualify for the exclusion, you must either be a resident of a foreign country or be physically present in a foreign country. Earnings from employment by the U.S. government don't qualify.

To qualify as a resident, you must reside in a foreign country for an uninterrupted period that includes the entire year (January 1 to December 31). So if you start working in London on March 31, 1998, you can't qualify for the exclusion under the entire-year rule, but you could possibly under the *physical presence test.* Brief trips back to the U.S. don't disqualify you from being a resident of a foreign country.

Under the physical presence test, you must be in a foreign county for 330 days during a 12-month consecutive period. If you weren't physically present or a bona fide resident for the entire year, the $72,000 exclusion has to be reduced based on the number of days you were out of the country.

To determine whether you meet the 330-day test, you may have to apply for an extension of time to file **(Form 2350, Application for Extension to File U.S. Income Tax Return).** Say you started to work in Paris on July 1, 1998; you won't know until July 1, 1999, if you meet the 330-day test for the 12-month period of July 1, 1998, to July 1, 1999.

You enter your foreign earnings on Form 1040 (line 7). Then you enter the amount of those earnings that you can exclude — plus your foreign housing deduction — as a negative number on line 21 and deduct it from your income.

If your foreign earned income was $72,000 or less and you earned it as an employee (you weren't self-employed), and you're not claiming a foreign housing exclusion or a deduction for moving expenses, the friendly folks at the IRS allow you to use Form 2555-EZ; the difference is 18 lines versus 48.

Life insurance

The death benefit paid to the beneficiary of a life insurance contract is exempt from tax. However, this exception doesn't apply to advance payments made to terminally or chronically ill taxpayers.

A limited portion ($180 a day or $65,700 annually) of an advance payment on a life insurance policy won't be subject to tax if paid to a terminally or chronically ill person. Unfortunately, here is where the law gets somewhat ghoulish. A terminally ill person is someone who is certified by a doctor as having a life expectancy under 24 months. A person is chronically ill if they can't perform at least two of their normal daily functions, such as eating, bathing, dressing, toileting, and so on. (Only the IRS could make such a distinction.) Amounts above $180 are also excludable if they are used to pay for long-term care. That's an oxymoron if we ever heard one. The tax lingo for these advanced payments is *viatical settlements.* Aren't you glad you took Latin in high school?

To get the name of viatical brokers or companies that advance money before the death of a policy holder, you can contact either the National Viatical Association at 800-741-9465, or the Viatical Association of America at 800-842-9811.

Line 22: Your total income

Whew! Are you ready to do the math? Don't be stubborn or proud; grab the calculator. Add lines 7 through 21 and put the final figure on line 22.

Chapter 7

Form 1040, Part Deux: Adjustments to Income Stuff

In This Chapter

▶ IRA deductions

▶ Student loan interest

▶ Medical savings accounts

▶ Moving expenses

▶ The self-employment tax write-off

▶ Keogh and SEP deductions and SIMPLE plans

▶ Penalty on early withdrawal of savings

▶ Alimony paid (that you deduct!)

Congratulations! If you're reading this chapter, you've probably made it through one of the more depressing parts of the tax return. Completing lines 7 through 22 is a bit like trying to count up the number of kindergarten students at the end of a field trip — it's hard to corral everyone, and the total keeps increasing. Despite the IRS calling this last section *Income,* most people just think of their employment earnings as income. If you've done lines 7 through 22, you now know that the IRS definition includes a whole lot more. Ugh!

The first step in the tax-slimming process is completing the *adjustments to income* section — adjustments are things that reduce the amount of income that can be taxed. It sure would be easier for you to understand if adjustments to income were simply called deductions from income. But no one ever said the IRS likes to make things simple. When you flip over your Form 1040, you'll see that there's another section that allows you to actually deduct things.

Adjusted Gross Income

In this section (see Figure 7-1), you'll be summing your adjustments to income (lines 23 through 31a) and subtracting them from your total income (line 22). The result of this subtraction is called your *adjusted gross income* (AGI). Your AGI is an important number, because it's used as the benchmark for calculating many allowable deductions — such as medical and miscellaneous itemized deductions — as well as the taxable amount of your Social Security income. In fact, if your AGI is too high in the eyes of the IRS, we're sorry to say that you may even lose the personal exemptions that you thought you were entitled to — the personal exemption that you can claim for yourself, your spouse, and your dependents. That's $2,700 for each of you.

An important thing to keep in mind is that you don't have to itemize your deductions on Schedule A to claim adjustments to income in this section. Everyone gets to make these adjustments!

Adjusted Gross Income If line 33 is under $30,095 (under $10,030 if a child did not live with you), see EIC inst. on page 36.	23 IRA deduction (see page 25)		23		
	24 Student loan interest deduction (see page 27)		24		
	25 Medical savings account deduction. Attach Form 8853		25		
	26 Moving expenses. Attach Form 3903		26		
	27 One-half of self-employment tax. Attach Schedule SE		27		
	28 Self-employed health insurance deduction (see page 28)		28		
	29 Keogh and self-employed SEP and SIMPLE plans		29		
	30 Penalty on early withdrawal of savings		30		
	31a Alimony paid b Recipient's SSN ▶		31a		
	32 Add lines 23 through 31a			32	
	33 Subtract line 32 from line 22. This is your **adjusted gross income** ▶			33	

For Disclosure, Privacy Act, and Paperwork Reduction Act Notice, see page 51.   Cat. No. 11320B   Form **1040** (1998)

Figure 7-1:
This section of Form 1040 may lower your taxes.

Here's the line-by-line rundown of the adjustments you may be able to make. The headings refer to line numbers where you plug your data into your 1040.

Line 23: You and your spouse's IRA deduction

Individual Retirement Accounts (IRAs) were established by Congress to allow taxpayers to establish a retirement plan on their own when they weren't covered by one at work. In the 1980s, Congress changed its collective mind and revised the law so that everyone could put away and deduct $2,000, even if he or she was covered by a retirement plan. Then — you guessed it — Congress did a back flip in 1986, and the law was modified again.

Now if our elected officials were serious about wanting people to contribute to retirement accounts, they would have made the IRA tax laws easy to understand. Well, they didn't, and the 1997 tax law changes made a bad situation worse. Your ability to take an *adjustment* or a tax-deductible IRA contribution is based not only on your income level, but also on whether you (and your spouse, if you're married) are already covered by some sort of retirement plan. We'll get to these issues in a minute. Before we do, you first need to determine whether you even have income that qualifies you for an IRA contribution. Read on.

Compensation needed to qualify for an IRA

If you don't earn employment income or receive alimony and just have income from something like investments, you are *not* allowed to contribute to an IRA, period. As explained in the next section, limits exist on the size of the IRA contribution that you can make if you *do* have employment income or alimony.

You may contribute to an IRA if you have at least some of the following types of compensation:

- ✔ Salary and wages
- ✔ Commissions and tips
- ✔ Self-employed earnings from your business — reduced by your contribution to your other retirement plan (Keogh or SEP) and the deduction allowed for one-half of the Social Security tax you have to pay as a self-employed person (see Chapter 8)
- ✔ Alimony paid to you

Congratulations! If you have income that qualifies you to contribute to an IRA, you've made it over the first hurdle.

Deductible IRA contributions

As a general rule, you claim a deduction for the contribution you are allowed to make to your IRA. Now for the exception to this general rule. If you or your spouse is covered by a retirement plan at work, your ability to claim a deduction may be reduced or eliminated. This doesn't mean you can't make a $2,000 nondeductible contribution or perhaps stash away $2,000 in a Roth IRA.

What to do if you're not covered by an employer's plan

If you aren't covered by a retirement plan where you work, you can make a fully deductible IRA contribution. You can skip this section on IRAs (see you later). But if your spouse is covered by a retirement plan, sorry, the next section is vital. You can't skip over it.

What to do if you're covered by an employer's plan

If you're filing as single and your modified adjusted gross income is $30,000 or less ($50,000 or less for married filing jointly), you're eligible to make a fully deductible IRA contribution. Modified adjusted gross income, it seems there's no end to terms like these. Although we explain it in all its glory later on in "How to figure partial IRA deductions," here's a short cut that most taxpayers can use. For 1040 filers your modified adjusted gross income is line 33 (your AGI) plus line 23 (your IRA deduction). For 1040A filers it's line 18 (your AGI) plus line 15 (your IRA deduction).

In 1999, the $50,000 limit jumps to $51,000 and gradually increases to $80,000 for joint filers by 2007. For singles, it's $31,000 in 1999 and on to $50,000 by 2005. See Chapter 21 for all the details.

Pause to catch your breath — here comes another big hurdle: If your income is above the $30,000 (single) or $50,000 (married) thresholds, or if you're covered by a retirement plan but your spouse isn't, or vice versa, and your joint income is more than $150,000, your ability to deduct an IRA contribution will be reduced or eliminated completely. We will explain how these income thresholds work against you in a minute. So how do you know whether you're *covered?* And what the heck is a *retirement plan?*

The simplest way to determine whether you're covered by an employer's retirement plan is to look at box 15 (the pension plan box) on your W-2 (the form that you receive early in the year from your employer that summarizes your previous year's earnings). If the pension plan box in box 15 is marked with an *X,* you're considered covered by some type of retirement plan. One of these boxes will be checked by your employer if your employer offers you any of the following:

- ✔ Pension, profit-sharing, stock bonus, or Keogh plans

- ✔ 401(k) plans

- ✔ Union retirement plans — 501(c)(18) plans for you Trivial Pursuit players!

- ✔ Qualified annuity plans

- ✔ Tax-sheltered annuities — also known as 403(b) plans

- ✔ Simplified Employee Pension (SEP-IRA) plans

- ✔ Retirement plans established by a federal, state, or local government

You're considered covered, or an active participant, even if you haven't earned the full right (known as *vesting*) to the benefits under your plan. If you switch employers during the year and one of the employers has a plan and the other doesn't, you're considered covered.

You're also considered covered by a plan when you are both salaried and self-employed, providing that you have your own Keogh, SEP, or SIMPLE Plan, and you aren't covered by a plan where you're employed. You are also considered covered by a plan if you are self-employed and have a Keogh, SEP, or SIMPLE plan.

If your employer offers you a retirement plan that you can contribute to, such as a 401(k) or 403(b), and you and your employer did not add any money to your account and no forfeitures were allocated during the tax year, you are *not* considered covered during the year. Thus, you could make a tax-deductible IRA contribution if your spouse also is not covered.

IRA planning tips

If you're currently completing your tax return for 1998, the IRA represents your last chance to make retirement contributions for 1998 (unless you had self-employment income that enables you to contribute to an SEP-IRA — see "Line 29: Keogh and self-employed SEP and SIMPLE plans," later in this chapter). Unfortunately, you can't go back now and make contributions to your employer's plan for last year.

If you have plenty of cash around, go ahead and make the IRA contribution. You have until April 15, 1999, and can still deduct it on your 1998 return. If you're tight on cash, it may be better to forgo making the IRA contribution for the last tax year. Looking forward, if you can contribute through your employer's plan, odds are quite high that you may make a higher tax-deductible contribution through that plan than through an IRA. Get signed up for your employer's retirement plan and start funneling money into it now! If you have self-employment income or don't understand how the employer retirement plans work, be sure to read Chapter 21 to learn all about the benefits of retirement plans.

Don't bother contributing to an IRA if you're already receiving Social Security benefits, are still earning employment income, and are covered (or considered covered) by an employer's retirement plan. Why? Because the paperwork is a nightmare. You need to complete the worksheets in Appendix B of Publication 590 *(Individual Retirement Arrangements)* to figure your IRA deduction as well as the taxable portion, if any, of your Social Security benefits. It's just too much of a hassle. If you're receiving Social Security, you're close to the age when you have to start withdrawing money from your IRA anyway. If you want to try to figure this out, good luck. The small tax savings won't be worth paying a tax advisor to figure it out for you.

Income limitations

If you're covered by a retirement plan where you work, all is not lost. You may still be able to take the tax deduction for an IRA contribution. However, *if* what's called your *modified adjusted gross income* (explained in the "How to figure partial IRA deductions" sidebar later in this chapter) *exceeds* the following thresholds (also pay attention to the filing status), you may not take the IRA deduction:

- ✔ At $40,000 and above, no deduction is allowed if you're single or a head of household. At $30,000 or less, you may take a full deduction for an IRA. If your modified AGI is between $30,000 and $40,000, you're entitled to a partial deduction.

- ✔ At $60,000 and above, no deduction is allowed if you're filing jointly or as a qualifying widow or widower. At $50,000 or less, you may take a full deduction for an IRA. If your income is between $50,000 and $60,000, you're entitled to a partial deduction.

- ✔ At $10,000 and above, no deduction is allowed if you're married filing separately. Below $10,000, a partial deduction is allowed. If you didn't live with your spouse for the entire year, you can ignore this rule. The single income limits apply.

- ✔ If you're married and you aren't covered by a pension but your wife is (or vice versa) and your joint income is below $150,000, you can take a full deduction for an IRA. If your joint income is between $150,000 and $160,000 you're entitled to a partial deduction. Above $160,000, no deduction is allowed.

If you can't take an IRA deduction or can take only a partial one, you can still make a nondeductible contribution to an IRA, as discussed later in this chapter. Although you don't get a deduction, the earnings on your contribution aren't subject to tax until the money is withdrawn. The compounding of your investment earnings over many years with deferred taxation has great value.

Starting in 1998, two new types of IRAs kick in, and a third type will be available in 1999. Although contributions aren't deductible, they do provide for tax-free earnings growth as well as tax-free withdrawals if certain conditions are met. Chapter 21 has all the details.

Contribution limits

The most that you can contribute for any year to your IRA is the *smaller* of the following:

✔ Your compensation (as we define in the previous section "Compensation needed to qualify for an IRA"), which you must include as income for the year

✔ $2,000

If you're married, your spouse may be able to contribute to an IRA as well. See the section "Your spouse's IRA deduction," later in this chapter.

 Peter is a real person who read his IRS instruction booklet and learned that he could contribute $2,000 to an IRA. He liked investing in mutual funds, so he set up three IRA accounts at three different mutual funds and contributed $2,000 to each one, for a total contribution of $6,000 for the year! The IRS computers discovered this glitch when the three mutual funds each reported under Peter's Social Security number that he had made this many contributions for the same tax year. Remember that the $2,000 limit is the maximum you can contribute regardless of whether your contributions are to one or more IRAs, or whether all or part of your contributions is deductible. (See the discussion of "Nondeductible IRA contributions (Form 8606)" in the next section.)

You should receive **Form 5498, Individual Retirement Arrangement Information** — it's like a little 1099 — or a similar statement from the custodian of your IRA by May 31, 1999. This form shows all the contributions you made to your IRA for 1998.

How to figure partial IRA deductions

You get a partial deduction

✔ If your modified adjusted gross income falls between $30,000 and $40,000 if you're single or between $50,000 and $60,000 if you're married filing jointly or a qualifying widow or widower, or

✔ If your modified adjusted gross income falls below $10,000 if you're married filing separately

If your modified adjusted gross income is above the phaseout limits, you aren't entitled to a deduction.

To figure your partial IRA deductions, you must first determine your modified AGI, which is your AGI from Form 1040 (line 33) or for 1040A filers (line 18). But the following deductions must be added back to this amount:

✔ Your IRA deduction

✔ Foreign earned income and housing deductions (this only applies to taxpayers who live and work abroad) per Form 2555 (see Chapter 6)

✔ The exclusion for Series EE U.S. savings bond interest (shown on Form 8815), explained in Chapter 10

✔ The exclusion for adoption assistance (Form 8839; see Chapter 8)

If you did not live with your spouse at any time during the year and you file a separate return, your filing status is considered single for this purpose.

1. Depending on your filing status, enter one of the following:

$40,000 — single or head of household
$60,000 — joint or qualifying widow or widower
$10,000 — married filing separately

1. _____

2. Enter your modified AGI   2. _____

3. Subtract line 2 from line 1   3. _____

4. Your IRA deduction   4. _____

If line 2 is larger than line 1, you aren't entitled to an IRA deduction — enter zero.

A. If line 3 is $10,000 or more, enter $2,000.

B. If line 3 is less than $10,000, multiply line 3 by 20% (.20). Round to the nearest $10. If the amount you arrive at is less than $200, enter $200. Don't ask why. These are the rules.

If you aren't covered by a pension but your spouse is or vice versa, enter $160,000 on line 1 and complete lines 1 through 4.

Nondeductible IRA contributions (Form 8606)

Although your deduction for an IRA contribution may be reduced or eliminated because of the adjusted gross income limitation, you may make nondeductible IRA contributions of up to $2,000 or 100 percent of your compensation, whichever is less. The difference between your allowable deductible contribution, which is entered on line 23, and your total contributions made, if any, is your nondeductible contribution.

If you can't deduct an IRA contribution, you may be wondering why or how you still contribute to an IRA. An astonishing number of taxpayers don't realize that you can still contribute to an IRA even if your contribution isn't deductible. And you may want to make nondeductible contributions, because the *growth* (from interest, dividends, and appreciation) on your contribution is sheltered from taxation inside the tax-friendly confines of an IRA, and the growth dollars won't be taxed until they're distributed to you years from now in retirement. The younger you are and the more years that your money can compound without taxation, the greater the value of this tax-deferred compounding.

For example, Alex is single. In 1998, he's covered by a retirement plan at work. His salary is $42,000, and his modified AGI is $45,000. Alex makes a $2,000 IRA contribution for that year. Because he's covered by a retirement plan and his modified AGI is over $40,000, he can't deduct his IRA contribution.

Because Alex can't deduct the $2,000 he contributed to the IRA, he should either designate his contribution as a nondeductible contribution by completing **Form 8606, Nondeductible IRAs — Contributions, Distributions, and Basis** or contribute $2,000 to the new Roth IRA that we discuss in Chapter 21. However, because the growth of his IRA — deductible or otherwise — is tax-sheltered, he's still wise to contribute to an IRA, especially if he's also contributed the maximum to his employer-sponsored retirement plans. See Chapter 15 for details on filling out Form 8606.

You must report nondeductible contributions to the IRS. Form 8606 must be filed to report nondeductible contributions even if you don't have to file a tax return for the year. If you're filing a Form 1040, you must attach Form 8606 to your 1040. There's a $50 penalty for not filing your 8606! Also, if your IRA contributions are more than the permissible amount, you must correct the overpayment, and you may be subject to a 6-percent penalty.

The Roth and other new IRAs

In addition to the four types of IRAs now in use — deductible IRAs, nondeductible IRAs, rollover IRAs for lump sums of your former employer's retirement plan, and medical savings accounts — the new law adds three new IRAs: The Roth and Education IRAs, which took effect on January 1, 1998, and Medicare Plus Choice MSAs, which come into being in 1999. See Chapter 21 for more information about the Roth and Medicare Plus Choice MSAs. Chapter 25 covers the Education IRA.

Roth IRAs

Here's the lowdown on Roth IRAs: You can contribute up to $2,000 to a Roth IRA, a deductible IRA, or a nondeductible IRA in any year, but you can only contribute to one of these. Your spouse can also contribute $2,000. Although you don't receive a deduction for your $2,000, the great feature of a Roth is that if you keep your dough in it for at least five years, the entire balance can be withdrawn tax-free when you retire. And just like a regular IRA, you have until April 15, 1999, to put away money for 1998.

A $2,000 deduction for a Roth can be made by single taxpayers with incomes below $95,000 but can't be made by singles with incomes exceeding $110,000. Between $95,000 and $110,000, the $2,000 is slowly phased out. For joint filers, the limits are $150,000 and $160,000. For example, Betsy and David, with a combined income of $175,000, file jointly. Because their income exceeds the $160,000 threshold, neither can contribute to a Roth IRA. Had Betsy's and David's income been $140,000, then both David and Betsy could have contributed $2,000 to a Roth.

Here is how the math for the phaseout works for single taxpayer with a modified AGI of $104,000 and a married couple with a $155,000 modified AGI:

	Single	Married
1. Income	104,000	155,000
2. Threshold	95,000	150,000
3. Subtract line 2 from 1.	9,000	5,000
4. Divide line 3 by the phaseout range ($15,000 if single, $10,000 if married).	$9,000/15,000	$5,000/10,000
5. Result	60%(.60)	50%(.50)
6. Maximum contribution	2,000	$2,000
7. Multiply line 5 by line 6.	$1,200	$1,000
8. Allowable Roth contribution (subtract line 7 from line 6)	$800	$1,000

If the amount in line 8 is less than $200 but above zero, you can contribute $200. Also, any result that isn't a multiple of $10 must be rounded to the next lowest $10. For example, $812 must be rounded down to $810.

Remember: The phaseout only comes into play when you're single and your income is between $95,000 and $110,000, or married with income between $150,000 and $160,000. Below $95,000 (single) or $150,000 (married), you don't have to worry about the phase-out. You are entitled to a full $2,000 contribution. Above $110,000 (single) or $160,000 (married), no contribution is allowed.

A distribution from a Roth isn't subject to the 10-percent early withdrawal penalty and tax if in addition to the five-year rule, it meets one of the following conditions:

- It's made on or after you reach 59¹/₂.
- It's made to a beneficiary (or your estate) after your death.
- It's made after you become disabled.

Withdrawals for the following purposes are subject to tax but not to the 10-percent early withdrawal penalty if you're under age 59¹/₂:

- To pay higher education expenses
- To purchase a first home (up to a $10,000 withdrawal allowed)

For the rules on higher education and first-time homebuyer expenses, go back to "Distributions before 59¹/₂," lines 15a and b, in Chapter 6.

Now for the five-year rule: The five-year clock doesn't start with the year in which you make the contribution. It starts with the year to which the contribution relates. For example, you contribute $2,000 in 1999 for 1998. Your holding period begins on January 1, 1998. If you contribute $2,000 for 1998, 1999, 2000, 2001, and 2002, the earliest you can make a tax-free withdrawal is 2003. Say the account was worth $25,000 on January 1, 2003. The entire $25,000 can be withdrawn tax-free; you don't have to wait five years every time you make a contribution.

If you don't keep your dough in an account for at least five years, the earnings you with-draw are subject to tax. The earnings don't get taxed until after you withdraw all your contributions. For example, say you put away $2,000 a year for three years. The account is now worth $7,500. If you withdraw the entire amount, only $1,500 is taxable or possibly subject to the 10-percent early withdrawal penalty. If you only withdraw $6,000, the entire withdrawal is tax and penalty free. It's only when you withdraw the $1,500 balance that you have to pay tax.

Five years means exactly that. Say John contributes $2,000 a year for four years starting in 1998. He dies in 2002 when the account is worth $12,000. If his beneficiary withdraws the $12,000 in 2002, the $4,000 gain will be taxed to the beneficiary. If John's beneficiary waits until 2003, the entire $12,000 gets withdrawn tax-free. The reason? Five years from January 1, 1998, doesn't roll around until January 1, 2003.

IRA conversions

Before we leave the Roth arena, you should know something about converting a regular IRA to a Roth IRA. You can do this without incurring the 10-percent early withdrawal penalty as long as the conversion is made within 60 days of the withdrawal from the regular IRA. The best way to accomplish this is to have your IRA go directly from one institution to the other.

You can only do a conversion if your income is under $100,000 and you are not married filing separately. There is no limit to the amount of money that can be converted. The drawback is that you must include the taxable amount in your income. For example, if you make nondeductible contributions of $10,000 to an IRA that's worth $25,000, you have to include $15,000 in your income. The $15,000 you have to include in your income isn't counted in figuring if you meet the under-$100,000 requirement. The minimum required distribution you have to take from a retirement or IRA plan because you're past 70 1/2 counts in determining the $100,000 threshold. After 2005, it won't.

Unlike a regular Roth's five-year holding period, a converted Roth's five-year holding period doesn't start with the year it relates to but with the year the conversion takes place. If a Roth contains both conversion and regular Roth contributions, the first money taken is deemed to be your regular Roth IRA contributions and the converted amounts come next (starting with the amounts converted first).

The five-year period starts with the year a contribution is made to a Roth. A subsequent conversion doesn't start a new five-year period. For example, if you're considering a conversion, open a Roth by April 15, 1999, for 1998. This starts the five-year holding period on January 1, 1998. A conversion made in 1998 falls under the January 1, 1998, starting date and can be taken out tax-free on January 1, 2003. However, 1999 is the year the five-year holding period starts to run for the purposes of determining if you're subject to the 10-percent early withdrawal penalty in case you make a withdrawal before you are 59 1/2.

Say you converted $50,000 from a regular IRA to a Roth in 1998 but discovered at the end of the year that your income exceeded $100,000. Oops! You can "undo" the conversion if you transfer the money back by the due date for filing your return (including extensions) for the year you made the conversion. If your filing date for 1998 is April 15, 1999 (meaning you didn't apply for an extension), you can correct your error regarding your 1998 conversion without any tax consequences if you make a trustee-to-trustee transfer back to a regular IRA by April 15, 1999. You also may want to do this if the stocks you own in the converted account took a nosedive — if, for example, the $50,000 you put in during 1998 is only worth $20,000 prior to April 15, 1999.

Taxpayers who convert a regular IRA to a Roth before January 1, 1999, could elect to spread the income they must report over four years. It was possible under the law as it was originally written for someone under the age of 59 1/2 to convert a regular IRA to a Roth, elect the four-year spread, and immediately make a withdrawal without incurring the 10-percent early withdrawal penalty. The 1998 tax act did away with this gimmick. Now, if you convert to a Roth, this scheme won't work.

If an account holder dies during the four-year period for reporting his income, any remaining amounts that have to be reported are included on his final return unless his spouse is the sole beneficiary of the Roth IRA account. In such cases, the spouse can elect to continue reporting the income over the remaining years. For example, say that George rolls over $40,000 from his IRA in 1998 and elects to report $10,000 a year in 1998, 1999, 2000, and 2001. He dies in 1999. The $30,000 must be reported on his final return. If he was married and left the account to his spouse, she could elect to report $10,000 a year for the remaining three years.

Education IRAs

A new higher education vehicle, Education Individual Retirement Accounts, was ushered in in 1998. We take a good, hard look at these accounts in Chapter 25, where you will see that these IRAs as well as state prepaid tuition plans are not effective ways to save for future college finances.

You can't contribute to both an Education IRA and a state tuition plan. Be sure to read Chapter 25 for more effective ways to save for your children's education.

Where to set up an IRA

Mutual fund companies, particularly no-load (commission-free) firms, are ideal choices. See Chapter 23 for more information.

Your spouse's IRA deduction

If your spouse is employed, the deductible amount of your spouse's IRA contribution goes on line 23 as well.

If your spouse is not employed, you can set up a spousal IRA and also contribute up to $2,000 for him (or her) for a total IRA deduction of $4,000.

Starting in 1998, a spouse not working outside the home can set up a deductible IRA even if his or her spouse is covered by a pension at work, provided the couple's income doesn't exceed $150,000. Between $150,000 and $160,000, a partial deduction is allowed. At $160,000, the deduction is eliminated. See the phaseout worksheet for joint filers under "Roth IRAs" in the previous section to determine whether you qualify for a partial deduction. If this phaseout works against you, don't overlook a nondeductible IRA.

The following example illustrates how to determine whether you qualify for an IRA deduction. Harvey is covered by 401(k) plan at work. His wife Judy isn't employed. The couple files jointly and has a combined income of $120,000. Judy may make a deductible IRA contribution to an IRA because she isn't covered by a pension plan and the couple's income is under $150,000. Harvey can't make a deductible IRA contribution because he's covered by a plan at a work, and as a couple, their income is beyond the threshold ($50,000–$60,000) for someone who is an active participant in a pension plan and is married and filing jointly.

If your spouse is employed

If your spouse is employed during the year — and each of you is under age 70$^1/_2$ at the end of the 1997 — you can both have IRAs. Each of you can contribute up to the $2,000 limit, unless your taxable compensation (or your spouse's) is less than $2,000. Qualifying income ranges are the same as those we explain earlier in this chapter in the section "Compensation needed to qualify for an IRA."

You or your spouse can choose to be treated as having no compensation for the year and use the rules for spousal IRAs. Generally, if one spouse has compensation of less than $2,000 for the year, a spousal IRA is more advantageous than a regular IRA.

For example, Michael and Lisa file a joint return for 1998. Michael earned $27,000, and Lisa earned $190. Lisa chose to be treated as having no compensation. Michael and Lisa can each contribute $2,000 to their respective IRAs for a total of $4,000.

If your spouse is not employed

If your nonworking spouse decides to set up his or her own IRA, the most that you can contribute is 100 percent of your taxable compensation, up to $4,000. You can divide your IRA contributions between your IRA and your spouse's IRA any way you choose, but you can't contribute more than $2,000 to either IRA. For example, if your salary is $3,500, you can contribute $3,500 — that is, $2,000 for you and $1,500 for your spouse, $1,500 for you and $2,000 for your spouse, or $1,750 for you and $1,750 for your spouse, but no more than $3,500 total. If your salary is over $4,000, the most you can contribute is $4,000.

If your spouse is younger than you, you're close to retirement age (70$\frac{1}{2}$), and all you can afford to contribute is $2,500, it makes sense to contribute $500 to your IRA and the larger $2,000 contribution to your spouse's IRA. That way, the money contributed continues to grow tax-free for a longer period before it must be withdrawn.

To contribute to a spousal IRA, you need to fulfill the following requirements:

✓ You must be married at the end of the tax year.

✓ Your spouse must not have reached age 70$\frac{1}{2}$ by the end of the year.

✓ You must file a joint return.

✓ You must have taxable compensation for the year.

✓ Your spouse must have no compensation — or must choose to be treated as having no compensation — for the year.

Spouses under age 70$\frac{1}{2}$

You can't make contributions to your own IRA for the year in which you reach age 70$\frac{1}{2}$ or in any later year. However, for any year you have compensation, you can continue to make contributions of up to $2,000 to your spouse's IRA until the year your spouse reaches age 70$\frac{1}{2}$.

Starting in 1998, penalty-free (but taxable) withdrawals will be permitted for college tuition and up to $10,000 cumulatively for first-time home buyers. A first home doesn't mean the first home you ever owned. It means you haven't owned a home within the last two years. You can also withdraw money before you are 59$\frac{1}{2}$ to pay the higher education bills for yourself, your spouse, your kids, or your grandkids. The withdrawal is taxable, but you escape the 10-percent penalty. There is no limit to withdrawals to pay higher education expenses. See Chapter 16, line 15a, for a complete explanation of the rules.

Line 24: Student loan interest deduction

You can deduct up to $1,000 of interest on a loan used to pay higher education and certain vocational school expenses (ask the vocational school whether it qualifies for this deduction if you have to borrow to pay the tab). The deduction gets increased to $1,500 in 1999, to $2,000 in 2000, and to $2,500 thereafter.

If you're single, the deduction quickly gets eliminated once your income hits $40,000 and disappears at $55,000. For joint filers, the deduction starts at the $60,000 income level, with the deduction getting wiped out at $75,000.

The beauty of the Student Loan Interest Deduction is that you don't have to itemize your deductions in order to claim it. You can claim the standard deduction (see Chapter 9) and this deduction as well. This should be of great benefit to recent graduates.

To take this deduction, you must meet the following requirements:

- ✔ The loan must be incurred to pay the higher education expenses of you, your spouse, or anyone you can claim as a dependent when you incur the debt.

- ✔ The expenses must be paid within a reasonable amount of time after the loan is taken out. We wish we could tell you what's reasonable, but you know how it is: The IRS knows what's reasonable when it sees it.

- ✔ You must be the person primarily responsible for the loan.

- ✔ The student must carry at least half the normal workload of a full-time student.

- ✔ Expenses for tuition, fees, room and board, books, and supplies qualify.

- ✔ Only interest paid during the first 60 months in which interest payments are required to be made qualifies. You can't get around this rule by refinancing the loan in order to restart the 60-month clock.

- ✔ Although the loan can be taken out at any time, the deduction only applies to that portion of the 60 months that comes after December 31, 1997; for example, if the 60-month clock begins on June 1, 1997, those months prior to January 1, 1998, do not qualify.

- ✔ Loans from related family members don't qualify for the deduction.

- ✔ Revolving lines of credit don't qualify unless you agree that the line will only be used to pay for education expenses.

Since loans are usually taken out by students because they can obtain lower interest rates, their parents won't be able to claim the deduction even if they make all the payments. That's because the parent didn't borrow the money. If the student is liable for the loan, the student can claim the interest deduction if they can be claimed as a dependent on someone else's return. And married couples have to file jointly to claim the deduction.

With all of these rules, high income taxpayers can probably do better with home equity loans (see Chapter 9).

Institutions making education loans are required to issue Form 1098-E, Student Loan Interest Payments, listing the interest and principal payments. Page 27 of your instruction booklet has a worksheet for 1040 filers to compute the phaseout amount. For 1040A filers, the worksheet appears on page 39.

Here's how the phaseout works:

		Single	Married
1.	Income	$43,000	$67,500
2.	Threshold amount	40,000	55,000
3.	Subtract line 2 from line 1.	3,000	7,500
4.	Phaseout range ($55,000 – $40,000 for singles, $75,000 – $60,000 joint filers)	15,000	15,000
5.	Divide line 3 by line 4.	$3,000/$15,000	$7,500/$15,000
6.	Result	20%	50%
7.	Maximum deduction	$1,000	$1,000
8.	Multiply line 7 by line 6.	$200	$500
9.	Allowable deduction (Subtract line 8 from line 7)	$800	$500

Line 25: Medical savings account deduction

You can set up a medical savings account (MSA) to pay your medical bills. This type of account, which is offered by insurance companies, is similar to an IRA. You can contribute and deduct up to $3,375 if married and $1,463 if single. A nifty feature of MSAs is that unlike an employer-provided flexible spending account (FSA), an MSA is not subject to the "use it or lose it" rule. Balances in the account can be carried over from year to year. The earnings on the account accumulate tax-free, and withdrawals to pay medical expenses aren't subject to tax. It's a lot like running your own insurance company, and best of all, you get to keep the profits.

Like regular IRAs, contributions to an MSA that are made before the April 15, 1999, filing date can be deducted on your 1998 return.

You can be covered only under one high-deductible plan. (Accident, disability, dental care, vision care, long-term care, medical supplemental insurance, and per diem plans that pay a fixed daily rate if you're hospitalized aren't considered additional plans.)

The non-reimbursed medical expenses that can be withdrawn free of tax are the ones that you could have deducted on your return as a medical expense if you itemized your deductions. What you can deduct as a medical expense is spelled out in Chapter 9. However, you can't make withdrawals to pay health insurance premiums except for continuation coverage required by federal law, long-term health care, or while you're unemployed.

Distributions from an MSA for non-medical expenses are subject to a 15-percent penalty, plus the tax on the distribution at your tax bracket. The penalty and income inclusion also apply if you pledge the account for a loan.

After age 65, you can withdraw funds from an MSA for any reason without paying the 15-percent penalty (but the funds are still taxable). Although not intended for this purpose, MSAs could potentially be looked at as additional retirement accounts.

The deduction is compiled on **Form 8853.** Starting in 1999, the deductible amounts are indexed for inflation.

Line 26: Moving expenses (Form 3903)

If you incur moving expenses because you have to relocate, you can deduct moving expenses for which your employer doesn't reimburse you. Self-employed individuals may also deduct their moving expenses and write the total on this line.

The place to deduct moving expenses is **Form 3903, Moving Expenses.** For a move to a foreign location, you have to use Form 3903-F. See Chapter 15 for more about filling out Form 3903.

Line 27: One-half of self-employment tax

If you're self-employed, you have to pay your own Social Security and Medicare taxes. This is one crummy drawback to being self-employed; if you worked for an employer, your employer would pay for half of your so-called self-employment tax. It's a little confusing because this tax is called a self-employment tax (not a Social Security and Medicare tax) — don't you wish the IRS would use English?

If you're self-employed and file Schedule C or Schedule C-EZ, or are a working partner in a partnership, or if you earned income for services you provided that you reported on line 21 of Form 1040 as miscellaneous income and you didn't incur any expenses in earning it, you have to file **Schedule SE, Self-Employment Tax.** That's the form you use to compute the Social Security and Medicare taxes you owe. See Chapter 15 for help with completing Schedule SE.

Now for some good news (yes, there is occasionally *some* good news when it comes to taxes). Half of the self-employment tax that you must pay is deductible. Complete Schedule SE and note the following: The amount on line 5 of Schedule SE is the amount of tax you have to pay, and it's carried over to Form 1040 (line 50) and added to your income tax that's due; half of what you have to pay — the amount on line 6 of Schedule SE — is entered on Form 1040 (line 27). This amount gets deducted from your income, thereby reducing the amount of tax you have to pay.

Line 28: Self-employed health insurance deduction

You can deduct 45 percent of your health insurance premiums from your income (in 1997, the deduction was 40 percent).

In 1999, the deduction increases to 60 percent. Based on your age, a portion of the premium for long-term care also qualifies for this deduction. For a quick study of this deduction, turn to "Insurance premiums" in Chapter 9's medical expense section.

A general partner (but not a limited partner), an independent contractor, or a shareholder in an S Corporation can also claim this deduction. For example, if the health insurance premiums for you and your dependents are $4,000, you can deduct $1,800 on line 28. The $2,200 balance is deducted on Schedule A (line 1) as a medical expense if you're itemizing your deductions.

Some married couples can deduct the whole amount. If your spouse is employed by you — even for a nominal salary — you may be able to deduct 100 percent of your family's medical expenses and not just 45 percent of your medical insurance premiums.

That's because self-employed people can pay and deduct an employee's family health insurance premiums as a business expense, even if the health insurance policy covers the owner as well; and if you set up a medical reimbursement plan, you may be able to deduct your family's other medical costs. A tax advisor can show you how to do this stuff. Or, for $175 a year, Bizplan can handle the whole thing for you (800-298-2923).

Two things make all this unattractive, however. You have to provide all employees with this coverage, and you (or the business) will incur a payroll tax expense on your spouse's salary.

Line 29: Keogh and self-employed SEP and SIMPLE plans

You can still open a self-employment retirement plan called a SEP in 1999 and deduct your contribution to it on your 1998 return. You have until August 15 to do this (or until October 15, 1999, if you have an extension until then).

As a self-employed person, you can set up a Keogh plan. Your contributions to the plan are not only deductible but are also exempt from tax until you start receiving benefits. But in order to make a Keogh contribution in 1999 that's deductible on your 1998 return, the plan had to be set up by December 31, 1998. (See Chapter 21 to learn about Keoghs.) If you already have a Keogh set up by the end of the tax year, see "Keogh contributions," later in this chapter.

As a general rule, employees who work less than 1,000 hours per year and employees who have been with you for less than two years don't have to be included in the plan. Check your plan document to see who needs to be covered by your plan. If you and your spouse are the only ones covered by the plan, you don't have to file an annual information return with the IRS until the plan's assets exceed $100,000. If you're subject to the filing requirements, file **Form 5500EZ;** if you have employees, use **Form 5500.**

If you forgot to set up a Keogh by December 31, 1998, you can't make a deductible contribution to it for 1998. But with a SEP, you can take a deduction for 1998 as long as you set one up and contribute to it by the due date for filing your 1998 return (which can be extended to October 15, 1999). Consider a SEP-IRA for the interim and establish a Keogh by December 31, 1999, so that you can switch over to funding a Keogh for 1999.

As of 1997, employers with fewer than 100 employees can establish what's known as SIMPLE plans. A cross between an IRA and a 401(k), a *SIMPLE plan* allows an employee to contribute up to $6,000 in pre-tax dollars with the employer matching a like amount. Unlike regular retirement plans, the nondiscrimination coverage rules don't apply. This means that the plan will qualify even if you as the owner are the only one who elects to participate. See Chapter 21 for more about SIMPLE and other small-business retirement plan options.

Keogh contributions

With a Keogh pension plan, you can contribute up to 25 percent of your earnings after deducting one-half of your self-employment tax and your Keogh contribution. The maximum amount of earnings that can be taken into account is $160,000. With a profit-sharing Keogh plan, you can only contribute up to 15 percent. Although 25 percent of $160,000 is $40,000, you're limited to a maximum deduction of $30,000. Once your earnings hit $196,689, you're at the $160,000 earnings limit ($196,689 minus your $30,000 Keogh contribution and one-half your self-employment tax of $6,689 equals $160,000). As a result of having to reduce your earnings by half of your self-employment tax and your Keogh contribution, the maximum rate on earnings before these adjustments works out to be 20 percent. The examples that follow illustrate the conversion percentages.

Example 1	
Earnings	$196,689
Less 50 percent of self-employment tax	$ 6,689
Balance	$190,000
Less 25 percent of $160,000 to a maximum of $30,000	$ 30,000
Maximum earnings base	$160,000

Example 2	
Earnings	$60,000
50 percent of self-employment tax	$ 4,238
Balance	$55,762
Keogh contribution (20 percent of $55,762)	$11,152
Maximum earnings base	$44,610

Twenty-five percent of $44,610 equals $11,152.

See Table 7-1, "Keogh and SEP Conversion Table," to determine your effective contribution rate based on the actual plan percentage that you choose to contribute.

Table 7-1	Keogh and SEP Conversion Table
Actual Plan Rate	*Effective Rate That You Contribute*
1%	.009901
2	.019608
3	.029126
4	.038462
5	.047619
6	.056604
7	.065421
8	.074074
9	.082569
10	.090909
11	.099099
12	.107143
13	.115044
14	.122007
15	.130435
16	.137931
17	.145299
18	.152542
19	.159664
20	.166667
21	.173554
22	.180328
23	.186992
24	.193548
25	.200000

SEP and Keogh contributions

The most you can contribute to a SEP or a Keogh profit-sharing plan is 15 percent of your net earnings from self-employment less one-half of your self-employment tax and your contribution to the SEP or Keogh sharing plan. This amount works out to be 13.0435 percent of your net earnings after the deduction for one-half of your self-employment tax. You don't have to make a contribution every year. Some years, you can skip making a contribution entirely or you can choose any contribution percentage up to 15 percent. The maximum amount of earnings that can be used to figure your contribution after deducting one-half of your self-employment tax and your SEP contribution is $160,000, and the maximum SEP or Keogh profit-sharing plan contribution is $24,000.

Example 1	
Earnings	$190,607
Less 50 percent of self-employment tax	$ 6,607
Balance	$184,000
Less SEP/Keogh contribution (13.0435 percent of $184,000)	$ 24,000
Maximum earnings base	$160,000

Fifteen percent of $160,000 amounts to $24,000, the maximum deductible SEP or profit-sharing Keogh contribution that can be made. Therefore, after your earnings reach $190,607, you're at the $24,000 limit. If you have employees, you simply multiply their salaries by 15 percent, if that's the percentage you selected. You don't have to do this calculation.

Example 2	
Earnings	$60,000
Less 50 percent of self-employment tax	$ 4,238
Balance	$55,762
Less SEP/Keogh contribution (13.0435 percent of $55,410)	$ 7,273
Maximum earnings base	$48,489

Fifteen percent of $48,489 equals your SEP/Keogh contribution of $7,273.

If you choose to put away 10 percent, subtract half of your Social Security tax from your earnings and multiply that by the effective rate: .090909.

Line 30: Penalty on early withdrawal of savings

If you withdraw funds from a savings account before maturity or redeem a certificate of deposit before it's due and you're charged a penalty, you can deduct it on your 1040 (line 30). You don't have to itemize your deductions to claim this deduction. You can deduct the entire penalty, even if it exceeds the interest income reported on the Form 1099-INT that you received. The penalty amount, if any, is shown in box 2 of the 1099, which the bank will send you by January 31, 1999.

Lines 31a and b: Alimony paid

The alimony you paid is deducted on line 31a; to the left of the amount, you have to enter your former spouse's Social Security number on line 31b. If you don't enter the number, you can expect to hear from the IRS because there is a $50 penalty for making this boo-boo, and your alimony deduction may be disallowed. If you paid alimony to more than one person, enter the total amount of alimony you paid on line 31a, enter the amount and Social Security number for each recipient on a separate schedule, and attach the schedules to your return.

You need to know what alimony is before you can deduct it as an expense. The alimony rules aren't simple, so hang in there.

This is alimony

Payments count as alimony only if *all* the following conditions are met:

- Payments are required by the divorce decree or a separation decree.
- The payer of alimony and its recipient don't file a joint return.
- The payment is in cash (including checks or money orders).
- The spouses who are separated or divorced are not members of the same household (see the sidebar "Members of the same household," later in this chapter).
- The payments are not required after the death of the spouse who receives the alimony.
- The payment is not designated as child support.

This is not alimony

Payments do not count as alimony if *any* of the following conditions are true:

- The payment is a noncash property settlement.
- The payments are a spouse's part of community income.
- The payments are destined to keep up the payer's property.
- The payments are not required as part of the separation or divorce settlement.

Rules and exceptions to alimony

Looks simple, you say? Sorry. The rules on alimony are one of the most complex areas of the law. The reason for this absurd complexity is that each party to a divorce is trying to achieve opposite goals. The payer usually wants to deduct every payment, and the recipient wants to pay as little tax as possible. So to keep everyone honest, more regulations breed more regulations!

Here's some more information that will help you plug in the right amount on line 11 for alimony received or line 31a for alimony paid.

Cash payments: A cash payment must be made in cash. (Makes sense, doesn't it?) Therefore, property settlements don't qualify. The transfer of a home or business is considered a property settlement.

Payments to a third party: Payments to a third party qualify as alimony if they are used in place of alimony and are requested in writing by your former spouse. These payments can be for medical expenses, housing costs, taxes, tuition, and so on.

Life insurance premiums: Life insurance premiums on your life insurance qualify as deductible alimony if the payment is required by the divorce or separation agreement and your former spouse owns the policy.

Mortgage payments: Mortgage payments are alimony if you must make mortgage payments (principal and interest) on a home jointly owned with your former spouse — and the terms of the decree or agreement call for such payments. You can deduct half of the total of these payments as alimony. Your spouse reports this same half as income. If you itemize deductions and the home is your qualified residence, you can include the other half of the interest portion in figuring your deductible interest.

Taxes and insurance: Tax and insurance payments qualify as alimony if you must make them on a home you hold as *tenants in common* — which means that your heirs get your share when you die. (The person you own the property with doesn't get your share.) You can deduct half of the tax and insurance payments as alimony, and your spouse reports this amount as income. If you and your spouse itemize deductions, you each may deduct one half of the real estate taxes. If the property is held as *tenants by the entirety* or as *joint tenants* (where the survivor gets it all), none of your payments for taxes and insurance qualify as alimony.

Minimum payment period: For alimony agreements executed in 1985 and 1986, annual payments in excess of $10,000 had to continue for at least six years. For agreements made after 1986, no minimum payment period exists.

Recapture: To keep people from disguising large divorce settlements as alimony, a recapture provision was enacted for agreements executed after 1986. *Recapture* means that you have to report as income part of what you deducted during the first two years that you started paying alimony. The recapture rule applies if your average payments decline in the first three years by more than $15,000.

For example, suppose that in year one and year two, you paid and deducted $25,000 in alimony, but in year three, you paid only $5,000. You triggered the recapture rules because your payment decreased by more than $15,000. See a tax expert. This is one area you shouldn't fool around with. However, recapture doesn't apply if your spouse dies or remarries or if your alimony payments are geared to a fixed percentage of your income and your income decreases.

Payments after death: Alimony payments must stop at your spouse's death. If you must continue to make payments after your spouse's death — because of the legalese included in the agreement — none of the payments that you made before or after death qualify as alimony that you can deduct.

Child support: A required payment that's specifically designated as child support under your divorce decree isn't deductible as alimony. Even if a payment *isn't* specially designated as child support, part of it will be considered child support if the payment is to be reduced when your child reaches a specified age, dies, marries, leaves school, or becomes employed.

For example, suppose that you're required to pay your spouse $2,000 a month. However, when your child reaches age 21, your payment will be reduced to $1,250. Only $1,250 of your $2,000 monthly payment is considered alimony, and the remaining $750 is considered nondeductible child support.

For *pre*-1985 divorce decrees, combined spouse and child support payments that are reduced when the child comes of age are treated as alimony. The IRS deemed this deal too good (of course) and thus changed the rules for agreements executed after 1984.

Members of the same household

You are members of the same household even if you and your spouse separate yourselves physically in your home (or in your tropical hut, just like Gilligan and the Skipper once did after they had a fight). However, payments made within one month of departure qualify as alimony. For example, suppose that on June 1, while you are still residing in the same residence with your spouse,

you make a support payment. If you move out by July 1, this payment is deductible. Any payments made prior to June 1 do not qualify, however. A technical exception exists, however. If you are not legally separated or divorced, payments made under a separation agreement or a support decree can qualify as alimony even if you are members of the same household.

Payments to nonresident aliens: Alimony paid to nonresident aliens is considered U.S. source income. This stipulation means that you have to withhold 30 percent for tax and send it to the IRS, just like your employer does with the tax withheld from your salary. Find out if the U.S. has a tax treaty with the country of your former spouse — under a number of tax treaties, alimony is exempt from withholding. See IRS Publication 901 *(U.S. Tax Treaties)* for some really interesting reading!

Line 32: Total adjustments

Go ahead, make your day. Add all the figures you have on lines 23 through 31a. This total represents your total adjustment — and we hope it's a big number! But alas, it may be zero. Don't despair; there are more deductions to come on the back of Form 1040.

Line 33: Adjusted gross income

The next step is subtracting the amount in line 32 from line 22 (the total income). The result is your adjusted gross income, which is one of those big tax terms that you hear a good deal about. Now you even know what it means!

The IRS must think that this is a pretty important number because the good people at the Department of the Treasury have designed an easy-to-find adjusted gross income line at the bottom of the 1040 (line 33) where you enter this amount before you turn to the back of the form. Congrats! You're halfway there! (But be sure to read the fine print on line 33 to see if you may qualify for the earned income credit.)

Chapter 8

The Rest of the 1040 and Other Yucky Forms

In This Chapter

▶ Tax computation time

▶ Credits you can take

▶ Other taxes to add on!

▶ Payments you already made

▶ Refund or amount you owe

*W*hen you turned the page of your 1040, you probably had that same sickening feeling that you had as a student when you turned the page on an exam — just to find more junk that you'd never finish before the bell rang! But we think that you can beat the bell this time if you take the 1040 line by line, relax, and let us help you. For some of you, the worst is over, for others, well, you've still got some nasty schedules ahead of you.

Tax Computation

You may think that because this section is entitled tax computation, you're going to calculate how much tax you owe or will be refunded and be on your merry way (see Figure 8-1). Wrong! What you're going to do here is calculate your taxable income — that is, the income that you actually owe tax on for the year. This isn't the finish line, however, because there may be some "Credits" (these are good because they reduce your tax bill) and some "Other Taxes" (these are obviously bad). Then you have to settle up with the IRS and figure in the "Payments" section whether you paid too much, too little, or just the right amount of tax during the year (yeah, that part will be a little like Goldilocks, the three bears, and the porridge-tasting stuff!).

Figure 8-1:
The Tax Computation section of Form 1040.

Form 1040 (1998)		Page 2
Tax and Credits	**34** Amount from line 33 (adjusted gross income)	**34**
	35a Check if: ☐ **You** were 65 or older, ☐ Blind; ☐ **Spouse** was 65 or older, ☐ Blind. Add the number of boxes checked above and enter the total here . . . ▶ **35a** ☐	
	b If you are married filing separately and your spouse itemizes deductions or you were a dual-status alien, see page 29 and check here . . . . . . ▶ **35b** ☐	
Standard Deduction for Most People	**36** Enter the **larger** of your **itemized deductions** from Schedule A, line 28, **OR standard deduction** shown on the left. **But see page 30 to find your standard deduction if you** checked any box on line 35a or 35b or if someone can claim you as a dependent . .	**36**
Single: $4,250	**37** Subtract line 36 from line 34	**37**
Head of household: $6,250	**38** If line 34 is $93,400 or less, multiply $2,700 by the total number of exemptions claimed on line 6d. If line 34 is over $93,400, see the worksheet on page 30 for the amount to enter .	**38**
	39 **Taxable income.** Subtract line 38 from line 37. If line 38 is more than line 37, enter -0- .	**39**
Married filing	**40** **Tax.** See page 30. Check if any tax from a ☐ Form(s) 8814 b ☐ Form 4972 . . ▶	**40**

Line 34: Adjusted gross income

This line is a piece of cake. To complete line 34 at the top of the back page, turn your return back over and copy the entry you made on line 33 — both lines are your adjusted gross income!

Line 35a

On line 35a, check the box if either you or your spouse is age 65 or older or blind. If you check one of those boxes and you are not itemizing your deductions, see Table 9-1 in Chapter 9 ("Over 65 or blind") to compute your increased standard deduction. If you're single or a head of household, your standard deduction gets increased by $1,050 if you're over age 65 or blind. If you're both over age 65 and blind, add $2,100 to your standard deduction. For all others, the standard deduction is increased by either $850 or $1,700. For example, if you and your spouse are over 65, add $1,700 to your $7,100 standard deduction. If one of you is blind, add $2,550 to the $7,100 amount.

Line 35b

If you're married filing separately and your spouse itemizes deductions, then you must too. If one claims the standard deduction, then both must.

Line 36

This section refers to what can be a complicated line, so don't make a quick decision between the two choices the IRS offers for "deductions." Either choice is good in the sense that the result reduces your taxable income — the income that you owe tax on. HOWEVER, and this is a big however, you may be cheating yourself if you automatically jump into the easier of the two choices and take the so-called "standard deduction."

The standard deduction is tempting because, without any complicated figuring, you simply take the deduction that corresponds to your filing status. For example, if you're filing as a single, you get to take a standard deduction of $4,250.

If your parent or someone else can claim you as a dependent, the standard deduction you are entitled to is limited. You're going to have to use the Table 9-2 worksheet for dependents in Chapter 9 ("Standard deduction for dependents") to figure your allowable standard deduction.

The other option for taking deductions, itemizing on Schedule A, takes a lot more work. Think of this path as the grass-roots deduction process because you must identify and tabulate numerous items to build enough deductions to exceed the standard one the IRS grants you. Otherwise, why would you make more work for yourself?

If you're in doubt about whether itemizing will save you money or what expenses you may actually itemize, jump over to Chapter 9 right now. Take a gander at the line items on Schedule A. Even if itemizing can't save you money for this year's return, you should educate yourself for the future about the deductions that are available. The major expenses that you may itemize include some home ownership expenses (mortgage interest and property taxes), state income taxes, medical and dental expenses that exceed 7.5 percent of your adjusted gross income, gifts to charity, casualty and theft losses that exceed 10 percent of your adjusted gross income, job expenses, and other miscellaneous things (that exceed 2 percent of your adjusted gross income).

Line 37: Subtract line 36 from line 34

After you've either completed Schedule A or elected to take the standard deduction, enter the result on line 36, and then subtract it from line 34 and enter the result on line 37. If your adjusted gross income is over $124,500 ($62,250 if married filing separately), your itemized deductions have to be reduced. Sorry! Refer to the worksheet at the end of Chapter 9 to reduce your itemized deductions if this situation applies to you.

Line 38: Exemptions

Multiply by $2,700 the number of exemptions you claimed on line 6d on the front side of your Form 1040. You already filled out line 6d by now (didn't you?), but in case you need to go back to make sure you grabbed all the exemptions that you are allowed, turn to the section "Figuring Personal and Dependent Exemptions" in Chapter 4.

Enter the result of your multiplication on line 38. For example, if you claimed four exemptions on line 6d, enter $10,800 (4 × $2,700) on line 38. Now you understand the financial benefits of your children — yeah, right!

Don't forget that if your income (line 34) exceeds the following amounts, your deduction for personal exemptions is limited. If you find yourself in this unenviable position — say, you're single and line 34 exceeds $124,500 — then turn to Chapter 4 to figure out how much you have to reduce your $2,700 exemption.

- ✔ Married filing separately — $93,400
- ✔ Single — $124,500
- ✔ Head of household — $155,650
- ✔ Married filing jointly or qualifying widow(er) — $186,800

Line 39: Taxable income

Hey, you get an easy math problem. Subtract line 38 from line 37 and enter the result on line 39. But if line 38 is more than line 37, you get to place 0 (that's a zero) on line 39. If this occurs, you could possibly have an NOL (that's net operating loss; see "More expenses than income" in Chapter 19). Now you've arrived at another tax landmark, your taxable income, which is your adjusted gross income minus your deductions (either standard or itemized) and minus your personal exemptions. This is the amount from which you will finally calculate your owed taxes.

Line 40: Tax

Here's where you finally calculate the total federal tax that you should pay based on your taxable income. If your taxable income is under $100,000, you figure your tax by finding the income bracket for your taxable income and filing status in the tax tables in the back of this book. If your income is over $100,000, you must use the tax rates for your filing status in the tax-rate schedules, which are also included. Suppose your taxable income is $111,400 (congratulations!); you just graduated to the Tax Rate Schedules. If you're single, it's Schedule X. Because your income is between $61,400 and $128,100, here's how to figure your tax:

		Tax
Taxable income	$111,400	
Less: Tax on $61,400 per Schedule X	$61,400	$13,897
Balance	$50,000	
Tax bracket for amount over $61,400	31% =	$15,500
Tax to be entered on line 40		$29,397

Capital gains tax worksheet

The new law reduced the maximum capital gains rate from 28 percent to 20 percent (10 percent for those in the 15-percent bracket). The rate for collectibles (art, and so on) is still at 28 percent. Remember that for depreciable real estate, the new rate is 25 percent on accelerated depreciation that's recaptured. If you find this capital gains stuff somewhat confusing, you're not alone. See Chapter 12 for an update course on the new capital gains rules.

The 1998 IRS Restricting and Reform Act did away with the confusion over charging different tax rates on capital gains depending on whether you held an investment for more than 12 or 18 months. Starting January 1, 1998, selling any asset that you've held for more than 12 months qualifies as a long-term capital gain that's subject to the lower maximum capital gains rates. However, some mutual fund investors in 1998 may discover that some of their capital gains are subject to the 28-percent rate because their funds are on a fiscal year that began in 1997 when the two holding periods had different rates. Thankfully, 1998 will be the last year that this quirk in the law applies. If line 39 places you in the 28-, 31-, 36-, or 39.6-percent tax bracket, use Part IV of Schedule D (see Chapter 12) to compute your tax. For example, suppose that you're single with a taxable income of $150,000 — which places you in the 36-percent tax bracket — and you have a $10,000 long-term capital gain. If you use the Tax Rate Schedule rather than computing your tax using Schedule D, you'll pay $3,600 on your capital gain instead of $2,000.

We offer two worksheets, Tables 8-1 and 8-2 later in this section, so that you can see whether your tax computation on Schedule D is correct or can decide that you want to skip that ugly section (Part IV) completely. Refer to Table 8-1 for 28-, 25-, and 20-percent gains, and refer to Table 8-2 for gains that are taxed at the 10-percent rate (because you're in the 15-percent bracket).

If you're eligible for the 10-percent rate, this doesn't mean that your entire gain is taxed at the 10-percent rate. Only that portion of your gain that would normally be taxed at 15 percent is taxed at 10 percent. Confused? Don't be. Here's an example to unravel the mystery. You're single and your taxable income without your $10,000 capital gain is $20,350. Five thousand dollars of your gain — which is the portion that brings you to the $25,350 level where you leave the 15-percent bracket — is taxed at 10 percent. The balance of your gain, which is $5,000, is taxed at the maximum 20-percent rate.

If you have a 28-, 25-, or 20-percent gain and line 39 is more than the following amounts, use Table 8-2. If line 39 without your capital gain is equal to or less than these amounts, use Table 8-3.

- ✔ Single — $25,350
- ✔ Married filing jointly or qualifying widow(er) — $42,350
- ✔ Married filing separately — $21,175
- ✔ Head of household — $33,950

Yes, we know that we're repeating this information, but it's important. So here's the worksheet. You're single with a taxable income of $101,400 and a capital gain of $40,000. By following this worksheet, you end up saving $4,400.

Table 8-1	Capital Gains Tax Worksheet (28, 25, or 20% Rates)	
1.	Enter the amount from line 39 of your 1040.	1. $101,400
2.	Enter the smaller amount of your net capital gain from Schedule D, lines 16 or 17.	2. $ 40,000
3.	If you're filing Form 4952 (that's the Investment Interest form; see "Line 13: Investment interest" in Chapter 9), enter the amount from line 4e of that form.	3. 0
4.	Subtract line 3 from line 2. If the amount is zero or less, stop here. Use the Tax Table or Tax Rate Schedule instead.	4. $ 40,000
5.	Subtract line 4 from line 1.	5. $ 61,400
6.	Figure the tax on the amount of line 5. Use the Tax Table or Tax Rate Schedule (for your particular case).	6. $ 13,897
7.	Multiply line 4 by whatever rate applies: 28% (.28), 25% (.25), or 20% (.20). (Example: $40,000 × 20%)	7. $ 8,000
8.	Add lines 6 and 7.	8. $ 21,897
9.	Figure the tax on the amount on line 1. Yes, use the Tax Table or the Tax Rate Schedules.	9. $ 26,297
10.	Enter the smaller of line 8 or line 9 here. Then enter this amount also on Form 1040 (line 40, in case you lost your place).	10. $ 21,897

For the 10-percent rate to apply (because your taxable income places you in the 15-percent bracket), line 39 (Taxable income) minus your capital gain has to be equal to or less than the following amounts:

- Single — $25,350
- Married filing jointly or qualifying widow(er) — $42,350
- Married filing separately — $21,175
- Head of household — $33,950

Table 8-2 has the worksheet for your rate. You're single with a taxable income of $30,350 and a capital gain of $8,000.

Table 8-2	Capital Gains Tax Worksheet (10% Rate)	
1.	Enter the amount from line 39 of your 1040.	1. $30,350
2.	Enter the smaller of your net capital gain from Schedule D, line 16 or 17.	2. $ 8,000
3.	If you're filing Form 4952 (that's the Investment Interest form; see "Line 13: Investment interest" in Chapter 9), enter the amount from line 4e of that form.	3. 0
4.	Subtract line 3 from line 2. If the amount is zero or less, stop here. Use the Tax Table or Rate Schedule instead.	4. $ 8,000
5.	Subtract line 4 from line 1.	5. $22,350

(continued)

Table 8-2 (continued)

6. Enter the appropriate amount: $25,350 (single), $43,500 (married filing jointly or qualifying widow or widower), $21,175 (married filing separately), or $33,950 (head of household).	6. $25,350
7. Subtract line 5 from line 6.	7. $ 3,000
8. Subtract line 7 from line 2.	8. $ 5,000
9. Figure the tax on line 5 . (Yes, use the Tax Table.)	9. $ 3,356
10. Multiply line 7 by 10% (.10).	10. $ 300
11. Multiply line 8 by 20% (.20).	11. $ 1,000
12. Add lines 9, 10, and 11.	12. $ 4,656
13. Figure your tax using the Tax Table.	13. $ 5,210
14. Enter the smaller of line 12 or 13. Then enter this amount on Form 1040 (line 40).	14. $ 4,656

Congratulations! You saved $554 by taking this 14-step math quiz.

The Kiddie Tax: Forms 8615 and 8814

Don't jump over to the next line quite yet. If you have children under age 14 who have investment income, you may need to complete some additional forms (see Chapter 15 for a discussion of Form 8615 and Form 8814).

Those tiny boxes on line 40: Forms 8814 and 4972

Form 8814, Parents' Election to Report Child's Interest and Dividends, is the form to use if you are electing to report your kids' investment income on your own return rather than having the kids file their own returns. See Chapter 15 for a detailed look at your choice.

Form 4972, Tax on Lump-Sum Distributions, however, is more common. If you decide to take all your money out of your employer's retirement plan in a lump sum, use this form to compute your tax under the 5- or 10-year averaging method. Using one of these averaging methods could save you a bunch of dough. Refer to Chapter 6 ("Lines 16a and 16b: Total pensions and annuities") for a complete discussion of this issue.

Credits

Now it's time for your credits — and each one has a nice form for you to fill out.

Line 41: Credit for child and dependent care expenses (Form 2441)

If you hire someone to take care of your children so that you can work, you're entitled to the credit that you figure on **Form 2441**. This credit may save you several hundred dollars. To be eligible, your child must be under the age of 13 or a dependent of any age who is physically or mentally handicapped. See Chapter 15 for information on Form 2441.

Line 42: Credit for the elderly or the disabled (Schedule R)

You use (and attach!) **Schedule R** for this credit. You are entitled to claim this credit (which could amount to as much as $1,125) if you are married and both you and your spouse are 65 or over — or both of you are disabled and any age. For single taxpayers, the maximum credit is $750. See Chapter 15 for a discussion of Schedule R and the reasons most people are ineligible for this credit. If you qualify, enter this credit on line 42.

Line 43: Child tax credit

Every child under age 17 on December 31 that you can claim as a dependent can cut your tax bill by $400. The child also must be a U.S. citizen or resident. In 1999, the credit jumps to $500. This credit reduces your tax bill dollar for dollar. Part of your credit gets whittled away, however, when your income exceeds $110,000 if filing jointly, $75,000 filing as single or head of household, and $55,000 if married filing separately. The credit gets reduced by $50 for every $1,000, or part thereof, that your income exceeds the above thresholds. The phaseout is on a per child basis. For example, for joint filers with one child, the credit is completely phased out when their income reaches $118,000. If they have two children, a complete phaseout of the credit won't occur until their income reaches $126,000.

A quick formula — for every $8,000 of income above the phaseout levels, you lose the $400 credit for one kid. At $16,000 you would lose the credit for two kids.

This new child tax credit comes in three varieties: The *Child Tax Credit* that most people find easy to compute; the *Additional Child Tax Credit* that comes into play when you have three or more kids and the regular Child Tax Credit exceeds your tax ; and the *Supplemental Child Credit* for those who can't use the regular Child Tax Credit because of claiming the Earned Income or Adoption Credit, for example. (And you don't need to have three or more kids to take advantage of this one, by the way.) To determine whether you qualify for the additional credit, you need to fill out **Form 8812, Additional Child Tax Credit.**

Why three variations of the same credit? Normally, the regular Child Tax Credit isn't refundable if the credit exceeds your tax. For example, if your tax is $700 and you're entitled to an $800 credit (2 kids x $400), sorry, no refund. But notice that we said normally. By filling out Form 8812, you may discover that you're entitled to the $100 difference.

To compute the child tax credit, use the worksheet on page 32 of your 1040 instruction booklet. Here's a plain English version.

Line 1: Based on the number of kids qualifying for the credit enter, the credit you are entitled to. One kid $400, two kids $800, and so on.

Line 2: Enter your AGI from line 34, Form 1040. If you are filing **Form 2555 or 2555EZ**, things get a little tricky. Add the amount of your foreign income and housing exclusion you deducted on line 21 of your Form 1040 to line 34 of your 1040 and enter the total here on line 2.

Line 3: Enter $110,000 if married, $75,000 if single or head of household, or $55,000 if married filing separately.

Line 4: If line 2 is less than line 3, check the No box and skip lines 4 and 5. Enter zero (-0-) on line 6 and go to line 7; if line 2 is more than line 3, check the Yes box and subtract line 3 from line 2.

Line 5: Divide line 4 by $1,000. If the result isn't a whole number, round it up to the next higher whole number. For example, round 4.25 to 5.

Line 6: Multiply the number on line 5 by $50.

Line 7: Subtract line 6 from line 1.

If line 6 is larger than line 1, stop here. You aren't entitled to the credit.

Line 8: Enter the amount of your tax from Form 1040, line 40.

Line 9: Here is where the supplemental or additional child tax credit comes into play because your child tax credit exceeds your tax after deducting other credits you are entitled to claim. You have to reduce your tax on line 8 by the other credits you are claiming.

If the amount on line 1 is $800 or less, check the No box and enter the amount of your credits on your 1040 for Credit for child and dependent care expenses (line 41), Credit for the elderly (line 42), and Education credits (line 44).

If line 1 is more than $800, you have to fill out the worksheet on Page 33 of your instruction booklet to compute how much of your Child Tax Credit you are entitled to because you are claiming other tax credits.

Line 10: Subtract line 9 from line 8. This is your tax after applying all tax credits to which you are entitled so you can determine the amount of the Child Tax Credit.

Line 11: Enter the smaller of line 7 or line 10 on line 11 and on Form 1040, line 43. This is your Child Tax Credit.

Line 44: Education credits (Form 8863)

In 1998, two new education credits kick in: the *Hope Scholarship Credit* and the *Lifetime Learning Credit*. Remember that credits reduce your tax, dollar for dollar. You claim both credits on **Form 8863, Education Credits (Hope and Lifetime Learning Credits)**.

The following sections provide a snapshot of how these credits work:

✔ **The Hope Scholarship Credit** provides a credit of $1,500 per student per year for the first two years of college. The credit is equal to 100 percent of the first $1,000 of tuition expenses (but not room, board, or books) and 50 percent of the next $1,000 of tuition paid. The credit can be claimed for you, your spouse, and your dependents. But if you earn too much, you won't be eligible. For married taxpayers (you must file jointly), the credit starts to phaseout at $80,000 of income and is completely lost at $100,000. For single taxpayers, the phaseout starts at $40,000 and is completely wiped out at $50,000.

The credit isn't available for anyone convicted of possession or distribution of a controlled substance. A student must carry at least one-half the normal course load.

✔ Starting June 30, 1998, you may be eligible for the **Lifetime Learning Credit,** a 20 percent credit on up to $5,000 of tuition expenses (but not room, board, or books) paid after that date. This credit is per family, not per student, as is the case with the Hope credit. If you don't use the $1,000 credit in one year, you can take the balance in another year until it's used. For example, if you have $1,000 in tuition expenses in

1998, you can claim a $200 credit. If you pay $4,000 in tuition in 1999, you can claim the balance of your $1,000 lifetime credit or $800. If your 1999 expenses were $5,000, your credit would still be limited to $800. Once you claim $1,000 in credits, that's it.

The same income limits and family-member restrictions that apply to the Hope credit also apply to this credit. Unlike the Hope credit, however, the student doesn't have to carry at least one-half the normal course load. Any course to acquire or improve job skills qualifies, but not courses involving sports or hobbies.

You can claim the Hope credit for one child and the Lifetime credit for another, but you can't claim both credits for the same student.

The IRS can check to see whether you're entitled to either the Hope or Learning credit because educational institutions are now required to issue **Form 1098-T,** which lists the student's name, Social Security number, the amount of tuition paid, whether the student was enrolled for at least half the full-time work load ,or whether the courses lead to a graduate level degree.

Line 45: Adoption credit (Form 8839)

You're entitled to a credit of up to $5,000 against your tax for adoption expenses. With the exception of foreign adoptions, the credit gets increased to $6,000 for the adoption of a child with special needs. This term includes a child with a medical, physical, mental, or emotional handicap; a child whose age makes him or her difficult to adopt; or a member of a minority group. A foreign child can't be considered a child with special needs. Here are the rules:

✔ If your adjusted gross income is $75,000 or less, you're entitled to the full credit. Between $75,000 and $115,000, the credit is phased out. At $115,000, it's gone.

✔ The child must be under 18 or physically or mentally incapable of self-care.

✔ Adopting your spouse's child doesn't qualify, nor does a surrogate parenting arrangement.

✔ Adoption expenses can't be paid with funds received from any federal, state, or local adoption program.

✔ The credit can't exceed your tax minus any credit for child and dependent care expenses (**Form 2441**), credit for the elderly or the disabled (Form 1040, **Schedule R**), and your tentative minimum tax (**Form 6251**).

✔ Any unused credit can be carried forward for five years until you use it up.

✔ Married couples must file a joint return. However, if you're legally separated for the last six months of the year, you're eligible to file a separate return and claim the credit.

✔ Except for the adoption of a child with special needs, the credit expires at midnight on December 31, 2001 (sounds like something right out of *Cinderella*).

The type of expenses that qualify for the credits include adoption fees, court costs, attorney fees, and other expenses directly related to adopting an eligible child.

In addition to the adoption credit, you exclude from your income up to $5,000 ($6,000 in the case of a child with special needs) of adoption expenses paid by your employer under an adoption assistance program. For example, you incur $10,000 in adoption expenses. You pay $5,000, and your employer pays $5,000 as part of an adoption assistance program. You're entitled to a $5,000 credit for the expenses you paid, and you're not taxed on the $5,000 paid by your employer.

As a practical matter, owners or principal shareholders of a business aren't eligible to participate in an adoption assistance program.

The credit is taken in the year following when the expenses are paid or in the year that the adoption becomes final. For example, you incur $6,000 of adoption expenses in 1998, of which you pay $4,000 in 1998 and $2,000 in 1999 when the adoption is finalized. You have to wait until 1999 to claim the credit, which is limited to $5,000. Had the adoption become final in 1998, you could claim the $5,000 credit in 1998 because you incurred all the expenses in 1998, even though some expenses weren't paid until 1999. With a foreign adoption, you can't claim the credit or the exclusion until the adoption becomes final. Adoption expenses paid in an earlier year are considered paid in the year the adoption becomes final.

Both the credit and the exclusion are computed on **Form 8839, Qualified Adoption Expenses.** The amount of the credit (line 10) gets entered on line 45 (Form 1040) or line 30 (Form 1040A). Any unused credit that can be carried forward to 1999 gets entered on line 11 of Form 8839. The phaseout income limits don't apply to carryovers. The phaseout is applied only once in the year that generated the credit.

The amount of taxable employer-provided adoption expenses is computed on Form 8839 in Part III. The taxable portion, if any on line 23, gets reported on line 7 whether you're filing Form 1040 or 1040A. Next to line 7, write AB for adoption benefit. How could you have a taxable benefit? Say your employer paid $7,000 in benefits but you were entitled to only a $4,000 exclusion because your income exceeded $75,000; $3,000 of the benefit would be taxable.

Line 46: Foreign tax credit (Form 1116)

Use **Form 1116** to figure this credit. If you are not itemizing your deductions, you have to claim the foreign tax you paid as a credit if you want to use it to reduce your tax.

Unfortunately, the computation of this credit is a killer — and even the IRS agrees. The instructions say that it should take you about $6\frac{1}{2}$ hours to read the instructions, assemble the data, and fill in the form. And that's with all the instructions in English (by and large) and all the parts included! Give it a whirl. If you hate number-crunching, a computer tax software program can help (refer to Chapter 2). If using a computer isn't your thing, see a tax advisor. Attach **Form 1116** to your return and bid it good riddance! You can either claim the foreign tax as a credit that you paid on line 46 or as an itemized deduction on Schedule A.

As a general rule taking the credit produces a larger savings. For more on foreign taxes, refer to "Line 8: Other taxes (foreign income taxes)" in Chapter 9.

You don't have to be a multinational corporation to pay foreign taxes. With more and more people investing in international mutual funds, the foreign tax credit is being used more than ever before to reduce investors' U.S. tax bills for their share of the foreign taxes paid by the fund.

The foreign tax credit can also be used for foreign taxes paid on income earned overseas that exceeds the $72,000 exclusion and the housing allowance. (See "Work overseas" in Chapter 30 for more on this tax credit.)

Starting in 1998, you can ignore the fiendish Form 1116 if your foreign tax is $300 or less ($600 for joint filers). On your 1998 return, simply enter the foreign tax you paid on line 46 if your foreign tax is less than these amounts. This simplified method of claiming the credit is available if the only type of foreign income you had was from dividends, interest, rent, royalties, annuities, or the sale of an asset.

Line 47: Other credits

The application of these credits is extremely limited, and few people are eligible for them. So, if you want to explore them further, you need to call the IRS (800-829-3676) and ask for the form and instructions. Sorry!

✔ **Form 8801, Credit for Prior Year Minimum Tax — Individuals and Fiduciaries**

✔ **Form 8396, Mortgage Interest Credit** (see the box on your 1040 by line 47)

  You may be eligible for this credit if you were issued a mortgage credit certificate by a state or local government agency. The maximum credit is $2,000. A good mortgage broker can assist you in qualifying for a state-sponsored mortgage loan so you can qualify for this credit.

✔ **Form 3800, General Business Credit:** This form includes a number of credits that qualify as general business credits. If you're claiming more than one of these general business credits, check the Form 3800 box on line 47 of your 1040 and attach Form 3800, claiming the credits you are eligible to claim. If you're claiming just one of these general business credits, check the Form (specify) box on line 47, fill in the form number, and attach that specific form. The following list includes the general business credits on **Form 3800**:

  • **Form 8834, Qualified Electric Vehicle Credit —** for all you environmentalists

  • **Form 3468, Investment Credit**

  • **Form 5884, Work Opportunity Credit**

  • **Form 6478, Credit for Alcohol Used for Fuel**

  • **Form 6765, Credit for Increasing Research Activities, or for Claiming the Orphan Drug Credit**

  • **Form 8586, Low-Income Housing Credit**

  • **Form 8830, Enhanced Oil Recovery Credit**

  • **Form 8826, Disabled Access Credit**

  • **Form 8835, Renewable Electricity Production Credit**

  • **Form 8845, Indian Employment Credit**

  • **Form 8846, Credit for Employer Social Security and Medicare Taxes Paid on Certain Employees' Tips**

  • **Form 8847, Credit for Contributions to Certain Community Development Corporations**

Residents of Washington, D.C. First-time home buyers in the district are entitled to a tax credit of up to $5,000 of the cost of the residence. This credit took effect on August 5, 1997, and is good until December 31, 2000. *First-time homebuyer* means that you didn't own a home within one year of the purchase of your new home. The credit is claimed on **Form 8859, District of Columbia First-Time Homebuyer Credit.**

The amount of the credit is reduced if your income is over $70,000 ($110,000 for joint filers). For every $1,000 above the threshold, the credit gets reduced by $250.

Lines 48 and 49: Simple addition and subtraction

Add lines 41 through 47 and put the sum here. (If you make a mistake, your grade will suffer.) Then subtract line 48 from line 40. If line 49 is greater than line 40, just enter 0.

Other Taxes

What! More taxes? Could be. Read the following sections to see if any of these taxes apply to you.

Line 50: Self-employment tax (Schedule SE)

If you earn income from being self-employed as well as from other sources, **Schedule SE** is used to figure another tax that you owe — the Social Security tax and Medicare tax. The first $68,400 of your self-employment earnings is taxed at 12.4 percent (this is the Social Security tax part). There isn't any limit for the Medicare tax; it's 2.9 percent of your total self-employment earnings. For amounts $68,400 or less, the combined rate is 15.3 percent (adding the two taxes together), and above $68,400 the rate is 2.9 percent. See Chapter 15 for information about filling out Schedule SE.

Line 51: Alternative Minimum Tax (Form 6251)

You would think that with all of the schedules and forms we've slogged through that you'd almost be done. Well, this line can prove to be a real bummer for some. This line refers you to yet another whole tax system — the Alternative Minimum Tax (AMT). The AMT is designed to snare higher income people who reduce their taxable income by claiming too many (from the perspective of the IRS) deductions. You need to figure your tax under the AMT system and compare it to the regular system on Form 1040. Guess what? You pay whichever one is higher.

You don't have to be Bill Gates to get clipped by the AMT. Although only 600,000 taxpayers are expected to be affected by the AMT, Congress' Joint Tax Committee expects the number to swell to 8.4 million by 2007. Unfortunately, a lot of these folks will be middle-income taxpayers. For example, one large middle-income family got hit with the AMT because their 12 personal exemptions, each currently worth $2,700, aren't allowed when figuring the AMT.

If you have any of the following types of deductions or income, you could be subject to the AMT. So get out your **Form 6251, Alternative Minimum Tax — Individuals,** and start calculating. The starting point is line 37 of your Form 1040 — your AGI after deducting your itemized deductions or standard deduction, but before you subtract your deductions for your personal exemptions in arriving at your taxable income. Enter the amount from line 37 on line 16 of Form 6251. From this amount, you have to add back the following items to arrive at your AMT income:

- Job expenses and miscellaneous itemized deductions (line 26 of Schedule A).
- Medical and dental expenses in excess of 10 percent of your income.
- Deductions for taxes (line 9 of Schedule A).
- Home equity mortgage interest not used to buy, build, or improve your home.
- Incentive stock options — the difference that you paid for the stock and what it was worth when you exercised the option. (See Chapter 12 for the lowdown on handling stock options.)
- Depreciation in excess of the straight-line method.
- Tax-exempt interest from private activity bonds issued after August 7, 1986.

Enter the preceding amounts on lines 1–14. Although the AMT was designed to make sure that the wealthy didn't escape paying a minimum amount by using loopholes and tax deductions, the 1993 tax law gave it more teeth. Nobody can say for certain, but our best estimate is that the AMT could grab people with incomes as low as $75,000, just like the family with the 12 exemptions that we discussed earlier in this section. And although the preceding items are most likely the ones that the average taxpayer will use to compute the AMT, a number of way-out items also go into figuring the AMT, such as intangible drilling expenses, circulation expenses, depletion, certain installment sales, passive activities and research, and experimental costs.

Is there any way to avoid the Alternative Minimum Tax? Defer those deductions and tax incentives that trigger the AMT or accelerate income so your deductions will be within the AMT limits. Unfortunately, this maneuver requires checking your income and deductible expenses periodically throughout the year. Investing in a tax software program or a tax advisor may help ease the burden.

We wish that we could provide you with a general guide on when your AMT will exceed your regular tax, thereby causing you to have to fork over the difference. Unfortunately, we can't. But here is the IRS rule: If your taxable income, combined with your personal exemptions and the items listed earlier in this section, exceeds the following amounts, you could end up paying the AMT:

- Married filing jointly and qualifying widow(er)s — $45,000
- Single or head of household — $33,750
- Married filing separately — $22,500

The AMT in brief

Here is a quick glance at how the AMT works.

	Regular Tax	AMT
Income	$150,000	$150,000
Deductions		
Taxes	<20,000>	0
Home Equity Interest (not used to improve your home)	<10,000>	0
Mortgage Interest	<20,000>	<20,000>
Charity	<5,000>	<5,000>
Job Expenses	<15,000>	0
Exemptions (5 × $2,700)	<13,500>	0
AMT Exemption		<45,000>
Taxable Income	$66,500	$80,000
Tax	$13,122	$20,800

The hapless taxpayer in this example has to cough up $20,800. That's $7,678 more than what his tax worked out to be under the regular method. You pay the higher of your regular tax or AMT. For simplicity, we didn't take into account all the various deduction phaseout amounts.

Starting in 1998, farmers no longer have to include certain installment sales when computing their AMT.

Line 52: Social Security and Medicare tax on unreported tip income (Form 4137)

If you worked in a restaurant that employed at least ten people and didn't report your share of 8 percent of the restaurant's income as tip income, your employer will do it for you. This amount (the difference between what you reported as tip income to your employer and your share of 8 percent of the restaurant's income), your allocated tips, is entered on box 8 of your W-2. The amount in box 8 isn't included in box 1 of your W-2 and has to be added to your total wages on Form 1040 (line 7). The Social Security tax that you owe on the amount in box 8 is computed on **Form 4137** and is entered on line 52.

When we say "your share of 8 percent of the restaurant's income," that doesn't mean that you're entitled to this income. What this means is that the IRS arbitrarily claims that the restaurant generated tip income equal to 8 percent of the restaurant's income. Box 8 of your W-2 is for your share of the total amount of tips.

If your employer wasn't able to collect from you all the Social Security and Medicare tax you owe on your reported tip income, box 13 of your W-2 will show that amount. Code A next to the amount in box 13 is for Social Security tax and Code B next to the amount in box 13 is for Medicare Tax. Enter the amounts in box 13 on Form 1040 (line 52), and to the left of the amount, write UNCOLLECTED TAX ON TIPS.

Line 53: Tax on qualified retirement plans (Form 5329)

The IRS should simply list **Form 5329** by the name IRA and Pension Penalties. Remember, if you take money out of an IRA or pension before you're 59½, you may owe a 10-percent penalty in addition to the tax on the amount that you withdraw. If you took out too little after reaching 70½, the penalty is 50 percent of the amount that you should have taken — based on your life expectancy — and what you actually withdrew or failed to withdraw. The penalty as computed on the Form 5329 is entered here for "other taxes." Refer to Chapter 6, "Line 15a and 15b: Total IRA distributions," for details on how to escape this penalty. You have a whole bunch of ways to escape, such as withdrawals for first-time home buyers and certain education expenses, as well as one or two others.

Line 54: Advance earned income credits

Enter the amount from box 9 of your W-2. If you're entitled to an EIC, you can file Form W-5 with your employer, and up to 60 percent of the credit can be added to your paycheck. This way you don't have to wait until the end of the year to get a refund (refer to Chapter 6, "Box 9: Advance EIC payment," and the following section "Line 59a: Earned income credit").

Line 55: Household employment taxes (Schedule H)

Even if you don't expect to hold high political office — or low political office — the provisions of the nanny tax can save you a tidy sum, as well as simplify the number and type of returns you have to file. The law covers housekeepers, babysitters, and yard-care workers, as well as nannies.

The nanny tax is figured on **Schedule H,** and the amount you owe is entered on line 55. If you didn't pay cash wages of $1,100 or more in 1998 or $1,000 or more in any calendar quarter, or didn't withhold any federal income tax, you can skip this form. If you paid more than $1,100 in wages in 1998 but less than $1,000 in any calendar quarter, you only have to fill out page 1 and enter the amount from line 8 of Schedule H onto line 55. If you paid more than $1,000 in any quarter, you have to fill out page 2 of the form and enter the amount from line 27 of Schedule H onto line 55. See Chapter 15 for more about filling out Schedule H.

Line 56: IRS pop quiz

Find your total tax by adding lines 49 through 55 and placing the amount here.

Payments

This is the section of the return where you finally, thankfully, get to tally up how much actual federal tax you paid during the year.

Line 57: Federal income tax withheld

Enter the amount from box 2 of your W-2 and your W-2G, 1099-DIV, and 1099-INT — as well as box 4 of your Form 1099-R — on line 57. Make sure that you don't overlook any tax withheld on a Form 1099.

Line 58: 1998 estimated tax payments

If you made estimated tax payments, fill in the total amount of the payments here. If you applied last year's overpayment to this year's return, don't forget to enter that amount, too! The IRS isn't kind enough to send you a reminder; you have to keep track yourself.

Remember, the IRS doesn't want to wait until April 15, 2000, to collect your 1999 tax. So, if you will owe money come next April 15, you must file quarterly estimates if 90 percent of your tax isn't being withheld from your income and you will owe more than $1,000.

Estimated tax payments are made on **Form 1040-ES, Estimated Tax for Individuals.** The form only requires your name, address, Social Security number, and the amount you are paying. For 1999 estimated payments, make sure that you use the 1999 1040-ES. See Chapter 15 if you need help filling out Form 1040-ES.

Line 59a: Earned income credit

The earned income credit is a special credit for lower-income workers. The credit is refundable — which means that if it exceeds your tax or if you don't owe tax, the IRS will send you a check for the amount of the EIC.

Unlike other credits, the EIC is no small piece of change. The credit can be as high $3,756. To qualify for the credit, your earned income must be less than the following amounts:

- ✔ $26,473 if you have one child
- ✔ $30,095 if you have two or more children

✔ $10,030 if you don't have any children and you are at least 25 (but under 65) and are not being claimed as a dependent by anyone else

Net self-employment income for the purposes of the EIC is your net earnings reduced by one-half of your self-employment tax on Schedule SE that you deducted on Form 1040 (line 28). If you lost money in your business as reported on Schedule C, you can deduct your loss from your other earned income.

Earned income doesn't include the following:

✔ Interest and dividends

✔ Social Security benefits

✔ Pensions or annuities

✔ Veterans' benefits

✔ Alimony or child support

✔ Unemployment insurance

✔ Welfare benefits

✔ Taxable scholarships or fellowships that were not reported on your W-2

In addition to your having to meet the earned income test, your child must meet the following tests:

1. **Relationship test**

   The child must be your son, daughter, adopted child, stepchild, or foster child.

2. **Residency test**

   Your child must have lived with you in your main home in the U.S. for more than six months. A foster child has to live in your home for the entire year. For a child who was born or died during the year, the residency test is met if the child lived with you for part of the year.

3. **Age test**

   Your child must be under 19 (or under 24 if a full-time student) or any age if permanently and totally disabled.

Figuring the earned income credit

If you meet all of the requirements, figuring the earned income credit is easy. No math is required. Just look up the credit you're entitled to for your earned income bracket in the Earned Income Credit Table. Read across to the appropriate column: no qualifying child, one child, or two children. For example, if your earned income is $12,260 and you have one qualifying child, you're entitled to an EIC of $2,271. Attach the EIC Schedule to your return and enter the credit on Form 1040 (line 59a).

A nice feature of this credit is that you don't have to wait until you file your return to claim it. If you're eligible for the credit, you can file **Form W-5, EIC (Advance Payment Certificate)** with your employer, and a portion of the credit will be added to your weekly paycheck. The advanced credit you received during the year is entered on box 9 of your W-2. You must enter the amount in box 9 on Form 1040 (line 54) and the EIC to which you're entitled on line 59a. For example, if you're entitled to an EIC of $1,200 and you received $500 throughout the year from your employer, $500 will be entered in box 9 of your W-2. The $500 is subtracted from your EIC of $1,200, and $700 will be refunded.

For individuals without children qualifying for the credit, you must, in addition to the income limit, have had a main home in the U.S. for more than six months, file a joint return if you are married, not be a dependent of another, and be at least 25 but under 65. You 1040 filers need to fill out and attach **Schedule EIC,** and enter the amount of nontaxable earned income on line 59b. To compute the credits, go to the EIC Table in your tax-instruction booklet. Based on your income and the number of qualifying children, read across for your earned income line to the amount of credit that you can claim.

Line 59b: Nontaxable earned income amount and type

Here's where the government wants to learn everything about you even if it isn't taxable. Depending on your income, the amount of your nontaxable income can either increase or decrease the credit you're entitled to. Sorry to leave you dangling, but that's how our tax system operates. Only by filling in the EIC worksheet in your 1040 instruction booklet will you discern whether this line hurts or helps you.

Nontaxable earned income includes:

✔ Voluntary salary deferrals, such as 401(k)s

✔ Combat pay

✔ Military personnel quarter and subsistence allowances

✔ Salary reductions under cafeteria plans (see fringe benefits)

✔ Housing allowances for the clergy

✔ The value of meals or lodging provided by your employer and for the convenience of the employer

✔ Excludable dependent care (line 18, Form 2441; or Schedule 2)

If you don't list your dependent's Social Security number on the EIC Form, you get NO credit. If investment income exceeds $2,300, NO credit. Investment income includes capital gains, interest, dividends, tax-exempt interest, and rental income after expenses.

Line 60: Additional child tax credit (Form 8812)

This is the refundable portion of the Child Tax Credit that we explained on line 43. To get part of the credit refunded, you to have file **Form 8812, Additional Child Tax Credit.**

Line 61: Extension request (Form 4868)

If you requested a four-month extension of time to file with **Form 4868,** enter the amount that you paid when you requested the extension. (You can find this form in the back of this book. Unbelievably, despite the millions of taxpayers who file for extensions each year, the IRS still doesn't include this form in the Form 1040 instruction booklet.)

Line 62: Excess Social Security and RRTA tax withheld

Line 62 applies only if you worked for two employers and your total wages were $68,400 or more. The maximum Social Security tax you are required to pay for 1998 is $4,240.80. So if $4,540.80 was withheld, $300 is entered on line 62. Box 4 of your W-2s contains the amount of Social Security tax that was withheld from your salary.

Line 63: Other payments

Here are a couple of the more obscure forms to wonder about:

- ✔ **Form 2439, Notice to Shareholders of Undistributable Long-Term Capital Gain:** Investors in mutual funds where the company didn't distribute your share of the long-term capital gains will receive this form. Enter the amount from line 2 of this form on line 63 and attach a copy of the form to your 1040. See Chapter 12 for information on how to handle the capital gains retained by the fund.

- ✔ **Form 4136, Credit for Federal Tax Paid on Fuels:** This form is for claiming credit for diesel fuels. There is a refundable credit for fuel used in non-highway vehicles. Bulldozers, forklifts, generators, and compressors used in your business qualify for the credit. Fuel used in motor boats doesn't qualify.

Line 64: Total payments

You enter the total of the payments (lines 57 through 63) on line 64 and hold your breath (or your nose).

Refund or Amount You Owe

Okay, this is it. Now comes the moment you've worked so hard for. Do you get money back? Do you pay? Read on and find out.

Line 65: The amount that you overpaid

If the amount of your total payments (line 64) is more than your total tax (line 56), subtract line 56 from line 64 (see Figure 8-2). The remainder is the amount you overpaid. Do you like that word "overpaid?"

Line 66: Amount that you want refunded to you

You can speed up the receipt of your refund by ten days to two weeks by having your refund wired to your account. That way you can ensure that it won't be lost or stolen. To do so, enter your routing number on line 66b. That's the nine-digit RTN in Figure 8-3. On line 66c, check the type of account: checking or savings. On line 66d, enter your account number. That's the DAN (Depositor Account Number) in Figure 8-3.

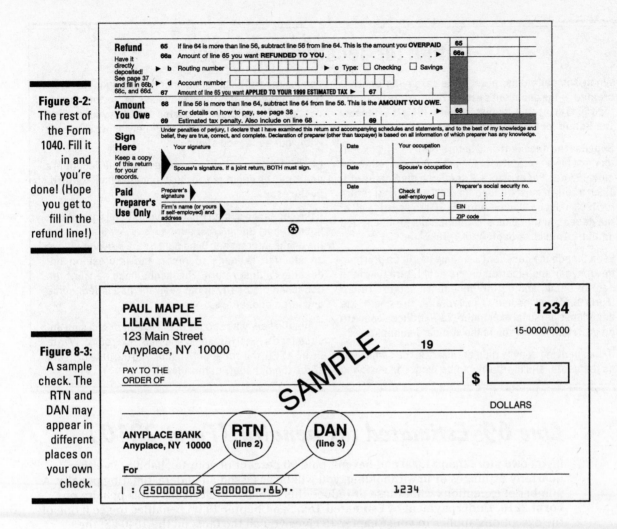

Figure 8-2:
The rest of the Form 1040. Fill it in and you're done! (Hope you get to fill in the refund line!)

Figure 8-3:
A sample check. The RTN and DAN may appear in different places on your own check.

Line 67: 1999 estimated tax

Here you indicate what amount of your refund you want applied to your 1999 (next year's) estimated tax. Once you make this selection and file your return, you can't change your mind and ask for it back. You have to claim it as a credit on your 1999 return.

Line 68: The gosh darn AMOUNT YOU OWE line

If your total tax (line 56) is larger than your total payments (line 64), subtract line 64 from line 56. This is the amount you owe. Sorry. Fill out **Form 1040-V, Payment Voucher,** that the IRS sends you.

If you want to charge what you owe on a credit card, go back to line 12 of the 1040EZ for the ins and outs of how to do this.

Return for deceased taxpayer

When someone dies, a separate taxpaying entity is created—the decedent's estate. If the estate has more than $600 in income, it must file **Form 1041, U.S. Income Tax Return for Estates and Trusts.**

Suppose the decedent died before April 15. The executor must file a tax return for the prior year as well as the current year. For example, if someone died on April 1, 1999, a return must be filed for 1998 and a final return for 1999 must be filed by April 15, 2000, reporting all of the deceased's income and deductions for the period January 1, 1999, through April 1, 1999.

Even though the decedent's income has to be prorated for the year and reported on the final return up to the date of death, and on the decedent's estate's return (Form 1041) for income received after the death, the decedent's personal exemption ($2,700) doesn't have to be prorated. Neither does the standard deduction.

If the surviving spouse didn't remarry in the same year as the death, a joint return can be filed. The surviving spouse reports all his or her income and deductions for the entire year and the deceased's up to the date of death. If you remarry in the same year that your spouse dies, you can file jointly with your new spouse, but not with your deceased spouse.

Medical expenses paid within one year of the decedent's death can be deducted on the decedent's final return or by the estate.

If the deceased owned E or EE savings bonds and chose not to report the interest during his or her lifetime, the tax on the interest has to be paid by the survivor unless an election is made to report the interest on the decedent's final return. This might make sense if the deceased died early in the year and had little income and large deductions.

Either the surviving spouse or the executor can sign the deceased's final personal income tax return. Write DECEASED, the decedent's name, and the date of death at the top of page 1 of the 1040.

Line 69: Estimated tax penalty (Form 2210)

If you owe more than $1,000 and haven't paid 90 percent of your tax liability in either quarterly estimates or in withholding, you will be assessed an underestimating penalty. A number of exceptions will excuse or reduce this penalty. You calculate this penalty on **Form 2210, Underpayment of Estimated Tax.** See Chapter 19 on penalties to see if one of the exceptions applies to you. Chapter 15 gives you all the facts on the 1040-ES, the estimated tax form, and the penalties that may apply if you don't fill it out.

Remember, the IRS doesn't want to wait until April 15, 1999, when you file your return, to collect your 1998 tax. You should have paid at least 90 percent of your tax by having tax withheld from your salary, pension, or IRA distributions — or by making estimated quarterly tax payments.

If you don't calculate this penalty yourself, the IRS does and will bill you for it. You don't want the IRS to prepare this form because the IRS will prepare it on the basis of your paying the maximum! A good tax software program will breeze through this form to see if you are eligible to have the penalty reduced or eliminated by one of the exceptions. The ability to calculate this form alone is worth the price of the software package.

No penalty will be assessed for any estimated tax payments that you failed to make as a result of the law that was enacted in 1996, 1997, or 1998 for provisions that took effect in 1998.

Finishing Up

Attach your W-2s, W-2Gs, 1099s where federal tax was withheld, and all schedules. If you owe money, make sure you write your Social Security number on the front of the check along with the notation 1998 Form 1040. Sign your return and mail it to the IRS Service Center for the area in which you live. (See the appendix for the correct address.) If you have to send a check, make it out to the Internal Revenue Service and not the IRS. If your check gets stolen, "IRS" can too easily be changed to "Mrs. Smith."

Part III
Filling Out Schedules and Forms

The 5th Wave   By Rich Tennant

"That? That's Schedule XIRS-1. We've never had to use it. But, if anyone actually discovers how to grow money on trees, Uncle Sam's got a form to get his fair share of the leaves."

In this part . . .

The plain old 1040 isn't just the plain old 1040 — it's really a souped up version that rides around with a number of schedules and forms, tailored to your specific tax situation. Naturally, these schedules and forms take after the 1040 in their complexity and potential for causing confusion. This part walks you through the schedules and forms that affect most taxpayers, with ways you may be able to take advantage of new tax cuts and tips that help you pay only what you really owe.

"Anyone may so arrange his affairs that his taxes shall be as low as possible; he is not bound to choose that pattern which will best pay the treasury; there is not even a patriotic duty to increase one's taxes."

— Learned Hand

Chapter 9
Itemized Deductions: Schedule A

● ●

In This Chapter

▶ Standard deductions versus itemizing

▶ Deductions for medical and dental expenses

▶ Deductions for taxes and interest you paid

▶ Deductions for gifts to charity and casualty and theft losses

▶ Deductions for job expenses and miscellaneous expenses

● ●

*I*f *Hamlet* were to be written today, we wonder if Shakespeare would have him lament, "To itemize or to take the standard deduction, that is the question." Forgive the Shakespearean reference, but that is indeed the question that must be answered.

The Decision: You've reached that point in preparing your return where this decision must be made. You totaled your income and subtracted your allowable adjustments to income. Now to arrive at your taxable income, you have to subtract your standard deduction and exemptions — or take the more difficult road and subtract your itemized deductions.

The Standard Deduction

If you're under 65, the standard deductions are as follows:

✔ Married filing jointly or a qualifying widow(er) — $7,100

✔ Head of household — $6,250

✔ Single — $4,250

✔ Married filing separately — $ 3,550

If you're married filing separately, you may claim the standard deduction only if your spouse also claims the standard deduction. If your spouse itemizes, you must also itemize. If you decide not to itemize your deductions, enter the standard deduction for your filing status on line 36.

Over 65 or blind

If you are blind or age 65 or above, the standard deduction is increased by $1,050 if you are single or a head of household, and it's increased by $850 if you are married filing jointly or a qualifying widow(er).

Instead of adding this extra deduction to your regular standard deduction, just check the appropriate blanks in the chart (see Table 9-1).

Table 9-1 Standard Deduction Chart for People Age 65 or Older or Blind

Check the number of boxes below. Then go to the chart.

You	65 or older ☐		Blind ☐
Your spouse, if claiming spouse's exemption	65 or older ☐		Blind ☐
Total number of boxes you checked		_____	

If Your Filing Status Is:	And the Total Number of Boxes You Checked Above Is:	Your Standard Deduction Is:
Single	1	$5,300
	2	$6,350
Married filing joint return or qualifying widow(er) with dependent child	1	$7,950
	2	$8,800
	3	$9,650
	4	$10,500
Married filing separate return	1	$4,400
	2	$5,250
	3	$6,100
	4	$6,950
Head of household	1	$7,300
	2	$8,350

If you're claiming an increased standard deduction, you can't use Form 1040EZ; you must use Form 1040A or Form 1040.

Standard deduction for dependents

If you can claim your child or dependent on your own or on another person's tax return, the dependent's standard deduction is limited to either $700 or to the individual's 1998 earned income plus $250 for the year (whichever amount is larger — but not more than the regular standard deduction amount of $4,250). So if you're helping your son or daughter prepare his or her return, use the worksheet in Table 9-2 to compute the standard deduction. If your dependent is 65 or older or blind, however, this standard deduction may be higher. Also use Table 9-2 to determine your dependent's standard deduction. Whether you're preparing your own return (as a child being claimed on your parent's return, for example) or you're preparing a return for a dependent that you're claiming, you must complete this worksheet. Otherwise, use the regular standard deduction.

Earned income includes wages, salaries, tips, professional fees, and other compensation that you received for services performed. It also includes anything received as a scholarship that counts as income.

An illustrated example of how to fill out the worksheet in Table 9-2 is provided in Chapter 5 under 1040EZ, line 5.

Table 9-2 Standard Deduction Worksheet for Dependents

If you are 65 or older or blind, check the boxes below. Then go to the worksheet.

You	65 or older ☐		Blind ☐
Your spouse, if claiming spouse's exemption	65 or older ☐		Blind ☐
Total number of boxes you checked		_____	

1. Enter your earned income. If none, go on to line 3.	1. _____
1A. Additional amount allowed in 1998	1a. $250
1B. Add lines 1 and 1A.	1b. _____
2. Minimum amount	2. $700
3. Compare the amounts on lines 1B and 2. Enter the larger of the two amounts here.	3. _____

4. Enter on line 4 the amount shown below for your filing status.
    Single, enter $4,250.
    Married filing separate return, enter $3,550.
    Married filling jointly or qualifying widow(er)
    with dependent child, enter $7,100.
    Head of household, enter $6,250.
	4. _____

5. Standard deduction.
a. Compare the amounts on lines 3 and 4.
    Enter the smaller of the two amounts here.
    If under 65 and not blind, stop here. This is your standard deduction.
    Otherwise, go on to line 5b.
	5a. _____

b. If 65 or older or blind, multiply $1,050 by the total number of blanks checked; if married or qualifying widow(er) with dependent child, use $850. Enter the result here.	5b. _____
c. Add lines 5a and 5b. This is your standard deduction for 1998.	5c. _____

Itemized Deductions

Some taxpayers simply compute their tax by using the standard deduction. If you have any doubt about being able to itemize and take more than the standard deduction, try itemizing and then use the higher of the two amounts. Does this advice make sense or what? That is, of course, unless you *want* the government to have more of your money.

Here's your itemized deduction shopping list:

✔ Medical and dental expenses that exceed 7.5 percent of your adjusted gross income (AGI)

✔ Taxes you paid

✔ Interest you paid

✔ Gifts to charity

✔ Casualty and theft losses

✔ Job-related, investment, and tax-preparation expenses that exceed 2 percent of your AGI

✔ Other miscellaneous itemized deductions not subject to the 2 percent limit. See line 27 later in this chapter for an in-depth analysis of these types of deductions.

You claim these deductions on Form 1040 with Schedule A. You carry the total on line 28 over to Form 1040 (line 36), where you subtract it from your AGI.

Separate returns and limits on deductions

If you are married and filing separately, both spouses have to itemize their deductions. One spouse can't use the standard deduction while the other itemizes. If you are divorced or legally separated, you are considered single, and you can itemize your deductions or claim the standard deduction no matter what your former spouse does. However, in itemizing your separate expenses, you can claim only those expenses for which you or your spouse are personally liable. For example, if a residence is in your former spouse's name and you paid the property taxes and the mortgage interest, you can't deduct them. However, if your divorce or separation agreement requires that you pay either the property taxes or the mortgage interest, then these payments can be deducted as alimony. Your former spouse reports payment as taxable alimony and is not allowed to deduct the mortgage interest, and real estate parts of the itemized deductions. Deciding who gets to deduct what when a couple divorces is almost as bad as dividing the property.

If you and your spouse are separated but don't have a decree of divorce or separate maintenance, you may be able to itemize or use the standard deduction and file as head of household. You can do this if you didn't live with your spouse during the last six months of 1998, and if you maintained a home for more than half of 1998 for yourself and a child that you are entitled to claim as a dependent.

But if you change your mind

Oops! Suppose that you discover you should have itemized after you already filed. Or even worse, suppose that you went to all the trouble to itemize but shouldn't have done so. Just amend your return by filing **Form 1040X, Amended U.S. Individual Income Tax Return.** But if you're married and you filed separately, you can't change your mind unless both you and your spouse make the same change. And if either of you must pay additional tax as a result of the change, you both need to file a consent. (Sorry, dear!) Remember that if one of you itemizes, the other no longer qualifies for the standard deduction.

Lines 1–4: Medical and Dental Costs

Your total medical and dental expenses (after what you were reimbursed by your health insurance policy) must exceed 7.5 percent of your adjusted gross income (lines 33 and 34 of your Form 1040). Both lines should be the same amount. If they aren't, your math is off. This detail knocks many people out of contention for this deduction. For example, if your adjusted gross income equals $30,000, you'd need to have at least $2,250 in medical and dental expenses. If you don't, you can cruise past these lines. (Because the threshold is so high, we hope, for your health's sake, that this is one deduction you *can't* take.)

You can deduct medical and dental expenses for you, your spouse, and your dependents, as well as the medical expenses of any person who is your dependent even if you can't claim an exemption for this person because he or she had income of $2,700 or more or filed a joint return, or your ex-spouse is claiming him or her as a dependent. You fill in the amounts on lines 1 through 4 on Schedule A (see Figure 9-1). This rule means you can deduct the medical expenses you paid for your child even though your ex-spouse is claiming him. For the purposes of the medical deduction, the child is considered the dependent of both parents (see the sidebar "Special cases — who gets the deduction?" later in this chapter).

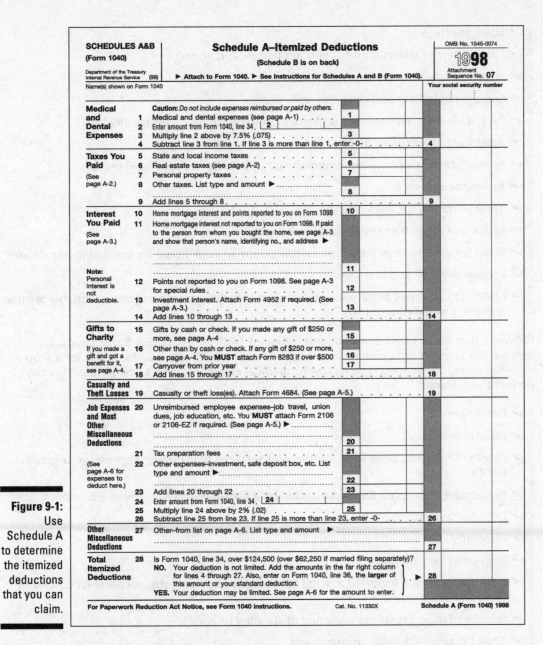

Figure 9-1: Use Schedule A to determine the itemized deductions that you can claim.

Medical and dental expense checklist

The following is a list of things that are deductible, so remember to save all those bills:

- Medical services (doctors, dentists, opticians, podiatrists, registered nurses, practical nurses, psychiatrists, and so on)

- Hospital bills

- Medical, hospital, and dental insurance premiums that you pay (but you can't deduct premiums paid by your employer); don't overlook premiums deducted from your paycheck

- Guide dog

- Wages and Social Security tax paid for worker providing medical care

- Birth control pills

- ✔ Legal abortion
- ✔ Special items (artificial limbs, contact lenses, and so on)
- ✔ Wages for nursing service
- ✔ Oxygen equipment and oxygen
- ✔ Part of life-care fee paid to a retirement home designated for medical care
- ✔ Treatment at a drug or alcohol clinic
- ✔ Special school or home for a mentally or physically handicapped person
- ✔ Ambulance service
- ✔ Transportation for medical care
- ✔ Drugs and medicines prescribed by a doctor
- ✔ Costs for medical equipment or modifications to your home for needed medical care
- ✔ Laboratory fees and tests
- ✔ Childbirth classes (but if your husband attends the classes as your coach, his portion of the fee isn't deductible)

Be aware that many medical and dental expenses can't be deducted. Surprisingly, a number of expenses that you make to improve your health, such as fees paid for a stop-smoking class, which should reduce your medical expenses, aren't deductible. You can't deduct these things:

- ✔ Diaper service
- ✔ Funeral expenses
- ✔ Health club or spa dues for activities and services that merely improve your general health
- ✔ Household help (even if recommended by a doctor)
- ✔ Life insurance premiums
- ✔ Maternity clothes
- ✔ Stop-smoking programs
- ✔ Medical insurance included in a car insurance policy covering all persons injured in or by the car
- ✔ Social activities (such as swimming or dancing lessons)
- ✔ Trips for general health improvement
- ✔ Nursing care for a healthy baby
- ✔ Weight-loss programs
- ✔ Over-the-counter medicines, toothpaste, toiletries, and cosmetics
- ✔ Surgery for purely cosmetic reasons (such as face lifts, tummy tucks, and so on) Plastic surgery required as the result of an accident is deductible.

Deductible travel costs

The cost of traveling to your doctor or a medical facility for treatment is deductible. If you use your car, you can deduct a flat rate of 10 cents a mile, or you can deduct your actual out-of-pocket expenses for gas, oil, and repairs. You can also deduct parking and tolls. You can't deduct depreciation, insurance, or general repairs.

Special cases — who gets the deduction?

Sometimes, when two or more people support someone, special rules apply to determine who can claim the medical expenses that were paid.

One tricky case is that of divorced and separated parents. A divorced or separated parent can deduct the medical expenses he or she paid for a child's medical costs — even if the child's other parent is entitled to claim the child as a dependent.

For the purposes of claiming medical expenses, a child is considered the dependent of both parents if all of the following conditions are met:

✔ The parents were legally separated or divorced or were married and living apart for the last six months of 1998.

✔ Both parents provided more than half the child's support in 1998.

✔ Either spouse had custody of the child for more than half of 1998.

Deductible travel costs to seek medical treatment aren't limited to just local auto and cab trips — a trip to see a specialist in another city also qualifies for the deduction. Unfortunately, though, transportation costs incurred when you're not going to and from a doctor's office or a hospital are a deduction the IRS likes to challenge (maybe because a lot of taxpayers tried to deduct as a medical expense travel to a warm climate, claiming health reasons!). The cost of transportation to a mild climate to relieve a specific condition is deductible — but the airfare to Arizona for general health reasons is not.

Trips to visit an institutionalized child have been allowed when the visits were prescribed by a doctor.

Another complicated case is that of a *multiple-support agreement* in which two or more people together provide more than half of a person's total support — but no one on his or her own provides more than half. Such an agreement allows *one* and only one of the individuals to claim the exemption for the person (even without providing more than half the support). If you are the person entitled to claim the exemption under the agreement, you can deduct the medical expenses you pay. But any other taxpayers who also paid medical expenses can't deduct them.

Meals and lodging

Your bill at a hospital is fully deductible. You may be able to deduct as a medical expense the cost of lodging not provided in a hospital while you're away from your home if you meet all the following requirements:

✔ The lodging is necessary for your medical care.

✔ The medical care is provided by a doctor in a medical facility.

✔ The lodging is not extravagant.

✔ There is no significant element of personal pleasure, recreation, or vacation involved in the travel.

The amount you can deduct as a medical expense for lodging can't exceed $50 a night for you and $50 a night for anyone accompanying you. Only meals that are part of a hospital bill are deductible.

Insurance premiums

Health insurance premiums that cover hospital, medical, and dental expenses; prescription drugs; and eyeglasses and the replacement of lost or damaged contact lenses are deductible as a medical expense. So is the monthly Part B Medicare premium that gets deducted from your Social Security check. If you're self-employed, don't overlook the opportunity to claim a direct deduction for 45 percent of your premium. (Take a peek at line 28 in Chapter 7.) Based on your age, a limited portion of the premium for long-term health care also is deductible.

Here are the deductible amounts for long-term health-care premiums:

Age	Deductible
40 or less	$210
more than 40, but not more than 50	$380
more than 50, but not more than 60	$7,770
more than 60, but not more than 70	$2,050
more than 70	$2,570

Reimbursements and damages

You must reduce your medical expenses by what you were reimbursed under your health insurance policy and from Medicare. Payments that you received for loss of earnings or damages for personal injury or sickness aren't considered reimbursement under a health insurance policy and don't have to be deducted from your medical expenses. If the total reimbursement you received during the year is the same as or more than your total medical expenses for the year, you can't claim a medical deduction.

If you are reimbursed in a later year for medical expenses you deducted in an earlier year, you must report as income the amount you received up to the amount you previously deducted as a medical expense. If you didn't deduct the expense in the year you paid it because you didn't itemize your deductions or because your medical expenses weren't more than 7.5 percent of your adjusted gross income, the reimbursement isn't taxable.

If you receive an amount in settlement of a personal injury suit, the part that is for medical expenses deducted in an earlier year is taxable if your medical deduction in the earlier year reduced your income tax.

In 1997, the IRS ruled that medical expenses or premiums paid by an employer for an employee's domestic partner or the domestic partner's dependent(s) are taxable to the employee and not a tax-free employee fringe benefit.

Special schooling

You can deduct as a medical expense the cost of sending a mentally or physically handicapped child or dependent to a special school in order to help him or her overcome a handicap. The school must have a special program geared to the child's specific needs. The total cost, transportation, meals, and lodging, as well as tuition, qualify. The types of schools that qualify are ones that do the following things:

✔ Teach Braille or lip reading

✔ Help cure dyslexia

✔ Treat and care for the mentally handicapped

✔ Treat individuals with similar handicaps

Nursing home

You can include in medical expenses the cost of medical care in a nursing home or home for the aged for yourself, your spouse, or your dependents. This deduction includes the cost of meals and lodging in the home if the main reason for being there is to get medical care.

You can't deduct the cost of meals and lodging if the reason for being in the home is personal (such as taking up residence in a retirement home). You can, however, include as a deductible medical expense the part of the cost that is for medical or nursing care.

Improvements to your home

You can deduct as a medical expense the cost of installing equipment and making improvements to your home in order to help treat a disease or ailment. For example, you can deduct the cost of an air conditioner because you suffer from allergies or asthma. But if the equipment or improvement increases the value of your home, your deduction is limited to the cost of the equipment or improvement minus the increase in the value to your home.

Be prepared to have a battle when making a large improvement to your home for medical reasons. Unless you go to the audit in a wheelchair with tears streaming down your cheeks, don't expect an overly sympathetic IRS. On the other hand, deductions for swimming pools have been allowed as a form of therapy in treating a severe ailment or disease. But improvements that merely help improve someone's general health (such as a hot tub or workout room) aren't deductible.

The increase-in-value test for a home doesn't apply to handicapped persons. Modifying stairs and doorways; building ramps, railings, and support bars; and adapting a home to the special needs of the handicapped are allowed. Chair lifts, but not elevators, are also part of the no-increase-in-value category.

Figuring your medical and dental deduction

Your deductible medical and dental expenses equal the total expenses that you've paid minus what you were reimbursed by your insurance policy. The result is then reduced by 7.5 percent of your adjusted gross income (AGI).

For example, suppose that your medical and dental expenses for the tax year were $4,500 and that your health insurance company reimbursed $500 of this. Thus, you had $4,000 of unreimbursed medical expenses. Enter this amount on line 1 of Schedule A. On line 2, you enter your AGI from Form 1040 (line 33). On line 3, you enter 7.5 percent of your AGI (suppose that your AGI is $40,000; you would enter $3,000 — that's $40,000 × .075). Subtract this amount from the medical expenses reported on line 1 of Schedule A and stick the remainder on line 4.

Lines 5–9: Taxes You Paid

As a general rule, you may deduct only the following tax payments made during the tax year:

- ✔ State and local income taxes
- ✔ Local real estate taxes
- ✔ State and local personal property taxes
- ✔ Other taxes (such as foreign income taxes)

Federal income and Social Security taxes are *not* deductible.

Line 5: State and local income taxes

This deduction consists of two elements: the amount of state and local taxes withheld from your salary, and what you paid in 1998 when you filed your 1997 state tax return. You'll find the amount of state tax withheld in box 18 on your W-2(s). If you made estimated state and local income tax payments in 1998, they are also deductible.

If you applied your 1997 refund on your state return as a payment against next year's state tax, that's also considered a deductible tax payment. However, you also have to report the amount as taxable income on Form 1040 (line 10).

Enter the total of your state and local tax payments from Boxes 18 and 21 of your W-2(s) on line 5 of Schedule A. Also enter on this line your state and local estimated income tax payments that you made in 1998. And don't forget to add the balance that you paid on your 1997 return. For residents of California, New Jersey, or New York, mandatory payments that you made to your state's disability fund are also deductible. So are disability payments to Rhode Island's temporary fund or Washington State's supplemental workers' compensation fund.

Line 6: Real estate taxes

You can deduct real estate taxes you paid during the year. If your monthly mortgage payment also includes an amount that's placed in escrow by the bank, you can't claim a deduction for that amount until the bank actually pays the local tax authorities. At the end of the year, the bank will send you a statement — probably called your Annual Mortgage Statement — indicating the amount that was paid to the local property tax collector. The statement usually lists the dates of the payments.

If you don't have a mortgage or you aren't escrowing your tax, you won't be making payments to the bank. You'll be making payments directly to the tax collector. So add up your canceled checks to figure the amount of tax you paid, and enter the amount on this line. (And if you don't have canceled checks, your problems are more serious than filling out Schedule A.)

Cooperative apartment

Tenants or stockholders of a cooperative housing corporation may deduct their share of the real estate taxes paid by the corporation. The corporation will furnish you with a statement at the end of the year, indicating the amount of the deduction you're entitled to claim.

Separate returns and real estate taxes

When a couple decides to file separate returns, deducting real estate taxes becomes a complicated matter. That's because the deduction is based on how title to the property is held. If the title is in your spouse's name and you paid the real estate taxes, neither of you can claim a deduction. If your payment is required as a result of your divorce or separation decree, the payment may qualify as an alimony deduction (see Chapter 7).

If property is owned by a husband or wife as *tenants by the entirety* or as *joint tenants* (which means the survivor inherits the other's share), either spouse can deduct the amount of taxes paid. If the property is held as *tenants in common* (each owner's share goes to his or her heirs at his or her death), each spouse may deduct his or her share of the taxes paid. However, the rules are somewhat different in community property states; see IRS Publication 555 *(Federal Tax Information on Community Property)*.

Special assessments

Water, sewer, and garbage pickup aren't deductible because they're considered nondeductible personal charges — and so are charges by a homeowners' association. Assessments by the local tax authorities to put in a new street, sewer system, or sidewalks aren't deductible. These types of assessments are added to the tax basis of your home. Either your annual mortgage statement from your bank or the tax collector's bill will indicate whether you're paying a special assessment or a real estate tax.

When you buy or sell real estate

When real estate is bought or sold, the buyer and the seller must apportion the real estate taxes between them. This stuff is done at the closing when the buyer and seller are furnished a settlement statement. For example, suppose that you paid $1,000 in real estate taxes for the year on January 1. On June 30, you sell the property. So at the time of settlement on your home sale, your settlement statement should reflect a payment or credit from the buyer for the property taxes you already paid for the remainder of the year. This is how the buyer pays you for the taxes you've effectively paid on his or her behalf for the remainder of the year when the buyer will be in the home. Therefore, you can only deduct the taxes you paid ($1,000) minus what the buyer reimbursed you ($500). That means you only deduct $500 in real estate taxes for the year on line 6 of Schedule A.

You can find this information on your settlement statement as well as in box 5 of **Form 1099-S, Proceeds from Real Estate Transactions.** The 1099-S is normally issued to you when you sell your home. However, under the new law not all home sales have to be reported on 1099-S. See Chapter 12 for more about this.

If the buyer pays back taxes (in other words, taxes that the property seller owed from the time he or she actually owned the home) at the closing or at a later date, they can't be deducted. They are added to the cost of the property. The seller can deduct back taxes paid by the buyer from the sales price when computing the profit that has to be reported on Schedule D (Form 1040). See Chapter 12 for information about handling the sale of your home.

The downside of property tax refunds and rebates

If you receive a refund or rebate in 1998 for real estate taxes you paid in 1998, you must reduce your itemized deductions that you're claiming for real estate taxes by the amount refunded to you. For example, if you paid $2,000 in property taxes during the year and also received a $300 refund because of a reduction in your tax that was retroactively granted, you may claim only $1,700 as the deduction for real estate taxes.

If you received a refund or rebate in 1998 for real estate taxes that you took as an itemized deduction on Schedule A in an earlier year, you must include the refund or rebate as income in the year you receive it. Enter this amount on your 1040 (line 21). In the unlikely event that your refund exceeds what you paid in taxes during the year, you need to include only the portion of the refund up to the amount of the deduction you took in the earlier year. For example, if you claimed a $500 deduction in 1997 and received a $600 rebate in 1998, only $500 of the rebate is taxable.

Line 7: Personal property taxes

Personal property taxes, both state and local, are deductible if the tax charged is based on the value of the personal property. Usually, you pay personal property taxes based on the value of your car and motorboat.

In most states, a registration fee is assessed on cars. These fees are not deductible unless the fees are based on the value of the car. The state organization that invoices you for this fee should state what portion, if any, of the fee, is based on the car's value.

Don't get confused. This section doesn't cover business taxes; they belong on Schedule C. And if you pay sales tax on the purchase of equipment, you can't deduct the sales tax separately. It's added to the cost of the asset, which is depreciated on Schedule C and E. And, finally, as much as you'd like to deduct your Social Security tax here, you can't.

Line 8: Other taxes (foreign income taxes)

You can deduct foreign taxes you paid (along with your state or local income taxes) as an itemized deduction on Schedule A, or you can claim a credit for foreign taxes by filing **Form 1116, Foreign Taxes.** *Note:* If your foreign income wasn't subject to U.S. tax (because it was excluded under the $72,000 foreign earned income allowance), you can't claim a deduction or a credit for any foreign taxes paid on the income that you didn't pay U.S. tax on.

In case you're asking yourself what foreign taxes have to do with you, the answer is that if you invested in a mutual fund that invests overseas, the fund may end up paying foreign taxes on some of your dividends. It seems more people are investing in these types of funds than ever before. If your mutual fund paid any foreign taxes, you'll find that information in box 6 of **Form 1099-DIV** that you received.

You can either deduct the foreign tax you paid on this line of Schedule A or claim a credit on Form 1040 (line 46). A deduction reduces your taxable income. A credit reduces the actual tax you owe. So if you're in the 28-percent tax bracket, claiming a deduction for $100 of foreign taxes will reduce your tax bill by $28. On the other hand, if you claim the $100 you paid as a foreign tax credit, you reduce your tax liability by $100, because credits are subtracted directly from the tax you owe.

So to the unsuspecting, claiming a foreign tax payment as an itemized deduction would appear to be a poor choice, because claiming the payment as a credit produces a greater tax saving. But have you ever tried to tackle Form 1116? The IRS estimates that it should take you over six hours to read the instructions and fill out the form.

If you have a tax software program, claim the payment as a credit. But if you don't have a software program and the amount of your foreign tax deduction is small, don't bother claiming it as a credit — simply write off the amount as a state and local tax deduction. If the amount is significant, you can tackle Form 1116 on your own, see a tax advisor, or buy a software program.

Starting in 1998, if the foreign tax you paid isn't more than $600 if married or $300 if single, and the only foreign income that you have is from investments, you can bypass Form 1116. Enter the foreign tax you paid on line 46.

Lines 10–14: Interest You Paid

The IRS allows you to deduct interest on certain types of loans. According to the IRS, acceptable loans include some (but not all) mortgage loans and investment loans. Interest incurred for consumer debt, such as on credit cards and auto loans — so-called *personal interest* — is no longer deductible. Business interest isn't deducted as an itemized deduction; it's deducted from your business income on Schedule C (see Chapter 11).

The 1986 tax act did away with the deduction for interest on taxes you owe. However, a number of court cases have allowed an interest deduction on income tax deficiencies related to business returns, Schedules C, F, and E. The IRS fights these deductions tooth and nail. Because this issue hasn't been resolved, determine your tolerance for picking a fight with the IRS if you want to proceed. If you do claim this interest deduction, claim it on the schedule it relates to: Schedule C, F, or E.

Lines 10–11: Home mortgage interest and points

You can deduct mortgage interest on your main home as well as a second or vacation home. Why two? We think it's because most representatives in Congress own two homes — one in Washington and one in their district! It doesn't matter whether the loan on which you are paying interest is a mortgage, a second mortgage, a line of credit, or a home equity loan. The interest is deductible as long as your homes serve as collateral for the loan.

Where are the data?

If you paid mortgage interest of $600 or more during the year on any one mortgage, you will receive a **Form 1098, Mortgage Interest Statement,** from your mortgage lender, showing the total interest you paid during the year. Enter this on line 10 of your Schedule A. Enter mortgage interest not reported on a 1098 on line 11. If you purchased a main home during 1998, Form 1098 reports the deductible points you paid. If you paid points that weren't reported on Form 1098, enter the amount on line 12. (If you paid less than $600 in mortgage interest, see your lender.)

You can deduct late payment charges as home mortgage interest. You will find these charges on your annual mortgage statement.

If you can pay down your mortgage more quickly than required, don't assume that doing so is not in your best financial interests just because of the deductions allowed for it (see Chapter 24).

Limitations on deductions

In most cases, you will be able to deduct all your home mortgage interest. Whether all of it is deductible depends on the date you took out the mortgage, the amount of the mortgage, and how the mortgage loan was used.

Interest on mortgage loans of up to $1 million taken out after October 13, 1987, to buy, build, or improve a first or second home is deductible. Your main home is the home you live in most of the time. It can be a house, a condominium, a cooperative apartment, a mobile home, a boat, or similar property. It must provide basic living accommodations including sleeping space, toilet facilities, and cooking facilities. Your second or vacation home is similar property that you select to be your second home.

In addition, interest on a home equity loan of up to $100,000 taken out after October 13, 1987, is deductible regardless of how the money is used. (Cut these amounts in half if you are married and file a separate return.) The proceeds of a home equity loan don't have to be used to buy, build, or improve your home. They can be used to pay off bills, pay college tuition, or take a vacation.

Interest on a home-improvement loan isn't deductible if it isn't a mortgage loan. The rule is simple: no mortgage, no interest deduction. So if a relative lends you money to buy a home, any interest that you pay isn't deductible unless the relative obtains a mortgage on the house.

Interest on mortgages of any size is tax deductible if you took out your mortgage before October 14, 1987, and you still retain that mortgage. If you've refinanced into a new mortgage since this magical date, you could be out of luck if you refinanced the mortgage for more than you owed prior to refinancing.

Interest on refinanced loans

If you refinanced a mortgage on your first or second mortgage for the remaining balance of the old mortgage, you're safe. If the interest on the old mortgage was fully deductible, the interest on the new mortgage is also fully deductible.

But, if you refinanced your old mortgage for more than its remaining balance, the rules on whether you can deduct all the interest on your new mortgage are crazy — the deductibility of the mortgage interest on the new loan depends on how you use the excess funds and the amount you refinanced. If the excess is used to improve, build, or buy a first or second home, and the excess plus all other mortgage loans is under $1 million, the interest on the new loan is fully deductible. If any of the excess of a new mortgage loan isn't used to build, buy, or improve your home, the excess is applied to your $100,000 home equity limit. If the excess is under $100,000, you're safe and it's fully deductible. The interest on the part that exceeds $100,000 is not deductible.

Points

The term *points* is used to describe certain up-front charges (pre-paid interest) that a borrower pays to obtain a mortgage. One point equals one percent of the loan amount financed. For example, if the loan is for $200,000, two points equal a $4,000 charge. You can deduct the amount you pay in points in 1998 if the loan was used to buy or improve your *main* residence.

Points on refinances

The points paid to refinance a mortgage on a main home aren't usually deductible in full in the year you pay them — even if the new mortgage is secured by your main home. However, if you use part of the refinanced mortgage to improve your main home and you pay the points instead of paying them from the proceeds of the new loan, you can deduct in full (in the year paid) the part of the points related to the improvement. But you must deduct the remainder of the points over the life of the loan. The points you pay on a second mortgage have to be deducted over the term of the loan.

For example, suppose that the remaining balance of your mortgage is $100,000. You take out a new mortgage for $150,000 and use $25,000 for improvements, $25,000 for personal purposes, and $100,000 to pay off the old loan. The points on the $25,000 used for improvements are deductible in 1998. The points on the remaining $125,000 balance of the new mortgage have to be written off over the term of the loan.

But here's a tip: Say that you refinanced your home three years ago and are writing off the points you paid over the 25-year term of the mortgage. If you refinance your mortgage again in 1998, the points remaining to be written off on your old mortgage can be written off in full in 1998. Enter this amount on line 12. The points on your new refinanced loan have to be deducted over the term of the new mortgage.

Seller-paid points

Sometimes, desperate times call for desperate measures. So if the seller pays the points that the buyer normally does, the buyer gets a double windfall. The buyer not only gets the seller to pay the points, but the buyer also gets to deduct them. The buyer also has to subtract the points deducted from the tax basis of the home. Although the seller paid the points, the seller can't deduct them. The points the seller paid are deducted from the selling price.

This crazy twist is retroactive to 1991. So if you are a buyer who had the seller pay the points on the purchase of your home but didn't deduct them, you can still do so by filing a **Form 1040X, Amended Return.** But you have to take this step before the three-year statute of limitations expires (see Chapter 19), or you can kiss any refund good-bye. When you file Form 1040X, write SELLER PAID POINTS on the upper-right corner of the form.

Line 12: Points not reported to you on Form 1098

If the points you paid, for some reason, were not reported on the 1098, based on the rules in the two preceding sections, you will have to compute this amount on your own. If the points were for your main house, you can deduct the amount for 1998. If it was refinancing for your second home, you have to deduct it over the term of the mortgage. Hunting for this information isn't all that difficult. When the loan was made, you were given a closing statement with the points you paid on it. Sometimes, it's referred to as an *origination fee*.

Line 13: Investment interest

When you borrow against the value of securities held in a brokerage account, the interest paid on what is referred to as a *margin loan* is deductible. This deduction, however, can't exceed your total investment income. If it does, the excess is carried forward and deducted from next year's investment income — or carried over to future years until it can be deducted. You use **Form 4952, Investment Interest,** to compute the deduction and carry over the result to Schedule A (line 13).

Investment income is income from interest, dividends, annuities, and royalties. It doesn't include income from rental real estate or from a *passive activity* (a passive activity is IRS jargon for a business deal or venture in which you are a silent partner). The following are not usually considered investment income:

✔ If you borrow money to buy or carry tax-exempt bonds, you can't deduct any interest on the loan as investment-interest expense. If 20 percent of your portfolio consists of tax-exempt bonds, 20 percent of your margin interest on your security account isn't deductible.

✔ Capital gains aren't usually considered investment income, but you can choose to treat capital gains as investment income. There is a trade-off, however. You have to reduce the amount of your capital gains eligible for the maximum long-term capital gain rate, which can be either 20 percent (10 percent if you're in the 15 percent bracket), 25 percent (for real estate), or 28 percent (for collectibles) — by the amount of your capital gains you are treating as investment income. Did you follow that?

For example, suppose that you have dividend income of $5,000, investment interest expense of $10,000, and a $20,000 long-term capital gain on stock you sold. You can deduct only $5,000 of your investment interest expense. The balance is carried over to 1999. However, if you treat $5,000 of your capital gain as investment income, you can deduct your entire investment interest expense of $10,000. But the amount of your $20,000 capital gain that is eligible for the 20 percent maximum rate on long-term capital gains is reduced to $15,000.

✔ Interest expense incurred in a passive activity such as rental real estate, an S Corporation, or a limited partnership isn't considered investment-interest expense. It can be deducted only from your passive-activity income.

Starting in 1998, you will be able to deduct up to $1,000 of student loan interest even if you don't itemize your deductions. The deduction is claimed as an adjustment to your income along with the other adjustments we discuss in Chapter 7, line 24.

Here's the fine print on student loan interest: Your income can't exceed $40,000 ($60,000 for joint filers); above these amounts, the deduction gets phased out. So at the $55,000 income level if you're single and the $75,000 income level if you're married, you can kiss this deduction goodbye. The maximum deduction jumps to $1,500 in 1999, $2,000 in 2000, and $2,500 in 2001.

Lines 15–18: Gifts to Charity

You can deduct your charitable contributions, but the amount of your deduction may be limited, and you must follow a number of strict rules. One good turn doesn't always deserve another!

After you understand the types of things you can and cannot deduct, completing this section is a snap. Qualifying contributions that you make by cash and check are totaled and entered on line 15, and those made other than by cash and check (for example, you donate your old *Taxe$ For Dummie$* books to charity when new editions come out) are entered on line 16.

If you make out a check at the end of the year and mail it by December 31, you can deduct your contribution even if the charity doesn't receive the check until January. If you charge a contribution on your credit card, you get to deduct it in the year you charged it — even if you don't pay off the charge until the following year.

If you signed up for a program where a percentage of your credit card purchases is donated to charity, remember to deduct what the credit card company paid on your behalf.

Qualifying charities

You can deduct your contributions only if you make them to a *qualified* organization. To become a qualified organization, most organizations (other than churches) must apply to the IRS. To find out whether an organization qualifies, just ask the organization for its tax exemption certificate.

Don't overlook your out-of-pocket expenditures

A commonly overlooked deductible charitable expense is your out-of-pocket expenses (money spent) incurred while doing volunteer work for a charity.

For example, you can deduct out-of-pocket expenses (such as gas and oil, but probably not rest-stop candy bars!) that are directly related to the use of your car in charitable work. You can't deduct anything like general repair or maintenance expenses, tires, insurance, depreciation, and so on. If you don't want to track and deduct your actual expenses, you can use a standard rate of 14 cents a mile to figure your contribution. You can deduct actual expenses for parking fees and tolls. If you must travel away from home in order to perform a real and substantial service, such as attending a convention for a qualified charitable organization, you can claim a deduction for your unreimbursed travel and transportation expenses, including meals and lodging. If you get a daily allowance *(per diem)* for travel expenses while providing services for a charitable organization, you must include as income the amount that is more than your travel expenses. Of course, you can deduct your travel expenses that are more than the allowance.

There's one restriction on these deductions: They're allowed only if there is *no significant amount* of personal pleasure derived from your travel. What is the limit the IRS sets on personal pleasure? Well, we can't find an IRS chart, but we can at least assure you that the IRS allows you to enjoy your trip without automatically disqualifying you from this deduction. The IRS doesn't mind if you decide to do some sightseeing, but you can't deduct expenses for your spouse or children who may accompany you. If you go to a church convention as a church member rather than as a representative of the church, you can't deduct your expenses.

You can deduct the cost and upkeep of uniforms that you must wear while doing volunteer work — as long as these uniforms are unsuitable for everyday use. A Boy or Girl Scout uniform, for example, would not be the type of clothing you would wear just anywhere!

If for some reason you doubt that an organization qualifies, you can check IRS Publication 78 *(Cumulative List of Organizations).* Most libraries have Publication 78. You also can call the IRS toll-free tax help telephone number (800-829-3676) to request this publication. If you're Internet-savvy, you can visit the IRS Web site at www.irs.ustreas.gov and go to the heading "Forms & Pubs" to get this publication. Nearly all the tax-exempt charities are listed.

Contributions that you make to the following charitable organizations are generally deductible:

- ✔ Religious organizations, including churches, synagogues, mosques, and so on
- ✔ Public park and recreational facilities
- ✔ Nonprofit schools
- ✔ Organizations such as CARE, the Red Cross, the Salvation Army, Goodwill Industries, the Girl and Boy Scouts, and so on
- ✔ War veterans' groups
- ✔ Your federal, state, and local government — if your charitable contribution is only for public purposes

Nonqualifying charities

Generally speaking, contributions or donations made to causes or organizations that just benefit the organization, as opposed to the greater society, are not deductible. The following are examples of organizations or groups to which you can't deduct contributions:

- Individuals

    Big surprise here! So don't try to deduct what you gave to your brother-in-law, because he doesn't count in the eyes of the IRS! The contribution can be to a qualified organization that helps needy and worthy individuals — like your brother-in-law.

- Social and sport clubs

- Members of the clergy who can spend the money as they wish

- Labor unions

- Groups that lobby for law changes (such as changes to the tax code!)

    The IRS does not want you to deduct contributions to organizations from which you may benefit — so include bingo and raffle tickets in this forbidden group.

- Political groups or candidates running for public office

- Foreign charities (but you can deduct contributions to a U.S. charity that transfers funds to a foreign charity — if the U.S. charity controls the use of the funds)

- Homeowners' associations

- Lottery ticket costs (gee, we wonder why not?)

- Dues paid to country clubs, lodges, orders, and so on

    But union dues are deductible as an itemized deduction subject to the 2 percent AGI limit on Schedule A.

- Tuition to attend private or parochial schools

This list can go on and on — didn't you suspect that a list of nonqualifying charities would be longer than a list of qualifying ones? — but we think you get the idea. So don't try to deduct the value of your blood donated at a blood bank, and don't even think about trying to deduct your contribution to your college fraternity or sorority!

Contributions of property

Generally, you can deduct the *fair market value* (FMV) of property given to a charity. FMV is the price at which property would change hands between a willing buyer and a willing seller. So if you bought a painting for $2,000 that's worth $10,000 when you donate it to a museum, you can deduct $10,000.

You can only use the FMV if — on the date of the contribution — the property would have produced a long-term capital gain or loss (property held one year or more) if it had been sold. If you donate property you held for less than a year, or you donate *ordinary income property,* your deduction is limited to your cost. Ordinary income property is inventory from a business, works of art created by the donor, manuscripts prepared by the donor, and capital assets held one year or less. Following are guidelines for deducting contributions of property:

- **If you contribute property with a fair market value that is less than your cost or depreciated value:** Your deduction is limited to fair market value. You can't claim a deduction for the property's decline in value since you acquired it.

- **If you have an asset that has declined in value:** Sell that asset to lock in the capital loss deduction (see Chapter 12) and donate the cash for an additional deduction.

    For example, suppose that you paid $12,500 for shares of a mutual fund that invested in Russia that are worth $6,000 today. If you donate the shares, all you can claim is a $6,000 charitable deduction. By selling the shares and donating the cash, however, not only will you be entitled to a $6,000 deduction, you also will have a $6,500 capital loss that you can deduct as well.

Contributions that are both qualified and nonqualified

If you receive a benefit from making a valid deductible contribution, you can deduct only the amount of your contribution that is more than the value of the benefit. For example, if you pay to attend a charity function such as a ball or banquet, you can deduct only the amount that is more than the fair market value of your ticket. You can also deduct unreimbursed expenses such as uniforms and actual automobile expenses, or use a standard rate of 14 cents per mile. Just subtract the value of the benefit you received from your total payment.

Ask the charity for a receipt that details the actual amount you contributed. Most charities are happy to provide this information. In fact, if the value of your contribution is $75 or more and that is partly for goods and services, the charity must give you a written statement informing you of the amount you can deduct. If you can't easily obtain a receipt, use an estimate based on something the IRS can't disagree with — common sense!

✔ **If you have an asset that has appreciated substantially in value:** Give the asset to the charity rather than sell the asset, get stuck for the tax, and donate the cash you have left. If you donate the asset itself, you get to deduct the full value of the asset, thereby escaping the tax.

Used clothing and household goods

Clean out those closets for next year so that you can save on your taxes! Hey, even Bill and Hillary Clinton took a deduction for this one! Used clothing — even used underwear, preferably washed — and household goods usually have a fair market value that is much less than the original cost. For used clothing, you claim the price that buyers of used items pay in used-clothing stores. See IRS Publication 561 *(Household Goods)* for information on the value of items such as furniture and appliances and other items you want to donate.

Cars, boats, and aircraft

If you contribute a car, a boat, or an aircraft, you may be able to determine its fair market value by using guides such as *blue books* that contain dealer sale or average prices for recent model years. These guides also give estimates for adjusting because of mileage and physical condition. The prices aren't official, however, and you can't consider a blue book as an appraisal of any specific donated property. But the guides are a good place to start.

Charitable deduction limits

All cash and noncash gifts are subject to some limits. Depending on whether you contributed cash or property, the amount of your deduction may be limited to either 30 or 50 percent of your adjusted gross income. Contributing cash to churches, associations of churches, synagogues, and all public charities, such as the Red Cross, for example, are deductible up to 50 percent of your AGI. Gifts of ordinary income property qualify for this 50-percent limit.

A 30-percent limit applies to gifts of capital gain property that has appreciated in value. In such instances, you can use the 50-percent limit — if you limit your deduction to your cost instead of using the FMV. For example, suppose that you donate a painting to a museum, a painting that cost you $10,000. It's currently worth $20,000. If you use the $20,000 value, your deduction for 1998 can't exceed 30 percent of your AGI. If you use the $10,000 value, you can deduct up to 50 percent of your AGI. The contribution has to be to a church or public charity, and you have to have owned the gift for at least one year. See Chapter 12 for the holding period rules.

The records you need: Part I

For contributions of $250 or more, you need a receipt from the charity — otherwise, you could have your deduction tossed out in the event of an audit. The receipt should indicate either the amount of cash you contributed or a description (but not the value) of any property you donated. The receipt must also indicate the value of any gift or services you might have received, and you must have the receipt by the time you file your return.

For cash contributions, a canceled check will suffice. But remember, if you donate cash or property valued at $250 or more, you also need a receipt. If you donate property, you need a receipt from the charity listing the date of your contribution and a detailed description of the property. Every donation is treated as a separate donation for applying the $250 threshold. You don't need a receipt for two $150 checks to the same charity.

If you contribute property worth more than $500, you have to attach **Form 8283, Noncash Charitable Contributions.** On the form, you list the name of the charity, the date of the gift, your cost, the FMV, and how you arrived at that value. If the value of the property you contributed exceeds $5,000, you need a written appraisal, and the appraiser also has to sign-off on Part III in Section B of Form 8283. The charity has to complete and sign Part IV of the form. A written appraisal isn't needed for publicly traded stock or nonpublicly traded stock worth $10,000 or less.

Line 17: (For the world's great humanitarians)

Line 17 is a pretty obscure line. The general rule for cash contributions is that they can't exceed 50 percent of your AGI. For gifts of property like stocks, bonds, and artwork, the amount can't exceed 30 percent of your AGI. So if you contribute more than the IRS permits as a deduction in one year, you can carry over the amount you couldn't deduct and deduct it within the next five years. Enter on line 17 the amount that you couldn't deduct from the last five years and want to deduct this year.

Line 19: Casualty and Theft Losses

We hope that you don't need to use this one. But if you do, and if you've come to view the Internal Revenue Service as heartless, this line may correct that impression. It's not — well, not completely. If you've suffered a casualty or theft loss, you will find that the IRS can be somewhat charitable. Unfortunately, as is the case with any unusual deduction, you've got to jump through quite a few hoops to nail it down.

After you determine whether your loss is deductible, get a copy of IRS **Form 4684, Casualties and Thefts,** on which you list each item that was stolen or destroyed. If your deduction ends up being more than your income — and it does happen — you may have what's known as a *net operating loss.* You can use this type of loss to lower your tax in an earlier or in a later year. This rule is an exception (of course!) to the normal rule that you must be in business to have a net operating loss.

Do you have a deductible loss?

Strange as it may seem, there has been extensive Tax Court haggling over what is and isn't a casualty. The phrase to remember is *sudden, unexpected, and unusual.* If property you own is damaged, destroyed, or lost as the result of a specific event that is sudden, unexpected, and unusual, you have a deductible casualty. Earthquakes, fires, floods, and storms meet this strict legal test.

But if you dropped a piece of the good china, if Rover chewed a hole in the sofa, if moths ate your entire wardrobe, or if termites gobbled up your brand-new backyard deck, you're doubly out of luck. You've suffered a nondeductible loss. These incidents don't meet the sudden-unexpected-unusual test.

Figuring the loss

Unfortunately, the amount of your deduction isn't going to equal the amount of your loss because the IRS makes you apply a deductible just as your auto insurer does. The IRS makes you reduce each individual loss by $100 and your total losses by 10 percent of your adjusted gross income. So if your adjusted gross income is $100,000 and you lost $11,000 when the roof caved in, your deduction is only $900. (That's $11,000 minus $100 minus 10 percent of your adjusted gross, or $10,000.)

That stipulation effectively wipes out a deduction for plenty of people. For those whose losses are big enough to warrant a deduction, though, the fun is just beginning. That's because your deduction is limited to either the decrease in the fair market value of your property as a result of the casualty, or the original cost of the property — whichever is lower.

Suppose that you bought a painting for $1,000 that was worth $100,000 when damaged by fire. Sorry. Your loss is limited to the $1,000 you paid for it. Now reverse it. You paid $100,000 for the painting, and thanks to the downturn in the market for black-velvet portraits of Elvis, it's worth only $1,000 right before it's destroyed. Your deductible loss is limited to $1,000. And you must apply this rule to each item before combining them to figure your total loss. (One exception is real estate. The entire property, including buildings, trees, and shrubs, is treated as one item.)

Because your loss is the difference between the fair market value of your property immediately before and after the casualty, an appraisal is usually the best way to calculate your loss. The only problem is that the appraiser can't see your property before the casualty, and any photographs or records you may have had probably went up in smoke or floated away. Therefore, it makes sense to videotape both the outside of the property and its contents, as well as expensive jewelry, and keep the tape in a safe deposit box, for example. You're not totally out of luck if you don't have before-and-after photos, though. A picture after the casualty and one showing the property after it was repaired comes in very handy when trying to prove the dollar value of your loss.

Casualty losses? You be the judge

Listen to this. A loss as the result of water damage to wallpaper and plaster seems like it ought to be deductible. Not according to the Tax Court, which ruled on such a case in the 1960s. The homeowner failed to prove that the damage came after a sudden, identifiable event. The water had entered the house through the window frames, and the damage could have been caused by progressive deterioration. Now suppose that a car door is accidentally slammed on your hand, breaking your diamond ring. The jewel falls from the ring and is never found. That lost diamond qualifies as a casualty. On the other hand, if your diamond merely falls out of its setting and is lost, there is no deduction. The number of cases like this is endless.

Proving a theft loss can be just as complex. The mere disappearance of cash or property doesn't cut it. You have to prove there was an actual theft. The best evidence is a police report — and your failure to file one could be interpreted as your not being sure something was stolen.

You should know that theft losses aren't limited to robbery — they also include theft by swindle, larceny, and false pretense. This very broad definition includes fraudulent sales offers or embezzlement. In one case, a New Yorker was even able to get a theft-loss deduction after handing over a bundle of money to fortune tellers. The reason? The fortune tellers were operating illegally.

The insurance effects

You've got casualty insurance? Great. But there are a couple of things you need to watch out for. First, if you expect to be reimbursed by your insurer but haven't seen any cash by tax-filing time, you've got to subtract an estimate of the expected reimbursement from your deductible loss. Second — and this sounds strange — you must reduce the amount of your loss by your insurance coverage even if you don't file a claim. Suppose that your loss is 100 percent covered by insurance, but you decide not to ask for a reimbursement for fear of losing your coverage. You can't claim a deduction for the loss. Only the amount of your loss that's above the insurance coverage would be deductible in that case.

If you're reimbursed by insurance and decide not to repair or replace your property, you could have a taxable gain on your hands. That's because the taxable gain is calculated by subtracting your cost from the insurance proceeds and not the property's fair market value. For example, imagine that your summer cottage, which cost $150,000 (the cost here refers to the cost of the building and excludes the land cost), burned to the ground. You get $190,000 in insurance money (the house's current FMV), giving you a fully taxable $40,000 gain.

To postpone the gain, you have to replace the property with a similar one, and it must be worth at least as much as the insurance money you received. If the new place is worth less than that, you must report the difference as a capital gain. In addition, you've got to replace the property within two years. The two-year period begins on December 31 of the year you realize the gain. If your home is located in a federally declared disaster area, you have four years, and you can generally get a one-year extension beyond that, if necessary.

Losses incurred in a presidentially-declared disaster area are subject to another special rule that can be a big help to your cash flow. You can choose to deduct the loss in either the current year or the preceding year. Turning back the clock with an amended return means that you can get a refund within 45 days — instead of waiting until the next year. This maneuver may also help if you were in a higher tax bracket last year.

Normally, you can't deduct the cost of repairing your property because the cost of fixing something isn't really a measure of its deflated fair market value. As with every IRS rule, however, this one has exceptions. You can use the cost of cleaning up or making a repair under the following conditions:

✔ The repairs are necessary to bring the property back to its condition before the casualty, and the cost of the repairs isn't excessive.

✔ The repairs take care of the damage only.

✔ The value of the property after the repairs is not — due to the repairs — more than the value of the property before the casualty.

Another point is worth knowing. With leased property, such as a car, the amount of your loss is in fact the amount you must spend to repair it. And, although appraisal fees aren't considered part of your loss, they count as miscellaneous itemized deductions.

The IRS is now required to accept appraisals to get a government-backed loan in a disaster area as proof of the loss. Additionally, the IRS can now extend the deadline for filing tax returns for up to 90 days in a presidentially-declared disaster area. If the IRS declares such a postponement, it can't charge interest during this period.

Lines 20–26: Job Expenses and Most Other Miscellaneous Deductions

Everybody likes to see a deduction that says something about "other." Oh goody, you think; here's my opportunity to get some easy deductions. Unfortunately, if you're like the vast majority of taxpayers, you won't get the maximum mileage out of these deductions. Why? Because the allowable items in this category tend to be small-dollar items. And you have to clear a major hurdle: You get a deduction only for the amount by which your total deductions in this category exceed 2 percent of your adjusted gross income. Here's how it works: If your adjusted gross is $50,000 and you have $1,500 of job-related expenses, only $500 is deductible. That's $1,500 minus $1,000 (2 percent of $50,000).

Line 20: Unreimbursed employee expenses

Even if you're not employed by Scrooge International — famous for offering few fringe benefits and not reimbursing job-related expenses — there's a good chance that you're spending at least some out-of-pocket money on your job. Ever take an educational course that helped you get ahead in your career? How about that home fax machine you bought so customers could reach you after hours? If your employer didn't pick up the tab, all is not lost. You can deduct those expenses — or at least a portion of them — from your taxes.

One word of caution: Just about every IRS rule regarding job-related expenses is subject to varying interpretations, which has made the IRS extremely inflexible as to what is and isn't deductible. On the other hand, the Tax Court, which ultimately decides disputes of deductibility, has a tendency to be more liberal than the IRS.

Job search expenses

Job search expenses are deductible even if your job search isn't successful. The critical rule is that the expenses must be incurred in trying to find a new job in the same line of work. So if you're looking to make a career change or seeking your first job, you can forget about this deduction. A taxpayer who retired from the Air Force after doing public relations for the service was denied travel expenses while seeking other employment in public relations. The way the IRS sees the world, any job he sought in the private sector would be considered a new trade or business.

Here are job search expenses that are considered deductible:

- ✔ Employment-agency and career-counseling fees
- ✔ Cost for placing situation-wanted ads
- ✔ Telephone calls
- ✔ Printing, typing, and mailing of resumes
- ✔ Travel, meals, and entertaining

Another time, the IRS held that, because a taxpayer had incurred a "substantial break" of more than a year between his previous job and his hunt for a new one, there was a lack of continuity in the person's line of work. No deduction. The IRS is unyielding when it comes to interpreting this rule. Fortunately, the Tax Court sees things differently, tending to consider such gaps as temporary.

If you're away from home overnight looking for work, you can deduct travel and transportation costs, as well as hotels and meals. The purpose of the trip must be primarily related to searching for a job, though. A job interview while on a golf outing to Palm Springs won't cut it. The IRS looks at the amount of time spent seeking new employment in relationship to the amount of time you are away.

Normally, you deduct job-related expenses on **Form 2106, Employee Business Expenses.** However, unless you're claiming job-related travel, local transportation, meal, or entertainment expenses, save yourself some trouble. You can enter the most basic job-hunting expenses directly on Schedule A (line 20) instead of having to fill out Form 2106. You can use the shorter Form 2106-EZ if you weren't reimbursed for any of your expenses and you simply claim the 32.5 cents per mile rate for your auto expenses.

Job education expenses

If you find that your employer demands greater technical skills, or the fear of being downsized has sent you back to the classroom, the cost of those courses is deductible (even if they lead to a degree) under the following conditions:

✔ You are employed or self-employed.

✔ The course doesn't qualify you for a new line of work.

✔ You already have met the minimum educational requirements of your job or profession.

✔ The course is required by your employer or state law, or the course maintains or improves your job skills.

The tax-free portion of up to $5,250 for employer-paid educational assistance has been reinstated retroactively from 1995 through May 31, 1997, and again for another three years to May 31, 2000. Refer to "What those boxes on your W-2 mean" in Chapter 6 for a detailed discussion of the new rules.

Like many other tax terms, "maintains or improves job skills" has consistently placed the IRS and taxpayers at odds. The intent of the law was to allow a deduction for refresher courses, such as the continuing education classes tax advisors have to take every year.

For example, an IRS agent was denied a deduction for the cost of obtaining an MBA, while an engineer was allowed to deduct the cost of his degree. The rationale: A significant portion of the engineer's duties involved management, interpersonal, and administrative skills. The court felt the engineer's MBA didn't qualify him for a new line of work and was directly related to his job. The IRS agent flunked this test. (There's something strangely satisfying about seeing the IRS turn on its own, isn't there?)

The general rule is that you must be able to prove by clear and convincing evidence how the course is helpful or necessary in maintaining or improving your job skills. So if you can clear that hurdle, here's what's deductible:

✔ Tuition and books

✔ Local transportation

✔ Travel and living expenses while away from home

Travel expenses are allowable if you must go abroad to do research that can only be done there. Travel and living expenses are also deductible when taking a course at a school in a foreign country or away from your home, even if you could have taken the same course locally. Unfortunately, you can't claim a deduction for *educational* trips. Let's say you're a French teacher who decided to spend the summer traveling in the south of France to brush up on your language skills. Nice try, says the IRS, but no deduction.

This year, two new education credits kick in for education expenses — the Hope Scholarship Credit and the Lifetime Learning Credit. Although the rules you have to meet to qualify for the credits are rather lengthy, we explain them in Chapter 8.

Miscellaneous job expenses

Just because your job requires you to incur certain expenses, it doesn't mean they are automatically deductible. So here's a rundown on what is generally deductible:

✔ Professional and trade-association dues

✔ Books, subscriptions, and periodicals

✔ Union dues

✔ Unreimbursed travel and entertainment (covered in detail in the next section)

✔ Uniforms and special clothing

✔ Medical exams to establish fitness

✔ Commuting expenses to a second job (moonlighting, are you?)

✔ Small tools and equipment

✔ Computers and phones

Deductions for computers and cellular phones are hardest to nail down. You must prove you need the equipment to do your job *because* your employer doesn't provide you with it or because the equipment at work isn't adequate or available. A letter from your employer stating that a computer is a basic requirement for your job isn't good enough. You must also establish that its use is for your employer's convenience and not yours.

For example, suppose that you are an engineer who, rather than staying late at the office, takes work home. You have a computer at home that is similar to the one in the office. Because the use of your computer isn't for the convenience of your employer, you can't claim a deduction. On the other hand, if you need a computer to use while traveling on business, it would be deductible because you now meet the convenience-of-your-employer requirement.

Fax machines, copiers, adding machines, calculators, and typewriters aren't subject to this rigid rule. You must, however, be able to prove that this equipment is job-related and not merely for your own convenience. Although the law requires that you keep a diary or record that clearly shows the computer's or cellular phone's percentage of business use, you don't have to keep a similar record for other office equipment. Be prepared, however, to prove that it is used mainly for business. With a fax machine, for example, it's worth keeping those printouts showing where your calls have been going and where they've been coming from.

We know, this is a crazy thing to ask; after all, are you going to write down every time you use a copier if the copies are for work or personal reasons? But that behavior is exactly what the law requires. Write your representative in Congress and tell him or her what you think. (You'll probably get a reply that says: "Really? When was that law passed?")

Just because your employer requires that you be neatly groomed doesn't mean the cost of doing so is deductible. An airline pilot can't deduct the cost of his haircuts, even though airline regulations require pilots to have haircuts on a regular basis.

Meeting the requirements and keeping the necessary records to deduct job-related expenses can become a part-time job. Unpleasant as it is, though, doing so will almost certainly slash your taxes and save you in the event you're audited.

Job travel (and entertainment!)

Probably no other group of expenses has created more paperwork than travel and entertainment expenses. Taxpayers may spend more time on the paperwork accounting for a business trip than they do planning for it. Unfortunately, this situation can't be changed. But at least we can help you deduct every possible expense in this area. So let's begin with the three basic rules regarding travel and entertainment expenses:

- ✔ You have to be away from your business or home to deduct travel expenses. (Makes sense, doesn't it?)
- ✔ You can deduct only 50 percent of your meal and entertainment expenses.
- ✔ You need good records.

Travel expenses that are deductible include taxi, commuter bus, and limousine fare to and from the airport or station — and between your hotel and business meetings or job site. You can also deduct auto expenses, whether you use your own car or lease (see "Line 10: Car and truck expenses" in Chapter 11), and the cost of hotels, meals, telephone calls, and laundry while you're away. Don't forget tips and baggage handling. Finally, remember the obvious deductions on airplane, train, and bus fare between your *tax home* and business destination.

Your tax home and travel expenses

Yes, we said tax home. This is where the situation gets a little tricky because, in order to be able to deduct travel expenses, you must be traveling away from your tax home on business. You are considered to be traveling away from your tax home if the business purpose of your trip requires that you be away longer than an ordinary working day — and you need to sleep or rest so you can be ready for the next day's business. Wouldn't it be nice if the law simply stated that you have to be away overnight?

Your *tax home* isn't where you or your family reside. Of course not. It's the entire city or general area in which you work or where your business is located. For example, suppose that you work in Manhattan but live in the suburbs. You decide to stay in Manhattan overnight because you have an early breakfast meeting the next morning. You aren't away from your tax home overnight; therefore, you can't deduct the cost of the hotel. The only meal expense you can deduct is the next morning's breakfast — if it qualifies as an entertainment expense.

At this point, you probably want to know how far away from your tax home you have to be. Unfortunately, there isn't a mileage count. When it comes to determining whether you're away from home overnight, the IRS uses that famous U.S. Supreme Court definition: "I can't define it, but I know it when I see it."

Also, your tax home may not be near where you live. For example, if you move from job to job without a fixed base of operation, each place you work becomes your tax home. And travel expenses aren't deductible. And if you accept a temporary assignment that lasts for more than a year, you have moved your tax home to the place of the temporary assignment. Sorry, no deduction.

Trips that mix business with pleasure

For travel within the U.S., the transportation part of your travel expenses is fully deductible even if part of it is for pleasure. For example, perhaps the airfare and cabs to and from the airport cost $700 for you to attend a business convention in Florida. You spend two days at the end of the convention playing poker with some old friends. Your transportation costs of $700 are fully deductible, but your meals and lodging for the two vacation days aren't.

Transportation costs for travel outside the U.S. have to be prorated based on the amount of time you spend on business and vacation. Suppose that you spend four out of eight days in London on business. You can deduct only 50 percent of your airfare and four days of lodgings and meals. Any other travel costs (such as taxis and telephone calls while you were conducting business) are deductible.

But this general rule for transportation expenses on travel abroad doesn't apply if you meet any of the following conditions:

- ✔ The trip lasts a week or less.
- ✔ More than 75 percent of your time outside the U.S. was spent on business. (The days you start and end your trip are considered business days.)
- ✔ You don't have substantial control in arranging the trip.

You are considered not to have substantial control over your trip if you are an employee who was reimbursed or paid a travel expense allowance, are not related to your employer, and are not a managing executive. Oh well, *c'est la vie.*

Weekends, holidays, and other necessary standby days are counted as business days if they fall between business days. Great! But if these days follow your business activities and you remain at your business destination for personal reasons, they are not business days.

For example, suppose that your tax home is in Kansas City. You travel to St. Louis where you have a business appointment on Friday and another business meeting on the following Monday. The days in between are considered tax-deductible business-expense days — you had a business activity on Friday and had another business activity on Monday. This case is true even if you use that time for sightseeing (going up in the Arch!) or other personal activities.

Trips primarily for personal reasons

If your trip was primarily for personal reasons (such as that vacation to Disney World), some of the trip may be deductible — you can deduct any expenses at your destination that are directly related to your business. For example, calls into work are deductible, as well as a 15-minute customer call in Fantasyland. But spending an hour on business does *not* turn a personal trip into a business trip to be deducted.

The records you need: Part II

As of October 1, 1995, you need a receipt for every travel and entertainment expense that exceeds $75. The amount had been $25 since 1962. Thankfully, someone at the IRS realized that something called inflation has occurred. No receipt, no deduction if you're audited. And a canceled check just won't cut it anymore. The receipt — or a separate diary entry — must also show the business purpose. Although you don't need a receipt if the amount is below $75, you still need an entry in your diary to explain to whom, what, where, when, and why. This $75 rule doesn't apply to your hotel bill. A hotel bill is required, regardless of the amount.

For entertainment, you need the name and location of the restaurant or the place where you did the entertaining; the number of people served or in attendance; the date and amount of the bill; and the business purpose, such as "Bill Smith, buyer for Company Z."

A hotel receipt has to show the name and location of the hotel; the dates you stayed there; and the separately stated charges for the room, meals, telephone calls, and so on.

Convention expenses

You can deduct your convention-travel expenses if you can prove that your attendance benefits your work. A convention for investment, political, social, or other purposes that are unrelated to your business isn't deductible. Non-business expenses (such as social or sightseeing costs) are personal expenses and aren't deductible. And you can't deduct the travel expenses for your family!

Your selection as a delegate to a convention doesn't automatically entitle you to a deduction. You must prove that your attendance is connected to your business. For conventions held outside North America, you must establish that the convention could be held only at that site. For example, an international seminar on tofu research held in Japan would qualify if that seminar was unique.

Entertainment: The 50-percent deduction

You can only deduct 50 percent of your entertaining expenses — and that includes meals. Starting in 1998, people in the transportation industry get a special break, so read on.

You may deduct business-related expenses for entertaining a client, customer, or employee. To be deductible, an entertainment expense has to meet the *directly-related* or *associated test*. That is, the expense must be *directly-related or associated* to the business you conduct. Under the directly–related test, you must show a business motive related to your business other than a general expectation of getting future business (what does the IRS think business entertainment is all about?). Although you don't have to prove that you actually received additional business, such evidence will help nail down the deduction. Don't panic! You can deduct goodwill entertaining and entertaining prospective customers under the *associated test*. You or your employee has to be present, and your entertaining has to be in a business setting. Because the IRS considers distractions at nightclubs, sporting events, and cocktail parties to be substantial, such events don't qualify as business settings. They do under the *associated* test.

If you have a substantial business discussion before or after entertaining someone, you meet the *associated* test. For example, suppose that after meeting with a customer, you entertain him and his spouse at a theatre and nightclub. The expense is deductible. Goodwill entertaining and entertaining prospective customers falls under the *associated* test. But handing a customer two tickets to the Super Bowl and telling him to have a good time doesn't cut it. The reason: There was no business discussion within a reasonable amount of time before or after the game. Entertainment includes any activity generally considered to provide amusement or recreation (a broad definition!). Examples include entertaining guests at nightclubs (and social, athletic, and sporting clubs), at theaters, at sporting events, on yachts, and on hunting or fishing vacations. If you buy a scalped ticket to an entertainment event for a client, you usually can't deduct more than the face value of the ticket. Country club dues aren't deductible; only the cost of entertaining at the club is. Meal expenses include the cost of food, beverages, taxes, and tips.

You can't claim the cost of a meal as an entertainment expense if you are also claiming it as a travel expense (this activity is known as *double-deducting*). Expenses are also not deductible when a group of business acquaintances takes turns paying for each other's checks without conducting any business.

With regard to gifts, you can't deduct more than $25 for a business gift to any one person during the year. A husband and wife are considered one person. So if a business customer is getting married, you can't give a $25 gift to each newlywed-to-be and expect to deduct $50.

Standard meal and hotel allowance — or "my city costs more than your city"

Instead of keeping records for your actual meal and incidental expenses (tips and cleaning), you can deduct a flat amount of $32 a day. You don't need to keep receipts with this method. But you do have to establish that you were away from home on business. If you travel to what the IRS considers a high-cost area, you can use $40 a day. (IRS

Publication 463 lists high-cost areas, and IRS Publication 1542 lists city-by-city per diem rates.) Employees as well as self-employed taxpayers can use the standard meal allowance. Taxpayers in the transportation industry (those involved in moving people and goods) can use a flat rate of $40 a day in the United States and $36 outside the United States.

Starting in 1998, people in the transportation industry covered by the U.S. Department of Transportation work rules get to deduct 55 percent of their meal expenses instead of the normal 50 percent limit. In later years, it will go to 80 percent. Airline pilots, the flight crew, ground crews, interstate bus and truck drivers, railroad engineers, conductors, and train crews are eligible for this break.

Instead of keeping records for your hotel and meal expenses, you can use a flat rate of $113 a day. You need to show only that the trip was for business. If you are traveling in what the IRS considers the high-cost location area, you can use $180 per day. Both rates are in addition to your transportation expenses, of course.

Unfortunately self-employed taxpayers can't use the flat per diem rates listed for hotel-and-meal expenses; only employees can. However, they can use the per diem rates for meals and submit their actual hotel bills.

If your employer's per diem reimbursement rate is equal to or less than the standard rate, no paperwork is necessary. That's what the standard rate is all about — to keep you from having to attach an accounting of your expenses when you file your return. If your actual expenses or your expenses using the standard meal allowance (your hotel bill plus the standard meal allowance) is more than your per diem allowance, you enter your actual expenses and per diem allowance on Form 2106. The excess of your expenses over your per diem allowance per Form 2106 gets deducted on Schedule A.

If your per diem allowance is more than the standard rate, the excess gets reported on your W-2. This amount is indicated in box 13 of your W-2 with the code **L**. If your expenses are more than the standard rate, you can deduct the excess. Enter your expenses and the amount shown in box 13 of your W-2 on Form 2106. The excess gets deducted on Schedule A.

You can find all the per diem rates on the IRS Homepage on the World Wide Web at www.irs.ustreas.gov.

The standard meal and hotel allowances don't apply to Alaska, Hawaii, Puerto Rico, or foreign locations, however. You can find the standard allowances for those locations in "The Maximum Travel per Diem Allowances for Foreign Areas" (published monthly), which you can order from the Government Printing Office (202-512-1800) — or you can call the State Department (703-875-7910) for the rate in a specific location.

You can't use the standard meal and hotel allowances if you are traveling for medical, charitable, or moving-expense purposes. The rate also can't be used if your employer is your brother or sister, half-brother or half-sister, ancestor, or lineal descendent. Finally, you can't use the standard allowance if your employer is a corporation in which you own ten percent or more. So many details!

What IRS form to use

What other form you attach to your Form 1040 depends on whether you are an employee or are self-employed:

- ✔ **If you are self-employed:** You deduct travel and entertainment expenses on **Schedule C** (line 24).

- ✔ **If you are employed:** You must use **Form 2106, Employee Business Expenses or 2106-EZ.**

For example, if you are paid a salary with the understanding that you will pay your own expenses, you claim these expenses on Form 2106 and then carry over the amount from line 10 of the 2106 to Schedule A (line 20) of your Form 1040 where the amount is claimed as an itemized deduction. Form 2106 also allows you to claim travel and entertaining costs that exceed your travel allowance or the amount for which you were reimbursed.

If you received a travel allowance, your employer adds the amount of the allowance to your salary, and it will be included in box 1 of your W-2. So if you received a travel allowance of $10,000 and spent $10,000, the $10,000 is not completely deductible because it's reduced by 2 percent of your AGI. For example, if your income is $100,000, you can deduct only $8,000 ($10,000 minus 2 percent of $100,000) of your travel expenses. If your income exceeds $124,500, or $62,250 if you are married filing separately, a portion of these deductions is reduced again.

Here's a neat hint: Instead of getting an allowance, have your employer reimburse you for actual expenses that you submit on an expense report. You won't have to file Form 2106, and you won't have to pay tax on the money that you never earned and lose part of your deductions due to silly rules like the 2-percent rule. Neat, huh?

Line 21: Tax preparation fees

You can deduct the fees paid to a tax preparer or advisor! You may also deduct the cost of being represented at a tax audit and the cost of tax-preparation software programs, tax publications, and any fee you paid for the electronic filing of your return.

Fees paid to prepare tax schedules relating to business income (Schedule C), rentals or royalties (Schedule E), or farm income and expenses (Schedule F) are deductible on each one of those forms. The expenses for preparing the remainder of the return are deductible on Schedule A.

Ready for another tax surprise? *Taxe$ For Dummie$* is deductible; so if you're in the 40-percent bracket, this book will cut your bill by $6.00 before you even leave the bookstore.

Line 22: Other expenses — investment, safe deposit box, and so on

You may be scratching your head as to how the IRS can throw in a line item here called "other expenses" when we're within the miscellaneous deduction category. The expenses that are most likely to help you on this line to build up to that 2-percent hurdle are fees you incur in managing your investments. Here's a rundown of deductible investment expenses:

- Financial periodicals
- Accounting fees to keep track of investment income
- Investment fees, custodial fees, trust administration fees, and other expenses you paid for managing your investments
- Investment fees shown in box 1e of Form 1099-DIV
- Safe deposit box rentals
- Trustee's fees for your IRA, if separately billed and paid
- Investment expenses of partnerships, S Corporations, and mutual funds. (You will receive a Schedule K-1 that will tell you where to deduct those expenses.)

You can't deduct expenses incurred in connection with investing in tax-exempt bonds. If you have expenses related to both taxable and tax-exempt income but can't identify the expenses that relate to each, you must prorate the expenses to determine the amount that you can deduct.

One of the benefits of all the lawyers here in America is that when you hire one for a variety of personal purposes, you may qualify to write off the cost. For example, you can deduct a legal fee in connection with collecting taxable alimony and for tax advice related to a divorce if the bill specifies how much is for tax advice and if the bill is determined in a reasonable way.

Part of an estate tax planning fee may be deductible. That's because estate planning involves tax as well as nontax advice. A reasonable division of the bill between the two will usually support a deduction for the portion attributable for tax advice. Legal costs in connection with contesting a will or suing for wrongful death aren't deductible. The same goes for financial planner fees you pay. The part that applies to tax advice is deductible.

You may deduct legal fees directly related to your job, such as fees incurred in connection with an employment contract or defending yourself from being wrongfully dismissed. You can deduct legal expenses that you incurred if they are business related or in connection with income-producing property.

A legal fee paid to collect a disputed Social Security claim is also deductible to the extent that your benefit is taxable. For example, suppose you paid a $2,000 fee to help collect your Social Security benefits. If 50 percent of your Social Security is taxable, you can deduct $1,000 (50 percent of the fee).

Lines 23–26: Miscellaneous math

Congratulations! You've slogged through one of the parts of the tax return that clearly highlights how politicians and years of little changes add up to complicated tax laws. We know you've spent a lot of time identifying and detailing expenses that fit into these ridiculous categories. As we warned you in the beginning of this section on job expenses and other miscellaneous deductions, you can deduct these expenses only to the extent that they exceed 2 percent of your adjusted gross income. Lines 23 through 26 walk you through this arithmetic.

Line 27: Other Miscellaneous Deductions

More miscellaneous deductions? You bet. These "other miscellaneous deductions" are different from those on lines 20 through 26 in that they aren't subject to the 2-percent adjusted gross income limit. Hooray, no convoluted math! These are 100 percent Grade A, no-fat deductions!

- **Gambling losses to the extent of gambling winnings:** Enter on line 27 of Schedule A.
- **Estate tax on income you received as an heir:** Enter on line 27 of Schedule A. You can deduct the estate tax attributable to income you received from an estate that you paid tax on. For example, suppose that you received $10,000 from an IRA account when the owner died. You included this amount in your income. The owner's estate paid $2,000 of estate tax on the IRA. You can deduct the $2,000 on line 27. It's called an *IRD deduction.* That's IRS lingo for *income in respect of a decedent,* which means the IRA owner never paid income tax on the money in the IRA.

✔ **Repayment of income:** If you had to repay more than $3,000 of income that was included in your income in an earlier year, you may be able to deduct the amount you repaid or take a credit against your tax. This is known as a "claim of right." (See Chapter 6 for help tackling this little gem.) However, if the repayment is less than $3,000, you must deduct it on line 22 of Schedule A.

✔ **Unrecovered investment in a pension:** If a retiree contributed to the cost of a pension or annuity, a part of each payment received can be excluded from income as a tax-free return of the retiree's investment. If the retiree dies before the entire investment is returned tax free, the unrecovered investment is allowed as a deduction on the retiree's final return. See line 16 in Chapter 6.

✔ **Work expenses for the disabled:** If you have a physical or mental disability that limits your being employed or that substantially limits one or more of your activities (such as performing manual tasks, walking, speaking, breathing, learning, and working), your impairment-related work expenses are deductible.

✔ **Impairment-related work expenses:** These expenses are allowable business expenses of attendant care services at your place of work and expenses in connection with your place of work that are necessary for you to be able to work. See IRS Publication 907 (*Information for Persons with Disabilities*) for more information.

If you're an employee, enter your impairment-related work expenses on line 10 of Form 2106. This amount is also entered on line 27 of Schedule A. And the amount that is unrelated to your impairment is entered on line 20 of Schedule A.

Line 28: Total Itemized Deductions

You've (thankfully) reached the end of Schedule A. Warm up that calculator again because you need to do some adding. Sum up the totals that you've written in the far right column on the schedule. You should be adding the amounts on lines 4, 9, 14, 18, 19, 26, and 27.

But wait! You can't just go ahead and enter that total on line 28. Why would the IRS allow you to do that after plowing through this difficult schedule? If your adjusted gross income (listed on line 34, which is the same as line 33 of your Form 1040) exceeded $124,500 for the year (or was above $62,250 if you're married filing separately), you're going to have to jump through more hoops because the IRS wants to limit your itemized deductions if you make this much money.

If your adjusted gross income is $124,500 or less for the year ($62,250 or less if married filing separately), you can call it quits now and simply write the total you calculated on line 28 of your Schedule A. Then you can enter this amount on line 36 of your Form 1040. Just make sure that the total of your itemized deductions is greater than the standard deduction (see the amounts at the beginning of the chapter).

If your income is above these limits, you've got more work to do. Read on. (We'd never accuse the IRS of living by that old adage, "You can never have enough of a good thing.")

Limit on itemized deductions

If your adjusted gross income exceeds $124,500 (or $62,250 if you are married filing separately), you have to reduce your total itemized deductions by 3 percent of your income above $124,500. Here's how it works: Say that your income is $144,500 and your total itemized deductions are $30,000. Because your income exceeds $124,500 by $20,000, you have to reduce your itemized deductions by $600 ($20,000 × 3 percent). Although you started with itemized deductions of $30,000, you can deduct only $29,400.

The 3-percent rule won't completely eliminate your itemized deductions because your deductions can't be reduced by more than 80 percent. So, in the preceding example, if your income was $1 million, you would still get to deduct $6,000 because your $30,000 in deductions can't be reduced by more than $24,000 ($30,000 × 80 percent).

So let's put this on paper in order to make it easier to do the math. Use the worksheet in Table 9-3 if your AGI exceeds $124,500 (married filing jointly) or $62,250 (married filing separately) to figure your allowable deductions.

Table 9-3	Itemized Deduction Worksheet		
		Sample	*Your Computation*
1. AGI line 33 (1040)		$150,000	1.
2. Enter $124,500 ($62,250 if filing separately)		$124,500	2.
3. Subtract line 2 from line 1		$ 25,500	3.
4. Total itemized deductions (Schedule A)		$ 20,000	4.
5. From Schedule A enter: Medical (line 4) Investment interest (line 13) Casualty loss (line 19) Gambling losses (line 28)		$ 10,000	5. _____ _____ _____ _____
6. Subtract line 5 entries from line 4		$ 10,000	6.
7. Multiply line 6 by 80%		$ 8,000	7.
8. Multiply line 3 by 3%		$ 765	8.
9. The smaller of lines 7 and 8		$ 765	9.
10. Your reduced itemized deductions: line 4 less line 9		$ 19,235*	10.

* This is the amount you're allowed to deduct. Now you can enter this amount on line 28 of Schedule A and carry it over to line 36 of your Form 1040. Just make sure that the total of your itemized deductions is greater than the standard deduction (see amounts at the beginning of this chapter).

You may be wondering why your medical and dental expenses, investment interest, casualty and theft losses, and gambling losses don't have to reduce these itemized expenses. The IRS doesn't limit or reduce your ability to write off these expenses so that they aren't subject to the 3-percent reduction rule. The IRS *does* want to limit your ability to deduct too much in the way of state and local taxes (including property taxes paid on your home), home mortgage interest, gifts to charity, job expenses, and miscellaneous deductions.

The net effect of the IRS tossing out some of these write-offs is that it raises the effective tax rate that you're paying on your income higher than what the IRS tables indicate. This may encourage you, for example, to spend less on a home or to pay off your mortgage faster (see Chapter 24), because you don't merit a full deduction.

What your neighbors are deducting

Table 9-4 shows the IRS statistics of the average deductions taken by taxpayers on their 1996 tax returns.

Table 9-4	Average Itemized Deductions (1996)			
AGI ($000)	*Medical*	*Taxes*	*Contributions*	*Interest*
$15–30	$4,498	$2,189	$1,339	$5,427
$30–50	$3,971	$3,055	$1,537	$5,873
$50–100	$5,997	$5,001	$2,025	$7,220
$100–200	$13,105	$9,544	$3,367	$11,023
Over $200	$37,1916	$35,386	$17,973	$22,258

Source: *Statistics of Income Bulletin,* The Internal Revenue Service

But you can't simply go ahead and claim the amounts listed in Table 9-4 — the IRS imposes penalties for doing that! And if your deductions exceed these amounts, you stand a greater chance of being audited. But at least you can see how your deductions match up with the norm.

Chapter 10

Interest and Dividend Income: Schedule B

. . . .

In This Chapter

▶ Interest income stuff

▶ Understanding your 1099-INT

▶ Dividend income stuff

▶ Understanding your 1099-DIV

▶ Foreign accounts and trusts

. . . .

Ah! More income — bring it on, you say? Remember that you're going to add it to the taxable income section. In this chapter, we go through Schedule B (see Figure 10-1). Can you find the form? It's a little IRS trick — Schedule B is on the back of Schedule A. After you do the math, transfer the interest income from line 4 on Schedule B to line 8a of the trusty Form 1040; the dividend income from line 6 on Schedule B goes on line 9 of Form 1040.

Year after year, many taxpayers dutifully complete Schedule B, file it with the rest of their return, and forget about it until they need to complete their next return. This particular schedule is a potential gold mine for reducing your future taxes. Why? Because you report on this schedule all the taxable interest and dividend income that you received during the year. If you complete this schedule and are in the higher tax brackets, many investments are tax-friendly. Be sure to check out Chapter 23 to find out all about them.

What you need to complete Schedule B are those 1099s (1099-INT and 1099-DIV) that banks, corporations, brokerage firms, and mutual fund companies send by January 31 of the following year. Make sure that you have one of these forms for each and every nonretirement account that you held money in during the tax year. If you're missing a form, get on the horn to the responsible financial institution and request it.

If you don't report all your interest or dividend income (or don't furnish the payer with your Social Security number), your future interest and dividend income is subject to backup withholding of 31 percent! To add insult to injury, about 18 months after filing your taxes, you'll receive a nasty notice called a CP-2501 listing the interest and dividends you didn't report. You'll end up owing interest and penalties in addition to the tax.

Although becoming ensnared in backup withholding is unpleasant, don't worry that the amounts withheld by financial institutions from your accounts and sent to the IRS are for naught. They simply represent a forced payment of your expected tax on your interest and dividends. You get "credit" for it on line 57, "Federal income tax withheld," on your Form 1040 (see Chapter 8 for more details). On Form 1040EZ, it's line 7; on Form 1040-A, it's line 35.

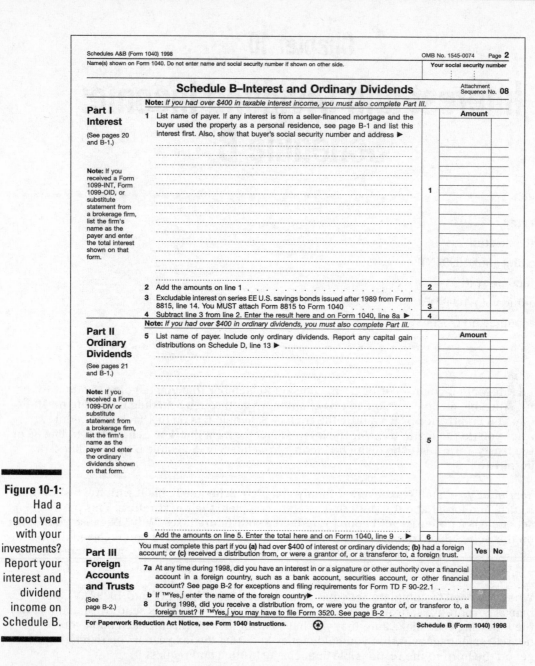

Figure 10-1:
Had a
good year
with your
investments?
Report your
interest and
dividend
income on
Schedule B.

Part I, Lines 1–4: Interest Income

In this first part of the schedule, you need to declare interest income that you earned during the tax year. Although this income can come from a variety of sources, as you'll soon realize, most of it is reported by large, impersonal financial institutions that will send you a computer-generated form, the **1099-INT, Interest Income**.

Before you complete the lines on Schedule B, we'd like to explain how to read your 1099-INT forms.

Understanding Form 1099-INT

You receive Form 1099-INT from the financial institution, such as a bank, that pays you interest. These forms aren't too difficult to read. The following are brief descriptions of little boxes and other stuff you find on your 1099-INT (see Figure 10-2).

Figure 10-2:
You receive Form 1099-INT from the institution that pays you interest.

	CORRECTED (if checked)		
PAYER'S name, street address, city, state, ZIP code, and telephone no.	Payer's RTN (optional)	OMB No. 1545-0112	
		1998 Interest Income	
		Form **1099-INT**	
PAYER'S Federal identification number	RECIPIENT'S identification number	1 Interest income not included in box 3 $	**Copy B For Recipient**
RECIPIENT'S name		2 Early withdrawal penalty $	3 Interest on U.S. Savings Bonds and Treas. obligations $	This is important tax information and is being furnished to the Internal Revenue Service. If you are required to file a return, a negligence penalty or other sanction may be imposed on you if this income is taxable and the IRS determines that it has not been reported.
Street address (including apt. no.)		4 Federal income tax withheld $	
City, state, and ZIP code		5 Foreign tax paid	6 Foreign country or U.S. possession
Account number (optional)		$	
Form **1099-INT**	(Keep for your records.)		Department of the Treasury - Internal Revenue Service

Don't assume that your 1099-INT forms are all correct. Big companies make mistakes, and they often cause taxpayers to pay more tax. Check your 1099-INT forms against your statements that you received throughout the year from the financial firm where you had the account paying the interest. If you receive an incorrect 1099-INT, ask the payer to issue a corrected one on the double!

The Taxpayer Bill of Rights requires that 1099s have the name, address, and telephone number of whom to contact in case the amount reported to the IRS is incorrect. Make sure you get a corrected one.

One problem with filing too early is that you might receive a corrected 1099-INT, which means that you will have to amend your return. And filing one return per year is more than enough for most of us!

The amount in box 1 and box 3 of the 1099-INT is the taxable interest that you have to report on line 1 of this schedule. But if you don't have more than $400 of total interest income for the tax year, you need not complete this part of Schedule B (you have to complete Part II, "Dividend Income," if you had more than $400 in dividend income). If you don't have more than $400 in interest, skip Part I and enter the total of your interest income on line 8a of Form 1040. Don't concern yourself with the rest of the boxes on your 1099-INT right now. As we breeze through this chapter, we'll let you know what to do with them.

Completing lines 1–4

Now that you've located and understand Form 1099-INT, you're ready to complete Part I of Schedule B.

Line 1: Taxable interest

Taxable interest includes interest you receive from bank accounts, interest income on loans you made to others, and interest income on loans from most other sources (anything except for municipal bond interest).

Taxable interest does not include interest on insurance dividends you leave on deposit with the Department of Veterans Affairs (for people who were in the armed services).

Interest that is taxed as dividends

Savings and loans, credit unions, savings banks, and money market funds often report the interest you earned as dividends. Report such interest as dividends; and instead of receiving a 1099-INT, you will receive a **1099-DIV, Dividends and Distributions**. Don't you think, sometimes, that everyone out there is trying to confuse you?

Gifts for opening an account

The value of that toaster you received is reported as interest on Form 1099-INT. Enjoy your toast!

Interest on life insurance dividends

This interest is taxable, but the dividends you receive aren't taxable until the total of all dividends received exceeds the total of all the premiums paid. Keep your annual dividend statements from your company in a file so that you can track that amount versus the premiums you paid.

Interest on EE U.S. savings bonds

If you don't have EE bonds, you may happily skip this line. (If you want to know about them, be sure to read Chapter 25.) You report the interest on EE bonds when you cash in the bonds. You can choose to report the interest every year instead of waiting to report all the interest earned on the bond when it is cashed in.

Reporting the interest every year may make sense if you have a child who has little or no income, because the first $700 of interest is exempt from tax (see Chapter 25). Attach a statement to your child's return saying that you elect to report the interest annually. If the interest is under $700, you're going to have to file a return even if one isn't required in order to make this election for the initial year. After that, as long as the interest is under $700, you don't have to file.

Series E bonds stop earning interest after 40 years; Series EE bonds stop earning interest after 30 years. (Series E was issued before 1980, and Series EE was issued after that.) You can avoid paying the tax on the accumulated interest at or before maturity by exchanging these bonds for HH bonds (see the next section, "U.S. H and HH bonds").

When the owner of an E or EE bond dies, the heir pays the tax when the bond is cashed in — unless the interest was reported on the decedent's final return. This choice makes sense if the owner of the bond died at the beginning of the year and had little or no income (and was in a lower tax bracket than the heir).

For example, if the owner died on January 10 and filed a return reporting the accumulated EE bond interest of $5,000, no tax would be added because the decedent is entitled to a standard deduction of $4,250 (if single) and a personal exemption of $2,700. On the other hand, if the heir is in the 31-percent tax bracket and had to report the $5,000 of accumulated interest when cashing in the bond, the tax would be $1,550.

U.S. H and HH bonds

H and HH bonds are issued only in exchange for E and EE bonds. Interest is paid semiannually, and you receive a Form 1099-INT from the government showing the amount of interest you must report. H bonds have a 30-year maturity, and HH bonds have a 20-year maturity. (In case you really want to know, H bonds were issued before 1980, and HH bonds were issued after that time.)

The amount of interest earned on the E or EE bonds that you exchanged is stated on the H or HH bonds. You report this amount when you cash in the H or HH bonds.

Joint returns, minors, and interest stuff

If your Social Security number is the one that's reported on the 1099-INT, the computers at the IRS check to see whether the interest from the 1099-INT is on your return. On a joint return, either your SSN or your spouse's number can be on the account because you're filing jointly.

But what about an account owned by you and someone other than your spouse (or if you're merely holding the money for someone else)? Suppose that only 50 percent of the $1,200 reported under your SSN is yours. Report the $1,200 on Schedule B, and on the line below,

subtract the $600 belonging to the other person. In the space for the name of the payer, write BELONGING TO NOMINEE. Enter the $600 as a negative number <$600>.

When a minor has an account, make sure that the minor's Social Security number is on the account. If he or she has more than $700 in interest, the minor must file a return. If under the age of 14 with interest and investment income exceeding $1,400, the excess is taxed at the parents' tax rate (find out more about the Kiddie Tax in Chapter 15).

U.S. Treasury bills

U.S. Treasury bills are short-term obligations of the U.S. government, issued at a discount. These bills mature in 1, 2, 3, 6, or 12 months. You report the interest in the year the bill matures, not when you purchase it.

For example, suppose that you purchase a $10,000 6-month T-bill for $9,700 in December 1998. You report the $300 of interest you earned when the bill matures in 1999. This maneuver is an excellent way to defer income to the next year.

Interest on U.S. Treasury bonds, notes, and bills is exempt from state tax.

Zero-coupon bonds

Zero-coupon bonds don't pay annual interest, but they are issued at a discount very similar to U.S. savings bonds. Each year, the bond increases in value equal to the amount of interest it is considered to have earned. In tax lingo, this is referred to as *original issue discount* (OID). Each year, the issuer or your broker will compute the amount of interest you have to report and send you a **Form 1099-OID**.

Interest on bonds bought or sold

When you buy a bond between the interest payment dates, you pay the seller the interest that was earned up to the sale date.

For example, suppose that on April 30 you buy a bond that makes semiannual interest payments of $600 on June 30. You must pay the seller $400 for the interest earned up to April 30. You report the $600 in interest that you received for the bond on Schedule B. On the line below, subtract the $400 of interest you paid the seller, and to the left of the $400 amount, write ACCRUED INTEREST PAID. Enter the $400 as a negative amount <$400>.

Tax refunds

Interest on tax refunds is taxable. This amount is shown in box 1 of your 1099-G.

Tax-exempt bonds

Interest on city and state bonds is exempt from tax. But you still must report it on Form 1040A (line 8b) or on Form 1040 (line 8b). Although the entry on line 8b is not added to your taxable income, it is used to determine the amount of your Social Security that may be subject to tax.

Most states have a provision that tax-exempt bonds are exempt from state income tax only if these bonds are issued by that state. For example, a New York State resident pays state tax on a tax-exempt bond issued by Ohio but doesn't pay state tax on a tax-exempt bond issued by New York.

Line 2: Total interest

Add all the amounts on line 1.

Line 3: U.S. savings bonds — education program

This is one tax shelter that most people are unaware of. Uncle Sam wants you to put money aside for your children's educations and provides you with a tax exemption to boot. All or part of the interest on U.S. savings bonds used to pay college tuition is exempt from tax under the following conditions:

- ✔ The U.S. savings bonds (Series EE) were issued after December 31, 1989.
- ✔ You are 24 years or older before the month in which you buy the bonds.
- ✔ The total redemption proceeds — interest and principal — don't exceed the tuition and fees paid for the year. (Room and board aren't considered tuition.)
- ✔ The tuition is for you, your spouse, or your dependents.

The amount of interest that can be excluded is reduced if your 1998 adjusted gross income meets the following requirements:

- ✔ Unmarried taxpayers with income of $52,250 or less are entitled to a full interest exclusion. Between incomes of $52,250 and $67,250, the exclusion is gradually phased out, and if income exceeds $67,250, there is no exclusion.
- ✔ For married people filing jointly, there is a complete interest exclusion if your income is under $78,350, with a phaseout range between $78,350 and $108,350.

The amount of interest that you can exclude is computed on **Form 8815, Exclusion of Interest from Series EE U.S. Savings Bonds Issued after 1989.** The amount of excludable interest is entered on Schedule B, line 3, and the total interest is listed on line 1. For example, suppose that you have $500 of excludable interest. You would enter this amount on lines 3 and 1.

Interest-free loans

Say you make an interest-free loan to someone. Guess what? The IRS assumes that the borrower paid you interest anyway. This is called *imputed interest.* The IRS imputes (states what the minimum rate should be). The borrower can deduct the interest he is considered to have paid if he uses the money to make an investment that produces income. You have to report as income the minimum amount of interest the IRS claims should have been charged. There's a second leg to this transaction: You're also considered to have made a gift of the interest for gift tax purposes. For the applicable minimum rates, go to the IRS Web page (www.irs.ustreas.gov). Loans with below-market rates of interest are also subject to this rule.

As with every other IRS rule, there are exceptions to this rule. Here they are:

- ✔ Loans under $10,000 aren't subject to the rule.
- ✔ For loans between $10,000 and $100,000, interest isn't imputed (that is, assumed to have been made) if the borrower's investment income for the year doesn't exceed $1,000. If this income exceeds $1,000, the imputed interest is limited to that amount of

the person's investment income. Say you lend your son $50,000. If his investment income is under $1,000, no interest is imputed (considered to have been paid). If his investment income is $1,200, that's all the interest you have to report, even if you should have charged him $4,000.

✔ Certain employee relocation loans to buy a new residence aren't subject to the interest-free loan rule that requires that a minimum rate be charged. See your company's employment benefits office or a tax advisor.

✔ If the loan exceeds $100,000 you have to deal with the imputed interest rule in its full glory.

Interest-free or a below-market-rate-of-interest loans usually occur when a family member taps you for money. In many cases, loans like these end up not being repaid (see Chapter 12, the section on "Nonbusiness bad debts"). If scaring someone off with the imputed interest rules doesn't work, try Shakespeare's "neither a borrower nor a lender be."

A lender reporting imputed interest or a borrower claiming an interest deduction must attach a statement to his return indicating how the interest was computed, the loan balance, the name of the borrower or lender, and the borrower's or lender's Social Security number. (If you're the borrower, it's the lender's and vice-versa.) That should also frighten most people.

Part II, Lines 5 and 6: Dividend Income

Well, we hope that you made a good bit of extra dough in Part I. Part II provides another opportunity to count your silver coins — er, we mean dividends. You find out about your dividends from another version of a 1099. You'll receive Form **1099-DIV, Dividends and Distributions** (see Figure 10-3), from the payer by January 31, 1999. If your 1099-DIV is incorrect, get the payer to correct it; otherwise, you may pay tax on income you never earned. You have to report all your dividend income on your return, or you'll be in big trouble.

The Taxpayer Bill of Rights requires that 1099s have the name, address, and telephone number of whom to contact in case the amount reported to the IRS is incorrect.

To report the income from jointly owned stock, follow the rules explained for reporting interest on a joint bank account in the sidebar "Joint returns, minors, and interest stuff," earlier in this chapter.

Figure 10-3: Form 1099-DIV shows you the dividends you reaped in 1998.

CORRECTED (if checked)			
PAYER'S name, street address, city, state, ZIP code, and telephone no.	1 Ordinary dividends $	OMB No. 1545-0110 **1998** Form **1099-DIV**	**Dividends and Distributions**
	2a Total capital gain distr. $		
PAYER'S Federal identification number / RECIPIENT'S identification number	2b 28% rate gain $	2c Unrecap. sec. 1250 gain $	**Copy B For Recipient**
RECIPIENT'S name	2d Section 1202 gain $	3 Nontaxable distributions $	This is important tax information and is being furnished to the Internal Revenue Service. If you are required to file a return, a negligence penalty or other sanction may be imposed on you if this income is taxable and the IRS determines that it has not been reported.
Street address (including apt. no.)	4 Federal income tax withheld $	5 Investment expenses $	
City, state, and ZIP code	6 Foreign tax paid $	7 Foreign country or U.S. possession	
Account number (optional)	8 Cash liquidation distr. $	9 Noncash liquidation distr. $	
Form **1099-DIV**	(Keep for your records.)	Department of the Treasury - Internal Revenue Service	

When is a dividend NOT a dividend?

Stock dividends and splits

Stock dividends and splits aren't taxable. You now own more shares! For example, suppose that you own 100 shares. If the stock is split two for one, you now own 200 shares. If you receive a 10-percent stock dividend, you now own 110 shares. Chapter 12 explains how you treat the shares you received when they are sold.

Life insurance dividends

Life insurance dividends aren't taxable until the total dividends received exceed the total premiums paid.

Watch out for corrected 1099s. If you file really early, you may need to file an amended return. (April 15 comes only once a year; it's best that way.)

Line 5: Name, payer, and amount

Schedule B, Part II, has a column for the name of the payer and a column for the amount of the dividend you received. Enter the name of the payer in the column that says to list the name of the payer. Enter the amount of the dividend you received in the column that says amount. For each 1099-DIV you received, enter the name of the payer and the amount received.

Line 6: Total dividends

This is the easy part. Total all the dividends you listed on line 5 and enter that amount on line 9 of your 1040.

Your 1099-DIV: Decoding those boxes

Here's what all those boxes on your 1099-DIV mean:

✔ **Box 1: Ordinary dividends.** Enter the total amount of your ordinary dividends on line 5. Make sure you list the payer's name to the left of the amount column.

If the total of your ordinary dividends doesn't exceed $400, skip Part II and enter the total on line 9 of Form 1040.

✔ **Boxes 2a and 2b: Capital gain distributions.** Capital gain dividends are no longer entered on Schedule B. Enter your capital gain dividends on Schedule D, line 13 (column f) — see Chapter 12.

Make sure you don't overpay the tax that's due on capital gains. The top rate is 20 percent (10 percent for folks in the 15-percent tax bracket). You can get the lowdown on all this by taking a look at line 40 in Chapter 8.

Some mutual funds with fiscal years beginning in 1997 and ending in 1998 might still have some capital gains dividends that are subject to the 28-percent rate. That's because in 1997, some security transactions were subject to a 28-percent tax if the security wasn't held for more than 18 months. The amount in box 2b gets entered on line 13 (column g) of Schedule D — see Chapter 12. After 1998, this quirk won't apply. Starting January 1, 1998, the capital gains rule applies to securities held for more than 12 months.

✔ **Box 3: Nontaxable distributions.** Nontaxable dividends and distributions aren't entered on your return. Nontaxable means exactly that. These distributions reduce the taxable amount of your shares when figuring your gain or loss when the shares are sold. For example, suppose that you purchased shares in a company or a mutual fund for $10,000, and you received $500 in nontaxable dividends. Your basis for determining gain or loss when you sell the shares is $9,500.

✔ **Box 4: Federal tax withheld.** Report your federal tax withheld on Form 1040 (line 57). On Form 1040EZ, it's line 7. On Form 1040A, it's line 35.

✔ **Box 5: Investment expenses.** This box refers to shares you own in funds not available to the public, so it doesn't apply to most people. We have yet to see a 1099-DIV with an entry in this box! (But it must be there for a reason!) If this box applies to you, it means that you own shares in a nonpublicly traded fund. You can deduct this expense as a miscellaneous itemized deduction on line 22, Form 1040 of Schedule B (see Chapter 9). Publicly traded funds don't pass investment expenses on to shareholders.

✔ **Box 6: Foreign tax paid.** If you own shares in a company or fund that was required to pay tax in a foreign country, your share of the tax is recorded in box 3. You can claim this amount as a credit against your tax as an itemized deduction. We discuss how to handle this in the section "Other taxes" in Chapter 9.

✔ **Box 7: Foreign country or U.S. possession.** This is easy. It states the country or U.S. possession where the tax was paid. You need this information when you fill out **Form 1116: Foreign Tax Credits.** See Chapter 8.

✔ **Boxes 8 and 9: Liquidating distributions.** You report these amounts (cash and noncash) on Schedule D (Capital Gains and Losses). If you have entries in these two boxes, see a tax advisor. And check out Chapter 12 to find out more about Schedule D.

Part III, Lines 7-8: Foreign Accounts and Trusts

If you have a foreign bank or security account, you have to check "yes" on line 7a of Schedule B and enter the name of the foreign country. However, if the average balance in the account in 1998 was under $10,000, you can check "no." But if you had more than $10,000 in a foreign bank or security account during the year, you have to file **Form TDF 90-22.1 Report of Foreign Bank and Financial Accounts** by June 30, 1999. On this form, you have to list where your account(s) are located, including the name of the bank, security firm, or brokerage firm; its address, and the account number.

If you're unique enough to have to deal with line 8, it means that you have a foreign trust. You have to check "yes" and complete **Form 3520** or **Form 926** (the trustee completes Form 3520-A). Good luck! (These forms are complicated; consider using a tax advisor.)

If you received a gift or inheritance from a foreigner in excess of $10,557 (this amount gets adjusted for inflation every year), you have to report it to the IRS, listing the foreigner's name and address. Report this information on **Form 3520**. The penalty for not filing is 5 percent for each month the return is not filed, up to a maximum of 25 percent of the amount received. Evidently, a lot of people were claiming that what they earned abroad was a gift. The amount you report to the IRS isn't taxable. The IRS does, however, want to know about it.

Chapter 11

Profit or Loss from Business: Schedule C

....

In This Chapter

▶ Using Schedule C-EZ

▶ Using Schedule C

▶ Reporting income

▶ Tallying and categorizing expenses

....

*R*unning your own firm really can be the American dream. In fact, the only thing better than working for yourself is knowing how to keep more of what you earn. It's like giving yourself an immediate raise at tax time.

If you're self-employed, you must report your income on Schedule C (or C-EZ), as well as your business expenses. You subtract your expenses from your income to arrive at your profit on which you have to pay tax.

Schedule C-EZ

Schedule C-EZ is a three-line form that's relatively EZ to complete. The requirement that your income must be less than $25,000 to use this form no longer applies. The only catch is that your deductible expenses can't exceed $2,500. You also can't use the C-EZ if you have a net loss from your business, and you can't deduct any expenses for the business use of your home.

If you qualify, have a go at it. After you fill in the easy background information in Part I, figure your net profit. To obtain an employer ID number, as required on line D, send a completed **Form SS-4, Application for Employer Identification Number,** to the IRS.

✔ Line 1: Fill in your income.

✔ Line 2: Fill in your expenses.

✔ Line 3: Subtract line 2 from line 1; this amount is your net profit.

You're done. Carry the profit over to Form 1040 (line 12). Unless you're a statutory employee (see Chapter 6), also carry the profit to Schedule SE so that you can calculate your self-employment tax.

Okay, you caught us. If you're deducting automobile expenses on line 2, you have to fill out Part III and answer five (maybe six) more questions so that the IRS can be sure that your expenses are legitimate. Four of those questions are yes/no questions. Don't you wish all IRS forms were like this?

Knowing what's taxable and what's deductible can, at times, be confusing. So read on. We take you by the hand to make sure that you don't miss a thing.

Schedule C

This schedule is not so EZ, but it isn't as bad as it looks (see Figure 11-1). In the rest of this chapter, we take you through the line-by-line instructions.

SCHEDULE C (Form 1040)	Profit or Loss From Business (Sole Proprietorship)	OMB No. 1545-0074
Department of the Treasury Internal Revenue Service (99)	► Partnerships, joint ventures, etc., must file Form 1065 or Form 1065-B. ► Attach to Form 1040 or Form 1041. ► See Instructions for Schedule C (Form 1040).	1998 Attachment Sequence No. 09

Name of proprietor | Social security number (SSN)

A Principal business or profession, including product or service (see page C-1) | **B** Enter NEW code from pages C-8 & 9 ►

C Business name. If no separate business name, leave blank. | **D** Employer ID number (EIN), if any

E Business address (including suite or room no.) ►
City, town or post office, state, and ZIP code

F Accounting method: **(1)** ☐ Cash   **(2)** ☐ Accrual   **(3)** ☐ Other (specify) ►

G Did you "materially participate" in the operation of this business during 1998? If "No," see page C-2 for limit on losses . ☐ Yes ☐ No

H If you started or acquired this business during 1998, check here . . . . ► ☐

Part I   Income

1	Gross receipts or sales. **Caution:** If this income was reported to you on Form W-2 and the "Statutory employee" box on that form was checked, see page C-3 and check here . . . . . ► ☐	1	
2	Returns and allowances	2	
3	Subtract line 2 from line 1	3	
4	Cost of goods sold (from line 42 on page 2)	4	
5	**Gross profit.** Subtract line 4 from line 3	5	
6	Other income, including Federal and state gasoline or fuel tax credit or refund (see page C-3) . . .	6	
7	**Gross income.** Add lines 5 and 6 . . . . ►	7	

Part II   Expenses. Enter expenses for business use of your home **only** on line 30.

8	Advertising	8		19	Pension and profit-sharing plans	19
9	Bad debts from sales or services (see page C-3) . .	9		20	Rent or lease (see page C-5):	
				a	Vehicles, machinery, and equipment .	20a
10	Car and truck expenses (see page C-3)	10		b	Other business property . .	20b
11	Commissions and fees . .	11		21	Repairs and maintenance . .	21
12	Depletion	12		22	Supplies (not included in Part III) .	22
13	Depreciation and section 179 expense deduction (not included in Part III) (see page C-4) .	13		23	Taxes and licenses	23
				24	Travel, meals, and entertainment:	
				a	Travel	24a
14	Employee benefit programs (other than on line 19) . . .	14		b	Meals and entertainment .	
15	Insurance (other than health) .	15		c	Enter 50% of line 24b subject to limitations (see page C-6) .	
16	Interest:					
a	Mortgage (paid to banks, etc.) .	16a		d	Subtract line 24c from line 24b	24d
b	Other	16b		25	Utilities	25
17	Legal and professional services	17		26	Wages (less employment credits) .	26
18	Office expense	18		27	Other expenses (from line 48 on page 2)	27

28	**Total expenses** before expenses for business use of home. Add lines 8 through 27 in columns ►	28	
29	Tentative profit (loss). Subtract line 28 from line 7	29	
30	Expenses for business use of your home. Attach **Form 8829**	30	
31	**Net profit or (loss).** Subtract line 30 from line 29.		
	• If a profit, enter on **Form 1040, line 12,** and ALSO on **Schedule SE, line 2** (statutory employees, see page C-6). Estates and trusts, enter on Form 1041, line 3.	}	31
	• If a loss, you MUST go on to line 32.		
32	If you have a loss, check the box that describes your investment in this activity (see page C-6).		
	• If you checked 32a, enter the loss on **Form 1040, line 12,** and ALSO on **Schedule SE, line 2** (statutory employees, see page C-6). Estates and trusts, enter on Form 1041, line 3.	}	32a ☐ All investment is at risk. 32b ☐ Some investment is not at risk.
	• If you checked 32b, you MUST attach **Form 6198.**		

For Paperwork Reduction Act Notice, see Form 1040 instructions.   Cat. No. 11334P   Schedule C (Form 1040) 1998

Figure 11-1: Schedule C, page 1.

Basic Information (A–D)

Lines A through D are pretty easy background stuff. To obtain an Employer ID Number, as required on line D, send a completed **Form SS-4, Application For Employer Identification Number,** to the IRS.

Accounting Method Stuff (F–H)

The two methods to report income are *cash* and *accrual.* With the cash method, you report income when it's actually received, and you deduct expenses when they're actually paid. However, there is (of course) one exception to this rule: If you charge an expense on a credit card, you deduct this expense in the year charged, even if you pay the charge in a later year. (So don't leave home without it!)

You must use the accrual method if you operate a business that has an inventory of merchandise, such as a clothing store. Under this method, you report income in the year that sales are made — even if the sales are billed or collected in a later year. You deduct expenses in the year that they're incurred, even if these expenses aren't paid until later. Under both cash and accrual methods, you report all income and expenses for the calendar year ending December 31.

If you have the choice, the cash method of accounting gives you more control over when your business sees a profit from year to year. For example, if next year looks like a slower year for you, perhaps because you plan to take a sabbatical, you may elect to push more income into next year. This plan will likely save you tax dollars because you should be in a lower tax bracket that next year. You can legally do this by delaying sending invoices until January, for example, that you would have mailed in December. Likewise, you may pay more of your expenses in December rather than waiting until January.

Part I, Lines 1–7: Income

Time to tally. This section wants you to find some *gross* things: gross sales, gross profits, and gross income.

Line 1: Gross receipts or sales

If you operate a service business, enter the income from fees that you actually collected (because you're reporting income under the cash method).

If you sell merchandise, you're required to use the accrual method, so enter here the total of all the sales that you billed your customers.

Line 2: Returns and allowances

If you had to return any fees, enter that amount here. If any customers returned merchandise, that amount also goes on this line, along with any discounts that those customers took.

Line 3: Subtraction quiz

All that you need to do on this line is subtract your returns and allowances (line 2) from your gross receipts and sales (line 1).

Line 4: Cost of goods sold

The IRS must think that you're an accountant; otherwise, the agency would simply say to subtract the cost of the merchandise that you sold from your sales to arrive at this figure. Services and other businesses that don't sell products don't have to put an amount on this line.

But because you aren't an accountant — thank heavens, you say? — you have to compute the cost of the merchandise that you sold in Part III (on the back of Schedule C). Part III is an eight-line schedule where you enter your beginning inventory, the merchandise that you purchased, the salary that you paid to your production workers (if you manufacture the product that you sell), and production supplies. You total all these expenses on line 40. From this total, you subtract your ending inventory to arrive at the cost of the goods that you sold. This amount goes back to line 4 (where you are right now!).

Remember, you can't deduct the cost of all the merchandise that you purchased during the year. You can deduct only the cost of merchandise that you sold. That's why you have to subtract your ending inventory, which is the stuff that you didn't sell. You get to deduct what's on hand when it's sold. You enter the amount of the merchandise you didn't sell (it's called *ending inventory*) on line 41. Your ending inventory gets carried over to your 1999 return. So don't forget to enter the amount from line 41 of your 1998 return.

The following example explains what this inventory business is all about. Say you own a retail furniture store. In 1998, you purchased two identical chairs, one for $1,200 and the other for $1,000. You sold only one chair (we hope business is better next year). Which one did you sell? The inventory method that you select determines that.

Under the *FIFO method* — First In, First Out — the first chair purchased is deemed the first one sold. If that's the $1,200 chair, then enter the cost of the $1,000 chair on line 41 because that's the one considered on hand at the end of the year. Under the *LIFO method* — Last In, First Out — the chair purchased last is deemed to be sold first. Under this method, the $1,000 chair is considered to be sold first, so enter $1,200 on line 41 because that's the cost of the chair that's considered the unsold one. Which method is better? In a period of rising costs, it's the LIFO method.

Line 33 also requires you to select the method that you used to value your inventory. Three methods are available — cost (box a), lower of cost or market (box b), and other (box c). Skip box c as it's too complicated. Most people check box a because it's the easiest. While the lower of cost or market can increase deductions if your inventory declines in value (you get to deduct the amount of the decline), it requires you to revalue your inventory every year. Once you select a valuation method, you can change it only with permission from the IRS.

Line 5: Gross profit

Hey, here's where you put the profit that you made on the merchandise that you sold. (Hopefully, this is a pleasant reminder of a successful year.)

Line 6: Other income

Just do what the schedule orders you to do — see page C-2 of the 1040 Booklet if you have any questions about other income. Some of the more common — and more obscure — examples of other income include the following:

✔ Federal and state gasoline or fuel tax credit

✔ Interest on accounts receivable

✔ Scrap sales

✔ Fee for allowing a company to paint an advertisement on the side of your building

Line 7: Gross income

This amount is usually the same as the amount on line 5. But if you had other items of income, such as a refund of a prior year's expense, enter that amount on line 6 and add it to the amount on line 5 to arrive at your gross income.

Part II, Lines 8–27: Expenses

Take a breath and get ready for all those wonderful lines split into two columns — so they'd all fit on one page!

Line 8: Advertising

On this line, enter the cost of any advertising that your business does to promote itself — for example, an ad in the Yellow Pages — as well as other forms of advertising including radio, newspaper, and promotional brochures and mailers.

Line 9: Bad debts from sales or services

If you use the accrual method to report income, you can write off losses when a customer doesn't pay a bill. But if you use the cash method, you can't — because you never recorded the income and paid tax on the money that your client owes. The rules regarding when cash-method taxpayers can write off a bad debt on a loan that they made are similar to those regarding when you can write off a personal loan that goes bad. We explain such things in "Nonbusiness bad debts" in Chapter 12.

Line 10: Car and truck expenses

If you plan to make an entry on this line, be sure to answer questions 43 through 47b in Part IV on the other side of Schedule C, commonly referred to as Page 2.

When you use your car for business, the expenses of operating your car are deductible. But remember that *using it for business* is the key phrase. You can compute this deduction by using either a flat rate of 32.5 cents per business mile, or you can keep track of actual expenses (gas, oil, repair, insurance, depreciation, and so on). Regardless of which method you use, you're supposed to keep a log or diary so that you can record the business purpose of your trips as well as the mileage ("Dear Diary. . . ."). You also have to record the odometer reading at the beginning and end of the year. You need all this information to be able to divide your expenses into personal and business use. But here's a word of caution: Whether you use the flat rate or tabulate your actual expenses, proving that you use your car 100 percent for business is just about impossible. Unfortunately, there's always some personal use!

You don't have to write down the miles that you travel every time you get in and out of your car. Making entries in your diary on a weekly basis meets the IRS requirement that you keep a record of your car's business use near or at the time of its use.

No help from Uncle Sam with commuting expenses

Commuting expenses between your home and office aren't deductible. These expenses are considered personal commuting expenses, no matter how far your home is from your office or place of work. And making telephone calls from your car while commuting or having a business discussion with a business associate who accompanies you doesn't turn your ride into a deductible expense (besides, you should be watching the road). And using your car to display advertising material on your way to the office doesn't count as business use of your auto, either. Finally, the cost of parking at your place of business isn't deductible — but the cost of parking when you visit a customer or client is.

If you use your car to call on clients or customers and don't have a regular office to go to, the mileage between your home and the first customer that you call on — as well as the mileage between the location of the last customer that you call on and your home — is considered commuting. If your office is in your home (which is a tough nut to crack — tax-wise anyway), you can deduct all your auto expenses for calling on clients or customers. Line 44 on the back of Schedule C asks you about the first-and-last-customer-of-the-day rule, but the IRS refers to it as *commuting.* The IRS wants you to enter on this line (44) the number of miles that you use your car when commuting.

Second job

If you moonlight after work, you can deduct the cost of getting from one job to the other. But transportation expenses going from your home to a part-time job on a day off from your main job aren't deductible. A meeting of an Armed Forces Reserve unit is considered travel to a second job, however. If the meeting is held on the same day as your regular job, it's deductible.

Temporary job site

If you have a regular place of business and commute to a temporary work location, you can deduct the cost of the daily round trip between your home and the temporary job site.

If you don't have a regular place of work (but ordinarily work at different locations in the general area where you live), you can't deduct the daily round trip between your home and your temporary job site. But if you travel to a job site outside your general area, your daily transportation is deductible. Sounds like a distinction without a difference, right? But if this exception applies to you, don't look a gift horse in the mouth.

You can deduct the business portion of the following: depreciation, leasing and rental fees, garage rent, licenses, repairs, gas, oil, tires, insurance, parking, and tolls.

If you're self-employed, you can deduct the business portion of interest on a car loan; if you're an employee, you can't. Fines for traffic violations aren't deductible, either — so slow down!

Standard mileage rate

Instead of figuring your actual expenses with those maddening depreciation computations, you can use a flat rate of 32.5 cents for every business mile. If you drove your car 15,000 miles for business, you'd be entitled to a $4,875 deduction. You claim this deduction on page 2 of **Form 2106, Employee Business Expenses.** On Form 2106, you multiply the business miles on line 13 by 32.5 cents and enter the result on line 22. You carry over this amount to line 1 of Form 2106, which, naturally enough, is on page 1. If you were reimbursed for any of your car expenses that weren't included in box 1 of your W-2 as taxable wages, a code L appears next to the amount of the reimbursement in box 13 of your W-2. You must deduct this amount from your auto expenses and enter it on line 7 of Form 2106.

Although Form 2106 is intended for employees who are deducting auto expenses, self-employed Schedule C filers will find Part II of the form helpful in computing their deductible automobile expenses.

If you choose the flat-rate, 32.5-cents-per-mile method, you can't claim any of your actual expenses, such as depreciation, gas, oil, insurance, and so on. If you want to use this method, you must choose it the first year that you start using your car for business. If you don't use the standard mileage rate the first year that you start using your car for business, you can't use the standard mileage rate in a subsequent year. But if you use the standard mileage rate the first year, you can switch to deducting your actual expenses, but you probably won't want to after you take a look at the rules in the IRS Publication 917 *(Business Use of a Car)*.

If you trade in your car, you can use the flat rate for both cars because you owned them at different times.

If you sell your car, you have to reduce its tax basis by the amount of depreciation built into the flat rate so that you can determine if you made a taxable profit or loss. There is a table (of course!) in IRS Publication 917 that shows you how to make this computation.

Sales tax can't be deducted separately — it's added to the car's tax basis for the purposes of determining the amount of depreciation that you're entitled to claim. If you're an employee, you can deduct personal property tax on your car if you itemize your deductions on Schedule A. (See "Line 7: Personal property taxes" in Chapter 9 for more info.) If you're self-employed, you deduct the business portion of your personal property tax on line 23 and the personal part on Schedule A.

Standard mileage rate or actual expenses?

You can deduct either the business portion of your actual expenses or use the standard rate of 32.5 cents per mile for your business miles (see the "Standard mileage rate" sidebar). If you choose to use the standard mileage rate, you must choose it in the first year that you start using your car for business. If you decide to use your actual expenses, you start off by deducting the amount of depreciation on your car that you're entitled to claim.

Depreciation

Computing the amount of depreciation on your car is mind-numbing. Unfortunately, the only way around this exercise in frustration is to use the 32.5-cent flat rate.

The IRS lumps automobiles into the *listed property* category of assets (they're subject to the 50-percent business use test) and gives cars a whole bunch of rules and regulations. Listed property is an IRS term for autos, telephones, computers, boats, and airplanes — items that the IRS suspects that you may use more for pleasure than for business. The IRS lists cars as a five-year property, which means that the IRS deems them to have a useful life of five years. Ready for the computation? Here goes.

If the business use of your car is 50 percent or more of its total use, you compute your depreciation (under MACRS — Modified Accelerated Cost Recovery System) according to what is known as the *half-year convention* (see Table 11-1).

The IRS limits the amount of depreciation that you can claim. The days of being able to write off a $90,000 car over three years are over. If, for example, you purchased a car in 1998 for $30,000, the maximum amount of depreciation that can you can claim in 1998 is $3,160, and then $5,000 in 1999, $2,950 in 2000, and $1,775 a year until the $30,000 is fully depreciated (which takes about 13 years). This formula, however, assumes that you use your car 100 percent for business. So if the business use of your car is less, the maximum yearly limits are reduced.

Table 11-1   Half-Year Convention for Auto Depreciation

Year	Yearly Percent	For a $30,000 Car if No Limit Is Applied	Maximum Yearly Limit
1-1998	20.00%	$6,000	$3,160
2-1999	32.00	9,600	5,000
3-2000	19.20	5,760	2,950
4-2001	11.52	3,456	1,775
5-2002	11.52	3,456	1,775
6-2003	5.76	1,728	1,775
	100.00%	$30,000	$1,775 in each succeeding year

Just when you thought all this rigmarole was bad enough, Congress — in its infinite wisdom — enacted the 40-percent rule. Under this rule, if you purchased more than 40 percent of all your business assets (including your auto) in the last quarter of 1998 (October to December), you don't use the depreciation percentages in Table 11-1. Instead, you must use the depreciation percentages known as the *mid-quarter convention* (see Table 11-2).

Table 11-2   Mid-Quarter Convention for Auto (and Computer) Depreciation

Year	First Quarter	Second Quarter	Third Quarter	Fourth Quarter
1	35.00%	25.00%	15.00%	5.00%
2	26.00	30.00	34.00	38.00
3	15.60	18.00	20.40	22.80
4	11.01	11.37	12.24	13.68
5	11.01	11.37	11.30	10.94
6	1.38	4.26	7.06	9.58

For example, you purchased a car for $20,000 in December (fourth quarter) and a computer for $10,000 in May (second quarter). Because both computers and autos are considered to have a five-year life for depreciation purposes, Table 11-2 shows the depreciation rates for both items. The percentage that you use to depreciate the computer in 1998 is 25 percent. Your auto depreciation schedule, however, looks like something else (see Table 11-3). Why? Because Table 11-3 alerts you that your yearly auto depreciation can't exceed the maximum amount in the table.

Table 11-3	Mid-Quarter Convention for Auto Depreciation		
Year	**Yearly % per the 4th Quarter Chart in Table 11-2**	**For a $20,000 Car**	**Maximum Yearly Limit**
1-1998	5.00%	$1,000	$3,160
2-1999	38.00	7,600	5,000
3-2000	22.80	4,560	2,950
4-2001	13.68	2,736	1,775
5-2002	10.94	2,188	1,775
6-2003	9.58	1,916	1,775
	100%	$20,000	$1,775 in each succeeding year

As a result of the 40-percent rule, your auto depreciation (in the previous example) comes to only $1,000 ($20,000 × 5 percent) because you started using the car in the fourth quarter. The depreciation for the computer amounts to $2,500 (10,000 × 25 percent) because you purchased it in the second quarter. In subsequent years, the yearly depreciation percentages would be 30 percent, 18 percent, 11.37 percent, and so on.

In 1999, you'd use 38 percent for the auto. But remember that although 38 percent comes to $7,600, you're limited to $5,000.

You can increase your 1998 depreciation deduction in the previous example from $1,000 to $3,160. You can accomplish this by electing to write off as a current expense part of the car's cost for the first year that the car was placed in service (when you started using it in your business). This procedure is known as *Section 179 depreciation*.

Section 179 allows you to write off, in one shot, up to $18,500 a year of the cost of a business asset you purchased during the year that you use in your business. However, because the asset in the preceding example is a car, you can't expense more than the yearly maximum depreciation limits for autos (listed property). In other words, regular depreciation plus Section 179 expensing can't exceed whatever the yearly maximum limit for depreciation of an auto. Because in the preceding example you're forced to use the 5-percent mid-quarter convention (the car was placed into service in the fourth quarter of the year), your depreciation deduction works out to be $1,000. However, you can kick this up to the $3,160 maximum by electing to expense part of the cost of the auto under the Section 179 expensing allowance. Phew! But on we go.

If you elect to use the Section 179 expensing method, you must reduce the basis of the car by the expensed amount ($20,000 − $3,160 = $16,840). The $16,840 becomes your new basis for depreciation in the coming years. Calculate depreciation from that point on, using $16,840 as your basis. Next year, you can deduct the maximum amount of depreciation for an auto placed in service in 1998, $5,000 in 1999, $2,950 in 2000, and $1,775 thereafter. If you started depreciating your car prior to 1998, Table 11-4 shows you the maximum yearly depreciation limits.

Table 11-4 Annual Depreciation Ceiling for Cars Placed in Service after 1986												
Year	**1987**	**1988**	**1989**	**1990**	**1991**	**1992**	**1993**	**1994**	**1995**	**1996**	**1997**	**1998**
1987	$2,560											
1988	4,100	$2,560										
1989	2,450	4,100	$2,660									

(continued)

Table 11-4 (continued)

Year	1987	1988	1989	1990	1991	1992	1993	1994	1995	1996	1997	1998
1990	1,475	2,450	4,200	$2,660								
1991	1,475	1,475	2,550	4,200	$2,660							
1992	1,475	1,475	1,475	2,550	4,300	$2,760						
1993	1,475	1,475	1,475	1,475	2,550	4,400	$2,860					
1994	1,475	1,475	1,475	1,475	1,575	2,650	4,600	$2,960				
1995	1,475	1,475	1,475	1,475	1,575	1,575	2,750	4,700	$3,060			
1996	1,475	1,475	1,475	1,475	1,575	1,575	1,675	2,850	4,900	$3,060		
1997	1,475	1,475	1,475	1,475	1,575	1,575	1,675	1,675	2,950	4,900	$3,160	
1998	1,475	1,475	1,475	1,475	1,575	1,575	1,675	1,675	1,775	2,950	5,000	$3,160
1999	1,475	1,475	1,475	1,475	1,575	1,575	1,675	1,675	1,775	1,775	3,050	$5,000
2000	1,475	1,475	1,475	1,475	1,575	1,575	1,675	1,675	1,775	1,775	1,775	$2,950
2001*	1,475	1,475	1,475	1,475	1,575	1,575	1,675	1,675	1,775	1,775	1,775	1,775

* and later years

To compute your annual depreciation deduction, first figure the maximum depreciation that you're allowed, assuming your car was used 100 percent for business. Then multiply that amount by the business-use percentage. For example, for a car that you started using in 1998, the maximum depreciation amount is $3,160. If you used your car 75 percent of the time for business, you can deduct $2,370 ($3,160 × 75 percent).

If the business use of your car is less than 50 percent, you must depreciate your car using the *straight-line method* under the *alternative depreciation system* (ADS) (see Table 11-5). Straight-line depreciation is relatively easy, right? Wrong, in this case. Remember, this is for a car with a business use of less than 50 percent, so the IRS makes you reduce the amount of depreciation that you're allowed under the straight-line method by the percentage of personal use.

Table 11-5   Straight-Line Method (ADS) for Auto Depreciation

Year	5-Year Property	Maximum Yearly Limit*
1	10%	$3,160
2	20	5,000
3	20	2,950
4	20	1,775
5	20	and 1,775 each succeeding year
6	10	and 1,775 each succeeding year

* Remember that this is the maximum deduction if your car was used 100 percent for business.

So if you used your car for business 40 percent of the time, the maximum depreciation allowed by law in the first year is $1,264 ($3,160 × 40 percent).

In the coming years, you calculate your depreciation deduction the same way. In years 2 through 5, you use a depreciation rate of 20 percent according to Table 11-5, and then 10 percent for year 6. Any depreciation that you can't claim in years 1 through 6 (because of the yearly maximum limits) is deducted in subsequent years at $1,775 a year less your personal use, until your car is fully depreciated.

All this auto depreciation stuff is almost enough to make you start using your feet to call on clients. But then, there's no depreciation allowance for shoes.

A tax software program can save you from all this mind-numbing number crunching.

Leased autos

If you lease a car rather than buy it, you're probably asking yourself why we waited so long to discuss how leased autos are deducted. The reason is that a special rule applies. This is your lucky day!

If you lease a car, you can deduct the rental payments. If the rental payments are, for example, $700 a month, enter $8,400 on line 24a of **Form 2106 Employee Business Expenses.** This sounds like a great deal. Why buy a car if the most that you can deduct in depreciation for a car purchased in 1998 is $3,160, when you can deduct $8,400 in rental payments? Don't celebrate yet.

Here's how the IRS gets back at you. Look at the line directly below line 24a. Yes, you see line 24b of Form 2106 — inclusion amount. Based on the value of the car that you're leasing, you have to reduce your rental payment by this inclusion. If you lease a car that's worth $30,500, you have to reduce your lease payments by $120. Every year of the lease, this amount increases. What's an inclusion amount? You don't want to know. But, fortunately, IRS Publication 917 *(Business Use of Your Car)* has a chart of the annual lease-inclusion amounts that are adjusted for inflation each year. The IRS thinks of everything. (Call 800-829-3676 to obtain a free copy of this publication.)

As you probably realize, even though you reduce your rental payments by the lease-inclusion amount, leasing still provides you with a larger deduction than purchasing. But lease payments that are payments toward the purchase price of a car aren't deductible. The IRS considers such leases a purchase contract because you end up owning the jalopy at the end of the lease. If you have such a lease agreement, you have to depreciate the car based on its value. As a result, you're back to the annual limit that you can claim for auto depreciation.

Line 11: Commissions and fees

The fees that you paid to sell your merchandise or to bring in new clients (as in referral fees) go on this line.

However, if you pay someone who isn't your employee more than $600 in a year, you have to file **Form 1099-MISC** with the IRS and send the person that you paid a copy of the form by January 31. IRS Publication 334 *(Tax Guide for Small Business)* explains how to comply with this requirement.

Line 12: Depletion

This line applies if your business deals with properties such as mines, oil and gas wells, timber, and exhaustible natural deposits. You can compute depletion two ways, and, of course, you want to use the one that produces the larger deduction. To be on the safe side, take a look at IRS Publication 535 *(Business Expenses)*.

Line 13: Depreciation

Depreciation is the annual deduction that enables you to recover the cost of an investment (that has a useful life of more than one year) in business equipment or in income-producing real estate. The word *depreciation* is itself enough to send most readers to the next chapter, we know, but just think of depreciation as a way of reducing your tax! Now, are you more excited about depreciation possibilities?

Unless you elect the special provision that allows you to deduct the first $18,500 of equipment or furniture used in your business (we explain this provision later in the chapter in "Your buying bonanza: The $18,500 deduction"), you have to write off your purchase of these assets over their useful life — as established by the IRS (see Table 11-6). You can't depreciate land and works of art. (So you can't depreciate your Van Goghs!) See Chapter 22 for a discussion of the pros and cons of depreciating versus taking an outright deduction.

If you're an employee claiming auto expenses, you claim the depreciation for the auto on **Form 2106, Employee Business Expenses;** Form 4562 isn't required. For rental income reported on Schedule E, use Form 4562 for property that you started renting in 1998. For property that you started renting before 1998, you don't need to file Form 4562.

Table 11-6	Useful Life
Type of Property	**Useful Life (Years)**
Computers and similar equipment	5
Office machinery (typewriters, calculators, copiers)	5
Autos and light trucks	5
Office furniture (desks, files)	7
Appliances (stoves, refrigerators)	7
Shrubbery	15
Residential buildings	27.5
Nonresidential buildings after 5/12/93	39
Nonresidential buildings before 5/12/93	31.5
Goodwill, customer lists, franchise costs, and covenants not to compete	15

To file (or not to file) Form 4562

You compute your depreciation deduction for business property that you started using in 1998 on **Form 4562, Depreciation and Amortization.** Carry the amount of depreciation that you calculate on this form over to line 13 of Schedule C.

For property that you started using prior to 1998, Form 4562 isn't required. On line 13 of Schedule C, just enter the amount that you're entitled to based on the useful life of the asset from the applicable schedule that we provide in this chapter. For example, if you want to depreciate an asset that has a five-year useful life, use Table 11-7. If you're depreciating cars, computers, or cellular phones, however, you must use Form 4562 because you can depreciate only the business portion of these items.

IRS depreciation percentages

To calculate the amount of depreciation that you're entitled to claim, glance at the IRS depreciation tables (Tables 11-7 through 11-10). For business property other than real estate, you'll notice that each table has two categories: *half-year convention* and *mid-quarter convention.* Usually, you use the half-year convention because the mid-quarter convention comes into play when the business assets you acquired and started using in the last three months of the year exceed 40 percent of all business assets that you placed in service during the year. Got that? Read on and follow the examples for both types of depreciation conventions.

Table 11-7 — MACRS (Modified Accelerated Cost Recovery System): 5-Year Property

Year	Half-Year Convention	First Quarter	Mid-Quarter Convention Second Quarter	Third Quarter	Fourth Quarter
1	20.00%	35.00%	25.00%	15.00%	5.00%
2	32.00	26.00	30.00	34.00	38.00
3	19.20	15.60	18.00	20.40	22.80
4	11.52	11.01	11.37	12.24	13.68
5	11.52	11.01	11.37	11.30	10.94
6	5.76%	1.38%	4.26%	7.06%	9.58%

Table 11-8 — MACRS: 7-Year Property

Year	Half-Year Convention	First Quarter	Mid-Quarter Convention Second Quarter	Third Quarter	Fourth Quarter
1	14.29%	25.00%	17.85%	10.71%	3.57%
2	24.49	21.43	23.47	25.51	27.55
3	17.49	15.31	16.76	18.22	19.68
4	12.49	10.93	11.97	13.02	14.06
5	8.93	8.75	8.87	9.30	10.04
6	8.92	8.74	8.87	8.85	8.73

Table 11-9 — MACRS: 15-Year Property

Year	Half-Year Convention	First Quarter	Mid-Quarter Convention Second Quarter	Third Quarter	Fourth Quarter
1	5.00%	8.75%	6.25%	3.75%	1.25%
2	9.50	9.13	9.38	9.63	9.88
3	8.55	8.21	8.44	8.66	8.89
4	7.70	7.39	7.59	7.80	8.00
5	6.93	6.65	6.83	7.02	7.20
6	6.23	5.99	6.15	6.31	6.48

Table 11-10 — Residential Rental Property (27.5-Year)

Use the row of the month of the taxable year placed in service.

	Year 1	Year 2	Year 3	Year 4	Year 5	Year 6
Jan.	3.485%	3.636%	3.636%	3.636%	3.636%	3.636%
Feb.	3.182	3.636	3.636	3.636	3.636	3.636
Mar.	2.879	3.636	3.636	3.636	3.636	3.636
Apr.	2.576	3.636	3.636	3.636	3.636	3.636

(continued)

Table 11-10 (continued)

Use the row of the month of the taxable year placed in service.

	Year 1	Year 2	Year 3	Year 4	Year 5	Year 6
May	2.273	3.636	3.636	3.636	3.636	3.636
Jun.	1.970	3.636	3.636	3.636	3.636	3.636
Jul.	1.667	3.636	3.636	3.636	3.636	3.636
Aug.	1.364	3.636	3.636	3.636	3.636	3.636
Sept.	1.061	3.636	3.636	3.636	3.636	3.636
Oct.	0.758	3.636	3.636	3.636	3.636	3.636
Nov.	0.455	3.636	3.636	3.636	3.636	3.636
Dec.	0.152	3.636	3.636	3.636	3.636	3.636

Half-year convention depreciation

Suppose that you're depreciating a computer that you purchased for $5,000 in 1998. First, you must look up its useful life. Computers have a useful life of five years, so use the depreciation percentages for 5-year property. Okay, easy enough so far.

Under the half-year convention for 5-year property (Table 11-7), you find 20 percent as the amount. For 1998, you're entitled to a $1,000 depreciation deduction ($5,000 × 20 percent). In 1999, you'd multiply the $5,000 cost by 32 percent for a deduction of $1,600. And then you use 19.20, 11.52, 11.52, and 5.76 percent in each of the succeeding years. Fun calculations, right? Based on the convention rules, the write-off period for stuff is one year longer than its useful life. That's because in the first year you're entitled to only a half-year's worth of depreciation. The half-year convention rule means that all assets are considered to have been purchased on July 1 — which entitles you to only half the normal amount of depreciation in the first year.

Mid-quarter convention depreciation

Remember that you must use the mid-quarter convention if the business property that you placed in service during the last three months of the year exceeds 40 percent of all your business property placed in service during the year.

For example, you bought a calculator for $500 on February 1, 1998, and a copier for $1,000 on October 1, 1998. Under the half-year convention, you're entitled to a depreciation deduction of $300 ($1,500 × 20 percent). But because more than 40 percent of all your business property was bought and placed into service the last three months of the year, you have to switch to the mid-quarter convention. So here's how you have to separately compute the depreciation for these two pieces of equipment.

Under the mid-quarter convention for 5-year property, for an asset purchased in the first quarter, the depreciation rate is 35 percent. Therefore, you're entitled to a $175 depreciation deduction ($500 × 35 percent) for the calculator. For the copier, you have to use the 5-percent rate for property bought during the fourth quarter ($1,000 × 5 percent), which entitles you to a $50 deduction.

The long and the short of all this is that by using the mid-quarter convention, you can claim only half the depreciation that you normally would. At this point, you're probably scratching the back of your head and wondering who thinks of these things. We must confess that we don't know either. Just play along.

Additions or improvements to property

An addition or improvement that you make to your property is treated as a separate item for the purposes of depreciation — regardless of how you depreciate the original asset. For example, you own a house that you've rented since 1984 and have been depreciating over 19 years (you were allowed to use that short of a useful life back then). And in 1998, you added a new roof. The roof has to be depreciated over 27.5 years and at the rate in the IRS depreciation tables. The depreciation tables reproduced in this chapter go up to only six years. For tables that go beyond six years, send for IRS Publication 534 *(Depreciation)*.

Your buying bonanza: The $18,500 deduction

Instead of computing depreciation by using the standard depreciation tables, you can elect to deduct up to $18,500 of the cost of business equipment that you purchased and placed into service in 1998. Actually, this isn't a one-time deduction; you can do this every year. One taxpayer that we know of liked this deduction so much that he deducted the same amount every year. Remember, however, that you have to spend up to $18,500 to get the write-off.

The 1999 limit jumps to $19,000 and then on to $25,000 in gradual increases.

For a car, the maximum that you can expense in 1998 is $3,160. Real estate doesn't qualify for this deduction, but furniture and refrigerators used in apartment buildings do. So if you bought office machinery, equipment, furniture, or a computer, reach for **Form 4562** and write off the whole thing on line 2 of Part I — provided the total cost doesn't exceed $18,500 — instead of hassling with those darn IRS depreciation percentage tables and convention rules. Unlike the mid-quarter convention rule that you're forced to use if you purchase most of your equipment in the last quarter of the year, you can write off the whole $18,500 — as long as everything was placed in service by December 31.

If you buy a few items, you can pick and choose which ones you want to write off completely and which ones you don't. If, for example, you spend $28,500 for office equipment, you can write off $18,500 and depreciate the $10,000 balance by using the 20-percent rate for a total depreciation deduction of $20,500 ($18,500 + $2,000). If you have two assets of equal value, but one depreciates over 5 years and the other over 15 years, write off the one with the longer depreciation first.

Now for the fine print (there always has to be some — this is a tax book, after all). If you're married filing separately, you can deduct only $9,250. If you buy equipment costing more than $200,000, the $18,500 that you're entitled to deduct is reduced dollar for dollar by the amount over $200,000. So if the total cost is $218,500 or more, you can kiss your $18,500 write-off good-bye; you have to wade through the depreciation tables to compute your depreciation. Have a nice time. The second rule regarding the $18,500 expensing is that this deduction can't produce a loss from all your business activities. Suppose that your consulting income — after all other expenses — is $10,000, and you bought $18,500 worth of equipment. You can expense only $10,000. The $8,500 balance carries over to the next year. If you have enough consulting income after your other expenses, you can deduct it then. If you don't, keep carrying it over until you do.

But there is a pleasant surprise. You can count all your earned income to determine if you pass the *no-loss test.* So in the preceding example, if you or your spouse had at least $8,500 in wages, you can deduct the whole $18,500.

Line 14: Employee benefit programs

Enter here the premiums that you paid for your employees' accident, health, and group term life insurance coverage — but don't count the cost of your own insurance benefits here. See "Line 28: Self-employed health insurance deduction" in Chapter 7 to find out how you may be able to deduct 45 percent of your personal health insurance premiums.

Line 15: Insurance (other than health)

Enter on this line the premiums that you paid for business insurance, such as fire, theft, robbery, and general liability coverage on your business property.

Line 16: Interest

Here you can deduct interest on business loans. If you took out a mortgage on your house and used the proceeds of the loan to finance your business, deduct the interest here — and not on Schedule A. If you borrowed money for your business from other sources, such as a bank or even your credit card, deduct the interest on those loans here as well.

For the adventuresome who want to deduct interest on an income tax bill, see "Interest You Paid" in Chapter 9.

Line 17: Legal and professional services

On this line, enter any fees that you paid for tax advice and for preparing tax forms related to your business, as well as legal fees regarding business matters.

Professional services include fees for accounting, engineering, and consulting work that you pay for.

If you pay someone more than $600 (your accountant or lawyer, for example), you have to provide them with **Form 1099-MISC** by January 31 — just like we told you to do with commissions that you deducted on line 11.

The IRS must love lawyers. Because starting in 1998, you must report all payments that you made to your lawyer — even for the reimbursement of expenses that you were billed. Additionally, the present exemption that payments made to corporations don't have to be reported to the IRS on Form 1099 no longer applies to lawyers. Know any good lawyer jokes?

Line 18: Office expense

Enter your costs for stationery, paper supplies, postage, printer toner, and other consumable items that you use in the operation of your office or business.

Line 19: Pension and profit-sharing plans

Enter your contribution to your employees' Keogh or SEP account(s). As for your own Keogh or SEP, enter that amount on Form 1040 (line 29).

Employers with fewer than 100 employees may establish what's known as SIMPLE retirement plans. These plans have none of the mind-numbing rules to follow or forms to file that regular retirement plans have. A SIMPLE plan can also cover the owner(s) of a farm (see Chapter 21 for more about SIMPLE plans and other small business retirement plans).

Lines 20a and b: Rent or lease

If you rented or leased an auto, machinery, or equipment, enter the business portion of the rental payments on line 20a. But if you leased a car for more than 30 days, you may have to reduce your deduction by an amount called the *inclusion amount* if your leased car's value exceeded:

Year Lease Began	Amount
1998	$16,100
1997	15,800
1996	15,500
1995	15,500
1994	14,600
1993	14,300
1992	13,700
1991	13,400
1987–90	12,800

See the section "Line 10: Car and truck expenses" to compile the inclusion amount. IRS Publication 917 *(Business Use of a Car)* has the lease inclusion table.

On line 20b, enter the rent you paid your landlord.

Line 21: Repairs and maintenance

Enter the cost of routine repairs — such as the cost to repair your computer — on this line. But adding a new hard disk isn't a repair; that cost must be depreciated over five years unless it qualifies for the special election to write off the first $18,500 of business assets.

A repair (as opposed to an improvement) keeps your equipment or property in good operating condition. A repair that also prolongs the life of your equipment has to be depreciated, so make the most of the $18,500 deduction instead of depreciating the cost over its useful life.

If you're confused about what qualifies as a repair and what qualifies as an improvement, you're not alone. Through the years, the Tax Court has been clogged with cases dealing with repairs as current write-offs versus improvements that have to be depreciated. We suggest that you contact a tax advisor to evaluate your specific situation.

Line 22: Supplies

If your company manufactures a product, you report factory supplies here. In other words, you deduct the cost of supplies that contribute to the operation of the equipment that you use in your office or business. For example, if you operate a retail store, you enter the cost of mannequins, trim, packaging, and other such items on this line.

Line 23: Taxes and licenses

Here you deduct your business taxes, such as Social Security and unemployment insurance taxes for your employees. You also enter the costs of permits and business licenses. You don't deduct on this line the Social Security tax that you pay because you're self-employed; you can deduct half of this tax on line 27 of your 1040 (see Chapter 7 for more on how this deduction works).

Lines 24a–d: Travel, meals, and entertainment

To find out what you can deduct for travel, meals, and entertainment, see the explanation in Chapter 9 (in the "Lines 20–26: Job Expenses and Most Other Miscellaneous Deductions" section). There's no point repeating all that stuff again here!

Line 25: Utilities

Can you imagine what this line is for? If you're thinking of electric and telephone bills, for example, you hit the nail on the head. However, if you're claiming a home office deduction (discussed in further detail later in this chapter), your utility costs belong on **Form 8829 Expenses for Business Use of Your Home** and not here.

Line 26: Wages

Enter here the wages that you paid your employees. Payments to independent contractors, however, should be deducted on line 27. Deduction of independent contractor expenses is a hot issue with the IRS. If someone works on your premises and under your control, he or she is probably your employee, and the rules about withholding taxes and Social Security apply. However, if treating these types of workers as independent contractors is standard in your industry (that is, at least 25 percent of your industry treats them this way) and you issue these workers a 1099 at the end of the year, you may have an escape hatch.

Line 27: Other expenses

On the reverse side of Schedule C is Part V, a schedule where you list your expenses whose descriptions defy the neat categories of lines 8–26. Here you can enter dues, subscriptions to related business periodicals, messenger services, overnight express fees, and so on.

Line 28: Total expenses

Addition time — add lines 8 through 27. This is what it costs to operate your business.

Line 29: Tentative profit (loss)

Subtract line 28 from line 7. If line 28 is more than line 7, you have a loss, and you enter it as a negative number. For example, if you lost $10,000, enter it as –$10,000.

Line 30: Form 8829

Yes, you can deduct home office expenses — but the rules are tough. You must use **Form 8829, Expenses for Business Use of Your Home,** to claim the deduction for the portion that you use for business. You can find a copy of this form in the back of this book, as well as detailed instructions for filling out the form in Chapter 15, along with the rules you must follow to nail down this deduction. You can't take a loss because of the home office deduction. You can, however, carry over an excess deduction amount to another year's tax return.

Because only a portion of your total mortgage interest and real estate taxes gets deducted as part of your home office expenses, don't forget to deduct the balance of your total mortgage interest that you entered on line 10(a) of Form 8829, as well as the balance of your total real estate taxes from line 11(a) of this form. Your mortgage interest balance goes on line 10 of Schedule A; the real estate taxes balance goes on line 6 of Schedule A.

Line 31: Net profit or (loss)

After you arrive at your net profit or loss, copy it onto Form 1040 (line 12) and then on Schedule SE (line 2) so that you can compute the amount of Social Security tax that you have to pay. See Chapter 8 to find out how to complete Schedule SE.

Lines 32a and b: At-risk rules

Suppose that you borrow money to go into business. The at-risk rules limit the amount of business losses that you can deduct on borrowed money that you're personally not liable to repay. For example, you need $20,000 to go into business. You invest $10,000, and your rich uncle gives you $10,000 with the understanding that you only have to pay him back if the business is successful. You lose the entire $20,000. You can only deduct the $10,000 that you personally invested in your business. See Chapter 13 ("Lines 27–31: Name . . . and so on!") for more details on the at-risk rules. Basically, if you're personally responsible for all the liabilities of your business, check box 32a.

If you aren't personally responsible, see a tax professional because the rules in this area are anything but clear or simple.

Operating Loss

Suppose that you start a business and it produces an operating loss. In other words, your costs — not just equipment, but rent, salaries, and other expenses — exceed your income. You may write off that loss against any other income that you and your spouse made that year.

And get this. If the loss is greater than your combined income in the current year, you can carry it back over each of the past two years and obtain a refund on the tax that you paid at that time. The loss still isn't used up by carrying it back? You can carry it forward to offset your income in the next 20 years. The carryback is mandatory unless you elect to carry it only forward. See Chapter 19 for information on amending a prior year's return and carrying back losses.

Losses incurred before January 1, 1998, can be carried back three years and forwarded for only 15 years. The three-year carryback still applies to the *net operating loss* (NOL) for losses incurred by small businesses in a presidentially declared disaster area. A small business is one that earned $5 million or less of income in each of the three preceding years. Farmers get to carry bad losses five years. See Chapter 14.

Keep in mind, however, that you can't operate a part-time business that continually loses money. This situation is known as a *hobby loss*. If you don't show a profit in at least three of every five consecutive years, you could have a fight — with the IRS — on your hands. You have to show a profit in at least three of every five consecutive years, or the IRS declares your business a hobby and disallows your losses. The IRS doesn't consider your enterprise a business if you have continuing losses. No business, no business deductions. Some taxpayers have challenged this rule in Tax Court and won. They were able to prove that they ran their enterprises like a business, anticipated making a profit, and didn't.

Chapter 12

Capital Gains and Losses: Schedule D

In This Chapter

▶ Tax basis background stuff

▶ Your introduction to Schedule D

▶ Short-term capital gains and losses

▶ Long-term capital gains and losses

▶ How to handle Form 4797 (if you need to)

▶ How to deal with the sale of your home, worthless securities, stock options, and bad debts

*I*f you sell a security, such as a stock, bond, or mutual fund (or another investment held outside a tax-sheltered retirement account), and you sell it for more than you paid for it, you owe capital gains tax on the profit. Conversely, when you sell an investment at a loss, the loss is tax deductible. Although it may seem unfair, a loss on the sale of your home, auto, jewelry, art, and furniture isn't deductible.

Schedule D is the place where you plug in your profit or loss on the following examples:

✔ Your coin or stamp collection

✔ Jewelry and art

✔ Stocks and bonds

✔ Your home (if you can't exclude all of the gain)

✔ Household furnishings

The new law reduced the maximum capital gain rate from 28 percent to 20 percent (10 percent for those in the 15-percent bracket). For assets purchased after 2001 and held for five years, you're entitled to an even lower rate of 18 percent (8 percent for taxpayers in the 15-percent tax bracket). These rates don't apply to collectibles. So if you find a priceless antique in grandma's attic, the maximum capital gains rate didn't budge; it's still 28 percent. There is one additional capital gains rate: 25 percent. When you sell depreciable real estate, part of the profit — equal to the depreciation that you deducted through the years — is taxed at 25 percent, and the balance of the profit is taxed at 20 percent.

Taxing all the depreciation at 25 percent only relates to real estate you started to depreciate after 1986. If you started to depreciate prior to 1987, part of the depreciation gets taxed at 25 percent and part at regular tax rates. Our advice: If you sell real estate that you started depreciating before 1987, see a tax pro.

Tax Basis Background

Before we jump into completing Schedule D, a little background is necessary on gains and losses and how to figure them. When you understand these concepts, Schedule D shouldn't be too difficult. If you already understand these key concepts, you can cruise on ahead to the instructions for completing Schedule D.

In order to determine if you sold something at a taxable gain or deductible loss, you first have to compute its tax basis. *Basis* is the tax system's way of measuring what you paid for your investment in stocks, bonds, or real estate, for example. In addition to helping you to calculate your capital gains and capital losses, your basis is also used to figure deductions for depreciation, casualty losses, and charitable gifts.

For example, if you purchase 100 shares of the Informed Investor's Mutual Fund at $40 per share, your cost basis is considered to be $4,000, or $40 per share. Simple enough. Now suppose that this fund pays a dividend of $2 per share (so you get $200 for your 100 shares) and that you choose to reinvest this dividend to purchase more shares of the mutual fund. If, at the time of the dividend payment, the fund has increased to $50 per share, your $200 dividend purchases four more shares. Now you own 104 shares. At $50 per share, your 104 shares are worth $5,200. But what's your basis now? Your basis is your original investment ($4,000) plus subsequent investments ($200) for a total of $4,200. Thus, if you sold all your shares now, you'd have a taxable profit of $1,000 (current value of $5,200 less the amount that you invested).

With a home, the basis works the same way. The tax basis of your home is increased for any improvements that you made and costs connected with purchasing the property — such as the fee that you paid the title company and your attorney. Any real estate broker's commission that you paid when you sold your home is also added to your tax basis, as well as any attorney and closing fees that you paid when you sold your home. To determine your profit (we hope that you had one), subtract your basis from the sales price. Make sure that you take more than a peek at "Use Schedule D When You Sell Your Home," later in this chapter, to see if you qualify for a $500,000 (couples) or $250,000 (if single) exemption from tax on the profit that can be claimed on the sale of a home.

If you own rental real estate, your basis is reduced by depreciation and any casualty losses that you may have deducted (see Chapter 23 for more details).

✔ **Property you purchased:** This tax basis is usually your cost increased by improvements or decreased by depreciation and casualty losses.

✔ **Property received as a gift:** To figure the basis of property that you received as a gift, you must know the donor's basis at the time the gift was made, its *fair market value* (FMV) at the time the gift was made, and any gift tax that the donor paid.

  • If the FMV at the time of the gift was *more than* the donor's basis, then your basis for figuring a gain or loss is the donor's basis.

    For example, suppose that your father gives you a gift of stock that cost him $5,000 but was worth $12,000 when he gave it to you. Your basis for figuring a gain or loss is $5,000.

  • If the FMV at the time of the gift was *less than* the donor's basis, your basis for figuring a gain is the donor's basis, and your basis for figuring a loss is the fair market value at the time of the gift.

In other words, the IRS says, "Heads we win, tails we win." For example, suppose that your father gave you stock that cost him (basis) $10,000, but was worth (FMV) $8,000 when he gave it to you. (Nice gift, huh?) If you sell the stock for $12,000, you have a $2,000 gain (sale price of stock $12,000 – $10,000 donor's basis). If you sell the stock for $7,000, you have a $1,000 loss (sale price of stock $7,000 – $8,000 FMV). If the sale price is between the FMV and the donor's cost ($8,000 and $10,000 in the example), you have neither a gain nor a loss. If your father paid gift tax when he gave you the gift, a portion of the gift tax that he paid is added to your basis.

✔ **Property that you inherited:** Your basis for figuring a gain or loss is usually the fair market value on the decedent's date of death. Sometimes — to save on taxes — the executor of an estate is allowed to use an alternative valuation date, which is six months after the date of death. When you inherit something, make sure that the executor gives you the estate tax valuation, because when you sell the asset, that figure will be your tax basis.

✔ **Property received for services:** The amount that you're required to include in your income becomes your basis. Suppose that for putting a deal together, you receive 100 shares of stock valued at $10,000. Because you had to pay tax on the value of the shares, your tax basis for the 100 shares is $10,000.

✔ **Property received in a divorce:** You use your spouse's basis. Generally, neither spouse is required to pay tax on property transferred as part of a divorce settlement.

See Chapter 3 for what to do if you received property or a stock as a gift or by inheritance and you don't have a clue as to its tax basis or FMV, or if you believe the values the donor or executor gave you are off the mark.

What Part of Schedule D?

Unfortunately the 1997 law wreaked havoc with this form. Whereas the old Schedule D had 19 lines, the 1998 version has 54.

Schedule D is now structured into four major parts (see Figure 12-1). Part I is for reporting short-term gains and losses. Part II is for reporting long-term gains and losses. (Part III summarizes the short- and long-term gains and losses. Part IV computes the maximum capital gains tax that you have to pay. The IRS now includes a Schedule D-1, which is continuation sheet for those of you with lots of gains and losses.)

If you hold property for one year or less, the gain or loss is *short term*. If you hold property for more than a year, the gain or loss is *long term*.

You list all your individual capital gains and losses on line 1 or 8. Line 1 is for short-term gains and losses, and line 8 is for long-term gains and losses.

Why the distinction? Because the IRS wants to make life complicated. The tax rates for long-term and short-term gains and losses differ. If your net capital gain is a long-term gain, depending on the type of asset and your tax bracket, the tax on the gain may be as low as 10 or 20 percent, but it can't exceed 28 percent. If the capital gain is short-term, the tax on it can be as high as the income tax brackets go (currently 39.6 percent at the federal level).

Thankfully, the 1998 law did away with the requirement that you had to hold an asset for more than 18 months to get the lowest capital gains rate. Since January 1, 1998, long-term gains have only one holding period — more than 12 months.

SCHEDULE D
(Form 1040)

Department of the Treasury
Internal Revenue Service   (99)

Capital Gains and Losses

▶ Attach to Form 1040.   ▶ See Instructions for Schedule D (Form 1040).
▶ Use Schedule D-1 for more space to list transactions for lines 1 and 8.

OMB No. 1545-0074

1998

Attachment
Sequence No. **12**

Name(s) shown on Form 1040

Your social security number

Part I   Short-Term Capital Gains and Losses–Assets Held One Year or Less

(a) Description of property (Example: 100 sh. XYZ Co.)	(b) Date acquired (Mo., day, yr.)	(c) Date sold (Mo., day, yr.)	(d) Sales price (see page D-6)	(e) Cost or other basis (see page D-6)	(f) GAIN or (LOSS) Subtract (e) from (d)	
1						

2 Enter your short-term totals, if any, from Schedule D-1, line 2	**2**			
3 Total short-term sales price amounts. Add column (d) of lines 1 and 2 . . .	**3**			
4 Short-term gain from Form 6252 and short-term gain or (loss) from Forms 4684, 6781, and 8824		**4**		
5 Net short-term gain or (loss) from partnerships, S corporations, estates, and trusts from Schedule(s) K-1		**5**		
6 Short-term capital loss carryover. Enter the amount, if any, from line 8 of your 1997 Capital Loss Carryover Worksheet		**6** ( )		
7 **Net short-term capital gain or (loss).** Combine lines 1 through 6 in column (f) . . . . ▶		**7**		

Part II   Long-Term Capital Gains and Losses–Assets Held More Than One Year

(a) Description of property (Example: 100 sh. XYZ Co.)	(b) Date acquired (Mo., day, yr.)	(c) Date sold (Mo., day, yr.)	(d) Sales price (see page D-6)	(e) Cost or other basis (see page D-6)	(f) GAIN or (LOSS) Subtract (e) from (d)	(g) 28% RATE GAIN or (LOSS) * (see instr. below)
8						

9 Enter your long-term totals, if any, from Schedule D-1, line 9	**9**				
10 Total long-term sales price amounts. Add column (d) of lines 8 and 9 . . .	**10**				
11 Gain from Form 4797, Part I; long-term gain from Forms 2439 and 6252; and long-term gain or (loss) from Forms 4684, 6781, and 8824		**11**			
12 Net long-term gain or (loss) from partnerships, S corporations, estates, and trusts from Schedule(s) K-1		**12**			
13 Capital gain distributions. See page D-2		**13**			
14 Long-term capital loss carryover. Enter in both columns (f) and (g) the amount, if any, from line 13 of your 1997 Capital Loss Carryover Worksheet . . .		**14** ( ) ( )			
15 Combine lines 8 through 14 in column (g)		**15**			
16 **Net long-term capital gain or (loss).** Combine lines 8 through 14 in column (f) . . . . ▶		**16**			

Next: Go to Part III on the back.

*28% Rate Gain or Loss includes **all** ™collectibles gains and lossesʃ (as defined on page D-6) and up to 50% of the eligible gain on qualified small business stock (see page D-5).

For Paperwork Reduction Act Notice, see Form 1040 instructions.   Cat. No. 11338H   Schedule D (Form 1040) 1998

Figure 12-1:
Schedule D,
page 1.

Property defined

Definitions are the spice of life for IRS agents. Here's an important one.

When most people refer to property, they mean real estate. But when the IRS talks about property, it could be anything that you own, such as a stock, bond, car, boat, or computer. So when you see the term *property* on a form, the government is talking about more than the old homestead.

Details for figuring short term or long term

In most cases, whether you've held a security or other asset for 12 months or more is obvious. Here are some details that may help in less clear cases.

For securities traded on an established securities market, you begin counting the days in your holding period the day after the trading date on which you bought the securities and stop on the trading date on which you sold them. For holding period purposes, ignore the settlement date — which is the date when you actually pay the broker for a purchase or get paid from the broker for a sale.

For property that you received as a gift, you're considered to have purchased the property on the same day

that the donor did — and not on the date of the gift — if you use the donor's tax basis as your basis. However, the holding period starts on the date of the gift if you sell it at a loss and you're required to use the fair market value of the property when it was given to you. Property inherited via someone's estate is treated as a sale of a long-term capital asset, even if you sold the shares or property the day after you received them. The one-year rule is ignored.

When you purchase assets such as stocks or bonds by exercising an option, the holding period starts the day after the option is exercised — and not on the day that you received or purchased the option.

Schedule D: Columns

After you determine whether the security that you sold goes in the short-term (Part I) or long-term (Part II) section, you're ready to work your way across the page. We must say that Schedule D is one of the least attractive IRS schedules. We'll walk you through an example and then explain how to complete the remaining line numbers.

Suppose that you sold 100 shares of General Motors stock for $4,000 on April 17, 1998. You had paid $6,000 for the shares on April 16, 1997. Therefore, you have a capital loss of $2,000. To figure out whether the loss is long- or short-term, start counting on April 17. The 17th of each month starts the beginning of a new month. Because you sold the shares on April 17, 1998 — one day over 12 months — the loss is long term. (Had you sold them on April 16 — exactly 12 months — the loss would have been short term.) Now plug the loss into Schedule D on line 8.

Column (a) Description of the property
100 shares of General Motors

Column (b) Date acquired
4-16-97

Column (c) Date sold
4-17-98

Column (d) Sales price
$4,000

Column (e) Cost or other basis
$6,000

Column (f) Gain or <loss> for entire year
<$2,000>

Column (g) 28% rate gain or <loss>

-0- If you were selling a collectible (art for instance), then this column would come into play. Column (g) informs the IRS that the gain in column (f) is subject to the 28 percent maximum capital gain and not the lower 20 or 10 percent rate.

When there is an entry in column (f) and no entry in column (g), it tells the IRS that the regular 20-percent maximum rate applies or that the maximum 10-percent rate applies if you're in the 15-percent tax bracket.

If you need more spaces because lines 1 and 8 can accommodate only four stock transactions, use Schedule D-1 to list the rest of your stock trades.

Figuring Your Profit or Loss

Now that you understand where the numbers go on the form, where the heck do you get the numbers? The following list tells you where:

- ✔ **Stocks and bonds:** If you sold a stock or bond, you will receive a **Form 1099-B, Proceeds from Broker and Barter Exchange Transactions,** or an equivalent from your broker by January 31, 1999. The IRS also gets a copy of this form. Form 1099-B lists the date of every sale and the amount after the broker's commission has been deducted. You enter this information on Schedule D. The IRS checks to see if it's correct. Just another friendly service by the folks at the IRS.

  A redemption or retirement of bonds or notes at their maturity is also considered a sale or trade and must be reported on Schedule D, whether or not you realized a gain or loss on the redemption. The tax basis is generally your purchase price plus the broker's commission. If you acquired the shares as a gift, your tax basis is the same as the donor's basis if you sold the shares at a gain, and the lower of the donor's basis or the FMV on the date of the gift if you sold the shares at a loss, plus any gift tax that was paid. If you inherited the shares, the basis is the FMV on the decedent's date of death. If you acquired the shares in exchange for services, the basis is the value that you had to pay tax on when you received the shares.

- ✔ **Stock dividends and splits:** If you receive additional stock as part of a nontaxable stock dividend or stock split, you must reduce the per-share basis (but not the total basis) of your original stock. You make this conputation by dividing the cost of the stock by the total number of shares that you now have. You must also reduce your basis when you receive nontaxable cash distributions because this transaction is considered a return on your investment.

  For example, suppose that in 1991 you bought 100 shares of ABC stock for $500, or $5 a share. In 1992, you bought 100 shares of ABC stock for $800, or $8 a share. In 1993, ABC declared a 2-for-1 stock split. You now have 200 shares of stock with a basis of $2.50 a share ($500 cost ÷ 200 shares) and 200 shares with a basis of $4 a share ($800 cost ÷ 200 shares).

  Or suppose that you purchased shares for $10,000 and received a $500 nontaxable dividend. Your tax basis is now $9,500 ($10,000 – $500).

- ✔ **Identifying shares:** If you buy and sell securities at different times in varying quantities and you can't definitely identify the securities that you sell, the basis of those sold is figured under the *first-in first-out method* — the first securities that you acquired are considered the first ones sold.

  If you bought 100 shares of GM at $30 and 100 at $50 and then sold 100 shares at $60, you would pay less tax if you used the shares that you purchased for $50 as your cost. You can do this stuff only if you specifically tell your broker to sell the shares purchased for $50; otherwise, you're deemed to have sold the 100 shares you bought at $30 per share.

✔ **Mutual fund shares:** When you sell shares of a fund, you can average the cost of the shares sold if they were bought at different times — or you can specifically identify the shares that you sold. Remember that the dividends used to purchase additional shares on which you paid tax every year increase your tax basis for determining a gain or loss when the shares are sold.

For example, suppose that you bought 1,000 shares of a fund for $10,000. Through the years, you received $5,000 in dividends that you used to buy additional shares. Your tax basis is $15,000 ($10,000 original cost plus the $5,000 of dividends received) for the shares that you now own.

You can use three methods to determine your tax cost, and your choice of which method to use depends on how your fund has performed and whether you want to pay taxes now (if you're in a lower bracket this year, for example) or later.

- The first way to determine your tax cost is the specific-share identification method. You simply decide which of your shares you want to sell, and make sure that you note it on the confirmation slip. For example, you bought 100 shares at $10 a share and another 100 shares for $20 a share. If you sell 100 shares, you can designate the 100 shares that cost $20 as being sold, thereby reducing your profit and the tax that you have to pay.

- The second method is called the first-in, first-out method, meaning that you always sell the shares that you've owned the longest period of time.

- The third and most complex option is the average-cost method. You must select either the single- or double-category option. With the single-category, you divide the amount that you paid for your shares (including reinvested dividends) by the number of shares that you own. Eureka! Average cost. Under this method, you're considered to have sold your long-term holdings first.

  The double-category method allows you to sell either your short-term or long-term holdings. You divide your shares into short- and long-term holdings at the time of the sale, and then you compute the average cost for each category.

✔ **Undistributed capital gains:** Here's an oddity that you shouldn't overlook. If your fund had capital gains that it didn't distribute to its shareholders, you can increase the tax cost of your fund's shares, which in turn reduces the tax that you eventually have to pay when you sell. We often see undistributed capital gains with technology and bio-tech funds. You'll be sent **Form 2439, Notice to Shareholders of Undistributed Long-Term Capital Gains.** You report your share of the undistributed gains and get a credit for the tax paid by the fund (entered on line 63, Form 1040), which is taxed at the 35-percent corporate rate. Your tax cost gets increased by the difference between the capital gain that was retained by the fund and the actual tax paid by the fund on your behalf. We bet that you thought that mutual funds represented the simplest way to invest in the market. This way of reporting the gain and the tax paid by the fund on your behalf puts you in the same position as if you actually received the capital gains, paid the tax, and reinvested the difference.

For capital gains retained by a mutual fund before August 6, 1997, you increase your tax cost (*basis* in IRS jargon) by a flat 65 percent of the capital gains retained by the fund. Here is the rule for dividends retained after August 6, 1997: Suppose that your fund retains $1,000 of your capital gain and pays $300 tax. You report the $1,000 as a capital gain dividend and get a $300 credit on your return for the tax paid by the fund. You also get to increase the tax basis of your fund by $700.

Now you have all the information that you need to tackle your 1998 Schedule D.

Part I, Lines 1 – 7: Short-Term Capital Gains and Losses — Assets Held One Year or Less

Line 1 should be a breeze if you fine-tuned your form skills in the preceding General Motors example. Now you use your very own short-term financial gains and losses as examples and complete the columns for line 1. If you have more than four items, you can list more on Schedule D-1.

Line 2: Enter your short-term totals, if any, from Schedule D-1, Line 2

Why the need for Schedule D-1? Because line 1 has space for only four trades. If you had more, enter them on Schedule D-1, add them all up, and enter the total sales price from Schedule D-1 in column (d) of this line. Enter the profit or <loss> that you computed on Schedule D-1 in column (f) on this line as well.

Line 3: Total short-term sales price amounts

Follow the instructions. Add column (d) of lines 1 and 2. Why? The IRS wants to compare the stock trades that you're reporting with the trades that your broker said you made and reported to the IRS on Form 1099-B

Line 4: Short-term gain from Form 6252, and short-term gain or <loss> from Forms 4684, 6781, and 8824

All these form numbers! Because these forms rarely apply to most people, you may as well use them to play the lottery. Seriously, most people are going to deal with only **Form 4684, Casualties and Theft** at some specific point in their lives. We cover this form in Chapter 9.

For those of you who are curious, **Form 6252** is for installment sales, **Form 8824** is for like-kind exchanges, and **Form 6781** is for commodity straddles. You can find more on Form 6252 later in this chapter; if the other two forms apply to you, we suggest that you consult a tax advisor. Enter the short-term gains or losses from these forms on line 4 of Schedule D.

Line 5: Net short-term gain or <loss> from partnerships, S Corporations, estates, and trusts from Schedule (s) K-1

Short-term gains or losses from a partnership, an S Corporation, an estate, or a trust are reported on a schedule called a K-1. On line 5, enter the short-term gain or loss as indicated on the K-1 (short-term gains and losses only; long-term gains and losses go to line 12).

Line 6: Short-term capital loss carryover

If you had more short-term losses than gains in previous years, the balance is called a *carryover*. If your short-term losses exceeded your long-term gains, you're allowed to deduct up to $3,000 of those losses against your other income and carry over the balance to future years. If you don't have any gains next year, you may deduct $3,000 on next year's Schedule D. You can keep carryover stuff until it's used up. For example, suppose that you had a $10,000 short-term loss in 1997 and no long-term gains or losses. You were allowed to write off $3,000 in 1997, and the $7,000 that you carried over to 1998 is entered on line 6.

Line 7: Net short-term gain or <loss>

Combine lines 1 through 6 in column (f) and enter the total here. Just a little more addition and subtraction to make your day complete.

Part II, Lines 8 – 16: Long-Term Capital Gains and Losses — Assets Held More than One Year

As you did in Part I, fill in the columns for your long-term gains and losses. Schedule D-1 is available to list all your trades in case you had more than can fit on line 8 of this form. This part has one more column than Part I. Why? To let the IRS know whether your gain is subject to the maximum 20-percent rate (it's 10 percent if you're in the 15-percent bracket or the 28-percent rate on collectibles).

When estates or heirs sell property that they inherited, they automatically get the long-term rate.

Line 9: Enter your long-term totals, if any, from Schedule D-1, Line 9

Just like you did on line 2 for short-term gains or losses, enter the totals of your long-term gains or losses from Schedule D-1 here. The total sales price goes in column (d). Enter your gain or <loss> in column (f) and the amount of your gain or loss that's subject to the 28-percent rate in column (g). This column is very important because it lets the IRS know whether your capital gain is subject to the 20-percent rate or 10-percent rate (if you're in the 15-percent tax bracket) or if your entire profit is going to be taxed at the 28-percent maximum rate because you sold a collectible — for example, an antique chair.

Line 10: Total long-term sales price amounts

Add column (d) of lines 9 and 10. The IRS compares this figure to determine whether you reported all the sales that your broker reported to the IRS. If this number doesn't agree with what your broker reported on Form 1099-B, you can expect to hear from the IRS in about 18 months that you didn't report all your sales and that you owe additional tax and interest.

Line 11: Gain from Form 4797; long-term gain from Forms 2439 and 6252; and long-term gain or <loss> from Forms 4684, 6781, and 8824

Here are some more lottery numbers. Everything that we said in line 4 applies here — plus **Form 2439, Notice to Shareholder of Undistributed Capital Gains,** and **Form 4797, Sales of Business Property.**

If you received a Form 2439, don't overlook the tax benefits that you're entitled to in the section on mutual funds in this chapter.

Form 4797, Sales of Business Property

The odds of having to complete any of those other nasty forms are thankfully small. But just in case you sell a business property, such as a building or an office copier, and have to deal with **Form 4797,** here are some tips to help you get through that form.

First of all, you should know that the reason for a separate form is that the tax treatment of this type of sale is extremely complex. So what's new? Long-term gains can be taxed as low as 10, 20, 25, or 28 percent, depending on your tax bracket and the type of asset, instead of at the regular rates, which can be as high as 39.6 percent. The government believes that the new maximum rates are too good a deal — many taxpayers were claiming a depreciation deduction on the real estate that they owned, as well as having any gain when they sold the property taxed at the lower capital gains rate. So the new maximum rate for the part of the profit equal to the depreciation deducted through the years is taxed at 25 percent. The balance of the profit is taxed at 20 (or 10) percent.

Here's how this depreciation rule for real estate works. Say you sold a building for $400,000 that you originally paid $200,000 for. Through the years, you claimed depreciation of $100,000, which reduces your tax basis for figuring your profit to $100,000. You have a $300,000 profit — $400,000 minus your cost ($200,000) reduced by your depreciation ($100,000). Of the $300,000 profit, the $100,000, representing deductions you took for depreciation, is taxed at 25 percent, and the $200,000 balance is taxed at 20 (or 10) percent. And you thought being Donald Trump was easy.

If you think this sounds complicated, you should know that this is the rule for real estate you started to depreciate after 1986. For depreciation claimed before 1987, part is taxed at the regular rate and part at 25 percent. Which part? See a tax professional.

The previous example explains why Form 4797 was invented. Generally, if you sell a business asset for a profit, the part of the gain that equals the depreciation deductions that you took through the years isn't taxed as a capital gain; it's taxed at your regular tax rate. The rule is worth repeating. With real estate, the part of the profit relating to the depreciation that you claimed is taxed at 25 percent. For all other property, depreciation is taxed at whatever your tax bracket is. To make this calculation, first you must figure out your tax basis of the property. Your basis is the price that you paid minus the total depreciation that you've taken over the years.

For example, suppose that you purchased machinery for $10,000 and that you used it in your business. In the three years that you owned it, you took depreciation deductions totaling $7,120. This step reduces your tax basis to $2,880 ($10,000 cost – $7,120 depreciation). Then you figure your profit. Your profit is the price that you sold the property for minus your tax basis. The next step is to figure out what part of that profit is to be taxed at regular rates and what part is to be taxed at capital gains tax rates. This procedure is known as *depreciation recapture* — IRS jargon for getting taxed at regular tax rates (as opposed to the capital-gain tax rates) on the part of the profit that equals the depreciation deductions that you took in previous years. Any amount of profit that's left over is taxed at the capital gains tax rates.

Perhaps you sold that same machinery (in the preceding example) for $5,880. Your profit is $3,000 ($5,880 sale price – $2,880 tax basis). You then subtract the depreciation deductions that you took ($3,000 – $7,120 = –$4,120). If you come up with a negative number, the full profit ($3,000) is taxed at your regular tax rate. On the other hand, if you sold the machinery for $11,000, your profit would be $8,120 ($11,000 sale price – $2,880 tax basis). Subtract the amount of depreciation that you claimed ($8,120 profit – $7,120 depreciation = $1,000). $7,120 (the amount of depreciation that you claimed) is taxed at your regular tax rate, and the $1,000 that's left over is taxed as a long-term capital gain (if you owned the machinery for more than one year).

For the purposes of depreciation, business property is divided into two types:

- ✔ Auto, business equipment, and machinery
- ✔ Real estate

All the depreciation deducted in the first category is recaptured if the property is sold at a gain. For real estate, depreciation is recaptured if there's a profit when it's sold, depending on whether you started to depreciate it before 1981 or between 1982 and 1986. Real estate that you started to depreciate after 1986 isn't subject to the recapture rules.

The depreciation recapture rules don't apply to business property sold at a loss. The loss is deductible from your income without limitation. The part of the profit that's recaptured and taxed at your regular tax rate is carried over from Form 4797 to Form 1040 (line 14). The long-term capital gain portion is carried over from Form 4797 to Schedule D (line 11). Use the long-term capital gain worksheet in Chapter 8 (in "Line 40: Tax") to make sure that you don't overpay.

This stuff may be more than you care to know about the sale of business property. But before you even contemplate the sale of business property, seek advice. If the amount involved is large, make sure that you get the best advice possible. See Chapter 2 for information about how to pick a good tax specialist.

Form 6252, Installment Sale Income

Here's the story on **Form 6252, Installment Sale Income.** Suppose that you sold a parcel of land for $60,000 in 1998. You paid $15,000 for it and will receive $10,000 in 1998 — and $10,000 a year for the next five years. You don't report the $45,000 profit that you made in 1998. You report a percentage of the profit as each installment is received.

You report the $10,000 that you receive every year on Form 6252, but you pay tax on only $7,500 of it, or 75 percent of what you received. (Your $45,000 profit is 75 percent of your $60,000 selling price.) The $2,500 that you don't pay tax on is the recovery of your cost. The $7,500 profit that you owe tax on is transferred to Schedule D.

Additionally, you can elect out of the installment method and report the entire gain in the year of sale. You may want to go this way if you have a great deal of itemized deductions that would be wasted because they're more than your income (or if you're in an Alternative Minimum Tax situation). See line 51, Chapter 8 for more about this tax.

If you have more deductions than income, you'll waste those excess deductions. Don't throw them out like garbage. For example, say that you have $10,000 in salary income, and personal exemptions and itemized deductions come to $55,000. You could report another $45,000 of income before you have to pay a dime in tax. So reporting all the income from an installment sale in the year of the sale would make sense in this example.

Line 12: Net long-term gain or <loss> from partnerships, S Corporations, estates, and trusts from Schedule(s) K-1

Line 12 is similar to line 5. You report long-term gains and losses as indicated on Schedule K-1 from partnerships, S Corporations, estates, and trusts on line 12.

Line 13: Capital gain distributions

Mutual fund distributions are reported on Form 1099-DIV. Capital gain distributions received from a partnership, an S Corporation, or an estate or trust are reported on a schedule called a K-1. You enter these distributions on line 13.

Some mutual funds with a fiscal year beginning in 1997 and ending in 1998 may have capital gains to which the old 18-month holding period (which was the law in 1997) may apply — for example, sales where the property was held more than 12 months but less than 18 months. These types of gains are subject to the maximum 28-percent rate and not the 20-percent rate. In column (g), you have to enter the part of your gain from column (f) that's subject to the 28-percent rate. Say that you have two capital dividends — one for $800 and one for $200 — that are subject to the 28-percent rate. Enter $1,000 in column (f) and $200 in column (g). This lets the IRS know that, of the $1,000 gain, $800 can't be taxed at a rate higher than 20 percent, and $200 can't be taxed at a rate higher than 28 percent.

Line 14: Long-term capital loss carryover

Enter on this line your long-term capital losses that you couldn't deduct in previous years because you didn't have any capital gains in those years. "Line 6: Short-term capital loss carryover" explains how to handle carryovers. Also enter your carryover loss in column (g). If you have a capital loss carryover, you apply it to your gains in the following order: 28-percent gains, then 25-percent gains, and then 20 (or 10) -percent gains. For example, you have a $5,000 1997 carryover loss. In 1998, you have a $10,000 gain that's subject to the 20 (or 10) -percent maximum rate and a $10,000 gain that's subject to the 28-percent rate. You apply the $5,000 loss to the 28-percent gain, so you end up with a $10,000 gain taxed at 20 (or 10) percent and a $5,000 net gain taxed at 28 percent.

Line 15: Combine lines 8 through 14 in column (g)

Just follow the instructions. Add lines 8 through 14 in column (g). It couldn't be easier, and besides, you're almost finished.

Line 16: Net long-term gain or <loss>

Combine the amounts from lines 8 through 14 in column (f). The addition and subtraction never seem to end.

Part III, Lines 17 and 18b: Summary of Parts I and II

Hey, this part should be easy, right?

Line 17: Combine lines 7 and 16

If this line is a loss, go to line 18. If it's a gain, enter the gain on Form 1040, line 13.

Line 18: Capital losses

If your capital losses exceed your capital gains as reported on line 17 of Schedule D, you can deduct up to $3,000 of that loss ($1,500 if you're married and filing separately) from your other income. Any remaining loss after deducting the $3,000 is carried over to the next year and applied to capital gains. If you don't have any gains in 1999, you can deduct $3,000 in 1999 and carry any remaining balance over to future years until you use up the loss.

For example, you and your spouse sold securities in 1998 that resulted in a capital loss of $7,000. You had no other capital transactions. On your joint 1998 return, you can deduct $3,000. You can carry over the unused part of the loss — $4,000 ($7,000 – $3,000) — to 1999. If your capital loss had been $2,000, your capital loss deduction would have been $2,000. You would have no carryover to 1999.

Note: Capital losses can't be carried over after a taxpayer's death. They're deductible only on the final income tax return. The capital loss limits ($3,000 a year) apply in this situation, too. A decedent's estate or heirs can't deduct his or her unused capital loss.

Don't overpay your capital gains tax

You can end up paying more than the maximum tax rate for long-term capital gains if you're not careful. If this occurs, your only defense is if the computer at the IRS picks up on it, recomputes your tax, and sends you a refund. But if the computer is lazy, this may not happen. If you discover that you made an error in paying this tax for your 1997 return, see Chapter 19 for information on how to file an amended return and get a refund.

So if you don't want to pay more than the new 10-, 20-, 25-, or 28-percent rates on your long-term gains, check to see if your taxable income for your filing status is over the amounts shown in Table 8-2 and 8-3 in Chapter 8, line 40. If your income is over the amounts in these tables, you will overpay your capital gains tax unless you use the appropriate worksheet in Table 8-2 or Table 8-3. You compute your tax on line 40.

If you don't use the worksheets in either Table 8-2 or 8-3, you will overpay the tax on your capital gain.

Use Schedule D When You Sell Your Home

A married couple can exclude up to $500,000 of the profit they made on the sale of their home. A single person is entitiled to a $250,000 exclusion from the capital gains tax.

To qualify:

- ✔ You or your spouse must have owned the residence within two of the past five years, and both of you must have used it as your primary residence for two out of the past five years; a vacation home can't meet this test.

- ✔ If you're single, the two-year ownership and use rule also applies; you must have owned and used the residence as your primary residence for two of the past five years.

Here's how the two-out-of-the-past-five-years rule works. The look-back starts on the date of the sale. For example, suppose that you sold your home on July 1, 1998. Between July 1, 1993, and July 1, 1998, you must have owned and used your home as your principal residence for any two years during this period. The periods don't have to be consecutive as long as they add up to two years.

The $500,000/$250,000 exclusion replaces the old once-in-a-lifetime $125,000 exclusion that was only available to taxpayers over 55. In addition to raising the exclusion limits, the new provision is more generous in another way: You may use it repeatedly, but not more often than every two years. Sales before May 7, 1997 — the date that the law changed — are ignored when figuring out if you meet the rule of not more than one sale every two years.

When determining the two-year ownership and use of your current home, you can count the periods of ownership and use of all prior residences with respect to a gain that was rolled over into your current home. Under the old law, you could defer paying the tax on your profit from selling your home if you reinvested what you received from the sale in a new home within two years. In case you're scratching your head over this one, here's how it works: You sold a home in 1996 and made a $50,000 profit that you rolled into your new home that you purchased in 1998 before the two-year rollover period ended. You want to sell your new home in 1999. You can count the years of ownership and use of the home that you sold in 1996 along with your current home when determining whether you meet the current two-year use and ownership rule.

The two-year rule is waived for both singles and couples when they have to sell their homes within two years because a new job requires them to move, or for health reasons, or for other unforeseen circumstances (you didn't like your neighbors?). Actually, the IRS is probably referring to a natural disaster or the loss of a job. If any of these exceptions apply, the exclusion is prorated.

Old law/new law tax tip

If you sold your home in 1998, you can claim either the $500,000 exclusion if married or the $250,000 exclusion if single.

But what about pre-1998 dates?

- ✔ If you sold your home prior to May 7, 1997 (including 1995 and 1996), and had a small profit but chose to pay tax on your profit (because you didn't want to waste the once-a-lifetime $125,000 exclusion that the old law allowed), you want to amend either your 1995 or 1996 return by claiming the $125,000 exclusion (if you were over 55). This will wipe out the

profit you reported and entitle you to a refund (see Chapter 19 to find out how to do this).

- ✔ If you sold your home before May 7 or before August 6, 1997, or if you had a binding contract to sell your home before August 6, 1997, and expected to defer the gain by buying a new home but didn't in the required 2- or 4-year period (because you were abroad), you have to amend your return for the year that the sale was made.

If your state hasn't adopted the new law, you have to report your profit under the old rules.

Tips for the newly widowed, married, or divorced

The ownership and use as a primary residence includes the period that a deceased spouse used and owned the residence.

The exclusion is available on an individual basis. This means that the $250,000 exclusion is available for the qualifying principal residence of each spouse for those who file jointly but live apart — not an uncommon arrangement these days. If you should marry someone who used the exclusion within the two-year period before your marriage, you're entitled to your $250,000 exclusion and vice versa.

If a residence is transferred in a divorce, the time that the ex-spouse owned the residence is taken into account to determine whether the ownership and use tests have been met.

For example, say you buy a house on September 1, 1997, for $350,000, and you sell it for $550,000 on September 1, 1998 (if we're going to make up a story, it costs nothing extra to make up a good one) when you move from New York to Los Angeles to start a new job. You're single. Because you owned the house for 12 months of the required 24-month period, you're entitled to one-half of the $250,000 exclusion or $125,000. This means that only $75,000 of your $200,000 profit is subject to tax.

The $500,000/$250,000 exclusion may have given you the idea that, because of the increased exclusion amount, you no longer have to keep records of your purchases or improvements. Although this premise may be true for a lot of people, it doesn't necessarily apply to everyone. Suppose that you're single and buy a house for $300,000. Because you don't know what you'll sell the house for in 20 years, you'd better hang on to the bills for any improvements. Suppose that you sell your house for $600,000 — a $300,000 profit — but you're entitled to only a $250,000 exclusion. Good records can help you reduce the profit even further.

Computing your profit

Computing the profit on the sale of your home is simple.

From the sales price, subtract the following expenses in connection with the sale:

- ✔ Real estate broker's commission
- ✔ Attorney fees
- ✔ Title closing costs
- ✔ Advertising costs

From the sales price after the expenses of the sale, subtract the following:

- ✔ Original cost of your castle
- ✔ Closing costs and attorney fees at the time of purchase
- ✔ Improvements

What constitutes an improvement? Anything that adds to the value of your house or prolongs its life. Drapery rods, venetian blinds, termite-proofing, and shrubbery all fit the bill. If you own a condo or co-op, your cost basis also includes special assessments to improve the building, such as renovating the lobby or installing a new heating system. Co-op owners get an additional boost, because the part of their maintenance charges that goes to paying off the co-op's mortgage can also be added to their cost.

From your profit, subtract the exclusion that you're entitled to. If you're single, it's $250,000; for couples, it's $500,000. If the exclusion exceeds your profit, you can stop right there because there's nothing more to do. You need not report the sale on your return; the entire profit is tax-free. If your profit exceeds the exclusion, you owe tax and have to report the sale on Schedule D. For example, your profit is $410,000, and you're entitled to a $250,000 exclusion. You have to report the sale and pay tax on $160,000.

On the other hand, if your profit is $410,000 and you're entitled to a $500,000 exclusion, you need not report the sale on your return.

If you have a loss, it's not deductible. Profits above the exclusion amounts are. We're sure that you've heard this before: "Heads they win, tails you lose."

Reporting a profit that exceeds the exclusion

You no longer report the sale of your home on Form 2119, Sale or Exchange of a Residence. The reason: The IRS did away with this form. The last year it was used was 1997. You have to report the sale of your residence on Schedule D only if the profit exceeds the exclusion that you're entitled to.

Normally, the purchaser (typically via the title company) reports the sale on **Form 1099-S, Proceeds from Real Estate Transactions.** If you're single and the sale is for $250,000 — or $500,000 or less for couples — and you meet the other requirements such as the two-year principal residence test, you can sign a certificate at the time of the sale so that a Form 1099-S doesn't have to be sent to the IRS.

Here's how you report the sale of your home on Schedule D if you are required to:

- ✔ **Line 8(a):** Residence

- ✔ **Line 8(b):** Date purchased

- ✔ **Line 8(c):** Date sold

- ✔ **Line 8(d):** Sales price

- ✔ **Line 8(e):** Cost

  Here's where you enter your original cost plus closing costs (don't forget your friendly lawyer's fee), improvements, sales commission, other expenses of the sale (closing costs), and the exclusion that you're entitled to — $500,000 if married; $250,000 if single.

- ✔ **Line 8(f):** Profit

  But make sure that you enter the $250,000 or $500,000 exclusion on line 8(e) along with all your costs.

If you used part of your home as an office or rented out your home, the exclusion doesn't apply to any depreciation that you claimed after May 6, 1997. For example, if you claimed $10,000 in depreciation after May 6, 1997, and you're entitled to a $500,000 exclusion and the gain on the sale of your home is $400,000, you can only exclude $390,000 of that gain. You owe tax on the $10,000 of depreciation claimed after May 6, 1997.

Following the home office and rental rules

If you used part of your home for business, only the profit on the part of your home that you used as your residence qualifies for the exclusion. You owe tax on the profit related to the part that you used for business. You report this profit on **Form 4797, Sales of Business Property,** which then gets carried over to Schedule D.

Here is how the rule works. Say you're married and you use part of your home (your study for instance, which comprises 20 percent of the total area of your home) as your office. You made $500,000 on the sale, 20 percent of which, or $100,000, is considered the sale of business property and 80 percent ($400,000) is the sale of your residence. Only the $400,000 portion is exempt from tax because it falls under the $500,000 exclusion.

But what if you didn't use your residence all the time as your office? Say you only used it for two years. This means you used your entire home as your principal residence for three out of the five past years. Congratulations, you meet the governing two-out-of-the-previous-five-years requirement. Good planning. You're entitled to the full $500,000 exclusion less the depreciation you claimed on the study after May 6, 1997.

Use Schedule D for Other Issues Involving Stocks (Worthless and Otherwise)

You can use Schedule D to handle such issues as worthless securities, wash sales, stock options, stock for services, and appreciated employer securities.

Worthless securities

Suppose that you felt certain that Company X was going to make a comeback, so you invested $15,000. But you were wrong. Not only has Company X failed to make this comeback, but its shares are no longer even being quoted in the morning's paper.

Great! So at least $15,000 is a write-off, right? No. The problem with this scenario is that you must be able to prove — with an identifiable event — that your investment is in fact *completely* worthless. Being partially worthless won't cut it. In one case, bondholders in a company canceled 30 percent of the face value of their bonds to keep the company afloat. But they couldn't deduct the portion of the debt that they canceled because their investment hadn't become completely worthless. Likewise, the fact that the shares of a company are no longer being quoted doesn't make them worthless.

We wish that we could tell you that convincing the IRS that you're entitled to write off your $15,000 investment is as easy as losing it. It's not — and this is an area of the law that's more confusing than most. You may think that bankruptcy, going out of business, liquidation, the appointment of a receiver, or insolvency indicates that your investment no longer had any value. But these events only prove that the company is in financial trouble, not that its shareholders won't receive anything in liquidation. In order to claim a deduction for worthless securities, your investment must be completely worthless.

When is an investment worthless? As a general rule, you can say that an investment is worthless when a company is so hopelessly insolvent that it ceases doing business or it goes into receivership, leaving nothing for its stockholders. If you're not sure, one source worth checking is **CCH** INCORPORATED (they also do the technical editing of this book). This outfit publishes an annual list of worthless securities as part of its "Capital Changes Reports." Most major brokerage firms and public libraries subscribe to this service, or you can reach the company directly at 800-TELL-CCH.

If proving when unmarketable shares in a company actually became worthless is so difficult, why not lock in a loss by finding some accomplice — the broker who sold them to you, for example — to take the shares off your hands for a penny apiece? Nice try, but no go. A number of taxpayers have attempted to structure "sales" in this fashion, but both the IRS and the Tax Court have denied the losses because these sales weren't considered legitimate. Instead, the taxpayers were told to hang on to their investments and deduct them only when they became certifiably worthless. In other words, they were back to square one.

Wash sales

Suppose that you own a stock that has declined in value. You think that it will recover, but you want to deduct the money that you lost. If you sell the stock and buy back the shares within 30 days of the sale, you can't deduct the loss. The loss is deducted when you sell the new shares.

Stock options

Stock options usually come in two varieties: *statutory options,* which have to meet certain IRS rules in order to qualify for special tax advantages, and *nonstatutory stock options,* which are also subject to special rules even though the tax savings aren't as great. Statutory stock options include incentive stock options and options under an employee stock purchase plan.

Incentive stock options (ISOs)

You aren't subject to tax when an incentive stock option is granted. You realize income or loss only when you sell the stock that you acquired by exercising the ISO.

You must exercise the option within 10 years from the date that it was granted. The option price has to be at least equal to the value of the stock on the day that the option was granted. For example, you can't receive an option to buy shares for $10 a share when the shares are selling for $18 a share. In any one year, you can't receive an option to buy shares that are worth more than $100,000 on the date that the option was granted. If you go over $100,000, the excess isn't considered an ISO, so read on until you get to the section "Nonstatutory stock options."

When you sell stock that you acquired by exercising an ISO, you have a long-term capital gain if you held the shares for more than one year from the date when you exercised the option and more than two years after the ISO was granted. For example, say you exercise an option for $15,000. You later sell the shares for $25,000. You have a long-term capital gain of $10,000 if you meet the one- and two-year rule. If you don't meet these rules, the $10,000 gain is divided into two parts. The difference between the exercise price and the value on the day that you exercised the option is taxed as ordinary income. The difference between the value on the day that you exercised the option and the value on the day that you sold the stock is treated as a capital gain (either short or long term). In the previous example, if the shares were worth $20,000 on the day that you exercised the option, then $5,000 of the gain would be taxed as ordinary income, and $5,000 (the difference between the sales price, $25,000, and the $20,000 value on the day the option was exercised) is taxed as a long-term capital gain.

Although the spread between the option price and the value on the day that you exercised the option isn't subject to tax for regular tax purposes, it is subject to the fiendish Alternative Minimum Tax (AMT). So take a peek at line 51 (AMT) in Chapter 8, or better yet, speak to a good tax pro.

The holding period for determining long- or short-term capital gains on shares acquired by exercising a stock option starts on the day after you exercise the option. We explain the holding period rules at the beginning of the chapter in the sidebar, "Details for figuring short term or long term."

Employee stock purchase plans

Employee stock purchase plans allow you to buy your company's stock at a discount. The discount isn't taxed until you sell the shares. If you hold the shares for more than two years after the option was granted and more than one year after you acquired the shares, the discount is taxed as ordinary income, and the difference between the value on the day that you acquired the shares is a capital gain (either short or long term). For example, you sold shares for $25,000 that you had purchased under an employee plan for $16,000. On the day that the options were granted, the shares were worth $18,000. Of the $9,000 gain, $2,000 ($18,000 – $16,000) is taxed at ordinary rates, and $7,000 ($25,000 – $18,000) is taxed as a capital gain, either short- or long-term.

If you sold the shares before the end of the two-year period, substitute the value of the shares on the day that you purchased them in place of the value when the option was granted to determine the ordinary income portion of the $9,000 gain. Suppose that the value of the shares on the day that you purchased them was $20,000. Of the gain, $4,000 ($20,000 – $16,000) is taxed as ordinary income, and the $5,000 balance ($25,000 – $20,000) is taxed as a capital gain. Is there a way around these maddening rules? Hold the shares for more than two years.

Nonstatutory stock options

Because nonqualified stock options don't have to meet any IRS rules, there are no restrictions on the amount of these types of options that may be granted. If a nonstatutory stock option doesn't have an ascertainable value when it's issued (which is usually the case for options that aren't traded on a stock exchange), no income is realized when you receive the option. When you exercise the option, you're taxed on the spread. For example, you exercise a $4,000 option to purchase stock trading at $10,000; you realize ordinary income of $6,000. Your tax basis for figuring a gain or loss when you sell the shares is $10,000. If the option has an ascertainable value, the value of the option is taxed as additional salary. For example, you receive an option to buy 100 shares that you can sell for $1,000 on the day that you receive the option. The bad news: You owe tax on the $1,000. The good news: When you exercise the shares, the $1,000 is added to the cost of the shares when determining whether you have a profit or loss when you sell the shares.

Stock for services

Stock for services is taxed as additional salary or fee income if you're an independent contractor. However, special rules apply as to when you have to report the income. If the stock is subject to restriction, you report as income the value of the stock when the restrictions are lifted. For example, a restriction may be that you have to work for the company for three years; otherwise, you forfeit the shares.

Even if the shares are subject to restrictions, you can elect to report the value of the shares as income in the year that you receive them. This is known as a *Section 83(b) election.* Why would you want to do this? Say that you receive shares in a start-up venture that have little value at the time you receive them. If you wait to report the value of the shares as income five years from now, when the restrictions are lifted and the shares are worth a great deal, you could be taxed at rates as high as 39.6 percent on the value at that time. On the other hand, if the shares are currently worth only a few thousand dollars, it would make sense to report the income now and pay a small amount of tax, because when you sell the shares after they've increased dramatically in value, the profit will be subject to the maximum 20 (or 10) -percent capital gain rate.

Appreciated employer securities

Many taxpayers overlook a special rule that applies when shares of the company that they work for are distributed to them as part of a lump sum distribution from a retirement plan. The value of the shares isn't subject to tax at the time that you receive them. Only the cost of the shares when they were purchased is. For example, shares of your employer's stock that you bought through your employer's retirement plan for $50,000 are now worth $200,000. Only the $50,000 is subject to tax when you receive the shares. If you sell the shares the following year for $225,000, you have to report a $175,000 capital gain that year.

If you don't hold the shares for more than one year, part of the gain is taxed as a short-term sale. In the previous example, if you didn't hold the shares for more than a year after they were distributed, $25,000 of the gain is short-term and $150,000 is long-term. The difference between the cost and the value on the day that they were distributed is treated as long term ($200,000 – $50,000), and the difference between the sales price and the value on the date of distribution is short-term ($225,000 – $200,000).

Use Schedule D for Nonbusiness Bad Debts

Suppose that you lent your best friend $2,500 on New Year's Eve, and you haven't seen him since New Year's Day. All is not lost. You can deduct the $2,500. This news comes as a surprise to many people, because usually you can deduct losses only on investment and business transactions. But you must be able to prove that there was a valid debt, that the debt is worthless, and that you previously paid tax on the money that you lent.

- **What is worthless?** As with securities, there must be some identifiable event — such as bankruptcy, legal action, or the disappearance of the debtor — to prove that you can't collect what you're owed. You don't necessarily have to sue the debtor or even threaten to take legal action. This is one of the few instances where the IRS is on your side, not your lawyer's!

- **The right to sue:** To prove that you have a valid debt, you should be able to show that you have a right to sue. This situation creates a special problem with loans to family members. The IRS tends to view such loans as gifts. So if you had your brother sign a promissory note and put up collateral when you lent him money, you could prevail if the IRS ever questioned whether it was a valid debt. Yet, as you probably know, most dealings between family members are done a little more casually than that. See the heading "Interest-free loans" in Chapter 10 for more on this painful subject.

- **Is the debt deductible?** Finally, to establish that a debt is deductible, you must have paid tax on what you lent. Suppose that you worked in a local bookstore in anticipation of being paid later. The bookstore went out of business, and you weren't paid. Sorry. Because you never received this income and didn't report it on your tax return, you're not entitled to a deduction if it's not paid.

You deduct nonbusiness bad debts on good old Schedule D as a short-term loss, regardless of how long the money was owed. If you don't have capital gains to offset the deduction, you can deduct $3,000 of the loss and carry over the balance to next year, just like with other investment losses. Additionally, you must attach a statement to your return explaining the nature of the debt; name of the debtor and any business or family relationship; date the debt became due; efforts made to collect the debt; and reason for determining that the debt is entirely worthless (only business debts can generate a deduction if they're partially worthless).

Don't confuse nonbusiness bad debts with business-related bad debts that can be deducted on your business tax returns. Refer to "Line 9: Bad debts from sales or services" in Chapter 11.

Chapter 13

Supplemental Income and Loss: Schedule E

- -

In This Chapter

▶ Defining supplemental income

▶ Completing Schedule E

▶ Discussing tax shelters

- -

on't let the words "Supplemental Income" throw you. That's just IRS-speak for the income you receive from rental property or royalties or through partnerships, S Corporations (corporations that don't pay tax; the owners report the corporations' income or loss on their personal tax returns), trusts, and estates. To report your rental or royalty income, you use Schedule E, which is laid out in the form of a profit or loss statement (income and expenses). From your income, you subtract your expenses. The remainder is your *net income,* the income that you have to pay taxes on. If you have a loss, the rules get a little sticky as to whether you can deduct it. (Isn't that a surprise?)

Remember that if you're a self-employed taxpayer receiving royalties, such as a musician, you use Schedule C. The information in this chapter applies to people who receive royalties and are not self-employed. For example, George Gershwin received royalties from *Porgy and Bess* and reported them on Schedule C. But he has passed away, and now his heirs receive royalties that must be reported on Schedule E.

You can input the income and expenses for up to three rental properties or royalty incomes (in columns A, B, and C) on Schedule E. If you have more than three entries, you can use as many Schedule Es as you need — but fill in the total for all the properties on only one Schedule E.

Part I: Income or Loss from Rental Real Estate and Royalties

If you receive rent or royalties, you should receive **Form 1099-MISC.** Box 1 is for rent, and box 2 is for royalties. (Even if you rent your summer home to the Queen of England, you report your rent and royalties separately.)

Line 1: Kind and location of each real estate property

On line A, enter the location. For example, two-family home, Albany, New York. The line provides enough room for listing three properties. If you have more than three properties, enter the additional properties on another Schedule E.

Line 2: Vacation home questions

Here, you're asked whether you used any of the properties listed on line 2A, 2B, or 2C, and for how long. For example, you may have rented out your beach home for July and August, but you used it in June and September. See the "Vacation homes" sidebar later in this chapter for information about vacation home expenses you can and can't deduct.

Lines 3–4: Income

Copy the amounts from your 1099-MISC onto lines 3 and 4 of Schedule E.

You may be wondering whether some unusual cases of rent are counted as income. Rent paid in advance, for example, is counted as rent. If you sign a lease in December 1998 and collect January's rent of $1,000, this amount is included in 1998's rent income on this schedule even though it applies to 1999's rent. Security deposits that you must return are not rental income. And if your tenant pays you to cancel the lease, the amount you receive is rent. It isn't considered a tax-free payment for damages. Although expenses paid by the tenant are considered rental income, you're entitled to deduct those expenses. Finally, if you're a good Samaritan and charge a relative or friend less than the fair rental value, your deductions for depreciation and maintenance expenses can't exceed the rent you collect.

Lines 5–18: Expenses

On these lines, you tabulate the amounts you're allowed to deduct. Now don't you wish that you were a better bookkeeper? If you have good records, you can save a tidy sum. The expense lines apply to both royalties and rents.

If you rent out half of a two-family house and you occupy the other half, for example, you can only deduct 50 percent of your expenses. If it's a three-family unit and you occupy one of the units, you can only deduct 66 percent of the expenses. Get the picture? But remember that the portion of your mortgage interest and property taxes that relates to the part you occupy gets deducted on Schedule A — see Chapter 9.

Line 5: Advertising

You're allowed to deduct the cost of newspaper ads, for example, if you had to run ads to find renters for your property. The same goes if you had building signs made.

Line 6: Auto and travel

Travel to inspect your rental property is deductible. But if you live in Buffalo and go to Florida in January to inspect a vacation home that you rent out part of the time, be prepared for a battle with the IRS. Refer to the guidelines for deducting travel in Chapter 9 ("Line 20: Unreimbursed employee expenses") and your auto in Chapter 11 ("Line 10: Car and truck expenses").

Line 7: Cleaning and maintenance

You can deduct your costs for cleaning and maintenance, such as your monthly fee for the window washer and your payment to the guy who tunes up your furnace before the cold weather sets in.

Line 8: Commissions

You can deduct commissions paid to a real estate broker to find a tenant. The norm is 5 to 10 percent.

Line 9: Insurance

We hope that you carry insurance to protect against your building burning down, lawsuits, and other perils such as floods and earthquakes. You get to deduct the cost of these policies. One tricky area to be aware of is if you pay for an insurance premium that covers more than one year. In this case, you deduct the portion of the premium that applies to each year's Schedule E. For example, suppose that in 1998 you pay a $900 premium that covers a three-year period. You deduct $300 in 1998, another $300 in 1999, and the final $300 in 2000.

Line 10: Legal and other professional fees

Legal fees incurred in the purchase of the property must be added to the cost of the building and deducted as part of your depreciation deduction (coming later). Legal fees for preparing a lease are deductible. And the part of your tax-preparation fee used to prepare this Schedule E is deductible.

Line 11: Management fees

You can deduct the costs of managing the property — collecting the rent, seeing to all the repairs, paying a management company (if you have one), and so on.

Line 12: Mortgage interest paid to banks (Form 1098)

This amount comes right off of **Form 1098, Mortgage Interest Statement,** which you get from the bank that holds the mortgage. The bank sends you this statement by January 31.

Line 13: Other interest

If the person you purchased the property from provided the financing and holds a mortgage on the property, the interest is entered here because this is where the interest that wasn't paid to financial institutions goes. All the fees you paid when you took out the mortgage are deducted over the duration of the loan. You also put the interest on a second mortgage here, as well as the interest on short-term installment loans for the purchase of appliances and other assets.

Unlike with a personal residence, points and fees to obtain a mortgage on rental property aren't deductible in the year you pay them. You must write off these amounts over the term of the loan and deduct them on this line. If you didn't receive a Form 1098, enter the interest you paid on this line.

For the adventuresome who want to deduct interest on an income tax bill, see "Interest You Paid" in Chapter 9.

Line 14: Repairs

Repairs are deductible in full. Improvements may be deducted over 27.5 years for residential property and over either 31.5 or 39 years, depending on when it was acquired, for commercial or nonresidential property (refer to Chapter 11 to obtain the rate of depreciation you can claim every year). A *repair* — such as fixing a leaky roof — keeps your property in good operating condition. It doesn't materially add to the value of the property or prolong its life. An *improvement,* such as adding an entire new roof, on the other hand, adds to the property's value or prolongs its life and thus is written off over its useful life.

Line 15: Supplies

You can deduct such things as cleaning supplies, light bulbs, and small items that you buy at a hardware store.

Line 16: Taxes

This line includes real estate taxes on the property. Additionally, if you employ a superintendent or a janitor, this is where you enter the Social Security and unemployment taxes that you have to pay. The bank holding the mortgage will send you an annual mortgage statement that gives you the tax information. The Social Security and unemployment taxes will be listed on your quarterly payroll tax return.

Line 17: Utilities

Why don't you just go ahead and enter your electric, gas, fuel, water, sewer, and phone costs for your property here? We would.

Line 18: Other

This is one of those catchall lines for things whose descriptions don't fit on the preceding lines. For example, you can enter costs such as gardening, permits, and any other expenses that you can't find a home for on lines 5–17.

Lines 19–26

Add lines 5 through 18 and enter the total on line 19. Then you get to do more figuring. Read on.

Line 20: Depreciation expense or depletion (Form 4562)

The tax law allows you to claim a yearly tax deduction for depreciation. You can't depreciate land. So, for example, you can depreciate only 85 percent of your cost (because, as a rule, at least 15 percent of a building's purchase price must be allocated to land). You can make this allocation based on the assessed value for the land and the building or on a real estate appraisal. You compute your depreciation deduction on **Form 4562, Depreciation and Amortization,** and you attach this form to your 1040 only if you first started to claim a deduction in 1998. If you claimed depreciation in an earlier year, the form isn't required. Compute the depreciation and enter the amount here. An annual depreciation rate schedule for residential real estate is available in Chapter 11. IRS Publication 534, *Depreciation,* has the depreciation schedule for commercial real estate.

Line 21: Total expenses

Add lines 19 and 20 and place the total on this line.

Line 22: Income or loss from rental real estate or royalty properties

The first part is just basic arithmetic. Go ahead and subtract line 21 from your income from line 3 or 4. If you have a positive number, you have, as the title of Schedule E announces, supplemental income; if your total is negative, you have a loss. On line 22, you'll notice a reference to Form 6198. This refers to the wonderful at-risk rules; don't concern yourself with these rules unless you were lucky enough to get a mortgage where you aren't personally liable for the payments.

Line 23: Deductible rental real estate loss (Form 8582)

If your real estate property showed a loss for the year (on line 22), you may not actually be able to claim that entire loss on your tax return. If you didn't show a loss, skip ahead to the next line.

Line 23 is where you enter how much of the loss on line 22 can be deducted. Rental real estate is considered a passive activity, and normally, you have to complete **Form 8582,**

Passive Activity Loss Limitations, to determine the portion, if any, that you're allowed to deduct. However, if you meet *all* the following conditions, you're spared from Form 8582 (keep your fingers crossed):

- ✔ Rental real estate is the only passive activity you're involved in. (Remember that passive activity is a business or investment where you act as a silent partner — you aren't actively involved.)

- ✔ You actively participated in making management decisions or arranged for others to provide services such as repairs.

- ✔ Your rental real estate loss did not exceed $25,000 — or $12,500 if you are married and filing separately.

- ✔ You didn't have rental or passive activity losses that you couldn't deduct in a prior year.

- ✔ If you are married and filing separately, you must have lived apart from your spouse for the entire year.

- ✔ Your modified adjusted gross income (see the following worksheet) is less than $100,000 (or $50,000 if you are married and filing separately).

If you meet all of the above six criteria, congratulations — you can skip the dreaded Form 8582 and write your deductible real estate loss right here on line 23.

If you have to fill out Form 8582 in order to compute your rental losses on Schedule E (line 22) because your modified AGI (adjusted gross income) is over the limit (or you were involved in other passive activities), you have to be familiar with tax-shelter rules and other rules that allow you to deduct up to $25,000 of losses from rental real estate that you actively manage.

If Form 8582 applies to you, oh taxpayer, you need a tax advisor!

Worksheet to determine whether you need to use Form 8582

This little worksheet helps you compute your modified AGI so that you can determine whether it's over the limits we just mentioned. If it is, off you go to Form 8582.

1. AGI from Form 1040 (line 33) $_____
2. Less: taxable portion of Social Security (line 20b) $_____
3. Subtract line 2 from line 1 $_____
4. Your IRA deductions (line 23) $_____
5. One-half of self-employment tax (line 27) $_____
6. Passive activity losses (line 17) $_____
7. Interest on Form 8815 $_____
8. Add lines 4–7 $_____
9. Add line 8 to line 3 = Modified AGI $_____

(If this line is under $100,000, or $50,000 if you are married and filing separately, you don't have to go to Form 8582 — as long as you meet the other five criteria we mention earlier.)

If you have only rental or royalty income or losses, you don't need to turn the page of your Schedule E. You're done! After you follow all those little instructions about what lines to add, take the amount from line 26 over to your 1040 (line 17).

But, if you must continue, bear up. You're halfway there.

The $25,000 exemption

Here's why that $100,000 modified AGI figure is so important. You can deduct up to $25,000 of the losses you incurred in rental real estate if you actively participate in the management of the property and own at least 10 percent — which means that you have to make management decisions regarding the approval of new tenants and rental terms, approving expenditures, and similar decisions. So if you turn an apartment or home that you own over to a real estate agent to rent and manage, the $25,000 loss-deduction rule doesn't apply. You might be able to pull off this deduction, though, if you reserve the right to approve all expenditures and improvements that have to be made.

Now for the ever-present exception to the general rule: If your income exceeds $100,000, the $25,000 limit is reduced by 50 cents for every dollar of income over $100,000. When your income reaches $150,000, the $25,000 allowance is completely phased out.

The loss that's phased out (the portion you can't deduct in any year) doesn't just disappear. You carry it over and enter it on line 2c of **Form 8582, Passive Activity Loss Limitations** (this is IRS speak for a tax shelter), to determine the amount of the carryover that's deductible in a future year. When you eventually sell the property, all your suspended losses can be deducted in the year of the sale. Later in this chapter, we explain all this again in greater deal in the section "The tax shelter rules."

The $25,000 figure is reduced to $12,500 if you are married filing separately and living apart from your spouse for the entire year; the phaseout begins at $50,000 of your AGI (not $100,000) and is completely phased out at $75,000.

If you lived with your spouse at any time during the year and are filing separate returns, you can't use the $12,500 exception (half of $25,000). Please don't ask us about the reason for this one. On Form 8582, you compute the portion of the $25,000 allowance you're entitled to.

Two other points are worth making. First, you must own at least 10 percent of the property. And second, to see whether your income exceeds $100,000 ($50,000 if you are married and filing separately), take your adjusted gross income from Form 1040 (line 33), but don't include any of the following:

- ✔ Any passive activity losses or income
- ✔ The taxable portion of your Social Security
- ✔ Deductible IRA contributions
- ✔ The deduction for one-half of your self-employment tax from Form 1040 (line 27)

Interest on U.S. savings bonds that you used to pay excludable tuition is included for purposes of determining the $100,000 amount.

IRS math quiz

Complete Part I of Schedule E by adding the positive amounts on line 22 and entering them on line 24. Then add royalty losses from line 22 and real estate losses from line 23, and enter the total on line 25. Finally, add the amounts on lines 24 and 25, and enter that total on line 26. Carry this total over to line 17 of Form 1040.

The tax shelter rules

If you rent out your vacation home or part of a two-family house, you're operating a tax shelter — and you always thought that tax shelters were something that only movie stars and high-income athletes got involved in!

In 1986, Congress decided to kill tax shelters and passed an anti-tax-shelter law. As a result, a loss from a _passive activity_ (that's what a tax shelter is now called in IRS jargon) can be deducted only if you have income from another passive activity. If you don't, the loss is _disallowed._ Disallowed losses are suspended and carried over to future years. If you have passive income (that's income from a shelter) next year, you can deduct the loss. If you don't have passive income next year, you keep carrying over the loss until you do, or until you sell the property or your interest in the tax shelter.

For example, suppose that you have a rental loss of $5,000 in 1998 and no other passive income. The loss is carried over to 1999. If in 1999, the property generates a $4,000 profit, you can deduct $4,000 of the suspended loss and carry over the $1,000 balance to 2000. If you sell the property in 2000, the $1,000 can be deducted — even if you don't have a rental income in 2000.

If you have two or more passive activities, you combine them to determine whether a loss in one can be used to offset a profit in another. For example, suppose that you own one building that you rent out at a $6,000 loss and another building that produces a $5,000 profit. You can use $5,000 of the $6,000 loss to offset the $5,000 profit from the second building, and the $1,000 balance is carried over to 1999.

Vacation homes

Determining the expenses you can deduct on a vacation home is no fun in the sun because you have to allocate the operating expenses based on how many days you rent your home and on how many days you use it. What's deductible and what's not are based on the following three mind-numbing rules:

Rule 1: If you rent your home for fewer than 15 days, you don't have to report the rent you collected, and none of the operating expenses are deductible. Your mortgage interest and real estate taxes are still deducted as itemized deductions.

Rule 2: If you rent your home for 15 or more days and your personal use of your home is more than the greater of 14 days or 10 percent of the total days it's rented, then the property isn't considered rental property, and the expenses allocated to the rental period can't exceed the rental income. The expenses that are allocated to the rental period, but which can't be deducted, are carried forward to future years. These expenses can be deducted to the extent of your future rental income or until you sell the property. If you have a profit on the rental of a vacation home, this rule doesn't apply.

In figuring the rental days, count only the days the home was actually rented. The days that you held the property out for rent, but it was not rented, don't count as rental days. After making this computation, you allocate your rental expenses based on the total number of days rented divided by the total number of rented days plus the days you used it. For example, suppose that your beach cottage was rented for 36 days and you used it for 36 days. In such a case, 50 percent of the operating expenses for the year would be allocated to the rental period, 36 days rented ÷ 72 days (36 rented and 36 personal days). Don't count any days you worked full-time to repair the property as personal days.

The Tax Court is on your side when it comes to deducting mortgage interest and taxes, which don't have to be allocated under the preceding formula. You can allocate this stuff on a daily basis. So, in the example, ten percent (36 rental days ÷ 365) of your taxes and mortgage interest would have to be allocated to the rental period. This process means that a larger amount of your other rental expenses can be deducted from your rental income and (better yet) you get to deduct 90 percent of your mortgage interest and taxes as an itemized deduction instead of 50 percent.

Rule 3: If the personal use of your residence doesn't exceed 14 days or 10 percent of the total days it's rented, then your vacation home is treated as rental property; if the total amount of your rental expenses exceeds your rental income, your loss is deductible if you have other passive income (or if the $25,000 special deduction allowance permits). You still have to allocate the expenses of running the property between personal and rental days.

Have a nice vacation.

If you have a passive activity loss, you compute the amount of the loss that can be deducted or that has to be carried over to future years on **Form 8582, Passive Activity Loss Limitations.** On this form, you combine your passive activity losses and income. If income exceeds losses, you have a deduction. If it doesn't, you have a suspended loss. But remember: If you sell the property, the loss, together with any suspended losses, is deductible.

Part II: Income or Loss from Partnerships and S Corporations

The average taxpayer finds page 2 of Schedule E the most daunting. On this page, you report income and losses from partnerships, S Corporations, estates, and trusts. Instead of the nice, long, symmetrical columns of page 1, Schedule E's flip side looks as if it was designed to confuse rather than clarify.

Partnerships and S Corporations aren't taxable entities. The income, gains, losses, and deductions of a partnership or an S Corporation are passed through to each partner or shareholder based on the ownership percentage. Instead of a 1099, each partner or shareholder receives a form called a K-1 that reflects the income, loss, or deduction that belongs on the return. For a partnership, it's **Form 1065 K-1;** for an S Corporation, it's **Form 1120S K-1.**

Lines 27–31: Name . . . and so on!

Now you have to deal not only with line numbers but also letters! Here's what you enter in the following columns for line 27:

(a) Enter the name of the Partnership or S Corporation.

(b) Enter "P" for Partnership or "S" for S Corporation.

(c) Put a check here if it's a foreign partnership.

(d) Scribble in the identification number for the partnership or S Corporation. (Hey, this is pretty easy so far!)

(e) and (f) Oops, we spoke too soon. Did you notice the question "Investment At Risk?" Here, you have to check "all is at risk" (e) or "some is not at risk" (f). The purpose of the at-risk rules is to prevent investors from deducting losses in excess of what they actually stand to lose.

This rule prevents you from investing $10,000 and deducting $30,000 if the partnership lost an additional $20,000 that you aren't personally responsible for. The K-1 that you receive indicates what you're at risk for (see item f). The at-risk rules are extremely complex. This is one area where we recommend that you see a tax advisor for help.

Passive income and loss

(g) The K-1 indicates a passive activity with a little check in the box — limited partner or publicly traded partnership. If you have a passive activity loss, enter the loss on Form 8582. You compute your allowable passive loss on **Form 8582, Passive Activity Loss Limitations** and then enter that amount in this column.

(h) Enter the income from the passive activity in this lovely column.

Refer to "The tax shelter rules" described earlier in this chapter for the definition of passive income and losses.

Nonpassive income and loss

(i) If you're a working partner in a partnership or a shareholder in an S Corporation, line 1 of the K-1 shows your share of the loss you're entitled to deduct. Enter that amount here.

(j) The wonderful K-1 also shows the amount of the partnership's or S Corporation's special depreciation that you get to deduct — line 9 of the K-1 for partnerships and line 8 for S Corporations. Enter it here.

(k) Enter the amount of income from Schedule K-1 in this column — it's the amount on line 1.

Part III: Income or Loss from Estates and Trusts

In this part, you enter income or loss from an estate or trust that you're a beneficiary of. You should receive a K-1 from either the estate or trust, and the K-1 also indicates income such as dividends, interest, and capital gains. Interest and dividends go on Schedule B (see Chapter 10), and capital gains go on Schedule D (see Chapter 12). It's the ordinary income or loss on the K-1 that goes on Schedule E. Maybe that's why the IRS gives us only two lines to work with in this part of the form — and that's down from *three* lines a couple of years back!

Lines 32–36: Name . . . and so on!

(a) Carefully enter the name of the estate or trust.

(b) Enter the identification number.

Passive income and loss

(c) Here you put the passive loss allowed from Form 8582.

(d) Enter the passive income from the K-1s and Form 8582.

Nonpassive income and loss

(e) and (f) Because most heirs or beneficiaries don't participate in the management of the estate or trust, it is very rare for an heir or beneficiary to have nonpassive income or loss.

Part IV: Lines 37–38: Income or Loss from Real Estate Mortgage Investment Conduits (REMIC)

If you've invested in a REMIC, which is a company that holds a pool of mortgages, you'll most likely receive interest on **Form 1099-INT, Interest Income** or **Form 1099-OID, Original Issue Discount.** But if you received **Form 1066, Schedule Q** from the REMIC, enter the amounts, names, and so on from that form on line 37. Add columns (d) and (e) and enter the total on line 38.

Part V: Summary

Unless you're a farmer and file Form 4835 (lines 39 and 41) or are a real estate professional (line 42), everything on Schedule E is pulled together on line 40. Do the math and transfer the amount to Form 1040 (line 17) and take a break. You deserve it.

If you rent out your farm, you report your rental income and expenses on **Form 4835, Farm Rental Income and Expenses.** Donald Trump — or rather, his accountant — is an example of one who has to fill out line 42, Reconciliation for Real Estate Professionals.

Chapter 14

Profit or Loss from Farming: Schedule F

• •

In This Chapter

▶ Figuring out Schedule F

▶ Reporting your income

▶ Tallying and categorizing all those expenses

▶ Understanding the special rules that apply only to farming

• •

Part of the responsibility of running a farm is reporting to the government how much income you receive when you sell your crop or livestock. Schedule F is the form you use to report this income, whether from operating a farm that produces livestock, dairy, poultry, fish, aquaculture products, bee products, fruit, or a truck farm (because produce isn't the only thing farmers raise and harvest). Even though Schedule F is titled "Profit or Loss from Farming," this form is also used to tell the IRS what you took in from operating a plantation, ranch, nursery, orchard, or oyster bed. Schedule F is not as bad as it looks. In this chapter, we take you through it, line by line.

Once upon a time all taxpayers could reduce their taxes by averaging their incomes over a number of years if their incomes suddenly shot up. All that ended in 1986. In 1998, farmers, but not other taxpayers, got a lucky break. If a farmer's income shoots up in 1998, farmers can once again reduce their taxes by averaging their incomes over the past three years. And thanks to the new law, you will not only be able to do this in 1998 but for all future years.

When you get to line 40 of your Form 1040 — the line where you compute your tax — use **Schedule J, Form 1040, Farm Income Averaging,** when computing your tax.

Basic Information (Lines A–E): Accounting Method Stuff

The first few lines of Schedule F look at your accounting method.

Lines A and B: Product and code. Lines A and B are the simplest part of the form. Suppose that you are a dairy farmer. On line A: Principal product, you write Milk. On line B: Principal agricultural activity code, write 112210. Where did the number on line B come from, you ask? The number comes from the list of Principal Agricultural Activity Codes found in Part IV on the reverse side of Schedule F. Code 112210 indicates that you're a dairy farmer.

Line C: Accounting method. The two accounting methods used to report income are the *cash* and the *accrual* methods. With the cash method, you report income at the time it is actually received, and you deduct expenses at the time they are actually paid. However, one exception exists to this rule (of course): If you charge an expense on a credit card, you can deduct this expense in the year you charged the purchase, even if you *pay* the charge in the following year. (So don't leave home without it.)

Most farmers use the *cash method* because it's the easier of the two methods. You total what you received and subtract what you paid. You don't need to figure out what you owe and who owes you. You don't need to determine your inventory at the end of the year (for crops or animals that you didn't sell). A slight exception to this rule exists as well, however. If you bought livestock or other items for resale, you must keep a separate record of the items that you didn't sell. These purchases can't be deducted until they are sold. And thanks to depreciation rules, farm structures and equipment can't be deducted in the year you paid for them. They have to be depreciated over their useful lives.

Under the *accrual method,* you report income in the year sales are made — even if the sales are billed or collected in a later year. You deduct expenses in the year in which the expenses are incurred, even if you don't pay these expenses until later.

Under both cash and accrual methods, you report all income and expenses for the calendar year ending December 31.

The cash method of accounting gives you more control over when your farm sees a profit from year-to-year. For example, if next year looks like a slower year for you, you may elect to claim more of your income in that next year. This will likely save you tax dollars, because you should be in a lower tax bracket that year (if it is, in fact, a less profitable year for you). You can legally shift your income by deferring sales or by delaying sending out bills until January (bills that you would have mailed in December, for example). Likewise, in order to lower your taxable income this year, you can pay more of your expenses in December rather than waiting until January.

If you are operating a farm and aim to produce a tax deduction (commonly referred to as a tax shelter) rather than a profit, you are required to use the accrual method.

Line D: Employer ID number. Enter your employer ID number on line D. If you don't have a number, complete **Form SS-4, Application For Employer Identification Number,** and send it to the IRS. When you get assigned a number, which only takes a couple of weeks, enter your number on line D.

Line E: Did you "materially participate"? If the sun isn't up when you start working on the farm each day, check yes. If you only show up on holidays and weekends to go horseback riding, check no. If you check no, you are operating a tax shelter and you probably won't be able to deduct any loss if the farm isn't profitable. In such cases, we advise consulting a tax advisor, and make sure that you see a good one. See Chapter 2 for more information on choosing a competent tax advisor. Chapter 13 explains how the tax shelter rules operate.

Part I, Lines 1–11: Income

Time to tally up your income. This section describes, line-by-line, the types of income you should enter on each line and how to complete the Income section of Schedule F. Wouldn't it be nice if you could just write down one simple number on one single line? No such luck. Hey, but who said farming (or paying taxes) was easy?

Line 1: Sales of livestock and other items you bought for resale

If you sold livestock that you bought for resale, enter the income you received on line 1. (For income you received from the sale of livestock that you *raised yourself,* just hold your horses. You'll have a chance to pony up *that* income amount on line 4, which we discuss momentarily.)

Line 2: Cost or other basis of livestock items reported on line 1

You must keep a careful record of *when* the animals you bought for resale were purchased (because you can only deduct the purchase price of those animals in the year that you sell them). For example, suppose that in 1997 you bought 10 cows for a total purchase price of $10,000, and you then sold the cows in 1998. You can't deduct the purchase price on your 1997 tax return; you deduct the $10,000 cost of these animals in 1998 — enter the amount on line 2.

Under the old law, the option to defer income to the next year could be used only in drought conditions. It now applies to all weather-related conditions, such as floods. See the sidebar "Livestock sales caused by weather-related conditions" later in this chapter.

Matching the cost with sales for resale reported on line 1 sounds a lot easier than it really is. For some types of livestock, figuring out which animals you purchased when can be tough. Think about it. Suppose that you're a poultry farmer who is continually buying baby chicks and raising others. When you sell 50 chickens, it's impossible to tell if the chickens you sold are the ones you raised or the ones you purchased (unless you're on a first-name basis with your chickens, or you use a teeny-tiny little branding iron on them). For this reason, poultry, fish, or other hard-to-differentiate livestock are exempt from the "which critter was purchased when" requirement. You can keep it simple — enter the income from the sale of this type of livestock on line 4. On line 34, enter the cost of the poultry, fish, and other such livestock that you purchased.

Don't use Schedule F to report income from the sale of animals held for *draft, breeding,* or *sport*. Income from the sale of these types of animals gets reported on **Form 4797, Sales of Business Property.** And because these animals are classified as business property, you can depreciate that Clydesdale, stud bull, or racehorse just as if it were a John Deere tractor.

Line 3: Subtraction quiz

All you do is subtract line 2 from line 1 and enter the total on line 3. So do it.

Line 4: Sales of livestock, produce, grains, and other products you raised

Line 4 is where you report the income from the sale of the products that you raise, grow, or produce. So if you're a dairy farmer, enter what you received from the sale of milk. If you also sold your corn and hay crop, tally up all your income and enter the total right here.

Lines 5a and b: Total Cooperative Distributions (Form 1099-PATR)

If you purchase farm supplies from a cooperative, you may receive income in the form of *patronage dividends,* which is fancy jargon for a *distribution of the cooperative's profits.* These payments are reported to you on **Form 1099-PATR.** You report patronage dividends on line 5a of Schedule F. However, dividends received from the purchase of *personal* family living items aren't taxable because the supplies weren't used in your business (that is, on your farm).

Livestock sales caused by weather-related conditions

If you sold more livestock (which includes poultry) than you usually do because of a weather-related condition such as a drought, you can postpone reporting some of your earnings until next year. Suppose that you normally sell 100 head a year, but because of a drought you sell 200 head of livestock for $300 a head. Of the $60,000 you receive, $30,000 can be reported in 1999 instead of reporting the entire $60,000 in 1998. The $30,000 you are allowed to postpone consists of the extra 100 head you sold at $300 a head.

To qualify for this postponement, the weather related area must be eligible for federal assistance. The income postponement includes sales that you made before the area became eligible for federal assistance, as long as the weather-related condition caused the sale. You have to be in the area; the animals don't.

To claim a postponement, list the following items in a statement:

- ✔ An election under 451(e) of the Internal Revenue Code to postpone a part of the income you received
- ✔ The date and location of the area eligible for federal assistance
- ✔ The number of animals sold in each of the three preceding years
- ✔ The number of animals you would have sold had it not been for the weather-related condition
- ✔ The total number of animals sold because of the weather-related condition
- ✔ A statement showing how you computed the amount you are postponing (as shown earlier in this section)

Attach this statement to your tax return.

Sometimes, a cooperative doesn't issue a dividend in the form of cash. It may issue a written *Notice of Allocation* or a *Per-Unit Retain Certificate* that can be redeemed in the future. If these certificates are qualified ones, you report them as income in the year you receive them; if they're nonqualified, you report the income in the year you redeem them.

Although you normally report dividends and distributions on Schedule B of Form 1040, Interest and Dividend Income, reporting cooperative distributions is an exception to this rule; you enter them on line 5. Enter the amounts from Form 1099-PATR (boxes 1, 2, 3, and 5) on line 5a; use 5b for the taxable amount. Remember, if the cooperative dividend was paid on purchases for nondeductible family living expenses, don't enter it on 5b. It's not taxable.

Lines 6a and b: Agricultural program payments

Normally, most payments you receive from the government under agricultural programs are taxable in the year you receive them. However, you don't have to pay tax on some of the payments received under certain cost-sharing conservation programs. The rules are rather nightmarish. Therefore, our advice is to seek the help of a tax professional who is experienced in this area. But for you die-hard do-it-yourselfers, IRS Publication 225, *(Farmer's Tax Guide),* which you can order by calling 800-829-3676, can walk you through the rules on this issue. It's not a light read, however.

If you received payments under a governmental agricultural program, that income is reported to you in box 7 on **Form 1099-G,** which you should receive by February 1, 1999. These payments may have come from a conservation program or payment-in-kind certificates. If you receive a payment-in-kind, you are entitled to a deduction for the material or supplies you receive (because you use those materials to operate your farm). Because you can sell commodity credit certificates and use them to pay price-support loans or other federal debts, you report the certificates as income in 1998 even if you don't use them until 1999.

No additional tax breaks are allowed for money received under feed assistance programs — all money you receive for feed assistance is taxable. If you didn't receive any cost-sharing payments, you should enter the same amount on line 6b that you entered on 6a.

Lines 7a–c: Commodity Credit Corporation (CCC) loans

Normally, you report income when you sell something such as your crop. However, if you pledge part or all of your crop to get a CCC loan, you can elect to report the loan proceeds in the year you receive the loan rather than in the year you sell the crop. We don't recommend doing this, however, because you could end up paying tax on a higher amount than the actual payments you received.

Our advice is to stay clear of electing to pay the tax on loan payments you receive in advance of selling a crop.

Lines 8a–d: Crop insurance proceeds and certain disaster payments

Crop insurance and disaster payments are taxable in the year they are received. But (there is always a but) because you are using the cash method of accounting, you can elect to postpone reporting income received from crop insurance or disaster payments until 1999. You do this by attaching a statement to your 1998 return that includes the following items:

- ✔ The statement that you are making this election pursuant to section 451(d) of the Internal Revenue Code
- ✔ A description of crops that were destroyed or damaged, the cause, and the date the damage was incurred
- ✔ What you received for each crop and from whom it was received

On lines 8a through 8d, you enter the following information about any income you receive from crop insurance or disaster payments:

- ✔ **8a:** Enter the amount received.
- ✔ **8b: Taxable amount:** This is usually the same as 8a. But remember, as previously explained, you can elect to report the payment next year.
- ✔ **8c:** If you are making an election to defer reporting the insurance or disaster payment until 1999, check this box.
- ✔ **8d:** Enter the amount you deferred from 1997. Next year, the difference between lines 8a and b gets entered here. The difference between lines 8a and 8b is the amount you are deferring to 1999.

Line 9: Custom hire (machine work) income

If you receive cash, services, or merchandise as payment for plowing your neighbor's field or renting out your tractor, jot down this amount on line 9 — the value of those items or services is taxable.

Line 10: Other income

Line 10 is where you enter every last dollar you earned from a whole bunch of miscellaneous activities, such as the following:

✔ **Cancellation of Debt:** For tax purposes, almost any debt that is canceled or forgiven must be included as income (see the sidebar, "Canceled or forgiven debts that aren't taxable," later in this chapter, for exceptions). Yes, the IRS is so hard-up, it even wants to collect from people who can't pay their bills. If the amount of canceled debt is more than $600, you should receive **Form 1099-C, Cancellation of Debt,** by January 31, 1999.

✔ **Bartering:** Suppose that you help a neighbor build a barn and you receive a horse in return for your work. The value of the horse must be reported as income. Even poor Jack of Beanstalk fame had taxable income when he traded his cow for those beans.

✔ **Refunds and reimbursements:** If you receive a refund on an item for which you took a deduction in a prior year, sorry — it's taxable. For example, suppose that you purchased feed in 1997 and took a deduction in that year. In 1998, however, you received a $500 refund. This refund also gets reported as income on line 10.

✔ **Soil, natural deposits, or timber sales:** If you remove and sell topsoil, fill dirt, gravel, or sand, you don't have to guess at all on this one — the proceeds on the sale of those items are taxable (although you can claim a *depletion deduction* if you own the timber for more than one year and elect to claim that the sale actually took place at the time the timber was cut). If you cut and sell some timber from your land (we're not talking about a major logging operation here), you include this income on line 10 as well. You can also deduct the cost of cutting and hauling the timber as an expense.

If you choose to claim a *depletion deduction,* you have to report the sale on **Form 4797, Sale of Business Property.** This can get rather tricky, so we recommend that you seek the advice of a professional tax advisor if you choose to get involved in this.

✔ **Rents and crop shares:** If you pasture someone else's cattle and take care of the cattle for a fee, include that income on line 10. But if you simply rent your pasture, the rent goes on Schedule E (see Chapter 13 for more information on Supplemental Income and Losses).

Normally, rent is reported on **Form 4835, Farm Rental Income and Expenses.** But because operating a farm is what you do for a living, report the rent on Schedule F. By reporting rental income on Schedule F, you get to pay more Social Security and Medicare tax (lucky you!). However, paying more now probably means that you will be able to collect more when you are old and gray.

If the rent you receive is paid as a share of the crop (rather than cash), you don't have to report the crop as income until you sell the crop or feed it to your animals. This is a good way to defer income to a later year.

✔ **Fuel tax credit and refunds:** If you claimed the cost of fuel as a deduction on line 21, any refund of federal excise taxes on that fuel is taxable. What the government has given now gets taken away.

✔ **Prizes:** If you win a cash prize at the county fair, include that income on line 10. The blue ribbon, however, isn't taxable.

Line 11: Gross income

The IRS couldn't have picked a better name for this line, after forcing you to snake your way through all the preceding lines. Add the amounts on lines 3 through 10 and enter the total amount on line 11.

Canceled or forgiven debts that aren't taxable

Guess what? Although most canceled debt must be claimed as income, a whole bunch of other canceled or forgiven debts are *not* taxable. Here's the list:

✔ **Gifts:** Suppose that your father lends you $7,500, and then a year later he tells you to forget it. A "loan" from a relative can be considered as a gift — and gifts aren't taxable.

✔ **Debt wiped out in a bankruptcy**

✔ **Price reductions:** Suppose that you buy seed and (after it is delivered to you) the seller then reduces the price — and sends you a rebate. Or perhaps your accountant reduces her bill because you may be having financial trouble. Even though you aren't bankrupt or insolvent, this type of debt forgiveness is not considered as income. Because you use the cash method of accounting, the payment of a business service would have been deductible if it had been paid.

✔ **Debt cancellation when you are insolvent:** Insolvency is when your liabilities exceed the value of your assets (even by one penny). If you are insolvent, you don't have to claim a portion of canceled debt as income — but only to the extent that you are insolvent. (Huh?) Here's where the math gets a bit tricky. Suppose that you are fortunate enough to get someone to cancel a $7,500 debt. Immediately before the cancellation, your assets are worth $75,000 and your liabilities total $80,000, which makes you insolvent to the tune of $5,000. In the case of the $7,500 canceled debt, you're not required to claim the $5,000 (the amount of insolvency) as income. Unfortunately, you do have to pay tax on the remaining $2,500. (Not a difficult situation to be in these days.)

Because the amount of income you have to report is based on the value of your assets, an accurate appraisal can save you a bundle. And it's not unusual for the difference between two appraisals on the same property to be as different as night and day. When seeking an appraisal, always remember — if you ask an appraiser how much two and two is and the appraiser responds "Am I buying or selling?" that's the guy you want to hire.

✔ **Farm debt:** Cancellation of farm debt isn't subject to tax either, provided that at least 50 percent of your income for the preceding three years comes from farming, and the person forgiving the debt isn't related to you, is not the person from whom you acquired the farm, or is not related to that person.

✔ **Contested liability:** The settlement of a contested liability is not considered income. For example, suppose that you are billed $10,000 for supplies that are so badly damaged you can't use them. If you contest that you owe nothing (because you are not liable for the cost of supplies you can't use), any cancellation of what you were billed is not considered as income.

If you receive a **Form 1099-C, Cancellation of Debt,** for debt that isn't subject to tax, our advice is to indicate the canceled debt on **Form 982, Reduction of Tax Attributes Due to Discharge of Indebtedness.** That way, the amount indicated on the 1099-G gets included on your return without your having to report it on any of the income lines on Schedule F. Everyone ends up happy — you and the IRS. When business or farming debt is canceled, the nontaxable portion of the cancellation must reduce any operating losses, tax credits, capital losses, and the tax basis of your depreciable property. Our recommendation: See a tax professional when it comes to debt cancellation.

Part II, Lines 12–34: Expenses

This part of Schedule F usually brings tears to your eyes as you take a hard look at what things cost.

Line 12: Car and truck expenses

One method to deduct vehicle expenses is to take a standard 32.5 cents per mile deduction. However, this method, the standard mileage deduction, can only be taken on cars or light trucks — and then only if you're claiming expenses on a single vehicle. If you're like most farmers, you have expenses on multiple light vehicles. Therefore, you can't use this simplified method; if you are using two cars or trucks, you are required to deduct your actual car and truck expenses. Sorry.

As a general rule, claiming your actual expenses will provide a larger deduction. You can deduct your expenses on the following items:

✔ Gas

✔ Oil

✔ Repairs

✔ License tags and fees

✔ Insurance

✔ Depreciation

You can only deduct vehicle expenses connected with actual business use, regardless of whether you take the standard mileage deduction or keep track of your expenses. For example, if a van is used 80 percent of the time for farm business and 20 percent for personal use, you can deduct only 80 percent of your actual expenses (or 80 percent of the miles you drove during the year, if you are using the standard 32.5 cents per mile rate). See Chapter 11 for more discussion on tracking expenses connected to car and truck use.

Line 13: Chemicals

On line 13, enter the total amount you paid for pesticides and herbicides.

Line 14: Conservation expenses

Want to see a farmer get really mad just before April 15? Just tell him that the $10,000 he spent to clear a pasture or cut diversion channels can't be deducted until he sells the land. Thankfully, though, these types of expenses are deductible if they are consistent with a government conservation program. But there is a limit. Conservation expenses can't exceed 25 percent of your total farming income. You can deduct the following conservation expenses:

✔ Leveling

✔ Grading

✔ Conditioning

✔ Terracing

✔ Contour furrowing

✔ Restoration of soil fertility

✔ Construction of diversion channels, drainage ditches, irrigation ditches, earthen dams, outlets, or ponds

✔ Eradication of brush

✔ Planting of windbreaks

Line 15: Custom hire (machine work) expenses

If you paid someone to spray your crop, plow a field, or harvest a crop, enter the amount you paid here. Tax auditors are trained to investigate this deduction to see if you're deducting land-clearing expenses or paying someone to build structures that have to be depreciated.

Remember two things: Land-clearing can only be deducted as a conservation expense, providing you make the election explained on line 14. And if you pay a custom hire more than $600, you have to file **Form 1099-MISC** with the IRS by February 28, 1999, and furnish a copy to the person you paid by January 31, 1999.

Line 16: Depreciation and Section 179 expense deduction

Depreciation is the annual deduction that allows you to recover the cost of your investment (which has a useful life of more than one year) in farm equipment and structures. The word depreciation in itself is enough to send most readers to the next chapter. We know, but just think of depreciation as a way of increasing your income! Now, are you more excited about depreciation possibilities?

Unless you elect the special provision that allows you to deduct the first $18,500 of equipment used on your farm (see the section on "Your Buying Bonanza: The $18,500 Deduction" in Chapter 11), you have to write off your purchase of these assets over their useful life — as established by the IRS (see Table 14-1). Land can't be depreciated. See Chapter 22 for a discussion of the pros and cons of depreciating versus taking an outright deduction.

Table 14-1	Farm Property Recovery Periods (Useful Lives)	
Type of Property (Assets)	*Useful Life (Years)*	
	GDS	ADS
Agricultural structures (single purpose)	10	15
Airplanes (including helicopters)[1]	5	6
Automobiles	5	5
Calculators and copiers	5	6
Cattle (dairy and breeding)	5	7
Communication equipment[2]	7	10
Computers and peripheral equipment	5	5
Cotton ginning assets	7	12
Drainage facilities	15	20
Farm buildings[3]	20	25
Farm machinery and equipment	7	10
Fences (agricultural)	7	10
Goats and sheep (breeding)	5	5
Grain bin	7	10
Hogs (breeding)	3	3
Horses (age when placed in service)		
Breeding and working (12 years or less)	7	10
Breeding and working (more than 12 years)	3	10
Racing horses (more than 2 years)	3	12
Horticultural structures (single purpose)	10	15
Logging machinery and equipment[4]	5	6
Nonresidential real property[5]	39	40
Office equipment (not calculators, copiers, or typewriters)	7	10
Office furniture or fixtures	7	10
Residential rental property	27.5	40

(continued)

Table 14-1 (continued)

Type of Property (Assets)	Useful Life (Years) GDS	ADS
Tractor units (over-the-road)	3	4
Trees or vines bearing fruits or nuts	10	20
Truck (heavy duty, unloaded weight 13,000 lbs. or more)	5	6
Truck (weight less than 13,000 lbs.)	5	5
Typewriter	5	6

[1] Not including airplanes used in commercial or contract carrying of passengers
[2] Not including communication equipment listed in other classes
[3] Not including single-purpose agricultural and horticultural structures
[4] Used by logging and sawmill operators for cutting of timber
[5] GDS is for property placed in service after May 12, 1993; for property placed in service before May 13, 1993, the recovery period is 31½ years

In Table 14-1, you notice two columns, GDS and ADS. GDS stands for *General Depreciation System*. Almost all farmers use this column. ADS stands for *Alternative Depreciation System*. You must use the ADS column when you start depreciating an asset in the year you elect out of the uniform capitalization rules. Talk about wanting to tear out your hair.

Livestock that you *purchase* for draft, breeding, dairy, or sport must be depreciated. If you *raise* this type of livestock, you can't depreciate them because you incurred no purchase cost.

Normally, buildings don't qualify for the $18,500 tax break. However, single-purpose agricultural or horticultural structures do qualify. An *agricultural structure* is one that is used to raise and feed livestock, breed chickens or hogs, or produce milk, feeder cattle, pigs, broiler chickens, or eggs. A greenhouse used for the commercial production of plants or mushrooms also qualifies as an agricultural structure.

The structure must be used only for the single purpose for which it was designed. For example, a hog pen will *not* qualify for the $18,500 maximum deduction if it is also used to house poultry. Using part of a greenhouse to sell plants also disqualifies you from claiming the deduction. But if you can't claim the immediate write-off under this rule, you are entitled to depreciation as explained in the following paragraphs.

Depreciating your car

Computing the amount of depreciation on your car can be mind-numbing. Unfortunately, the only way around this exercise in frustration is using the 32.5 cents per mile flat expense rate.

Automobiles are lumped by the IRS into the *listed property* category of assets (they are subject to the 50-percent business-use test), and the IRS has given cars a whole bunch of rules and regulations. *Listed property* is an IRS term for assets that include automobiles, telephones, computers, boats, and airplanes — items that the IRS suspects you may be using more for pleasure than for business. The IRS lists cars as five-year property, which means that the IRS deems them to have a useful life of five years. Ready for the computation? Here goes.

If the business use of your car is 50 percent or more, your depreciation is computed under MACRS (Modified Accelerated Cost Recovery System) according to what is known as the half-year convention (see Table 14-2).

Table 14-2		Half-Year Convention for Auto Depreciation	
Year	**Yearly Percent**	**For a $30,000 Car**	**Maximum Yearly Limit**
1-1998	15.00%	$4,500	$3,160
2-1999	25.50%	$7,650	$5,000
3-2000	17.85%	$5,355	$2,950
4-2001	16.66%	$4,998	$1,775
5-2002	16.66%	$4,998	$1,775
6-2003	8.33%	$2,499	$1,775
Total	100%	$30,000	$1,775 in each succeeding year

So, for a $30,000 car purchased in 1998, the maximum amount of depreciation that you can claim on your 1998 return is $3,160. In 1999, you get to claim a $5,000 depreciation deduction, $2,950 in 2000, and $1,775 a year until the $30,000 is fully depreciated (which will take around $13^{3}/_{4}$ years). This formula, however, assumes that the car is being used 100 percent for business. So, if the business use is less, the maximum yearly limits have to be reduced. You may be forced to use Table 14-4, mid-quarter convention, which is explained later in this chapter.

To file (or not to file) Form 4562

You compute your depreciation deduction on **Form 4562, Depreciation and Amortization,** for business property you started using in 1998. Carry the amount of depreciation you calculated on this form over to line 16 of Schedule F.

For property you started using prior to 1998, Form 4562 isn't required. Just enter the amount on line 16 of Schedule F. However, if you are depreciating cars, computers, or cellular phones, you must use Form 4562 because only the business portion of these items can be depreciated.

IRS depreciation percentages

To figure the amount of depreciation you are entitled to claim, glance at the IRS depreciation tables (see Tables 14-2 through 14-7). For business property other than real estate, notice that each table has two categories: half-year convention and mid-quarter convention. Usually you use the half-year convention. The mid-quarter convention comes into play when the farm assets you acquired and started using in the last three months of the year exceed 40 percent of all your business property that you place in service during the year. Got that? Read on and follow the example for both types of depreciation conventions.

Half-year convention depreciation

Suppose that you are depreciating a computer that you purchased for $5,000 in 1998; first look up its useful life in Table 14-1. Computers have a useful life of five years, so use the depreciation percentages for five-year property. Okay, easy enough so far.

Under the half-year convention for five-year property (see Table 14-4), you find 15 percent as the amount. For 1998, you are entitled to a $750 depreciation deduction ($5,000 × 15%). In 1999, you multiply the $5,000 cost by 25.5 percent for a deduction of $1,275. And then you use 17.85, 16.66, 16.66, and 8.33 percent in each of the succeeding years. Fun calculations, right? Based on the convention, note that the write-off period for stuff is one year longer than its useful life. That's because in the first year you're entitled to only a half-year's worth of depreciation. The half-year convention rule means that all assets are considered to have been purchased on July 1 — which entitles you to only half the normal amount of depreciation.

Mid-quarter convention depreciation

You must use the mid-quarter convention if the business property you placed in service during the last three months of the year exceeds 40 percent of all your business property placed in service during the year.

For example, suppose that you bought a calculator for $500 on February 1, 1998, and a copier for $1,500 on October 1, 1998. Under the half-year convention, you're entitled to a depreciation deduction of $300 ($2,000 × 15%). But because more than 40 percent of all your business property was bought and placed into service during the last three months of the year, you have to switch to the mid-quarter convention. So here's how you must compute the depreciation for these two pieces of equipment.

Under the mid-quarter convention for five-year property (see Table 14-4) for an asset purchased in the first quarter, the depreciation rate is 26.25 percent. Therefore, you're entitled to a $131.25 depreciation deduction ($500 × 26.25%) for the calculator. For the copier, you have to use the 3.75 percent rate for property bought during the fourth quarter ($1,500 × 3.75%), which entitles you to a $56 deduction. In 1999, use 22.13 percent for the calculator and 28.88 percent for the copier.

The long and the short of all this is that if you are forced into using the mid-quarter convention, you get less than half the depreciation in the first year that you normally would.

For farm property you started depreciating in 1987 and 1988, you must use different depreciation tables than the ones shown here. The other tables allow you to take larger deductions in the earlier years and smaller ones in the later years. Whatever depreciation rate you are required to use, at the end of three, five, seven, or ten years, and so on, you get to write off the entire asset. You can obtain the depreciation tables for assets you started to depreciate before 1989 by calling the IRS for Publication 946 (*How To Depreciate Property*).

Table 14-3		MACRS: Three-Year Property			
Year	**Half-Year Convention**	**First Quarter**	**Mid-Quarter Convention**		
			Second Quarter	**Third Quarter**	**Fourth Quarter**
1	25.00%	43.75%	31.25%	18.75%	6.25%
2	37.50%	28.13%	34.38%	40.63$	46.88%
3	25.00%	25.00%	25.00%	25.00%	25.00%
4	12.50%	3.12%	9.37%	15.62%	21.87%

Table 14-4		MACRS: Five-Year Property			
Year	**Half-Year Convention**	**First Quarter**	**Mid-Quarter Convention**		
			Second Quarter	**Third Quarter**	**Fourth Quarter**
1	15%	26.25%	18.75%	11.25%	3.75%
2	25.5%	22.13%	24.38%	26.63%	28.88%
3	17.85$	16.52%	17.06%	18.64%	20.21%
4	16.66%	16.52%	16.76%	16.56%	16.40%
5	16.66%	16.52%	16.76%	16.57%	16.41%
6	8.33%	2.06%	6.29%	10.35%	14.35%

Table 14-5 | | **MACRS: 7-Year Property** | | |

Year	Half-Year Convention	First Quarter	Mid-Quarter Convention Second Quarter	Third Quarter	Fourth Quarter
1	10.71%	18.75%	13.39%	8.04%	2.68%
2	19.13%	17.91%	18.56%	19.71%	20.85%
3	15.03%	13.68%	14.58%	15.48%	16.39%
4	12.25%	12.16%	12.22%	12.27%	12.87%
5	12.25%	12.16%	12.22%	12.28%	12.18%
6	12.25%	12.16%	12.22%	12.27%	12.18%
7	12.25%	12.16%	12.23%	12.28%	12.19%
8	6.13%	1.52%	4.58%	7.67%	10.66%

Table 14-6 | | **MACRS: 10-Year Property** | | |

Year	Half-Year Convention	First Quarter	Mid-Quarter Convention Second Quarter	Third Quarter	Fourth Quarter
1	7.5%	13.13%	9.38%	5.63%	1.88%
2	13.88%	13.03%	13.59%	14.16%	14.72%
3	11.79%	11.08%	11.55%	12.03%	12.51%
4	10.02%	9.41%	9.82%	10.23%	10.63%
5	8.74%	8.71%	8.73%	8.75%	9.04%
6	8.74%	8.71%	8.73%	8.75%	8.72%
7	8.74%	8.71%	8.73%	8.75%	8.72%
8	8.74%	8.71%	8.73%	8.74%	8.72%
9	8.74%	8.71%	8.73%	8.75%	8.72%
10	8.74%	8.71%	8.73%	8.74%	8.71%
11	4.37%	1.09%	3.28%	5.47%	7.63%

Table 14-7 | | **MACRS: 20-Year Property** | | |

Year	Half-Year Convention	First Quarter	Mid-Quarter Convention Second Quarter	Third Quarter	Fourth Quarter
1	3.75%	6.563%	4.688%	2.813%	0.938%
2	7.219%	7.088%	7.148%	7.289%	7.430%
3	6.677%	6.482%	6.612%	6.742%	6.872%
4	6.177%	5.996%	6.116%	6.237%	6.357%
5	5.713%	5.546%	5.658%	5.679%	5.880%
6	5.285%	5.130%	5.233%	5.336%	5.439%
7	4.888%	4.746%	4.841%	4.936%	5.031%
8	4.522%	4.459%	4.478%	4.566%	4.654%
9	4.462%	4.459%	4.463%	4.460%	4.458%
10	4.461%	4.459%	4.463%	4.460%	4.458%

For years 11 through 21, see IRS Publication 946 *(How To Depreciate Property)*. For property with a 27¹/₂-year life (residential real estate), see Table 11-10 in Chapter 11.

Line 17: Employee health and benefit programs

Enter on line 17 the premiums you paid for your employees' accident, health, and group term life insurance coverage — but not the cost of your *own* health insurance.

Your personal health insurance premiums are not deducted on Schedule F. Fifty-five percent of *your* health insurance gets deducted on Schedule A as a medical expense. You can claim the other 45 percent on line 28 of Form 1040 as a direct deduction against your income. See Chapter 7 to find out how you may be able to deduct 45 percent of your personal health insurance premiums directly from your income. In 1999, the percentage jumps to 60 percent.

Line 18: Feed purchased

On line 18, enter the total cost of livestock feed you purchased during the year.

Your expenses for prepaid feed (along with other prepaid farm supplies) can't exceed 50 percent of your *other* deductible farm expenses. For example, suppose that in 1998, you expended $10,000 on fertilizer, feed, and seed you plan to use in 1999. Your other deductible farm expenses in 1998 total $18,000. Therefore, your allowable 1998 deduction for prepaid farm supplies can't exceed $9,000 (that's 50 percent of $18,000). The other $1,000 that you can't deduct in 1998 can be deducted in 1999, when you actually put the supplies to use.

The 50 percent rule doesn't apply if a change occurred in your farming operation that was caused by an extraordinary event such as a flood, a drought, or other catastrophe. One other rule: The prepayment can't be a *deposit* that can be refunded. It has to be a nonrefundable payment against a binding contract to take delivery of the feed or supplies.

Line 19: Fertilizer and lime expenses

Although you have to report as income the value of fertilizer and lime that you receive under a government program, the good news is that, because you are using these items on your farm, you are also entitled to claim the value of these items as a deduction. Enter the expenditure for these items on line 19. The rule for prepaid items (discussed in the preceding section) also applies to fertilizer and lime.

Line 20: Freight and trucking expenses

You don't have to be a tax expert to figure out what goes here. The cost of operating your own truck goes on line 12. You can't deduct fines for overloading a truck, even if unintentional.

Line 21: Gasoline, fuel, and oil

Gasoline for operating a car or truck goes on line 12. This line is for tractor gas, grease, oil, antifreeze, kerosene, and coal for heaters, brooder stoves, lanterns, and tank heaters. This is what they mean by fuel. Fuel to heat your personal residence isn't deductible unless you use part of it for business. But more on that later.

Line 22: Insurance (other than health)

Insurance premiums to protect your buildings, livestock, grain, crops, equipment, and supplies from loss or damage are deductible. Premiums for workers' compensation insurance and liability insurance are also included on line 22.

Suppose that a horse wanders onto your property, falls down a drainage ditch, and has to be destroyed. If you don't have liability insurance, guess who would need to hire a lawyer? Our advice is to protect yourself with liability insurance, and to also carry adequate fire, theft, robbery, and crop insurance. Although you can't deduct the insurance premiums paid for your residential insurance, if you use a portion of your home for business purposes, you can then deduct that portion of the premium.

Insurance premiums that you pay in advance can only be deducted in the year they apply. For example, suppose that on January 1, 1998, you paid a three-year insurance premium of $1,500. Of that prepaid amount, $500 gets deducted in tax year 1998, $500 in 1999, and $500 in tax year 2000. Business interruption insurance can also be deducted. But any amount paid under the policy is fully taxable.

Lines 23a and b: Interest expense

Most farm interest is deductible; that includes interest on the mortgage on your farm, as well as the interest on loans used to buy farm equipment and farm supplies. As a general rule, the IRS divides interest into the following categories:

- Trade or business interest
- Investment interest
- Interest on a residence
- Personal interest

Deduct trade or business interest on Schedule F; include mortgage interest and interest on other business debts that you may incur while running your farm.

Of the other types of interest, investment interest is deducted on **Schedule A, Itemized Deductions.** What's investment interest? Suppose that you open a margin account at Merrill Lynch to trade commodities. The interest you pay is categorized as investment interest. Investment interest can be deducted only to the extent of your investment income. However, if you trade farm commodities as part of your farm operation, the investment interest rules don't apply. Interest on a residence is also deducted on Schedule A.

Personal interest, such as credit card interest and personal loans, can't be deducted. But what if you borrow $30,000 and use $10,000 to buy farm equipment and $20,000 to buy a car that is strictly for personal use? You have to make an allocation. The interest on the $10,000 used to buy farm equipment is deductible; the interest on the $20,000 used to buy the car is not deductible. For more information on deducting interest, see Chapter 9.

Line 24: Labor hired

On line 24, enter the amount you paid in cash wages — that is, the total amount you pay your employees *before* you withhold income tax, Social Security, and Medicare taxes. The cost of any meals and lodging that you provide is not considered wages, which means that employees don't have to pay tax on it. However, *you* are allowed to deduct those costs as a valid "other expense." On line 34, you can deduct the cost of food you buy for your employees.

Any cash allowance that you give employees to buy meals is considered part of their wages. Normally, you can deduct only 50 percent of the cost of meals (see entertainment expenses in Chapter 11).

If more than half of all the employees to whom you provide meals are furnished the meals for what the law calls "the convenience of the employer," then all the meals you furnish your employees are fully deductible. No 50-percent "haircut." Farmers meet this "convenience" test.

If you pay your employees *in-kind,* you can deduct (as a labor expense) the value of the goods they received. For example, suppose that you give an employee a horse worth $1,500 as payment for painting your barn. You can then deduct the $1,500 as a labor expense. However, remember that you must also report (as income) the $1,500 as if you sold the horse to your employee, because bartering is a taxable event.

The wages you paid and the income tax, Social Security, and Medicare taxes that you are required to withhold are reported to the government on **Form 943, Employer's Annual Tax Return for Agricultural Employees.** This form must be filed by January 31, 1999. Most likely, you're going to have to deposit the Social Security and Medicare taxes along with the income tax you withheld prior to filing Form 943. All this is explained in IRS Publication 51 Circular A *(Agricultural Employer's Tax Guide).*

The wages you pay to a child under the age of 18 are not subject to Social Security and Medicare taxes. So, as long as the child's wages total less than $4,250 (the standard deduction for tax year 1998), the child won't have to pay any tax at all (as long as that $4,250 is the child's *only* source of income). And better still, you get to deduct the $4,250 as a labor expense. The only requirement is that the amount you pay for the child's services must be reasonable. For example, you can't claim that you paid your three-year-old $4,250 to clean out the barn. And because the standard deduction is tied to the rate of inflation, every year it goes up by about $100 or so.

Line 25: Pension and profit-sharing plans

On line 25, enter the amount you contributed to your employees' Keogh and SEP (Simplified Employee Pension) account(s). As for your own Keogh or SEP, enter that amount on Form 1040, line 29 (see Chapter 7 for information on deducting your own contributions to your retirement accounts). A relatively new type of retirement plan called a SIMPLE retirement plan is available to employers with fewer than 100 employees. These plans have none of the mind-numbing rules to follow or forms to file that regular retirement plans have. A SIMPLE plan can also cover the owner(s) of a farm. See Chapter 21 for more information on retirement accounts.

Lines 26a and b: Rent or lease expense

On line 26a, enter the amount that you paid to rent farm machinery and tractors.

If you lease equipment under the condition that you *own the equipment at the end of the lease,* the IRS considers this a *conditional sales contract,* which isn't really a lease. A conditional sales contract is considered a purchase — you must depreciate the cost of this equipment rather than deducting the lease payments as a business expense.

If you rent a farm, you can deduct the rental payments that cover the land, buildings, and so on, but you can't deduct the amount that represents the fair rental value of the farm house in which you live. However, if you use part of your home for business, you *can* deduct that portion. For more on deducting home office expenses, see Chapter 11.

If you pay rent in the form of crop shares, you can't deduct the value of the crops as rent, even though you are required to send the landlord a **Form 1099-MISC** (if the value of what you paid was more than $600). Only the rent that you paid in cash gets deducted on line 26.

Line 27: Repairs and maintenance

Repairs are deductible in full. Improvements must be depreciated. How can you tell the difference between a repair and an improvement? An *improvement* extends the useful life of something. A repair doesn't. Fixing a leak is a repair. Replacing a roof is an improvement. When does a repair move into the category of an improvement? This is something the IRS and taxpayers often go to court over. There is no easy answer.

Line 28: Seeds and plants purchased

Line 28 is one of the simplest lines on the form — just enter the amount you paid for seed and plants. If you prepaid for seed or plants that you will use the following year, you may be able to deduct only a portion of that expense this tax year. See the rules regarding prepaid seed in the "Line 18: Feed purchased" section, earlier in this chapter.

Line 29: Storage and warehousing

Nothing tricky here. Enter the amount you paid the grain elevator operator and other storage and warehousing expenses.

Line 30: Supplies purchased

Baling wire, oil for lamps, shovels, and other types of supplies used around a farm get deducted here.

Line 31: Taxes

Line 31 is where you deduct real estate, your share of the Social Security and Medicare taxes *you* had to fork over on the wages you paid (not the amount you *withhold* from the employee's check; that withholding gets reported on Form 943, Form W-3, and the employee's Form W-2), and personal property taxes on farm business assets. You can deduct half the amount you pay on your own Social Security tax. However, that amount is deducted on line 27, Form 1040, not on Schedule F. See Chapter 7 for more information on how to pay your Social Security tax.

The real estate taxes you paid on the part of your farm that you use as your home are deducted on **Schedule A, Itemized Deductions** and not on this line. State income taxes also get deducted there. Sales taxes paid on the purchase of farm equipment can't be deducted separately. Sales taxes are added to the total cost of the equipment, which then gets depreciated.

Some states grant a sales tax exemption for farm equipment and supplies. Check with your state's revenue office.

Line 32: Utilities

On line 32, deduct your utility expenses. For example, you can deduct your water expenses for irrigation and other farm use, electricity to run farm equipment, and your telephone (to the extent it's used for business). However, if some of these items are used for your farm residence as well, that portion of your utility bill is considered a personal expense and can't be deducted.

Line 33: Veterinary, breeding, and medicine

On line 33, tally up your expenses for veterinary and breeding fees, medicines, vaccines, culling chickens, dehorning, and testing cattle.

Lines 34a–f: Other expenses

Congratulations! You made it to the last line on which you have to make entries. On line 34, put deductions for expenses that you couldn't find a home for on lines 12 through 33, such as accounting, dues, bookkeeping, commissions, office supplies, government milk assessments, business travel, and entertainment.

Personal clothing isn't deductible. The IRS has been known at times to disallow a deduction for overalls or work clothes because a farmer couldn't convince the tax auditor that it wouldn't be appropriate to wear the overalls into town. If you get to line 34f and run out of space, attach a schedule of additional expenses, write `See expenses from attached schedule`, and enter the total of those expenses on line 34f.

Line 35: Total expenses

Time for an addition quiz: Add up lines 12 through 34f; then enter the amount of your total farm expenses on line 35.

Line 36: Net farm profit or loss

An additional math test: Subtract your total expenses (line 35) from your total income (line 11). If you come up with a positive number, guess what? You've made a profit! Enter the amount of your net profit on line 36, copy the amount onto Form 1040, line 18, and also onto Schedule SE, line 1. (Schedule SE is used to compute your Social Security and Medicare tax.)

If you have a loss (line 35 is larger than line 11), then subtract line 11 from line 35. Enter this amount in brackets. For example, enter a $10,000 loss as [$10,000]. Enter this amount on Form 1040, line 18, and on Schedule SE, line 1.

Lines 37a and b: At risk

If you have a loss and are personally liable to pay back every dime you borrowed to go into business, check line 37a. If not, check line 37b and schedule an appointment with a tax professional. The rules are complex regarding the deduction of losses when you have no economic risk.

Tax Issues Specific to Farmers

Unfortunately, you still have to cope with a few additional things that we explain in the following sections.

Estimated taxes

The IRS doesn't want to wait until April 15 to collect what you owe. If two-thirds of your income was from farming in 1997 and 1998, you have to make an estimated income tax payment by January 15, 1999, or file your return (including your full tax payment) by March 1, 1999. If you don't make an estimated payment, you will be charged a penalty equal to current market interest rates. The penalty is computed on **Form 2210-F, Underpayment of Estimated Tax by Farmers and Fishermen.**

The amount of your required estimated tax payment is $66^2/_3$ percent of your 1998 actual tax *or* 100 percent of your 1997 tax, whichever is the smaller amount. For example, suppose that your 1998 tax is $10,000 and your 1997 tax was $1,000. Because your 1997 tax of $1,000 is smaller than $6,667 (two-thirds of your 1998 tax of $10,000), you have to pay only $1,000 on January 15, 1999. You pay the balance, $9,000, when you file on April 15.

If you are hearing about all this for the first time, sorry. Mark your January 2000 calendar so this won't happen again when you file your 1999 return.

Operating at a loss

When operating any business, you must show a profit in a least three of every five consecutive years or the IRS will term your business a hobby and disallow your losses, a situation known as *hobby losses.* If you're breeding horses, training, showing, or racing them, however, you must make a profit in *two out of seven* years in order to keep the tax collector away. The IRS does not consider your enterprise a business if you have continuing losses — no business, no business deductions.

However, if your farm does incur a net loss in 1998, you can write off that loss against any other income you and your spouse made that year. And get this — if the loss is greater than your combined income in the current year, you can carry the loss back over each of the past five years and obtain a refund on the tax you paid at that time. The loss still isn't used up by carrying it back? You can carry the loss *forward* to offset your income in the *next* 20 years. See Chapter 19 for more information on amending a prior year's return and carrying back losses.

For losses incurred before 1998, the carryback was three years. If the losses weren't used up by offsetting income in the three preceding years, they could be carried forward for 15 years. For nonfarmers and for casualty losses, a mishmash of rules governs whether the carryback should be two years as opposed to three years. See Chapter 19 for more details.

Your Social Security tax

This tax is commonly referred to as the self-employment tax. See line 52, Chapter 8, to find out how to compute this and take a deduction for half of what you pay in Social Security tax.

Farmers have an optional method for computing this tax. The computation is made in Part II of Schedule SE.

Here's how it works. If your gross income (from line 11 on Schedule F) is $2,400 or less, you can report two-thirds of your gross income as your *net farm income from self-employment*. Remember, you use this amount to compute your Social Security tax (not for figuring the amount on which you pay income tax). For example, suppose that your gross income was $1,800 and your net income (profit) was $500 — you can elect to report $1,200 (2/3 of $1,800) as your self-employment income, for the purpose of computing your Social Security tax. (However, you still pay income tax only on the $500 net income that you earned.)

If your gross income from farming is more than $2,400 and your net income (profit) is less than $1,737, you may elect to report $1,600 as your self-employment earnings, on which your Social Security tax will be computed. Why do all this?

- ✔ You receive credit for Social Security coverage.

- ✔ Your dependent child care deduction and earned income credit increase with this method.

Investment credits

The law allows an *investment credit,* which is similar to a direct payment of tax, for what you spent on reforestation or to rehabilitate historic structures and buildings placed in service before 1936. For reforestation, the law allows a credit for up to $10,000 of these expenditures. If you rehabilitate a historic structure, you can take an investment credit equal to 20 percent of your expenses. The *energy credit* equals 10 percent of what you spend installing solar or geothermal energy-producing equipment. These credits are computed on **Form 3468, Investment Credit.**

Fuel credits

You can claim a credit for the off-highway use of fuels on your farm. The credit is computed on **Form 4136, Credit for Federal Tax Paid on Fuels.** After July 1, 1998, this credit applies to kerosene. *Note:* The definition of *off-highway use* doesn't apply to motor boats. The credit is equal to 13 cents for every gallon of gas used on your farm.

You can buy dyed diesel fuel tax-free for use on a farm. Ask the vendor for an exemption certificate. Fill it out, hand it back to him, and watch the price drop 24.4 cents a gallon.

Sale of a farm or equipment

The sale of a farm or farm equipment gets tricky — you must consider many different factors, such as recapture of depreciation, credits, and basis (cost) adjustments to the property being sold. These types of sales are reported on **Form 4797, Sales of Business Property.** For more information on capital gains, see Chapter 12.

Installment sales

Cash-method farmers who use the installment method for reporting the sale of farm property don't have to take installment sales into account when determining whether they're subject to the Alternative Minimum Tax. See line 51 in Chapter 8 if you're subject to this fiendish tax because you're claiming too many deductions.

Chapter 15
Other Schedules and Forms to File

Most taxpayers need to file a variety of other tax schedules and forms to accompany their 1040s. These documents are tailored to specific tax situations. For example, for nondeductible IRAs, you need Form 8606. We know it's a chore. But think of the process this way: As a general rule, the more yucky the schedules, the more you reduce the amount of tax you pay. This chapter presents a brief overview of the major forms that taxpayers need to file, with tips for filling out the trickier lines. We discuss them in alphabetical and numeric order.

Form 1040-ES, the Estimated Tax Form

If you're self-employed or have income, such as retirement benefits, that isn't subject to withholding, you should be making quarterly estimated tax payments on Form 1040-ES. On average, a third of what you earn isn't yours. (It's depressing, we know.) You're only its temporary custodian until mid-April. But if you keep too much in custody — that is, you don't have enough withheld — that "third of what you earn" is subject to a penalty if you don't pay in enough. What's enough? Read on.

You must pay in at least 90 percent of your tax during the year. But if not paying in 90 percent leaves a balance of less than $1,000, you don't need to make quarterly estimates. For example, your 1998 tax is $3,000. Ninety percent amounts to $2,700. Your withholding comes to $2,600, which is less than 90 percent of your tax. Because you owed less than $1,000 when you filed, no estimated payments were required. For 1999, you'll have to make quarterly estimated payments if you expect to owe more than $1,000 when you file on April 15, 2000.

You make estimated tax payments on **Form 1040-ES, Estimated Tax for Individuals.** The form requires only your name, address, Social Security number, and the amount that you're paying. For 1999 estimated payments, make sure that you use the 1999 1040-ES. Enter the amount of your estimated payments on line 58 of Form 1040 when you file your annual return.

For example, suppose that you're self-employed. Your 1998 tax is $7,000, and your self-employment tax is $3,000 — a total of $10,000. The law requires that you make estimated tax payments of 90 percent of your estimated 1999 tax or 100 percent of your 1998 tax. So if you expect your 1999 total tax to be the same amount that it was in 1998 (that is, $10,000), you must make quarterly estimates of $2,250 (90 percent of $10,000 ÷ 4), with 10 percent, or $1,000, coming due in April 2000. However, if you make quarterly estimates of $2,500 (100 percent of your 1998 tax), and your actual 1999 tax comes to $25,000, no penalty will be assessed. Because you paid 100 percent of your 1998 tax ($10,000), you can wait until April 15, 2000, to pay the $15,000 balance.

If your 1998 income is more than $150,000, you have to make estimated tax payments equal to 105 percent of your 1998 tax to escape a 1999 underestimating penalty if your 1999 tax turns out to be substantially more than your 1998 tax. For example, suppose that your 1998 tax was $100,000. Because your 1998 income was more than $150,000, you had to make estimated payments of at least $105,000. Therefore, even if your 1999 tax turns out to be $200,000, you had to make estimated payments of only $105,000 (105 percent of your 1998 tax) and can wait until April 15, 2000, to pay the $95,000 balance without incurring any penalty.

The only way that you can escape the penalty for not making the quarterly payments is to know the rules. If you got burned by this penalty on your 1998 return, don't let it happen in 1999. When you file your 1998 return on April 15, 1999, you also need to make your first quarterly estimated payment for 1999. The three additional payments are due June 15, 1999; September 15, 1999; and January 15, 2000.

You use Form 1040-ES (1999) to compute your 1999 estimated tax payments. It comes with four vouchers that must accompany your checks so that you get credited for your payments.

But before you fill in the vouchers that are due April 15, 1999; June 15, 1999; September 15, 1999; and January 15, 2000; you have to figure out how much you have to pay. That's why the first part of the form contains a worksheet. It's sort of a mini tax return so that you can figure out your 1999 tax and how much you have to pay in quarterly installments. Because you're making an estimate, you can adjust future estimated payments if your income for the balance of the year moves up or down.

If your income has been pretty consistent and you end up paying the same amount of tax every year, enter the amount of tax from line 56 of your 1040 (or line 34 of your 1040A) on line 13c of the worksheet. Divide this amount by four and enter this amount on line 17. This amount is what you have to pay every quarter. But if you want to keep a little more money in your pocket, you can get away with paying only 90 percent of this amount. But as we explained previously, a fail-safe method is to pay 100 percent of your 1998 tax. Then, no matter what your tax turns out to be, the IRS can't access a penalty if your estimated tax is off by a mile. If your 1998 tax turns out to be $100,000, you can wait to pay the $90,000 balance on April 15, 2000, without incurring a penalty. However, if your 1998 income is more than $150,000, this "fail-safe" method works only if you pay in 105 percent of your 1998 tax when making your 1999 estimated payments.

If the tax that you pay every year is pretty consistent, you have to pay in only 90 percent. For example, your 1998 tax is $10,000. You're required to pay in only $9,000 in quarterly installments of $2,250, and you can wait to pay the $1,000 balance come next April. And remember, if you end up owing less than $1,000 because enough tax is taken out of your salary or pension, you don't have to make quarterly estimated payments. You can pay the balance that you owe when you file.

We know that we're repeating ourselves. But if you can't base your 1999 estimated income on what you earned in 1998 because it's too up and down, or if you also have to pay self-employment tax, are on salary, and have tax withheld or your deductions will change, can you guess what we're about to say? Get a software program. But because you laid out good money for this book, here's how to complete the estimated tax worksheet.

Line 1: Enter your 1998 income or what you expect to earn in 1999.

Line 2: Enter your standard deduction or your itemized deductions for 1999. If you expect them to be the same, enter the amount from line 36 of your 1040.

Line 3: Subtract line 2 from line 1.

Line 4: Enter your exemptions. Multiply the amount that you claimed on line 6(d) of your 1040 by $2,700. This amount will actually be a little higher in 1999 because exemptions get increased every year by the annual rate of inflation. Remember, this figure is an estimate, and we're trying to take you through this form in the quickest and simplest way.

Line 5: Subtract line 4 from line 3. This figure is your taxable income.

Line 6: Figure your tax on line 5 by using the tax rate schedules that come with the 1040ES for 1999, which are included in the back of this book. You figure your tax the same way that you did when you prepared your 1998 return. For a quick refresher course, go back to line 40 in Chapter 8.

Line 7: Additional taxes. On this line, enter the 10-percent penalty that you expect to pay because you're under 59$\frac{1}{2}$ and plan to tap into your IRA in 1999. If you don't expect to have any weird kind of financial transactions, enter zero on this line.

Line 8: Add lines 6 and 7. It's getting easier.

Line 9: Enter the tax credit that you're entitled to — child tax credit, child care, earned income, and foreign tax credits are the most common ones. The child tax credit for 1999 is $500 per child.

Line 10: Subtract line 9 from line 8.

Line 11: Enter your 1999 self-employment tax. We cover how to compute this tax later in this chapter, so jump to "Schedule SE: Self-Employment Tax Form" if you need a quick review. That's how you pay your Social Security tax if you're self-employed.

Line 12: Skip this line. It applies only in the most unusual circumstances.

Line 13a: Add lines 10 through 12.

Line 13b: We took care of this credit on line 9, so you can ignore this line.

Line 13c: Subtract line 13b from 13a. You should end up with the same amount as on line 13a. **This figure is your 1999 estimated tax.**

Lines 14a and 14b: Here's where you have an option. You can pay either 100 percent of your 1998 tax (line 34 of your 1998 Form 1040A or line 56 of your 1998 Form 1040) or 90 percent of line 13c. The choice is yours. Using your 1998 tax is the fail-safe method because you pay no penalties if you're off by a mile. Remember, if your 1998 income was more than $150,000, you have to pay in 105 percent of your 1998 tax to use the fail-safe method.

Line 14c: Enter the amount that you want to pay — the 90 percent amount from line 14a, or 100 or 105 (if your 1998 income was more than $150,000) percent of your 1998 tax from line 14b.

Line 15: Enter the amount of tax that you expect to have withheld from your salary or pension.

Line 16: Subtract line 15 from line 14c. This amount is what you have to pay.

Line 17: Divide line 16 by four to figure out what you have to pay every quarter. However, if you skipped the first payment on April 15, 1999, you have to divide line 16 by three, because now you have to make 3 payments: June 15, September 15, and next January 15. If you're making two payments because you missed both the April 15 and June 15 payments, divide line 16 by two and get your money in on September 15 and January 15.

The payment vouchers: Enter your name, address, and Social Security number as well as the amount you're paying on the voucher that you submit. Also, put your Social Security number on your check with the notation 1999 1040 ES. Make your check out to the Internal Revenue Service and mail it, along with the voucher, to the address on the last page of the 1040-ES.

Don't mail your payment to the Service Center where you file. Use the pre-addressed envelopes that the IRS sent you. If you're using your own envelopes, be sure to mail your check and payment voucher to the address shown on the Form 1040-ES instructions for the place where you live.

Form 2441, Child and Dependent Care Expenses

If you hire someone to take care of your children so that you can work, you're entitled to the credit that you figure on **Form 2441**. This credit may save you several hundred dollars. To be eligible for the credit, your child must be under the age of 13 or a dependent of any age who is physically or mentally handicapped.

✔ Line 1 of Form 2441 requires that you report the name, address, Social Security number or Employer Identification number (EIN) of the person or organization providing the care, and the amount that you paid to the provider.

  If your nanny or baby-sitter is off the books, you can't claim this credit. However, if your annual payment to any one individual is less than $1,100, you're not liable for the payment of Social Security taxes for your child care provider. See "Schedule H: Nanny Tax" later in this chapter for the nanny tax rules.

  If you didn't receive dependent care benefits from your employer, you need to complete only Part II in addition to line 1. If you did receive these benefits, you have to complete Part III on the back of the form. Employer-provided dependent care benefits are noted in box 10 of your W-2.

✔ On line 2, enter the amount that you paid your nanny or baby-sitter. However, you can't enter more than $2,400 for one child or $4,800 for two or more children.

✔ On line 3, enter the amounts from line 2, keeping in mind the $2,400 limit for one child and $4,800 limit for two or more kids.

✔ On line 4, enter your earned income; enter your spouse's earned income on line 5, and on line 6, enter the smaller of lines 3, 4, or 5. On line 7, enter your adjusted gross income (AGI) from line 34 of your 1040.

✔ Based on your AGI, use the chart just below line 8 to find out what percentage of line 6 can be claimed as a credit. For example, if your amount on line 7 was over $28,000, you're entitled to a credit equal to 20 percent of the amount entered on line 6. Enter that percentage on line 8, and do the math to get the figure on line 9. Copy that number over to line 41 on the 1040. 1040A filers have a separate form for this credit — Schedule 2, Form 1040A — and should enter the credit on line 26 of the 1040A.

Many states also allow a credit for child and dependent care expenses. New York, for example, allows the same credit as the IRS does. Check with the tax office in your state to find out what credit, if any, you'll be allowed.

Looking ahead, find out whether your employer offers you the ability to have money deducted from your paycheck — before taxes — into a dependent-care spending account. You may be able to do this in the future and save even more tax dollars instead of taking this credit (you can't do both).

If your employer has a day care plan or provides day care services, the reimbursement from your employer for day care costs or the value of the day care services that your employer provides is taxable if the amount that you enter on line 10 of the Form 2441 is above $5,000. Where does the line 10 number come from? Box 10 of Form W-2.

To determine whether any portion of the amount below $5,000 is taxable, you have to complete Part III of Form 2441. The portion of tax-free child care benefits that you received reduces the amount of child care and dependent care expenses eligible for the child care credit.

Form 3903, Moving Expenses

If you incur moving expenses because you have to relocate for your job, you can deduct moving expenses for which your employer didn't reimburse you. Self-employed individuals may also deduct their moving expenses. And, unlike other deductible expenses, this deduction isn't subject to varying interpretations. It's subject to two mathematical tests. The first one: The distance between your new job location and your former home must be at least 50 miles more than the distance between your former home and your former job location. Let us run this by you one more time:

        A. Miles from your old home to new work place   _____

        B. Miles from your old home to old work place   _____

        C. Subtract line B from line A   _____

If line C is more than 50 miles, you're entitled to a moving-expense deduction.

The second test requires that you remain employed on a full-time basis at your new job location for at least 39 weeks during the 12-month period immediately following your arrival. In other words, you can't claim a deduction unless you pass the distance test and satisfy the employment-duration requirement.

The rule is even tougher on self-employed people. To get the deduction, you must work in the same new job for 78 weeks (that's a year and a half) during the 24 months after your arrival. To save you this bit of math, a part-time job doesn't satisfy the 39- or 78-week test.

If you work outside the U.S., you're eligible for a special exemption: You can deduct expenses for a move to a new home in the U.S. when you permanently retire. The move doesn't have to be related to a new job. This exemption also applies to a survivor of someone who worked outside the U.S.

Meals, temporary living expenses, and expenses incurred in the sale or lease of a residence are no longer deductible. You may deduct only the cost of moving your household goods and personal effects from your former residence to your new one, plus travel and lodging costs for you and members of your household while traveling to your new residence. Lodging before the move or on the day of arrival doesn't count, nor do meals while on the road. These are the federal rules. Some states allow a deduction for moving expenses — your state rules may or may not be similar to the federal rules.

The place to deduct moving expenses is **Form 3903, Moving Expenses.** For a move to a foreign location, you have to use **Form 3903-F.** If you haven't met the 39- or 78-week test by the time that you file your return, don't worry. You're still allowed to claim the deduction if you expect to meet the test. However, if it turns out that you fail the 39- or 78-week test, you must report the deduction as income on next year's tax return. No fun at all.

But you've lucked out with Form 3903; it's only five lines to get through! Here's what you do:

Line 1: Enter the cost of transporting and storing your household goods and personal effects.

Line 2: Enter the travel and lodging expenses for you and members of your household from your old home to your new home. If you use your car, you can claim 10 cents a mile plus tolls and parking.

Line 3: Add lines 1 and 2 (your total moving expenses).

Line 4: Enter the amount that your employer reimbursed you for your moving expenses. You can find this amount in box 13 of your Form W-2 with a code P next to it. If you weren't reimbursed by your employer, box 13 will have nothing in it, so put zero on line 4 of Form 3903.

Line 5: Subtract line 4 from line 3. The result is the amount of your deductible 1998 moving expenses. Now enter this amount on your Form 1040 (line 26).

If line 3 is less than line 4, subtract line 3 from line 4 and include the amount on line 7, Form 1040 "wages etc." The reason? If you receive a reimbursement from your employer that's larger than your expense, you have to pay tax on the difference. If this is the case, make no entry on line 5.

Form 8606, for Nondeductible IRAs

If you made nondeductible contributions to your IRA, not all the money that you withdraw is taxable. To compute what's taxable, you have to fill out **Form 8606, Nondeductible IRAs — Contributions, Distributions, and Basis.**

Form 8606 is important if you made or are making nondeductible contributions or if you're taking money out of an IRA that you made nondeductible contributions to. This form tells you how much money you have to pay tax on every time you withdraw money from your nondeductible IRA account.

Line 1: Enter your 1998 nondeductible IRA contribution, including the dough that you put in between January 1, 1999, and April 15, 1999. Enter your $2,000 contribution on this line if you meet any of the following criteria:

✔ You're doing the $2,000 maximum because you're covered by a pension plan where you work and you earned more than $50,000 if married or $30,000 if single.

✔ You can't do any part of a Roth IRA because your income exceeds $150,000 (couples) or $110,000 if single.

If only a portion of your contribution qualifies for an IRA deduction or a Roth IRA and you elect to have the remaining balance treated as a nondeductible contribution, enter that amount here. For example, you want to put away $2,000. But because you're single and covered by a plan and your income is $35,000, only half of your $2,000 qualifies for the deduction; so, on line 23 of Form 1040 or line 15 of Form 1040A, enter $1,000. Now enter the $1,000 balance here on line 1. But, you have more than one choice when selecting an IRA. You could also do a $1,000 deductible IRA and a $1,000 Roth IRA. Or a $2,000 Roth IRA.

Line 2: Here's where you enter the total of all the nondeductible IRA contributions that you made in prior years. Where do you get this info? Line 12 from your 1997 Form 8606.

Line 3: This is the really easy part of the form. Add lines 1 and 2, and enter the total here.

If you didn't withdraw any money from this IRA, enter the amount from line 3 on line 12. Sign and date the form, and attach it to your return. Nothing else is required.

If you withdrew any money from your nondeductible IRA, you have to tackle lines 4 through 13. They may look complicated, but they really aren't. Just a lot of adding and subtracting, so get your calculator ready.

Line 4: If you made your nondeductible contribution for 1998 between January 1, 1999, and April 15, 1999, you have to enter that amount again on this line. Why? In order to determine how much of your withdrawal is taxable, you have to compare the total of all your nondeductible contributions that you made through December 31, 1998, with the value of your IRA on this date. You know the rules. Apples to apples!

Line 5: Subtract line 4 from line 3. This amount is the total of all your nondeductible contributions through December 31, 1998.

Line 6: Enter the value of all your IRAs on December 31, 1998.

Line 7: Enter what you withdrew only in 1998.

Line 8: Add lines 6 and 7. This amount is what your IRAs would have been worth on December 31, 1998, if you hadn't withdrawn any money.

Line 9: Get out your calculator. Divide line 5 by line 8. Don't panic; we don't leave you dangling over this computation. Here's a hypothetical situation. Say your nondeductible contribution on line 5 is $10,000. The value of your IRAs on line 6 is $90,000, and according to line 6, you withdrew $10,000 in 1998. Line 8 is $100,000 (the total of lines 6 and 7). Now divide line 5 ($10,000) by line 8 ($100,000). The answer: 10 percent. Enter this amount on line 9.

Line 10: Multiply line 7 (the $10,000 that you withdrew in 1998) by line 9 (10 percent). In the example, if you came up with $1,000, you got it right. This amount is the portion of the $10,000 that you withdrew that you don't have to pay tax on.

Line 11: Subtract line 10 from line 5. In our example, this amount is $9,000. The IRS refers to this amount as your tax basis, which is nothing more than IRS lingo for the remaining balance of the nondeductible money that you put into your IRA that you don't have to pay tax on when it comes out. Whoo!

Line 12: If you made an entry on line 4, add it to line 11. If you didn't make an entry on line 4, copy the amount from line 11 on line 12.

Line 13: Subtract line 10 ($1,000) from line 7 ($10,000) and enter the difference ($9,000) here. This amount is the portion of your withdrawal that you have to pay tax on. Enter this amount on line 15b, Form 1040, or on line 10b, Form 1040A.

Sign and date the form and attach it to your return.

You must file Form 8606 to report nondeductible contributions even if you don't have to file a tax return for the year. If you file a Form 1040, you must attach Form 8606 to your 1040. There is a $50 penalty for not filing your 8606! Also, if your IRA contributions are more than the permissible amount, you may be subject to a 6-percent penalty, plus you must correct the overpayment.

Forms 8615 and 8814, the Kiddie Tax

If you have children under age 14 who have investment income, you may need to complete Form 8615 or Form 8814. Once a child reaches age 14, the kiddie tax doesn't apply — the child pays whatever his or her tax rate is.

Form 8615 is the form that you use if your child files his or her own return; use **Form 8814** if you elect to report your kids' investment income on your return. See the sidebar, "Why your 3-year-old may be in the 39.6 percent tax bracket," for more on making this election.

Here's how the kiddie tax works. If a child has $2,400 in interest income, for example, the first $700 is exempt from tax. The next $700 is taxed at the child's tax rate (15 percent), which comes to $105. But, because you're required to compute the tax using the tax tables, the actual figure comes to $107, and the remaining $1,000 is taxed at the parent's rate. So if the parent is in the 31-percent tax bracket, the kiddie tax amounts to $310 ($1,000 × 31 percent) plus the child's portion of $107 for a total bill of $417.

Children whose investment income is over $700 must file a return, but if their income is under $1,400, they can file their return using the less complicated Form 1040A. If they don't have any taxable investment income (you invested the money that their grandparents gave them in tax-exempt bonds), they don't have to file a return until their earned income, such as income from a part-time job, exceeds $4,250. Unless your child was 14 by the end of 1998, here's how to compute the kiddie tax. Enter your Social Security number and taxable income on Form 8615. Add the amount of your child's investment income that's in excess of $1,400 to your taxable income. You recompute your tax, and the difference between the tax on your return and the recomputed figure is the kiddie tax. A good tax software program can save you all this math (refer to Chapter 2).

But if you don't have a tax software program and your child's investment income in excess of $1,400 is $1,000, add the $1,000 to your taxable income. Now you compute your tax on this amount. For example, if the tax on this amount is $9,310 and the tax on your return is $9,000, the $310 difference is the kiddie tax. Enter that amount plus $107 (the tax on the $700 that isn't exempt from tax, per the tax tables) on your child's return on Form 1040 (line 40); you should also check the box marked 8615. If your kid gets stuck for the kiddie tax, you have to use Form 1040 when filing his or her return. The computation of the kiddie tax on Form 8615 doesn't affect the tax that you have to pay. Your taxable income is used only to determine the tax rate for your kid's income above $1,400. It only feels like you're being taxed twice.

But there's more. (There always is.) If you and your spouse file separate returns, you enter the larger of either your or your spouse's taxable income on Form 8615. If you're separated or divorced, the parent who has custody of the child for the greater part of the year uses his or her taxable income when completing Form 8615. But if you and your spouse live apart and qualify to file as unmarried (single or head of household), the custodial parent's taxable income is used on Form 8615.

And it gets worse (as it always seems to)! If you have two or more kids, you enter the total of all their investment income on Form 8615. The kiddie tax is computed and allocated among them. For example, suppose that your daughter's investment income in excess of $1,400 is $3,000, and your son's is $2,000; you enter $5,000 on each child's Form 8615. Then each child's share of the total kiddie tax is allocated. Your daughter's share is three-fifths of the tax, and your son's share is two-fifths.

Why your 3-year-old may be in the 39.6-percent tax bracket

Once upon a time, if you were in the 70-percent tax bracket (rates were that high before 1981), it made sense to make a gift of investment property to your children because the income that the property produced would be taxed at the child's tax rate — which could have been as low as 11 percent. But that was in the good old days (if you think there's something nostalgic about 70-percent tax rates). This tax savings scheme ended in 1986. Nowadays, if a child is under the age of 14, all investment income over $1,400 is taxed at the parent's tax rate — which could be as high as 39.6 percent. The reason for the change is to remove the incentive for higher income earners to transfer lots of money to their kids just to save tax dollars by benefiting from lower tax brackets.

By now you're looking for a way to avoid having to file a separate tax return because your child has $1 over $700. Is there a way, you ask? Yes. If your child has investment income of only $7,000 or less and it's all from interest and dividends, you can report the income on your return by filing Form 8814. That's $7,000 for each child. But we don't recommend this course of action because if you pick this method, the kiddie tax is higher than it would be on the child's return, and yours could be as well. To learn more about the smartest ways to invest in your child's name, read Chapter 25. The $7,000 threshold is indexed for inflation.

Form 8829, Expenses for Business Use of Home

Yes, you can deduct home office expenses — but the rules are tough. You must use **Form 8829, Expenses for Business Use of Your Home,** to claim this deduction. You can find a copy of this form in the back of this book.

You may also be able to derive some nice tax savings from your home. If you use part of your residence for business, you can deduct the mortgage interest, real estate taxes, depreciation, insurance, utilities, and repairs related to that part of your house. The same applies to renters as well. It sounds simple, but here comes the fine print. To claim a home office deduction, you must use your home on a regular and exclusive basis as either a place where you meet with customers or clients or as the principal place where you carry on your business.

As if this requirement isn't bad enough, in 1993 the U.S. Supreme Court added an additional pair of tests — *relative importance* and *time spent*. Now you must compare the relative importance of the work done at all business locations — and that includes yours as well as that of your customers.

Suppose that you're a sales representative who spends 40 hours a week calling on customers and 10 hours in your home office, scheduling appointments and maintaining business records. Your home office is not your principal place of business. That's because calling on customers is of primary importance and your home office, although essential, is less important. If the relative importance comparison doesn't identify a principal place of business, you then compare the time spent at each location. You spend most of your time outside your home office providing a service or calling on customers? You can kiss this deduction good-bye.

If you use a portion of your home to store inventory or samples, the rules have been eased. Say that you sell cosmetics and use part of your study to store samples. You can deduct expenses related to the portion of your study used to store the cosmetics, even if you use the study for other purposes. (Hang on for one more year because, starting in 1999, you'll be able to deduct a home office — even if your home office is used only to conduct administrative or management activities. So, in the previous example of the sales representative, a home office deduction will be allowed.)

This deduction can't produce a loss. For example, suppose that your business income is $6,000. You have $5,000 in business expenses and home office expenses of $1,500 (of which $1,000 is for the percentage of your mortgage interest and real estate tax allocated to the use of the office). First, you deduct the interest and taxes of $1,000, which leaves a balance of $5,000 for possible deductions. Then you deduct $5,000 of business expenses, which brings your business income to zero. The remaining $500 of your home office expenses can't be deducted, but you can carry it over to the next year. If you don't have sufficient income to deduct the $500 next year, you can carry it over again.

In order to fill out Form 8829 correctly if you're a renter, you first have to determine your total rent — including insurance, cleaning, and utilities. Then you deduct the portion used for business. If you rent four rooms and one room is used for business, you're entitled to deduct 25 percent of the total. (If the rooms are the same size, you can use this method. If not, you have to figure out the percentage on a square-footage basis.)

For homeowners, you compute the total cost of maintaining your home, depreciation, mortgage interest, taxes, insurance, repairs, and so on. Then deduct the percentage used for business. Gardening can't be deducted!

Measuring your home office

Complete lines 1 through 7 on Form 8829 to find out how much of your home you used *exclusively* for your business.

- **Line 1:** Enter the area, in square feet, of the part of your home that you used for business: for example, 300 square feet.

- **Line 2:** To determine the percentage of your home that you used for business, enter the total area, in square feet, of your home: for example, 1,500 square feet.

- **Line 3:** Divide line 1 by line 2 and enter the result as a percentage here. In the earlier example, you would enter 20 percent (300 ÷ 1,500). Keep this percentage handy; it's the percentage of the expenses for the whole house — such as interest, real estate taxes, depreciation, utility costs, and repairs — that you use on Form 8829 to determine your deduction.

- **Line 7:** Unless you use your home as a day care facility, you can skip lines 4 through 6 and enter your deduction percentage from line 3 onto line 7.

Figuring your allowable home office deduction

Lines 8 through 34 on Form 8829 involve mega-computations — much more than our space allows. In this section, we take you through some of the basics, but we suggest that you consult a tax advisor or IRS Publication 587 *(Business Use of Your Home)* for additional information.

- **Line 8:** Enter the amount from line 29 of your Schedule C (this is what you earned after expenses). Your home office deduction can't exceed this amount.

- **Lines 9 through 20, column (a):** Expenses that apply exclusively to your office go in this column. Repairs and maintenance, such as painting your office, are two such items.

✔ **Lines 9 through 20, column (b):** Enter your expenses that apply to the entire house on these lines. The IRS refers to them as *indirect expenses*.

If you rent, instead of own, your home, the rent that you paid goes on line 20, column (b). Gardening and lawn care aren't deductible.

✔ **Lines 21 through 34:** It's number crunching time — enough to make us wonder who came up with this form!

✔ **Line 34:** This is your allowable deduction. Carry it over to line 30 on Schedule C.

Determining your home office's depreciation allowance

You also have to apply your home office deduction percentage (from line 7 of Form 8829) to your home's depreciation allowance. This section includes a line-by-line breakdown of the appropriate part on Form 8829.

Line 35: Your home's value

Here's where you compute your depreciation deduction. You get to write off the percentage of your home that you claim as a home office (in our earlier example, 20 percent) over either $31^1/2$ or 39 years, depending on when you set up your office. Usually, residential property is written off over $27^1/2$ years, but because the office is used for business, it's considered business property and has a longer life.

Enter what you paid for the home (including the original and closing costs, as well as any improvements to the property) on this line.

Line 36: Land not included

Because you can't deduct land, you have to subtract the value of the land that your home sits on from the cost of your home in order to get the net cost of the house. A value of 15 percent for the land is a safe subtraction.

Line 37: Basis of building

Subtract line 36 from line 35. This amount is the basis of your home after subtracting the value of the land that you can't depreciate.

Line 38: Business portion of your home

Multiply line 37 by your home office deduction percentage from line 7. In our continuing example, that's the 20 percent of the house used for business that you can write off.

Line 39: Depreciation percentage

If you set up your office before May 12, 1993, it's a $31^1/2$-year write-off. Use Table 15-1 to determine your depreciation percentage.

Table 15-1			$31^1/2$-Year Depreciation Schedule for Business Use of Home									
Use the column for the month of the year that you set up your office.												
Year	**Jan**	**Feb**	**Mar**	**Apr**	**May**	**Jun**	**Jul**	**Aug**	**Sep**	**Oct**	**Nov**	**Dec**
1	3.042%	2.778%	2.513%	2.249%	1.984%	1.720%	1.455%	1.190%	0.926%	0.661%	0.397%	0.132%
2–7	3.175%	3.175%	3.175%	3.175%	3.175%	3.175%	3.175%	3.175%	3.175%	3.175%	3.175%	3.175%

For years 8 and beyond, use the depreciation table in IRS Publication 587 *(Business Use of Your Home)*.

If you set up your office after May 12, 1993, the write-off is over 39 years. Use Table 15-2 to determine your depreciation percentage.

Table 15-2	39-Year Depreciation Schedule for Business Use of Home											
Use the column for the month of the year you set up your office.												
Year	Jan	Feb	Mar	Apr	May	Jun	Jul	Aug	Sep	Oct	Nov	Dec
1	2.461%	2.247%	2.033%	1.819%	1.605%	1.391%	1.177%	0.963%	0.749%	0.535%	0.321%	0.107%
2–39	2.564%	2.564%	2.564%	2.564%	2.564%	2.564%	2.564%	2.564%	2.564%	2.564%	2.564%	2.564%

For example, if you set up your office in June 1998, enter 1.391 percent on line 39 of Form 8829. Every year thereafter you use 2.564 percent.

Line 40: Depreciation allowable

Multiply line 38 by line 39. This is your depreciation deduction based on the business use of your home. Enter this amount here on line 40 and on line 28 of this form as well.

Deducting what's left

Remember, you can't take a loss because of the home office deduction. You can, however, carry over an excess deduction amount to another year's tax return.

On lines 41 and 42, you compute the amount of your home office deduction that you couldn't deduct. You get to deduct it in future years, providing that you have enough income.

On Schedule A, don't forget to deduct the balance (in our example, 80 percent) of your total mortgage interest that you entered on line 10(a) of Form 8829, as well as the balance of your total real estate taxes from line 11(a) of this form. Your mortgage interest balance goes on line 10 of Schedule A; the real estate taxes balance goes on line 6 of Schedule A.

Form W-4, Employee Withholding

If you owe a bundle to the Internal Revenue Service for 1998, chances are you aren't withholding enough tax from your salary. Unless you don't mind paying a lot on April 15, you need to adjust your withholding in order to avoid interest and penalties if you can't pay what you owe when it's due. We include a worksheet to help your through the morass of IRS instructions on the back of your W-4 (see Table 15-3).

Table 15-3	Worksheet for Completing Your 1999 W-4
	Amount
1. Enter your 1999 estimated itemized deductions. If you're claiming the standard deduction, enter 0 on lines 1 and 3, and skip to line 4.	$_____
2. Enter $7,100 if you're filing jointly, $6,350 if head of household, $4,300 if single, or $3,550 if married filing separately.	$_____

	Amount

3. Subtract line 2 from line 1. $_____

4. Enter adjustments to your income (IRA contributions, alimony, and so on). $_____

5. Add lines 3 and 4. $_____

6. Divide line 5 by $2,500 (drop fractions). For example, if line 5 is $8,775 ÷ $2,500, which equals 3³/₅, enter 3 on line 6. _____

7. New child tax credit. If you're single and your income is less than $47,000 ($60,000 if married), enter 1 on line 7 for each child that you can claim the credit for. If you're single and your income is between $47,000 and $80,000 ($60,000 and $115,000 if married), enter 1 if you have two or three kids eligible for the credit, or enter 2 if you have four or more kids. $_____

8. Enter the number of personal exemptions you are entitled to claim for yourself, your spouse, and your dependents. For example, if you are married and have two kids, enter 4. $_____

9. Add lines 6, 7, and 8. This is the number of exemptions that you're entitled to claim on line 5 of your W-4. $_____

As you fill out this worksheet, remember: If you're married and both you and your spouse work, you need to factor in the "marriage penalty," which assures that together you'll owe more than two unmarried people who have the same incomes. The marriage penalty is one of those family-unfriendly facts of the tax code, and in our experience, it's the single greatest cause of underwithholding.

To make sure that your W-4 reflects the marriage penalty, you have to adjust your withholding allowances.

Too many exemptions?

If you claimed more than ten withholding exemptions on your **Form W-4, Withholding Allowance Certificate,** or if you earned more than $200 per week and claimed an exemption from all withholding, your employer *must* submit the W-4 to the IRS.

If the IRS determines that you overstated the number of exemptions that you're entitled to, it will either notify your employer that your withholding certificate is inaccurate or ask you for written verification of why you believe you're entitled to the extra exemptions that you claim. If the IRS asks you for this information, it sends you **Form 6355, Worksheet to Determine Withholding Allowances.** Form 6355 is three pages long and is more detailed than the W-4 that you completed.

If, after reviewing Form 6355, the IRS determines that you aren't entitled to the number of exemptions that you claimed, it notifies your employer to disregard your W-4 and to withhold tax based on the number of exemptions you're entitled to. This edict remains in effect until the IRS approves a new W-4. To get approval to change the number of your exemptions, you must file a new W-4 with your employer, who again submits the W-4 to the IRS. You also must attach a written statement explaining why you're requesting a change.

If you don't have a reasonable basis for the number of exemptions that you claimed, you'll be assessed a $500 penalty any time you attempt to claim more exemptions than you are entitled to. A simple error or an honest mistake won't result in a penalty. Phew!

First, on a sheet of paper, write down the salary of the lower-paid spouse. Next to the salary figure, write the number of allowances that you show on line 9 of the worksheet in Table 15-3.

✔ For every $5,000 of wages (up to $60,000), you subtract one allowance. The lower-paid spouse makes $40,000? You cut eight allowances.

✔ For every $10,000 of wages between $60,000 and $110,000, you slice another allowance.

For those who would rather not wade into this, the computer program Turbo Tax can do it for you.

Schedule H: Nanny Tax

You figure the nanny tax is on **Schedule H,** and enter the amount that you owe on line 55 of the 1040.

✔ If you paid cash wages of $1,100 or more during the year, or withheld federal income tax (you're not required to withhold tax but you may want to accommodate your employee's request to do so), you have to fill out only page 1 and enter the amount from line 8 of Schedule H onto line 55 of Form 1040.

✔ If you paid more than $1,000 in any quarter, you have to fill out page 2 of the form and enter the amount from line 27 of Schedule H onto line 55 of Form 1040.

Even if you don't expect to hold high political office — or low political office — the provisions of the nanny tax can save you a tidy sum, as well as simplify the number and type of returns that you have to file. The law covers housekeepers, baby-sitters, and yard-care workers, as well as nannies.

Prior to the nanny tax, which is retroactive to January 1, 1994, household employers had to file quarterly reports and pay Social Security taxes if they paid household help more than $50 in a quarter. Now you don't have to withhold and pay Social Security taxes unless you pay a domestic worker more than $1,100 during the year. (If you're just learning about the change in the law and didn't pay more than $1,000 in 1995, 1996, or 1997, but filed quarterly returns, you can get your money back by filing **Form 843, Claim for Refund and Request for Abatement.** After April 15, 1999, you can no longer collect any 1995 tax that you incorrectly overpaid. See Chapter 19 to find out more about the statute of limitations on refunds.)

Here are two important provisions about the nanny tax that you should be aware of:

✔ You don't have to pay Social Security tax for domestic employees under the age of 18, regardless of how much you pay them. (Under the age of 18 means that the employee is under that age for any portion of the year.) The exemption doesn't apply if the principal occupation of the employee is household employment.

✔ You don't have to file quarterly payroll tax forms. Any Social Security, Medicare, or federal unemployment (FUTA) taxes, as well as income taxes that you choose to withhold, can be paid when you file your return in April.

Beginning in 1998, however, your withholding or estimated tax payments must be enough to cover the Social Security, Medicare, and FUTA taxes that you owe, or a penalty will be assessed.

Although the nanny tax simplifies your IRS filings, you still have to keep filing quarterly state unemployment tax returns, unless your state elects to conform to the IRS method of filing annually.

Schedule H looks more formidable than it really is. Here's the lowdown on what it's really about:

✔ If you paid your household help less than $1,100 in 1998 and didn't withhold any income tax, you don't have to file this form.

✔ If you paid someone more than $1,100 but no more than $1,000 in any one quarter (that's a three-month period — January, February, and March, and so on), you only have to fill out Part I.

For example, suppose that you pay someone $60 a week. That's $780 a quarter and $3,120 for the year. You only have to answer questions A, B, and C on the form and fill out the eight lines in Part I. It's strictly simple math stuff. You have to multiply the $3,120 in cash wages that you paid by the 12.4 percent Social Security rate as well as the 2.9 percent Medicare tax rate. You add both of these taxes together on line 8 of the form and carry this amount over to line 55 of Form 1040. Sign and date the form at the bottom of page 2 and attach it to your return.

Don't forget that you also have to furnish your employee with a W-2 stating the amount that you paid, as well as the amount of Social Security, Medicare, and income tax you withheld. Withholding income tax is optional on your part. One further chore: You have to file a copy of the W-2 and Form W-3 (if more than one W-2 is being filed) with the Social Security Administration in Wilkes-Barre, Pennsylvania, by February 28, 1999. Your employees must get their W-2s by January 31.

✔ If you paid someone employed in your home more than $1,000 in any quarter, you have to fill out Parts II and III because not only do you owe Social Security and Medicare taxes, but you also have to pay federal unemployment tax. This tax is commonly referred to as FUTA.

A good tax software program is the best way to go if you have to fill out Parts II and III because a heck of a lot of adding, subtracting, and multiplying is involved.

Check with your state tax department to find out whether you have to register and pay state unemployment tax on a quarterly basis. Also check with your insurance broker to see if your homeowner's insurance covers domestic employees or if you need a separate workers' compensation policy. Don't play fast and loose in this area. If your nanny gets hurt or injured, you may have to pay a bundle if you don't have insurance coverage.

The immigration law requires that you verify that every new employee is eligible to work in the U.S. You do this by completing **Form I-9, Employment Eligibility Verification.** You can get this form from the Immigration Service (800-744-0777). The form doesn't get filed. Hang onto it in case someone from the Immigration Service should knock on your door.

Schedule SE: Self-Employment Tax Form

If you earn income from being self-employed as well as from other sources, use Schedule SE to figure another tax that you owe — the Social Security tax and Medicare tax. The first $68,400 of your self-employment earnings is taxed at 12.4 percent (this is the Social Security tax part). The Medicare tax doesn't have any limit; it's 2.9 percent of your total self-employment earnings. For amounts $68,400 or less, the combined rate is 15.3 percent (adding the two taxes together), and for amounts above $68,400, the rate is 2.9 percent.

Your self-employment earnings may be your earnings reported on the following:

- ✔ **Schedule C** (line 31)
- ✔ **Schedule C-EZ** (line 3)
- ✔ **Schedule K-1** (line 15a), **Form 1065** — if you're a partner in a firm
- ✔ **Schedule F** (line 36)
- ✔ **Form 1040** (line 21) — your self-employment income that you reported as miscellaneous income

You can use Section A of Schedule SE, called the short worksheet, if you have only self-employment income. If you're self-employed and also are employed by someone else, you have to use the long form; otherwise, you'll pay more Social Security than you're required to because Social Security tax has already been withheld from your salary. To prevent this disaster, enter the total of the amounts from boxes 3 and 7 of your W-2 on line 8a of page 2 of Schedule SE. (And if you file **Form 4137** on unreported tips, enter the amount from line 9 of that form on line 8b of Schedule SE.)

Now for some good news. (Yes, occasionally there is some good news when it comes to taxes.) Half of your self-employment tax is deductible. Complete Schedule SE and note the following: The amount on line 5 of Schedule SE is the amount of tax that you have to pay, and you carry it over to Form 1040 (line 50) and add it to your income tax that's due; enter half of what you have to pay — the amount on line 6 of Schedule SE — on Form 1040 (line 27).

Wouldn't it be nice if this form simply said `If you are self-employed, use this form to compute how much Social Security and Medicare tax you have to pay`? Paying this tax ensures that you'll be entitled to Social Security when you're old and gray.

You have three choices when filling out this form:

- ✔ **Section A — Short Schedule SE:** This section is the shortest and easiest one to complete — 6 lines. But if you were employed on a salary basis and had Social Security tax withheld from your wages, you will pay more self-employment tax than you're required to if you use the short schedule. Moonlighters beware.

- ✔ **Section B — Long Schedule SE:** Use this part of the form if you received wages and are also self-employed. Suppose that you have wages of $30,000 and have $50,000 in earnings from your business. If you use the Short Schedule SE, you'll end up paying Social Security tax on $80,000 when the maximum amount of combined earnings that you're required to pay on is only $68,400. You pay Medicare tax, however, on the entire $80,000.

  This section is not all that formidable. But here again, a good tax software program automatically sees to it that you don't end up paying more Social Security tax than you have to.

- ✔ **Part II — Optional method:** If your earnings are less than $1,600, you can elect to pay Social Security tax on at least $1,600 so that you'll build up Social Security credit when you become 65.

Here's the lowdown on Section A — Short Schedule SE:

Line 1: If you're not a farmer, you can skip this line. If farming is your game, enter the amount from line 36 of Schedule F (F is for farming) or line 15a, Form 1065, Schedule K-1 for farm partnerships.

Line 2: Enter the total of the amounts from line 31, Schedule C; line 3, Schedule C-EZ; and line 15a, Schedule K-1 (for partnerships). This is how each partner pays his or her Social Security tax, and the miscellaneous income reported on line 21 is what you have to pay Social Security tax on. What kind of income do you have to pay on? Directors' fees, notary public fees, finders' fees, and commissions.

What's not subject to self-employment tax? Jury duty, forgiveness of a debt even if you owe tax on it, rental income, executor's fees, prizes and awards, lottery winnings, and gambling winnings — unless gambling is your occupation.

Line 3: A breeze. Add lines 1 and 2.

Line 4: Multiply line 3 by 92.35 percent (.9235). Why? If you were employed, your employer would get to deduct its share of the Social Security tax that it would have to pay, and so do you. Or you can think of it this way: Paying self-employment tax of 15.3 percent on 92.35 percent of your earnings is a lot better than having to pay on 100 percent. So don't ask any more questions. Do the math and be thankful for small favors.

Line 5: If line 4 is less than $68,400, multiply line 4 by 15.3 percent (.153) and enter that amount on line 50 of Form 1040. For example, if line 4 is $10,000, multiply it by 15.3 percent, and you get $1,530.

If line 4 is more than $68,400, multiply it by 2.9 percent (.029) and add that amount to $8,481.60. (This is the maximum amount of Social Security tax that you're required to pay.) For example, if line 4 is $70,000, multiply that amount by .029, which comes to $2,030. Now add this amount ($2,030) to $8,482 ($8,481.60 rounded to the nearest dollar) for a grand total of $10,512. Enter this amount on line 50 of Form 1040. (The 2.9 percent is your Medicare tax.)

Line 6: Multiply line 5 by 50 percent. You can deduct this amount ($5,256) on line 27 of your 1040.

Schedule R: Credit for the Elderly or the Disabled

You use (and attach!) **Schedule R** for this credit. You're entitled to claim this credit (which could amount to as much as $1,125) if you're married and both you and your spouse are 65 or over — or both of you are disabled and any age. For single taxpayers, the maximum credit is $750.

But wait, there are requirements that make most people ineligible for this credit: You have to reduce the amount of the income that's eligible for the credit by the nontaxable portion of your Social Security and other pension and disability benefits. Also, if your income is over $7,500 (if you're single) or $10,000 (if you're married), the amount of your income that's eligible for this credit is reduced further. Yup. The long and short of all this interesting information is that after completing this two-page form, most people will discover that they aren't entitled to claim this credit.

If you find that your credit is zero, try this step: Instead of struggling with the form, you can have the IRS figure the credit for you. Fill out page 1 of the form, which asks questions about your age, filing status, and whether you're disabled. Attach the form to your return, and on Form 1040 (line 42), write CFE (an acronym for credit for the elderly) on the dotted line. *Remember:* Always check the computation for a form that you asked the IRS to calculate to make sure that the IRS's computation is right. The IRS isn't infallible.

The amount of the credit is 15 percent of the following base amounts:

- ✔ $5,000 if you're single, head of household, or a qualifying widow(er)
- ✔ $5,000 if you're filing jointly and only one of you is over 65 or disabled
- ✔ $7,500 if you're filing jointly and both of you are over 65 or disabled, or one of you is over 65 and the other is under 65 and disabled
- ✔ $3,750 if you're married filing separately and are 65 or older (or disabled) and didn't live with your spouse in 1998

Additionally, the base amount is reduced by the amount of your Social Security income that isn't subject to tax and one-half of the excess of your adjusted gross income that exceeds one of the following:

- ✔ $7,500 if you're single, head of household, or a qualifying widow(er)
- ✔ $10,000 if you're married filing jointly
- ✔ $5,000 if you're married filing separately and lived apart from your spouse for all of 1998

For example, suppose that your adjusted gross income (AGI) is $20,000, you have nontaxable Social Security of $2,000, and you and your spouse are over 65.

Base amount	$7,500
Nontaxable portion of Social Security	$2,000
AGI	$20,000
Reduction limit	$10,000
Excess	$10,000
One-half of excess	$5,000
Reduced base amount ($7,500 – $5,000 – $2,000)	$500
Credit (15% of $500)	$75

Enter the $75 credit on line 42 of Form 1040. The credit can't exceed your tax. So if your tax is $60 and the credit is $75, the $15 difference isn't refundable. If you're claiming the credit because you're under 65 and disabled, your doctor must complete and sign Part II on page 1 of Form 1040, Schedule R.

Part IV
Audits and Errors: Dealing with the IRS

The 5th Wave   By Rich Tennant

"And just how long did you think you could keep that pot o'gold at the end of the rainbow a secret from us, Mr. O'Shea?"

In this part . . .

Good news and bad news arrive via the U.S. Postal Service. One letter that you hope doesn't find its way to you is an official, thin envelope from the IRS announcing that you've won their special drawing. Perhaps you were hoping that the return that you hadn't filed wouldn't be missed. Maybe you're a law-abiding citizen and can't understand why the tax folks are hassling you again. You might choose to ignore the IRS's queries, but we don't recommend making the IRS angry.

In this part, you learn how to deal with just about everything the IRS can throw at you during the year. If you didn't file in time or couldn't pay all your taxes, we provide a shoulder to cry on as well as sound counsel for how to make things better.

"There is one difference between a tax collector and a taxidermist — the taxidermist leaves the hide."

— Mortimer Caplan

Chapter 16

The Dreaded Envelope I: IRS Notices

In This Chapter
- ▶ Feeling popular (with the IRS crowd)
- ▶ Deciphering nutty notices
- ▶ Understanding assessment and nonassessment notices
- ▶ Keeping the IRS's hands off your property and salary

Greetings!

Now that the military draft is over, Americans no longer receive notices from their government bearing such a salutation. A different government agency, the Internal Revenue Service, now provides you with equally unpleasant news. Did you know that you have a 35-percent chance of receiving a notice from the IRS stating that you failed to report all your income, filed late, didn't pay what you owed, or made an error in preparing your return? Maybe you even committed a combination of these infractions!

Getting an envelope in the mail from the IRS strikes fear in the hearts and souls of even the most confident and honest taxpayers. In some cases, the mistakes taxpayers make are easily fixed. An IRS computer, in one of the IRS's ten regional service centers, automatically generates a notice when it spots an inaccuracy. The good news is that this system is cost-effective for the IRS because it brings in billions more tax dollars. The bad news for you is that these notices are often ambiguous, intimidating, and (in some cases) wrong!

Finding Strength in Numbers

If you think that you received an IRS notice simply because you're unlucky, you may be mistaken. Winning the IRS notice lottery is easy, and you're hardly in exclusive company! Each year, the Internal Revenue Service issues the following items:

- ✔ 34 million penalty notices

- ✔ 2.6 million notices informing taxpayers that they didn't report all their income

- ✔ 2 million notices to taxpayers stating that they failed to file a tax return

- ✔ Tens of millions of notices to taxpayers, the exact number not being quantifiable, that they either failed to pay what they owed or made a mistake in preparing their tax returns

Every year, approximately 12 million beleaguered taxpayers write back saying that the notices they receive are either incorrect or unclear.

In dealing with the IRS, or with any large bureaucracy, persistence and patience count. The importance of this strategy can't be stressed enough. The only thing that you must not do is give up or become discouraged. "I shall overcome" should be your motto.

One of the biggest headaches in dealing with the IRS is that the agency can be big and impersonal. That's why this part of the book provides you with suggested strategies and sample response letters developed from the decades of experience that have helped our clients deal with those daunting IRS notices. These strategies and letters work. When an IRS form can work better and faster than a letter, we include that form and suggest using it.

All the letters and IRS forms contained in this book may be copied for your personal use. On the sample letters, items that you must fill in are enclosed in brackets.

Understanding the IRS Notice Process

If you never had a pen pal, you have one now. And you don't even have to write back — the letters just keep coming. However, this pen pal doesn't like being ignored. This pen pal doesn't get mad — this pal (the IRS) just takes your money.

Receiving your typical notice

The notice system usually starts with the issuance of a notice of adjustment, a **CP-2501** (an income verification notice), a **CP-2000, We're Proposing to Change Your Return;** a **CP-13, We Changed Your Account;** or a 30-day letter (notifying you of the results of an audit). If you fail to respond to this notice, if the IRS isn't satisfied with your reply, or if you fail to exercise your appeal rights, a Statutory Notice of Deficiency is issued. Remember that adjustments merely correcting a math or processing error — or assessing a penalty — don't require the issuance of a Statutory Notice. Why the big deal over this kind of notice? The law requires a Statutory Notice if the IRS is demanding more than your return revealed that you owed. We get into what you should do when you receive a Statutory Notice in "Receiving a Statutory Notice of Deficiency," later in this chapter.

When the IRS makes an assessment, the amount of that assessment — plus penalties — is entered into the service center's computer under your Social Security number. The service center then sends three notices, at approximately five-week intervals, over a 15-week period. All three notices ask for payment within ten days.

The first notice is either **Form CP-13, We Changed Your Account,** or **Form CP-14, Request For Payment.** CP-13 states the reasons for the change, such as math errors, penalties assessed, plus interest and adjustments for payments you claim you made but the IRS hasn't received or can't apply to your account. Form CP-14 is sent if no errors are being corrected (for example, you sent your return with a balance owing). The second notice is either a **Form 501, Reminder** or a **Form 71-A, Reminder of Unpaid Tax.** The third and final notice is **CP-504, We Intend to Levy — Respond Now,** which is sent by certified mail (the law requires that it be sent this way before the IRS starts seizing property or salary). This notice informs you that if payment isn't received within 30 days, the IRS has the right to seize your property and garnish your wages. (Remember, the IRS defines property as more than just your residence; it likes to drool over your car, boat, and investments, too.) Ouch! You can expect to receive a CP-504 about 10 weeks after the first notice. Before this recent change, the IRS sent four notices before it got tough.

Now for some good news: You now can appeal a levy or lien notice. When you do, the IRS must stop all collection activity while your appeal is pending. Don't confuse a notice stating that the IRS intends to levy or file a lien with the real McCoy. Notices of intent are designed to scare you, and they do a pretty good job of that. See "Appealing a lein or levy" later in this chapter for more information.

If you receive a Final Notice and can't pay what you owe, see Chapter 19 to review your options. If you haven't paid the balance or contacted the IRS to arrange payment within ten days, the contact section of the Automated Collection System (ACS) takes over, unless the IRS has what's known as *levy source information* — that is, the IRS knows where it can get its cash; it knows where to find your property or income. In that case, a Notice of Levy will be issued against your salary and bank accounts, for example. The contact section handles cases where the payment of tax can't be satisfied by levy. The ACS contacts you by telephone, and if it can't get you to pay, the ACS turns the case over to a revenue officer.

Business taxpayers in arrears will be contacted by phone after receiving two bills over a period of 11 weeks.

Deciphering a notice

Don't panic! If you're like most taxpayers, you'll look at the notice, see a dollar figure, and decide it's too painful to look at the notice again. Check again; the dollar figure might be a refund — but it isn't likely.

One critical bit of advice: The computers at the service centers won't tolerate being ignored. Maybe they hooked you by error, but there's no satisfying them until they reel you in, or until you convince the IRS that the computers made an error. To do so, you must respond quickly to a notice. Otherwise, you severely prejudice your appeal rights and end up with no recourse but to pay the tax and forget the whole thing — or to pay the tax and then try to get your money back. This isn't as impossible as it seems. We tell you how to get back what is rightfully yours in Chapter 18.

Every notice contains the following:

- ✔ Date of the notice
- ✔ Taxpayer Identification number — your Social Security or Employer Identification number (make sure that it's yours)
- ✔ Type of tax form
- ✔ Tax period — the year
- ✔ Document locator number (DLN) in the upper-right corner (every notice and payment that you make to the IRS is assigned a DLN; this number allows the IRS to trace every transaction)
- ✔ Penalties charged
- ✔ Interest charged
- ✔ Amount owed
- ✔ Tax payments you made

Both you and the IRS are able to track any missing tax payment by a long series of numbers printed on the back of your check. The first fourteen numbers make up the DLN; the next nine are your Social Security number, followed by a four-letter abbreviation of your name. The next four numbers are the year the payment was applied (9712 means the year ending December 1997), and the last six digits record the date the payment was received.

Be careful about making a payment with a check drawn on a money market or line of credit account. These checks may not be returned in your monthly statement, so you won't have them as proof of tax payment. Getting a copy from the bank is usually as difficult as getting the bank to raise its passbook savings account interest rate.

Unfortunately, not every notice provides all the information necessary to precisely determine what went wrong — IRS notices are famous for their lack of clarity. Our favorite is a client's notice that indicated that either an error was made, or that an outstanding balance existed, or that not all the payments listed on the return were made, or that a penalty was being assessed. The notice went on to promise that a separate notice (which, by the way, never came) would explain which explanation applied.

All is not lost if you receive an IRS notice that, after careful inspection, is not understandable. Call the IRS at the telephone number indicated on the notice or at 800-829-1040 and request a transcript of your tax account (which takes about three to five days to arrive). This printout lists every transaction posted to your account. With this additional information, you should be able to understand why you were sent the notice.

If the transcript of your tax account fails to clarify why you received the notice in the first place, write to the IRS and ask it to provide a better or more exact explanation. To find out how to do this, see Chapter 18.

Assessing Assessment Notices

Assessment notices usually inform you of one of the following situations:

- ✔ You weren't given credit for all the tax payments you claim you made.
- ✔ You made a math error or used the wrong tax table or form.
- ✔ You filed a return but neglected to pay what you owed.
- ✔ You agreed to the results of a tax examination.
- ✔ You owe a penalty.

General assessment notice — Form CP-22A

The IRS uses Form CP-22A to inform you that your refund is being reduced or eliminated (or that it's being applied against an outstanding balance) because of one of the reasons from the preceding list. The IRS also intercepts refunds to pay nontax governmental debts, such as defaults on student loans and nonpayment of child support. The IRS refund interception program is discussed in greater detail in Chapter 18.

The IRS also sends Form CP-22A to assess a penalty for filing or paying late, failing to make timely estimated tax payments, failing to report all your income, or overstating credits or deductions on your return. Watch out!

Income verification notice — Form CP-2501

A few years ago, a convict serving prison time sent the IRS 1099s stating that the prosecutor and judge who sentenced him received $900,000 in income. Can you imagine the face of the prosecutor when he found out the IRS wanted another $200,000 in taxes? You can now sue in Federal Court if this happens. The lesson: Don't believe that the IRS is automatically correct in its assessment of your income.

Generally, all 1099s must include the name, address, and telephone number of whom to contact in case the 1099 is incorrect, and the IRS must investigate the disputed 1099.

Income verification notices ask you to explain differences between the income and deductions you claimed on your return — such as mortgage interest — and the income and deductions reported to the IRS by banks, your employer, and brokerage firms. Your salary is reported to the IRS on Form W-2, and all other income is reported to the IRS by the payer on Form 1099. The IRS *assumes* that the information reported to it on these forms is correct and that you made a mistake on your return. If you ignore an income verification, you will receive a **Form CP-22A, Statement of Change to Your Account,** that bills for penalties, interest, and additional tax. If income tax was withheld, the CP-22A reflects that situation.

One of the quickest ways we know to become separated from your money is to ignore one of these nice little notices. If the notice you receive is wrong or unclear, you need to notify the IRS. To find out how to do this, see Chapter 18.

In 1995, CP-2501 and CP-2000 notices picked up a cool $3.4 billion from 2.7 million taxpayers. If you fail to report all your income, you can expect to receive a CP-2501 and CP-2000 within 18 to 24 months after filing your return. Of the CP-2501 and CP-2000 notices sent, another 1.8 million went to people who didn't file, asking why they didn't file. (You can't refer to these 1.8 million nonfilers as taxpayers.)

An IRS notice can be wrong for many reasons:

- The income that the IRS says you didn't report is exempt from tax.

- The income that the IRS says you failed to report is not yours. For example, you opened a bank account for your child or for a relative, and you inadvertently gave the bank your own Social Security number.

- The IRS counted the income twice. Perhaps you reported interest income on a schedule other than the proper one. Or your broker reported your total dividends to the IRS as having been paid by the broker, while you reported those dividends on your return according to the names of the corporations that paid them.

- You reported income in the wrong year. Maybe someone paid you at the end of the year, but you didn't receive this income until the beginning of the next year — and you reported it in that year.

If you think that the IRS's conclusions about your return are wrong, turn to Chapter 18 to find out how to respond to IRS notices.

We're proposing changes to your return — CP-2000

This form cuts right to the chase. It assumes that the information the government received regarding your income and that doesn't appear on your return is correct. No questions are asked about whether this information is correct or not. The IRS assumes it's correct, and you're billed for additional tax and interest.

Backup withholding notice

As a trade-off for repeal of the short-lived mandatory withholding on interest and dividends, Congress enacted a system of backup withholding if you fail to furnish a payer of taxable income with your Social Security number. The IRS also notifies the payer that backup withholding should be started if you failed to report interest and dividend income on your tax return.

If the IRS determines that backup withholding is required, the payer is informed to withhold tax at the rate of 31 percent. What type of income most often gets hit for this type of withholding? Interest and dividends, payments of more than $600 per year in the course of business, gross proceeds that a broker reports in a barter exchange, and annual royalties in excess of $10 are usually targeted.

Backup withholding usually applies only to interest and dividend income. Other payments, however, are subject to withholding if you fail to provide the payer with your Social Security number. The IRS doesn't notify you that you're subject to backup withholding — it instead notifies the payer, who is required by law to notify you.

By notifying your local Taxpayer Advocate — the IRS problem-solving official (see Chapter 18) — you can stop backup withholding under certain circumstances:

✔ You did not underreport your income.

✔ You did underreport — but you paid the tax, interest, and penalties on the unreported income.

✔ The backup withholding will cause you undue hardship, and the underreporting probably will not happen again.

If you get hit with backup withholding, file all your returns for delinquent years, start reporting all your income, or pay what you owe. If you do this, the IRS will automatically stop backup withholding on January 1 if everything is in order by the proceeding October 15.

Withholding allowances notice — Form 6355

We have to be a little technical here, but please stay with us through this bit of IRS paperwork. If you claimed more than ten withholding exemptions on your **Form W-4, Withholding Allowance Certificate,** or if you earned more than $200 per week and you claimed an exemption from all withholding, your employer *must* submit the W-4 to the IRS. If the IRS determines that you overstated the number of exemptions you're entitled to, it will either notify your employer that your withholding certificate is inaccurate or ask you for written verification of why you believe you're entitled to the extra exemptions you claimed.

If the IRS asks you for this information, it will send you **Form 6355, Worksheet to Determine Withholding Allowances.** Form 6355 is three pages long and is more detailed than the W-4 that you completed.

If, after reviewing Form 6355, the IRS determines that you aren't entitled to the number of exemptions claimed, it will notify your employer to disregard your W-4 and to withhold tax based on the number of exemptions you're entitled to. This edict remains in effect until the IRS approves a new W-4. To get approval to change the number of your exemptions, you must file a new W-4 with your employer, who again submits the W-4 to the IRS. You also must attach a written statement explaining the reason for requesting a change.

If you don't have a reasonable basis for the number of exemptions claimed, you will be assessed a $500 penalty. A simple error or an honest mistake will not result in a penalty. Phew!

Annually, the IRS receives about 600,000 W-4s claiming either more than ten exemptions or a complete exemption from withholding. All these W-4s get screened, of course. The IRS contacts about 42 percent of the taxpayers submitting these W-4s and sends them a Form 6355 or **Form 6450, Questionnaire to Determine Exemption From Withholding.**

Hardship, IRS style

If backup withholding creates a hardship — that is, you need the dough to live on — you can request that it be stopped. IRS regulations state that undue hardship exists in several forms. For example, you are under hardship if backup withholding — when combined with other withholding and estimated tax payments — produces a substantial overpayment of tax. Or perhaps your ability to pay medical expenses would be affected. Maybe you rely upon the interest and dividend income to meet basic living expenses, or you live on a modest fixed income. You're also a hardship case if you've filed a bankruptcy petition or if you're an innocent spouse who had no knowledge of your mate's failure to report all income. See Chapter 4 for more information on this last topic.

Every October 15, the IRS makes a determination on hardship cases and other cases where backup withholding should be stopped, such as where there is no underreporting of interest and dividends or the underreporting has been corrected. If the IRS decides in your favor, backup withholding stops on January 1 of the following year. There are two exceptions to the January 1 rule, however: If the IRS determines that there was no underreporting or that you would suffer undue hardship, the IRS notifies you and informs the payer either not to start backup withholding or to stop backup withholding within 45 days of its determination.

Are you still with us? To bring you back to life after that stuff, here's the story of why we have all these forms for withholding. A few years back, all the workers from an assembly line in a Michigan auto plant claimed an exemption from withholding; they didn't file returns for that year. It took some time, but the IRS put a stop to those shenanigans!

Federal tax lien notice — Form 668 (F)

A *statutory lien* automatically goes into effect when you neglect or refuse to pay the tax the IRS demands. This type of lien attaches to all property that you own. A statutory lien is sometimes referred to as a *secret lien* because its validity doesn't depend on its being filed as a matter of public record.

Because a statutory lien places the rights only of the IRS ahead of yours, the IRS will usually file a Notice of Lien in order to place itself first in line before your other creditors. (No cutting in line, please!) A federal tax lien covers all of a taxpayer's property, including real estate, cars, bank accounts, and personal property. These liens are filed in accordance with state law, usually with the county clerk, town hall, or court where the taxpayer lives.

You should be aware that credit agencies routinely pick up liens that have been filed against you. After a credit agency has this information, your credit is marked lousy. Even if paid, a lien stays on your credit history for seven years.

Although the law requires that the IRS release a lien within 30 days after it has been paid, the IRS doesn't always comply. Upon paying the tax, you should secure **Form 669-B, Certificate of Discharge of Property for Federal Tax Lien Under Section 6325(b)(2)(A) of the IRC,** from the revenue officer who filed the lien.

The Taxpayer Bill of Rights (discussed in Chapter 18) tells you what to do when the IRS fails to release a lien. The IRS is liable for damages if it fails to release an erroneous lien or a lien that has been paid.

Property levy notice — Form 668-A

A Notice of Levy is used to seize your property, and that includes your bank and brokerage accounts. You can kiss your money good-bye 30 days after this levy is served. A Notice of Levy usually isn't issued until after the IRS has exhausted all other possible collection procedures, however. The IRS does make an effort to contact you in order to try to arrange a payment schedule, and it usually sends at least three notices. Remember, you filed a tax return indicating where you work, where you bank, and where you have other assets!

You may be interested to know that some assets are exempt from levy:

- A taxpayer's principal residence — unless personally ordered in writing by a district director or an assistant district director (the head IRS official for your district), or if the collection of tax is in jeopardy.

- 85 percent of unemployment benefits.

- Tools and books of a taxpayer's trade, business, or profession up to $3,125. (After 1998, this amount is adjusted annually for inflation.)

- Schoolbooks. (The IRS doesn't want you to stop studying!)

- Court-ordered child support payments.

- Wearing apparel.

- $6,250 worth of furniture and personal effects. (After 1998, this amount gets adjusted annually for inflation.)

- Undelivered mail.

- 85 percent of worker's compensation and non-means-tested welfare payments.

- Military service disability payments.

Although pension, Keogh, and IRA benefits aren't exempt from levy, it's IRS policy that they will be levied upon judiciously — these plans were established for a taxpayer's future welfare. This policy statement also mandates that pension benefits totaling less than $6,000 annually will not be levied upon. Social Security benefits aren't exempt from levy.

Wage levy notice — Form 668-W(c)

Form 668-W(c), Notice of Levy on Wages, Salary and Other Income, is used to seize wages. It's a six-part form served on your employer. Whereas a Notice of Levy (see the preceding section) attaches only to property held by a third party (such as a bank) at the time the levy is issued, a wage levy is a continuing one — it applies to all wages, salaries, and commissions owed, as well as to future wages, salaries, and commissions.

Continuous levies that apply to what you'll receive in the future and only apply to wage levies also apply to 15 percent of unemployment and workers' compensation benefits as well as non-means-tested welfare payments. The meek won't inherit the world. The IRS will.

But part of every taxpayer's wages is exempt from levy. This exemption is equal to a taxpayer's standard deduction plus the number of personal exemptions he or she is entitled to, divided by a 52-week year. Therefore, in 1998, a married taxpayer entitled to four exemptions (husband, wife, and two children) would be entitled to a weekly exemption of $344, computed as follows:

Standard deduction	$ 7,100
Personal exemptions (4 × $2,700)	$10,800
	$17,900

$$17,900 \div 52 = \$344 \text{ per week}$$

The $17,900 is the 1998 amount. In 1999, it will be adjusted for inflation, and the $344 exemption from levy in the example will be increased to about $356. Don't spend it all in one place.

A taxpayer claims the amount of the exemption from levy to which he or she is entitled on **Form 668-W(c), Part 6, Statement of Exemptions.** If you don't fill out Part 6 and return it to your employer so it can be sent to the IRS, your employer is required to compute your exemption as married filing separately with one exemption, which works out to only $120 a week. (Yikes — better fill out Part 6!) The amount of wages that can be exempted can be increased for the amount of court-ordered child support payments.

If by levying your wages the IRS pushes you below the poverty level or you wind up not being able to meet your basic living expenses, see "When you can't pay your taxes" in Chapter 19 in order to free yourself from this forced slavery.

Handling Nonassessment Notices

The IRS usually issues a nonassessment notice to inform you of one of the following situations:

- You forgot to sign a return.
- You failed to attach a W-2.
- You omitted a form or schedule.
- You didn't indicate filing status.

But I never got Part 6 of Form 668-W(c)!

If your employer fails to furnish you with Part 6 of Form 668-W(c), send the following statement to the IRS revenue officer (you can find the agent's name, address, and telephone number on the notice, or your employer can give you this information):

[date]

Re: [your name]

[Social Security number]

Dear [revenue officer's name]:

In connection with the Notice of Levy that was served on my employer, please be advised that I am married and entitled to claim the following personal exemptions on my tax return:

1. Myself

2. My spouse, [his or her name and Social Security number]

3. My children, [their names, ages, and Social Security numbers]

4. My court-ordered child support payments that amount to [$] weekly

Very truly yours,

[your name]

If you receive this notice, simply write across the notice in bold lettering: INFORMATION REQUESTED IS ATTACHED. Then attach the requested information to the notice and return it to the IRS in the envelope provided. After you provide the IRS with the requested information, the matter is usually closed — unless the information submitted conflicts with information previously reported on the return. If this situation occurs, the IRS will send a notice that assesses additional tax, interest, and possibly a penalty, or that instructs you to contact a particular person at the IRS.

A notice correcting a refund due to you (usually made on Form CP-22A) shouldn't be viewed as a nonassessment notice, however. Just because a notice doesn't demand that you write a check, don't think that the IRS isn't billing you for something. Quite often, the IRS reduces a refund when it assesses additional tax or penalties.

Paying interest on additional tax

Starting with 1998 returns, the IRS must send a notice of additional tax due within 18 months of the date you file your return. If the IRS doesn't send such a notice, it must stop charging interest after 18 months and until 21 days after it sends the notice.

This provision doesn't cover all notices, so here's what you should know about this 18-month rule:

 ✔ Your return had to be filed on time — otherwise, you don't get a suspension of interest.

 ✔ The failure to file or to pay penalties isn't covered by this rule.

 ✔ Additional tax due as the result of an audit isn't covered.

So what is covered? Say you forgot to report $1,000 of income on your 1998 return that you filed August 15, 1999 (assuming that you obtained a four-month extension), and the IRS didn't send a notice until September 1, 2001. You owe interest from April 15, 1999 (filing an extension doesn't stop the running of interest from the original due date) through February 15, 2001 (18 months from August 15, 1999). Interest is suspended from February 15, 2001 through September 21, 2001 — 21 days from the September 1, 2001 date of the notice.

Receiving a delinquent tax return notice

A word of caution: You should treat a delinquent tax return notice as seriously as it sounds. If your tax return is delinquent, you may be contacted by mail, by telephone, or in person. Remember that the IRS has the right to issue a summons commanding you to appear with your tax records and explain why you didn't file a tax return.

Failure to file a tax return or returns could involve possible criminal violation of the Internal Revenue Code. Usually, the IRS isn't terribly interested in prosecuting individuals who haven't filed and who don't owe a substantial amount of tax. The IRS is, however, very interested in prosecuting prominent individuals because these prosecutions make good headlines. Extra! Extra! Read all about it!

If you file late returns — even in response to an IRS inquiry — and don't owe a substantial amount of tax (what's considered substantial is known only to the IRS), the IRS probably will accept the return and assess a penalty for late payment and possibly fraud.

If you don't reply to a delinquent return notice, the IRS can take one of the following steps:

 ✔ Refer the case to its Criminal Investigation Unit.

 ✔ Issue a summons to appear.

✔ Refer you to the Audit Division.

✔ Prepare a "substitute" return.

If the IRS decides to prepare a "substitute" return for you, it will use the information that it has on you in its master file. The IRS prepares a substitute return using the married filing separately tax table, the standard deduction, and one exemption.

Having the IRS prepare your return is the quickest way we know of for you to become separated from your money. Unlike having a tax return prepared by a tax advisor, no fee is involved when the IRS prepares a substitute return. The only charge is the amount of tax that you will unnecessarily pay. Remember, the IRS isn't interested in saving you money.

Although you may have a valid reason for not filing (such as illness or insufficient income), or the IRS may have lost or misplaced your return — notwithstanding the fact that this type of error is something that the IRS is reluctant to admit — any taxpayer who receives a delinquent return notice should consider seeking the services of a *qualified* tax advisor (see Chapter 2).

Why not beat the IRS to the punch? The IRS has an official policy of not prosecuting anyone who files a return prior to being contacted and makes arrangements to pay what is owed. Penalties and interest, however, will be assessed.

Appealing the results of an audit

The IRS issues **Form 4549-A, Income Tax Examination Changes,** and **Form 1902-B, Report of Individual Tax Examination Changes,** after an audit has been completed. Form 4549-A spells out any adjustments to income and expenses that have been made, as well as any penalties and interest that are due.

These notices are often referred to as *30-day letters.* Within 30 days after receipt of an audit notice, you must agree to the adjustment, submit additional information explaining why an adjustment shouldn't be made, or request a hearing before the Appeals Division.

If you disagree with the proposed adjustment, and the amount of tax is more than $25,000, a written protest must be filed. IRS Publication 556 *(Examination of Returns, Appeal Rights, and Claims for Refund)* is extremely helpful in preparing a protest. Consider retaining a tax advisor when protesting large sums.

Taxpayers can make appeals to the Appeals Office, whose purpose is to settle disputes. The IRS agent who examined your return has no authority to take into account the time and expense to the IRS, as well as the possibility that the IRS may lose in court. An appeals officer can. Approximately 85 percent of all cases referred to the Appeals Office are settled.

If the amount involved is less than $2,500, the IRS doesn't require a written statement. You merely tell the IRS agent that you want to appeal. For amounts between $2,500 and $25,000, you have to submit a brief written statement of the disputed issues and why you feel your deduction should be allowed. This requirement only applies to field audits. Adjustments resulting from an audit at an IRS office don't require a written appeal. But we advise you to prepare one anyway.

The IRS also issues a 30-day letter if you fail to show up for an audit. In such an instance, the examining agent will review your return and make adjustments to both income and deductions that he or she deems warranted.

If you receive a 30-day letter because you failed to show — even if you missed the audit because you never received the original notice scheduling it — contact the agent at the number given on the letter and schedule an audit appointment. If you make a new appointment within 30 days, the examining agent or appointment clerk will place a hold on your adjusted return (that is, it won't be processed), pending the outcome of the rescheduled audit.

After completion of the audit, the IRS issues a new notice of income tax changes that supersedes the preceding one. If you agree to the audit changes and sign off on the changes, you can pay what you owe at that time, or you can wait to be billed.

Appealing a lien or levy

Within 30 days of receiving a notice that a lien has been filed against you, you have the right to request an appeal. You can also appeal an IRS notice to levy your salary or property, because under the new law, the IRS must notify you in writing, at least 30 days prior to levying, of your right to appeal the levy. At the appeal hearing, you can raise any issue relevant to the action the IRS is taking. You can request innocent spouse relief, ask for an installment agreement, or make an offer-in-compromise. You can't raise an issue that was raised at a prior hearing. You can even challenge the underlying tax liability that the IRS is trying to collect. For example, say you ignored a prior IRS notice, and now the IRS wants its dough. You can only challenge the underlying amount of tax due if you didn't receive a Statutory Notice of Deficiency (explained in the next section) or you didn't have a prior opportunity to dispute the tax liability.

Appeals are made to the IRS Office of Appeals. If your appeal is rejected, you can appeal to the U.S. Tax Court. If for some reason the Tax Court lacks jurisdiction, you can appeal to a federal district court.

Unfortunately, this right to appeal only applies to IRS collection action initiated after January 17, 1999.

Receiving a Statutory Notice of Deficiency

Although a notice (such as one proposing income tax changes, or a CP-13 or CP-14) informs a taxpayer that additional tax is due, the IRS can't legally enforce the collection of additional tax until a Statutory Notice of Deficiency — often referred to as a *90-day letter* — is sent to a taxpayer by certified mail at the taxpayer's last known address.

A Statutory Notice of Deficiency isn't required if additional tax is due because of a math error. Statutory notices are generally required only if additional tax is due as the result of the IRS adjusting a taxpayer's income, deductions, or credits from what was originally reported on the tax return. Unless a petition is filed with the U.S. Tax Court in Washington within 90 days of receipt of a Statutory Notice, the IRS can initiate collection action at the end of the 90-day period. If you file a petition with the Tax Court, you can delay all collection action until 60 days after the court renders its decision. If you live outside the United States, the 90-day period is extended to 150 days.

The address of the Tax Court is included on the notice, but we give it to you here anyway, just in case:

> 400 Second Street, N.W.
> Washington, D.C. 20217

The notice will indicate when the 90-day period expires. If your petition gets lost in the mail or arrives late, you're out of luck. However, a certified mail, FedEx, DHL, Airborne, or UPS receipt showing that the petition was sent to the Tax Court within the 90-day period will save the day.

Chapter 17

The Dreaded Envelope II: Audits

*O*n a list of real-life nightmares, most people would rank tax audits right up there with having a tooth pulled without Novocain. The primary trauma of an audit is that it makes many people feel like they're on trial and are being accused of a crime. Don't panic.

First of all, you may be one of the tens of thousands of taxpayers whose return is audited at random. No, the IRS isn't headed by sadists. Random audits help the IRS identify common areas on tax forms where taxpayers make mistakes or fail to report income. Second, you may be audited simply because a business that reports tax information on you, or someone at the IRS, made an error regarding the data on your return.

About 12 percent of audited returns are left unchanged by the audit — that is, the taxpayers don't end up owing more money. In fact, if you're the lucky sort, you may be one of the rare individuals who actually gets a refund because the audit finds a mistake in your favor!

Unfortunately, it's more likely that you'll be one of the roughly 88 percent of audit survivors who end up owing more tax money. The amount of additional tax that you owe in interest and penalties hinges on how your audit goes.

What You Should Know about Audits

Most people would agree that not knowing what to expect in a situation is what's most terrifying. And this is even more true when dealing with the IRS. Here's what you need to know about audits:

✔ You don't have to attend your audit. An enrolled agent, CPA, or attorney can go in your place.

✔ If at anytime during the audit you feel hopelessly confused or realize that you're in over your head, you can ask that the audit or interview be suspended until you can speak to a tax pro. When you make this request, the IRS must stop asking questions and adjourn the meeting so you can seek help and advice.

✔ The burden of proof is on you. You're considered to be guilty until proven innocent. Unfortunately, that's how our tax system operates. However, if you and the IRS end up in court, the burden of proof switches to the IRS, provided you meet the IRS's substantiation and record-keeping requirements and present credible evidence. What all this means is that you can't just sit in court and say "Prove it" to the IRS.

✔ Unless a routine examination reveals the likelihood of unreported income, the IRS can't conduct a financial status audit by demanding that you fill out **Form 4822, Statement of Annual Estimated Personal and Family Expenses** so the IRS can determine how you lived on the income reported on your return.

Surviving the Three Types of Audits

Thankfully, only three types of audits exist: office audits, field audits, and correspondence audits. Statistical audits are a thing of the past. With all three types of audits, maintaining good records is the key to survival. (Chapter 3 tells you what to do if you're audited and can't produce the needed evidence. If you haven't already taken out the trash and lost all your evidence, you can also refer to Chapter 3 for help filing and organizing the documents you may need.)

Office audits

An office audit is held at the IRS. The IRS informs a taxpayer that it is scheduling an office audit by sending a notice numbered 904. The front of this notice lists the date of the audit, and the back lists the items that the IRS wants to examine.

The audit date isn't chiseled in granite. If you can't gather the information necessary to substantiate the items the IRS is questioning, you can request a postponement. As a general rule, the IRS grants you only two postponements, unless you can demonstrate a compelling reason for an additional delay, such as an illness or the unavailability of certain tax records.

If you need more time but can't get an additional postponement, go to the audit with the records you have, put on your most confident face, and calmly inform the tax examiner that you need more time to secure the documents you need in order to substantiate the remaining items the IRS is questioning. The tax examiner then prepares a list of the additional items the IRS needs to complete the audit, together with a mailing envelope so that you can mail copies of the requested documents to the IRS.

Deciding where your audit happens

Both field and office audits are conducted in the district where a return was filed. This practice may create a burden if you live in one district and are employed or have your businesses located in another. For example, if you work or your business is located in Manhattan and you live in Connecticut, you normally would be contacted by the examination branch in Connecticut. If your tax records are in Manhattan or you spend most of your time there, you can request that the examination be transferred to the Manhattan District.

Besides gaining the convenience of having the audit conducted where either your records, your advisor, or your business is located, you also get a little more time to pull together your tax data.

To transfer an audit from one district to another, first call the IRS auditor and tell him or her why you want to transfer the audit to a different district. The transfer usually takes two to three months. The IRS also requires that you request the transfer in writing.

The following note will suffice when requesting that a tax examination be transferred from one IRS district to another:

[your address]

[date]

District Director

[address of district that issued exam notice]

Re: [your name and your Social Security number]

[exam year]

Dear District Director:

Because my tax records are located in [ex. Manhattan] and I spend most of my time there, I respectfully request that the audit you have scheduled be transferred to the [ex. Manhattan] District.

You may contact me during business hours at [telephone number]. Thank you in advance for your prompt attention to this request.

Very truly yours,

[your name]

Enclosed: Copy of exam notice

Never mail originals. If the additional documents don't lend themselves to easy explanation through correspondence, then schedule a second appointment to complete the audit.

Most office audits are concerned with employee business expenses, itemized deductions such as medical expenses, charitable contributions, tax and interest-expense deductions, miscellaneous itemized deductions, deductions for personal exemptions, and moving-expense deductions. Lately, the IRS has expanded office audits to include small-business returns, income from rental property, and income from tips and capital gains.

If the IRS is trying to verify your income, it may want to know about your lifestyle.

How will the IRS find out about your lifestyle? You'll tell them, that's how. Auditors are trained to control the interview. They feign ignorance, use appropriate small talk, use "silence" and "humor" appropriately, and avoid overtly taking notes so as not to distract the taxpayer, and they pay attention to the taxpayer's nonverbal language. The IRS even has a form to flush out lifestyle information, **Form 4822, Statement of Annual Estimated Personal and Family Expenses,** which — thank heaven — the IRS can now only spring on you when a routine examination has established the likelihood of unreported income. The form asks all about your expenses, from groceries to insurance — anything you and your family would spend money on as consumers. We don't know what it is about this form, but when the IRS shoves it under someone's nose, a lot of taxpayers can't resist the urge to respond, "I'll show them what it costs to live in this country." What most people are unaware of is that you're under no obligation to fill out this form. The law only requires you to fill out and file a tax return. Statistical research has revealed that the IRS can collect more tax by examining sources of income than by examining deductions. If you operate a small business or have rental income, be prepared to explain where every deposit into your bank account came from.

Field audits

Field audits are conducted at a taxpayer's place of business. These audits focus on business returns and complex individual returns. If you file Form 1040, Schedule C, you're a likely candidate for a field audit.

Again, be prepared to verify the source of every deposit into your bank account. Field agents are required to survey both your preceding and subsequent years' tax returns to determine whether similar items are treated in a consistent manner. If an audit results in a significant increase in tax, you are now suspect, and the revenue agent will audit your subsequent years' tax returns (which normally are only surveyed).

An office audit specifies what items will be examined from the very beginning of the process. Not so with a field audit — revenue agents have a great deal of discretion as to what items they review and to what depth they review the items. Count on having to verify gross income, travel and entertainment expenses, gifts, automobile expenses, commissions, payments to independent contractors, and any expenses that appear large in relation to the size of your business.

Revenue agents may examine each and every deduction or merely select a month or two of expenses and examine them on a sample basis. If they don't turn up any discrepancies, an agent will accept the rest of the expenses for that category as correct.

Correspondence audits

Correspondence audits are exactly what the name suggests. The IRS conducts correspondence audits completely by mail and limits these audits to a few key areas of individual returns, such as itemized deductions, casualty or theft losses of less than $2,000, employee business expenses of less than $1,000, IRA and Keogh plan payments, dependency exemptions, child care and earned income credits, deductions for forfeited interest on early withdrawals from savings accounts, and exclusion from income of disability payments. Income items may also be examined by a correspondence audit.

If you're ever the proud subject of a correspondence audit, the IRS gives you a return envelope in which to submit your documents, canceled checks, bills, and statements to substantiate the items the IRS questions. Again, *never* send original documents — only copies. It's crucial that you retain the originals in case you have to stare down further inquiries.

When it comes to substantiating any deduction, the burden of proof is on you. If what you must substantiate is complex or requires a detailed explanation, you can ask for an interview in which you can explain in person.

Statistical audits

Since 1995, the IRS no longer conducts TCMP audits (TCMP is an acronym for Taxpayer Compliance Measurement Program). The IRS conducted these audits to gather statistical information that can be used to determine pockets of noncompliance. Nevertheless, you should know that the IRS still conducts random audits; they just aren't known as TCMP audits.

For a TCMP audit, the IRS randomly selected 1,000 freelance writers (or any other group of individuals or businesses), for example, in order to measure the degree of tax compliance for that industry, trade, or profession. On the basis of these audits, the IRS National Office determined which areas required stricter or greater enforcement efforts.

Although TCMP audits accounted for only $1/2$ of 1 percent of all audits in any year, they also were the most detailed. The IRS, for example, even requested birth certificates of a taxpayer's kids to prove that the parent was entitled to claim them as dependents.

How the IRS selects returns for audit

A computer program called the Discriminant Function System (DIF) selects returns for audits. This program scores each return for potential error based on IRS criteria. IRS personnel then screen the returns and select those most likely to have mistakes. They also look for returns that will result in significant additional taxes being assessed when they're audited.

Some returns are selected for audit as the result of an IRS project, such as one targeting waiters not reporting all their tip income, or another focusing on tax shelters.

Returns are also selected by examining claims for refunds and by matching information documents, such as Forms W-2 and 1099, with returns.

Questioning Repetitive Audits

It is IRS policy *not* to examine an individual's tax return if the taxpayer has been examined for the same issue(s) in either of the two preceding years and the audit resulted in no (or only a small) tax change. However, this policy doesn't apply to business returns or individual returns that include a **Schedule C, Profit or Loss from Business** or **Schedule F, Profit or Loss from Farming.**

If you receive a notice of audit questioning the same item(s) questioned in a previous audit, call the agent and inform him or her that the IRS audited the same issue(s) in one of the two prior years with little or no change in tax. (And do note that the IRS has never bothered to define *little.* Changes of less than a few hundred dollars in tax, however, should meet this criteria.) The examining agent will ask you to furnish proof. Mail the examiner a copy of the IRS notice that your prior return was accepted without change, or mail the notice that adjusted your return.

 If you can't document that the IRS is questioning items that it *already* questioned — with no change in tax — in one of the two preceding years, the lack of documentation doesn't mean that you can't get the current examination canceled. Just inform the examining agent by telephone about the prior year's tax examination. The agent will postpone the audit and request your tax account records from the two preceding years. If the transcript of your tax account in the IRS computer supports your contention, the IRS will cancel the audit.

Getting Ready for an Audit

Preparing for an audit is sort of like preparing for a test in school: The IRS informs you of which sections of your tax return the agency wants to examine so that you know what to "study." The first decision you face when you get an audit notice is whether to handle it yourself or to turn to a tax advisor to represent you. Hiring representation costs money but saves you time, stress, and possibly money.

If you normally prepare your own return and are comfortable with your understanding of the areas being audited, represent yourself. If the IRS is merely asking you to substantiate deductions, you'll probably do all right on your own. However, make sure you read "What You Should Know about Audits," earlier in this chapter.

What constitutes substantiation may at times involve a somewhat complicated interpretation of the law and its accompanying regulations. If the amount of tax money in question is small compared to the fee you'd pay a tax advisor to represent you, self-representation is probably the answer. However, if you're likely to turn into a babbling, intimidated fool and are unsure of how to present your situation, hire a tax advisor to represent you.

Two tax-audit myths debunked

#1. If you file at the last minute or get an extension of time to file, you won't be audited because your return will get lost in the crowd.

Wrong! The audit selection, unseen by human eyes, is done by computer.

#2. Don't use the gummed mailing label showing your name and address that the IRS sends. If you do, you will increase your chances of being audited.

Wrong! The weird numbers on this label are used by the IRS for data processing purposes only, not for deciding whether your return should be audited.

Who can represent you in an audit?

The IRS permits three types of individuals to fully represent taxpayers before the IRS: enrolled agents, certified public accountants, and attorneys. All three are bound by IRS rules of practice. (Tax preparers can represent you at an audit but not in any appeals beyond that.)

Enrolled agents (EAs) become enrolled to practice before the IRS by passing a two-day written examination administered by the IRS in which their knowledge of the tax code is tested. Alternatively, they must have at least five years of experience as an IRS tax auditor. Attorneys

and certified public accountants are the other two groups permitted to represent taxpayers before the IRS. Many states have continuing education requirements for CPAs and attorneys. The IRS requires that EAs also meet continuing education requirements.

Probably the best way to find a qualified tax professional is to ask a relative or friend for a recommendation of someone whose level of service and performance the relative or friend is more than satisfied with. To figure out which of these tax practitioners may be best suited to help you in an audit, be sure to read Chapter 2.

Even if you choose to represent yourself and find yourself over your head in an audit, you've got a backup. At any time during the examination — such as when you feel a dizzy sensation — the Taxpayer Bill of Rights allows you to request that the audit be suspended until you have time to consult with either an enrolled agent, a certified public accountant, or an attorney. When you make this request, the IRS agent must stop asking questions or requesting documents until you are properly represented.

But if you do decide to handle the audit yourself, get your act together sooner rather than later. Don't wait until the night before to start gathering receipts and other documentation. You may discover, for example, that you can't find certain documents.

You need to document and be ready to speak with the auditor about the areas the audit notice said were being investigated. Organize the various documents and receipts in folders. You want to make it as easy as possible for the auditor to review your materials. *Don't* show up, dump shopping bags full of receipts and paperwork on the auditor's desk, and say, "Here it is — *you* figure it out."

Don't bring documentation for parts of your return that aren't being audited, either. Besides creating more work for yourself, you're required to discuss only those areas mentioned in the audit letter.

Whatever you do, *don't ignore your audit request letter*. The Internal Revenue Service is the ultimate bill-collection agency. And if you end up owing more money (the unhappy result of most audits), the sooner you pay, the less interest and penalties you'll owe.

Winning Your Audit

Two people with identical situations can walk into an audit and come out with very different results. The loser can end up owing much more in taxes and have the audit expanded to include other parts of the return. The winner can end up owing less tax money. Here's how to be a winner.

✔ **Treat the auditor as a human being.** This obvious advice isn't always practiced by taxpayers. You may be resentful or angry about being audited. You're a busy person with better things to do with what little free time you have, so you might be tempted to gnash your teeth and tell the auditor how unfair it is that an honest taxpayer like you had to spend scores of hours getting ready. You might feel like ranting and raving about how the government wastes too much of your tax money or that the party in power is out to get you.

Bite your tongue.

Believe it or not, most auditors are decent people just trying to do their jobs. They are well aware that taxpayers don't like seeing them. But you don't have to bow before them, either — just relax and be yourself. Behave as you would around a boss you like — with respect and congeniality.

✔ **Stick to the knitting.** You're there to discuss *only* the sections of your tax return in question. The more you talk about other areas or things that you're doing, the more likely the auditor will probe into other items.

✔ **Don't argue when you disagree.** State your case. If the auditor wants to disallow a deduction or otherwise increase the tax you owe and you don't agree, state only once why you don't agree. If the auditor won't budge, don't get into a knock-down, drag-out confrontation. He or she may not want to lose face and will only feel inclined to find additional tax money — that's the auditor's job. Remember that you can plead your case with several layers of people above your auditor. If that course fails and you still feel wronged, you can take your case to Tax Court.

✔ **Don't be intimidated.** Just because IRS auditors have the authority of the government behind them, that doesn't make them right or all-knowing. The audit is only round one. If you disagree with the results, you have the right to appeal.

✔ **Appeal the results of an audit, if necessary.** If you're dissatisfied with the results of an audit, refer to the section "Results of an audit notice: Form 4549" in Chapter 16 to figure out how to make an appeal.

✔ **Go to Tax Court.** If you receive a Statutory Notice of Deficiency, you have 90 days to appeal your case. If you don't appeal, the IRS can enforce collection on the 91st day. Refer to the section "Receiving a Statutory Notice of Deficiency" at the end of Chapter 16.

Understanding the Statute of Limitations on Audits

The IRS must make any assessment of tax, penalties, or interest within three years from the due date for filing a tax return. If the IRS grants you an extension of the filing deadline, the statute of limitations is extended to include the extension period. If the due date falls on a legal holiday or a Saturday or Sunday, the due date is postponed to the next business day.

Here's how the statute of limitations works: The IRS must make an assessment regarding a 1998 tax return by April 15, 2002, three years from the April 15, 1999, due date. *After this date, the IRS can make no demand for additional tax.* If a return is filed after the due date, the three-year period starts on the date the return was filed. However, if you filed your return on or before April 15, 1999, the three-year statute of limitations still expires on April 15, 2002.

If more than 25 percent of the income required to be reported is omitted from a return, the statute of limitations extends to six years. No statute of limitations runs on a false or fraudulent return. Thus, if a false or fraudulent return was filed, there's no time limit on when the government can assess additional tax. The same goes for *not* filing a return; there's no time limit.

Your state tax return and the IRS

The IRS and 48 states have an agreement calling for the exchange of information about taxpayers. Only Nevada and Texas haven't signed on. Under these agreements, individual states and the IRS notify each other about taxpayers who failed to file returns and when either a state or the IRS has adjusted a taxpayer's taxable income.

The tax laws of most states provide that if the IRS has adjusted your tax return, you must file an amended state income tax return with that state within 30 to 90 days of the IRS's adjustment. The amended state return must reflect the adjustments made by the IRS, and you must pay any additional tax plus interest. If an amended return isn't filed, your state's tax collector, upon receiving notice of the adjustments from the IRS, will send a demand for additional tax and interest, and possibly a penalty for not notifying the state within the required time frame.

Extending the statute of limitations

If the statute of limitations is about to expire and you haven't resolved your problems with the IRS, you'll be asked to agree to extend the statute of limitations. If you don't agree, the IRS will immediately assess your tax based on the information it has. The only way to stop the IRS from forcing you to pay the tax is to file a petition with the Tax Court within a 90-day period. Although IRS Publication 1035 *(Extending the Assessment Period)* explains this process, our advice is to see a professional if you ever get into water *this* hot.

The statute of limitations on tax collection is . . .

Ten years — period. After that, the IRS can't collect a dime. The ten-year assessment period starts on the day the IRS receives your return only if no adjustments are made to the return. However, if the government increases your tax or makes an adjustment, the ten years runs from the date of the additional assessment.

If the ten-year period is about to expire, the IRS usually attempts to extend the period by getting you to sign **Form 900, Tax Collection Waiver.** More often than not, the IRS will threaten to seize everything under the sun that you own unless you agree to sign. Here's when you absolutely need professional help — and not just any tax advisor but someone who is an expert and specializes in these types of cases. Ask people that you trust for suggestions of people to contact.

After December 31, 1999, the IRS may not ask a taxpayer to extend the statute of limitations if it hasn't issued a levy. If you have an installment in force when the 10 years expires, the terms of the agreement allow the IRS to extend the statute of limitations for the period of the agreement plus 90 days.

This provision doesn't prohibit the IRS from suing to reduce the tax claim to a judgment, which gives the IRS more time to collect what a taxpayer owes. Such suits, however, are rare.

Chapter 18

Fixing Mistakes the IRS Makes

. . . .

In This Chapter

▶ Demystifying IRS mistakes

▶ Responding to notices

▶ Mastering the generic response form

▶ Dealing with a nonresponsive IRS

▶ Finding a lost refund

. . . .

Get out your boxing gloves! Just kidding. It's best to leave your boxing gloves and attitude somewhere else — you definitely don't want to antagonize the IRS. When you're dealing with a bureaucracy and bureaucrats, you don't want them to be angry. Remember, they have the power to bring you to your knees. This is true whether you're dealing with an entry-level clerk, a phone assistant, or a manager.

Most tax problems arrive uninvited, unannounced, and when you least expect them. Unfortunately, most people don't have a clue how to legally, swiftly, and inexpensively get Uncle Sam off their backs. Stay tuned as we explain how to fix a variety of problems caused by the IRS — without breaking a sweat or an IRS employee's limbs!

Although reluctant to admit it, the IRS does make mistakes. In fairness to the IRS, collecting taxes from more than 100 million individuals and businesses under an extraordinarily complex tax system is, to say the least, difficult. The number of errors can appear to be limitless, but most errors occur for simple reasons.

Pointing the Finger: Common IRS Flubs

We wish that we could explain why the IRS can't get it right the first time. We can't. But we can give you an idea of the number of mistakes made, the types of mistakes, and the action you can take. We also can — and do! — offer tips to keep you away from the IRS paper trail.

The IRS processes just over a billion transactions a year. So, math wizards, what does an error rate of, say, one percent translate into? A hundred, you say. Wrong! Try adding seven zeroes to that figure. Now, what do you have? 10 million errors — way to go, that's right; take the rest of the day off.

That's a whole bunch of errors. The following is a long list of the types of flubs the IRS can make:

✔ **Misapplied payments:** The IRS may not have posted tax payments that you made to your tax account (under your Social Security number). Payments are sometimes posted to the wrong year or type of tax. Perhaps the IRS did not properly post over-payments from a preceding or subsequent year.

✔ **Misunderstood date:** The IRS may claim that you didn't file or pay tax on time. Computers at a service center may not acknowledge that the due date for filing or paying fell on a legal holiday or on a Saturday or Sunday and may therefore blame you for filing late, when in fact you filed on the first business day following a legal holiday or a Saturday or Sunday. Or perhaps you had a valid extension of time to file, but the IRS said that you filed your tax return late.

✔ **Wrong Social Security/ID number:** A data processing clerk may incorrectly input your Social Security number, or you may have been assigned two numbers. Because all data on a joint return is recorded under the Social Security number of the spouse whose name is listed first, any payments or credits that the other spouse made may not be posted under the first spouse's number. This situation frequently occurs when taxpayers file jointly for the first time or when a taxpayer files separately after having filed jointly in a prior year.

✔ **Wrong income:** Income earned by another person may be inadvertently reported under your Social Security number. This often happens when a taxpayer opens a bank account for a child or another relative.

✔ **Exempt income:** Money you earned on your IRA, on a Keogh, on a pension account, or from municipal bond interest, was reported to the IRS as being taxable.

✔ **Income double-counted:** Income earned from a taxpayer's business or profession may have been recorded as income from wages — or vice versa — and the IRS moved the income to the line or schedule on the taxpayer's return where it correctly belongs. That's okay, but sometimes the IRS does this *without* removing the income from the line or schedule where it was first incorrectly entered!

✔ **Lost return:** The IRS or the U.S. Postal Service may have lost your return and payment, leaving you in the unenviable position of having to prove the timely filing of the return. Hope you made a copy!

✔ **Partially corrected error:** The service center may have corrected only one of the errors that was previously made. For example, an IRS error may be corrected, but the penalties and interest that were incorrectly charged were not removed.

✔ **Data processing error:** A computer bug — or another unexplained phenomenon — may have caused a notice to be issued stating that a math error on your return was made where no error exists. Or someone may have failed to input all the data from the schedules attached to your return into the IRS computer.

Data processing errors are common with **Form 2210, Underpayment of Estimated Tax by Individuals and Fiduciaries,** where a taxpayer claims an exemption from the penalty for underestimating the amount of his or her required estimated tax payments. This kind of error usually causes the IRS either to assess a penalty when it shouldn't have or to issue a refund for the underestimating penalty that the taxpayer has paid.

✔ **Incorrect 1099:** The IRS may receive an incorrect Form 1099 from a bank or brokerage firm — either the amount of income reported on the form is wrong or the income isn't yours.

Fixing IRS Mistakes: Fight Fire with Fire

There is elegance in simplicity when corresponding with the IRS. Keep to the point. No letter should be longer than one page. A half page gets even quicker results. Remember, the tax examiner reviewing your inquiry could have little experience in the area you're writing about. Such people are, however, extremely conscientious in performing their duties. You stand a better chance of achieving the results you want by making their jobs as easy as possible. Don't succumb to the temptation to go into a narrative on how unfair our tax system is or how you are paying more than your fair share. Save that stuff for your representative in Congress.

Your letter to the IRS should contain the following items — and nothing more:

✔ Vital facts: name, mailing address, Social Security number on the tax return, and the year of the disputed tax return.

✔ Document locator number (DLN), type of tax, and a copy of the notice you received — refer to "Deciphering a notice," in Chapter 16, to find out what the heck a DLN is.

✔ What type of mistake the IRS made.

✔ What action you want the IRS to take.

✔ Copies of the documents necessary to prove your case — canceled checks, corrected Form 1099s, mailing receipts — but never send the originals.

Address your letter to the Adjustments/Correspondence (A/C) Branch at the service center that issued the notice. You should note the type of request you are making at the extreme top of the letter — REQUEST TO ADJUST FORM [form number]. Use the barcoded envelope that was sent with the notice to mail your letter.

Include a simple thank you and the telephone number where you can be reached if the tax examiner has any questions. Telephone contact between you and the tax examiner can take weeks off the Adjustments/Correspondence process. See Figure 18-1 for an example of a generic Dear John, er, we mean Dear IRS, letter. This example addresses an adjustment to be made to form CP-2000.

Figure 18-1: Here's how to compose a Dear IRS letter that gets right to the point.

Request to Adjust Form CP-2000

[your address]
[date]

Adjustments/Correspondence Branch
Internal Revenue Service Center
[address]

Re: [your name, Social Security
number]
[tax year, DLN]

Dear IRS:
I have received your notice dated [date], in which you claim that I failed to report [$] of interest on my tax return.

Please be advised that your notice, a copy of which is enclosed, is incorrect. The interest that you claimed I earned was in fact earned on my daughter's bank account. Her Social Security number is [number], which should have been given to the bank, instead of mine, when the account was opened.

Please adjust your notice to reflect that no additional tax is due. Thank you for your prompt attention to this request. I can be reached at [phone number] should you require any additional information.

Very truly yours,
[your name]

Upon receipt of your letter, the A/C Branch will stop the computer from sending further notices until the matter is resolved. If your problem can't be resolved in seven days, you will be sent a letter indicating when it can be resolved. If you receive a second notice, don't be alarmed. This delay isn't unusual. The IRS doesn't move all that fast.

If 30 days go by and you haven't heard from the IRS or you receive a third notice, see the section "Getting Attention When the IRS Ignores You," later in this chapter.

Sending a Simple Response to a Balance Due Notice

If you receive a *balance due notice* for a tax that has already been paid, simply mark the front of the notice: THIS BALANCE HAS BEEN PAID. SEE REVERSE SIDE OF NOTICE FOR PAYMENT INFORMATION. PLEASE REMOVE ALL PENALTIES AND INTEREST CHARGES THAT WERE ASSESSED.

The information that the IRS requires to properly credit your payment can be obtained from the back of your canceled check. On the back of the check, you will notice the date, the location of the IRS service center, where it was endorsed, and the serial number stamped on it.

If any of this information isn't legible or you can't readily cull it from the back of the check, simply photocopy the check (front and back) and send the photocopy — along with the notice — in the envelope provided. Write across the notice: THIS HAS BEEN PAID — COPY OF CHECK ENCLOSED.

Sending Generic Responses to Generic Notices

If you're like us, you probably dislike form letters with a passion. At times, however, you have no choice but to fight fire with fire. To simplify things, we have included an all-purpose generic response letter (see Figure 18-2).

You can use this letter simply by inserting any one of the following responses to frequent IRS errors. In order to keep it simple, we list the IRS error you want to address as the heading, and the response you can use appears right below it in quotes. We also include some explanatory text without quotes.

Misapplied payments

"Enclosed is a copy of my canceled check, front and back, showing that the tax was paid."

Misunderstood due date

Here are several solutions to common problems with due dates:

Figure 18-2:
You can get down-and-dirty with the IRS folks by using this battle-proven generic letter. Just insert the correct generic paragraph from the appropriate section where indicated.

Generic Response Letter

Request to adjust Form [number]
[your address]
[date]

Adjustments/Correspondence Branch
Internal Revenue Service Center
[address]

Re: [your name, Social Security number]
[tax year, DLN, Form number]

Dear IRS:

I am in receipt of your notice dated [date] (copy enclosed). Please be advised that your notice is incorrect.

[Insert generic paragraph(s) we have provided pertaining to one of the issues to be corrected.]

I would appreciate your adjusting the notice that you sent me now that you have the information contained in this letter that was previously unknown to you.

I would also appreciate your abating any penalties and interest that were incorrectly assessed.

I thank you in advance for your prompt attention to this request. I can be reached at [number] should you have any questions.

Very truly yours,
[your name]

Due date for filing or paying fell on Saturday, Sunday, or legal holiday

"Please be advised that your notice incorrectly penalizes me for filing/paying late. The due date for filing/paying fell on a [Saturday], and I made payment/filed on the next business day. Enclosed is a copy of my check dated [date], which is dated the date of the extended due date, as allowed by law. The serial number on the back of the check clearly indicates that the IRS negotiated my check on [date].

"Please correct your records to reflect that my return/payment was timely and remove all penalties and interest that were charged."

If you don't have a mailing receipt and you know your return was mailed on time, you may have to request a copy of the envelope in which you mailed your return from the service center before requesting an adjustment. Your mailing envelope becomes a permanent part of your return.

Valid extension of time to file

"Your notice incorrectly assesses a penalty for late filing. Enclosed is a copy of my extension that granted me an extension of time to file until [date]. I filed my return prior to the expiration of the extension on [date]."

"Please correct your records by removing the penalties and interest that were incorrectly assessed."

Enclose a copy of any canceled check that may have accompanied the extension and refer to the check in the letter.

Late filing

If you mailed your return on time with a balance due that you didn't pay — and the IRS sent a notice demanding the balance plus an erroneous late filing penalty — be prepared for lengthy correspondence with the IRS. If you don't have a postal mailing receipt, you will have to write to the service center and request a copy of the mailing envelope in which your tax return was mailed so that you can check the postmark.

"Your notice incorrectly assessed a late filing penalty in the amount of [amount]. Please be advised that my return was timely filed on [date]."

"By checking the postmark on the envelope in which my return was mailed, you will see that I didn't file late and therefore no penalty should be assessed. I would appreciate your sending me a copy of my mailing envelope when responding to this inquiry."

If the IRS can't locate your envelope (which sometimes happens) or the envelope bears a crazy, illegible postmark date, you have a problem. If this is the only time you were notified that you filed your return late, you will have to request that the penalty be abated due to reasonable cause — and due to your record of always filing on time. (We hope that you've always filed on time.) For more on reasonable cause, see Chapter 19.

Starting in 2000, if you file on time and enter into an agreement to pay in installments, the late payment penalty gets reduced from 0.5 percent a month to 0.25 percent a month while you're making payments. See "When You Can't Pay Your Taxes" in Chapter 19. The total late payment penalty that can be charged can't exceed 25 percent of the tax owed.

Wrong income

"The income on which you claim I owe additional tax per your notice is not my income. The bank/broker/insurance company [or whatever] incorrectly reported the income that was earned on this account as belonging to me. This account, in fact, belongs to my [mother, for example], who reported it on her tax return for the year in question. Her Social Security number is [123-45-6789]."

"Enclosed, please find a copy of my [mother's] tax return and a statement from her stating that the balance in the account you question belongs to her. I have instructed the bank to correct its records. Please correct yours so that my tax account shows that no tax is owed your agency."

Exempt income

We are constantly amazed when we review returns that clients prepared themselves. One of the things that crops up all the time is how often they pay tax on income they don't have to. Here are two prominent examples and the appropriate response when the IRS sends a bill for tax due on tax-exempt income.

Keogh — IRA

"The income on which you claim I owe additional tax is income earned from my [Keogh or IRA] account and is exempt from tax. Enclosed is a copy of my year-end statement of that account. Please note that the number of this account is the same as the number that appears on your notice. Please correct your records so my tax account shows that no additional tax is owed your agency."

Municipal bonds

"The income on which you claim I owed additional tax is exempt municipal bond interest. Enclosed is a corrected statement from my broker/bank that clearly identifies that the amount of income reported on your notice is tax-exempt municipal bond interest. Please correct your records so that my tax account shows that no tax is owed your agency."

Income double-counted

"The interest income you claim I failed to report on my tax return for the year in question was, in fact, reported on Schedule C of my return (copy enclosed). By adjusting Schedule B (Interest and Dividend Income) of my tax return without adjusting my Schedule C, you are requiring me to pay tax on the same item of income twice by double-counting it. Please correct your records so my tax account reflects that no tax is owed your agency."

Lost return

This is a tough one. But one secret that the IRS hates to admit is that it frequently loses or misplaces tax returns. The IRS even has a form letter when this happens. The letter requests that you send a duplicate. Unfortunately, when you do, you're likely to receive a follow-up notice saying that the IRS received the duplicate, but that it was filed late!

Refund return

"Enclosed is a copy of my return that your notice claimed was not filed. Please be advised that this return, which indicated a refund due, was filed on [date]."

If you have a postal mailing receipt, enclose a copy of it.

If your return was mailed by someone other than yourself, or if another person saw you mail your return, get a statement to that effect and enclose it. (Of course, if the person that you asked to mail your return forgot, you can always try to get him or her to pay your late filing penalty.)

Balance Due return

"Enclosed is a copy of the return that your notice (copy enclosed) dated [date] claimed was not filed. Please be advised that my return was mailed on [date]. However, as of this date, my check number [number] dated [date] that accompanied my tax return hasn't been returned to me by my bank.

"I call your attention to Estate of Wood, 92TC No.46 case in which the court held that a timely mailed return is presumed to have been received by the IRS.

"I would appreciate your correcting your records to reflect that this return was timely filed. If you would be kind enough to send me a bill for the balance I owe without reference to any penalties, I will remit full payment on receipt of your bill."

If you, in fact, included a check for the balance due with your return that has now been lost, don't forget to ask your bank to stop payment on the check. You don't want to have to write the IRS again when it credits two payments to your tax account. Plus, you can send the stop payment order with your letter to the IRS as proof that everything was lost.

Enclose any proof of mailing that you have.

Lost check

"Please be advised that my check, number [number], dated [date], was attached to my return that I filed on [date]. Because my check still hasn't been returned by my bank, I am placing a stop payment on it and have issued a new check for the same amount as the original check, which I have enclosed. Kindly abate the interest that you charged on your notice. It would be unfair to charge me interest because your agency can't locate my check."

Tax assessed after statute of limitations

By filing a **Form 911, Taxpayer Application for Assistance Order,** or TAO, you put the IRS on notice that it could be liable for damages and costs up to $1,000,000 resulting from its reckless and intentional behavior in dunning you. If the IRS's actions on or after July 22, 1998, are merely negligent, you can collect damages and costs up to $100,000. TAOs are covered under the Taxpayer Bill of Rights in Chapter 19. This form is filed with the office of the IRS's Taxpayer Advocate in your area. You can get a copy of Form 911 by calling 800-TAX-FORM. The downside of filing this form is that the statute of limitations is extended while this application is pending.

To cover all bases, write to the Adjustments/Correspondence Branch at the service center that issued the assessment.

"Please be advised that your assessment for additional tax, penalties, and interest was issued in violation of the statute of limitations. The time for making an additional assessment for the year in question expired on [date].

"Please remove this assessment from my tax account, along with any interest or penalties that were charged. The assessment you made is in direct violation of the law. An assessment must be made within three years after the return is filed. This assessment doesn't comply with that requirement."

Refer to "Understanding the Statute of Limitations on Audits" in Chapter 17 for more on the statute of limitations.

Partially corrected error

"Please make the following adjustment [insert] as requested in my original letter of [date] (copy enclosed) that your current notice [date] failed to adjust."

At this point, you may want to refer the matter to the local Taxpayer Advocate Office. (See "Getting Attention When the IRS Ignores You," later in this chapter.)

Erroneous refund

Remember what your mother told you about keeping money that doesn't belong to you? She was right, of course — maybe because she had to deal with the IRS. As a practical matter, if you want to save yourself a great deal of time corresponding with the IRS, deposit the check, but don't spend the money (sorry). You ultimately will receive a bill for it. You can also send it in, if you want to get rid of it.

You returned a refund check

"Enclosed is a refund check that was incorrectly issued to me."

Return the check to the service center where you filed your return, not to the Treasury Department office that issued the check. Send this letter by certified mail.

You didn't return a refund check sent to you by mistake

"Your notice demanding interest on a refund sent to me in error is assessed in violation of the law. I discovered the error only when I received your notice demanding repayment. I call your attention to the fact that Section 6404(e)(2) of the Internal Revenue Code states that no interest may be charged if a taxpayer who receives an erroneous refund of $50,000 or less repays it when the IRS demands payment. Enclosed please find my check in the amount of the tax that was incorrectly refunded. Please correct your notice by removing the interest that you shouldn't have charged me."

If this approach doesn't work, you should contact the IRS Taxpayer Advocate in your area.

Data processing error

This problem is probably the most difficult to cope with.

"Your notice incorrectly states that [choose appropriate problem(s)]:

    (a) a mathematical error was made.

    (b) I used the wrong tax table in computing my tax.

    (c) I incorrectly claimed a credit.

"Please be advised that I rechecked my return and do not believe that any error was made. Enclosed is a copy of my return. Please review it and advise me exactly where you think an error was made.

"I thank you in advance for your prompt attention to this request."

Incorrect 1099

Use (a) or (b) when appropriate.

    (a) "Your notice incorrectly claims that I failed to report all the income I received from [name].

(b) "Please be advised that the 1099 information that you received
from [name] is incorrect.

"I enclose a copy of a corrected 1099 that [name] has issued to me.

"I would appreciate your adjusting my tax account to reflect the information contained in the corrected 1099. When this is done, you will
readily see that no additional tax is due."

Always try to get the 1099 corrected and send along a copy of the new one. The 1099 lists the
name, address, and telephone number of whom you should contact if the 1099 is wrong.

Wrong year

"The miscellaneous income your notice claims I failed to report for the
year in question was not received until the following year and was reported on that year's return (copy enclosed). Additionally, I am enclosing a copy of my bank statement for the month in which this income was
received. You will notice that this bank statement bears the following
year's date."

Never received prior notices

"Your records don't have my correct address, which is probably why I
never received your prior notices. Please send me copies of these notices so that I can determine whether the most current notice that I
enclose is correct. If it is, I will pay the amount I owe upon receipt
of the notices I request. If it is not correct, I will contact you. I
thank you in advance for your prompt attention to this request."

To speed up this process, call the IRS at the number indicated on the notice and request
copies of the prior notices. Also, send the IRS **Form 8822, Change of Address.** If all this
fails, see how to get a transcript of your tax account from the IRS in Chapter 3 under "Lost
Tax Returns."

Call the IRS for a copy of your tax account. This document will reveal all postings made by
the IRS for tax, interest, penalties, and payments.

Getting Attention When the IRS Ignores You

At times, it seems that a black hole ravages every IRS Service Center, devouring loads of
taxpayer correspondence. Naturally, the IRS won't respond right away in these cases. If
this happens to you, the IRS has a special office that handles these problems: the office of
your local Taxpayer Advocate.

Getting to know your local Taxpayer Advocate

Since 1977, the local Taxpayer Advocate Office has been the complaint department of the
IRS. There is an advocate in every one of the 33 IRS districts, as well as at each of the 10
service centers. An advocate's function is to resolve taxpayer problems that can't be
resolved through normal channels.

The National Taxpayer Advocate who is appointed by the Secretary of the Treasury
oversees all functions of the local Taxpayer Advocates and their employees. Both the

National and local Taxpayer Advocates operate independently from the IRS and report directly to Congress. The purpose behind this independence is to provide taxpayers with a "customer friendly" problem-solving office. Being independent of all other IRS offices enables the office of the local advocate to cut through red tape.

Local Taxpayer Advocates don't interpret tax law, give tax advice, or provide assistance in preparing tax returns. But they do resolve procedural, refund, notice, billing, and other problems that couldn't be fixed after one or more attempts by a taxpayer. A local advocate can abate penalties, trace missing tax payments, and credit them to a taxpayer's account. An advocate can also approve replacement refund checks for originals that were either lost or stolen, release a lien, and — of greatest importance — stop IRS collection action.

Meeting the criteria for a Taxpayer Advocate case

The local Taxpayer Advocate accepts cases for a variety of reasons. The following cases are certain to be considered:

✔ You call or write the IRS about a problem. After 30 days, you contact the IRS again, but the IRS still ignores you.

✔ You file your return expecting a nice refund, but after 60 days, you're still waiting. You contact the IRS, but nothing happens.

✔ You receive a letter from the IRS promising to respond to your particular inquiry by a certain date, but the IRS forgets about you.

Established IRS procedures often fail to correct a problem — but don't count on the local advocate to be overly charitable. If the advocate won't take your case, he or she will refer it to the IRS office that should have handled it from the start.

Contacting the local Taxpayer Advocate

Except in emergency cases, such as when a levy has been filed although the taxpayer owes the IRS no money, taxpayers should write to the advocate in the district where they reside. Your letter should contain the following:

✔ A complete description of the problem

✔ Copies of the fronts and backs of canceled checks (if applicable)

✔ A signed copy of your tax return (if applicable)

✔ Copies of all notices received from the IRS

✔ Copies of previous letters written to the IRS regarding this problem

✔ The number of phone calls you made to the IRS, whom you spoke with, the dates, and what was discussed

✔ Any other documents or information that might help the advocate expedite the resolution of this problem

✔ A telephone number where you can be reached during the day

In an emergency situation, you should contact the office of the local Taxpayer Advocate by phone. When you do call, an advocate can immediately take a variety of actions. For example, the advocate can issue a **Form 911, Taxpayer Application for Assistance Order (TAO),** if a notice of levy has been incorrectly issued.

The IRS toll-free phone number (800-829-1040) can direct you to the office of your local advocate.

If the Advocate takes your case

Taxpayer Advocates and their employees are committed to resolving your problem in seven working days. If they can't, you will be informed, usually by telephone, when you can expect the problem to be resolved. Most cases are closed in 30 days or less. If an advocate asks for certain information and it isn't sent, the case won't be held open indefinitely. After two weeks, it will be closed, in which case you must make a new Taxpayer Advocate contact. An advocate closes a case by writing to the taxpayer and explaining what corrective action has been taken, if any. (If no corrective action can be taken, the advocate's letter offers an explanation.)

Finding Your Refund When It Doesn't Find You

If you didn't receive your refund, you may be one of about 100,000 taxpayers whose refund checks are returned to the IRS by the U.S. Postal Service. According to the IRS, these checks are undeliverable because of incorrect addresses or because the taxpayer moved and failed to leave a forwarding address. So if you move, make sure that you notify the IRS by filing **Form 8822, Change of Address.** That way, you'll be sure to get your refund.

The actual figures on how many taxpayers never receive their refund checks are substantially higher when one takes into account the refund checks that are either lost or stolen. There are also a number of other reasons why a taxpayer may not have received a refund. For example, the refund could have been used to offset another year's tax bill or to pay what was owed on a delinquent student loan or past-due child support.

How to locate your refund

Yes, there is a lost-and-found department. You can find out the status of your refund by using the IRS automated TeleTax System. By dialing 800-829-4477 on a touch-tone phone, you will be prompted through a series of computerized instructions.

Refund inquiries shouldn't be made until at least six weeks from the date the return was filed. It takes about that much time for the IRS to process a tax return and program the information into TeleTax. Only after the IRS inputs the information on your return into its computer can you find out about the status of your refund.

If a mistake was made, the refund may have to be processed manually, which may take an additional four to six weeks. Whatever the reason for the delay, the TeleTax System usually explains it. TeleTax also informs you of the date your refund check was mailed or when it will be mailed.

If it has been more than ten days to two weeks since the date a refund check was scheduled to be mailed and you still haven't received it, the check was probably lost or stolen. If this is the situation, you can do one of three things:

- Fill out **Form 3911, Taxpayer Statement Regarding Refund,** and send it to the service center where you filed. This one-page form asks whether you ever received the check, or whether you received it and lost it. Allow four to six weeks for processing.

- Contact the office of your local Taxpayer Advocate. See "Getting Attention When the IRS Ignores You," earlier in this chapter, for more information.

- Contact the IRS refund section at 800-829-1040. You'll have the opportunity to speak to an IRS employee instead of a machine.

Uncashed refund checks

You must cash a refund check within 12 months. If your refund check isn't cashed within the required 12-month period, it doesn't mean that you're not entitled to your refund. You are. A new refund check will have to be issued and the uncashed one returned to the IRS. This procedure can be accomplished by filing **Form 3911, Taxpayer Statement Regarding Refund,** with the service center where you filed your return. Across the top of the form, insert: THE ENCLOSED REFUND CHECK CANNOT BE CASHED; 12 MONTHS HAVE PASSED SINCE IT WAS ISSUED. PLEASE ISSUE A REPLACEMENT CHECK.

You aren't entitled to additional interest on a replacement check because you failed to deposit or cash your refund. But you are entitled to interest if the IRS is late in issuing your refund. See the very next section.

Interest on refunds

If the IRS doesn't issue your refund within 45 days of filing your return, it must pay you interest. So if you file by April 15 and you don't receive your refund by May 30, interest is due.

Refunds and estimated tax payments

If you requested that your refund be applied to next year's tax, you can't change your mind and subsequently request a refund. You can get your overpayment back only by taking credit for it on next year's tax return. No interest is paid on an overpayment of tax credited to next year's tax bill.

Joint refunds

When married couples have divorced or separated, or when a dispute exists as to how much of the refund each is entitled to, Revenue Ruling 80-7 provides a formula for determining each spouse's share of the refund. Again, this is one of those times when consulting a tax advisor is a must. If the parties can't decide how to divide the refund, either spouse may request that the IRS issue a separate refund check by filing **Form 1040X, Amended U.S. Individual Income Tax Return,** and making the computation required by Revenue Ruling 80-7. The IRS will accept a joint 1040X with only one signature from a divorced or separated taxpayer requesting a separate refund check. The worksheet on the back of **Form 8379, Injured Spouse Claim and Allocation,** will guide you through the computation. Attach this form to your amended return. The refund belongs to the spouse whose income, deductions, and tax payments produced the refund. Filing jointly doesn't change who is entitled to the refund. Filing jointly only determines the amount of tax a couple has to pay.

Revenue Ruling 80-7 must be modified for taxpayers residing in community property states (California, Nevada, New Mexico, Arizona, Idaho, Washington, Louisiana, and Texas).

Joint estimated payments

Where joint estimated payments have been made and a husband and wife file separate returns, the estimated payments may be divided in any manner the couple sees fit. However, if a couple can't agree on how estimated payments are to be divided, the payments will be divided in the same manner as joint refunds, as required by Revenue Ruling 80-7.

Deceased taxpayer

If a refund is due a deceased taxpayer, **Form 1310, Statement of Person Claiming Refund Due a Deceased Taxpayer,** must be attached to the return unless the surviving spouse files a joint return. If the form isn't attached, the IRS will send back the return along with Form 1310. The refund will be processed once the IRS receives Form 1310.

Statute of limitations

To get a refund, you must file a return within three years of its due date, including extensions of time to file (or within two years from the date tax was paid, if later). After that time, you forfeit the refund. A return filed before the due date is considered to have been filed on the due date. For example, if the due date for filing a return is April 15, 1998, an amended return must be filed by April 15, 2001. After that date, no refund will be allowed.

If the April 15, 1998, filing date was extended to August 15, 1998, an amended return must be filed by August 15, 2001. Your acceptance of a refund doesn't bar a future claim for a refund if you subsequently discover that you made a mistake in computing the amended return and now realize that you're entitled to an even greater refund than you computed on your amended return.

The statute of limitations is suspended when a person is financially disabled — a disability renders him or her unable to manage financial affairs. This change was brought about by the case of a senile taxpayer who erroneously overpaid the IRS $7,000, and a timely (within three years) refund claim wasn't filed. Assuming that adequate proof of a medical disability can be provided, this taxpayer under the new law can get back the $7,000 that was overpaid.

Given the number of taxpayers who have aging parents, a word of caution is required. This rule doesn't apply where a taxpayer's spouse, or another person such as a guardian, is authorized to act on the disabled taxpayer's behalf regarding financial matters. So where there is an "authorized person," the normal three-year statute of limitations rule prevails regardless of the taxpayer's "financial disability." The IRS believes that the person looking after the disabled person's financial affairs should be bound by the same three-year rule that everyone else has to follow. How disabled does someone have to be? The disability or impairment must be expected to result in death, or has or is expected to last continuously for at least a 12-month period.

Erroneous refunds

If you receive an erroneous refund and don't repay it, the IRS can't use a lien or levy to enforce collection. Its only remedy is to sue you or to issue a deficiency notice. The IRS can't charge interest on erroneous refunds under $50,000. For more on this, see Chapter 19.

Refund offset program

If the IRS intercepts a joint refund and only one spouse owes for support, a government debt, or back taxes, the IRS must notify the other spouse of the action that must be taken to get its share of the refund. The IRS can't keep the entire refund. The nonobligated spouse must file **Form 8379, Injured Spouse Claim and Allocation,** to claim his or her share of the refund. Revenue Ruling 80-7 explains how to divide the refund. In 1996, the IRS intercepted 2.1 million refunds as part of this program. Yes, Big Brother is watching.

Just remember: To err is human, to forgive divine. And we never accused the IRS of not being human.

Chapter 19

Fixing Your Own Mistakes

In This Chapter

▶ Fixing bad returns

▶ Making a deal with the IRS

▶ Abating penalties and interest

▶ Understanding your Taxpayer Bill of Rights

*W*e all make mistakes. To make them is human; to admit that they're our fault is not, typically, human. In most cases, the sooner you fix a problem, the happier and less poor you'll be. In some cases, you need to complete more paperwork; in others, you have to speak with and cajole IRS employees. Regardless, here's our advice for how to do it now, do it right, and be done with it!

Amending a Return

Through the years, when taxpayers discovered that they failed to claim a deduction or credit in a prior year, they often asked whether they could claim that deduction in the current year. They couldn't, and you can't, either.

TAX CUT

If you discover that you forgot to claim a deduction and the statute of limitations hasn't expired, you have to file an amended return. Similarly, if you discover that a deduction was improperly claimed, you must file an amended return and pay any additional tax plus interest.

Not surprisingly, more amended returns are filed when the flow of funds is going in a taxpayer's direction rather than in the government's. Although this isn't a startling discovery, it has more to do with *letting sleeping dogs lie* than with people's honesty. It will take a sociologist to properly address this issue, and we aren't quite qualified to pull it off.

If you forgot to claim a deduction in a prior year, you must file an amended return within three years from the date of filing your original return, or within two years from the time the tax was paid, whichever is later. **Form 1040X, Amended U.S. Individual Income Tax Return,** is used to correct a prior year's tax return.

Suppose that you file your 1998 return on April 15, 1999. If you want to amend this return, you must do so by April 15, 2002. However, if you filed your return on or before April 15, 1999, the three-year statute of limitations still expires on April 15, 2002. If you had an extension of time to file until October 15, 1999, the three-year period starts to run from that date.

This three-year rule is suspended for anyone suffering from a disability that renders him unable to manage his financial affairs. This provision enables such taxpayers to recover tax that was erroneously overpaid in instances where the three-year statute of limitations would normally bar a refund. However, when a taxpayer's spouse or another person such as a guardian is authorized to act on the disabled taxpayer's behalf, this new rule doesn't apply. The IRS believes that the person looking after the disabled person's financial affairs should be bound by the same three-year rule that everyone else has to follow. How disabled does someone have to be? The disability or impairment must be expected to result in death, or it must have lasted or be expected to last for more than a year.

In most cases, filing an amended return doesn't affect the penalty for underestimating your tax. For example, suppose that you were assessed a $1,000 penalty for underpayment of your estimated tax. Your amended return is for half the tax on your original return. The $1,000 underestimating penalty can't be reduced. This is one mistake that can't be amended.

Amended returns are also useful for changing how you reported an item on your original return. You can change your mind in the following situations:

- ✔ You filed separately but now want to file jointly. It is important to note that you *cannot* do this in reverse — you can't switch to filing separately if you originally filed jointly.

- ✔ You want to switch between five- and ten-year averaging on paying tax on a lump-sum retirement payment.

- ✔ You want to change from itemizing your deductions to claiming the standard deduction, or vice versa.

- ✔ You reported something incorrectly. This situation may occur if you claimed a deduction or an exemption of income to which you weren't entitled. An example could be when a noncustodial parent incorrectly claimed an exemption for a child or claimed head of household filing status.

Some decisions to treat an item in a certain manner are irrevocable, such as using the straight-line depreciation method and taking a net operating loss forward instead of backward.

More expenses than income

An amended return is permitted if you incur a *net operating loss* (NOL). You have an NOL if you lost money (in a business or profession) that exceeds all your other income. You can carry back an NOL to offset your taxable income in the two previous years, and this action will entitle you to a refund. If the NOL is not used up by carrying it back, it can be carried forward for 20 years until it is used up.

Additionally, when filing your return for the NOL year, you can elect to carry the NOL forward instead of having to amend your returns for the two preceding years. This choice may make sense when your income or tax rates are rising. The reverse would be true if tax rates are declining. Remember, make sure that you really want to carry the NOL forward, because you can't change this election by filing an amended return.

You need **Form 1045, Application for Tentative Refund,** to carry back an NOL. This form can be used only if it is filed within one year of the year you had the NOL. If it isn't, **Form 1040X, Amended U.S. Individual Income Tax Return,** must be used.

The number of years that NOLs could be carried back changed in 1998. Before then, NOLs could be carried three years instead of two to obtain a tax refund. The carryforward, however, was limited to 15 years.

The three-year carryback rule has been retained for casualty and theft losses as well as for NOLs attributable to losses in a presidentially-declared disaster area for the owner of a small business (providing that the person's income for each of the proceeding years was under $5 million). Farmers are entitled to a 5-year carryback of a NOL (see Chapter 14).

The tax benefit rule

Usually, if you deduct an expense in one year and part or all of that expense is reimbursed in a subsequent year, you have to report the reimbursement as income. For example, suppose that you deducted $10,000 in medical expenses in 1997 and were reimbursed $3,000 by your insurance company in 1998. You have to report the $3,000 in 1998.

However, if the original deduction didn't result in a tax savings, you don't have to report the reimbursement. For example, you may receive a state tax refund for a year in which you claimed the standard deduction instead of itemizing your deductions — you don't have to report the refund.

When You Can't Pay Your Taxes

"If you can't pay," goes the old saw, "you can owe." That's certainly the way the Internal Revenue Service looks at things. Taxpayers currently owe the IRS almost $200 billion in back taxes, an amount that increases at the rate of $15 billion a year.

If you're one of the millions of Americans who can't pay all they owe, you've got four options:

- ✔ You can pay it off in installments, which 2.6 million taxpayers are currently doing.

- ✔ You can put it off until you have more money.

- ✔ You can try to convince the IRS to take less than it wants. In 1996, the IRS accepted 27,673 of these offers.

- ✔ You can file for bankruptcy — in the absolute worst-case scenario.

Whatever you do, don't confuse filing and paying. More people get into hot water because they mistakenly believe that they should put off filing until they can pay. If you are one of the 5 to 10 million nonfilers that the IRS is currently looking for, file your return as soon as possible — even if you can pay only part of what you owe. Owing the IRS money is expensive. Eight-percent interest compounds daily on the balance you owe, in addition to a late-payment penalty of half a percentage point per month. This adds up to big bucks! Every month you're late in filing, you have to tack on an extra 5-percent penalty, up to a maximum of 25 percent.

At first, the IRS comes after you through the mail. If you owe money, either from the findings of an audit or because you simply couldn't pay it all on April 15, you'll get three notices from the IRS at five-week intervals; the second one is threatening in tone. If you didn't pay everything you owe on April 15, the third and last letter will arrive by certified mail around July 4.

Suppose that you allow all three letters to go by without paying any money. Your account is now considered delinquent and is forwarded to the IRS Automated Collection System (ACS), which means you'll start getting telephone calls demanding payment — at home and, if the IRS can't reach you at home, at work, at your club, anywhere the IRS has a number for you. Although the IRS is trying to be a friendlier place, the agency is anything but congenial when demanding payment. If the ACS isn't successful in getting you to pay up, your account may be transferred to an IRS revenue officer, who will contact you in person.

If you owe more than $100,000, your file will be sent to a revenue officer immediately instead of to the nice folks at ACS who contact people by phone.

In many cases, the agency already has what it refers to as *levy source information.* Your file won't go to an agent. The IRS will place a levy on your assets or salary, or it may seize your property. Remember, if you file a return, the government knows where your income comes from and how much you make. Not only does the IRS know about your assets from your tax return, but it also has the right to get more information about you from credit and governmental agencies, such as the Department of Motor Vehicles, the Passport agency, and the U.S. Postal Service. It can make you pay in more ways than one. And every time you make a payment, the IRS makes a permanent record of your bank account.

To avoid that hassle, if there's any way you can get the money together, send a partial payment when filing your return, a partial payment with the first and second notices, and the balance (including interest and penalties) with the third notice.

When the IRS sends a bill for under $100,000, you have 21 interest-free days to pay it. If the amount you owe is over $100,000, you have ten *business* days before you're charged interest.

The IRS must notify you of your right to request an appeal 30 days prior to levying your salary or property. You then have 30 days from that date to request an appeal. See Chapter 16 for more information about appealing liens and levies.

Requesting an installment agreement

In some cases, people need more time to pay what they owe. If you need more time, you can request to pay in installments by attaching **Form 9465, Installment Agreement Request,** to your return or to any of the notices you receive and sending it to the IRS Service Center where you file or to the center that issued the notice. We include Form 9465 in the back of this book. You also can request an installment agreement by telephoning the IRS Taxpayer Services office. This number is in the telephone directory. It's also printed on the notice you receive.

If you owe less than $10,000 and can pay off what you owe in 36 months, the IRS is required by law to grant your request to pay in installments. However, there are some strings attached. Over the past five years, you had to have filed and paid your tax on time. Even if this rule knocks you out of contention, it is IRS policy to automatically grant installment agreements when the amount owed is under $10,000 and can be paid off in 36 months. When you make this request, a mailing will come from the IRS saying your request has been accepted and telling you where to send the money. You won't have to provide a financial statement, but you will have to sign **Form 433-D, Installment Agreement.** Nor will a federal tax lien be filed — that's no small matter, because a tax lien can affect your credit rating for seven years, even if you pay off your tax liability in a shorter period of time. There's a $43 charge for an installment agreement and a $24 charge for reinstating an agreement you defaulted on.

Be careful not to fall behind in your payments, or you may have to apply for an installment plan all over again. If you can't make a payment, contact the IRS. You stand a good chance of being able to skip a payment if you have a plausible reason. Although the IRS isn't all that charitable, it reserves its wrath for taxpayers who ignore the agency.

Installments get trickier if you owe more than $10,000 or want to stretch your payments over more than 36 months. You can either use Form 9465 or go straight to the IRS, either by mail or by phone. (A representative, such as an enrolled agent, a CPA, or an attorney, can make this request on your behalf.) You'll need to file a financial statement listing your assets, liabilities, and monthly income and expenses, which is submitted on **IRS Form 433-F, Collection Information Statement for Individuals.** Use Form 433-A if you're self-employed. For a business, use Form 433-B.

You can appeal the rejection of request for an installment agreement to the IRS Appeals Office (see Chapter 16).

Starting in 2000, if you filed your return on time and enter into an installment agreement, the late-filing penalty gets reduced from 0.5 percent a month to 0.25 percent a month while you're making your payments. The total late-payment penalty that can be charged can't exceed 25 percent of the tax owed. On $10,000 of tax owed, this reduction amounts to a $25-per-month savings.

After reviewing the form, the IRS will recommend one of the following courses of action, or a combination of them. The IRS may tell you to

✔ Make immediate payment by liquidating some of your assets.

✔ Obtain a cash advance from a credit line.

✔ Borrow against the equity in any assets you may have, such as your residence.

✔ Make an installment agreement.

There is a fifth option: If there's just no way you can pay, the IRS will stop bothering you for the money. Yes, if you get the fifth option, the IRS will prepare **Form 53, Report of Taxes Currently Not Collectible,** and you'll be off the hook for a while. But the IRS will contact you every 9 to 12 months for a new financial statement, to see whether your financial condition has changed. Remember, the IRS has ten years to collect what you owe before the statute of limitations on collections expires.

Making an offer

What if you think there's no way you'll ever be able to pay it all off? The IRS, believe it or not, often takes partial payment. First, you need to fill out **Form 656, Offer in Compromise.** This is a one-page form that requires you to complete only three lines in addition to your name, address, and Social Security number. You merely state the amount you can pay in relation to your net worth and give the simple statement, `I cannot pay these taxes`, as the reason for making the offer. Then comes the hard part — you also have to supply a financial statement, **Form 433-A.** And, unlike the application for an installment plan, this financial statement will be audited, not merely reviewed.

If you discover that you don't owe the tax, and the IRS claims you do, you can make an offer based on *doubt of liability*. You simply state that you do not owe this tax.

An Offer in Compromise is a matter of public record and, if accepted, may come with strings attached. You may have to agree that, for a period of years, perhaps as many as five, you will pay more than you offered should your financial condition improve. An aging Joe Louis had to accept such terms, in case he ever started earning millions again by going back into the boxing ring.

Who are candidates for Offers in Compromise? All types of taxpayers: senior citizens with few or no assets or in poor health, spendthrifts who earned large sums of money and squandered it, athletes and actors whose earning potential has diminished, casualties of downsizing, and people whose relatives are reluctant to leave them money because of their tax problems.

You can appeal an offer that is rejected. While an offer is pending, the IRS is prohibited from levying your salary or property.

Declaring bankruptcy

If things are really dire, you may decide that declaring personal bankruptcy is the only way out. When you file a bankruptcy petition, it puts a legal stop to all IRS collection action, and the government can no longer garnish your salary or seize your property. Income taxes that are more than three years old are forgiven.

You can recover up to $1 million in damages if the IRS willfully violates the bankruptcy law's prohibition against seizing your salary or property.

Even if your tax liability isn't completely wiped out in bankruptcy court, as often happens, the IRS won't have as much power over you anymore. For example, you don't have to get IRS approval on an installment plan. If the bankruptcy court allows your repayment plan because the bankruptcy judge finds it fair and equitable, the IRS has to accept it.

Remember that bankruptcy is a drastic step and shouldn't be undertaken unless you're guided by an attorney experienced in this area. Bankruptcy damages your credit report, but with all the liens the IRS has filed, your credit is already damaged. Generally, personal income taxes that are more than three years old from the original due date, and more than two years old from the actual filing date, can be wiped out in a bankruptcy and become what is known as *dischargeable debt*. However, in a Chapter 13 filing, the two-year filing rule doesn't apply. The tax only has to be more than three years old.

Planning ahead to avoid these problems

The best defense is to make adequate provisions for paying your taxes in the first place. Routinely review your withholding allowances (Form W-4) to make sure that the proper amount of tax is being withheld from your salary. (See Chapter 15 if you need help determining how much to withhold.) If you're self-employed or have income that isn't subject to withholding, you should be making quarterly estimated payments using Form 1040-ES.

Estimated taxes

The penalty for underestimating your tax may be abated because of a casualty, disaster, or another unusual circumstance. The penalty can also be abated by filing **Form 2210, Underpayment of Estimated Tax,** if you meet one of the following conditions:

✔ You paid 100 percent of your 1997 tax. To escape the penalty for 1999, you will have to pay 105 percent of your 1998 tax if your 1998 income exceeded $150,000.

✔ You met the 90-percent tax payment requirement.

If you have income that isn't subject to withholding, the IRS doesn't want to wait until April 15 to be paid. The agency wants you to pay what you owe in quarterly estimates. The penalty kicks in if you owe $1,000 or more when you file your return, and you haven't made tax payments equal to 90 percent of your tax during the year.

✔ You filed a return for the previous year that showed no tax liability.

✔ You retired at age 62 or later, or became disabled, and your underpayment was due to reasonable cause.

✔ If you operate a seasonal business or didn't earn your income evenly throughout the year, you may be able to reduce or eliminate the penalty by using the annualized income installment method. Not many taxpayers use it because of its complexity, but if you think it will save you money, IRS Publication 505 (*Withholding and Estimated Tax*) explains how it works. For example, say you earned nothing for 11 months and then had income in the 12th month. You were required to make only one estimated payment instead of four.

To get the penalty waived, attach an explanation to Form 2210 along with any documentation that will prove you shouldn't be charged a penalty. See lines 58 and 69 in Chapter 8 for details about this fiendish penalty.

Abating a Penalty

Although the Internal Revenue Code contains about 150 penalties, some are more common than others. The most common penalties include:

- Accuracy errors (the IRS defines accuracy errors as either negligence or disregard of the rules)
- Failure to file
- Failure to pay
- False Withholding Exemption Certificate (Form W-4)
- Underestimating tax

Many taxpayers who receive a penalty notice believe that a penalty wouldn't have been charged unless it was correct, and they simply pay it. After all, penalties are asserted on official-looking documents. Never think that any notice is correct. This is the primary requirement for making sure that you don't pay what you don't owe.

In 1996, the IRS assessed 34 million penalties for a total of $13.2 billion; 4.2 million penalties totaling $5.7 billion were abated for reasonable cause or because they were improperly assessed. Taxpayers can look to several sources — the Internal Revenue Manual, court cases, IRS Rulings and Announcements, and the regulations to the Internal Revenue Code — to determine whether they meet the definition of reasonable cause. Penalties are never deductible. Because some penalties are considered an addition to the tax you have to pay, interest is computed on the total amount due — tax plus penalties.

The Internal Revenue Manual (IRM)

The Internal Revenue Manual is the IRS bible. It contains the rules that IRS employees must follow in applying the law (not that it helps you any if they don't). According to the manual, the following situations constitute reasonable cause for abating a penalty:

- Your return was mailed on time but was not received until after the filing date, regardless of whether or not the envelope bears sufficient postage.
- Your return was filed on time but was received by the wrong IRS office.
- You relied upon erroneous information provided to you by an IRS officer or employee.
- Your return was filed late due to death or serious illness of the taxpayer, or to the death or illness of a family member.
- You were unavoidably away on the filing date.
- Your place of business, residence, or business records were destroyed due to fire or other casualty.
- You applied to the IRS district director for proper tax forms prior to the filing deadline — but these forms were not furnished in sufficient time.
- You presented proof of having visited an IRS office before an IRS expiration date for filing returns in order to secure information on how to properly complete your return — but you were not able to meet with an IRS representative.
- You were unable, for reasons beyond your control, to obtain the records necessary to determine the amount of tax due, or, for reasons beyond your control, you weren't able to pay. For example, you couldn't get your money out of a bankrupt S&L to pay your taxes, or your account was attached by a lien or court order. Perhaps you earned money in a foreign country that you couldn't convert into dollars, or a person who was needed to cosign a check was ill or away.

Reasonable cause — an important definition

With the exception of fraud penalties, just about every penalty can be abated for what is known as reasonable cause. The IRS defines reasonable cause as follows:

"If the taxpayer exercised ordinary business care and prudence and was nevertheless unable to file or pay within the prescribed time, then the delay is due to reasonable cause."

✔ Your tax advisor incorrectly advised you that you didn't need to file a return, even though you provided him or her with all the necessary and relevant documents, or the advisor prepared the return incorrectly.

Your ignorance of the law may be considered reasonable cause for a late return if other factors, such as a situation in which you are filing a return for the first time, support this contention. However, you must demonstrate that you exercised ordinary care and prudence.

Court cases that define reasonable cause

The following court precedents can be handy to know when dealing with the IRS. Precedents are good things because they act like rules that the IRS will obey. You can use these arguments when appropriate. The IRS should listen. But be careful: When you start citing court cases (look for the italicized text in the sections that follow so you can identify the court case), the eyes of IRS officials (or anyone else, for that matter) may start to glaze over.

Ignorance

The taxpayer's limited education and business experience, together with his reliance on the advice of an attorney, caused his failure to file to be due to reasonable cause. *C.R. Dexter,* 306 F. Supp 415.

Litigation

The taxpayer's late filing was due to reasonable cause when litigation was necessary to determine the taxability of income received. *F.P. Walker* (CA-9), 326 F. 2nd 261 (nonacq).

Timely mailed and presumed received

Even though a taxpayer didn't have a certified or registered mailing receipt, the Tax Court held that the IRS is presumed to have received a timely mailed return when a postal official testified that she had accepted and postmarked the envelope prior to the due date of the return. The Court found it a mere coincidence that the taxpayer's state return hadn't been received by the state tax authority either. *Estate of Wood,* 92 TC 793. One could safely infer that the court would have been equally convinced if an employee or other individual had given the same testimony.

Return executed but misplaced

Tax returns were signed and given to an employee whose duty was to mail the returns. Instead, the employee by error then placed the returns in a file together with copies of the returns of many other corporations. When the IRS sent a notice a year later, the error was discovered and the returns were filed at that time. *Bouvelt Realty,* 46 BTA 45.

Return misplaced by the IRS

The Commissioner failed to refute the taxpayer's evidence that the tax returns were timely filed but misplaced by the IRS. *J.J. Carlin,* 43 TCM (CCH) 22.

Mailing of return on time

The IRS asserted that a return due on the 15th had not been received for filing until the 17th. The corporate officer who had mailed the return had died, and because of the Commissioner's failure to produce the envelope in which the return was mailed, it was held that no penalty should attach. *Capento Securities Corp.,* 47 BTA 691 (Nonacq) Aff'd CA-1.

Honest belief

The taxpayer's honest but mistaken belief that an extension of time to file allowed him to delay the filing of his tax return until he had sufficient funds to pay his tax constituted reasonable cause for the late filing of his tax return. *M.S. Alba,* DC, East.Dist.MO.No.80-764.

In another case, a taxpayer — while separated from her husband — attached her W-2 to a joint return that she gave back to her husband to file. The honest belief that the return was filed didn't constitute willful neglect. *E. Barker,* 22 TCM 634.

Illness

The taxpayer's illness and hospitalization constituted reasonable cause for failure to file a tax return. *C. Freeman,* 40 TCM 1219, Dec. 37,236 (M).

Reliance on accountant

Where a corporate taxpayer selects a competent tax expert, supplies him with all necessary information, and requests him to prepare proper tax returns, the taxpayer has done all that ordinary business care and prudence can reasonably demand. *Haywood Lumber & Mining Co. vs. Comm.,* (CA-2) 178 F.2nd 769.REV'D CA-2.

Excuses that won't fly

The dog-ate-my-taxwork excuse won't work, nor will these:

Delegation of authority

In a landmark case, the Supreme Court held that the reliance on an attorney as to the filing date of a return didn't constitute reasonable cause. *R.W. Boyle, SCT. 105 S. Ct. 687.* A qualified tax advisor's incorrect advice as to whether a tax return should be filed constitutes reasonable cause, but his or her mistaken advice as to the correct date a return must be filed does not.

But subsequent to *U.S. vs. Boyle,* a disabled taxpayer's reliance on an attorney to timely file a return was considered reasonable cause. *C. Brown vs. U.S.,* 57 AFTR 2d (M.D. Tenn. 1985).

Incarceration

The Tax Court rejected a taxpayer's claim that incarceration constituted reasonable cause. *R. Llorente,* 74 TC 260.

IRS rulings and announcements

Taxpayers are amazed when they discover that most of the rules they must follow are created by the IRS — not by Congress. That's because most tax laws include the following language: "in accordance with rules and regulations to be promulgated by the Secretary of the Treasury" — meaning that the Treasury Department makes and enforces the rules. Therefore, you must pay special attention to IRS rulings and announcements — there's a whole lot of promulgating going on.

Partnership returns — Rev. Proc. 84-35

If a partnership is composed of ten or fewer partners and each of the partners reports his or her share of the partnership's income and deductions, the partnership won't be charged a penalty for not filing its return.

Erroneous advice given by IRS employees over the telephone

According to IRS Information Release IR-88-75, incorrect advice given over the telephone by an IRS employee may constitute reasonable cause. The only problem with this is how you prove that you called the IRS and received erroneous advice. The IRS will consider that a taxpayer received incorrect advice over the telephone if a taxpayer provides the following information:

- Whether the taxpayer tried to find the answer to the question in IRS forms, instructions, or publications
- The questions asked and the specific facts given to the IRS employee
- The answer the taxpayer received
- The IRS employee's name
- The date and time of the call

If you're reading this provision for the first time, it's probably too late. But please use it the next time you call the IRS for advice.

IRS criteria in determining reasonable cause

This IRS ruling spells out the criteria for reasonable cause. Here they are:

- Do the taxpayer's reasons address the penalty that was assessed?
- Does the length of time between the event that caused the late filing and the actual filing negate the fact that the taxpayer attempted to correct the situation in a timely fashion?
- Does the continued operation of a business after the event that caused the taxpayer's noncompliance negate the taxpayer's excuse?
- Should the event that caused the taxpayer's noncompliance or increased liability have been reasonably anticipated?
- Was the penalty the result of carelessness, or does the taxpayer appear to have made an honest mistake?
- Has the taxpayer provided sufficient detail (dates, relationships) to determine whether he or she exercised ordinary business care and prudence? Is a nonliable individual being blamed for the taxpayer's noncompliance? What is the nature of the relationship between the taxpayer and this individual? Is the individual an employee of the taxpayer or an independent third party, such as an accountant or a lawyer?

✔ Has the taxpayer documented all pertinent facts?

✔ Does the taxpayer have a history of being assessed the same penalty?

✔ Does the amount of the penalty justify closer scrutiny of the case?

✔ Could the taxpayer have requested an extension or filed an amended return?

Critical to getting the IRS to accept your reasons for late filing or paying is the time frame between the event that was clearly beyond your control and the date of your ultimate compliance with your obligation to file or pay. What the IRS considers to be an acceptable amount of time between these two events is based on the facts and circumstances in each case. Figure 19-1 shows a reasonable cause sample letter.

Sample Reasonable Cause Letter

Request to abate penalty
[your name and address]
[today's date]

Adjustments/Correspondence Branch
Internal Revenue Service Center
[address]

Re: [your name]
[Social Security number]
[tax year]

Dear IRS:

I am in receipt of your notice of [date] in which you asserted a late filing and payment penalty in the amount of [penalty $] plus interest on this amount of [interest $].

Please be advised that my late filing and payment were due to reasonable cause and, according to tax law, should be abated.

On [date], I was ill with [illness]. I was hospitalized and didn't recover sufficiently until [date]. When I was well enough to assemble the data necessary to file a return and pay what was owed, I immediately did so. Enclosed is a letter from my physician confirming the nature of my illness and the length of my recovery, as well as the hospital bill.

Regulation 301.6651-1(c) provides that:

"If a taxpayer exercised ordinary business care and prudence and was nevertheless either unable to file the return or pay within the prescribed time, the delay is due to reasonable cause."

Thank you in advance for your prompt attention to this request. If you require further clarification of any point, I can be reached at [number].

Very truly yours,

[your name]

Enclosed: Form CP-22A (Statement of Change to Your Account)
Letter from physician and hospital

Figure 19-1:
A sample reasonable cause letter.

Penalty appeals

If the Adjustments/Correspondence Branch (see Chapter 18) rejects your request to have a penalty abated, you may appeal. Every service center has a penalty appeals unit. The A/C Branch notice informing taxpayers that their request was rejected will also inform them of their appeal rights and how to exercise them.

Payment of the penalty is not a prerequisite to requesting an appeal. There is no official IRS form for requesting this type of appeal. Although some appeals within the IRS need not be in writing, this one must. Your original letter requesting an abatement can be used with one simple modification: Your opening sentence should state that you are requesting an appeal from a tax examiner's determination (which you are enclosing) that you failed to establish reasonable cause.

Some IRS offices require that the tax and interest be paid before they will consider a penalty abatement. Although no specific law requires this, the IRS is famous for making up its own rules.

You may want to include any additional reasons that constitute reasonable cause, or any documentary evidence, such as your passport showing that you were out of the country, medical records stating that you were ill, a statement from a third party who saw you mail the return on time, or a police or insurance report showing that the loss of your records was due to a theft or other casualty. These documents, if available, should have been sent with the original abatement request. Hold nothing back!

At times, for inexplicable reasons, tax examiners take the position that a taxpayer should have quickly estimated his income and filed a return based on this estimate. In such instances, you should point out that the event that you considered reasonable cause prevented you from preparing an estimate.

It is IRS policy that no collection action will be taken while a penalty appeal is pending — unless the case has already been assigned to a collection officer who has determined that the appeal was requested solely to postpone or delay payment. If you're being bugged for the penalty, contact the office of your local Taxpayer Advocate in order to get the IRS Collection Division off your back. A Taxpayer Advocate has authority to do this.

Be patient when requesting an abatement of a large penalty or when appealing a penalty abatement decision. The process is not speedy.

Abating Interest

Whereas the IRS has the power to abate a penalty for reasonable cause, it doesn't have — as a general rule — the authority to abate interest. But like every IRS rule, there are some limited exceptions when interest *can* be abated.

When interest is incorrectly charged

If interest was assessed after the expiration of the statute of limitations or was assessed illegally, then it's probably correct to assume that the underlying tax was also incorrectly assessed. If this is the case, then the interest, as well as the tax, can be abated.

Interest and tax that were incorrectly or illegally assessed may be abated in one of two ways. You can use **Form 911, Taxpayer Application for Assistance Order,** or you can write to the Adjustments/Correspondence Branch at the service center (or district office) that issued the notice. Figure 19-2 shows a sample letter with two possible reasons.

You can collect damages when the IRS willfully or negligently collects tax that isn't owed.

Sample Letter

[your name and address]
[today's date]

Internal Revenue Service Center
[address]

Re: [your name]
[Social Security number]
[tax year]

Dear IRS:

I respectfully request that you abate the tax assessment in the amount of [amount] that your agency made by error pursuant to the enclosed notice.

Reason (1): Section 6404(e) specifically allows for the abatement of tax that was assessed as the result of an IRS mathematical or clerical error.

Reason (2): Your assessment was made after the three-year statute of limitations had expired. Such assessments are prohibited by law.

I may be reached by telephone during the day at [number] should you require any further information.

Very truly yours,

[your name]

Enclosed: Copy of notice

Figure 19-2:
A sample letter to abate interest.

Erroneous refunds

The IRS is required to abate interest on a demand for repayment of a refund issued in error. In order for this rule to apply, the refund must be less than $50,000, and the taxpayer must be in no way responsible for causing the refund. On an erroneous refund, the IRS can charge interest only from the point in time when it demanded repayment and not for the period prior to the taxpayer being asked to repay it.

For example, suppose that you should have received a $100 refund, but instead, you received a $1,000 refund. No interest may be charged on the $900 for the period of time you held the money. If interest is assessed on the $900, the filing of **Form 843, Claim for Refund and Request for Abatement,** will get back the interest that you paid.

IRS delays

The Tax Reform Act of 1986 gives the IRS the authority to abate interest on any tax deficiency when an IRS official fails to perform a *ministerial act* and instead moves at a snail's pace in handling routine matters. (In this case, a ministerial act has nothing to do with performing the prescribed rituals of your favorite religious institution; the IRS official must appropriately and in a timely manner perform the prescribed rituals of your "favorite" government agency.) The IRS has the right to abate interest, but it is not compelled to do so. When the failure to perform a ministerial act has occurred, interest is required to be abated from the time when the IRS first contacted you, not from the due date of your tax return, which normally is the case.

Here's how the IRS has decided whether interest can be abated:

✔ You moved from one state to another. Your return was selected for audit. You request the audit to be transferred to your new location, and the transfer is approved. But the IRS delays in transferring your case. Interest *can* be abated.

✔ An audit reveals that additional tax is due. You and the IRS have agreed on the amount of additional tax due, but the IRS delays in sending you a bill. Interest *can* be abated.

✔ You deducted a loss from a tax shelter that is being audited. It takes a long time to complete the audit of the shelter. Interest *can't* be abated.

✔ The agent auditing your return is assigned to a training course, and, during the training course, no work is done nor is the audit reassigned to a different agent. Interest *can't* be abated. Sounds crazy, doesn't it?

Congress thought it was crazy, too. Starting with 1997 returns filed in 1998, interest can be abated because of the types of IRS staffing problems indicated in the previous two bullet points.

Form 843, Claim for Refund and Request for Abatement, is used to abate interest where the IRS has caused a delay. Check box 4a (Interest Caused by IRS Errors and Delays). Be forewarned, though: Getting interest abated on an IRS delay is a tough nut to crack.

Starting with 1997 tax returns, the IRS has the authority but, again, is not compelled to abate interest when managerial acts cause delay. Delays by the IRS caused by loss of records, transfer of personnel, extended illness, leave, or training are now a cause for abating interest. Unfortunately, this rule doesn't apply to 1996 returns filed in 1997 or to earlier returns.

When the IRS doesn't send a bill

When you sign off on the results of a tax examination or notice of proposed adjustments to your return, the IRS must send you a bill for payment within 30 days. If it doesn't, the agency can't charge interest until a bill is sent. Use Form 843 to abate any interest charges after the 30-day period.

When the IRS sends a bill

If the amount owed is under $100,000, you have 21 interest-free days to pay it. If the amount you owe is over $100,000, you have 10 *business* days before you're charged interest.

The 18-Month Rule

Starting with 1998 returns, the IRS must send a notice of additional tax due within 18 months of filing your return. If it doesn't, it has to stop charging interest after 18 months and until 21 days after it sends a notice.

Not all IRS notices are covered by this provision. For example, audit notices aren't. See Chapter 16 for the ins and outs of how this provision works.

The Taxpayer Bill of Rights

This great republic was founded on the principle that taxation without representation is tyranny. But if you've ever had a run-in with the IRS, you know that taxation *with* representation isn't so hot either. To feed its insatiable appetite for spending, Congress has given the IRS almost unlimited authority to collect taxes — an authority that, sadly, can be abused in all sorts of horrible ways.

A few years ago, lawmakers decided to do something about the monster they had created. Responding to a flurry of taxpayer horror stories, in 1988 Congress enacted the so-called Taxpayer Bill of Rights. The idea: to lay out in writing what the IRS can get away with when collecting your money, and what you can do to fight back.

Now, whenever you get a notice of any kind from the IRS, you get a four-page summary of the Taxpayer Bill, entitled "Your Rights as a Taxpayer." This remarkably readable document explains how to appeal an IRS decision, suggests where you can get "free information," and assures you that you are entitled to "courtesy and consideration" from IRS employees. Reading it, you could almost get the impression that the IRS is a friendly place that only wants what's best for you. That assumption, of course, would be a terrible mistake.

It's not that the original Taxpayer Bill of Rights is worthless. On the contrary, it contains two very significant points:

✔ At any time during an audit or interview, you may ask to speak with an enrolled agent, attorney, or CPA. The IRS must stop what it's doing and let you do so.

✔ The IRS may not take money or property from you on the same day that you comply with a summons. In other words, the IRS can't demand that you appear and then seize your car when you get to its office — something that used to happen a lot.

Despite those important rights, the original Taxpayer Bill of Rights left much to be desired — in too many cases, it allowed the IRS *itself* to interpret your rights. It's like having the same person as prosecutor, judge, and jury.

The Taxpayer Bill of Rights — Parts 2 and 3

Our complaint with the original Taxpayer Bill of Rights was that it didn't have teeth. Now it does. But not a full set. And, unlike in the Rocky movies, the Taxpayer Bill of Rights 2 that became law on July 30, 1996, and Part 3, which came about when the IRS was overhauled in 1998, don't see to it that the underdog always wins. Here's what the new-and-improved Taxpayer Bill of Rights does for you:

✔ Abates the penalty for failing to deposit payroll taxes for first-time filers of employment tax returns.

✔ Allows you to file a joint return after a separate return has been filed without having to pay the full joint tax. This starts with 1997 returns (not 1996 returns filed in 1997).

✔ Allows the return of levied property, including your salary, if you have an installment agreement to pay what you owe and it would be a hardship (you can't pay your bills) not to return it. Under the old rules, once the IRS "glommed" your dough, it couldn't return it.

✔ Requires that 1099s have the name, address, and telephone number of whom to contact in case the reported amount is incorrect and needs investigating.

✔ Shifts the burden to the IRS to prove its position was substantially justified when you prevail in a suit with the IRS. If the IRS position was not substantially justified, you can collect for legal fees and court costs from the IRS. Under the old rule, *you* had to prove that the IRS's position was *not* substantially justified.

✔ Requires that the IRS, upon a taxpayer's request, make every reasonable effort to contact private creditors when a Notice of a Tax Lien has been withdrawn.

The bill also includes the following helpful provisions:

✔ If a few people, namely the owners or officers of a business, are personally responsible for payment of taxes that were withheld from their employees' salaries and one of these individuals pays more than his share, that person can sue to recover that amount from the others. The IRS is now obliged to tell what each person paid and what the IRS is doing to collect what is owed from the others.

✔ The IRS must notify taxpayers if it receives a payment that can't be applied against what is owed instead of merely depositing the check and holding it in limbo.

✔ If you owe the IRS, the IRS must send you at least an annual bill so you know where you stand. The statement must include a detailed computation of the interest charged.

✔ For taxes that are jointly owed by you and your ex-spouse, you can ask the IRS what it is doing to get your ex-spouse to pay the tax, and you have the right to be told how much has been paid. Because of possible hostility towards an ex-spouse, the IRS won't reveal the spouse's home or business address.

✔ The *innocent spouse rules* have been made more lenient in a number of ways. Relief can also be obtained on an apportioned basis. See Chapter 4.

✔ If the IRS doesn't send a notice adjusting a taxpayer's return within 18 months, it must stop charging interest after 18 months and until 21 days after a notice is sent. See Chapter 16, because not all IRS notices are covered under this rule.

✔ You can collect up to $1 million in damages if the IRS acts with reckless or intentional disregard of the rules in collecting tax. If the IRS is merely negligent, the limit is $100,000. Starting with 1997 tax returns (not 1996 returns filed in 1997), the IRS has the authority but, again, is not compelled, to abate interest because of delays on the part of the IRS. Delays caused by loss of records, transfer of personnel, extended illness, leave, or training are now a cause for abating interest.

✔ If someone issues you a fraudulent 1099, you can sue for damages (up to $5,000).

✔ Proof under the timely-mailing-is-filing rule requires that a document or return had to be sent by either certified or registered mail. Using FedEx, DHL, Airborne, or UPS is now the equivalent to sending a return or document by certified or registered mail.

A mailing receipt that you receive from the post office other than for certified or registered mail isn't considered valid proof of meeting the timely-mailing-is-timely-filing rule.

✔ Financial status audits to scrutinize a taxpayer's lifestyle are only allowed when a routine examination has established a likelihood of unreported income. See Chapter 17.

✔ Taxpayers have a 30-day period to appeal a lien or levy. See Chapter 16.

✔ The rejection of an Offer in Compromise or a request for an installment agreement can be appealed.

✔ While an Offer in Compromise or a request for an installment agreement is pending or on appeal, the IRS can't levy against a taxpayer.

Part V
Year-Round Tax Planning

The 5th Wave   By Rich Tennant

"Death and taxes _are_ for certain, Mr. Dooley; however, they're not mutually exclusive."

In this part . . .

Taxes are not a financial island unto themselves. Just about every major financial decision you make involves a tax angle and has tax consequences. With just a little bit of knowledge and advance planning, you can make your money work much harder for you. In fact, the worse you are at managing your finances, the more money you can put back into your pocket, if you learn how to make tax-wise financial decisions. This part helps you make the most of your money year-round. Just don't forget that it's here!

"The avoidance of taxes is the only intellectual pursuit that still carries any reward."

— John Maynard Keynes

Chapter 20

Tax-Wise Personal Finance Decisions

Taxes build and fix roads and bridges, allow local libraries to stay open year 'round — and pay for the pensions of members of Congress who have been forced to resign. These are some of the many "benefits" that we derive from our tax dollars!

But what do you really get out of taxes?

Most people get headaches from completing their annual tax returns and feel terribly disorganized because they have better things to do during the year than keep all those receipts and records they may need come April. And if that isn't enough, most of us become a bit perturbed when we see how little money is left over for *us* after Uncle Sam and state and local governments take their share.

Fitting Taxes into Your Financial Puzzle

You probably work hard for your money. Between actual hours in the office and commuting, you may well spend 50 hours per week on job-related activities. That's about 2,500 hours per year. Think about that number — 2,500 hours per year, *year after year after year,* spanning several decades.

That's a lot of time spent working to earn money.

Now, how much time do you spend learning and figuring out how to make the most of this money? Yeah, we thought so — are you blushing?

Directing your personal finances involves much more than simply investing money. It includes making all the pieces of your financial life fit together. And, just like designing a vacation itinerary, managing your personal finances means developing a strategy to make the best use of your limited dollars.

Taxes are a large and vital piece of your financial puzzle. The following list shows some of the ways that tax issues are involved in making sound financial decisions throughout the year:

✔ **Spending:** The more you spend, the less you'll be able to take advantage of the many benefits in our tax code that require you to have money to invest in the first place. For example, you need money to purchase real estate, which offers many tax benefits (see Chapter 24). And because taxes are a hefty portion of your expenditures (probably one of your top items), a budget that overlooks tax reduction strategies is doomed to failure. Unless you have wealthy, benevolent relatives, you're resigned to a lifetime of working if you can't save money.

✔ **Retirement accounts:** In no other aspect of your financial situation do taxes play a greater role than contributing to retirement accounts. Taking advantage of these outstanding tax-reduction opportunities could mean tens, perhaps even hundreds, of thousands more dollars in your pocket come retirement time. Who says there are no free lunches? See Chapter 21 for more information on retirement accounts.

✔ **Investing:** Many tax angles enable you to invest wisely. In addition to investing in stocks, bonds, and mutual funds, you may also invest in real estate and your own business. It isn't enough to choose investments that generate healthy rates of return. What matters is not *what you make* but *what you keep* — after paying taxes. Understand and capitalize on the many tax breaks available to investors. Chapter 23 covers investing and taxes.

✔ **Protecting your assets:** Some of your insurance decisions also affect the taxes you pay. You'd think that after a lifetime of tax payments, your heirs would be left alone when you pass on to the great beyond — wishful thinking. Estate planning may enable less in taxes to be siphoned off from your estate. See Chapter 26 to find out more about estate planning.

Taxes infiltrate many areas of your personal finances. Often, people make important financial decisions without considering taxes (as well as other important variables). Although this chapter shows you that taxes are an important component to factor into your major financial decisions, *taxes should not drive or dictate the decisions you make.*

Sometimes, in an obsession to minimize or avoid taxes, people make decisions that are counterproductive to achieving their long-term personal and financial goals. Consider the case of Dave, a former IBM manager.

Dave was with IBM from the early days and retired in the mid-1980s. He had accumulated a great deal of IBM stock outside tax-sheltered retirement accounts — stock that Dave was reluctant to sell because he would have to pay capital gains tax. So he held onto it. IBM was the Rock of Gibraltar and would keep on growing. Anyway, if IBM got into trouble, the whole country would be in the hopper, or so Dave thought.

Unfortunately for Dave, IBM's fortunes did change for the worse, and its stock plummeted precipitously — down by more than 70 percent after Dave's retirement (meanwhile, the overall stock market was surging to ever greater heights). Dave had a large chunk of his total assets — about half — tied up in IBM stock, so its plunge took Dave's dreams of a financially comfortable retirement with it.

Dave had planned to sell his stock someday, so he was going to have to pay the tax eventually. Although — generally speaking — it's better to postpone paying taxes, in Dave's case, it was a mistake to postpone selling the IBM stock, because he had half his money invested in it. It would have been prudent for Dave to sell off at least some of the stock so he could better diversify his portfolio.

It's important to note that we aren't saying with the benefit of 20/20 hindsight that Dave should have dumped a stock that declined in value. The point is that he had such a large chunk of his money in one stock — and that's a risky proposition for a retiree, no matter how solid the company may appear.

Taxing Mistakes

Even if some parts of the tax system are hopelessly and unreasonably complicated, there's no reason why you can't learn from the mistakes of others to save yourself money. With this goal in mind, we list the most typical tax blunders that people make when it comes to managing their money.

Not saving and investing through retirement accounts

All the tax deductions and tax deferrals that come with accounts such as 401(k)s and IRAs were put in the tax code to encourage people to save for retirement. So why not take advantage of the benefits? You probably have your reasons or excuses, but most excuses for missing out on this strategy just don't make good financial sense. Most people underfund retirement accounts because they simply spend too much and because retirement seems so far away. Many people also mistakenly believe that retirement account money is totally inaccessible until they're old enough to qualify for senior's discounts. See Chapter 21 to find out all about retirement accounts.

Ignoring tax considerations when investing money

Suppose that you have some stock you want to unload so that you can buy a new car. You figure out which of your stocks or stock mutual funds is currently riding high but also seems to have the poorest future prospects. You sell this stock at a significant profit and feel good about your financial genius. But, come tax time, you may feel differently.

Don't forget to factor the taxes due from the sale of investments (except those in retirement accounts) into all your decisions about what you sell and when you sell it. Your tax situation should also factor into what you invest outside retirement accounts. If you're in a relatively high tax bracket, you probably don't want investments that pay much in taxable distributions such as interest and dividends, which only add to your tax burden (unless you're holding a tax-free type of investment). See Chapter 23 for more details on the tax considerations of investing.

Not buying a home

In the long run, owning a home should cost you less than renting. And because mortgage interest and property taxes are deductible, the government, in effect, subsidizes the cost of home ownership. And, even if the government didn't help you with tax benefits when buying and owning a home, you'd still be better off owning over your adult life. Why? Because as a renter, all of your housing expenses are exposed to inflation, unless you have a great rent-controlled deal. So treat yourself to your own abode. And don't let the lack of money for a down payment stand in your way — many ways exist to buy real estate with very little money up front. See Chapter 24 to find out about real estate and taxes.

Ignoring the financial aid tax system

The college financial aid system in this country assumes that the money you save outside tax-sheltered retirement accounts is available to pay educational expenses. As a result, middle- and upper-income families who save money *outside* instead of *inside* retirement accounts qualify for far less financial aid than they otherwise would. So in addition to normal income taxes, an extra financial-aid "tax" is effectively exacted. Be sure to read Chapter 25, which talks about the right and wrong ways to save and invest for educational costs.

Seeking and getting advice after a major decision

Too many people seek out information and hire help *after* making a decision, although we all know that it's generally wiser and less costly to seek preventive help ahead of time. Before making any major financial decisions, educate yourself. The book you're holding in your hands can help answer most of your questions.

If you're going to hire a tax advisor to give advice, do so *before* you make your decision(s). (Read Chapter 2 for tips on finding a good tax advisor.) The wrong move when selling a piece of real estate or when taking a large sum from a retirement account can cost you thousands of dollars in taxes!

Not withholding the right amount of taxes

If you're self-employed or earn significant taxable income from investments outside retirement accounts, you should be making quarterly tax payments. Likewise, if during the year, you sell a major asset at a profit, you may need to make a quarterly tax payment. Some self-employed people dig themselves into a perpetual tax hole. They get behind in their tax payments during their first year of self-employment and are always playing catch-up. They don't have a human resources department to withhold taxes from their pay, and they fail to submit estimated quarterly tax payments. Don't be a "should've" victim. People often don't discover that they "should've" paid more taxes during the year until after they complete their return in the spring — or get a penalty notice from the IRS and their state. Then they have to come up with a sizable sum all at one time.

To make quarterly tax payments, call 800-TAX-FORM and order a copy of IRS **Form 1040-ES, Estimated Tax for Individuals.** (We include one in the back of this book.) This form explains how to calculate quarterly tax payments — the IRS even sends you payment coupons and envelopes in which to send your checks. We walk you through the essentials of completing this form in Chapter 15.

Although we — and the IRS — want you to keep up with your taxes during the year, *we* don't want you to overpay. Some people have too much tax withheld during the year, and this overpayment can go on year after year. Although it may feel good to get a sizable refund check every spring, why should you loan your money to the government interest-free? If you work for an employer, complete a new W-4 form to adjust your withholding. We've been kind enough to include one in the back of the book. Complete the W-4 and turn it in to your employer. If you're self-employed, complete **Form 1040-ES, Estimated Tax for Individuals.** (See Chapter 15 for instructions on completing your W-4.)

If you know that you would otherwise spend the extra tax money that you're currently sending to the IRS, then this forced-savings strategy may have some value. But you can find other, better ways to make yourself save. You can set up all sorts of investments, such as mutual funds (see Chapter 23), to be funded by automatic contributions from your paycheck (or from a bank or investment account). Of course, if you *prefer* to loan the IRS more money — interest-free — go right ahead.

Not taking legal deductions

In most cases, folks miss out on perfectly legal deductions because they just don't know about them. Ignorance is not bliss when it comes to your income taxes . . . it's costly. If you aren't going to take the time to discover the legal deductions available to you (you bought this book, so why not read the relevant parts of it?), then spring for the cost of a competent tax advisor at least once. You can also try one of the user-friendly software packages we recommend in Chapter 2.

Fearing an audit, some taxpayers (and even some tax preparers) avoid taking deductions that they have every right to take. Unless you have something to hide, this oversight is expensive and silly. Remember that a certain number of returns are randomly audited every year, so even when you don't take every deduction to which you're legally entitled, you may get audited anyway! And how bad is an audit, really? If you read Chapter 17, you can find out how to deal with your audit like a pro. An afternoon with the IRS is not as bad as you think. It may be worth the risk of claiming all the tax breaks you're entitled to if you consider the amount you can possibly save over the years.

Ignoring the timing of events you can control

The amount of tax you pay on certain transactions can vary, depending on the timing of the transactions. If you're nearing retirement, for example, you may soon be in a lower tax bracket. To the extent possible, you should delay and avoid claiming investment income until your overall income drops, and you should take as many deductions or losses as you can *now* while your income is still high. Following are two tax-reducing strategies that you may be able to put to good use when you can control the timing of either your income or deductions: income shifting and bunching or shifting deductions.

Income shifting

Suppose that your employer tells you in late December that you're eligible for a bonus. You learn that you have the option of receiving your bonus in either December or January. Looking ahead, if you're pretty certain that you will be in a higher tax bracket next year, you should choose to receive your bonus in December. (Refer to Chapter 1 to find out about your tax bracket.)

Or suppose that you run your own business and operate on a cash accounting basis and think that you'll be in a lower tax bracket next year. Perhaps you plan to take time off to be with a newborn or take an extended trip. You can send out some invoices later in the year so that your customers won't pay you until January, which falls in the next tax year.

Shifting or bunching deductions

When you total your itemized deductions on Schedule A (see Chapter 9), if the total is lower than the standard deduction, then you should take the standard deduction. This itemized deduction total is worth checking each year, because you may have more deductions in some years than others, and you may occasionally be able to itemize.

Because you can control when you pay particular expenses that are eligible for itemizing, you can *shift* or *bunch* more of them into the select years when you have enough deductions to take advantage of itemizing. Suppose that, because you don't have many itemized deductions this year, you use the standard deduction. Late in the year, however, you feel certain that you'll itemize next year because of large medical expenses that you expect to incur. It makes sense, then, to shift and bunch as many deductible expenses as possible into next year. For example, if you're getting ready to make a tax-deductible donation of old clothes and household goods to charity, wait until January to do so.

In any tax year that you're sure that you won't have enough deductions to be able to itemize, shift as many itemizable expenses as you can into the next tax year. If you don't know what types of expenses you can itemize, be sure to peruse Chapter 9.

Be careful if you use your credit card to pay expenses. These expenses must be recognized for tax purposes in the year in which the charge was made on the card, not when you actually pay the credit card company.

Not using tax advisors effectively

If your financial situation is complicated, it's usually a mistake to go it alone and rely only on the IRS booklets to figure your taxes. The IRS instructions certainly aren't going to highlight opportunities for tax reductions, and these instructions are often hopelessly complicated. Start by reading the relevant sections of this book.

You also have the option of hiring a competent tax advisor. You can figure out taxes for yourself, or you can pay someone to figure them out for you. Doing nothing is not an advisable option!

If you're overwhelmed with the complexity of financial decisions, get advice from tax and financial advisors who sell their time and nothing else. Protect yourself by checking references, clarifying the total expected fees up front, and confirming exactly what advice, analysis, and recommendations the advisor will provide for the fees charged. If your tax situation is complicated, you'll probably more than recoup a preparer's fee, as long as you take the time to hire a good one (see Chapter 2 for tips on hiring help).

Remember that it's most beneficial to use a tax advisor when you're faced with new tax questions or problems. If your tax situation remains complicated, or if you know that you would do a worse job on your own, by all means keep using a tax preparer. But don't pay a big fee year after year to a tax advisor who simply fills in the blanks. If your situation is unchanging or is not that complicated, consider hiring and paying someone to figure out your taxes one time. After that, go ahead and try completing your own tax return.

Why People Make Poor Tax Decisions

When bad things happen, it's usually for a variety of reasons. And so it is with making financial blunders that cause you to pay more tax dollars. The following sections describe some common culprits that may be keeping you from making tax-wise financial maneuvers.

"Financial planners" and brokers' advice

Wanting to hire a professional to help you make better financial decisions is a logical and sensible inclination, especially if you're a time-squeezed person. But if you pick a poor planner or someone who isn't a financial planner but a salesperson in disguise, watch out!

Unfortunately, more than 90 percent of the people who call themselves financial planners, financial consultants, or financial advisors actually work on commission, which creates enormous conflicts of interest for impartial, unbiased, and objective financial advice.

Brokers and commission-based financial planners (who are also therefore *brokers*) structure their advice around selling you investment and other financial products that provide *them* with a commission. As a result, they tend to take a narrow view of your finances and frequently ignore the tax and other consequences of financial moves. Or they may use the *supposed* tax benefits of an investment they're eager to sell you as a reason for you to buy it. It may be a tax benefit for someone, but not necessarily for you in your specific situation.

The few planners who work on a *fee basis* primarily provide money-management services and charge 1 to 2 percent per year of the money they manage. Fee-based planners have their own conflicts of interest as well, because all things being equal, they want you to hire them to manage *your money*. Therefore, they can't objectively help you decide if you should pay off your mortgage and other debts, invest in real estate or a small business, or invest more in your employer's retirement plan. In short, they have a bias against financial strategies that take investable money out of their hands.

Be especially leery of planners, brokers, and money-managing planners who lobby you to sell investments that you've held for a while and that show a profit. If you sell these investments, you may have to pay a hefty tax burden. (See Chapter 23 for more insight on how to make these important investing decisions.)

Advertising

Another reason you may make tax missteps in managing your personal finances is advertising. Although many reputable financial firms with terrific products advertise, the firms that spend most heavily on advertising often are those with inferior or downright lousy offerings.

Responding to most ads is usually a bad financial move, whether the product being pitched is good, bad, or so-so, because the company placing the ad typically is trying to motivate you to buy a specific product. The company doesn't care about your financial alternatives, whether its product fits with your tax situation, and so on. Many ads try to catch your attention with the supposed tax savings that their products generate.

Advice from publications

You read an article that recommends some investments. Tired of not taking charge and making financial decisions, you get on the phone, call an investment company, and — before you know it — you've invested. You feel a sense of relief and accomplishment. You've done something.

Come tax time, you get all these confusing statements detailing dividends and capital gains that you must report on your tax return. *Now* you see that these investment strategies generate all sorts of taxable distributions that add to your tax burden. And you may be saddled with additional tax forms to complete by April 15. You wish you had known.

Articles in magazines, newspapers, Internet sites, and newsletters can help you stay informed, but they can also cause you to make ill-advised financial moves that overlook tax consequences. Writers have limited space and often don't think about the big picture or the ways their advice could be misunderstood or misused. Even worse is that too many writers don't know the tax consequences of what they write about. Find out about tax-wise investing in Chapter 23.

Overspending

Far too many tax guides go on and on and on, talking about this tax break and that tax break. The problem is that in order to take advantage of many of the best tax breaks, you need to have some money to invest. If you spend all that you earn, as most Americans do, you miss out on many terrific tax benefits that we tell you about in this book. And the more you spend, the more taxes you pay, both on your income and on the purchases you make (through sales taxes).

Just like losing weight, spending less *sounds* good, but most people have a hard time budgeting their finances and spending less than they earn. Perhaps you already know where the fat is in your spending. If you don't, it's a real eye-opener to figure out where all your monthly income is going. The task takes a little bit of detective work — looking through your credit card statement and your checkbook register to track your purchases and categorize your spending.

Financial illiteracy

Lack of education is at the root of almost all personal financial blunders. You may not understand the tax system and how to manage your finances because you were never taught how to manage them in high school or college.

Financial illiteracy is a widespread problem not just among the poor and undereducated. Most people don't plan ahead and educate themselves with their financial goals in mind. People react — or worse — do nothing at all. You may dream, for example, about retiring and never having to work again. Or perhaps you hope that someday you can own a house or even a vacation home in the country.

You need to understand how to plan your finances in order to accomplish your financial goals. You also need to understand how the tax system works and how to navigate within it to work toward your objectives.

If you need more help with important personal financial issues, pick up a copy of *Personal Finance For Dummies,* 2nd Edition, (IDG Books Worldwide, Inc.) written by one of us — Eric Tyson.

Chapter 21
Retirement (Tax-Reduction) Accounts

• •

In This Chapter

▶ Understanding the virtues of contributing to retirement accounts
▶ Comparing the different types of retirement accounts
▶ Addressing withdrawals and other taxing retirement account issues

• •

Saving and investing through retirement accounts is one of the simplest and best ways to reduce your tax burden. Unfortunately, most people can't take advantage of these plans because they spend too much of what they make. So not only do they have less savings, they also pay higher income taxes — a double whammy. And don't forget, the more you spend, the more sales tax you pay on purchases.

In order to take advantage of the tax savings that come with retirement savings plans, you must first spend *less* than you earn. Only then can you afford to contribute to these plans.

Retirement Account Benefits

For some baby boomers and Generation Xers, age 65 may seem like the distant future. For many people, it's not until middle age that some warning bells start to stimulate thoughts about what money they'll live on in the golden years.

The single biggest mistake people at all income levels make with retirement accounts is not taking advantage of them. In your 20s and 30s (and for some in their 40s and 50s), it seems a whole lot more fun to spend and live for today and postpone saving for the future. But assuming that you don't want to work your entire life, the sooner you start to save, the less painful it is each year, because your contributions have more years to compound. Each decade you delay contributing approximately doubles the percentage of your earnings you should save to meet your goals. For example, if saving 5 percent per year in your early 20s would get you to your retirement goal, waiting until your 30s may mean socking away 10 percent; waiting until your 40s, 20 percent . . . it gets ugly beyond that!

So the longer you wait, the more you'll have to save and, therefore, the less will be leftover to spend. As a result, you may not meet your goal, and your golden years may be more restrictive than you hoped.

We use this simple lesson to emphasize the importance of considering *now* the benefits you achieve by saving and investing in some type of retirement account.

Contributions are (generally) tax-deductible

Retirement accounts are misnamed. They sound unpalatable to most people, particularly the youngsters among us. Saving for retirement is like eating a dozen plain rice cakes for dinner: It may be healthier and help you to live longer, but you want to live *life* — not live for retirement.

Retirement accounts should really be called tax-reduction accounts. If they were, people might be more excited about contributing to them. For many people, avoiding higher taxes is the motivating force that gets them to open the account and start the contributions.

If you're a moderate income earner, you probably pay about 35 percent between federal and state income taxes on your last dollars of income (see Chapter 1 to identify your tax bracket). Thus, with most of the retirement accounts described in this chapter, for every $1,000 you contribute to them, you save yourself about $350 in taxes in the year that you make the contribution. Contribute five times as much, or $5,000, and whack $1,750 off your tax bill!

Tax-deferred compounding of investment earnings

After money is placed in a retirement account, any interest, dividends, and appreciation add to the amount of your account without being taxed. You get to defer taxes on all the accumulating gains and profits until you withdraw the money, presumably in retirement. Thus, more money is working for you over a longer period of time.

Your retirement tax rate need not be less than your employed rate for you to come out ahead by contributing money to retirement accounts. In fact, because you defer paying tax and you have more money compounding for you over more years, you can end up with more money in retirement by saving inside a retirement account even if your retirement tax rate is higher than it is now.

Some people fret that their taxes will increase when they retire. Although it could happen, the following simple example shows you why your time is better spent worrying about more important issues — like whether you have enough tortilla chips and salsa for your weekend visitors.

Consider the case of a 40-year-old woman earning $35,000 per year who pays 35 percent in federal and state taxes on her last dollars of income. She contributes 10 percent, or $3,500, this year to a retirement savings plan, thereby decreasing her current year's taxes by $1,225. Assume that the money she contributes earns an average annual rate of return of 8 percent until she withdraws the money at age 65. After paying taxes at the same rate on her withdrawal at age 65 as she pays today, she'll have about $15,580 left. If she hadn't saved this money through a retirement plan, she would have had only $8,080 at age 65.

Now suppose that her career takes off and she earns more money (and pays more taxes) as she gets closer to retirement. How high would her retirement tax rate have to be before she should regret having saved in the retirement account? She would have to pay about 67 percent in taxes on the retirement account withdrawals to be worse off. In other words, her tax rate would have to nearly double for her to be worse off by delaying paying taxes on her income contributed to the retirement account — an unlikely occurrence.

And remember this: You may get an added bonus from deferring taxes on your retirement account assets if you're in a lower tax bracket when you withdraw the money. You may very well be in a lower tax bracket in retirement because most people have less income when they're not working.

Note: If you're near retirement and already have money in a tax-sheltered type of retirement account (for example, at your employer), by all means continue to keep it in a tax-sheltered account if you leave. You can accomplish this goal, for example, by rolling the money over into an IRA account. If your employer offers good investment options in a retirement plan and allows you to leave your money in the plan after your departure, consider that option, too.

You can save less money and spend more

That's right! Because of all the terrific tax benefits you get by saving and investing in retirement accounts, you end up with more money now than if you had saved the money elsewhere.

Retirement account penalties for early withdrawal

One objection that some people have to contributing to retirement accounts is the early withdrawal penalties. Specifically, if you withdraw funds from retirement accounts before age 59$\frac{1}{2}$, you not only have to pay income taxes on the withdrawals, but you also may pay early withdrawal penalties — typically 10 percent in federal and state charges. (There's a 25-percent penalty for withdrawing from a SIMPLE plan within the first two years, which will decrease to 10 percent thereafter.)

The penalties are there for good reason: to discourage people from raiding retirement accounts. The system is built to save people from their bad habits. Remember, retirement accounts exist for just that reason — saving toward retirement. If you could easily raid them without penalties, the money would be less likely to be there when you need it during your golden years.

If you have an emergency, such as catastrophic medical expenses or a disability, you may be able to take early withdrawals from retirement accounts without penalty. And thanks to the 1997 tax law changes, under certain conditions (which are spelled out later in this chapter), you may withdraw funds from particular retirement accounts free of penalties (and in some cases even current income taxes) for educational expenses or a home purchase.

What if you just run out of money because you lose your job? Although you can't bypass the penalties, if you're earning so little income that you need to raid your retirement account, you'll surely be in a low tax bracket. So even though you pay some penalties to withdraw retirement account money, the lower income taxes that you pay on withdrawal — as compared to the taxes you would have incurred when you earned the money originally — should make up for most or all of the penalty.

Also know that if you get in a financial pinch while you're still employed, some company retirement plans allow you to borrow against a portion of your cash balance. Just be sure that you can repay such a loan — otherwise, your "loan" becomes a withdrawal and triggers income taxes and penalties.

Another strategy to meet a short-term financial emergency is to withdraw money from your IRA and return it within 60 days to avoid paying penalties. We don't generally recommend this maneuver because of the taxes and potential penalties invoked if you don't make the 60-day deadline.

If your only "borrowing" option right now is a high-interest credit card, you should save three to six months' worth of living expenses in an accessible account before funding a retirement account to tide you over in case you lose your income. Money market mutual funds are an ideal vehicle to use for this purpose.

You may be interested to know that if good fortune comes your way and you accumulate enough funds to retire "early," you have a simple way around the pre-age-59$\frac{1}{2}$ early withdrawal penalties. Suppose that at the young age of 50, you retire and want to start living off some of the pile of money you've stashed in retirement accounts. No problem. The IRS graciously allows you to start withdrawing money from your retirement accounts free of those early withdrawal penalties. To qualify for this favorable treatment, you must commit to make withdrawals for at least five continuous years, and the amount of the withdrawal must be at least the minimum required based on your life expectancy.

Types of Retirement Accounts

If you earn employment income (or receive alimony), you have the option to put money away in a retirement account that compounds without taxation until you withdraw the money. And in most cases, your contributions are tax-deductible. The following sections discuss the major types of "IRS-approved" retirement accounts and explain how to determine whether you are eligible for them.

Employer-sponsored plans

You should be thankful that your employer values your future enough to offer these benefits. Also be grateful that your employer has gone to the trouble of doing all the legwork of setting up the plan, including, in most cases, selecting investment options. If you were self-employed, you'd have to hassle with setting up your own plan and choosing a short list of investment options. All you have to do with an employer plan is save enough to invest, and allocate your contributions among the few investments offered.

401(k) plans

For-profit companies generally offer 401(k) plans. The silly name comes from the section of the tax code that establishes and regulates these plans. The 401(k) generally allows you to save up to $10,000 per year (for 1998). Your employer's plan may have lower contribution limits, though, if not enough employees save enough in the company's 401(k) plan. Your contributions to a 401(k) are generally excluded from your reported income and thus are free from federal and, in some cases, state income taxes, but not from Social Security and Medicare taxes (and from some other state employment taxes).

Some employers don't allow you to start contributing to their 401(k) plan until you've worked for them for a full year. Others allow you to start contributing right away. Some employers also match a portion of your contributions. They may, for example, match half of your first 6 percent of contributions (so in addition to saving a lot of taxes, you get a free bonus from the company). Check with your company's benefits department for your plan's details.

Smaller companies (those with fewer than 100 employees) can consider offering 401(k) plans, too. In the past, it was prohibitively expensive for smaller companies to administer 401(k)s. If your company is interested in this option, contact a mutual fund organization, such as T. Rowe Price, Vanguard, or Fidelity, or a discount brokerage house such as Charles Schwab or Jack White (see Chapter 23). In some cases, your employer may need to work with a separate plan administrator, in addition to one of these investment firms.

403(b) plans

Many nonprofit organizations offer 403(b) plans to their employees. As with a 401(k), your contributions to these plans are federal and state tax-deductible. The 403(b) plans often are referred to as tax-sheltered annuities, the name for insurance-company investments that satisfy the requirements for 403(b) plans. For the benefit of 403(b) retirement-plan participants, no-load (commission-free) mutual funds can also be used in 403(b) plans.

Nonprofit employees are generally allowed to contribute up to 20 percent or $10,000 of their salaries, whichever is less. Employees who have 15 or more years of service may be allowed to contribute beyond the $10,000 limit. Ask your employee benefits department or the investment provider for the 403(b) plan (or your tax advisor) about eligibility requirements and details about your personal contribution limit.

If you work for a nonprofit or public-sector organization that doesn't offer this benefit, make a fuss and insist on it. Nonprofit organizations have no excuse not to offer a 403(b) plan to their employees. Unlike a 401(k) plan, 403(b) plans have virtually no out-of-pocket set-up expenses or ongoing accounting fees. The only requirement is that the organization must deduct the appropriate contribution from employees' paychecks and send the money to the investment company handling the 403(b) plan. If your employer doesn't know where to look for good 403(b) investment options, send them to Vanguard (800-662-2003), Fidelity (800-343-0860), or T. Rowe Price (800-492-7670), all of which offer good mutual funds and 403(b) plans.

SIMPLE plans

Employers in small businesses have yet another retirement plan option, known as the SIMPLE-IRA. SIMPLE stands for Savings Incentive Match Plans for Employees. SIMPLE-IRAs have a contribution limit of $6,000 per year. Relative to 401(k) plans, SIMPLE plans are expected to make it easier for employers to reduce their costs thanks to easier reporting requirements and fewer administrative hassles.

Employers must make small contributions on behalf of employees, however. Employers can either match, dollar-for-dollar, the employee's first 3 percent contributed or contribute 2 percent of pay for everyone whose wages exceed $5,000. Interestingly, if the employer chooses the first option, the employer has an incentive not to educate employees about the value of contributing to the plan because the more employees contribute, the more it costs the employer. And, unlike a 401(k) plan, greater employee contributions don't enable higher-paid employees to contribute more.

Self-employed plans

If you work for yourself, you obviously don't have an employer to do the legwork to set up a retirement plan. You need to take the initiative. Although establishing a plan means work for you, you can select and design a plan that meets *your* needs. You can actually do a better job than many companies do; often, the people setting up a retirement plan don't do enough homework, or they let some salesperson sweet talk them into commission-laden investments.

Your trouble will be rewarded — self-employment retirement plans generally allow you to sock away more money on a tax-deductible basis than most employers' plans do.

If you have employees, you're required to make contributions comparable to the company owners' (as a percentage of salary) on their behalf under these plans. Some part-time employees (those working fewer than 500–1,000 hours per year) and newer employees (less than a few years of service) may be excluded. Not all small-business owners know about this requirement — or they choose to ignore it, and they set up plans for themselves but fail to cover their employees. The danger is that the IRS and state tax authorities may, in the event of an audit, hit you with big penalties and disqualify your prior contributions if you have neglected to make contributions for eligible employees. Because self-employed people and small businesses get their taxes audited at a relatively high rate, messing up in this area is dangerous. The IRS has a program to specifically audit small pension plans.

Don't avoid setting up a retirement savings plan for your business just because you have employees and you don't want to make contributions on their behalf. In the long run, you build the contributions you make for your employees into their total compensation package — which includes salary and other benefits like health insurance. Making retirement contributions need not increase your personnel costs.

To get the most from your contributions as an employer, consider the following:

- ✔ Educate your employees about the value of retirement savings plans. You want them to understand, but more importantly, you want them to appreciate your investment.

- ✔ Select a Keogh plan that requires employees to stay a certain number of years to vest in their contributions and allows for "Social Security integration" (see the discussion in the upcoming section on Keogh plans).

- ✔ If you have more than 20 or so employees, consider offering a 401(k) or SIMPLE plan, which allows employees to contribute money from their paychecks.

SEP-IRAs

Simplified Employee Pension Individual Retirement Account (SEP-IRA) plans require little paperwork to set up. They allow you to sock away about 13 percent (13.04 percent, to be exact) of your self-employment income (business revenue minus expenses) up to a maximum of $24,000 (for 1998) per year. Each year, you decide the amount you want to contribute — there are no minimums. Your contributions to a SEP-IRA are deducted from your taxable income, saving you big-time on federal and state taxes. As with other retirement plans, your money compounds without taxation until withdrawal.

Keoghs

Keogh plans require a bit more paperwork to set up and administer than SEP-IRAs. The appeal of certain types of Keoghs is that they allow you to put away a greater percentage (20 percent) of your self-employment income (revenue less your expenses), up to a maximum of $30,000 per year.

Another appeal of Keogh plans is that they allow business owners to maximize their contributions relative to employees in two ways that they can't with SEP-IRAs:

- ✔ Keogh plans allow *vesting schedules,* which require employees to remain with the company a specified number of years before they earn the right to their full retirement account balances. Vesting refers to the portion of the retirement account money that the employee owns. After a certain number of years, you become fully vested and, therefore, own 100 percent of the funds in the retirement account. If an employee leaves prior to being fully vested, he loses the unvested balance, which reverts to the remaining plan participants.

- ✔ Second, Keogh plans allow for *Social Security integration.* Integration effectively allows those in the company who are high-income earners (usually the owners) to receive larger percentage contributions for their accounts than the less highly-compensated employees. The logic behind this idea is that Social Security taxes top out after you earn more than $68,400 (for 1998). Social Security integration allows you to make up for this ceiling.

Just to make life complicated, Keoghs come in four main flavors:

- ✔ **Profit-sharing plans:** These plans have the same contribution limits as SEP-IRAs. So why would you want the headaches of a more complicated plan when you can't contribute more to it? Profit-sharing plans appeal to owners of small companies who want to use vesting schedules and Social Security integration, which cannot be done with SEP-IRA plans.

- ✔ **Money-purchase pension plans:** You can contribute more to these plans than you can to a profit-sharing plan or SEP-IRA. The maximum tax-deductible contribution here is the lesser of 20 percent of your self-employment income or $30,000 per year.

Although allowing for a larger contribution, no flexibility is allowed on the percentage contribution you make each year with a money purchase pension plan. Thus, these plans make the most sense for high-income earners who are comfortable enough financially to know that they can continue making large percentage contributions.

If the simplicity of the money-purchase pension plan appeals to you, don't be overly concerned about the consequences of some unforeseen circumstance that may make you unable to make the required contribution. You can amend your plan and change the contribution percentage starting the next year. And, as long as you have a reason, the IRS generally allows you to discontinue the plan altogether. Prior contributions can remain in the Keogh account; you can even transfer them to other investment companies if you like. Discontinuing the plan simply means that you won't be making further contributions. You don't lose the money. However, if you have employees, you need to notify them and vest them 100 percent.

Usually, the reason people reduce contributions is that their business income drops off. The silver lining to your shrinking income is that Keogh plan contributions are set as a percentage of your earnings. So less income means proportionately smaller dollar contributions.

✔ **Paired plans:** These plans combine the preceding profit-sharing and money-purchase plans. Although it requires a little more paperwork to set up and administer, a paired plan takes the best of both individual plans.

You can attain the maximum contribution possible (20 percent) that you get with the money-purchase pension plan but have some of the flexibility that comes with a profit-sharing plan. For example, you can fix your money-purchase pension plan contribution at 8 percent and contribute anywhere from 0 to 12 percent of your net income to your profit-sharing plan. Thus, in any given plan year, you may contribute as little as 8 percent of your net income and as much as 20 percent.

✔ **Defined-benefit plans:** These plans are for people who are able and willing to put away more than $30,000 per year. As you can imagine, only a very small percentage of people can afford to do this. Consistently high-income earners older than age 45 to 50 who want to save more than $30,000 per year in a retirement account should consider these plans. If you're interested in defined-benefit plans, you need to hire an actuary to crunch the numbers to calculate how much you can contribute to such a plan.

Individual Retirement Accounts (IRAs)

A final retirement account option is an Individual Retirement Account (IRA).

The 1997 tax law made significant changes to the IRA laws and options. Specifically, two new types of IRAs — Roth IRAs and Education IRAs — were added to the already-too-long list of Americans' retirement account options. Plus, a variety of existing IRA rules were altered, such as the conditions for making penalty-free withdrawals. More on the new rules in a moment.

Because your IRA contributions may not be tax deductible, contributing to an IRA generally makes sense only after you've exhausted contributing to other retirement accounts, such as the employer and self-employed based plans discussed earlier that allow for tax-deductible contributions.

"Regular" IRAs

Anyone with employment (or alimony) income can contribute to a "regular" or "standard" IRA — in other words, the original type of IRA before Congress monkeyed with the laws and created more IRA flavors. You may contribute up to $2,000 each year.

If you don't earn $2,000 a year, you can contribute as much as you'd like (and can afford) up to the amount of your employment or alimony income. If you're a nonworking spouse, you're also eligible to put $2,000 per year into a so-called spousal IRA.

Your contributions to an IRA may or may not be tax-deductible. For tax year 1998, if you're single and your *adjusted gross income* (AGI) is $30,000 or less for the year, you can deduct your IRA contribution in full. If you're married and file your taxes jointly, you're entitled to a full IRA deduction if your AGI is $50,000 per year or less. *Note:* These AGI limits will increase in future tax years (more details in a moment).

If you make more than these amounts, you can take a full IRA deduction if and only if you (or your spouse) are not an *active participant* in any retirement plan. The only way to know for certain whether you're an active participant is to look at your W-2 form, that smallish (4 x 8½-inch) document your employer sends you early in the year to file with your tax returns. Little boxes in box 15 on the W-2 form indicate whether you're an active participant in a pension or deferred-compensation plan. If either of these boxes is checked, you're an active participant.

Effective tax year 1998 and beyond, married couples with adjusted gross incomes of $150,000 or less will no longer find themselves disqualified from taking a tax deduction for an IRA contribution because one person is an *active participant* in an employer's retirement plan. At an AGI between $150,000 and $160,000, a partial deduction is allowed. At an AGI of $160,000 or more, no IRA deduction is allowed for spouses of active retirement account participants.

If you're a single-income earner with an adjusted gross income above $30,000 but below $40,000, or part of a couple with an AGI above $50,000 but below $60,000, you're eligible for a partial IRA deduction, even if you're an active participant. The size of the IRA deduction that you may claim depends on where you fall in the income range. For example, a single income earner at $35,000 is entitled to half ($1,000) of the full IRA deduction because his or her income falls halfway between $30,000 and $40,000.

A couple earning $52,500 loses just a quarter of the full IRA deduction amount because their incomes are a quarter of the way from $50,000 to $60,000. Thus, the couple can take a $1,500 IRA deduction. (Refer to Chapter 7 to find out how to calculate your exact deductible IRA contribution.)

The 1997 tax law changes have scheduled over the years ahead a gradual rise in the AGI ceiling for fully deductible IRA contributions. Table 21-1 shows how the schedule breaks down. (Remember that these figures represent the beginning of a $10,000 phaseout range. In 1998, for example, IRA deductibility phases out between $30,000 and $40,000 for single taxpayers.)

Table 21-1	The Adjusted Gross Income Ceiling for IRA Contributions	
Tax Year	**Singles**	**Married Filing Jointly**
1998	$30,000	$50,000
1999	$31,000	$51,000
2000	$32,000	$52,000
2001	$33,000	$53,000
2002	$34,000	$54,000
2003	$40,000	$60,000
2004	$45,000	$65,000

Tax Year	Singles	Married Filing Jointly
2005	$50,000	$70,000
2006	$50,000	$75,000
2007 and beyond	$50,000	$80,000

IRA account holders are now allowed to withdraw up to $10,000 from their IRAs for a first home purchase (as defined as not having owned a home in the past two years) and to withdraw funds for college expenses for a family member (child, spouse, the IRA holder, and grandchildren).

Even if you can't deduct a portion or all of a $2,000 IRA contribution because you're already covered by another retirement plan and your adjusted gross income is greater than the limits in Table 21-1, you can still contribute the full $2,000 to an IRA as long as you had that much employment income during the year. Many people think that they can't make the contribution if they can't deduct it. This misunderstanding is common among people who used to contribute to IRAs before the tax law changes of 1986. (Before 1986, anyone could deduct his or her IRA contributions, but lots of restrictions on deductions were added in 1986.)

An IRA contribution that is not tax-deductible is called, not surprisingly, a *nondeductible* IRA contribution. (We've never accused the IRS of being creative.) The benefit of this type of contribution is that the money can still compound and grow without taxation. For a person who plans to leave contributions in the IRA for a long time (a decade or more), this tax-deferred compounding may make nondeductible contributions worthwhile. However, before you consider making a nondeductible IRA contribution, be sure to read about the newer IRAs (such as the Roth IRA) that may offer benefits more to your liking.

If you end up making a nondeductible IRA contribution, you may wonder how the IRS will know not to tax you again on those portions of IRA withdrawals (because you've already paid income tax on the nondeductible contribution) in retirement. Surprise, surprise, you must fill out another form, **Form 8606,** which you file each year with your tax return to track these nondeductible contributions (find this form in the back of this book). If you haven't filed your 1998 tax form yet, you may still make your IRA contribution.

Why so many different types of retirement accounts?

The different types of retirement accounts — 401(k)s, 403(b)s, SEP-IRAs, Keoghs, regular IRAs, Roth IRAs, and SIMPLE — and the unique tax laws governing each are enough to drive taxpayers and some tax preparers insane. The complexity of the different rules is another reason that otherwise well-intentioned folks don't bother with these accounts. Depending on which accounts you use, you may be able to contribute much more or much less than your neighbor (we discuss these inequities later in this chapter).

As with the other complicated parts of our tax laws, retirement account regulations have accumulated over the years. Just like the stuff that you toss into your spare closet, attic, basement, or garage, the regulations just keep piling up. No one really wants to deal with the mess.

Our neighbors to the north in Canada have a retirement account system that we could learn from. In Canada, they have but one account — it's called the Registered Retirement Savings Plan (RRSP). Everyone with employment income can establish this account and contribute up to 18 percent, or up to a maximum annual total contribution of $14,500 — simple, equitable, and easy to understand. Why don't we do it? Go talk to the boneheads in Congress who brought us this "simple, equitable, and easy" tax system you're reading about!

Roth IRAs

For years, some taxpayers and tax advisors (and book authors and financial counselors) have complained about the rules and regulations on regular IRAs. The income limits that allowed for taking an IRA deduction were set too low. And if they couldn't take a tax deduction on a contribution, many people were unmotivated to make a nondeductible contribution because earnings on the contribution would still be taxed upon withdrawal. (Granted, the tax-deferred compounding of earnings is worth something — especially to younger people — but that's a more complicated benefit to understand and value.)

So, rather than addressing these concerns by changing regular IRAs, Congress decided to make things even more complicated by introducing another whole IRA known as the Roth IRA, named after the Senate Finance Committee chairman who championed these new accounts. Perhaps if congressional representatives couldn't name accounts after themselves, removing some of the incentive to continue creating new retirement accounts, we might someday have real tax reform!

The Roth IRA, also known as the IRA Plus, allows, beginning in tax year 1998, for up to a $2,000 annual contribution for couples with adjusted gross incomes (AGIs) under $150,000 and for single taxpayers with AGIs under $95,000. The $2,000 limit is reduced for married taxpayers with AGIs above $150,000 ($95,000 if single) and is eliminated for couples with AGIs above $160,000 ($110,000 for singles).

Although this new IRA doesn't offer a tax deduction on funds contributed to it, it does offer benefits not offered by regular IRAs and some other retirement accounts. The distinguishing feature of the Roth IRA is that the earnings on your contributions aren't taxed upon withdrawal as long as you are at least age 59^1/$_2$ and have held the account at least five years.

Retirement account inequities

If you don't have access to a retirement plan through your place of employment, you can try lobbying your employer to set up one — or you can look elsewhere for a job that offers this valuable benefit. Failing these options, you have a right to be angry about the inequities in terms of access to tax-deductible retirement accounts.

To put everyone on more equal footing, those who work for employers without retirement savings plans should be allowed to contribute more to their IRAs. It isn't fair that people who work for companies that have no retirement savings plans can deduct only $2,000 per year from their taxable income for an IRA. In some cases, they may not be able to deduct anything!

Consider an example of two households that each have annual employment income of $50,000. One household has access to a 401(k) plan, but the other household has no access to retirement plans other than an IRA. The household with the 401(k) can put away and deduct from its taxable income thousands of dollars more per year than the household with just the IRA.

The inequity can be even greater with higher-income earners. A self-employed person, for example, making $100,000 per year can sock away a tax-deductible $20,000 per year. Those who earn $150,000+ per year may be able to save $30,000, perhaps even more, if they establish defined-benefit plans and other types of plans.

These inequities have persisted because of the federal government's budget deficit. Allowing more people to make larger tax-deductible contributions to retirement accounts would reduce government revenue in the short-term.

Tax deductions for retirement savings are included in the tax system to encourage people to provide for their own retirement. It's hypocritical and inequitable for the government and our tax laws to stress the importance of saving for retirement and not give people equal access to do so.

Should you convert your regular IRA to a Roth IRA?

If the Roth IRA's tax-free withdrawals of accumulated earnings appeal to you, you may be interested to know that the new tax laws allow taxpayers with adjusted gross incomes of less than $100,000 to transfer money in a regular IRA to a Roth IRA without having to pay any early withdrawal penalties. The catch (you knew there'd be one) is that you must pay income tax on the amount transferred.

Whether you'll come out ahead in the long run by doing this conversion depends largely on your time horizon and retirement tax bracket. The younger you are and the higher the tax bracket you think that you'll be in

when you retire, the more the conversion makes sense. On the other hand, if you drop into a lower tax bracket in retirement, as many retirees do, you're probably better off keeping the money in a standard IRA account.

Of course, if you can't afford to pay the current income tax you'll owe on the conversion, then don't do it. And, again, remember that a future Congress could reverse some of the benefits of the Roth IRA. Thus, we generally don't advise many people to convert a regular IRA into a Roth IRA.

An exception to the age-59$\frac{1}{2}$ rule is made for first time home buyers who can withdraw up to $10,000 from a Roth IRA to apply to the purchase of a principal residence. Remember, however, that your Roth IRA must be in existence for five years before you're allowed an income-tax-free withdrawal for a home purchase. (Penalty-free withdrawals for a first home purchase will be permitted from a regular IRA; however, you will still owe income tax on the accumulated earnings withdrawn.)

Another attractive feature of the Roth IRA: For those not needing to draw on all their retirement accounts in the earlier years of retirement, the Roth IRA, unlike a standard IRA, does not require distributions after the account holder passes age 70$\frac{1}{2}$.

Before you go running out to contribute to a Roth IRA, keep in mind that the lack of taxation on withdrawn earnings is in no way guaranteed for the future. Although Congress can giveth tax benefits, Congress can also taketh them away. If the government is running large deficits in future years, turning around and taxing Roth IRA withdrawals would offer one way to increase tax revenues.

Consider contributing to a Roth IRA if you've exhausted your ability to contribute to tax-deductible retirement accounts and you aren't allowed a tax deduction for a regular IRA contribution because your adjusted gross income exceeds the deductibility thresholds. Sorry, but you can't contribute $2,000 in the same tax year to both a regular IRA and a Roth IRA; the sum total of your standard and Roth IRA contributions may not exceed $2,000 in a given year.

To set up a Roth, you and the financial institution must execute **Form 5305-R, Roth Individual Retirement Trust Account.** For a custodial account, you must complete **Form 5305-RA, Roth Individual Retirement Custodial account.** (Neither form gets attached to your return. Keep the form in a safe place in case the IRS ever wants to look at it.) What's the difference between the two types of accounts? At most banks and brokerage firms, you set up a custodial account. Trust accounts don't restrict the type of assets you can invest in.

Medical savings accounts

Effective tax year 1997, the government started testing Medical Savings Accounts (MSAs) that allow self-employed people and employers with an average of 50 or fewer employees (during the past two years) to put money away on a pretax basis toward medical expenses.

The maximum amount that eligible employees may contribute each year is limited to 65 percent of that individual's health insurance plan deductible or 75 percent of the family's deductible. Contributions to an MSA can be made through tax year 2000.

MSAs have some bizarre limitations and rules. Contributions to MSAs can only be made for individual health plans with yearly deductibles between $1,500 and $2,250 and maximum out-of-pocket limits not exceeding $3,000 and family plans with deductibles of between $3,000 and $4,500 and maximum out-of-pocket limits not exceeding $5,500.

Unlike health care dollars put into an employer's flexible benefit plan, if you don't use the money contributed to the MSA, you can simply let it continue to grow and then use it in the future. However, if you withdraw the money before age 65 and don't use it for medical expenses (unless you have a disability or die), you'll owe a 15-percent federal penalty tax as well as regular income tax plus any penalties assessed by your state.

To date, few major investment firms, such as the better mutual fund companies, offer MSAs. As with any other type of investment account, be sure to examine the fees on these accounts and the merits of the investment options each company offers before investing.

For tax years 1999 through the end of 2002, seniors on Medicare will be able to contribute money to a Medicare MSA.

Education IRAs

Congress wasn't content to add just Roth IRAs to the new list of IRA flavors, so they created a third type of IRA known as the Education IRA. These accounts are misnamed because they have nothing to do with retirement. They are tax-sheltered vehicles to allow parents to save for their children's educational costs.

Although Education IRAs offer some benefits, they also come with serious potential drawbacks. Read Chapter 25, which deals with important taxes relating to kids, for an explanation of the pros and cons of the Education IRAs.

Annuities

If you've contributed the maximum amount allowable to all the previously mentioned retirement accounts for which you are eligible, then you may want to consider annuities. Annuities, like IRAs, allow your capital to grow and compound without taxation. You defer taxes until withdrawal. Annuities carry the same penalties for withdrawal prior to age $59\frac{1}{2}$ as do IRAs (although unlike all other retirement accounts except a Roth IRA, you aren't forced to begin withdrawals at age $70\frac{1}{2}$; you may leave the money in an annuity to compound tax deferred for as many years as you desire).

And, unlike an IRA that has a $2,000 annual contribution limit, you can deposit as much as you want in any year in an annuity — even $1 million if you have it! As with a so-called nondeductible IRA, you get no up-front tax deduction for your contributions. Thus, consider an annuity only after fully exhausting your other retirement account options.

What exactly is an annuity? Well, annuities are peculiar investment products — contracts, actually — that are backed by insurance companies. If you, the annuity holder (investor), die during the so-called accumulation phase (that is, prior to receiving payments from the annuity), your designated beneficiary is guaranteed to receive the amount of your original investment.

I need how much for retirement?

On average, most people need about 70 to 80 percent of their preretirement income to maintain their standard of living throughout retirement.

For example, if your household earns $40,000 per year before retirement, you'll likely need $28,000 to $32,000 (70 to 80 percent of $40,000) per year during retirement to live the way that you're accustomed to living.

Remember that 70 to 80 percent is just an average. You may need more or less. If you currently save little or none of your annual income, expect to have a large mortgage payment or growing rent in retirement, or anticipate wanting to travel and do other expensive things in retirement, you may need 90 percent, perhaps even 100 percent, of your current income to maintain your standard of living in retirement.

On the other hand, if you now save a high percentage of your earnings, are a high-income earner, expect to own your home free of debt by retirement, and anticipate leading a modest lifestyle in retirement, you may be able to make do with 60 percent of your current income.

If you've never thought about what your retirement goals are, looked into what you can expect from Social Security (stop laughing), or calculated how much you should be saving for retirement, now's the time to do it. *Personal Finance For Dummies*, 2nd Edition, written by Eric Tyson and published by IDG Books Worldwide, goes through all the necessary details and even tells you how to come up with more to invest and how to do it wisely.

Because annuities carry higher fees (which reduce your investment returns) due to the insurance that comes with them, you should first make the maximum contribution that you can to an IRA, even if it isn't tax-deductible. Also, only consider annuities if you plan to leave the money in the annuity for at least 15 years or more. The reason: It typically takes that long for the tax-deferred compounding of your annuity investment to make up for the annuity's relatively higher annual fees, as well as the fact that, upon withdrawal, the earnings on an annuity are taxed at ordinary income tax rates, which are higher than the more favorable long-term capital gains tax rates. If you don't expect to keep your money invested for 15 to 20 plus years, you should do better by simply investing your money in "tax-friendly" investments in nonretirement accounts (see Chapter 23).

Taxing Retirement Account Decisions

In addition to knowing about the different types of retirement accounts available and the importance of using them, we know that you're going to have other problems and questions. It's not that we're so darn smart, but our clients have trained us! Here are the sticky issues you may be struggling with, along with our recommendations.

Prioritizing retirement contributions

If you have access to more than one type of retirement account, prioritize which accounts to use by what they give you in return. Your first contributions should be to employer-based plans that match your contributions. After that, contribute to any other employer or self-employed plans that allow tax-deductible contributions. If you've contributed the maximum possible to tax-deductible plans or don't have access to such plans, contribute to an IRA (read the previous section, "Individual Retirement Accounts," about choosing between a regular IRA and a Roth IRA).

If you've maxed out on contributions to an IRA or don't have this choice because you lack employment income, consider an annuity or tax-friendly investments (see Chapter 23).

We hate to bring it up, but some spouses worry about whether the bulk of their retirement account contributions will end up in the other spouse's account. You may be concerned about this situation because of the realities of a potential divorce.

You should also know that in a divorce, money in retirement accounts (regardless of how much is in which person's name) can be divided up like the other assets. But rather than worrying about the possibility of divorce, how about investing in the effort to make your relationship stronger in order to avoid this problem? If you dislike paying taxes, you're going to hate a divorce wherein you could face a 50-percent "tax rate" — that's the amount of your combined assets your spouse could walk away with!

Or perhaps you're sure that your spouse doesn't read books like this one and may make big investing mistakes. You can handle this second worry by educating yourselves and by making decisions together where your retirement money is concerned.

Transferring existing retirement accounts

With employer-maintained retirement plans, such as 401(k)s, you usually have limited investment options. Unless you are the employer or can convince the employer to change, you're stuck with what is offered. If your employer offers four mutual funds from the Lotsa Fees and Lousy Performance Fund Company, for example, you can't transfer this money to another investment company.

After you leave your employer, however, you generally have the option of leaving your money in the employer's plan or transferring it to an IRA at an investment company of your choice. The process of moving this money from an employer plan to investments of your choice is called a *rollover.* And you thought you weren't going to be reading anything fun today!

When you roll money over from an employer-based retirement plan, never take personal possession of the money. If your employer gives the money to you, the employer must withhold 20 percent of it for taxes. This situation creates a tax nightmare for you because you must then jump through more hoops when you file your return. You should also know that you need to come up with the extra 20 percent when you do the rollover because you won't get the 20 percent back that your employer withheld in taxes until you file your tax return. If you can't come up with the 20 percent, you have to pay income and maybe even excise taxes on this money as a distribution. Yuck!

After you leave the company, you can move your money held in SEP-IRAs, Keoghs, IRAs, and many 403(b) plans (also known as *tax-sheltered annuities*) to nearly any major investment firm you please. Moving the money is pretty simple. If you can dial an 800 number, fill out a couple of short forms, and send them back in a postage-paid envelope, then you can transfer an account. The investment firm to which you're transferring your account does the rest. Here's the lowdown on how to transfer retirement accounts without upsetting Uncle Sam or any other tax collector:

1. **Decide to which investment firm you would like to move the account.** When investing in stocks and bonds, mutual funds are a great way to go. They offer diversification and professional management, and they're low-cost.

2. **Call the 800 number of the firm you're transferring the money to and ask for an *account application* and *asset transfer form* for the type of account you're transferring — for example, SEP-IRA, Keogh, IRA, or 403(b).** The reason for allowing the new investment company to do the transfer for you is that the tax authorities impose huge penalties if you do a transfer incorrectly. It's far easier and safer to let the company to which you're transferring the money do the transfer for you. If they screw it up (good investment firms won't), they're liable.

3. **Sit by your mailbox every day until the forms arrive.** After they do, complete the account application and asset transfer form. Completing this paperwork for your new investment firm opens your new account and authorizes the transfer.

If you have questions or problems, the firm(s) to which you're transferring your account have armies of capable employees waiting to help you. Remember, these firms know that you're transferring your money to them, so they normally roll out the red carpet.

4. **Mail the completed account application and asset transfer forms to your new investment company.** Transferring your existing assets typically takes a month to complete. If the transfer isn't completed within a month, get in touch with your new investment firm to determine the problem.

If your old company isn't cooperating, a call to a manager there may help to get the ball rolling. The unfortunate reality is that too many investment firms will cheerfully set up a new account to *accept* your money on a moment's notice, but they will drag their feet, sometimes for months, when it comes time to *relinquish* your money. If you need to light a fire under their behinds, tell a manager at the old firm that you're sending letters to the local Better Business Bureau, National Association of Securities Dealers (NASD), and the Securities and Exchange Commission (SEC) if they don't complete your transfer within the next week.

Taking money out of retirement accounts

Someday, hopefully not until you retire, you'll need or want to start withdrawing and enjoying the money that you socked away in your retirement accounts. Some people, particularly those who are thrifty and good at saving money (also known, by some, as cheapskates and tightwads), have a hard time doing this.

You saved and invested money in your retirement accounts to use at a future date. Perhaps you're in a pinch for cash and the retirement account looks as tempting as a catered buffet meal after a day of fasting. Whatever the reason, here's what you need to consider *before* taking the money out of your retirement accounts.

When should you start withdrawing from retirement accounts?

Most people start withdrawing funds from retirement accounts *when* they retire. This option may or may not be the best financial decision for you. Generally speaking, you're better off postponing drawing on retirement accounts until you need the money. The longer the money resides inside the retirement account, the longer it can compound and grow, tax-deferred. But don't wait if postponing means that you must scrimp and cut corners — especially if you have the money to use and enjoy.

Suppose that you retire at age 60 and, in addition to money inside your retirement accounts, you have a bunch available outside as well. If you can, you're better off living off the money outside retirement accounts *before* you start tapping the retirement account money.

If you aren't wealthy and have saved most of the money earmarked for your retirement inside retirement accounts, odds are you'll need and want to start drawing on your retirement account soon after you retire. By all means, do so. But have you figured out how long your nest egg will last and how much you can afford to withdraw? Most folks haven't. It's worth taking the time to figure how much of your money you can afford to draw on per year, even if you think that you have enough.

Few people are wealthy enough to consider simply living off the interest and never touching the principal, although more than a few people live like paupers so that they can do just that. Many good savers have a hard time spending and enjoying their money in retirement. If you know how much you can safely use, you may be able to loosen the purse strings.

One danger of leaving your money to compound inside your retirement accounts for a long time — after you're retired — is that the IRS will require you to start making withdrawals by April 1 of the year *following* the year you reach age 70½. It's possible that because of your delay in taking the money out — and the fact that it will have more time to compound and grow — you may need to withdraw a hefty chunk per year. This procedure could push you into higher tax brackets in those years that you're forced to make larger withdrawals.

This forced distribution no longer applies to people who are working for a company and also does not apply to money held in the newer Roth IRAs discussed earlier in this chapter. Self-employed individuals still have to take the distribution.

If you want to plan how to withdraw money from your retirement accounts in order to meet your needs and minimize your taxes, consider hiring a tax advisor to help. If you have a great deal of money in retirement accounts and have the luxury of not needing the money until you're well into retirement, tax planning will likely be worth your time and money.

Naming beneficiaries

With any type of retirement account, you're supposed to name beneficiaries who will receive the assets in the account when you die. You usually name primary beneficiaries (your first choices for receiving the money) and secondary beneficiaries — who receive the money in the event that the primary beneficiaries are also deceased when you pass away.

The designations aren't cast in stone; you can change them whenever and as often as you desire by sending written notice to the investment company or employer holding your retirement account. Note that many plans require spousal consent to the naming of a beneficiary other than the spouse.

Do the best that you can in naming beneficiaries, and be thankful that you don't have to designate someone to raise your children in your absence! You should also know that you can designate charities as beneficiaries. If you want to reduce the amount of money that's required to be distributed from your retirement accounts annually, name beneficiaries who are all at least ten years younger than yourself.

Life expectancy and your IRA

If you are self-employed or retired from a company, on April 1 of the year following the year you turn 70½, you have to make some important decisions about how the money will come out of your regular IRA (this policy is not applicable to Roth IRAs discussed earlier in this chapter). The first choice: whether you receive yearly distributions based on your life expectancy or based on the joint life expectancies of you and your beneficiary. If your aim is to take out as little as possible, you'll want to use a joint life expectancy. That choice will stretch out the distributions over a longer period.

Next, you have to decide how you want your life expectancy to be calculated. By using the method known as *term-certain,* you pick the current IRS estimate of your life expectancy and then reduce it by one year every year. So if the IRS figures that you'll live 23.1 years this year, next year you'd divide the balance of the account by 22.1, and so on. See IRS Publication 590 on the wonderful subject of calculating your life expectancy.

Under the second method, known as *recalculation,* you go back to the IRS tables in Publication 590 and look up your new life expectancy each year. Over time, this method has you taking out a little less money per year than by using the term-certain approach. (According to the IRS tables, your life expectancy doesn't decrease by a full year every 12 months.)

But the recalculation method has some serious drawbacks. Namely, if one spouse dies, only the survivor's life expectancy is used. When you both die, the entire balance must be paid out by the end of the next year to whomever is next in line for the money. That rule could mean a big tax bill for whomever is getting the balance of your account — presumably an heir. If you use the term-certain approach, the heir gets to keep taking money out in dribs and drabs, just as you had been doing. To us, the term-certain method is the clear winner.

The IRS allows you to calculate the required minimum distribution based on the joint life expectancy of you and your oldest named beneficiary. However, you can't use a difference of greater than ten years for a non-spouse. If a non-spouse is named as the beneficiary and is more than ten years younger, for tax purposes of calculating required withdrawals, they are considered to be just ten years younger than you. Maybe that's why some rich, older men like marrying younger women!

Perplexing pension decisions

As discussed earlier in the chapter, if you've worked for a larger company for a number of years, you may have earned what is known as a *pension benefit*. This term simply means that upon attaining a particular age, usually 55 to 65, you can start to receive a monthly check from the employer(s) you worked for. With many pension plans today, you earn ("vest") a benefit after you have completed five years of full-time work.

Make sure that you keep track of the employer(s) where you have earned pension benefits as you move to new jobs and locations. Mail address changes to your previous employers' benefits departments. If they lose track of you and you forget that you've earned a benefit, you could be out a great deal of money.

What age to start?

With some plans, you may be able to start drawing your pension as early as 50 years of age — as long as you have worked enough years somewhere. The majority of plans, however, won't give you payments until age 55 or 60. Some plans even make you wait until age 65.

If you don't have a choice as to at what age you want to start drawing benefits, that situation surely simplifies things for you. Before you get perplexed and overwhelmed if you do have options, remember one simple thing: Smart actuaries have created the choices available to you. Actuaries are the kinds of people that score 800s (a perfect score, in case you forgot) on their math SATs. These folks work, eat, breathe, and sleep numbers.

The choices you confront show you the younger you elect to start drawing benefits, the less you are paid. Conversely, the longer you can wait to access your pension, the more you should receive per month. That said, here are some pointers:

 ✔ Some pensions stop offering higher benefits after you reach a certain age — make sure that you don't delay starting your benefits after you've reached this plateau. Otherwise, make your decision as to at what age to start drawing benefits based on when you need the money and/or can afford to retire. Run the numbers or hire a competent tax or financial advisor.

 ✔ If you're still working and earning a healthy income, think twice before starting pension benefits — these pension benefits are likely to be taxed at a much higher rate. You're probably going to be in a lower income tax bracket after you stop working.

 ✔ If you know that you're in poor health and will not live long, consider drawing your pension sooner.

It's not worth your time attempting to calculate which age option will lead to your getting more money. So many assumptions, such as the rate of inflation and the number of years you'll live, are beyond your abilities to accurately predict. The actuaries have done their homework on these issues, and that's why the numbers vary the way they do.

Which payment option for you married folks?

Besides deciding at what age you'll elect to start receiving benefits, if you're married, you may have other choices, such as how much money you'll receive when you begin your pension benefit versus how much your spouse will receive if you pass away.

Before we dig into these choices, remember, actuaries are smart — don't make your selection based on age differences between you and your spouse. For example, if you're married to someone much younger, you may be tempted to choose the pension option that maximizes the amount your spouse receives upon your death because you're likely to pre-decease your spouse. However, each person's pension options already reflect the age differences between spouses, so don't waste your time with this line of thinking. Remember those smart actuaries.

Although the actuaries know your age and your spouse's age, they don't know or care about your ability and desire to accept financial risk. Pension options differ from one another in how much money you can receive now versus how much your spouse is guaranteed to receive in the event that you die first. As with many things in life, there are tradeoffs. If you want to ensure that your spouse continues to receive a relatively high pension in the event of your passing, you must be willing to accept a smaller pension payment when you start drawing the pension.

The actuaries also don't know about your current health. All things being equal, if you're in poor health due to a chronic medical problem when you choose your pension option, lean toward those that provide your spouse with more.

The following are some of the typical options, which are ranked in order of providing the most to the fewest dollars at the beginning of retirement. The first choices, which provide more cash in hand sooner, are the riskiest from the standpoint of surviving spouses. The latter choices, which offer less cash in hand today, are the least risky for surviving spouses:

- **Single Life Option:** This option pays benefits only as long as the pensioner (person who earned the pension benefit) is alive. *The survivor receives nothing.* The single life option offers the highest monthly benefits but is also the riskiest option. For example, the pensioner receives $1,500 per month for as long as he or she is alive. The spouse receives nothing after the pensioner's death. Only consider this option if you have sufficient assets for your spouse to live on in the event of your dying early in retirement.

- **Ten Years' Certain Option:** This option pays benefits for at least ten years, even if the pensioner passes away within the first ten years of drawing the pension. The pensioner continues to receive benefits for as long as he or she lives, even if he or she lives more than ten years. For example, a pensioner receives $1,400 per month for at least ten years until his or her death. The spouse then receives nothing.

- **50 Percent Joint and Survivor Option:** With this option, the survivor receives 50 percent of pensioner's benefit after his or her death. For example, a pensioner receives $1,350 per month. Upon the pensioner's death, his or her spouse receives a reduced benefit of $675 per month.

- **²/₃ Joint and Survivor Option:** With this option, the survivor receives 66 percent of the pensioner's benefit after his or her death. For example, a pensioner receives $1,310 per month. Upon the pensioner's death, his or her spouse receives a reduced benefit of $865 per month.

- **75 Percent Joint Survivor Option:** With this option, the survivor receives 75 percent of the pensioner's benefit after his or her death. For example, a pensioner receives $1,275 per month. Upon the pensioner's death, the spouse receives a reduced benefit of $955 per month.

- **100 Percent Joint and Survivor Option:** With this option, the survivor receives 100 percent of the pensioner's benefit after his or her death. For example, a pensioner receives $1,200 per month. Upon the pensioner's death, the spouse also receives $1,200 per month.

Choosing the best pension option for you and your spouse is not unlike selecting investments. What's best for your situation depends on your overall financial circumstances and desire, comfort, and ability to accept risk. The Single Life Option is the riskiest and should be used only by couples who don't really need the pension — it's frosting on the financial cake — and are willing to gamble in order to maximize benefits today. If the surviving spouse is very much dependent on the pension, select one of the survivor options that leaves a high benefit amount after the pensioner's death.

Beware of insurance salespeople and "financial planners" (who also sell life insurance and are therefore brokers and not advisors) who advocate that you purchase life insurance and take the Single Life Option. They argue that this option enables you to maximize your pension income and protect the surviving spouse with a life insurance death benefit if the pensioner dies. Sounds good, but the life insurance expense outweighs the potential benefits. Choose one of the survivor pension options that effectively provides life insurance protection for your survivor. This method is a far more cost-effective way to "buy" *life* insurance.

Chapter 22

Small Businesses and Tax Planning

*W*hether *you* are your entire company or you have many employees for whom you're responsible, running a business can be one of the most frustrating, exhilarating, rewarding — and financially punishing — endeavors of your adult life.

Many Americans fantasize about being their own boss. Tales of entrepreneurs becoming multimillionaires focus our attention on the financial rewards without teaching us about the business and personal costs associated with being in charge.

The biggest challenges business owners face are the personal and emotional ones. It's sad to say, but these challenges rarely get discussed among all the glory tales of rags-to-riches. Major health problems, divorces, the loss of friends, and even suicides have been attributed to the passions of business owners consumed with winning or overwhelmed by their failures. Although careers and business success are important, if you really think about it, at best these things should be no higher than fourth on your overall priority list. Your health, family, and friends can't be replaced — but a job or business can.

Business owners know the good and the bad. Consider all the activities that your company has to do well in order to survive and succeed in the rough-and-tumble business world. You have to develop products and services that the marketplace will purchase. You have to price your wares properly and promote them. What good is a better mousetrap if you're the only one who knows about it? After you've successfully developed offerings that meet a need, new worries begin: competitors. Your success will likely spur imitators.

Even though you never desired a career in real estate, you may nevertheless find yourself reading the fine print in lease contracts and evaluating office space. Perhaps you must struggle with the decision of whether to continue operating out of that spare bedroom or to pony up for some office space. If that worry isn't enough, you need to read trade and professional journals to keep current with changes in your field. Although you never wanted to be a human resource manager, you need to know about the right ways to hire, train, and retain good employees. And you soon may need to become an expert on insurance and other employee benefits.

With money flowing into and out of your coffers, you need to keep appropriate records documenting your income and expenses. Otherwise, preparing your business's tax return will be a frustrating endeavor. Getting audited under these circumstances could produce a never-ending nightmare. And, unlike working for a corporation, owning a small business makes *you* fully responsible for ensuring that the right amount of tax is withheld and paid on both the state and federal level.

Real versus bogus businesses and the hobby loss rules

This chapter is about how small-business owners can make tax-wise decisions while running their businesses. It is *not* about how to start up a *sideline business* for the primary purpose of generating tax deductions.

Unfortunately, some self-anointed financial gurus claim that you can slash or even completely eliminate your tax bill by setting up a sideline business. They say that you can sell your services while doing something you enjoy (something legal, of course). The problem, they argue, is that — as a regular wage earner who receives a paycheck from an employer — you can't write off many of your other (that is, personal) expenses. These hucksters usually promise to show you the secrets of tax reduction if you shell out a few too many bucks for their audiotapes and notebooks of inside information.

"Start a small business for fun, profit, and huge tax deductions," one financial book trumpets, adding that "the tax benefits alone are worth starting a small business." A seminar company that offers a course on "How to Write a Book on Anything in 2 Weeks . . . or Less!" (we must be doing something wrong!) also offers a tax course entitled, "How to Have Zero Taxes Deducted from Your Paycheck." This tax seminar will tell you how to solve your tax problems: "If you have a sideline business, or would like to start one, you're eligible to have little or no taxes taken from your pay." Gee, sounds good. Where do we sign up?

Suppose that you're interested in photography. You like to take pictures when you go on vacation. These supposed tax experts will tell you to set up a photography business and start deducting all your photography-related expenses: airfare, film, the utility bills and rent for your "home dark room," and restaurant meals with potential clients (that is, your friends). Before you know it, you've wiped out most of your taxes.

Sound too good to be true? It is. Your business spending must be for the *legitimate* purpose of generating an income. According to the IRS, a sideline activity that generates a loss year in and year out is not a business but a "hobby."

Specifically, an activity is considered a hobby if it shows a loss for three or more of the past five tax years. (Horse racing, breeding, and so on is considered a hobby if it shows a loss for six or more of the past seven tax years.) Certainly, some businesses lose money. But a real business can't afford to do so year after year and still remain in business. Who likes losing money unless the losses are really just a tax deduction front for a hobby?

If the hobby loss rules indicate that you're engaging in a hobby, the IRS will disallow your claiming of the losses. In order to challenge this ruling, you must convince the IRS that you are seriously attempting to make a profit and run a legitimate business. The IRS will want to see that you're actively marketing your services, building your skills, and accounting for income and expenses. The IRS also wants to see that you aren't having too much fun! If you're deriving too much pleasure from an activity, in the eyes of the IRS, the activity must not be a real business!

The bottom line is this: You need to operate a legitimate business for the purpose of generating income and profits — not tax deductions. If you're thinking that it's worth the risk of taking tax losses for your hobby year after year because you won't get caught unless you're audited, think again. The IRS audits an extraordinarily large number of small businesses that show regular losses.

This chapter can at least help you to make tax-wise decisions that will boost your business profits and comply with the myriad tax regulations that annoy many entrepreneurs like yourself. Read *Small Business For Dummies* by Eric Tyson and Jim Schell (IDG Books Worldwide, Inc.) for more information about successfully running your business.

Getting and Staying Organized

If you're thinking of starting a business or are already in the thick of one, you need to keep a proper accounting of your income and expenses. If you don't, when it comes time to file the necessary tax forms for your business, you won't be able to complete them accurately.

Besides helping you over the annual tax-filing hurdle, you want accurate records so that you can track the financial health and performance of your business during the year. How are your profits running? Can you afford to hire new employees? Analyzing your monthly or quarterly business financial statements can help you answer these important business questions.

Here's a final reason to keep good records: The IRS may audit you, and if they do, you'll be asked that dreaded question: "Can you prove it?" Small-business owners who file **Schedule C Profit or Loss From Business** with their tax return are audited at a much higher rate than other taxpayers. Although that dubious honor may seem like an unfair burden to business owners, the IRS targets small businesses for good reason — more than a few small-business owners bend the tax rules, and many areas exist where small-business owners can mess up.

The following sections cover the key tax-organizing things that small-business owners should keep in mind.

Leave a trail

When it comes time to file your annual return, you want the documentation that enables you to figure your business income and expenses. At a minimum, set up some file folders into which you can collect receipts and other documentation — perhaps one folder for tabulating your income and another for compiling your expenses. Computer software may help you with this chore as well, but you must still go through the hassle of learning a new program and then continually entering the data. (QuickBooks by Intuit, which is designed for small-business owners, is a good choice.)

It doesn't matter whether you use file folders, software, or a good old-fashioned shoebox to collate this important financial information. What does matter is that you keep records of expenses and income.

Odds are very good that you'll lose or misplace some of those little pieces of paper needed to document your expenses. Thus, one big advantage of charging expenses on a credit card or of writing a check is that these transactions leave a paper trail. This trail makes it easier to total your expenses come tax time and deal with being audited when you need to prove your expenses.

Just remember to be careful if you use a credit card, because you may buy more things than you can really afford. Then you're stuck with a lot of debt to pay off. On the other hand (as many small-business owners know), it's difficult to find lenders when you need money. (Using the credit on a low-interest-rate credit card can be an easy way for you to borrow money without shamelessly begging a banker for a loan.)

Likewise, leave a trail with your revenue. Depositing all your receipts in one account will help you come tax time or should you ever get audited.

Separate business from personal finances

One of the IRS's biggest concerns is that as a small-business owner, you'll try to minimize your business profits (and therefore taxes) by hiding business income and inflating your business expenses. Uncle Sam thus looks suspiciously at business owners who use personal checking and credit card accounts for business transactions. You may be tempted to use your personal account this way (because it's a hassle to open separate accounts — not because you're dishonest). Take the time to open separate accounts. It not only makes the feds happy but also makes your accounting easier.

Please don't make the mistake of thinking that paying for an expense through your business account proves to the IRS that it was a legitimate business expense. If they find that the expense *was* truly for personal purposes, the IRS will then really dig into your business's financial records and see what other shenanigans are going on.

Keep current on income and payroll taxes

When you're self-employed, you're responsible for the accurate and timely filing of all taxes owed on your income. Without an employer and a payroll department to handle the paperwork for withholding taxes on a regular schedule, you need to make estimated tax payments on a quarterly basis.

If you have employees, you also need to withhold taxes on their incomes from each paycheck they receive. And you must make timely payments to the IRS and to the appropriate state authorities. In addition to federal and state income tax, you need to withhold and send in Social Security and any other state or locally mandated payroll taxes as well as annually issue W-2s for each employee and 1099-MISCs for each independent contractor paid $600 or more. Got a headache yet?!

For paying taxes on your own self-employment income, you can obtain **Form 1040ES, Estimated Tax for Individuals,** from the back of this book. This form comes complete with an estimated tax worksheet and the four payment coupons to send in with your quarterly tax payments. It's amazing how user-friendly government people can be when they want our money. The form itself has some quirks and challenges, but you'll be happy to know that we explain how to complete Form 1040ES in Chapter 15.

To discover all the amazing rules and regulations of withholding and submitting taxes from employees' paychecks, ask the IRS for **Form 941.** Once a year, you also need to complete **Form 940** for unemployment insurance payments to the feds. And, unless you're lucky enough to live in a state with no income taxes, don't forget to call for your state's estimated income tax package.

If you aren't going to keep current on taxes for yourself and your employees, hire a good tax advisor who will force you to jump through the necessary tax hoops. (Refer to Chapter 2 for advice on selecting a tax advisor.) Many small businesses have been ruined by falling behind in taxes. When you hire employees, for example, you're particularly vulnerable to multiple tax land mines. Payroll companies and tax advisors are there for a reason, so use them selectively. They take care of all the tax filings for you, and if they screw up, they pay the penalties. Check with a tax advisor you trust for the names of reputable payroll companies in your area.

Minimizing Your Small-Business Taxes

Every small business has to spend money to make money. Most businesses need things like phone service, paper, computers and printers, software, a bottle of extra-strength aspirin, and a whole bunch of other things you probably never thought you'd be purchasing.

But don't spend money on business stuff just for the sake of generating tax deductions. In some cases, business owners we know buy all sorts of new equipment and other gadgets at year's end for their business so that they can reduce their taxes. Although we endorse reinvesting profits in your business and making your company more efficient, keep in mind that the more you spend, the less you earn — the same as with your personal finances. Remember, there's nothing wrong with paying taxes. In fact, it's a sign of business success!

What follows is an overview of what to do and what not to do in order to spend tax-wisely for your business.

Depreciation versus deduction

When you buy equipment such as computers, office furniture, bookshelves, and so on, each of these items is supposed to be *depreciated* over a number of years. Depreciation simply means that each year, you get to claim as a tax deduction a portion of the original cost of purchasing an item, until you depreciate it all. Depreciation mirrors the declining value of equipment as it ages.

For example, suppose that you spend $3,000 on computer equipment. According to the IRS, computer equipment is to be depreciated over five years. Thus, each year you can take a $600 deduction for depreciation of this computer if you elect straight-line depreciation (which is defined in Chapter 11).

By expensing or deducting (by using what's called a *Section 179 deduction*) rather than depreciating, you can take as an immediate deduction the entire $3,000 you spent on computer equipment (unless it contributes to your business showing a loss or a larger loss). As a small-business owner, you can take up to a $19,000 deduction for tax year 1999 for purchases of equipment for use in your business.

It's tempting to want to expense the full amount of equipment immediately, but that action isn't always the best thing to do. In the early years of your business, for example, your profits may be low. Therefore, because you won't be in a high tax bracket, the value of your deductions is limited. Looking ahead — if you have reason to be optimistic about your future profits — you may actually save tax dollars by choosing to depreciate your purchases. Why? By delaying some of your tax write-offs until future years (when you expect to be in a higher tax bracket because of greater profits), you save more in taxes.

Cars

If you use your car for business, you can claim a deduction (refer to the "Line 10: Car and truck expenses" section in Chapter 11 for details). The mistake that some business owners (and many other people) make is to buy an expensive car. This purchase causes two problems. First, the car may be a waste of money that could be better spent elsewhere in the business. Second, the IRS limits how large an annual auto expense you can claim for depreciation.

The IRS gives you a choice of how to account for business automobile expenses. You can either expense a standard mileage charge (32.5 cents per mile for tax year 1998) *or* keep track of the actual operating expenses (such as gas, insurance, repairs, and so on), plus take depreciation costs.

For cars that were *placed in service* (bought or began to be used in the business) after 1986, depreciation is done over five years. If you bought a car in 1998, for example, the maximum amount of depreciation that you can take is $3,160 in the first year, $5,000 in the second year, $2,950 in the third year, and $1,775 in the fourth and following years until the car is depreciated down to nothing. The way the math works out, you are effectively limited by these caps if you spent more than about $15,800 on a car in 1998.

With expensive cars, the mileage expense method will probably shortchange your deduction amounts for auto usage. Now you have another reason not to spend so much on a car! If you buy a reasonably priced car, you won't need to go through the headache of tracking your actual auto expenses (in addition to not wasting money) because the mileage expense method will probably lead to a larger deduction. It's so much easier just to track mileage and use the mileage expense method.

Be aware that auto dealers increasingly push automobile *leasing*. For the auto dealers and salespeople in the showrooms, leases have the marketing appeal of offering buyers a monthly payment that's often lower than auto loan payments — without the perceived noose around the neck of a large car loan. Don't be fooled. If you do your homework and hunt for a good deal on a car, buying with cash is the best way to go. Borrowing with an auto loan and leasing are much more expensive (leasing generally being the highest cost) and encourage car buyers to spend more than they can afford.

Travel, meal, and entertainment expenses

The IRS has clamped down on writing off travel, meal, and entertainment expenses because so many business owners and employees abuse the policy by trying to write off nonbusiness expenses. Some books, seminars, and unscrupulous tax preparers have effectively encouraged this abuse.

Be honest — not only because it's the right thing to do, but also because the IRS looks long and hard at expenses claimed in these areas. Travel must be for a legitimate business purpose. If you take a week off to go to Hawaii, spend one day at a business convention, and then spend the rest of the time sight-seeing, you may have a great time — but only a portion of your trip expenses may be deductible.

Shifting income and expenses

Many small-business owners elect to keep their business accounting on what's called a cash basis. This choice doesn't imply that all the business's customers literally pay in cash for goods and services or that the business owners pay for all expenses with cash. *Cash basis accounting* simply means that, for tax purposes, you recognize or report income in the year it was received, and expenses in the year they were paid.

By operating on a cash basis, you can control the amount of profit (income minus expenses) that your business reports for tax purposes from year to year. If your income fluctuates from year to year, you can lower your tax burden by doing a little legal shifting of income and expenses.

Suppose that you recently started a business. Assume that you have little, but growing, revenue and somewhat high start-up expenses. Looking ahead to the next tax year, you can already tell that you'll be making more money and will likely be in a much higher tax bracket (refer to Chapter 1 for the personal income tax brackets). Thus, you can likely reduce your tax bill by paying more of your expenses in the next year. Of course, you don't want to upset any of your business's suppliers, but

many of your bills could be paid January 1 of the next year instead of late December of the preceding year. *(Note:* Credit card expenses are recognized as of the date you make the charges, not when you pay the bill.)

Likewise, you can somewhat control when your customers pay you. If you expect to make less money next year, simply don't invoice customers in December of this year. Wait until January so that you receive more of your income next year. Be careful with this revenue-shifting game. If a customer mails you a check in December, the IRS laws don't allow you to hold the check until January and count the revenue then. After you receive payment, it must be recognized for tax purposes as revenue.

One final point limits who can do this revenue and expense two-step. Sole proprietorships, partnerships, S Corporations, and personal service corporations (which we discuss later in the chapter) generally can shift revenue and expense. On the other hand, C Corporations and partnerships that have C Corporations as partners may not use the cash accounting method if they have annual receipts over $5 million per year.

One exception exists: If you extend a business trip to stay over on a Saturday in order to qualify for a lower airfare — and you save money in total travel costs by extending your stay — you can claim the extra costs incurred to stay over through Sunday. If your spouse or friend tags along, his or her costs most definitely are *not* deductible.

Only 50 percent of your business expenses for meals and entertainment are deductible. (The deduction was 80 percent before 1994.) In addition, the IRS no longer allows any deductions for club dues (such as health, business, airport, or social clubs), entertainment facilities (such as executive boxes at sports stadiums), apartments, and so on. (Refer to Chapter 11 for more details.)

Home alone, or outside office space?

If you have a truly small business, you may have a choice between setting up an office in your home or getting outside office space. Many financial and nonfinancial considerations play into this decision. At home, are you going to have the discipline to get to work, or will you be tempted to sleep until 10 a.m., watch soap operas, and play solitaire on your computer? Will you argue with your spouse, who expects you to pick up the dry cleaning, go grocery shopping, and play with the family pets because you're *at home?*

And then there's the issue of being home alone, where the social highlights of the day may be greeting the postal carrier and having lunch with your cat or dog. (Although, compared to lunch with some of the bosses you may have had, lunch with a pet may be a welcome relief!)

The financial and tax sides of the home office decision actually are not important — certainly not nearly as important as many business owners make them out to be. Why? First, the cost of office space you rent or purchase outside your home is an expense that can be deducted on your business tax return. With a home-based office (if you own your home), you already get to claim the mortgage interest and property taxes as deductions on your personal tax return. So don't set up a home office thinking that you'll get all sorts of extra tax breaks. You'll qualify for some minor ones (such as deductions for utilities, repairs, and insurance) for the portion of your home devoted to business. Refer to Chapter 11 for more details.

The one extra home-based office deduction that you can take if you're a homeowner is *depreciation*. (See Chapter 24 to find out more about the other tips to avoid paying taxes on the profits from the sale of your home.)

If you don't need to move into a larger apartment or home to accommodate your business, then you may feel that your current home provides "free" office space. This situation may be true. However, if your home is larger than you need, you *could* move to a smaller, less expensive home!

Try as best you can to make your decision about your office space based on the needs of your business and your customers, along with your personal preferences. If you're a writer and don't need fancy office space to meet with anyone (or to impress anyone), working at home may be just fine. On the other hand, one writer we know rents space because, at home, he has munchkins running around who can't understand why daddy has to work. If you operate a retail or service business that requires lots of customers to come to you, getting outside office space is probably the best choice for all involved — and the most legal way to go as well. Check with the governing authorities of your town, city, and county to learn what regulations exist for home-based businesses in your area.

Independent contractors versus employees

If you really want to give yourself a headache, read the tax laws applying to the classification of people that a business hires as either employees or independent contractors. If a business hires an employee, the business is required to withhold federal and state taxes and then send the taxes to the appropriate tax authorities. The government likes the employee arrangement because independent contractors (as a group) tend to pay less in taxes by underreporting their income. Contractors are also entitled to take more business deductions than are allowed for regular employees.

If a business hires independent contractors to perform work, the contractors are responsible for paying all their own taxes. However, business owners are now required to file **Form 1099** with the IRS and some state tax agencies. On Form 1099, you report the amount of money paid to contractors who receive $600 or more from the business. This form allows the IRS to keep better tabs on contractors who may not be reporting all their income.

Unless a company offers benefits to an employee (insurance, retirement savings plans, and so on), a hired hand should prefer to be an independent contractor. Contractors have more leeway to deduct business expenses, including the deduction for a home office. Contractors can also tax-shelter a healthy percentage of their employment income in a self-employed retirement savings plan, such as a SEP-IRA or Keogh (see Chapter 21 for more details on retirement accounts). However, one additional *expense* for contractors is their obligation to pay the full share of Social Security taxes (although they can then deduct half as a tax deduction), whereas an employer would pay half the Social Security and Medicare taxes on behalf of the employee.

So how do you, as the business owner, decide whether someone should be classified as a contractor or as an employee? Some cases are hard to determine, but the IRS has a set of guidelines to make most cases pretty clear cut.

The classic example of the *independent contractor* is the professional service provider, such as legal, tax, and financial advisors. These people are considered contractors because they generally train themselves and — when hired — figure out how they can accomplish the job without much direction or instruction from the employer. Contractors usually perform work for a number of other companies and people, and they typically hire any others they need to work with them.

All in the family

If you hire family members to perform real work for fair wages, you may be able to reduce your tax bill. If your children under the age of 18 are paid for work performed, they're probably in a much lower tax bracket than you are. And, if they're working for you, the parent, they need not pay any Social Security tax like you do. You can even get your kids started on investing by taking some of their earnings and helping them to choose some investments or contribute some of their earnings to an Individual Retirement Account.

If you earn more than the family member you're paying, your child/employee may be in a lower tax bracket. Thus, as a family, you may pay less in total taxes. But you can't simply pay a family member for the sole purpose of reducing your family's taxes. The family member you're paying must be doing legitimate work for your business,

and you must be paying a reasonable wage for the type of work being done.

If you earn more than the $68,400 cap (in 1998) for full Social Security taxes, hiring a family member may lead to more Social Security taxes being paid by your family. Why? If you earn more than $68,400, you don't pay Social Security taxes on the amount above $68,400. If you instead pay a family member for working in the business and that person is earning less than the $68,400 threshold, then, as a family, you'll end up paying more in total Social Security taxes. Although it's true that earning more helps you qualify for more Social Security benefits come retirement, given the future of the Social Security system, your family member will be lucky to get back all of what he or she is paying into the system.

On the other hand, *employees* usually work for one employer and have set hours of work. For example, a full-time secretary hired by a business would be considered an employee because he or she takes instructions from the employer regarding when, where, and how to do the assigned work. Another indication of employee status is whether the secretary's presence at the work site is important for completing the assigned work.

What do you do if your situation falls in between these two types, and you're perplexed about whether the person you're hiring is a contractor or employee? Ask a tax advisor or contact the IRS for their handy-dandy **Form SS-8, Determination of Employee Work Status.** Complete the form, mail it in, and let the IRS make the call for you. That way, the IRS can't blame you — although you may rightfully feel that you're letting the fox guard the henhouse!

Insurance and other benefits

A variety of insurance and related benefits are tax-deductible to corporations for all employees. These benefits include the following:

- Health insurance

- Disability insurance

- Term life insurance (up to $50,000 in benefits per employee)

- Dependent care plans (up to $5,000 per employee may be put away on a tax-deductible basis for child care and/or care for elderly parents)

- Flexible spending or *cafeteria* plans, which allow employees to pick and choose the benefits on which to spend their benefit dollars

If the business is *not* incorporated, the business owner(s) can't deduct the cost of the preceding insurance plans for themselves — but they can deduct these costs for employees.

For tax years 1998 and 1999, self-employed people can deduct 45 percent (it will increase to 50 percent in 2000) of their health insurance costs for themselves and their covered family members. This provision of the tax code expired at the end of 1993, but Congress revived it in 1994. If you didn't take this deduction in 1995 or 1996, go back and amend your return now.

Also, as we explain in Chapter 27, the percentage of self-employed health insurance costs that may be deducted will increase until it eventually hits 100 percent in the year 2007.

Retirement plans

Retirement plans are a terrific way for business owners and their employees to tax-shelter a healthy portion of their earnings. If you don't have employees, regularly contributing to one of these plans is usually a no-brainer. If you have employees, the decision is a bit more complicated but is still often a great idea. Self-employed people may contribute to Keoghs, Simplified Employee Pension Individual Retirement Accounts (SEP-IRAs), or SIMPLE plans. Small businesses with a number of employees should also consider 401(k) plans. We discuss all these plans in detail in Chapter 21.

To Incorporate or Not to Incorporate

Starting a business is hard enough between mustering up the courage and swinging it financially. Many business owners meet their match trying to decide what should be a reasonably straightforward issue: whether to incorporate. Just about every book that addresses the subject (or just about every lawyer or accountant who advises business owners) steers clear of giving definitive answers.

In some instances, the incorporation decision is complicated, but in most cases, it need not be a difficult choice. Taxes may be important to the decision but aren't the only consideration. This section presents an overview of the critical issues to consider.

Liability protection

If you're one of the millions of small-business owners in America, the chief reason to consider incorporation is for purposes of *liability protection.* Attorneys speak of the protection of the *corporate veil.* Don't confuse this veil with insurance (or with the veil a bride normally wears on her wedding day). You don't get any insurance when you incorporate. You may need or want to buy liability insurance instead of (or in addition to) incorporating. Liability protection doesn't insulate your company from being sued, either.

When you incorporate, the protection of the corporate veil provides you with the separation or division of your *business* assets and liabilities from your *personal* finances. Why would you want to do that? Suppose that your business is doing well and you take out a bank loan in order to expand. The next year, however, the government enacts a regulatory change that makes your services or product obsolete. Before you know it, your business is losing money and you're forced to close up shop. But if you can't repay the bank loan because of your business failure, the bank shouldn't be able to go after your personal assets if you're incorporated.

Unfortunately, many small-business owners who need money find that bankers ask for a *personal guarantee,* which negates part of the liability protection that comes with incorporation. Also, if you play financial games with your company (such as shifting money out of the company in preparation for defaulting on a loan), a bank may legally be able to go after your personal assets. You must adhere to a whole host of ground rules and protocols to prove to the IRS that you're running a bona fide company. For example, you need to keep corporate records and hold an annual meeting — even if it's just with yourself!

A business can be sued if it mistreats an employee or if its product or service causes harm to a customer. But the owner's personal assets should be protected if the business is incorporated and meets the other "tests" for being a legitimate business.

Before you call your neighborhood lawyer or your state offices to figure out how to incorporate, you should know that incorporating takes time and costs money. So if incorporating doesn't offer some benefits to outweigh the hassles and costs, you shouldn't do it. Likewise, if the only benefits of incorporating can be better accomplished through some other means (such as purchasing insurance), save your money and time and don't incorporate.

Liability insurance — a better alternative if you can get it

Before you incorporate, ask yourself (and perhaps others in your line of business or advisors who work with businesses like yours) what actions could cause you to be sued. Then see if you can purchase insurance to protect against these potential liabilities. Insurance is superior to incorporation because it pays claims.

Suppose that you perform professional services but make a major mistake that costs someone a lot of money — or worse. Even if you're incorporated, you can still be sued. If you're incorporated and someone successfully sues you, your company has to cough up the dough. This situation not only costs a great deal of money, but can also sink your business. Only insurance can cover such financially destructive claims.

You can also be sued if someone slips and breaks a bone or two. To cover these types of claims, you can purchase a property or premises liability policy from an insurer.

Accountants, doctors, and a number of other professionals can buy liability insurance. A good place to start searching for liability insurance is through the associations that exist for your profession. Even if you aren't a current member, check out the associations anyway — you may be able to access any insurance they may provide without membership, or you can join the association long enough to get signed up. Incorporating doesn't necessarily preclude insuring yourself also. Both incorporating and covering yourself with liability insurance may make sense in your case.

Corporate taxes

Corporations are taxed as entities separate from their individual owners. This situation can be both good and bad. Suppose that your business is doing well and making lots of money. If your business is not incorporated, all the profits from your business are taxed on your personal tax return in the year that those profits are earned.

If you intend to use these profits to reinvest in your business and expand, incorporating can potentially save you some tax dollars. If your business is incorporated (as a regular or so-called *C Corporation*), the first $75,000 of profits in the business should be taxed at a lower rate in the corporation than on your personal tax return (see Table 22-1). One exception to this rule is personal service corporations, such as accounting, legal, consulting, and medical firms (which pay a flat tax rate of 35 percent on their taxable incomes).

Another possible tax advantage for a corporation is that corporations can pay — on a tax-deductible basis — for employee benefits such as health insurance, disability, and up to $50,000 of term life insurance. The owner is usually treated as an employee for benefits purposes. (Refer to the "Insurance and other benefits" section earlier in this chapter for more details.) Sole proprietorships and other unincorporated businesses can usually only take tax deductions for these benefit expenses for employees. Benefit expenses for owners who work in the business aren't deductible.

Table 22-1	1998 Corporate Tax Rates for Regular (C) Corporations
Taxable Income	*Tax Rate*
$0–$50,000	15%
$50,001–$75,000	25%
$75,001–$100,000	34%
$100,001–$335,000	39%
$335,001–$10,000,000	34%

Resist the temptation to incorporate just so you can have your money left in the corporation, which may be taxed at a lower rate than you would pay on your personal income (see Chapter 1 for the personal income tax rates). Don't be motivated by this seemingly short-term gain. If you want to pay yourself the profits in the future, you could end up paying *more* taxes. Why? Because you pay taxes first at the corporate tax rate in the year your company earns the money. Then you pay taxes *again* on these profits (this time on your personal income tax return) when you pay yourself from the corporate till in the form of a dividend.

Another reason not to incorporate (especially in the early days of a business) is that you can't immediately claim the losses for an incorporated business on your personal tax return. You have to wait until you can offset your losses against profits. Because most businesses produce little revenue in their early years and have all sorts of start-up expenditures, losses are common.

S Corporations

Subchapter S Corporations, so named for that part of the tax code that establishes them, can offer some business owners the best of both worlds. You get the liability protection that comes with being incorporated, and the business profit or loss passes through to the owner's personal tax returns. So if the business shows a loss in some years, the owner may claim those losses in the current year of the loss on the tax returns. If you plan to take all the profits out of the company, an S Corporation may make sense for you.

The IRS allows most — but not all — small businesses to be S Corporations. In order to be an S Corporation in the eyes of the almighty IRS, a company must meet *all* the following requirements:

- Be a U.S. company
- Have just one class of stock
- Have no more than 75 shareholders (who are all U.S. residents or citizens and are not partnerships, other corporations, or, with certain exceptions, trusts)

Limited liability companies (LLCs)

Just in the past generation, a new type of corporation has appeared. Limited liability companies (LLCs) offer business owners benefits similar to those of S Corporations but are even better in some cases. Like an S Corporation, an LLC offers liability protection for the owners. LLCs also pass the business's profits through to the owner's personal income tax returns.

Limited liability companies have fewer restrictions regarding shareholders. For example, LLCs have no limits on the number of shareholders. The shareholders in an LLC can be foreigners, and corporations and partnerships can also be shareholders.

Compared with S Corporations, the only additional restriction LLCs carry is that sole proprietors and professionals can't always form LLCs (although Texas allows this). All states now permit the formation of LLCs, but most state laws require you to have at least two partners and not be a professional firm.

Other incorporation issues

Because corporations are legal entities distinct from their owners, corporations offer other features and benefits that a proprietorship or partnership doesn't. For example, corporations have shareholders who own a piece or percentage of the company. These shares can be sold or transferred to other owners, subject to any restrictions in the shareholders' agreement.

Corporations also offer *continuity of life,* which simply means that corporations can continue to exist despite the death of an owner — or the owner's transfer of his or her share (stock) in the company.

Don't incorporate for ego purposes. If you want to incorporate in order to impress friends, family, or business contacts, you should know that few people will be impressed or even know that you're incorporated. Besides, if you operate as a sole proprietor, you can choose to operate under a different business name ("doing business as" or *d.b.a.*) without the cost — or the headache — of incorporating.

If you're in doubt

If you've weighed the pros and cons of incorporating and you're still on the fence, our advice is to keep it simple. Don't incorporate. Remember that after you incorporate, it takes time and money to un-incorporate. Start off as a sole proprietorship and then take it from there. Wait until the benefits of incorporating — for your particular case — outweigh the costs and drawbacks of incorporating.

Where to get advice

If you're totally confused about whether to incorporate because your business is undergoing major financial changes, getting competent professional help is worth the money. The hard part is knowing where to turn, because it's a challenge to find one advisor who can put all the pieces of the puzzle together. And be aware that you may get wrong or biased advice.

Attorneys who specialize in advising small businesses can help explain the legal issues. Tax advisors who do a lot of work with business owners can help explain the tax considerations. If you find that you need two or more advisors to help make the decision, it may help to get them together in one room with you for a meeting — which may save you time and money (unless your tax and legal advisors spend too much time schmoozing each other for client referrals).

Investing in Someone Else's Business

Putting money into your own business (or someone else's) can be a high-risk but potentially high-return investment. The best options are those you understand well. If you hear about a promising business opportunity from someone you know and trust, do your research and make your best judgment. The business may well be a terrific investment. But keep in mind that people are always willing to take more risk with other people's money than with their own — and that many well-intentioned people fail at their businesses.

A relatively new provision in the tax law applies a low 14-percent capital gains rate to profits realized from investments held for five or more years in new stock issued by small businesses (*small* being defined as businesses with gross assets at or less than $50 million). With the maximum long-term federal capital gains rate now at 20 percent, this provision offers some additional relief on small-business investments. So if you have a knack for identifying up-and-coming entrepreneurs, you may be able to make rewarding investments that aren't too taxing.

Before investing in a project, ask to see a copy of the business plan. Talk to others (who aren't involved with the investment!) about the idea and learn from their comments and concerns. But don't forget that many a wise person has rained on the parade of what turned out to be a terrific business idea.

Avoid *limited partnerships* and other small-company investments pitched by brokers, financial planners, and the like. They want you to buy limited partnerships because they earn hefty commissions from the sales. If you want a convenient way to invest in businesses and earn tax breaks, buy some stock mutual funds inside a retirement account.

Buying or Selling a Business

If you're buying or selling an existing business, consider getting the help and advice of competent tax and legal advisors.

If you're a buyer, good advisors can help you inspect the company you're buying and look for red flags in the financial statements. Advisors can also help structure the purchase to protect the business you're buying — and to gain maximum tax benefits.

If you're a seller, your advisors can help you prepare your business for maximum sale value and minimize taxes from the sale price.

If your business is worth a lot, make sure you read the chapter on estate planning, because hefty taxes may be owed upon your death if you don't structure things properly. Your heirs may be forced to sell your business to pay estate taxes! See Chapter 26 for more information on estate planning.

Chapter 23

Your Investments and Taxes

• •

In This Chapter

▶ Understanding tax-friendly investment strategies

▶ Comprehending tax ramifications of reinvesting and dollar-cost averaging

▶ Knowing which tax-favored "investments" to favor and which to avoid

▶ Deciding what, when, and how to sell investments

• •

*I*f you have money to invest, or if you're considering selling current investments that you hold outside the tax-friendly confines of a retirement account, income tax should be an important factor in your decision. But tax considerations alone should not dictate how and where you invest your money and when you sell. You should also weigh issues such as your desire (and the necessity) to take risks, your personal likes and dislikes, and the number of years you plan to hold on to the investment.

Note: This chapter focuses on tax issues relating to investments in mutual funds, stocks, bonds, and other securities. Other chapters in this part of the book cover tax matters for investing in real estate or small businesses, investing for your children's future, and protecting your assets from estate taxes.

Tax-Slimming Investment Techniques

Lots of folks invest their money in ways that increase their tax burdens. In many cases, they (and sometimes their advisors) don't consider the tax impact of their investment strategies.

For investments that you hold inside *tax-sheltered* retirement accounts such as IRAs and 401(k) plans (discussed in detail in Chapter 21), you don't need to worry about taxes. This money isn't generally taxed until you actually withdraw funds from the retirement account. Thus, you should never invest money that's inside retirement accounts in other tax-favored investments, such as tax-free money market funds and bonds (discussed later in this chapter).

You are far more likely to make tax mistakes investing in assets held *outside* retirement accounts. Consider the many types of distributions produced by nonretirement account investments that are subject to taxation:

✔ **Interest:** Bank accounts, for example, pay you interest that is fully taxable generally at both the federal and state levels. Bonds (IOUs) issued by corporations also pay interest that is fully taxable. Bonds issued by the federal government, which are known as *Treasury bonds,* pay interest that is *federally* taxable.

✔ **Dividends:** When you invest in *stock* (shares of company ownership), many companies share some of their profits with you as a shareholder in the form of dividends. As with interest on a bank account, these dividends are fully taxable.

> ✔ **Capital gains:** The profit from the sale of an investment at a price higher than the purchase price is known as a *capital gain*. Capital gains are generally federally and state taxable. As we explain in the sidebar "The impact of the lowered capital gains tax rates," later in this chapter, a different series of tax rates applies to capital gains.

A common mistake many people make is not choosing the best type of security in which to invest, given their tax bracket. Here are some guidelines for choosing the best type of investment, based on your federal tax bracket:

> ✔ **31-percent or higher federal tax bracket:** If you're in one of these high brackets, you should definitely avoid investments that produce taxable income. For tax year 1998, the 31-percent federal bracket started at $61,400 for singles and $102,300 for married couples filing jointly.

> ✔ **28-percent federal tax bracket:** If you invest outside retirement accounts, in most cases, you should be as well or slightly better off in investments that do not produce taxable income. This may not be the case, however, if you're in tax-free money market and bond funds whose yields are depressed due to high operating expenses.

> ✔ **15-percent federal tax bracket:** Investments that produce taxable income are generally just fine. You'll likely end up with *less* if you purchase investments that produce tax-free income because these investments yield less than comparable taxable ones even after factoring in the taxes you pay on those taxable investments. When you're investing your money, it's not the *return* that your investment earns that matters; what matters is the return you actually get to keep *after* paying taxes. The following sections describe some of the best investment choices you can make to reduce your overall tax burden.

Pay off high-interest debt

Many folks have credit card or other consumer debt, such as auto loans, that costs 8, 9, 10 percent or more per year in interest. Paying off this debt with your savings is like putting your money in an investment with a guaranteed tax-free return that's equal to the interest rate you were paying on the debt. For example, if you have credit-card debt outstanding at a 15-percent interest rate, paying off that loan is the same as putting your money to work in an investment with a guaranteed 15-percent annual return. Remember that the interest on consumer debt is *not* tax-deductible, so you would actually need to earn *more* than 15 percent on your other investments in order to net 15 percent after paying taxes.

If you still aren't convinced that paying off consumer debt is a great "investment" (if you have the cash to do so), consider this: Banks and other lenders charge higher rates of interest for consumer debt than for debt on investments (such as real estate and business). Debt for investments is generally available at a lower rate of interest, and it's tax-deductible. Consumer debt is not only hazardous to your long-term financial health (because you're borrowing against your future earnings), but it's also more expensive.

In addition to ridding yourself of consumer debt, paying off your mortgage quicker may make sense, too. This financial move isn't *always* the best one because the interest rate on mortgage debt is lower than that on consumer debt and is usually tax-deductible. For more details on home mortgage decisions, see Chapter 24.

Fund your retirement accounts

Make sure that you take advantage of opportunities to direct your employment earnings into retirement accounts. If you work for a company that offers a retirement savings plan such as a 401(k), try to fund it at the highest level you can manage. If you earn self-employment income, look into SEP-IRAs and Keoghs. See Chapter 21 for all the details on retirement accounts.

The impact of the lowered capital gains tax rates

Just to make matters even more complicated, the IRS doesn't tax all distributions equally. The complication in this case, however, can save you some money.

Effective January 1, 1998, a long-term capital gain, which is the profit (sales proceeds minus purchase price) on a security that you own more than 12 months, is taxed on a different tax-rate schedule. Short-term capital gains (securities held one year or less) are taxed at your ordinary income tax rate.

Tax laws passed in 1997 reduced the federal tax rate on long-term capital gains from 28 percent to 20 percent for holding periods of more than 12 months and to 18 percent beginning in the year 2006 for assets bought on or after January 1, 2001, and held for more than five years. For investors in the lowest federal income tax bracket — 15 percent — the long-term capital gains tax is lowered to 10 percent for assets held more than 12 months and 8 percent beginning in the year 2001 for assets held for more than five years.

Notwithstanding the perverse gambling-like enjoyment some people derive from trading, the sane strategy of buying and holding — which reduces trading costs and the likelihood of being whipsawed by fluctuating investment values — makes even more sense now.

When investing outside of retirement accounts, investors who frequently trade their investments (or who invest in mutual funds that do the same) should seriously reconsider these strategies and holdings. With longer-term capital gains being taxed at even lower tax rates now, trading that produces short-term gains (from investments held 12 months or less), which are taxed at ordinary income tax rates, penalizes higher bracket investors the most.

You can choose when to sell most investments. Thus, you can control when you realize the profit (capital gains) on your investments. If you're a high-tax-bracket investor, hold on to your nonretirement investments for more than 12 months to get favorable long-term capital gains treatment.

In addition to the possibility that the IRS wants to make our tax lives more difficult, there is some logic behind the lower long-term capital gains tax. Some argue that this lower tax encourages investment for long-term growth. On the other hand, some complain that it's a tax break for the affluent.

You get two possible tax bonuses by investing more of your money in retirement accounts. First, your contributions to the retirement accounts come out of your pay before taxes are figured, which reduces your overall tax burden. Second, the earnings on the investments inside the retirement accounts compound without taxation until withdrawal. Funding retirement accounts makes particular sense if you're currently in a high tax bracket and can allow the money to compound over many years (at least 10 years, preferably 15 to 20 years or more).

If you need to save money *outside* retirement accounts for short-term purposes such as buying a car or a home, by all means, don't do all your saving inside sometimes difficult and costly to access retirement accounts. But if you accumulate money outside retirement accounts with no particular purpose in mind (other than that you like seeing the burgeoning balances), why not get some tax breaks *too* by contributing and investing through retirement accounts? Because your investments can produce taxable distributions, investing money outside retirement accounts requires greater thought and consideration. This is another reason to shelter more of your money in retirement accounts.

Use tax-free money market and bond funds

If you're in a high enough tax bracket (federal 28 percent to 31 percent, or higher), you may find that you come out ahead with tax-free investments. Tax-free investments yield less than comparable investments that produce taxable earnings. But the earnings from tax-free investments *can* end up being greater than what you're left with from taxable investments *after* paying required federal and state taxes. See the sidebar "Determining whether tax-free funds pay more," later in this chapter, to find out how to compare the yields.

Tax-free *money market funds,* offered by mutual fund companies, can be a better alternative to bank savings accounts that pay interest (which is subject to taxation). The best money market funds pay higher yields and give you check-writing privileges. If you're in a high tax bracket, you can select a *tax-free* money market fund, which pays dividends that are free from federal and/or state tax. You can't get this feature with bank savings accounts.

Unlike bank savings accounts, money market mutual funds aren't insured by the FDIC (Federal Deposit Insurance Corporation). For all intents and purposes, though, money market funds and bank accounts have equivalent safety. The lack of FDIC insurance should not concern you, because fund companies haven't failed. And in those rare instances when a money fund's investments have lost value, the parent company has infused capital to ensure no loss of principal on the investor's part.

Just as you can invest in a tax-free money market fund, so too can you invest in tax-free bonds via a tax-free *bond mutual fund.* These funds are suitable for higher tax bracket investors who want an investment that pays a better return than a money market fund without the risk of the stock market. Bond funds are intended as longer-term investments (they offer daily liquidity but fluctuate in value).

Companies offering competitive yields on tax-free money market funds and bond funds are Vanguard (800-662-7447), USAA (800-531-8181), and Fidelity (800-544-8888). Fidelity's Spartan series funds generally require higher minimums to open ($10,000 or more versus the other firms' $3,000).

Invest in tax-friendly stock mutual funds

Too often, when selecting investments, people mistakenly focus on past rates of return. We all know that the past is no guarantee for the future. But an even worse mistake is choosing an investment with a reportedly high rate of return without considering tax consequences. Many people investing in stock mutual funds outside of retirement accounts make this mistake.

Numerous mutual funds effectively reduce their shareholders' returns because of their tendency to produce more taxable distributions (dividends and capital gains). Many mutual fund investors are affected by taxable distributions, because more than half the money in mutual funds resides outside tax-sheltered retirement accounts.

Historically, however, many mutual fund investors and publications have not compared the tax-friendliness of similar mutual funds. Just as you should avoid investing in funds with high sales commissions, high annual operating expenses, and poor relative performance, you should also avoid tax-unfriendly funds when investing outside of retirement accounts.

When comparing two similar funds, most people prefer a fund that averages returns equaling 14 percent per year rather than a fund earning 12 percent. But what if the 14-percent-per-year fund causes you to pay a lot more in taxes? What if, after factoring in taxes, the 14-percent-per-year fund nets just 9 percent, while the 12-percent-per-year fund nets an effective 10-percent return? In that case, you'd be unwise to choose a fund solely on the basis of the higher reported rate of return.

All stock mutual fund managers buy and sell stocks during the course of a year. Whenever a mutual fund manager sells securities, any gain or loss from those securities must be distributed, by year's end, to the fund shareholders. Securities sold at a loss can offset those liquidated at a profit. If a fund manager has a tendency to cash in more winners than losers, significant capital gains distributions can result.

What's a mutual fund?

Mutual funds are one of the best, if not *the* best, investment vehicles ever created. Why? Because good mutual funds take most of the hassle and cost out of figuring out which securities (stocks, bonds, and so on) to invest in. A mutual fund offers tremendous diversification because the fund managers typically invest in dozens of securities from companies in many different industries. Mutual funds allow you to have your money managed by the best money managers in the country — some of the same folks who manage money for the already rich and famous. And, mutual funds can help you meet many different financial goals.

Mutual funds, which you can purchase from the comfort of your own living room BarcaLounger, can pay you a better rate of return over the long haul than a dreary and boring bank or insurance company account. *No-load* (no commission) funds can be bought directly from the mutual fund company without a broker (and therefore without sales commissions). Fund operating fees, which are deducted from your returns, are quite reasonable at the larger and more successful fund companies. You can purchase great funds that charge from 0.2 to 1.0 percent (annually) of the amount you have invested. That amount works out to just $2 to $10 per year per $1,000 you invest through the fund.

Mutual funds, like all investments, carry their own unique risks that you need to be aware of before you leave the seemingly safe havens of banks and insurers. For example, funds that invest in stocks and bonds fluctuate in value along with overall changes in the stock and bond markets. If you don't know good funds or how to put together and manage a fund portfolio that meets your needs, pick up a copy of *Mutual Funds For Dummies,* 2nd Edition, by Eric Tyson (published by IDG Books Worldwide, Inc.).

Choosing mutual funds that minimize capital gains distributions, especially short-term capital gains distributions that are taxed at the higher ordinary income tax rates rather than the favored long-term capital gains rates we discuss earlier in this chapter, can help investors defer and minimize taxes on their profits. By allowing their capital to continue compounding, as it would in an IRA or other retirement account, fund shareholders receive a higher total return.

Long-term investors benefit the most from choosing mutual funds that minimize capital gains distributions. The more years that appreciation can compound in a mutual fund without being taxed, the greater the value to the fund investor. If you focus your stock fund investing inside retirement accounts, you need not worry about capital gains distributions. You can find the historic capital gains distribution information on a fund by examining its prospectus.

In addition to capital gains distributions, mutual funds produce *dividends* that are subject to normal income tax rates. Again, all things being equal, nonretirement account investors in high tax brackets should avoid funds that tend to pay a lot of dividends.

Investors who purchase mutual funds outside tax-sheltered retirement accounts should also consider the time of year they purchase shares in funds, in order to minimize the tax bite. Specifically, investors should try to purchase funds *after* rather than just before the fund makes the following types of distributions:

- **Capital gains distributions:** December is the most common month in which mutual funds make capital gains distributions. If making purchases late in the year, investors may want to find out whether and when the fund may make a significant capital gains distribution. Often, the unaware investor buys a mutual fund just prior to a distribution, only to see the value of the fund decline. But the investor must still pay income tax on the distribution. The December payout is generally larger when a fund has had a particularly good performance year.

✔ **Dividend distributions:** Many stock funds that pay reasonably high dividends tend to pay out dividends quarterly — typically on a March, June, September, December cycle. Try to avoid buying shares of these funds just before they pay. Make purchases early in each calendar quarter (early in the months of January, April, July, and October). Remember that the share price of the fund is reduced by the amount of the dividend and the dividend is taxable.

Don't get *too* concerned about *when* funds make distributions, because you can miss out on bigger profits by being so focused on avoiding a little bit of tax. If you want to be sure of the dates when a particular fund makes distributions, call the fund.

Mutual fund managers of actively managed portfolios, in their attempts to increase their shareholders' returns, buy and sell individual securities more frequently. However, this trading increases the chances of a fund needing to make significant capital gains distributions. *Index funds,* by contrast, are mutual funds that invest in a relatively fixed portfolio of securities. They don't attempt to beat the market averages or indexes. Rather, they invest in the securities to mirror or match the performance of an underlying index. Although index funds cannot beat the market, they have the following advantages over actively managed funds:

✔ Because index funds trade much less than actively managed funds, index fund investors benefit from lower brokerage commissions.

✔ Because significant ongoing research need not be conducted to identify companies in which to invest, index funds can be run with far lower operating expenses. All factors being equal, lower brokerage and operating costs translate into higher shareholder returns.

✔ Because index funds trade less, they tend to produce lower capital gains distributions. For mutual funds held outside of tax-sheltered retirement accounts, this reduced trading effectively increases an investor's total rate of return. Thus, index mutual funds are tax-friendlier.

The Vanguard Group (800-662-7447), headquartered in Valley Forge, Pennsylvania, is the largest mutual fund provider of index funds. Vanguard also offers a series of Tax-Managed mutual funds, which are index funds that seek to maintain even lower capital gains distributions. What makes Vanguard's Tax-Managed funds even more tax-friendly is that whenever its fund managers need to sell securities because of changes in the index or shareholder redemptions, the manager makes sure to offset capital gains by selling some securities with losses. The fund can achieve this result because the fund managers have the flexibility to temporarily deviate slightly from the underlying index.

Consider reinvesting and dollar-cost averaging

If you make small purchases in a particular nonretirement account investment over time, you increase your accounting complexity and tax-filing headaches. For example, if you buy shares in a mutual fund, you'll be asked if you want the dividends and capital gains paid out to you as cash or reinvested into buying more shares in the fund. Increasing numbers of individual companies allow you to reinvest dividends on individual stock holdings. These plans are known as *dividend reinvestment plans,* or DRIPs. Some discount brokers also offer this service for free for individual stocks.

If you're retired or need to live off your investment income, receiving cash payments probably works best. If you don't need the money, reinvesting dividends allows your money to continue compounding and growing in the investment. Although reinvesting complicates your tax situation because you're buying shares at different times at different prices, the benefits should outweigh the hassles. (But please take note: You still must pay current taxes on reinvested distributions in nonretirement accounts.)

Another investing approach is *dollar-cost averaging,* which can also cause tax headaches when you sell investments held outside of retirement accounts. Dollar-cost averaging simply means that you're investing your money in equal chunks on a regular basis, such as once a month. For example, if you have $60,000 to invest, you can choose to invest $2,000 per month until it's all invested, which takes a few years. The money that awaits future investment isn't lying fallow. You keep it in a money-market-type account, where it earns a bit of interest while it waits its turn.

The attraction of dollar-cost averaging is that it enables you to ease a large chunk of money into riskier investments instead of jumping in all at once. The possible benefit is that if the price of the investment drops after some of your initial purchases, you can buy more later at a lower price. If you had dumped all your money at once into an investment and then the value dropped like a stone, you'd kick yourself for not waiting.

The flip side of dollar-cost averaging is that if your investment of choice appreciates in value, you may wish that you had invested your money faster. Another possible drawback of dollar-cost averaging is that you may get cold feet as you continue to invest money in an investment that's dropping in value. Many people who are attracted to dollar-cost averaging (out of fear of buying before a price drop) may be scared to continue "boarding a sinking ship."

Dollar-cost averaging is most valuable when the money you want to invest represents a large portion of your total assets, and you can stick to a schedule. It's best to make your contributions automatic so that you're less likely to chicken out. If you aren't investing a lot of money, or the amount is a small portion of your total holdings, don't bother with dollar-cost averaging.

If you buy an investment via dollar-cost averaging or dividend reinvestment at many different times and prices, accounting is muddied as you sell blocks of the investment. Which shares are you selling: the ones you bought at a higher price, or the ones you bought at a lower price?

Determining whether tax-free funds pay more

As discussed earlier in this chapter, if you're in the federal 31-percent tax bracket, you will *usually* come out ahead in tax-free investments. If you're in the federal 28-percent tax bracket, you may or may not earn more in tax-free investments.

In order to do the comparison properly, factor in federal as well as state taxes. For example, suppose that you call Vanguard and the representative tells you that the Prime Portfolio money market fund currently yields 5.5 percent. The yield or dividend on this fund is fully taxable.

Further suppose that you're a resident of the great state of California — home to beautiful beaches and rumbling earthquakes — and that Vanguard's California money market fund currently yields 3.5 percent. The California tax-free money market fund pays dividends that are free from federal *and* California state tax. Thus, you get to keep all 3.5 percent that you earn. The income you

earn on the Prime Portfolio fund, on the other hand, is taxed.

So here's how you compare the two:

Yield on tax-free fund ÷ yield on taxable fund

.035 (3.5%) ÷ .055 (5.5%) = 0.64

In other words, the tax-free fund pays a yield of 64 percent of the yield of the taxable fund. Thus, if you must pay more than 36 percent (1.0 − 0.64) in federal and California state tax, you net more in the tax-free fund (see Chapter 1 for details on how to determine your federal and state tax rate).

If you do this analysis comparing some funds today, be aware that yields *do* change. The difference in yields between tax-free and taxable funds widens and narrows a bit over time.

For record-keeping purposes, save your statements detailing all the purchases in your accounts. Most mutual fund companies, for example, provide year-end summary statements that show all transactions throughout the year. Be sure to keep these statements. For purchases made in recent years and in the future, fund companies should also be able to tell you what your average cost per share was when you need to sell your shares.

Tax-Favored Investments to Avoid

Investment and insurance brokers and "financial planners" (who sell products, work on commission, and are therefore salespeople) love to pitch investment products that supposedly save you on your taxes. In all cases, you have better options available. Most of the time, the salesperson won't examine your entire financial situation. Therefore, the salesperson may sell you an inappropriate or lousy investment that pays (the salesperson!) hefty commissions. The following sections discuss the main investments these commission-driven folks try to sell you — along with the reasons why you shouldn't buy them.

Limited partnerships

Limited partnerships (LPs) sold through brokers and financial planners should be avoided at all costs. They are fundamentally inferior investment vehicles. That's not to say that no one has ever made money on one, but they are burdened with high sales commissions and ongoing management fees that deplete your investment. You can do better elsewhere.

Limited partnerships invest in real estate and a variety of businesses, such as cable television and cellular phone companies. They pitch that you can get in on the ground floor of a new investment opportunity and make big money. They also usually tell you that while your investment is growing at 20 percent or more per year, you get handsome dividends of 8 percent or so each year. Sound too good to be true? It is.

Many of the yields on LPs have turned out to be bogus. In some cases, partnerships have propped up their yields by paying back investors' original investment (principal) — without clearly telling them, of course. The other LP hook is the supposed tax benefit. The few loopholes that did exist in the tax code for LPs have largely been closed. (Amazingly, some investment salespeople hoodwink investors into putting their retirement account money — which is already tax-sheltered — into LPs!) The other problems with LPs overwhelm any small tax advantage, anyway.

The investment salesperson who sells you this type of investment stands to earn a commission of up to 10 percent or more — so only 90 cents, or less, of your dollar actually gets invested. Each year, LPs typically siphon off another few percentage points for management fees and other expenses. Most partnerships have little or no incentive to control costs. In fact, the pressure is to charge *more* in fees to enrich the managing partners.

Unlike with a mutual fund (which you can sell if it isn't performing), with LPs you can't vote with your dollars. If the partnership is poorly run and expensive, you're stuck. LPs are *illiquid.* You can't get your money out until the partnership is liquidated, typically seven to ten years after you buy in.

The only thing *limited* about a limited partnership is its ability to make you money. If you want to buy investments that earn profits and have growth potential, stick with stocks (preferably using mutual funds), bonds, real estate, or your own business.

Cash-value life insurance

Life insurance should *not* be used as an investment, especially if you haven't reached the maximum allowable limit for contributing money to retirement accounts. Agents love to sell cash-value life insurance for the high commissions they earn. Life insurance that combines life insurance protection with an account that has a cash value is usually known as *universal, whole,* or *variable life.*

It's true that the cash value portion of your policy grows without taxation until you withdraw it. But if you want tax-deferred retirement savings, you should *first* take advantage of retirement savings plans, such as 401(k)s, 403(b)s, SEP-IRAs, and Keoghs, which give you an immediate tax deduction for your current contributions. These accounts also allow your investments to grow and compound without taxation until withdrawal.

Money paid into a cash-value life insurance policy gives you no up-front tax breaks. If you've exhausted contributing to tax-deductible retirement accounts, you may find that a nondeductible IRA and then, possibly, variable annuities can provide tax-deferred compounding of your investment dollars (see Chapter 21). Some company retirement plans also allow you to make nondeductible contributions, the benefit of which is that your investment earnings compound without taxation over the years.

The only real financial advantage cash-value life insurance offers is that, with proper planning, the proceeds paid to your beneficiaries can be free of estate taxes. You need to have a fairly substantial estate at the time of your death to benefit from this feature. And numerous other, more cost-effective methods exist to minimize your estate taxes (see Chapter 26 for more details on estate planning).

Load mutual funds and the like

Load mutual funds aren't funds that send firearms with their marketing materials. *Load* simply means sales commission — and that means that up to 8.5 percent of your investment dollars are siphoned off to pay some broker a commission. Although mutual funds are good investment vehicles, you shouldn't have to pay a sales commission or load. Loads are additional and unnecessary costs that are deducted from your investment money. Load funds don't perform any better than no-load (commission-free) funds. Why should they? Commissions are paid to the salesperson, not to the fund manager.

Another problem with buying load funds is that you miss out on the opportunity to objectively assess whether you should buy a mutual fund at all. For example, maybe you should pay off debt or invest somewhere else. But salespeople almost never advise you to pay off your credit cards or mortgage, or to invest through your company's retirement plan instead of investing through them.

Salespeople who sell mutual funds usually push other stuff as well. Limited partnerships, life insurance, annuities, futures, and options hold the allure of big commissions. Salespeople tend to exaggerate the potential benefits and to obscure the risks and drawbacks of what they sell — they often don't take the time to educate investors.

✔ In addition to load mutual funds, you may be pitched to buy a *unit investment trust* or *closed-end fund.* For the most part, these funds are similar to other mutual funds, and they also pay brokers' commissions.

✔ Beware of brokers and financial planners selling bogus no-load funds, which are actually load funds that simply hide the sales commission.

You may be told something along the line that — as long as you stay in a fund for five to seven years — you won't have to pay the back-end sales charge that would apply upon sale of the investment. This claim may be true, but it's also true that these funds pay investment salespeople hefty commissions. The brokers are able to receive this commission because the fund company charges you high ongoing operating expenses (usually 1 percent more per year than the best funds). So one way or another, these salespeople get their pound of flesh (that is, their commissions) from your investment dollars.

Invest in no-loads and avoid load funds and investment salespeople. The only way to be sure that a fund is truly no-load is to look at the prospectus for the fund. Only in the prospectus, in black and white and without marketing hype, must the truth be told about sales charges and other fund fees. Never buy an investment without looking at its prospectus.

Annuities

Annuities are a peculiar type of insurance and investment product — sort of a savings-type account with slightly higher yields that are backed by insurance companies.

Insurance agents and financial planners working on commission happily sell annuities to anyone with money to invest. The problem is, annuities are suitable for a relatively small number of people with money to invest. If annuities do make sense for you, you can buy no-load (commission-free) annuities by bypassing salespeople and dealing directly with mutual fund companies.

The major selling hook of annuities is the supposed tax savings. "Why pay taxes each year on your investment earnings?" the agent or financial planner will say. As in other types of retirement accounts, money that's placed in an annuity compounds without taxation until withdrawal. However, unlike most other types of retirement accounts — 401(k)s, SEP-IRAs, and Keoghs — your contributions to an annuity give no up-front tax deductions. (Read Chapter 21 to find out more about retirement account options.) The only income tax benefit, as with cash-value life insurance, is that the earnings compound without tax until withdrawal. Thus it makes sense to consider contributing to an annuity only after you fully fund your tax-deductible retirement accounts.

Because annuities carry higher annual expenses due to the insurance that comes with them, they generally make sense only if you have many years to allow the money to compound. So annuities are *not* appropriate if you are already in retirement or near retirement. Also, the new lower tax rate on long-term capital gains (which we discuss earlier in this chapter) also makes investing money in annuities relatively less attractive than simply investing in tax-friendly nonretirement account holdings. All earnings on an annuity are taxed upon withdrawal at ordinary income tax rates whereas with a nonretirement account investment, much of your profits could be deferred into lower taxed long-term capital gains.

Under the old tax laws, many investors needed to keep money in an annuity at least 10 to 15 years for the benefits to outweigh the costs. Under the new law, add at least five more years to that time horizon so that the benefit of tax-deferred compounding outweighs an annuity's higher annual operating expenses and possibly higher income taxes upon withdrawal.

Selling Decisions

After you've owned a stock, bond, or mutual fund for a while, you may kick around the idea of selling some or all of it. Taxes should factor into the decision when you consider selling investments that you hold outside tax-sheltered retirement accounts. If the investments are inside retirement accounts, taxes aren't an issue because the accounts are sheltered from taxation (unless you're withdrawing funds from the accounts — see Chapter 21 for the details). In most cases, you need not waste your money or precious free time consulting a tax advisor. In the sections that follow, we outline the concepts that you should apply to your selling situation.

Selling selected shares

Before we get into specific types of investment decisions you're likely to confront, we must deal with a rather unpleasant but important issue: accounting methods for security sales. Although this stuff gets a little complicated, with some minimal advance planning, you can acquire sound methods to reduce your tax burden.

If you sell *all* the shares of a security that you own, you can ignore this issue. Only if you sell a portion of your shares of a security should you consider *specifying* which shares you're selling. Suppose that you own 200 shares of stock in Intergalactic Computer Software, and you plan to sell 100 shares. You bought 100 of these shares ten years ago at $50 per share, and then another 100 shares two years ago for $100 per share. Today, the stock is worth $150 per share. What a savvy investor you are!

Which 100 shares should you sell? The IRS gives you a choice, from a tax accounting standpoint. You can identify the *specific* shares that you sell. You may opt to sell the last or most recent 100 Intergalactic shares you bought, which would minimize your tax bill — because these shares were purchased at a higher price. At the time you want to sell the shares through your brokerage account, identify the shares you want to sell by noting the original date of purchase and/or cost of those shares. So in the case of your Intergalactic stock holdings, simply tell your broker that you wish to sell the 100 shares that you bought two years ago (give the date) at $100 per share. The broker should include this information on the confirmation slip you receive for the sale.

The other method of determining *which* shares you're selling is the method the IRS forces you to use if you don't specify *before* the sale which shares are to be sold — the *first-in-first-out* (FIFO) method. FIFO is not a dog with a funny name; it is an accounting term that means that the first shares you sell are the first shares that you bought. Not surprisingly, because most stocks appreciate over time, the FIFO method leads to paying more tax sooner. In the case of Intergalactic, FIFO means that the first 100 shares sold are the first 100 shares that you bought (the ones you bought ten years ago at the bargain basement price of $50 per share).

Although you'll save taxes today if you specify that you're selling the shares that you bought most recently, don't forget (and the IRS won't let you) that when you finally sell the other shares, you'll then owe taxes on the *larger* profit you realize from those shares. The longer you hold these shares, the greater the likelihood that their value will rise, realizing a larger profit for you (although you end up paying more taxes). Of course, the risk always exists that the IRS will raise tax rates in the future or that your particular tax rate will rise. If you sell some of your investment holdings, keep your life simple by considering selling all your shares of a specific security. That way, you don't have to hassle with all this accounting rigmarole for tax purposes.

In order to choose or *specify* which shares you are selling, you must select them before you sell. If you don't, the IRS says that you must use the FIFO method. You may wonder how the IRS knows whether you specified which shares before you sold them. The IRS doesn't know. But if you're audited, the IRS will ask for proof.

Selling securities with (large) capital gains

Of course, no one likes to pay taxes. But if an investment you own has appreciated in value, someday you will have to pay tax when you sell (unless you plan on passing the investment onto your heirs upon your death — see Chapter 26 on estate planning).

Capital gains tax applies when you sell a security at a higher price than you paid for it. As we explain earlier in this chapter, the capital gains rate is potentially lower than the tax rate you pay on ordinary income (such as from employment earnings or interest on bank savings accounts). Odds are, the longer you hold securities such as stocks, the greater the capital gains you'll accrue, because stocks tend to appreciate over time. Suppose that your parents bought you 1,000 shares of XYZ company stock ten years ago, when it was selling for $10 a share (your folks probably didn't, but let's pretend). Today, it's selling for $20 per share; but you also vaguely recall that the stock split two-for-one a few years ago, so now you own 2,000 shares. Thus, if you sell XYZ stock for $40,000 today, you'd have a capital gain of $30,000 on which to pay taxes. So why would anyone want to sell?

The answer depends on your situation. For example, if you need the money for some other purpose — buying a home, taking a year-long trip around the world — and the stock is your only source of funds, go for it. If you can't do what you want to do without selling, don't let the taxes stand in the way. Even if you pay state as well as federal taxes totaling some 35 percent of the profit, you'll have lots left over. Before you sell, however, do some rough figuring to make sure that you have enough to accomplish what you want.

What if you hold a number of stocks? In order to diversify and meet your other financial goals, all you have to do is prioritize. Give preference to selling your largest holdings (total market value) that have the smallest capital gains. If some of your securities have profits and some have losses, sell some of each to offset the profits with the losses. (Gains and losses on securities held one year or less are taxed at your ordinary income tax rates — see Chapter 12 for more details.)

Don't expect to obtain objective, disinterested tax-wise advice regarding what to do with your current investments from a stock broker or from most financial planners. If they earn commissions from the products they sell, their bias will be to tell you to sell. Even though some financial planners don't get commissions, they can't charge fees on what they aren't managing. If you need objective help with these "sell versus hold" decisions, turn to a competent tax or financial advisor who works on an hourly basis.

Selling securities at a loss

Perhaps you own some turkeys in your portfolio. If you need to raise cash for some particular reason, you may consider selling some securities at a loss. Don't hold on to an investment just because its value now is less than when you paid for it. Waiting until its value rises to what you originally paid is a natural, but silly, human desire. Selling a loser now frees up your money for better investments. Losses can also be used to offset gains (investments sold at a profit) — as long as both offsetting securities were held for more than 12 months (long-term) or both were held for 12 months or less (short-term). The IRS makes this delineation because long-term gains and losses are taxed on a different rate schedule than short-term gains and losses (see Chapter 12 for more information about capital gains).

Both short-term and long-term losses can be deducted against ordinary income, subject to limitations. If you want to sell securities at a loss, be advised that you can't claim more than $3,000 in short-term or long-term losses on your federal tax return in any one tax year. If you sell securities with losses totaling more than $3,000 in a year, the losses must be carried over to future tax years. This situation not only creates more tax paperwork, but also delays realizing the value of deducting a tax loss. So try not to have *net losses* (losses plus gains) that exceed $3,000 in a year.

Stock options and taxes

Some companies grant particular employees *stock options*. If you're the proud holder of this type of option, congratulations! You're either an important employee or work for a company that believes in sharing the success of its growth with its employees.

If you have stock options, sometimes known as *incentive stock options,* you face a number of important decisions that can have significant tax consequences. Basically, stock options grant you the right to buy shares of stock from your employer at a predetermined price. For example, suppose that you take a job with Wal-Mart and the company tells you that, after December 31, 1999, you may "exercise the right" to purchase 1,000 shares of its stock at $25 per share.

In the years ahead, you and other Wal-Mart employees help the company to continue growing and expanding. By the end of 1999, the Wal-Mart stock price has risen to $50 per share. Thus, because your options enable you to buy Wal-Mart stock for $25 per share and it's now at $50 per share, you have a profit on paper of $25,000 (1,000 shares × $25 profit per share)!

To realize this profit, you must first exercise your option (your company benefits department can tell you how). After you are the proud owner of the shares, you can sell them if you want to. However — and this is a big however — if you sell the shares within a year of having exercised the options, you will owe ordinary income tax on the profit. If you hold the shares for more than 12

months, then you will pay the lowest possible long-term capital gains tax, which may be a bit less. You may also be subject to the Alternative Minimum Tax (AMT). See Chapter 8 to find out more about this tax.

If you're a high-income earner, it's normally to your advantage to hold on to your exercised stock options for at least more than 12 months so that you qualify for the favorable capital gains tax treatment. The risk in waiting to sell is that your profits shrink as the stock price drops.

If you aren't a high-income earner and waiting to sell offers no tax advantage, selling your shares as the shares become exerciseable is usually prudent. It's somewhat dangerous to have too much of your wealth tied up in the stock of your employer. Remember, your *job* is already on the line if the company's success wanes.

Nonstatutory stock options are a bit different type of option. With these, you must pay tax on the options either when you receive them (if you can determine their fair market value) or when you exercise them. You must also pay income tax on the difference between the fair market value of the stock at the time you exercise the option *minus* the value of the option on which you pay tax. After you exercise the option, the decision on when to sell (and the tax consequences) is the same as for incentive stock options. If you don't know which type of option your employer offers, ask the benefits department.

Some tax advisors advocate doing *year-end tax-loss selling.* The logic goes that if you hold a security at a loss, you should sell it, take the tax write-off, and then buy it (or something similar) back. Sounds good in theory, but when you eventually sell the shares that you bought again at the lower price, you'll owe tax on the increased price anyway. (If you sold other stocks during the year at a profit, tax-loss selling to offset these taxable gains makes more sense.) But many people who sell an investment that has declined in value don't want to buy the same investment again. This reluctance can cause other investment blunders. For example, if you bought some stocks back in the summer of 1987, the first few months of ownership probably brought new meaning to the next season of the year: fall. Although your stocks probably plummeted 30 percent or more, it wasn't because of your poor stock-picking ability. You simply got caught in the U.S. stock market downdraft. You'll make a bad situation worse by panicking and selling at reduced price levels just to take a tax loss. If anything, consider doing the opposite — take advantage of the sale and buy more!

If you do decide to sell for tax-loss purposes, be careful of the so-called *wash sale* rules. The IRS doesn't allow deduction of a loss for a security that you sell if you buy that same security back within 30 days. As long as you wait 31 or more days, no problem. If you're selling a mutual fund, you can easily sidestep this rule simply by purchasing a fund similar to the one you're selling.

Mutual funds and the average cost method

In America, you never have a shortage of choices — so why shouldn't it be the same with accounting methods? When you sell shares in a mutual fund (this information doesn't apply to money market funds, which don't fluctuate in value), the IRS allows you an additional method — the *average cost method* — for determining your profit or loss for tax purposes.

If you bought shares in chunks over time and/or reinvested the fund distributions (such as from dividends) into more shares of the fund, tracking and figuring what shares you're selling can be a real headache. So the IRS allows you to take an average cost for all the shares you bought over time.

Be aware that after you elect the average cost method, you can't change to another method for the remaining shares. If you plan to sell only some of your fund shares, and it would be advantageous for you to specify that you're selling the newer shares first, choose that method (as we describe in the "Selling selected shares" section, earlier in this chapter).

If you own a security that has ceased trading and appears worthless (or even if you've made a loan that hasn't been repaid — even if to a friend), you can probably deduct this loss. See Chapter 12 for more information on what situations are deductible and how to claim these losses on your annual tax return.

Selling securities whose costs are unknown

When you sell a security or a mutual fund that you've owned for a long time (or that your parents gave you), you may not have any idea what the security originally cost (also known as its *cost basis*). If you could only find the original account statement that shows the original purchase price and amount. . . .

If you can't find that original statement, start by calling the firm where you purchased the investment. Whether it's a brokerage firm or mutual fund company, they should be able to send you copies of old account statements. You may have to pay a small fee for this service. Also, increasing numbers of investment firms (particularly mutual fund companies) automatically calculate and report cost basis information on investments that you sell through them. The cost basis they calculate is generally the average cost for the shares that you purchased. See Chapter 3 for more ideas on what to do when original records aren't available.

Chapter 24
Real Estate and Taxes

. . . .

In This Chapter

▶ Home ownership tax breaks

▶ The home buying decision and taxes

▶ Mortgage quandaries

▶ Strategies for keeping the IRS at bay when selling your house

▶ Tax considerations when investing in real estate

. . . .

Tax benefits are a significant reason why many people, especially people in the real estate business — such as real estate agents, bankers, mortgage brokers, and others in the lending business — engage in plugfests for property ownership.

Buying a home or investing in real estate *can* provide financial and psychological rewards. And tax breaks can help reduce the cost of owning real estate. On the other hand, purchasing and maintaining property can also be time-consuming, emotionally draining, and financially painful.

Don't make the mistake of looking at someone's property that's worth $200,000 today (bought 20 years ago for $40,000) and assume that real estate investment, and the tax benefits it offers, is the inside track to wealth creation. Consider the expenditures the owner likely made over the years, such as fixing plumbing and electrical problems, updating appliances, replacing the roof, and repainting. And then consider the annual carrying costs — the interest alone over the life of the mortgage can total more than the original purchase price of the property! Of course, when you buy and sell real estate, you have transaction costs, such as real estate broker's commissions, loan fees, and title insurance. Also, don't forget that $40,000 sounds cheap, but 20 years ago when the cost of living was much lower, 40 grand actually bought a great deal.

Don't get us wrong — we aren't saying that real estate isn't a good investment. Over the long-term, real estate, like stocks, is generally a good investment. However, we don't want you to mistakenly assume that real estate is a better investment than what it really is.

Real Estate Tax Breaks

Just as contributing money to retirement accounts (refer to Chapter 21) yields tax breaks, so does buying a home and investing in other real estate. Our tax system favors property ownership because of the widely held belief that owners take better care of their property when they have a financial stake in its future value. Arguing with this logic is difficult if you have visited almost any government-subsidized tenement.

All the powerful real estate lobbies also contribute to the addition and retention of real estate tax benefits in our tax code. Builders, contractors, real estate agents, the banking industry, and many other real-estate-related sectors have an enormous financial stake in the American hunger to own and improve properties.

You should understand the tax aspects of home ownership and investing in other real estate so that you can make the most of these tax-reduction opportunities. Making wise real estate moves requires that you also know how to fit real estate decisions into your overall financial picture. After all, you have limited income and other options on which to spend your money.

Don't make the mistake of depending on those involved in the typical real estate deal to help you see the bigger picture. Remember that these folks make their livings off your decision to buy real estate, and the more you spend, the more they make.

We know that you can't wait to uncover the real estate tax breaks that are available for the taking. But before we get to them, we kindly ask that you never forget two important caveats to gaining these property tax advantages:

✔ You have to *spend* money on real estate — acquiring property, paying the mortgage and property taxes over the years, and improving the property while you own it — to even be eligible for the tax breaks. As you see in this chapter, if you earn a high enough income or make the wrong financial moves, you may not be able to claim some of the real estate tax benefits available.

✔ Always remember that you aren't the only one who knows that the U.S. tax code offers these real estate tax breaks. What difference does that make? Remember that the price of real estate in the United States reflects the fact that buyers and sellers know about the tax deductions. This is a major reason why so many people are willing to pay sums with many zeroes for a piece of the American Dream. Other countries that don't offer tax breaks for home ownership, such as Canada, have comparatively lower prices, because buyers can't afford to pay higher prices when they can't bank on a tax deduction to help subsidize the cost.

The following sections offer an overview of the tax goodies available to homeowners in the United States. The benefits are similar to, but different from, the tax benefits for rental or income property owners, which are discussed later in this chapter.

Mortgage interest and property tax write-offs

When you buy a home, you can claim two big ongoing expenses of home ownership as tax deductions on Schedule A of Form 1040. These expenses consist of your property taxes and the interest on your mortgage.

You're allowed to claim mortgage-interest deductions on a primary residence (where you actually live) and on a second home for mortgage debt totaling $1,000,000. You're also allowed to deduct the interest on a home equity loan of up to $100,000 (see Chapter 9).

Property taxes are also fully deductible on Schedule A, whether you purchase a $15,000 one-room shack in an unpopulated rural area without electricity or a multimillion-dollar mansion on several acres overlooking the ocean.

Home office deductions

When you run your business out of your home, you may be able to take additional tax deductions beyond the mortgage interest and property taxes you already claim as a homeowner. Refer to "Home alone, or outside office space?" in Chapter 22 for a discussion of this issue.

What if politicians took away real estate tax breaks?

If the folks in Washington, who make and forever change our tax laws, yanked away the current tax goodies for real estate, the result would be a depressing effect on U.S. property values. There's not much argument about this outcome. By removing real estate's tax breaks, politicians would effectively raise the cost of property ownership.

In recent years, there's been a movement afoot for "tax reform." Some of the proposals on the table would disallow several of the tax deductions currently allowed for real estate. This is not the first time these ideas have been discussed, and it surely won't be the last.

But it's highly unlikely that politicians will take away home-ownership tax breaks. Property owners, who make up the majority of voters, would likely bounce the offenders out of office, and real estate lobbyists are also a powerful force to reckon with.

Capital gains exclusion

Normally, when you make an investment in a stock or business, for example, and you later sell it for a profit (also known as a *capital gain*), you owe tax on the profit. Some real estate, however, receives special treatment in this regard.

Under the 1997 capital gains tax changes pertaining to the sale of a primary residence, the amount of profit from a house sale that can be excluded from tax has been increased significantly: up to $250,000 for single taxpayers and up to $500,000 for couples filing jointly. Moreover, to take advantage of this tax break — unlike under the old house-sale rules — house sellers need not be over a particular age or buy a replacement residence of equal or greater value to the one just sold.

So, if you're longing to move to a less costly housing market, you're largely free of tax constraints to do so. This new provision also benefits empty nesters and others nearing or in retirement, who want to buy a less costly home and free up some of their home equity to use toward retirement.

If you want to sell appreciated rental property, the new house-sale rules may benefit you as well. How? By moving into a rental property and making it your primary residence for at least two years, you can shield the property's profits from taxation. (Obviously, this strategy is only feasible for certain types of properties that you would be willing/able to live in. Also, it doesn't apply to appreciation you take after May 7, 1997 — see Chapter 12.)

If you move from your house, rent it out for a period of time, and then sell it, the IRS may consider that you have converted your home from a primary residence to a rental property. Thus, you may lose the privilege of excluding tax on the profit from the sale. The only exception: You actively tried to sell the house after you moved and only rented it temporarily to help defray the costs of keeping it until you sold it.

Purchasing Your Own Pad

It really doesn't matter why you're thinking of buying a home. This type of decision is seldom motivated by financial considerations alone. Whether your five-story walkup has lost its Bohemian appeal or you can't get the paint stains off the kitchen floor, that's a good enough reason to buy a home.

Dealing with "excess" housing profits

Although the new house-sale laws benefit many, the law does have a negative twist. If you live in an area with inexpensive real estate, you may find this difficult to believe: Some longer-term homeowners, especially in the higher-cost sections of the country, may have profits in excess of the new law's limits ($250,000 for singles and $500,000 for couples).

For those in that admittedly enviable position, the new law offers no escape hatch. At the time of sale, single homeowners with accumulated profits (which also include those profits rolled over, under the old tax laws, from previous sales) greater than $250,000 and couples with profits greater than $500,000 must pay capital gains tax on the excess.

When they start to bump up against the maximum amounts that can be shielded from capital gains taxation, long-term homeowners and those buying expensive homes may want to consider selling and moving, even if it's within the same neighborhood.

Those whose homes have appreciated well in excess of the limits may want to consider, if possible, holding their homes until their deaths, at which point, under current tax laws, the IRS wipes the capital gains slate clean.

Also keep in mind that although relatively few homeowners today have housing profits in excess of these seemingly high limits, the limits are fixed and aren't scheduled to increase with inflation. Thus, in the years ahead, increasing numbers of homeowners will be affected by the limits.

Financially speaking, you really shouldn't buy your own place unless you anticipate being there for at least three years, and preferably five years or more. Many expenses accompany buying and selling a property, such as the cost of getting a mortgage (points, application and credit report fees, and appraisal fees), inspection expenses, moving costs, real estate agents' commissions, and title insurance. And remember — most of these expenses are *not* tax-deductible; at best, they can only be added to your home's tax basis. To cover these transaction costs plus the additional costs of ownership, a property needs to appreciate a fair amount before you can be as well off financially as if you had continued renting. A property needs to appreciate about 15 percent just to offset these expenses, even factoring in the tax benefits that homeowners enjoy.

If you need or want to move in a couple of years, counting on that kind of appreciation is risky. If you're lucky (that is, if you happen to buy before a sharp upturn in housing prices), you may get it. If you aren't, you'll probably lose money on the deal.

Some people are willing to buy a home even when they don't expect to live in it for long because they plan on turning it into a rental when it's time to move on. Holding rental property can be a good long-term investment, but don't underestimate the responsibilities that come with rental property. (Rent the movie *Pacific Heights* and talk to friends and colleagues who have been landlords.)

Renting's okay; you're okay if you rent

Don't believe that you aren't a success if you aren't a homeowner. And as we discuss earlier in this chapter, don't feel pressured to buy a home because of the tax breaks or because that's what everyone else is doing. Remember that the value of those tax breaks is reflected in the higher U.S. home prices versus the lower home prices in other countries where real estate owners don't get tax deductions.

House losses aren't deductible

Some homeowners have learned firsthand in the past generation that real estate prices go down as well as up.

If it's time for you to sell your house and move on, you may be disappointed to learn that you can't deduct the loss if your house sells for less than you bought it. If you lose money investing in the stock market, on the other hand, these losses are usually deductible (refer to Chapter 23). Although you may feel it's unfair that home ownership losses are not tax-deductible, don't forget that you're already getting many other tax perks from your home. You get to deduct mortgage interest and property taxes.

Some financially successful long-term renters include people who pay low rent — either because they've made sacrifices to live in a smaller rental, for example, or live in a rent-controlled building. One advantage of low rental costs is that you may be able to save more money. If you can consistently save ten percent or more of your earnings, you will probably meet your future financial goals, house or no house.

Another advantage of being a long-term renter is that you won't have a great deal of money tied up in your home. Many homeowners enter their retirement years with a substantial portion of their wealth in their homes. As a renter, you can have all your money in financial assets that you can probably tap into far more easily.

Some renters are tempted to invest in a property elsewhere and rent it to others or use it when they want. Make sure that you read the sections later in this chapter that discuss investment property and second homes. This decision is neither straightforward nor simple.

Exploring the tax savings in home ownership

To quickly determine your monthly tax savings from home ownership, try this simple shortcut: Multiply your marginal federal tax rate (discussed in Chapter 1) by the total monthly amount of your property taxes and mortgage. (Technically, not all your mortgage payment is tax-deductible; only the portion of the mortgage payment that goes to interest is tax-deductible. However, in the early years of your mortgage, the portion that goes toward interest is nearly all the payment. On the other hand, your property taxes will probably rise over time, and you can also earn state tax benefits from your deductible mortgage interest and property taxes.)

To figure out more precisely how home ownership may affect your tax situation, try plugging some reasonable numbers into your tax return to *guesstimate* how your taxes may change. You can also speak with a tax advisor.

When you buy a home, make sure that you refigure how much you're paying in income tax, because your mortgage interest and property tax deductions should help lower your tax bill. Many home buyers skip this step, and they end up getting a big tax refund the next year. Although getting money back from the IRS may feel good, it means that at a minimum, you made an interest-free loan to the IRS. In the worst case, the reduced cash flow during the year may cause you to accumulate debt or miss out on contributing to tax-deductible retirement accounts. If you work for an employer, ask your payroll/benefits department for **Form W-4** (see Chapter 15 for information about how to fill this out). If you're self-employed, you can complete a worksheet that comes with **Form 1040-ES** (see the back of this book for a copy, and turn to Chapter 15 for help filling it out).

Keep track of your tax bracket

When you first consider purchasing a home or purchasing a more expensive home, it usually pays to plan ahead and push as many so-called itemizable deductions as you can into the tax year in which you expect to buy your home.

For example, suppose that this year you're using the standard deduction because you don't have many itemized deductions. You decide late in the year that you'll probably buy a home in the coming year. Because you'll have mortgage interest and property taxes to write off, you'll probably be able to itemize next year. It makes sense, then, to collect as many deductible expenses as possible and shift them into next year. For example, if the solicitations surrounding the December holidays prompt you to contribute to charities, you can wait until January to donate. Take a look at the deductible items on Schedule A (discussed in Chapter 9) to determine what else you may want to postpone paying.

Also, be aware that your income tax bracket may change from year to year. Thus, when possible, you can choose to pay more or less of some itemizable expenses in one year versus another. Suppose that you receive your annual property tax bill in the fall of the year, and it's payable in two installments. You must pay one installment before the end of the year, whereas you have until the next spring to pay the other installment. If for some reason you expect to be in a lower tax bracket next year — perhaps you're going to take a sabbatical and will earn less income — you may choose to pay the entire property tax bill before the current year ends. In this case, the property tax deduction has greater value to you in the current year because you're in a higher tax bracket.

Be sure to read Chapter 1, which explains how to figure your current and future expected tax bracket for planning purposes to minimize your taxes.

Deciding how much to spend on a home

If you fall in love with a home and buy it without looking at your monthly expenditures and long-term goals, you may end up with a home that dictates much of your future spending. Real estate agents and mortgage lenders are more than happy to tell you the maximum that you are qualified to borrow. They want your business, and the more money you spend, the more they make. But that doesn't mean that you should borrow the maximum.

Typical is the advice of this real estate broker who also happens to write about real estate:

"The first step is to find out what price you can afford to buy. The easiest way to do this is to make an appointment with a loan agent or a mortgage broker."

Easy, yes. Will this get you the right answer? Probably not. Like real estate agents, mortgage brokers tell you the maximum loan you can qualify for. This amount is not necessarily what you can "afford." Remember, mortgage and loan agents get a commission based on the size of your loan. It isn't part of their job description (nor generally their expertise) to take into consideration what your other financial goals and needs are, such as saving for retirement.

In addition to analyzing your retirement planning, other questions you should ask yourself before you buy may include whether you spend (and want to continue spending) on fun stuff, such as travel and entertainment. If you want to continue your current lifestyle (and the expenditures inherent in it), be honest with yourself about how much you can really afford to spend as a homeowner.

Often, first-time home buyers are apt to run into financial trouble because they don't know their spending needs and priorities and don't know how to budget for them. Buying a home can be a wise decision, but it can also be a huge burden. Some people don't decrease their spending as much as they should based on the large amount of debt they just incurred. In fact, many homeowners often spend even more on all sorts of gadgets and furnishings for their homes. Many people prop up their spending habits with credit. For this reason, a surprisingly large percentage of people — some studies say about half — who borrow additional money against their home equity use the funds to pay other debts.

Don't let your home control your financial future. Take stock of your overall financial health — especially in terms of retirement planning if you hope to retire by your mid-60s — *before* you buy property or agree to a particular mortgage.

Tracking what you spend on your home

Although it may be a bit of a hassle, it's in your best interest to document and track when you spend money improving your property. For tax purposes, you can add the cost of these improvements to your original purchase price for the home. So, when you someday sell the property, you get to reduce your profit, for tax purposes, accordingly. Keep in mind that under the new tax laws, most people won't owe capital gains tax from the sale of a house. Single people can make a $250,000 profit, and married couples filing jointly can receive $500,000 in profit without paying tax on the proceeds of the sale. However, you should still track your home improvement expenditures because it's impossible to know while you're living in your home if your future sale, which could be many years off, could trigger capital gains tax. Who knows how much real estate will appreciate in the interim or what changes could happen to the tax laws.

When you sell your house, you'll need to report to the IRS, on **Schedule D, Capital Gains and Losses,** the selling price of the house and how much you spent improving it. Therefore, we strongly advise setting up a simple file folder, perhaps labeled "home improvements," into which you deposit receipts for your expenditures.

The challenging part for most people is simply keeping the receipts separate. Another challenge is to correctly distinguish between spending on *improvements,* which the IRS allows you to add to your cost of the home, and spending for *maintenance and repairs,* which you can't add to the original purchase price of the home.

Improvements include expenses such as installing an alarm system, adding or remodeling a room, planting new trees and shrubs in your yard, and purchasing new appliances. These improvements increase the value of your home and lengthen its life. Maintenance and repairs include expenses such as the cost of hiring a plumber to fix a leaky pipe, repainting, repairing a door so that it properly closes, and recaulking around your bathtub to prevent leaks.

It's interesting to note that if you hire a contractor to do the home improvements, the IRS allows you to effectively add the cost of the contractor's time (the labor charges) into the overall improvements that reduce your home's profit for tax purposes. On the other hand, if you elect to do the work yourself, you gain no tax benefit for your sweat. You cannot add in a cost for the value of your time — the IRS assumes that your time isn't worth anything — you work for free! Now you may have another reason to hire someone to do the work for you.

Also, don't forget to toss into your receipt folder the *settlement statement*, which you should have received in the blizzard of paperwork you signed and received when you bought your home. Don't lose this! This valuable piece of paper itemizes many of the expenses associated with the purchase of your home. You can add many of these expenses to the original cost of the home and reduce your taxable profit when it comes time to sell. Also keep proof of other expenditures that the settlement statement may not document, such as inspection fees that you paid when buying your home.

Tread carefully if you purchase a vacation home

Part of the allure of a second or vacation home is the supposed tax and financial benefits. Even when you qualify for some or all of them, tax benefits only partially reduce the cost of owning a property. We've seen more than a few cases in which the second home is such a cash drain that it prevents its owners from contributing to and taking advantage of tax-deductible retirement savings plans.

If you can realistically afford the additional costs of a second home, we aren't going to tell you how to spend your extra cash. But please don't make the all-too-common mistake of viewing a second home as an investment. The way most people use them, they aren't.

Investment real estate is property that you rent out. Most multiple homeowners rent their property out very little — ten percent or less of the time. As a result, second homes are usually money pits.

If you don't rent out a second home property most of the time, ask yourself whether you can afford such a luxury. Can you accomplish your other financial goals — saving for retirement, paying for your primary residence, and so on — with this added expense? Keeping a second home is more of a consumption than an investment decision if you don't rent it out. Most people can't afford this extraordinary luxury.

Also, be aware that if your vacation home appreciates in value, the IRS doesn't allow you to sell this type of home without taxation of your capital gains, as they do with primary residences (see the discussion earlier in this chapter).

Reporting revenue if you rent a room

The IRS allows you to rent your home or a room in your home for up to 14 days each year without having to declare the rental income and pay income taxes on it. Rental of your home or a portion thereof for more than 14 days requires that you report the income when you file your annual tax return. You can declare rental income by filing Schedule E. (Refer to Chapter 13 for more information.)

Tax-Wise Mortgage Decisions

The largest expense of property ownership is almost always the monthly mortgage payment. In the earlier years of a mortgage, the bulk of the mortgage payment covers interest that is generally tax-deductible. In this section, we discuss some important mortgage decisions and how to factor taxes, and your financial circumstances, into making intelligent decisions.

15-year or 30-year mortgage?

There are, unfortunately, thousands of mortgage options. Fixed-rate and variable-rate mortgages come with all sorts of bells and whistles. The number of permutations is mind-numbing.

From a tax perspective, one of the most important mortgage selection issues is whether to take a 15-year or 30-year mortgage. To afford the monthly payments, most home buyers need to spread the loan payments over a longer period of time, and a 30-year mortgage is the only option. A 15-year mortgage requires higher monthly payments because you pay it off more quickly.

Even if you can afford these higher payments, taking the 15-year option may not be wise. The money for making extra payments doesn't come out of thin air. You may have better uses for your excess funds. What you're really asking, if you're considering whether you should take a 30-year or a 15-year mortgage, is whether you should pay off your mortgage slowly or quickly. And the answer isn't as simple as you may think.

First, think about *alternative uses* for the extra money you're throwing into the mortgage payments. What's best for you depends on your overall financial situation and what else you can do with the money. If you elect the slow, 30-year mortgage payoff approach, and you blow the extra money on a new car, for example, you're better off paying down the mortgage more quickly. In that case, take the 15-year version. (If you need to buy a car in the future, saving in a money market fund so that you don't need to take out a high-cost car loan makes sound financial sense.)

But suppose that you aren't so frivolous with your extra money. What if you take the extra $100 or $200 per month and contribute it to a retirement account instead. That step may make financial sense. Why? Because additions to 401(k)s, SEP-IRAs, Keoghs, and other types of retirement accounts are tax deductible (refer to Chapter 21).

If you dump that $200 into a retirement account, you get to subtract that $200 from the income on which you pay taxes. If you're paying 35 percent in federal and state income taxes, you shave $70 (that's $200 multiplied by 35 percent) off your tax bill. (You're going to pay taxes when you withdraw the money from the retirement account someday. In the meantime, the money that would have gone to taxes is growing on your behalf.) If you elect a faster payoff mortgage (15-year mortgage), when you add that $200 more to your mortgage payment, you get *no* tax benefits.

With kids, you have an even greater reason to fund your retirement accounts before you consider paying down your mortgage at a faster rate. Under current rules for determining financial aid for college expenses, money in your retirement accounts is not counted as an asset (see Chapter 25).

If you're uncomfortable investing and would otherwise leave the extra money sitting in a money market fund or savings account, or worse, if you would spend it, you're better off paying down the mortgage. Take the 15-year approach. If the investments in your retirement account plummet in value, the impact of the tax-deferred compounding of your capital may be negated. Paying off your mortgage quicker, on the other hand, is just like investing your money in a sure thing — but with a modest rate of return.

In most cases, you get to deduct your mortgage interest on your tax return. So if you're paying 8-percent interest, it really may cost you only around 5 to 6 percent after you factor in the tax benefits. If you think that you can do better by investing elsewhere, go for it. Remember, though, that you owe income tax from profits on your investments held outside of retirement accounts. You aren't going to get decent investment returns unless you're willing to take risks. Investments such as stocks and real estate have generated better returns over the long haul. These investments carry risks, though, and are not guaranteed to produce any return.

If you *don't* have a burning investment option, it's usually wise to pay down your mortgage as your cash flow allows. If you have extra cash and have contributed the maximum allowed for retirement accounts, you may want to invest in real estate or perhaps a business. You have to decide whether it is worth the extra risk to make a particular investment instead of paying down your mortgage.

How large a down payment?

What if you're in the enviable and fortunate position of having so much money that you can afford to put down more than a 20-percent down payment? Perhaps you're one of those wise people who don't want to get stretched too thin financially, and you're buying a less expensive home than you can afford. How much should you put down?

Some people, particularly those in the real estate business (and even some tax and financial advisors), say that you should take as large a mortgage as you can for the tax deductions — that is, don't make a larger down payment than you have to. This is silly reasoning. Remember, you have to pay out money in interest charges to *get* the tax deductions.

Again, what makes sense for you depends on your alternative uses for the money. If you're considering other investment opportunities, determine whether you can expect to earn a higher rate of return than the interest rate you'll pay on the mortgage.

During this century, stock market and real estate investors have enjoyed average annual returns of around 10 percent per year (just remember the past doesn't guarantee the future). So if you borrow mortgage money at around 8 percent today, you may come out ahead by investing in these areas. Besides possibly generating a higher rate of return, other real estate and stock investing can help you diversify your investments, which is always good.

Of course, you have no guarantee that you can earn 10 percent each year. And don't forget that all investments come with risk. The advantage of putting more money down for a home and borrowing less is that paying down a mortgage is essentially a risk-free investment (as long as you have emergency money you can tap).

If you prefer to limit the down payment to 20 percent and invest more elsewhere, that's fine. Just don't keep the extra money (beyond an emergency reserve) under the mattress, in a savings account, or in bonds that provide returns lower than the mortgage is costing you.

Should I take out a home equity loan?

This special type of mortgage loan allows you to borrow against your home in addition to the mortgage you already have (a first mortgage). The allure of home equity loans today is simple. Borrowing against real estate is relatively low-cost and (usually) tax deductible to boot. Generally, the interest on a home equity loan of up to $100,000 is tax deductible (refer to Chapter 9).

The problem, however, with home equity loans is that they allow, and even encourage, people to overspend. It's no wonder that many people have them (and, in some cases, for frivolous reasons), because they can be as easy to use as credit cards — you can access some home equity loans simply by writing a check to pay for vacations, new living room furniture, and other things. Borrowing against your home makes financial sense in some cases — for example, when you decide to build an addition to your home instead of selling the house to buy a larger one. The question then becomes should you take out a second mortgage or refinance the first one?

Taking out a second mortgage is usually an inferior option for a long-term loan. Second mortgages or home equity loans have higher interest rates than comparable first mortgages. They're also riskier from a lender's perspective, because the primary mortgage lender gets first dibs if you file bankruptcy or the property ends up in foreclosure.

A home equity loan may be beneficial if you need more money for just a few years or if your first mortgage is at such a low interest rate that refinancing to get more cash would be as costly — otherwise, avoid home equity loans.

Refinancing decisions and taxes

If your loan has a higher rate of interest than loans currently available, you may save money by refinancing. To save money by refinancing a mortgage, you have to spend money and time. So you need to crunch a few numbers, and factor taxes in, to determine whether refinancing makes sense for you.

Because refinancing almost always costs money, it's a bit of a gamble whether you can save enough to justify the cost. Ask your mortgage lender or broker how soon you can recoup the refinancing costs, such as appraisal expenses, loan fees and points, title insurance, and so on.

For example, if the refinance costs you $2,000 to complete and reduces your monthly payment by $100, the lender or broker typically says that you can save back the refinance costs in 20 months. This prediction isn't accurate, however, because you lose some tax write-offs if your mortgage interest rate and payments are reduced. You can't simply look at the reduced amount of your monthly payment (mortgage lenders like to look at that reduction, however, because it makes refinancing more attractive).

If you want a better estimate but don't want to spend hours crunching numbers, take your tax rate as specified in Chapter 1 (for example, 28 percent) and reduce your monthly payment savings on the refinance by this amount. If your monthly payment drops by $100, you *really* save only around $72 a month after factoring in the lost tax benefits. So you recoup the refinance costs in 28 months ($2,000 of refinance costs divided by $72) — not 20 months.

If you can recover the costs of the refinance within a few years or less, go for it. If it takes longer, refinancing may still make sense if you anticipate keeping the property and mortgage that long. If you estimate that you need more than five to seven years to break even, refinancing is probably too risky to justify the costs and hassles.

When you refinance, don't forget to change the amount of tax you pay during the year. See the section "Exploring the tax savings in home ownership," earlier in this chapter, for more information on how to change your tax withholding.

Besides getting a lower interest rate loan, another reason people refinance is to pull out cash from the house for some other purpose. This strategy can make good financial sense, because under most circumstances, mortgage interest is tax deductible. If you're starting a business or buying other real estate, you can usually borrow against your home at a lower cost than on a business or rental property loan. (If you are a high-income earner, you may lose some of the tax deductibility of your home mortgage interest deductions — refer to the limitations on itemized deductions as explained in Chapter 9.)

If you've run up high-interest consumer debt, you may be able to refinance your mortgage and pull out extra cash to pay off your credit cards, auto loans, or other costly credit lines, thus saving yourself money. You can usually borrow at a lower interest rate for a mortgage and get a tax deduction as a bonus, which lowers the effective borrowing cost further. Consumer debt, such as auto loans and credit cards, is not tax deductible.

Borrowing against the equity in your home can be addictive. An appreciating home creates the illusion that excess spending isn't really costing you. Remember that debt is debt, and you have to repay all borrowed money. In the long run, you wind up with greater mortgage debt, and paying it off takes a bigger bite out of your monthly income. Refinancing and establishing home-equity lines also costs you more in loan application fees and other charges (points, appraisals, credit reports, and so on).

Selling Your House

As discussed earlier in this chapter, a homeowner can realize large profits (capital gains) when selling his house. Whenever you sell a house, you must file **Schedule D, Capital Gains and Losses,** with Form 1040 from the same tax year in which you sell your house. However, neither you nor the IRS receive **Form 1099-S** from the firm handling the sale of your house unless the gross sale price exceeds $500,000 (for married couples) or $250,000 for an unmarried seller.

Here are some common concerns affecting house sales that have important tax angles.

Not wanting to sell at a loss

Many homeowners are tempted to hold on to their properties when they need to move if the property is worth less than when they bought it or if the real estate market is soft, especially because the loss isn't tax-deductible. We don't recommend this strategy. It probably isn't worth the hassle of renting out your property or the financial gamble to hold on to the property.

You may reason that in a few years, the real estate storm clouds will clear, and you can sell your property at a higher price. Here are three risks associated with this way of thinking:

- ✔ First, you can't know what's going to happen to property prices in the next few years. They may rebound, but they can also stay the same or drop even further. *A property generally needs to appreciate at least a few percentage points each year just to make up for all the costs of holding and maintaining it.* So, in every additional year you hold the property that it doesn't appreciate at least a few percentage points, you're losing more money.

- ✔ If you haven't been a landlord, don't underestimate the hassle and headaches associated with the job. Being a long-distance landlord is even more of a challenge. You can always hire someone to manage your property, but that approach creates costs, too — usually about 6 percent of the monthly rental income.

- ✔ After you convert your home into a rental property, you need to pay capital gains tax on your profit when you sell (the only exception is if you temporarily rent your home while you're still actively trying to sell it). This tax wipes out much of the advantage of having held on to the property until prices recovered. (If you want to be a long-term rental property owner, you can, under current tax laws, do a *tax-free exchange* into another rental property after you sell.)

We understand that it's not much fun to sell a house that hasn't made you any money. But too many homeowners make a bad situation worse by holding on to their homes for the wrong reasons after they move. No one wants to believe that they're losing money. But the money is already lost. Many people who hold on rub salt into their real estate wounds. If and when the value of the property you're waiting to sell finally increases, odds are other properties you'd next buy will have increased as well. Unless you'll have no down payment to buy your next home, or you want to keep such a property as a long-term investment, holding on to a home you move from is usually not wise.

House sales, taxes, and divorce?

A divorce complicates many personal and financial issues. Real estate is no different. In the past, if ownership of a home that has appreciated in value were transferred between spouses because of a divorce, capital gains tax was owed. Fortunately, this is no longer one of the additional costs of divorce. Transfers of property between spouses aren't taxed if the transfers are made within one year of divorce (and both spouses are U.S. residents or citizens).

If you're selling your house because of a divorce, *when* you sell the house can have significant tax ramifications. If you agree to sell the house in the divorce settlement, you can each make up to $250,000 in profit before any tax is levied.

Wanting to convert a home into rental property

One advantage to keeping your current home as an investment property after you move is that you already own it. Locating and buying a property takes time and money. Also, you know what you have with your current home. If you go out and purchase a different property to rent, you're starting from scratch.

On the other hand, don't consider converting your home into a rental when you move unless this decision really is a long-term proposition. As we discuss in the preceding section, selling rental property has tax consequences.

As we explain later in the chapter, one of the tax benefits of rental real estate is the depreciation deduction. As your property ages, the IRS allows you to write off or deduct from your rental income for the "wearing out" of the building. Although this deduction helps reduce your taxes, be aware that you may not be able to deduct as much for depreciation expenses when you convert your home to rental property as you can on a rental bought separately. If your home has appreciated since you bought it, the IRS forces you to use your original (lower) purchase price for purposes of calculating depreciation. To make tax matters worse, if your home has declined in value since you originally purchased it, you must use this lower value, at the time you convert the property, for purposes of depreciation.

If the idea of keeping the home you move from as a long-term investment appeals to you, take stock of your overall financial situation *before* you make the final call. Can you afford to purchase your next home given the money that's still tied up in the home you're considering keeping as a rental? Can you afford to contribute to tax-deductible retirement plans, or will the burden of carrying two properties use up too much of your cash flow? Will your overall investments be well diversified, or will you have too much of your money tied up in real estate (perhaps in one area of the country)?

Real Estate Investing

For most people, the only real estate they own or consider owning is the home in which they live. If that's all you desire, we aren't going to push you into the business of investing in and managing rental property. It's a great deal of work, and other investments are certainly available, such as mutual funds (that own stocks), that are far more convenient and just as profitable.

But some people just have that itch to own something tangible. Real estate is, well, *real,* after all. You can fix it up, take pictures of it, and drive your friends by it!

Deciding whether real estate investing is for you

Whether you should invest in real estate versus other investments, such as stocks, bonds, or mutual funds, depends on many factors. The first and most important question to ask yourself is whether you're cut out to handle the responsibilities that come with being a landlord. Real estate is a time-intensive investment — it isn't for couch potatoes. Investing in stocks can be time-intensive as well, but it doesn't have to be if you use professionally managed mutual funds. Conversely, you can hire a property manager with real estate experience to reduce your workload. But the time required to own and oversee rental property can still be significant.

An often-overlooked drawback to investing in real estate is that you earn no tax benefits while you're accumulating your down payment. Rental property is usually a cash drain, as well, in the first few years of ownership. Retirement accounts, on the other hand, such as 401(k)s, SEP-IRAs, Keoghs, and so on (discussed in Chapter 21) give you immediate tax deductions as you contribute money to them. Although real estate offers many tax deductions, as we discuss earlier in the chapter, the cost of real estate reflects the expected tax breaks. So don't invest in real estate because of the tax deductions. Exhaust contributing to retirement accounts before considering property as an investment.

A final consideration with regard to whether real estate investing is for you: If you think that you have an excellent understanding of real estate and how to improve its value, you have reason enough to invest in it.

Enjoying rental property tax breaks

When you purchase property and rent it out, you're essentially running a business. You take in revenue — namely rent from your tenants — and incur expenses from the property. You hope that, over time, your revenue exceeds your expenses so that your real estate investment produces a profit (cash flow, in real estate lingo) for all the money and time you've sunk into it. You also hope that the market value of your investment property appreciates over time. The IRS helps you make a buck or two through a number of tax benefits. The major benefits follow.

Operating expense write-offs

In addition to the deductions allowed for mortgage interest and property taxes, just as on a home in which you live, you can deduct on your tax return a whole variety of other expenses for rental property. Almost all these deductions come from money that you spend on the property, such as money for insurance, maintenance and repairs, and food for the Doberman you keep around to intimidate those tenants whose rent checks are always "in the mail."

But one expense — depreciation — doesn't involve your spending money. Depreciation is an accounting deduction that the IRS allows you to take for the overall wear and tear on your building. The idea behind this deduction is that, over time, your building deteriorates and needs upgrading, rebuilding, and so on. The IRS tables now say that for residential property, you can depreciate over 27$\frac{1}{2}$ years; for nonresidential property, 39 years. Only the portion of a property's value that is attributable to the building(s) — and not the land — can be depreciated.

For example, suppose that you bought a residential rental property for $300,000 and the land is considered to be worth $100,000. Thus, the building is worth $200,000. If you can depreciate your $200,000 building over 27$\frac{1}{2}$ years, that works out to a $7,272 annual depreciation deduction.

If your rental property shows a loss for the year (when you figure your property's income and expenses), you may be able to deduct this loss on your tax return. If your *adjusted gross income* (as defined in Chapter 7) is less than $100,000 and you actively participate in managing the property, you're allowed to deduct your losses on operating rental real estate — up to $25,000 per year. Limited partnerships and properties in which you own less than ten percent are excluded. (Refer to Chapter 13 for more details.)

To deduct a loss on your tax return, you must *actively participate* in the management of the property. This rule doesn't necessarily mean that you have to perform the day-to-day management of the property. In fact, you can hire a property manager and still actively participate by doing such simple things as approving the terms of the lease contracts, tenants, and expenditures for maintenance and improvements on the building.

Good versus bad real estate investments

You can invest in real estate in a number of ways. The traditional and best method is to purchase property in an area that you've researched and are familiar with. Single-family homes and multi-unit buildings generally work best for most investors. Make sure that you do your "due diligence." Have the property professionally inspected and secure adequate insurance coverage.

If you want a stake in real estate but don't want the responsibilities and hassles that come with being a landlord, consider *real estate investment trusts* (*REITs*). REITs offer the benefits of property ownership without the headaches of being a landlord. REITs are a collection of real estate properties, such as shopping centers, apartments, and other rental buildings. REITs trade as securities on the major stock exchanges and can also be bought through mutual funds such as Fidelity Real Estate and Cohen & Steers Realty Shares.

Be careful, though; some real estate investments rarely make sense because they're near-certain money losers. Many investors get sucked into these lousy investments because of the supposed high-expected returns and tax breaks. Limited partnerships, for example, that are sold through stock brokers and financial planners who work on commission are burdened by high sales commissions and ongoing management fees, as well as illiquidity (refer to Chapter 23).

Time shares are another nearly certain money loser. With a time share, you buy a week or two of ownership, or usage, of a particular unit, usually a condominium in a resort location. If you pay $8,000 for a week (in addition to ongoing maintenance fees), you're paying the equivalent of more than $400,000 for the whole unit year-round, but a comparable unit may sell for only $150,000. All the extra mark-up pays the salespeople's commissions, administrative expenses, and profits for the time-share development company.

If you make more than $100,000 per year, you start to lose these write-offs. At an income of $150,000 or more, you can't deduct rental real estate losses from your other income. People in the real estate business (for example, agents and developers) who work more than 750 hours per year in the industry may not be subject to these rules. (Refer to Chapter 13 for more information.)

You start to lose the deductibility of rental property losses above the $100,000 limit whether you're single or married filing jointly. You can carry the loss forward to future tax years and take the loss then, if eligible. This policy is a bit unfair to couples because it's easier for them to break $100,000 with two incomes than for a single person with one income. Sorry — this is yet another part of the marriage tax penalties!

Rollover of capital gains on rental or business real estate

Suppose that you purchase a rental property and nurture it over the years. You find good tenants and keep the building repaired and looking sharp. You may just find that all that work wasn't for naught. The property may someday be worth much more than you originally paid for it.

However, if you simply sell the property, you owe taxes on your gain or profit. Even worse is the way the government defines your gain. If you bought the property for $100,000 and sell it for $150,000, you not only owe tax on that difference, but you also owe tax on an additional amount, depending on the property's depreciation. The amount of depreciation that you deducted on your tax returns reduces the original $100,000 purchase price, making the taxable difference that much larger. For example, if you deducted $25,000 for depreciation over the years that you owned the property, you owe tax on the difference between the sale price of $150,000 and $75,000 ($100,000 purchase price minus $25,000 depreciation).

Tax credits for low-income housing and old buildings

If you invest in low-income housing or particularly old commercial buildings, the IRS grants you special tax credits. The credits represent a direct reduction in your tax bill because you're spending to rehabilitate and improve these properties. The IRS wants to encourage investors to invest in and fix up old or run-down buildings that likely would continue to deteriorate otherwise.

The amounts of the credits range from as little as 10 percent of the expenditures to as much as 90 percent,

depending on the property type. The IRS has strict rules governing what types of properties qualify. Tax credits may be earned for rehabilitating nonresidential buildings built in 1935 or before. "Certified historic structures," both residential and nonresidential, also qualify for tax credits. See **IRS Form 3468** to learn more than you care to about these credits.

All this tax may just motivate you to hold on to your property. But you *can* avoid paying tax on your profit when you sell a rental property by "exchanging" it for a similar or "like-kind" property, and thereby rolling over your gain. (You may not receive the proceeds — they must go into an escrow account.) The rules, however, are different for rolling over profits (called *1031 exchanges,* for the section of the tax code that allows them) from the sale of rental property than for a primary residence.

Under current tax laws, the IRS continues to take a broad definition of what *like kind* property is. For example, you can exchange from undeveloped land into a multiunit rental building.

The rules for properly doing one of these 1031 exchanges are complex. Third parties are usually involved. Make sure that you find an attorney and/or tax advisor who is expert at these transactions to ensure that you do it right.

Real estate corporations

When you invest in and manage real estate with at least one other partner, you can set up a company through which you own the property. The main reason you may want to consider this action is liability protection. A corporation can reduce the chances of lenders or tenants suing you.

Refer to the discussion in Chapter 22 about incorporating, the different entities under which you may do business, and the pros and cons of each.

Chapter 25

Kids and Taxes

● ●

In This Chapter

▶ Tax and financial costs and benefits of a second income

▶ Social Security numbers and other child tax goodies

▶ Taxes, financial aid, and educational expenses

▶ The kiddie tax system

● ●

C loth diapers or disposables? Which is better for your baby's bottom? Are you adding to landfills by using disposables? But what about all those harsh chemicals used to clean the cloth diapers?

When should you send your youngster to preschool? And to which school? Should you move in order to live in a better school district? And can you afford to move, or will it cause you to work so many hours that you'll rarely spend time with your child? If you stay put, will your child end up in the junior high like the one in the next town over where last year a kid brought a gun to school and shot another student?

And what about toys? You want your baby to be stimulated and have fun, but the toys need to be at least somewhat educational. And then you have to worry about the safety issue. Is your baby going to get hurt when some part comes loose?

Raising children involves lots of decisions and trade-offs. Many new parents are surprised at the financial and tax consequences of having kids. We wrote this chapter so that you can spend more time enjoying the first smile, first step, first word, and the first high-five.

Bringing Up Baby

Although kids can cost a lot of money, the expenses, or thousands of diaper changes during the infant years, rarely deter people from wanting a family. And for good reason — kids are wonderful, at least most of the time. They're our future. (If you don't have kids, who do you think is going pay your future Social Security benefits?)

Raising a family can be the financial equivalent of doing a triathlon and can stretch and break the budgets of even those who consider themselves financially well off and on top of things. Taxes are an important factor in a number of kid-related issues. Here's our take on some important tax issues that you may confront before conception and in the early years of raising a baby.

Costs and benefits of the second income

In addition to less sleep at night and frequent diaper changing, children mean increased spending. At a minimum, expenditures for food and clothing increase. Although you may have less time to shop for yourself, causing your personal spending to decrease, you're likely to spend more on housing, insurance, day care, and education. And don't forget the host of not-so-incidental incidentals. Toys, art classes, sports, field trips, and the like can rack up big bills, especially if you don't control what you spend on them.

One of the most challenging decisions that new parents face is whether to work full-time, part-time, or not at all. We mean work at a paying job, that is — parenting is the lowest paid but potentially most rewarding job there is. The need or desire to work full-time is obvious — doing so brings more money home. However, you may rightfully feel that working full-time prohibits you from playing as active a role in raising your children as you would like. As you consider the additional expenses of raising children, you may also need to factor in a decrease in income.

Financially speaking, taxes can have a big impact on the value or benefit of working full-time, especially for two-income couples. Remember that the tax brackets are set up so that the last dollars of earnings are taxed at a higher rate (refer to Chapter 1). So if you decide whether or not to work full-time by simply looking at the salary that your employer quotes you as the total value of that second income (for example, $30,000), you're making a potentially big personal and financial mistake.

Take the case of Ron and Mary, a nice couple who struggled with how to handle their work schedules after the birth of their first child. They both worked full-time. Mary, a marketing manager, earned $55,000 per year, and Ron, a schoolteacher, made $32,000 per year. Ron was considering working part-time or not at all so that he could be at home with their daughter. Because of Ron and Mary's prior financial commitments, such as their home mortgage, they believed that they couldn't afford for Ron to work less than full-time.

Ron and Mary took a closer look at their finances and taxes and started to see things a little differently. Taxes took a whopping 40 percent of Ron's income, so his take-home pay was just $19,200 per year, or $1,600 per month. Then they added up all the additional costs of both parents working full-time: day care, a second car, more meals eaten out, and so on. When they totaled up all these extra costs in addition to the taxes, which could be eliminated if Ron didn't work at all or worked on a greatly reduced basis, they figured that Ron was effectively contributing about $300 per month from his full-time job — or about $1.80 per hour!

Ultimately, because of his low after-tax effective hourly income, Ron decided to quit his job and work part-time at home. This solution gave the family the best of both worlds — a more involved dad and husband and some income without most of the extra costs that come with a second job. And because Ron was able to work part-time, he and his wife were able to earn some tax credits (discussed in the "Dependent care tax credit" section, later in this chapter) for part-time day care for their daughter.

Of course, people enjoy other benefits of working besides income. But examine taxes and other expenses on that second income to ensure that you're making your financial decision to work based on complete and accurate information.

Getting Junior a Social Security number

When a child is born, he or she may be a bundle of joy to you, but to the federal government and the IRS, Junior is just a number — more specifically, a Social Security number. The IRS allows you to claim your children as dependents on your tax return. For tax year 1998, each child is "worth" a $2,700 deduction as your dependent. So if you're in

Teaching kids about taxes and money

Show your kids your paystub! Although you probably haven't shown what you earn to your parents, best friends, and perhaps even your spouse, sharing with your children what you earn and what you pay in taxes can be highly educational. This information gets kids thinking about the realities of living within a set income.

Your paystub helps kids see not only what you earn each month, but also how much goes out for expenses like taxes. You can then have discussions about the costs of rent and mortgages, utilities, food, and everything else. Your children may better understand your financial constraints, and they'll be well on the road to financial literacy, prepared for the day when they'll be responsible for earning money, paying taxes, and meeting monthly bills. You aren't doing them (or yourself) any favors by keeping them in the dark.

In the absence of information, children have no conception of the amount their parents earn. Some have outrageously inflated ideas of how much their parents make — this misconception is often especially true for children whose parents eagerly fulfill their requests for purchases.

the 28-percent federal tax bracket, each child saves you a cool $756 in federal taxes. Not bad, but the deduction isn't going to cover much more than the cost of diapers for the year. *(Note:* As we discuss in Chapter 4, high income earners may have this wonderful deduction reduced or even eliminated.)

To claim your child as a dependent on your tax return, he or she must have a Social Security number. You also need a Social Security number for your child if you want to establish investment accounts in your child's name (although you may not want to after you understand the drawbacks to doing so, which we discuss later in this chapter).

The IRS requires a Social Security number because people were inventing children — you know, telling the IRS they'd just had twins when the closest they actually came to becoming parents was baby-sitting their best friend's kid one evening!

If you need **Form SS-5, Application for a Social Security Card**, simply call the Social Security Administration (800-772-1213) and ask them to mail you one. Fill it out and mail it ASAP. After all, how many times in your child's life do you get to save more than $700 per year just by spending two minutes filling out a government form?

Child care tax goodies

In addition to the extra personal deduction that you can take with each new child and the tax savings that come with that deduction, you should also be aware of the tax perks (for child care and related expenditures) that may save you thousands of dollars.

Dependent care tax credit

If you hire child care assistance for your youngster(s), you may be able to claim a tax credit on your annual return (which you claim on **Form 2441**). To be eligible for this credit, you (and your spouse, if you're married) must work at least part-time, unless you're a full-time student or you're disabled. Your kid(s) must be under the age of 13 or physically or mentally disabled.

The nanny tax

Someday you may want to run for or be nominated to an important public office. If you hire a nanny to take care of your child, you're best off to legally withhold and file the taxes necessary for employing help. Zoè Baird, President Clinton's original nominee for Attorney General, and Michael Huffington, failed Senate candidate in California, didn't withhold and file these taxes, and the press found out. Baird was nixed, and Huffington's blunder helped sink his floundering political ship.

Even if you aren't planning to run for political office someday, you need to know that you're legally required to withhold Social Security and other taxes if you have household employees who are earning $1,000 or more in a tax year. You can now do this through the filing of your annual tax return, and — surprise, surprise — it requires another form (**Schedule H**). Refer to the section on household employment taxes in Chapter 15 to find out how to report your so-called nanny tax.

In addition to complying with the law on employee withholdings, you also benefit because you may be allowed to take advantage of tax breaks if the employee helps with child care. The employee benefits, of course, by building up Social Security credits — and these credits qualify an employee for monthly retirement income payments. These credits also qualify the employee for disability benefits and qualify the employee's dependents for survivor's benefits.

In addition to paying the taxes for household help on your annual tax return, you also need to pay unemployment tax for any household employee to whom you paid $1,000 or more per calendar quarter. Request **Form 940, Employer's Annual Federal Unemployment Tax Return,** from the IRS to do so. Some states have similar requirements, so contact your state's employment tax office for information. This unemployment tax can be paid on Form 1040 (see Chapter 15).

Because a credit is a dollar-for-dollar reduction in your taxes owed, it may save you hundreds of tax dollars each year. And you not only count child care expenses toward calculation of the tax credit, but you also may be able to count the cost of a housekeeper or even a cook if the expense benefits your kids.

As we discuss in the preceding section, tax and other considerations will influence your desire as a parent to work outside the home. *Working at least part-time makes you eligible for this tax credit. If you elect to be a full-time mom or dad, you aren't eligible for the dependent care tax credit.*

If your employer offers a dependent care assistance plan (discussed in the following section), you may be able to reduce your taxes by taking advantage of that benefit rather than the dependent care tax credit. Your tax credit is reduced or eliminated if you use your employer's dependent care plan spending account. To find out more about how to claim this credit on your annual tax return, refer to Chapter 15.

Dependent care spending accounts

Increasing numbers of employers offer flexible benefit or spending plans. These plans allow you to choose among a number of different benefits, such as health, life, and disability insurance; vacation days; and dependent care expenses.

These plans allow you to put away money from your paycheck on a pretax basis, which you can then use to pay for child care expenses. Doing so saves you federal, state, and even Social Security taxes. These plans allow you to put away up to $5,000 per year ($2,500 for those of you who are married filing separately). The exact amount that you can put away depends on the specifics of your employer's plan.

Dependent care spending accounts are a "use it or lose it" benefit. If you aren't able to spend the money for child care expenses in the current tax year, at the end of the year the IRS forces you to forfeit all the unused money. So be careful not to go overboard and contribute more than you are certain to use.

As we mention in the preceding section, your participation in your employer's dependent care assistance plan reduces your tax credit. You can't do both. If you're in the federal 28-percent tax bracket and higher, you should be able to save more in taxes by using your employer's plan than by taking the credit on your tax return. The only way to know for sure is to run the numbers.

The dependent care tax credit and spending accounts that we discuss in this section can also be used to pay for the costs of taking care of other dependents, such as an ill or elderly parent. Refer to Chapter 15 and your employer's employee benefits manual for more information.

Child Tax Credit

Every child under the age 17 on December 31 that you can claim as a dependent can cut your tax bill by $400. In 1999 it jumps to $500. If you have three or more kids and your total child tax credits exceed your tax bill, part of the credit may be refundable. The credit is reduced by $50 for every $1,000 or fraction thereof of income above $75,000 for singles, $55,000 for married couples filing singly, or $110,000 for couples filing jointly.

This credit comes in three varieties: The regular Child Tax Credit; the Additional Child Tax Credit for use when you have three or more kids and the regular Child Tax Credit exceeds your tax, and the Supplemental Child Credit that you can use when you're ineligible to use the regular Child Tax Credit because you're claiming other credits, such as the Earned Income or Adoption credit. See Chapter 8 for information about how to compute and claim this credit.

Taxes and Educational Expenses

What do taxes have to do with educational expenses? A surprising amount. How you invest money that will pay for educational expenses can have an enormous impact on your family's taxes, ability to qualify for financial aid, and overall financial well being.

The (hidden) financial aid tax system

The financial aid system (to which parents apply so that their children are eligible for scholarships, grants, and loans) treats assets differently when held outside rather than inside retirement accounts. Under the current financial aid system, the value of your retirement plans is *not* considered an asset. Thus, the more money you stash in retirement accounts, the greater your chances of qualifying for financial aid and the more money you qualify for.

Most new parents don't place their savings in retirement accounts. Many nonwealthy parents make the mistake of saving and investing money in a separate account for their child (perhaps even in the child's name) or through some other financial product, such as a life insurance policy. Why is this a mistake? Because they end up being taxed at a much higher level than if they had employed other savings strategies.

Most important, parents should be saving and investing through retirement accounts that give significant tax benefits. Initial contributions to a 401(k), 403(b), SEP-IRA, Keogh, or other retirement accounts (described in Chapter 21) are usually tax deductible. An additional and substantial benefit is that after the money is placed in these accounts, it grows and compounds without taxation until withdrawal.

When a millionaire's kid gets more financial aid than a middle-class family's

What's truly amazing and sad about the way the current financial aid system works is that some affluent people who don't really need aid can get more than those who aren't nearly as financially well off. Here's a real case that, although somewhat extreme, is not that unusual. This story highlights the shortcomings of the current procedures used to determine financial need.

Kent, a doctor who earned $200,000 per year, and his spouse Marion, a housewife, had a son who applied for and received financial aid. By the time their son was ready to apply to college, Kent had quit working as a physician and was earning little money while doing some part-time teaching. However, he had more than $1,200,000 in his retirement savings plan, which he had accumulated over his years of work. Being savvy financial managers, Kent and Marion had little

money invested and available outside tax-sheltered retirement accounts. Because the financial aid system ignores retirement accounts in its analysis, and because Kent's income was modest at the time his son applied for aid, the family got significant aid.

On the other hand, Rick and Liz, full-time employees with a combined income of $50,000, and their daughter received no financial aid. Why? Because Rick and Liz had been saving money in their daughter's name. By the time she was ready to apply for college, she had about $25,000 saved. Rick and Liz had also accumulated some other modest investments outside retirement accounts, but they only had about $30,000 put away in retirement accounts. Because of the assets available outside retirement accounts and their current income, they were deemed not needy enough for aid.

Therefore, it doesn't make sense to forgo contributions to your retirement savings plans in order to save money in a taxable account for Junior's college fund. If you do, you pay higher taxes both on your current income and on the interest and growth of this money. In addition to paying higher taxes, money that you save *outside* retirement accounts, including money in the child's name, is counted as an asset and reduces your child's eligibility for financial aid. Thus, you're expected to contribute more to your child's educational expenses.

Generally, the worst approach to saving for college costs is saving money in your child's name. Colleges expect a much greater percentage of money in your child's name (35 percent) to be used for college costs than money in your name (6 percent). This is the hidden financial aid tax. (Don't assume that you can't qualify for aid — a fair amount of it, both loans and grants, is available without regard to financial need.) If you plan to apply for financial aid, it's best to save money in your name rather than in your child's name (in a *custodial account*).

Note: As we discuss later in the chapter, if you're affluent enough that you expect to pay for your kid's entire educational costs, investing through custodial accounts can save on taxes. Prior to your child reaching age 14, the first $1,300 of interest and dividend income is taxed at your child's income tax rate rather than yours. After age 14, *all* income generated by investments in your child's name is taxed at your child's rate.

Education IRAs: Tread carefully

Effective in 1998, Education IRAs may be established for each child, and contributions of up to $500 per child per year may be made until the child reaches age 18. The $500 contribution limit is above and beyond the $2,000 limit that a wage earner may contribute to a traditional or Roth IRA (which we discuss in Chapters 7 and 21).

Contributions to an Education IRA aren't tax deductible; however, investment earnings can compound and be withdrawn free of tax as long as the funds are used to pay for college costs and, in the year of withdrawal, the new Hope and Lifetime Learning Credits aren't claimed for the student (see the sidebar "The new educational tax credits" for more on these new credits).

However, before running out to contribute to an Education IRA, be aware that it isn't clear at this early date how college financial aid officers are going to treat this type of savings. Although the decision probably won't please most parents, financial aid officers will most likely treat funds placed in an Education IRA either as a child's asset, which reduces financial aid by 35 percent for each dollar in the child's name, or as a prepaid tuition plan, which reduces aid dollar for dollar.

So, unless you're affluent enough to pay for the full cost of your children's college education without any type of financial aid, hold off on contributing to these new IRAs until it's clear how financial aid offices are going to treat them. If you're affluent, you yourself may not be eligible to contribute to these new Education IRAs. The full $500 per child may only be contributed to an Education IRA for couples with adjusted gross incomes (AGIs) under $150,000 and single taxpayers under $95,000. The $500 limit is reduced for married taxpayers with an AGI above $150,000 ($95,000 if single) and eliminated if the AGI is above $160,000 ($110,000 for singles).

Here are some of the rules concerning contributions and withdrawals from an Education IRA.

- ✔ For joint filers with an income between $150,000 and $160,000, the $500 gets phased out and eliminated when their combined incomes exceed $160,000. For single filers, the phaseout is between $95,000 and $110,000. Above the $110,000 income level, singles aren't allowed to make contributions.

- If you earn more than these thresholds and want your kids to have Education IRAs, there's a loophole. Simply have someone else, such as a grandparent, who isn't earning more than the threshold amounts make the Education IRA contribution on your behalf.

- ✔ The tax-free exclusion of the earnings isn't available on a distribution from the IRA in the same year that a Hope or Lifetime Earning Credit is claimed.

- ✔ Contributions to the account must be made before the child reaches 18.

- ✔ The money in the account can't be used to invest in a life insurance policy.

- ✔ When the beneficiary reaches 30, any balance must be distributed to the beneficiary, and any earnings must be included in his or her income. However, prior to reaching 30, the beneficiary may transfer or roll over the balance to another beneficiary who is a member of his or her family. The distribution must be made within 30 days of the beneficiary's 30th birthday or within 30 days of his or her death.

- ✔ No contribution may be made in a year that a contribution is made to a state tuition program for the child (see "Avoid prepaid and qualified state tuition programs" later in this chapter for more information).

- ✔ Any part of a distribution that must be included in income because it wasn't used to pay college expenses is subject to a 10-percent penalty unless paid as a result of death or disability.

Here's an example of how the earnings on an Education IRA get taxed: Grandma and grandpa contributed $600 to Chloe's account. It is now worth $1,000. Chloe withdraws the $1,000 but only uses $750 to pay college expenses. Because only 75 percent of the distribution ($750÷1,000) was used to pay her college expenses, only 75 percent of the $400 of earnings ($300) is exempt from tax. Chloe must pay tax on the $100 balance. If she had used the entire $1,000 to pay her college expenses, the entire $400 of earnings would be exempt from tax. One additional point: The $100 that Chloe had to pay tax on is subject to a 10-percent penalty.

The new educational tax credits

The 1997 tax law changes included a number of perks for parents with minor children. In addition to an out-right tax credit just for having children under the age of 17 (which we discuss in Chapter 5), the new laws also contain tax credits to assist some parents with the often high costs of education. We say "some" because the credits are phased out for single tax filers with adjusted gross incomes between $40,000 and $50,000, and married couples filing jointly with adjusted gross incomes between $80,000 and $100,000 (these phaseout ranges will increase with inflation beginning in the year 2002).

The first of the two credits — the Hope Scholarship Credit — allows, beginning in 1998, up to a $1,500 tax credit toward tuition and fees in each of the first two years of college (beginning in the year 2002, these amounts will increase along with inflation).

The second credit — the Lifetime Learning Credit — allows up to a 20-percent credit in tuition and fee expenses paid after June 30, 1998 (after the year 2002, the credit increases to up to 20 percent of $10,000 of expenses). The Lifetime Learning Credit can be used toward undergraduate and graduate education and toward course work that upgrades job skills.

If a taxpayer claims either of these credits in a tax year, the taxpayer is not eligible for withdrawing money without taxation from an Education IRA. Also, the Hope Scholarship Credit may not be taken in a year when the Lifetime Learning Credit is used.

Chloe can elect to waive either the $400 or $300 exclusion from tax in the above examples because she decided to claim the Hope or Lifetime Learning credits instead of claiming an exclusion from tax on the withdrawal from her Education IRA. In this case, the 10-percent penalty wouldn't apply because she chose to include the earnings she withdrew in her income.

Eligible higher education expenses include tuition, fees, books, supplies, and equipment to obtain a bachelor's degree, an associate's degree, or a graduate-level or professional degree, whether on a full-time, half-time, or less than half-time basis. However, room and board expenses only qualify as higher education expenses if the student carries at least one-half the normal workload.

Minimizing your taxes and paying for college

Socking money away into your tax-sheltered retirement accounts helps you reduce your tax burden and may help your children qualify for more financial aid. However, accessing retirement accounts before age 59¹/₂ incurs tax penalties.

So how do you pay for your children's educational costs? There isn't one correct answer, because the decision depends on your overall financial situation. Here are some ideas that can help you meet expected educational expenses as well as minimize your taxes:

✔ **Don't try to do it all yourself.** Unless you're affluent, don't even try to pay for the full cost of a college education for your children. You can't afford it. You and your child will, in all likelihood, have to borrow some money.

✔ **Apply for aid, regardless of your financial circumstances.** A number of loan programs, such as Unsubsidized Stafford Loans and Parent Loans for Undergraduate Students (PLUS), are available even when your family is not deemed financially needy. Only Subsidized Stafford Loans, on which the federal government pays the interest that accumulates while the student is still in school, are limited to those students deemed financially needy.

In addition to loans, a number of grant programs are available through schools and the government, as well as through independent sources. Specific colleges and other private organizations (including employers, banks, credit unions, and community groups) also offer grants and scholarships. Some of these have nothing to do with financial need.

✔ **Save in your name.** If you've exhausted your retirement account contributions, it's fine to save money that you're earmarking to pay for college. Just do it in your name.

✔ **Get your kids to work.** Your child can work and save money to pay for college costs during junior high, high school, and college. In fact, if your child qualifies for financial aid, he or she is expected to contribute a certain amount to education costs from employment held during the school year or summer breaks and from his or her own savings. Besides giving the student a stake in his or her own future, this training encourages sound personal financial management down the road.

✔ **Borrow against your home equity.** If you're a homeowner, you can borrow against the equity (market value less the outstanding mortgage loan) in your property. Doing so is usually best because you can borrow against your home at a relatively low interest rate, and the interest is generally tax-deductible. (Refer to Chapter 9 for information on tax-deductibility rules.)

✔ **Borrow against your company retirement plans.** Many larger firms' retirement savings plans, such as 401(k)s, allow borrowing. Just make sure that you are able to pay the money back. Otherwise, you'll owe big taxes for a premature distribution.

If your parents want to gift money to your children for college expenses, it's generally better if the money is kept in your name; otherwise, have the grandparents keep the money until the kids are ready to enter college.

Taxes on Your Kiddies' Investments

As we mention earlier, parents of all different financial means must be aware of the financial aid implications of putting money into an account bearing a child's name. If you haven't read the section "Taxes and Educational Expenses" earlier in this chapter, please read it before you jump into investing money in your children's names.

Parents used to have a significant tax incentive to transfer money into their children's names, because the earnings on those investments were taxed at the child's tax rate. In 1986, the tax rules changed, however, and this benefit was greatly reduced. Also as a result of these tax law changes, increasing numbers of children need to file tax returns. (Actually, parents normally do the paperwork.)

Kiddie taxes for children under age 14

Prior to reaching the magical age of 14, kids have a special tax system that applies to them. Specifically, the first $650 of *unearned income* (income from interest and dividends on investments) that a child earns is not taxed at all. It's tax-free! In contrast, *earned income* is considered income earned from work. For example, the money that Macaulay Culkin of *Home Alone* fame earned from his blockbuster movies was earned income. (We hear that Macaulay is having a tougher time finding work these days.) Refer to Chapter 8 to find out when you need to file a tax return for your child.

The next $650 of unearned income for this age set is taxed at the federal level at 15 percent. Everything over $1,300 is taxed at the parent's income tax rate. The system is set up in this fashion to discourage parents from transferring a lot of assets into their children's names, hoping to pay lower taxes.

Because the first $1,300 of unearned income for the child is taxed at such a low rate, many parents are tempted to transfer some money into the child's name to save some income taxes. Quite a number of financial books and advisors recommend this strategy. Consider this passage referring to transferring money to your children, from a tax book written by a large accounting firm:

> "Take advantage of these rules. It still makes sense to shift some income-producing assets to younger children."

Wrong! As we discuss in "The (hidden) financial aid tax system," earlier in this chapter, this short-sighted desire to save a little in taxes today can lead to your losing out on significant financial aid later. And what about your limited discretionary income? You don't want to put money in your child's name if it means that you aren't fully taking advantage of your retirement accounts.

Only consider putting money into an account bearing your child's name if

✔ You expect to pay for the full cost of a college education yourselves and not apply for or use any financial aid, including loans that aren't based on financial need.

✔ You're comfortable with the notion that your child will have legal access to the money at age 18 or 21 (depending upon the state in which you live) if the money is in a custodial account in the child's name. At that age, the money is legally your child's, and he or she can blow it on something other than a college education.

After all the caveats and warnings, if you're still thinking about putting money into an account bearing your child's name, consider buying tax-friendly investments that won't generate significant tax liabilities until after the child turns 14. (Refer to Chapter 23 for tax-friendly investment ideas.) As you see in the following section, after your kids turn 14, all income they earn is taxed at their rate, not yours.

You can also buy investments in your name and then transfer them to your child's name after Junior turns 14. (Each parent is limited to gifting $10,000 to each child per year.) That way, if the investment declines in value, you can take the tax loss; if the investment turns a profit, you should save on your taxes by transferring the investment to your child and having your child pay tax on it after turning 14. This strategy won't work if your child is like Macaulay Culkin and in a higher tax bracket than you are!

Children 14 and older: Adults to the IRS

Although your gangly teenager may still be wearing braces, using acne cream, and spending two hours a day on the phone, to the IRS he or she is a warm-blooded, tax-paying adult, just like you, as soon as he or she turns age 14. Because most 14-year-olds don't earn a great deal of income, taxes on their investments don't need to be a concern. However, the same negative financial aid considerations we discuss earlier in the chapter apply to money held in their name versus yours.

Tax-wise and not-so-wise investments for educational funds

You will hear many sales pitches for "tax-wise" investments to use for college savings. Most aren't worthy of your consideration. Here's our take on the best, the mediocre, and the worst.

Double-what bonds?

Among the many forms of bonds (debt) that our fine government issues are *EE* (double "E") bonds. These are one of the many classes of Treasury bonds issued by that national organization with a penchant for borrowing money. You may hear about these as a suggested investment for children's college expenses.

EE bonds purchased after 1989 have a unique tax twist if you use the sales proceeds to pay for educational tuition and fees. (Room and board and other education-related costs are not covered.) The interest earned on the bonds is fully exempt from federal taxation (interest on all Treasury bonds is already state tax-free) as long as two other requirements are met:

- The purchaser of the bond must be at least 24 years of age.

- At the time the bonds are sold to pay for educational tuition and fees, the holder of the bond may not have adjusted gross income in excess of $65,850 if single or $106,250 if married and filing a joint return.

Just to make matters more complicated, even if you are somehow able to know years in advance what your income will be when your toddler has grown into a college-bound 18-year-old, you've gotta file yet another tax form, **Form 8815**, to claim the exclusion of the interest on EEs from federal taxation. And don't forget that not a year goes by without Congress messing with the Federal tax laws. So the income requirements for the tax exemption can change.

You should also know that EE bonds generally pay a lower rate of interest than other, simpler Treasury bonds. The yield or interest rate on EE bonds is also a chore to understand. You must hold these bonds for at least five years in order to receive the return. The return is equal to 85 percent of the average yield payable on five-year Treasury notes during the period held, or 4 percent, whichever is higher.

Regardless of how the EE bond proceeds are used, taxation of the interest on them is deferred until they're cashed. Although in most cases this tax deferment is beneficial, don't forget that children under age 14 can earn $650 of interest tax-free every year. So if you buy the bond and register it in your child's name, he or she may end up actually paying more in taxes when the bonds are cashed in, because all the interest income will be recognized at once. Buying the bond in your child's name, however, may hurt his or her chances of obtaining financial aid.

Our advice: Don't waste your time on these needlessly complicated bonds. They are testimony to the absurdly complicated tax code and government rules. You're better off investing in mutual funds that offer some growth potential. But if we haven't dissuaded you, make sure that you buy these bonds from the Federal Reserve Bank in your area and hold them in an account with the Federal Reserve so that you'll always get a statement on your account and won't lose track of the bonds when you're no longer being paid interest!

Mutual funds are ideal

Mutual funds, which offer investors of all financial means instant diversification and low-cost access to the nation's best money managers, are an ideal investment when you are saving money for educational expenses. Refer to Chapter 23 for a discussion of the tax-wise ways to invest in funds.

Think twice about Treasury bonds

Treasury bonds issued by the federal government are often recommended by many tax and financial books as a college investment. We aren't enthusiastic about some of these (see the sidebar "Double-what bonds?"). Zero-coupon Treasuries are particular tax headaches. Zero-coupon Treasuries are sold at a discount to their value at maturity instead of paying you interest each year. Guess what? You still have to report the effective interest you're earning each year on your tax return. And just to give you a headache or pad your tax preparer's bill, this implicit interest needs to be calculated. Yuck!

Don't bother with cash value life insurance

Life insurance policies that have cash values are some of the most oversold investments to fund college costs. The usual pitch is this: Because you need life insurance to protect your family, why not buy a policy that you can borrow against to pay for college? Makes sense, doesn't it? Insurance agents also emphasize that the cash value in the policy is growing without taxation over time. Although this part of their sales pitch is true, you have better alternatives.

The reason you shouldn't buy a cash value life insurance policy is that, as we discuss earlier in this chapter, you're better off contributing to retirement accounts. These investments give you an immediate tax deduction that you don't receive when you save through life insurance. Because life insurance that comes with a cash value is more expensive, parents are more likely to make a second mistake — not buying enough life insurance coverage. If you need and want life insurance, you're better off buying lower-cost term life insurance.

Make sure your money grows

An investment that fails to keep you ahead of inflation, such as savings or money market accounts, is another poor investment for college expenses. You need your money to grow in order to afford educational costs down the road. The interest on these accounts is also taxable, which doesn't make sense for many working parents.

Avoid prepaid and other qualified state tuition programs

State tuition programs that allow you to put away an unlimited amount of money on a nondeductible basis to pay tuition as well as room and board are another oversold device to save for college. The earnings aren't taxed until you start withdrawing money for college. Distributions from a qualified state tuition program used to pay college expenses qualify for the Hope and Lifetime Learning credits.

Some states that don't have an income tax have prepaid tuition plans. A number of states have alternative education incentives, such as college savings bonds, credits or deductions for tuition paid, or waiver of penalties for early withdrawals from 401(k) plans used to pay higher education expenses.

Prepaid tuition plans and other such programs should generally be avoided. A few states have developed plans to enable you to pay college costs at a specific school (calculated for the age of your child). The allure of these plans is that by paying today, you eliminate the worry of not being able to afford rising costs in the future.

This logic doesn't work for several reasons. First, odds are high that you don't have the money today to pay in advance. If you have that kind of extra dough around, you're better off using it for other purposes (and you're unlikely to worry about rising costs anyway). You can invest your own money — that's what the school's going to do with it anyway. Besides, how do you know which college your child will want to attend and how long it may take Junior to get through?

Chapter 26
Estate Planning

Among the dreariest of tax and financial topics is the issue of what happens to your money when you die. Depending on how your finances are structured, you (actually, your estate) may get stuck paying *estate taxes* when you die.

Unfortunately, the time when the grim reaper pays a visit can't be predicted. This scenario doesn't mean that we all need to participate in complicated estate planning. To the contrary — if your assets aren't substantial, a few simple moves may be all you need to get your affairs in order.

Estate planning takes time and money, which are precious commodities for most of us. Whether it's worthwhile to spend your time and money on estate planning depends on your personal and financial circumstances, both now and in the near future.

We know that your days are just packed with excitement, and you bound out of bed most mornings, racing off to a job that you love. Who can blame you for not wanting to plan for the day when you won't see the sun rise? Unlike filing your annual tax return, arranging your financial affairs for your death is easy to put off. Unfortunately, if you don't spend some time on estate planning, your family and others who are close to you will pay the price when you're gone. Do you really want the government to get all that money?

Will I Owe Estate Taxes?

With all the warnings about the enormous estate taxes that may be owed upon our deaths, you may think that owing estate taxes is a common problem. It isn't. But some insurance agents, attorneys, and estate planning "specialists" use scare tactics to attract prospective clients, often by luring them to free estate-planning seminars. What better way to find people with money to invest!

In tax year 1998, an individual at his or her death can pass $625,000 to a beneficiary without federal estate taxes. On the other hand, a couple, *if* they have their assets, wills, and trusts properly structured (as discussed later in this chapter), can pass $1.25 million to beneficiaries without federal estate taxes. Because most people are still trying to accumulate enough money to someday retire or take a trip around the world, it's hardly a normal problem for folks to have this much cash lying around when they die.

And, if those amounts don't seem large enough to you, the 1997 tax bill allows people in the years ahead to pass more of their estates on to their children and other heirs free of federal estate taxes. Gradually through the year 2006, the amount that a deceased person may leave to her heirs will increase from the 1998 figure of $625,000 to $1 million (see Table 26-1). Thus, married couples making use of bypass trusts will eventually be able to shield $2 million from federal estate taxes. (Qualifying small-business owners are also getting a higher exemption from federal estate tax, allowing them to pass on up to $1.3 million of interest in their small business.)

Table 26-1	Allowable Amount That Can Be Passed to Heirs Free of Federal Estate Tax
Year	Federal Estate-Tax-Free Amount
1998	$625,000
1999	$650,000
2000	$675,000
2001	$675,000
2002	$700,000
2003	$700,000
2004	$850,000
2005	$950,000
2006	$1,000,000

Unless you die prematurely, whether your assets face estate taxes depends on the amount of your assets that you use up during your retirement, unless you already possess great wealth. How much of your assets are used up depends on how your assets grow over time, as well as how rapidly you spend money.

To calculate the value of your estate upon your death, the IRS totals up your assets and subtracts your liabilities. Assets include your personal property, home and other real estate, savings and investments (such as bank accounts, stocks, bonds, and mutual funds held both inside as well as outside retirement accounts), and life insurance death benefits (unless properly placed in a trust as we describe later in this chapter). Your liabilities include any outstanding loans (such as a real estate mortgage), bills owed at the time of your death, legal and other expenses to handle your estate, and funeral expenses.

If you're married at the time of your death, all assets that you leave to your spouse are excluded from estate taxes, thanks to the *unlimited marital deduction* (which we discuss later in this chapter). Also, any charitable contributions or bequests that you dictated in your will are deducted from your assets before calculating your *taxable estate*.

How High Are Estate Taxes?

Under current tax law, at your death, if your estate totals more than $625,000, you may owe federal estate taxes. The tax rates are fairly hefty (see Table 26-2).

Table 26-2	Federal Estate Taxes on Estates in Excess of $625,000
Value of Estate	**Tax Rate**
$ 625,000 – $ 750,000	37%
$ 750,001 – $ 1,000,000	39%
$ 1,000,001 – $ 1,250,000	41%
$ 1,250,001 – $ 1,500,000	43%
$ 1,500,001 – $ 2,000,000	45%
$ 2,000,001 – $ 2,500,000	49%
$ 2,500,001 – $ 3,000,000	53%
$ 3,000,001 – $10,000,000	55%
$10,000,001 – $21,040,000	60%
Over $21,040,000	55%

States can also levy additional estate and inheritance taxes. Most states don't; they simply share in the federal taxes that the IRS collects from each estate.

Some states have elected to assess their own estate taxes and, therefore, do not share in the federal estate taxes collected. Not surprisingly, such states opt out of the federal tax-sharing so that they can assess and collect an even higher rate of estate tax than they would receive from the federal government. Thus, if you live in one of those states, your estate taxes will be higher due to the additional state levy.

Some states also impose an inheritance tax.

Reducing Expected Estate Taxes if You're Rich

You have your work cut out for you as you search around and try to educate yourself about estate planning. You can find many attorneys and non-attorneys selling estate planning services, and you can encounter lots of insurance agents hawking life insurance. All are more than happy to sell you their services. Most people don't need to do fancy-schmancy estate planning with high-cost attorneys. We give you the straight scoop on what, if anything, you should be concerned with now and at other junctures in your life, and we tell you the conflicts of interest that these "experts" have in rendering advice.

Thanks to all the changes in the tax laws and the thousands of attorneys and tax advisors working to find new ways around paying estate taxes, a dizzying array of strategies exist to reduce estate taxes — including taking up residence in a foreign country! We start with the simpler stuff and work toward the more complex.

Gifting

There's nothing wrong with making, saving, and investing money. But someday, you have to honestly look at yourself in the mirror and ask, "For what purpose?" It's easy to rationalize hoarding money — you never know how long you'll live or what medical expenses you may incur. Besides, your kids are still paying off their VISA cards and don't seem to know a mutual fund from an emergency fund. (Not that you'd want to be judgmental of your kids or anything!)

Gifting options

You have options in terms of what money or assets you gift to others. Start with cash or assets that haven't appreciated since you purchased them. If you want to transfer an asset that has lost value, consider selling it first; then you can claim the tax loss on your tax return and transfer the cash.

Be careful to avoid gifting assets that have appreciated greatly in value. Why? Because if you hold such assets until your death, your heirs receive what is called a *stepped-up basis.* That is, the IRS assumes that the effective price your heirs "paid" for an asset is the value on your date of death — this wipes out the capital gains tax that is otherwise owed when selling an asset that has appreciated in value.

A more complicated way to gift money to your heirs and still retain some control over the money is to set up a *Crummey Trust.* (Its name has nothing to do with the quality of the trust.) Although the beneficiary has a short window of time (a month or two) to withdraw money that's contributed to the trust, you can verbally make clear to the beneficiary that, in your opinion, leaving the money in the trust is in his or her best interest. You can also specify, in the trust document itself, that the trust money be used for particular purposes, such as tuition. Some of the other trusts we discuss later in this chapter may meet your needs if you want more control over the money you intend to pass to your heirs.

Current tax law allows you to gift up to $10,000 per individual and organization each year to as many people and organizations — such as your children, grandchildren, best friends, or favorite charities — as you desire (no tax forms required). If you're married, your spouse can do the same. The benefit of gifting is that it removes the money from your estate and therefore reduces your estate taxes. Even better is the fact that all future appreciation and income on the gifted money also is removed from your estate, because the money now belongs to your gift recipient.

Upon your death, your money has to go somewhere. By directing some of your money to people and organizations now, you can pass on far more later because you'll be saving anywhere from 37 to 60 percent in estate taxes. Plus, while you're alive, you can experience the satisfaction of seeing the good that your money can do.

You can use gifting to remove a substantial portion of your assets from your estate over time. Suppose that you have three children. You and your spouse can both give each of your children $10,000 per year for a total gift of $60,000 per year. If your kids are married, you can make an additional $10,000 gift to their spouses for another $60,000 per year. You can also gift an unlimited amount to pay for current educational tuition costs and medical expenses. Just be sure to make the payment directly to the organization charging the fees.

The annual tax-free gifting limit of $10,000 per recipient will be indexed to inflation beginning in 1999.

Leaving all your assets to your spouse

Tax laws wouldn't be tax laws without exceptions and loopholes; here's another one: If you're married at the time of your death, any and all assets that you leave to your spouse are exempt from estate taxes normally due upon your death. In fact, you may leave an unlimited amount of money — millions and millions of dollars if you have it — to your spouse. Hence, the name *unlimited marital deduction.* Assets that count are those willed to your spouse or for which he or she is named as beneficiary (such as retirement accounts).

Paying some gift taxes now to avoid estate taxes later

You can gift up to $10,000 tax-free per person and per organization per year to as many people or organizations as you like. However, you can gift more than $10,000 in a year to your heirs.

If you have substantial assets now (several million dollars, for example), and you're worried that your advancing age may prohibit you from moving the money out of your estate quickly enough to get down to the $625,000 limit, you may be able to pass on more money to your heirs by transferring a larger lump sum of money now. This strategy is particularly useful if you wish to focus your gifting to one or two people.

Suppose that you want to gift $1,100,000 to your son — why can't you be *our* parents? — and you do it this year.

You'll owe the IRS gift tax. So you write the IRS a check. By doing this, you accomplish two positives for maximizing how much you pass to your son and other heirs:

✔ You transfer $1,100,000 to your son and avoid accumulating more growth on that money in your estate. (Remember, unless your money is growing inside tax-deductible retirement accounts, that growth is taxable.)

✔ Because you pay the gift tax out of your estate, you reduce your taxable estate by the amount of the gift tax.

(*Note:* Technically, you must live three years following the gift for your heirs to avoid paying estate tax on it.)

Although leaving all your assets to your spouse is a tempting estate-planning strategy for married couples, this strategy can backfire. The surviving spouse may end up with an estate tax problem upon his or her death because he or she will have all the couple's assets. (See the following section for a legal way around this issue, appropriately called a *bypass trust*.) You face three other less likely but potential problems:

✔ You and your spouse could die simultaneously.

✔ The unlimited marital deduction is not allowed if your spouse isn't a U.S. citizen.

✔ Some states don't allow the unlimited marital deduction, so be sure to find out about the situation in your state.

Establishing a bypass trust

As we discuss in the previous section, a potential estate tax problem is created upon the death of a spouse if all of his or her assets pass to the surviving spouse. When the surviving spouse dies, only $625,000 (for tax year 1998) can be passed on free of federal estate taxes.

If you have substantial assets, you and your spouse can each take advantage of the $625,000 estate-tax-free rule and pass to your heirs a total of $1.25 million estate-tax-free. By shielding an additional $625,000 from estate taxes, you save your heirs nearly $250,000 in estate taxes. How? Each of you can arrange a *bypass trust* (also known as *credit shelter* or *exemption equivalent*) in your will.

Upon the death of the first spouse, assets held in that spouse's name go into a trust. The surviving spouse and/or other heirs can still use the income from those assets and even some of the principal. They can receive 5 percent of the value of the trust or $5,000, whichever is greater, each year. They can also draw additional principal if it's needed for educational, health, or living expenses. Ultimately, the assets in the bypass trust pass to the designated beneficiaries (usually, but not limited to, children).

For a bypass trust to work, you will likely need to rework how you hold ownership of your assets (for example, jointly or individually). You may need to individually title your assets so that each spouse holds $625,000 in assets in order for each to take full advantage of the $625,000 estate tax-free limit.

In the years ahead, as the 1997 tax law changes are phased in, bypass trusts will become even more valuable. As the amount that an individual can pass on free of estate taxes is raised to $1 million by the year 2006, a married couple will be able to pass on a total of $2 million free of estate taxes when they use a bypass trust.

Buying cash-value life insurance

Two major types of life insurance exist. Most people who need life insurance — and who have someone dependent on their income — should buy *term* life insurance, which is pure life insurance: You pay an annual premium for which you receive a predetermined amount of life insurance protection. If the insured person passes away, the beneficiaries collect; otherwise, the premium is gone. In this way, term life insurance is similar to auto or homeowner's insurance.

The other kind of life insurance, called *cash-value* life insurance, is probably one of the most oversold financial products in the history of Western civilization. Cash-value policies (whole, universal, variable, and so on) combine life insurance with a supposed savings feature. Your premiums not only pay for life insurance, but some of your dollars are also credited to an account that grows in value over time, assuming that you keep paying your premiums. On the surface, this sounds potentially attractive.

It's true that life insurance, when bought and placed in an irrevocable life insurance trust (which we discuss later in this chapter), receives special treatment with regard to estate taxes. Specifically, the death benefit or proceeds paid on the policy upon your death can pass to your designated heirs free of estate taxes. (Some states don't allow this.)

People who sell cash-value insurance — that is, insurance salespeople and other life insurance brokers masquerading as "estate planning specialists" and "financial planners" — too often advocate life insurance as the best, and only, way to reduce estate taxes. But the other methods we discuss in this chapter are superior in most cases.

Insurance companies aren't stupid. In fact, they're quite smart. If you purchase a cash-value life insurance policy that provides a death benefit of say $1 million, for example, you have to pay substantial insurance premiums, although far less than $1 million. Is that a good deal for you? No, because the insurance company invests your premium dollars and earns a return just as you would have if you had invested the money yourself instead of buying the life insurance.

Over the years, between the premiums you pay on your life policy and the returns the insurance company earns investing your premiums, the insurance company is able to come up with more than $1 million. Otherwise, how could they afford to pay out a death benefit of $1 million on your policy? If the insurance company can do it, so can you.

Using life insurance as an estate planning tool is beneficial if your estate includes assets that you don't want to subject to a forced sale to pay estate taxes after you die. For example, small-business owners whose businesses are worth millions may want to consider cash-value life insurance under specialized circumstances. If your estate will lack the other necessary assets to pay expected estate taxes and you don't want your beneficiaries to be forced to sell the business, you can buy life insurance to pay expected estate taxes.

If you want to get advice on whether life insurance is an appropriate estate-planning strategy for you, don't expect to get objective information from anyone who sells life insurance.

Among the best places to shop for cash-value life insurance policies are the following:

- **USAA** (800-531-8000)
- **Ameritas** (800-552-3553)
- **Wholesale Insurance Network** (800-808-5810)

Setting up trusts

If estate planning hasn't already given you a headache, understanding the different types of trusts should. A *trust* is a legal device used to pass to someone else the management responsibility and, ultimately, ownership of some of your assets. We discuss some trusts earlier in this chapter, such as bypass, Crummey, and life insurance trusts; here, we talk about some other trusts you may hear about when you do estate planning.

Living trusts

A *living trust* effectively transfers assets into a trust. If you use a *revocable living trust,* you control those assets and can revoke the trust whenever you desire. The advantage of a living trust is that upon your death, assets can pass directly to your beneficiaries without going through probate. *Probate* is the legal process for administering and implementing the directions in a will. Living trusts keep your assets out of probate but, in and of themselves, do nothing to help you deal with estate taxes. (Living trusts can contain bypass trusts and other tax-saving provisions.)

Don't get seduced into buying cash-value life insurance for the wrong reasons

Cash-value policies are aggressively pushed by insurance salespeople because of the high commissions (50 to 100 percent of the first year's premium paid by you) that insurance companies pay the agents.

These policies are expensive ways to purchase life insurance. Because of their high cost (about eight times the cost of the same amount of term life insurance), you're more likely to buy less life insurance coverage than you need — that's the sad result of the insurance industry pushing this stuff. The vast majority of life insurance buyers need more protection than they can afford to buy with cash-value coverage.

Agents know which buttons to push to get you interested in buying the wrong kind of life insurance. Insurance agents will show you all sorts of projections that imply that after the first 10 or 20 years of paying your premiums, you'll have such a large cash value in your policy that you won't need to pay more premiums to keep the life insurance in force. The only reason that you may be able to stop paying premiums is that you've poured too much extra money into the policy in the early years of payment. Remember that cash-value life insurance costs eight times as much as term.

Insurance agents also argue that your cash value grows tax-deferred. But if you want tax-deferred retirement savings, first take advantage of retirement savings plans (such as 401(k)s, 403(b)s, SEP-IRAs, and Keoghs), which give you an immediate tax deduction for your current contributions in addition to growth without taxation until withdrawal. Money paid into a cash-value life policy gives no up-front tax breaks to you. If you've exhausted the tax-deductible plans, then variable annuities or a nondeductible IRA can provide tax-deferred compounding of your investment dollars (see Chapter 21).

Life insurance tends to be a mediocre investment anyway. The insurance company quotes you an interest rate for the first year only. After that, the rate is up to the company's discretion. If you don't like the future interest rates, you can be penalized for quitting the policy. Would you invest your money in a bank account that quoted an interest rate for the first year only and then penalized you for moving your money in the next seven to ten years?

Property and assets that are owned in joint tenancy or inside retirement accounts — such as IRAs or 401(k)s — and have designated beneficiaries generally pass to heirs without going through probate. (Many states also allow a special type of revocable trust for bank accounts called a *Totten* trust, which insulates the bank accounts from probate, as well. Such trusts are established for the benefit of another person, and the money in the trust is paid to the beneficiary upon the account holder's death.)

Probate is a lengthy, expensive hassle for your heirs. Attorney probate fees can run around 5 to 7 percent of the value of the estate. In addition, your assets become a matter of public record as a result of probate. In addition to saving you on probate fees and maintaining your financial privacy, living trusts are also useful in naming someone to administer your affairs in the event that you become incapacitated.

You can't escape the undertaker or the lawyers. It costs money and time to set up a trust and transfer property in and out. Thus, living trusts are likely to be of greatest value to people who are age 60 and older, single, and own assets worth more than $100,000 that must pass through probate (including real estate, nonretirement accounts, and business). Small estates may actually be less expensive to probate in some states than the cost and hassle of setting up a living trust.

Charitable trusts

If you're feeling philanthropic, charitable trusts may be for you. With a *charitable remainder trust,* you or your designated beneficiary receives income from assets you donate to a charity. At the time of your death, or after a certain number of years, the principal is donated to the charity and is thus removed from your taxable estate. A charitable remainder trust makes especially good sense in cases where a person holds an asset he or she wishes to donate that has greatly appreciated in value. By not selling the asset before the donation, a hefty tax on the profit is avoided.

In a *charitable lead trust,* the roles of the charity and beneficiaries are reversed. The charity receives the income from the assets for a set number of years or until you pass away, at which point the assets pass to your beneficiary. You get a current income tax deduction for the value of the expected payments to the charity.

Getting advice and help

The number of people who will happily charge you a fee or sell you some legal advice or insurance far exceeds the number actually qualified to render objective estate-planning advice. Attorneys, accountants, financial planners, estate planning specialists, investment companies, insurance agents, and even some nonprofit agencies stand ready to help you figure out how to dispense your wealth.

Most of these people and organizations have conflicts of interest and lack the knowledge necessary to properly do sound estate planning for you. Attorneys are biased toward drafting legal documents and devices that are more complicated than you may need. Insurance agents and financial planners who work on commission try to sell you cash-value life insurance. Investment firms and banks want you to establish a trust account that requires that the assets be managed through them in the future.

Although the cost of *free* estate-planning seminars is tempting, you get what you pay for — or worse.

Wills

Wills — legal documents that detail your instructions for what you want done with your personal property and assets upon your death — won't save you on taxes or on probate. Wills are, however, an estate-planning basic that most people should have but don't. Most of the world doesn't bother with wills, because laws and customs divvy up a person's estate among the spouse and children or other close relatives.

The main benefit of a will is that it ensures that your wishes for the distribution of your assets are fulfilled. If you die without a will (known in legalese as *intestate*), your state decides how to distribute your money and other property, according to state law. Therefore, your friends, more-distant relatives, and favorite charities will probably receive nothing. For a fee, the state will appoint an administrator to supervise the distribution of your assets.

If you have little in the way of personal assets and don't really care who gets your possessions and other assets (state law usually specifies the closest blood relatives), you can forget about creating a will. You can save yourself the time and depression that inevitably accompanies this gloomy exercise.

If you have minor (dependent) children, a will is necessary to name a guardian for them. In the event that you and your spouse should both die without a will, the state (courts and social service agencies) decides who will raise your children. Therefore, even if you cannot decide at this time who would raise your children, you should *at least* appoint a trusted guardian who could decide for you.

Living wills and medical powers of attorney are useful additions to a standard will. A living will tells your doctor what, if any, life-support measures you would accept. A medical power of attorney grants authority to someone you trust to make decisions with a physician regarding your medical care options. These additional documents are usually prepared when a will is drawn up.

Start the process of planning your estate by looking at the big picture first. Talk to your family members about your financial situation. Many people never take this basic but critical step. Your heirs likely have no idea what you're considering or what you're worried about. Conversely, how can you develop a solid action plan without understanding your heirs' needs and concerns? Be careful not to use money to control or manipulate other family members.

For professional advice, you need someone who can objectively look at the big picture. Attorneys and tax advisors who specialize in estate planning are a good starting point. Ask the professionals you're thinking of hiring if they sell life insurance or manage money. If they do, they can't possibly be objective and likely aren't sufficiently educated about estate planning, given their focus.

For preparation of wills and living trusts, check out the high-quality software programs on the market. Legal software may save you from the often difficult task of finding a competent and affordable attorney. Preparing documents with software can also save you money.

Using legal software is generally preferable to using fill-in-the-blank documents. Software has the built-in virtues of directing and limiting your choices and keeping you from making common mistakes. Quality software also incorporates the knowledge and insights of the legal eagles who developed the software. As to the legality of documents that you create with software, remember that a will, for example, is made legal and valid by the proper signing of documents by you and your witnesses. An attorney preparing a document is *not* what makes it legal. If your situation isn't unusual, legal software may work well for you. Here are two good software packages worth considering:

Estate planning from the grave

It should go without saying that not everyone does the right type of estate planning before they pass on. Some people die before their time, and others just can't seem to get around to the planning part, even if they're in failing health.

Although it's impossible for a person to do any further planning after he's dead and gone, that person's heirs may legally take steps that can, in some cases, dramatically reduce estate taxes. Some legal folks call these steps "postmortem planning." Here's an example of how it works.

Suppose that Peter Procrastinator never got around to planning for the distribution of his substantial estate. When he died, all of his estate was to go to his wife. No dummy, his wife hired legal help so that she could

disclaim, or reject, part of Peter's big estate. Why would she do that? Simple, so that part of the estate could immediately go to their children. If she hadn't disclaimed, Peter would have missed out on his $625,000 estate tax exclusion. By disclaiming, she possibly saved her kids more than $200,000 in estate taxes.

The person doing the disclaiming, in this case Peter's wife, may not direct to whom the disclaimed assets will go. Peter's will or other legal documents specify who is second-in-line. Otherwise, state law dictates who is next in the receiving line. Disclaimers are also irrevocable, must be made in writing, and are subject to other IRS rules and regulations. A knowledgeable executor and attorney can help you with disclaiming.

✔ For will preparation, check out WillMaker by Nolo Press. In addition to enabling you to prepare wills (in every state except Louisiana), WillMaker can help you prepare a *living will* and *medical power of attorney* (as we discuss earlier in the chapter).

✔ Nolo's Living Trust software enables you to create a living trust that serves to keep property out of probate in the event of your death (remember that it does *not* address the issue of estate taxes). Like wills, living trusts are fairly standard legal documents that you can properly create with the guidance of a top-notch software package. The Living Trust package also advises you to seek professional guidance for your situation, if necessary.

If you want to do more reading on estate planning, pick up a copy of *Plan Your Estate* by attorney Denis Clifford (Nolo Press). If you have a large estate that may be subject to estate taxes, it's probably worth your time and money to consult an attorney or tax advisor who specializes in estate planning.

Part VI
The Part of Tens

In this part . . .

These short chapters can be read anytime you have a few spare minutes, and they're packed with information that somehow needs to stand out. We highlight, for example, the ten most important changes in the tax laws affecting your 1998 and future returns. In this part, you can also learn about the ten best ways to avoid an audit, find answers to ten other important tax questions, and even discover the top ten ways to reduce your taxes that you or your friends may overlook.

If you have your own idea for a list of Ten Tax somethings, send us the idea. If we publish the list you suggest in our next edition of *Taxe$ For Dummie$,* we'll send you next year's edition — free!

"The wisdom of man never yet contrived a system of taxation that would operate with perfect equality."

— Andrew Jackson

Chapter 27
Ten Important Tax Law Changes

•••

1 n August of 1997, Congress passed and President Clinton signed into law The Taxpayer Relief Act of 1997. If ever there was a misnamed piece of legislation, this was it!

Sure, the vast majority of the changes would lead to tax reductions. However, comprehending and complying with the new laws takes real time and in some cases money to hire professional tax help. All this for an average per taxpayer benefit estimated at a mere $70! Averages, of course, can be deceiving. Some people, especially more moderate-income earners and those with minor children may derive far more than a $70 benefit. Higher income earners with little saved or invested stand to benefit the least. Many of the new tax perks are phased out, in IRS speak (wiped out in our terminology), at higher income levels.

Before the ink was dry on the 1997 tax bill, Congress and the IRS started tinkering and interpreting what the new laws would mean for all of us. In this chapter, we highlight the ten biggest tax law changes affecting your 1998 and future years' tax returns. Read it and reap the rewards!

Roth individual retirement accounts (IRAs)

This is the first tax year in which a single taxpayer with an adjusted gross income (AGI) under $95,000 and joint filers with an AGI under $150,000 can contribute up to $2,000 per year to a Roth IRA. (The amount that can be contributed is reduced for singles with AGIs up to $110,000 and married couples filing jointly with an AGI up to $160,000, and is completely eliminated for those with AGIs above these thresholds).

What the heck is a Roth IRA, you may be asking, and how the heck is it different from a regular IRA? The new Roth IRA (named after the chairman of the Senate Finance Committee who was its chief proponent) doesn't offer a tax deduction on funds contributed to it; however, it does offer benefits not provided by other retirement accounts, including regular IRAs. The biggest benefit of the Roth IRA is that all the earnings on your contributions aren't taxed upon withdrawal as long as you're at least age 59$^1/_2$ and your account is at least five years old. Another benefit that appeals to some taxpayers is that unlike funds in a regular IRA, those in a Roth don't have to be withdrawn beginning in the year following the tax year in which the account holder reaches age 70$^1/_2$.

Before you run out to fund a Roth IRA, though, peruse Chapter 21 to make sure that you're taking advantage of the best retirement account options available to you. It's still generally best to fund accounts that offer up-front tax breaks before considering a Roth IRA.

Reduced capital gains tax rate

The tax rate on long-term *capital gains* (that is, the profit from selling a nonretirement account investment for a higher price than it was bought for) is reduced from 28 percent to 20 percent for higher tax bracket investors. To qualify for this new, lower tax rate, you must hold the investment for more than 12 months. For those in the 15-percent income tax bracket, the capital gains tax rate for investments held more than 12 months drops to 10 percent.

Beginning in the year 2006, the capital gains rate for higher tax bracket investors drops even further — to 18 percent — for investments held at least five years. For those in the 15-percent income tax bracket, the new five-year rate drops to 8 percent, effective in the year 2001.

Fortunately, in 1998, Congress had the good sense to do away with the third tier of capital gains rates for investments held between 12 and 18 months, for which the old maximum capital gains tax rate of 28 percent applied. Under the 1997 tax law changes, you had to hold an investment more than 18 months to qualify for the lowest long-term capital gains rate. See Chapter 23 to find out all about the new rules and how to select tax-wise investments for the years ahead. Chapter 12 explains how to calculate and report your capital gains (and losses) when you file your federal income tax return.

At the time this book goes to press, Congress is yet again considering monkeying with the capital gains tax laws. It seems that some in Congress are worried about spending the new-found budget surpluses (how about paying off a portion of the five trillion in debt, folks?). Specifically under consideration is a further reduction in the long-term capital gains rate to 15 percent for the higher tax bracket investors and to 7.5 percent for those in the 15-percent federal tax bracket. However, with all the fireworks over the Clinton scandals, further tax law changes may be delayed due to excessive television appearances by congressional publicity hounds discussing the Monica "affair" with Geraldo and Larry King.

Tax-free house-sale profits

If you plan to retire soon, or if you have a smaller family now that the kids have left the nest, or if you simply want to move to a less costly housing market, the new rules are virtually tailor-made for you. Under the new house-sale rules, single people may exclude from federal tax up to $250,000, and couples up to $500,000, of profit. And, unlike under the old house-sales rules, you need *not* buy a replacement residence or buy a replacement residence of equal or greater value within two years of the closing of the sale of your previous house.

Not everyone is better off under this new tax law. Some homeowners, particularly those who live in high cost areas and have owned their homes for many years, have gains exceeding the $250,000 or $500,000 limits. If they sell, they'll owe tax on whatever profits exceed their applicable exclusion limit. (Under the old laws, such homeowners could have avoided taxation by simply buying a replacement residence of equal or greater value than the one sold.) See Chapter 24 for a discussion of how to best capitalize on these new house-sale rules.

Credit for minor children

In tax year 1998, a $400 credit (raised to $500 in tax year 1999 and beyond) per child under the age of 18 will help parents with a small portion of the costs of having and raising children. This credit, however, as with many of the tax perks in the new tax laws, is phased out for higher income earners: single parents with an adjusted gross income in excess of $75,000 and married couples filing jointly with an adjusted gross income exceeding $110,000 lose $50 of the credit for every $1,000 above these amounts. This income ceiling is another reason parents should consider making the "educational investment" of spending more time at home with the kids rather than working more hours and losing so much to taxes.

Educational tax breaks

The new laws create two tax credits for educational expenses: the Hope Scholarship Credit and the Lifetime Learning Credit. These credits are only fully available to single income earners with adjusted gross incomes of less than $40,000 (partial credits are allowed for those with incomes up to $50,000) and married couples filing jointly with adjusted gross incomes of less than $80,000 (partial credits are allowed for those with combined incomes of up to $100,000).

Also, beginning in 1998, parents may contribute up to $500 per child per year to a new type of tax-sheltered investment account called an Education IRA. Although contributions to the Education IRA aren't tax deductible, investment earnings can compound and be withdrawn free of tax as long as the funds are used to pay for college costs and the tax credits just mentioned aren't taken that same year. See Chapter 25 for the specifics on these new provisions.

Approach the Education IRA with caution. Although it's not yet clear how college financial aid officers are going to treat these accounts, contributing to Education IRAs will probably reduce a family's eligibility for financial aid.

Enhanced tax breaks for small-business owners

Over the next decade, the amount of a self-employed person's health insurance premiums that are deductible will increase to 100 percent (see Table 27-1). As in the past, in order to take this deduction, your business must show a profit for the year.

Self-employed people can now put money away on a pretax basis into a medical savings account (MSA) to pay for out-of-pocket health care costs with a high-deductible medical insurance plan (see Chapter 22). And, last but not least, new tax laws loosen up the restrictions on deducting expenses for a home office (see Chapter 11 for all the details).

Table 27-1	The Amount of a Self-Employed Person's Health Insurance That Is Tax-Deductible
Tax Year	**Deductible Percentage**
1998	45%
1999–2001	60%
2002	70%
2003 and after	100%

Better IRA withdrawal rules

Except for a few situations having mostly to do with emergencies such as a major illness and unemployment, tapping into an IRA account before age $59^{1}/_{2}$ (called an "early withdrawal") triggers a hefty 10-percent federal income tax penalty (in addition to whatever your state charges).

Beginning with tax year 1998, however, you'll be allowed to make a penalty-free early withdrawal from your IRA for two specific expenses. First-time home buyers may withdraw up to $10,000. Amounts may also be withdrawn for qualified higher education costs.

Early withdrawals from IRA accounts are still subject to regular income tax in the year of withdrawal. The one exception is for withdrawals from a Roth IRA for a first-time home purchase. As long as the Roth IRA account is at least five years old, this withdrawal is both penalty-free and federal income tax-free.

The new Roth IRA accounts are also exempt from the normal retirement account requirement to begin taking minimum distributions at age $70^{1}/_{2}$ if you aren't working. See Chapter 21 for all the details on retirement accounts.

Estate tax law changes

Gradually over the coming years, the amount that a deceased person may leave to heirs will increase to $1 million. And qualifying small-business owners will have a new, higher exemption to allow them to pass on up to $1.3 million of interest in their small business free of federal estate tax.

Also, the amount that may be gifted free of taxation, currently set at $10,000 per recipient, will be indexed to inflation beginning in tax year 1999. See Chapter 26 for a complete explanation of all the new estate tax law changes.

(Small) increased taxpayer rights

In 1998, the IRS, through congressional hearings, got quite a bit of negative press. After hearing from individual taxpayers who felt that they were put through the wringer by the tough guys down at IRS central, Congress decided to come to the rescue and give taxpayers more protection and rights. We have to chuckle a bit at all this — after all, Congress was the organization that created all these ambiguous and cumbersome tax laws in the first place.

Here are the major provisions that will supposedly benefit taxpayers (we say supposedly because the actual benefit is often far, far less than meets the eye):

- **Burden of proof falls (more) on the IRS.** Unlike the criminal justice system, which operates under the logic that when charged with a crime, you're presumed innocent until you're proven guilty, our tax system has operated under the reverse, perverse logic that you're guilty until you prove yourself innocent. However, to benefit from being presumed innocent until the IRS proves otherwise, your tax disagreement must actually land in court, and you must meet other requirements, including having good records and having been cooperative and compliant to that point.

- **Taxpayers have new protections regarding collections.** In recent years, the IRS got itself into trouble with the way they handled certain tax collections. In some cases, taxpayers experienced unjustified and confrontational seizure of property and other assets, even for small amounts of tax owed. Now, for example, the IRS needs a court order to sell someone's home and needs a higher level of approval within the IRS to seize someone's business.

- **Innocent spouse rules are enhanced.** As we discuss in Chapter 4, married couples heading toward divorce don't always cooperate about money and taxes. The tax bill passed in 1998 beefs up a spouse's ability to file separately while still married to avoid being held responsible for the other spouse's tax negligence. Although this may sound attractive, we fear that this will increase total costs for both spouses, especially if you factor in additional divorce lawyer wrangling over tax liabilities. See Chapter 4 for more details.

- **Advice given by tax advisors to taxpayers is confidential.** With legal matters, what a client tells his attorney is largely confidential. With tax issues, that same standard of confidentiality hasn't been applied to what a taxpayer tells his preparer or advisor. Now it is, at least with respect to advice, but the new confidentiality doesn't extend to documents.

Chapter 28

Ten Frequently Asked Tax Questions

O ver the years, a great number of people have asked us all sorts of tax questions. We've also noted the conspicuous absence of some questions that people should ask — sometimes you don't know what to ask because you don't know what you don't know. We also realize that there are some questions that more of you would really like to ask but don't feel comfortable asking. We answer all of these questions for you right now in the privacy of your own home.

If I can't make (or already missed) the deadline for filing my return and paying what I owe, what do I do?

Don't panic, but get on the stick. And unless you lost your records in a fire or some other documented catastrophe (your dog eating them doesn't count), you'll owe interest and penalties if you miss the April 15 filing deadline as well as owe taxes. Every day you delay coming clean, the more it's going to cost you as the interest and penalties mount.

If it's before midnight on April 15, you're in luck. Join 6 million other people and get yourself an additional four months to procrastinate by filing **Form 4868.** (You can find this form in the back of our book — you'd think that the IRS would put this form in its booklet because this is a form many people realize they need at the last minute. But the IRS doesn't.) You need not have a good excuse for the extension — you get it even if you were too busy having fun.

If you file an extension, you're still obligated to pay the tax that you owe. Because you haven't completed your tax return (that's why you need the extension, right?), you won't know how much you owe. You're going to have to estimate. Better to overestimate and send them a bit more than you think that you need to.

If you don't have the money to pay your taxes, it's far better to contact the IRS and tell them your situation. The IRS is actually understanding and will work out a payment plan (with interest, of course). Refer to Chapter 19 for tips on what to do if you can't pay. If you don't have the necessary records to prepare your return, refer to Chapter 3.

How can I know that I'm not overlooking deductions?

Educate yourself. You don't know what you're missing until you know what goodies are available. This book, particularly Parts II, III, and V, can help you see the light. If you're currently working with a tax preparer and aren't confident of his or her capabilities, consider getting a second opinion by taking your past couple of tax returns to another preparer and seeing whether other tax-reduction opportunities can be uncovered. Tax-preparation software (see Chapter 2) may help you as well.

How long do I have to keep my tax forms?

Easy one. The quick answer is three years from your official filing date (usually April 15). But check out Chapter 3 for a few exceptions to this rule — remember, the IRS loves exceptions to the rules.

If I forgot to deduct something in a prior tax year, may I go back and fix my mistake now?

It depends on what you forgot and how long ago you filed your return. Unfortunately, one of the best deductions available, for retirement accounts, can't be claimed on an amended return (unless the money was legally contributed by the time you filed your return). Other oversights you made in reporting your income, deductions, and expenses can generally be handled on **Form 1040X, Amended U.S. Individual Income Tax Return.** Call the IRS at 800-TAX-FORM for a copy of Form 1040X, or find the form in the back of this book.

You must file your amendments within three years from April 15 of the year you filed the original return. (If you filed after April 15 because you got an extension, count the three years from the date you actually filed your completed return.) Refer to Chapter 19 to find out how to amend your return.

Why do I pay so much in taxes?

We actually pay less in taxes than people in most developed countries. It's easy to over-look all the stuff our tax dollars pay for, such as national defense, roads, bridges, schools, libraries, police departments, Social Security income, and retiree health care benefits — and $600 toilet seats!

The best — and legal — way to reduce your taxes is to master the strategies that we discuss in this book, some of which can be applied when preparing your annual return (Parts II & III) and others that involve advance planning (Part V).

Some taxes, such as sales taxes, can be reduced by simply spending less money. Besides saving you tax dollars, this approach can boost your savings account. If you're like most Americans, you probably aren't saving enough anyway. Now you have another reason to cut your spending. A double bonus!

It's tempting to want to blame the government for high taxes. Effecting change through government is slow and unlikely. But if you can change your financial behaviors, that's where you can save big tax dollars. Your ability to take advantage of most tax-saving maneuvers hinges on your consistently spending less than you earn so that you have cash to invest.

Haven't they closed all the tax loopholes?

Yes, it's true that many of the financial schemes concocted to reduce taxes have been eliminated by changes in the tax laws over the past decade. This elimination of many loopholes has put a number of investment salespeople and *creative* financial planners out of business. Thankfully, this has reduced the likelihood of your being hoodwinked into buying some bad investments. Fewer loopholes create a more level playing field. Most of the tax-reduction strategies we discuss in this book are open to people of any economic means.

Why do the wealthy and corporations pay so little in taxes?

This myth is perpetuated by those rare but highly publicized cases where — because of large write-offs — affluent people and mighty corporations appear to slide by without paying their fair share of taxes. Yet, the truth is that the highest-income earners typically pay more in taxes than most of us earn in a year! The top 1 percent of all income earners pay 25 percent of all federal taxes. That's why so many of these folks moan and complain about how much they pay in taxes. (The polite ones complain to their tax and financial advisors, lest others think that they're ungrateful for their high incomes!)

The only way a person or company with a big income can end up paying less in taxes than a person or company with a smaller income is if a great deal of money is spent on tax-deductible stuff, such as mortgage interest, property taxes, and reinvesting in business.

These perfectly legal write-offs are available to anyone, regardless of income. In fact, low-income earners have tax deductions, such as the earned income tax credit, that others can't take. Also, a wealthy person can't deduct the mortgage interest on anything larger than a $1,100,000 first mortgage.

It's true that the wealthy and corporations can afford to employ tax advisors to keep their tax bills to a minimum. But what they do to reduce their taxes still has to be legal. Cheating is illegal for all taxpayers, and the IRS audits those with the deepest pockets most often.

Shouldn't I buy real estate to reduce my taxes?

You can write off mortgage interest and property taxes on most pieces of real estate (for more details, see Chapter 24). This type of write-off can help, but you shouldn't buy real estate *because* of these tax breaks. You should own a home because you need a place to live long-term. Besides, owning should cost you less than paying an ever-escalating rent over the years.

Real estate property sellers aren't stupid. The tax benefits available on homes are factored into the current selling prices. This is one of the reasons why real estate is so expensive.

How can I avoid a last-minute scramble for documents?

One of the easiest tax headaches to avoid is the search for tax forms at midnight on a rainy Sunday night. We include in the back of this book the tax forms you're most likely to need. (You're welcome.) You can also pick up the forms the next time you're at the local post office or library, or you can call the IRS at 800-829-3676. Another easy way to avoid the midnight search is to use some of the tax-preparation software we recommend in Chapter 2. It's also your responsibility to take care of your personal forms, like your W-2s.

If you have access to the Internet, you can download the tax forms you need (for free!) from the IRS's World Wide Web page (start browsing at www.irs.ustreas.gov) or file transfer site (ftp.fedworld.gov). You need an Adobe Acrobat text reader (download it for free from the IRS's Web page or from Adobe's Web page at www.adobe.com, or call Adobe at 800-272-3623). Simply download the form you need and print it; the IRS will happily accept the form when you file your return.

Setting up a filing system can be a big time-saver if you experience the missing-form syndrome. If you have limited patience for setting up neat file folders and you lead an uncomplicated financial life (that is, you haven't saved the receipts that you need for tax purposes throughout the year), you can confine your filing to January and February. During those months, you find in the mailbox your tax booklets from the IRS and your state tax authority, along with tax summary forms on wages paid by your employer (W-2), investment income (1099), and home mortgage interest (1098). Find a file folder or big envelope and label it something easy to remember — "1999 Taxes" is a brilliant choice — and then dump all these forms in as they arrive. When you're ready to crunch numbers, just open the file or envelope and away you go. See Chapter 3 for more organizing tips.

Why does my brother-in-law get a larger tax refund than I do?

Because you aren't your brother-in-law. Seriously, though, a large refund is not a sign of victory over the IRS. In fact, it's more likely a sign of failure. Large refunds result from having paid the IRS too much in taxes during the year. You essentially give the federal government an interest-free loan when you overpay your taxes during the year and wait until the next spring to get your money back. If your brother-in-law pays little in the way of taxes relative to his income, he probably takes advantage of all the tax breaks we tell you about in this book. Good thing you got the book!

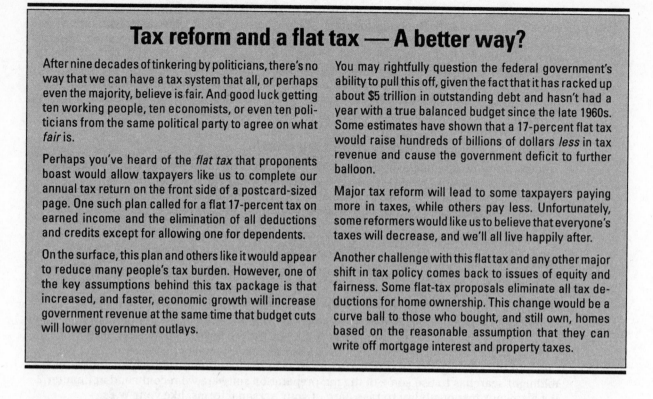

Tax reform and a flat tax — A better way?

After nine decades of tinkering by politicians, there's no way that we can have a tax system that all, or perhaps even the majority, believe is fair. And good luck getting ten working people, ten economists, or even ten politicians from the same political party to agree on what *fair* is.

Perhaps you've heard of the *flat tax* that proponents boast would allow taxpayers like us to complete our annual tax return on the front side of a postcard-sized page. One such plan called for a flat 17-percent tax on earned income and the elimination of all deductions and credits except for allowing one for dependents.

On the surface, this plan and others like it would appear to reduce many people's tax burden. However, one of the key assumptions behind this tax package is that increased, and faster, economic growth will increase government revenue at the same time that budget cuts will lower government outlays.

You may rightfully question the federal government's ability to pull this off, given the fact that it has racked up about $5 trillion in outstanding debt and hasn't had a year with a true balanced budget since the late 1960s. Some estimates have shown that a 17-percent flat tax would raise hundreds of billions of dollars *less* in tax revenue and cause the government deficit to further balloon.

Major tax reform will lead to some taxpayers paying more in taxes, while others pay less. Unfortunately, some reformers would like us to believe that everyone's taxes will decrease, and we'll all live happily after.

Another challenge with this flat tax and any other major shift in tax policy comes back to issues of equity and fairness. Some flat-tax proposals eliminate all tax deductions for home ownership. This change would be a curve ball to those who bought, and still own, homes based on the reasonable assumption that they can write off mortgage interest and property taxes.

Why should I work so hard if I have to pay all these taxes?

Here's a question more of you should be asking, especially two-income families. Although we don't want to get into trouble by suggesting that someone may not be spending enough time at home with the kids, couples pay a very high effective rate of tax on the second income. That second-income earner may be making only the minimum wage when you factor in all the commuting costs, lunches out, work-clothing expenses, child care expenses, and so on. Of course, there are other benefits to working besides money. But you have to ask yourself whether commuting traffic jams and office politics are really worth the minimum wage!

Most people don't make the most of their money. We work hard at earning money but not at educating ourselves about how to make it stretch further. That's why you owe it to yourself to read Part V of this book.

Chapter 29
Ten Proven Ways to Avoid Audits

. . . .

*1*f you've never been audited, you probably fall into one of these categories: You aren't old enough yet, you haven't made gobs of money, or you're just plain lucky. The fact is that many taxpayers do get audited during their adult lives. It's just a matter of time.

Even well-meaning and humble authors of well-meaning and humble tax-advice books aren't exempt. One of us, Eric, has stared down an audit and says that the audit wasn't too bad — sort of like preparing for an exam . . . in a course you aren't taking for credit!

You can take some common-sense steps (honesty being the star of the show) to reduce your chances of winning this most unwelcome lottery. After all, instead of wasting your day in some IRS office, you want to make sure that you have sufficient time for jury duty or to run down to the Department of Motor Vehicles to renew your driver's license.

Dot your i's and cross your t's

Audit your own return *before* you send it in. If the IRS finds mistakes through its increasingly sophisticated computer-checking equipment, you're more likely to get audited. They figure that if they find obvious errors, some not-so-obvious ones lurk beneath the surface. So your undotted i's and uncrossed t's are probably more likely than ever to make some computer beep at IRS Central (beeps are bad).

Have you included all your income? Think about the different accounts you had during the tax year. Do you have interest and dividend statements for *all* your accounts? Finding these statements is easier if you've been keeping your financial records in one place. Check your W-2s and 1099s against your tax form to make sure that you wrote the numbers down correctly.

Don't forget to check your math. Have you added, subtracted, multiplied, and divided correctly? Are your Social Security number and your address correct on the return? (Just use that handy-dandy, preprinted label the IRS gives you with your federal return — as long as *it* is accurate.) Did you sign and date your return?

These infractions will not, on their own, trigger an audit. In some cases, the IRS simply writes you a letter asking for your signature or the additional tax you owe (if the math mistake is not too fishy or too big). In some rare instances, they even send a refund if the mistake they uncover is in the taxpayer's favor — really! Regardless of how they handle the mistake, it can be a headache to clear up, and, more importantly, it can cost you extra money.

Declare all your income

When you prepare your return, you may be tempted to shave off a little of that consulting income you received in the form of a check. Who will miss it, right? The IRS will, that's who.

Thanks largely to computer cross-checking, the IRS has many ways to find unreported income. Be particularly careful if you're self-employed; anyone who pays you more than $600 in a year is required to file a Form 1099, which basically tells the IRS how much you received.

If you knowingly hide income, you'll be drawn and quartered. Only kidding. But you will face substantial penalties and, depending on the amount, criminal prosecution. That wouldn't be a picnic, especially if you can't afford to hire F. Lee Bailey.

Don't itemize, and if you do, be honest

People who itemize their deductions on Schedule A are far more likely to get audited because they have more opportunity and temptation to cheat. By all means, if you can *legally* claim more total deductions by using Schedule A than you can with the standard deduction (this deduction stuff is all spelled out in Chapter 9), we say "itemize, itemize, itemize." Just don't try to artificially inflate your deductions.

On the other hand, if it's basically a toss-up between Schedule A and your standard deduction, it's safer to take the standard deduction, which the IRS can't challenge.

Earn less money

At first glance, this may seem like an odd statement, but there really are costs associated with affluence. One of the costs of a high income — besides higher taxes — is a dramatic increase in the probability of getting audited. If your income is more than $100,000, you have about a 1 in 20 chance each year of being audited. But you have less than a 1 in 100 chance if your income is under $50,000. You see, there *are* advantages to earning less!

If you manage to pile up a lot of assets and don't enjoy them in retirement, your estate tax return — your "final" tax return — is at great risk of being audited. Do you think a 1 in 20 or 1 in 100 chance is bad in the audit lottery? More than 1 in 7 estate tax returns are audited by Uncle Sam. Nearly half of estate tax returns for estates of $5 million plus are audited. Why? Because big bucks are at stake. The IRS collects an average of more than $100,000 for each estate tax return it audits! So enjoy your money while you're alive or pass it along to your heirs in the here and now — otherwise, you may have trouble passing it along in the there and later!

Don't cheat

It may have taken the IRS a while to wise up, but now the government is methodically figuring out the different ways that people cheat. The next step for the IRS — after they figure out how people cheat — is to come up with ways to catch the cheaters. And with the enormous size of the federal debt outstanding, the pressure on the IRS to produce more revenue is huge. Cheaters beware!

Also, the IRS offers rewards for informants. If you're brazen enough to cheat and the IRS doesn't catch you, you may not be home free yet. Someone else may turn you in. So be honest — not only because it's the right thing to do but also because you'll probably sleep better at night knowing that you aren't breaking the law.

Tax protesters take note

Why should you take note? Because the IRS may. The IRS may flag returns that are accompanied by protest notes. Threats are bad, too — even if they're meant in fun (humor is not rife at the IRS, we suspect). The commandment is: Thou shalt not draw attention to thyself.

The protest issue is interesting. During congressional hearings, tax protesters stand up and tell members of Congress that the income tax is unconstitutional. They say they have proof. If we can get our hands on the proof, we'll include it in the next edition of this book. In the meantime, pay your taxes and resist the temptation to send along a cranky letter with your tax returns and payments.

Stay away from back-street refund mills

This advice doesn't apply to the majority of tax-preparation firms, but unfortunately, some firms out there fabricate deductions. Run away — as fast as you can — from tax preparers who tell you, after winking, that they have creative ways to reduce your tax bill, or those who base their fees on how many tax dollars they can save you. Be careful if you hire a tax preparer, and refer to Chapter 2 for how to find a top-quality tax preparer.

Be careful with hobby losses

Some people who have full-time jobs also have side businesses or hobbies with which they try to make a few bucks. But be careful if you report the side business as showing a loss year after year on your tax forms. Filers of **Schedule C, Profit or Loss from Business**, are at greatest risk for audits.

Here's an example. You like to paint surreal pictures, and you even sold one in 1993 for $150. But since then you haven't sold any paintings (the surreal market has bottomed out). Nevertheless, you continue to write off your cost for canvas and paint. The IRS will take a close look at that record, and you may be a candidate for an audit.

Don't be a nonfiler

The IRS has a special project with a mission to go after the estimated five to ten million nonfilers. Lest you think that the IRS does things in small ways, the IRS has assigned hundreds of agents to this project. Again, when you get caught — which is just a matter of time — in addition to owing back taxes, interest, and big penalties, you could also face criminal prosecution — gulp — and end up serving time in the slammer. So keep a clear conscience, continue to enjoy your freedom, and file your tax returns. And, remember, better late than never!

Work for an employer and don't cut corners if you don't

People who are self-employed have more opportunities to make mistakes on their taxes — or to creatively take deductions — than company-payroll wage earners. As a business owner, you're responsible for self-reporting not only your income but also your expenses. You have to be even more honest when dealing with the tax authorities, because the likelihood of getting audited is higher than average.

There's nothing wrong with being self-employed. But resist the temptation to cheat, because you're far more likely to be scrutinized and caught as a self-employed worker.

Don't disguise employees as independent contractors

This maneuver is covered by another IRS project. You remember the old barb: You can't put a sign around a cow that says, "This is a horse." You don't have a horse — you have a cow with a sign around its neck. Okay, we're reaching a bit . . . but the point is this: Just because you call someone an independent contractor doesn't mean that this person is not your employee. If you aren't sure about the relationship, refer to Chapter 22.

Carry a rabbit's foot

Try as you may to be an obedient taxpayer, you can get audited simply because of bad luck. Every year, the IRS audits thousands of people at random. Although such an under-taking may seem like a colossal waste of time to a tax neophyte like yourself, this effort provides the IRS with valuable information about the areas of tax returns where people make the most (or least) mistakes — and about the areas where people like to cheat!

So, if you do get an audit notice, don't assume that you did anything wrong. However, be prepared for your audit — see Part IV of this book.

(Did you notice how many items we included in this Part of Tens chapter? Okay, it's eleven, but we didn't know whether you thought the last one was particularly helpful; if you did find it helpful, call it a bonus tip.)

Chapter 30

Ten Commonly Overlooked Tax-Reduction Opportunities

$\cdots\cdots\cdots\cdots\cdots\cdots\cdots\cdots\cdots\cdots\cdots\cdots\cdots$

*T*his chapter presents a short list of some of the more commonly overlooked opportunities to reduce individual income taxes.

The income tax you pay is based on your taxable income minus your deductions. We start first with overlooked ways to minimize your taxable income. Then we move on to often-ignored deductions. We don't want you to be like all those people who miss out on perfectly legal deductions simply because they don't know what they can and what they can't deduct. Here are ten overlooked ways to reduce your income tax burden.

Break up with your banker

Out of apathy or lack of knowledge of better options, far too many people keep extra cash dozing away in their neighborhood bank. Yes, the bank has a vault and sometimes friendly tellers who may greet you by name, but banks also characteristically pay relatively lousy rates of interest. It's fine to keep your household checking account at the local bank, but you're throwing away free interest if you keep your extra savings money there. The better money market mutual funds often pay substantially greater interest than bank savings accounts and offer equivalent safety. And if you're in a high tax bracket, money market funds come in tax-free flavors. Refer to Chapter 23 to find out more about tax-friendly investments.

Invest in wealth-building assets

During your working years, while you're earning employment income, you probably don't need or want taxable income from your investments because it can increase your tax bill. Focus on investments that offer growth potential and offer little in the way of current taxable income. Real estate, stocks, and small-business investments fit the bill. These investments offer the best long-term growth potential, although you need to be able to withstand dips and sags in these markets. Most of the return that you can earn with these investments comes from appreciation in their value, making them tax-friendly because you are in control and can decide when to sell and realize your profit.

Fund "tax reduction" accounts

Even better than investments that appreciate are those that don't cause you any tax liability. When you funnel your savings dollars into retirement accounts, such as a 401(k), 403(b), SEP-IRA, Keogh, or IRA, your money compounds without taxation over the years. Even if the investments you hold inside these accounts pay out taxable dividends, no tax is owed. If you think that saving for retirement is boring, consider the tens of thousands of tax dollars these accounts can save you during your working years. If you don't use these accounts to save and invest, you may very well have to work many more years to accumulate the reserves necessary to retire. Refer to Chapter 21 to find out more.

Work overseas

You've always wanted to travel overseas. If you go to work for a time in a foreign country with low income taxes, you may be able to save big-time on income taxes. For tax year 1998, IRS tax laws allow you to exclude $72,000 of foreign-earned income (whether working for a company or on a self-employed basis) from U.S. income taxes. To qualify for this income tax exclusion, you must work at least 330 days (about 11 months) of the year overseas or be a foreign resident. You claim this income tax exclusion on IRS **Form 2555.**

If you earn more than $72,000, don't worry about being double-taxed on the income over this amount. You get to claim credits for foreign taxes paid on your U.S. tax return on **Form 1116, Foreign Tax Credit.** Perhaps to give you more time to fill out this form and others, the IRS gives Americans working abroad two extra months (until June 15) to file their tax returns.

The $72,000 limit on overseas income, thanks to the tax law passed in 1997, will increase $2,000 per year until it reaches $80,000 per year. (In the year 2008, the limit will be raised with increases in the cost of living.)

As with many things in life that sound too good to be true, this pot of overseas gold has many catches. First, many of the places you've romanticized about traveling to and perhaps living in — such as England, France, Italy, Sweden, Germany, and Spain — have higher income tax rates than ours. Also, this tax break is not available to U.S. government workers overseas.

Look at the whole package when deciding whether to work overseas. Some employers throw in a housing allowance and other benefits. Some companies understand the tax breaks and reduce your pay accordingly. Be sure to consider other costs of living overseas, both financial and emotional. Expect to pay sky-high prices for fresh produce in the Middle East, and budget for bigger phone bills to call loved ones in the States.

Check whether you can itemize

The IRS gives you two methods to determine your total deductions. Deductions are just what they sound like: You subtract them from your income before you calculate the tax you owe. So the more deductions you take, the smaller your taxable income — and the smaller your tax bill. You get to pick the method that leads to the largest total deductions — and thus, a lower tax bill. But sometimes the choice is not so clear, so be prepared to do some figuring.

Taking the *standard* deduction usually makes sense if you have a pretty simple financial life — a regular paycheck, a rented apartment, and no large expenses, such as medical bills, moving expenses, or loss due to theft or catastrophe. Single folks qualify for a $4,250 standard deduction, and married couples filing jointly get a $7,100 standard deduction for 1998.

The other method of determining your allowable deductions is to *itemize* them on your tax return. This painstaking procedure is definitely more of a hassle, but if you can tally up more than the standard deduction amounts, itemizing saves you money. Schedule A of your 1040 is the page for summing up your itemized deductions, but you won't know whether you have enough itemized deductions unless you give this schedule a good examination (refer to Chapter 9).

If you total your itemized deductions on Schedule A and the total is less than the standard deduction, take the standard deduction without fail. The total for your itemized deductions is worth checking each year, however, because you may have more deductions in some years than others, and you may occasionally be able to itemize.

Because you can control when you pay particular expenses that are eligible for itemizing, you can *shift* or *bunch* more of them into the select years when you have enough deductions to take full advantage of itemizing. For example, suppose that you're using the standard deduction this year because you just don't have many itemized deductions. Late in the tax year, though, you feel certain that you'll buy a home sometime during the next year. Thanks to the potential write-off of mortgage interest and property taxes, you also know that you'll be able to itemize next year. It makes sense, then, to shift as many deductible expenses as possible into the next year.

Trade consumer debt for mortgage debt

Suppose that you own real estate and haven't borrowed as much money as a mortgage lender would currently allow (given the current market value of the property and your financial situation). And further suppose that you've run up high-interest consumer debt. Well, you may be able to trade one debt for another. You probably can refinance your mortgage and pull out extra cash to pay off your credit card, auto loan, or other expensive consumer credit lines. You can usually borrow at a lower interest rate for a mortgage, thus lowering your monthly interest bill. Plus, you may get a tax-deduction bonus because consumer debt — auto loans, credit cards, credit lines — is not tax-deductible, but mortgage debt generally is. Therefore, the effective borrowing rate on a mortgage is even lower than the quoted rate suggests.

Don't forget that refinancing your mortgage and establishing home equity lines involve application fees and other charges (points, appraisals, credit reports, and so on). You must include these fees in the equation to see whether it makes sense to exchange consumer debt for more mortgage debt.

This strategy involves one big danger: Borrowing against the equity in your home can be an addictive habit. We've seen cases in which people run up significant consumer debt three or four distinct times and then refinance their home the same number of times over the years in order to bail themselves out. At a minimum, continued expansion of your mortgage debt handicaps your ability to work toward other financial goals. In the worst case, easy access to borrowing encourages bad spending habits that can lead to bankruptcy or foreclosure on your debt-ridden home.

Consider charitable contributions and expenses

If you itemize your deductions on Schedule A, you can deduct contributions made to charities. For example, most people already know that when they write a check for $50 to their favorite church or college, they can deduct it. Yet many taxpayers overlook the fact that they can also deduct expenses on work done for charitable organizations. For example, when you go to a soup kitchen to help prepare and serve meals, you can deduct your transportation costs to get there. You just need to keep track of your bus fares or driving mileage. The IRS currently allows a deduction of 14 cents per mile. You can also deduct the fair market value of donations of clothing, household appliances, furniture, and other goods to charities — many of these charities will even drive to your home to pick up the stuff. Just make sure to keep some documentation: Write a detailed list and get it signed by the charity (refer to Chapter 9).

Review your personal property and state taxes

If you don't currently itemize, you may be surprised to learn that your personal property and state income taxes are itemizable. If you must pay a fee to the state to register and license your car, you can itemize the expenditure as a deduction (line 8 on Schedule A, "Other Taxes"). The IRS allows you to deduct only the part of the fee that relates to the value of your car, however.

The state organization that collects the fee should be able to tell you what portion of the fee is deductible. If it's a user-friendly organization, it even shows this figure (for a fee) on your invoice. What service!

Maximize miscellaneous expenses

A number of so-called *miscellaneous expenses* are deductible on Schedule A. Most of these relate to your job or career and managing your finances. These expenses are deductible to the extent that, in sum, they exceed 2 percent of your adjusted gross income (see Chapter 9):

✔ **Educational expenses:** You may be able to deduct tuition, books, and travel costs to and from classes if your education is related to your career. Specifically, you can deduct these expenses if your course work improves your work skills. Continuing education classes for professionals may be deductible. If the law or your employer requires you to take courses to maintain your position, these courses are also deductible. But educational expenses allowing you to change or to move into a new field or career are not deductible.

✔ **Job search and career counseling:** After you obtain your first job, you may deduct legitimate costs related to finding another job within your field. For example, suppose that you're a chef in a steak house in Chicago, and you decide you want to do stir-fry in Los Angeles. You take a crash course in vegetarian cooking and then fly to L.A. a couple of times for interviews. You can deduct the cost of the course and your trips — *even if you don't ultimately change jobs.* If you hire a career counselor to help you figure everything out, you can deduct that cost, too. On the other hand, if you're burned out on cooking and decide that you want to become a professional volleyball player in L.A., that's a new career. You may get a better tan, but you won't generate deductions from changing jobs.

✔ **Unreimbursed expenses related to your job:** If you pay for your own subscriptions to trade journals to keep up-to-date in your field, or if you buy a new desk and chair to ease back pain, you can deduct these costs. If your job requires you to wear special clothes or a uniform, you can write off the cost of purchasing and cleaning them, as long as the clothes aren't suitable for wearing outside of work.

If you buy a computer for use outside the office at your own expense, you may be able to deduct the cost of the computer if it's for the convenience of your employer, or if it's a condition of your employment (and is used more than half the time for business). Union dues and membership fees for professional organizations are also deductible.

✔ **Investment and tax-related expenses:** Investment and tax-advisor fees are deductible, as are subscription costs for investment-related publications. Accounting fees for preparing your tax return or conducting tax planning during the year are deductible, as are legal fees related to your taxes. If you purchase a home computer to track your investments or prepare your taxes, you may be able to deduct part of that expense, too.

Double-check your self-employment expenses

If you're self-employed, you already deduct a variety of expenses from your income before calculating the tax that you owe. If you buy a computer or office furniture, you can deduct those expenses (sometimes they need to be gradually deducted or *depreciated* over time). Salaries for your employees, office supplies, rent or mortgage interest for your office space, and phone expenses are also generally deductible.

Although more than a few business owners cheat on their taxes, some self-employed folks don't take all the deductions they should. In some cases, people simply aren't aware of the wonderful world of deductions. For others, large deductions raise the risk of audit. Taking advantage of your eligible deductions makes sense and saves you money. It's worth the money to hire tax help — either by using a self-help book like this one or by paying a tax professional to review your return one year.

Appendix A

Reaching Out to the IRS

● ●

*E*instein was fond of saying that the most complicated thing he ever encountered was the income tax. Evidently, he considered the theory of relativity to be simple mathematics in comparison. So if you go through a bottle of aspirin when filling out your forms, you're in good company. **Medical Disclaimer:** If you are filling out your tax forms all in one day, don't finish off the bottle!

This appendix is our attempt to give you as much detailed "where to find it and where to send it" type of information as we can so that you don't have to run all over the place to get what you need. To that end, we have phone numbers, we have addresses, we have tips, and we have warnings. Enjoy!

IRS Tax Forms and Publications

Some of the things that your tax dollars help provide are tax forms and information publications. Only the most commonly used forms come with your annual IRS 1040 booklet. In the back of this book, we provide many of the forms you'll likely need to complete your tax return. But we also give you a list of other forms that are sometimes needed. So get your money's worth! Call 800-TAX-FORM to get more forms and publications than you ever wanted in your life. (Be prepared for a busy signal. Lots of folks call this number. If you have Internet access, the Web site at www.irs.ustreas.gov may be faster.)

If you're in a pinch for time and can't wait for some oddball form by mail, you have other options. You can obtain forms by:

✔ Visiting a local IRS office

✔ Lumbering over to your local library

✔ Going to other government offices

✔ Boogying to some banks

✔ Trying tax preparation software (see Chapter 2)

✔ Downloading the forms to your personal computer from an online service or the Internet (see Chapter 2)

Individual Tax Forms

Form 1040
U.S. Individual Income Tax Return (if you itemize or have income of $50,000 or more or income from oddball sources)

Form 1040A
U.S. Individual Income Tax Return

Form 1040EZ
Income Tax Return for Single and Joint Filers With No Dependents

Form 1040NR
U.S. Nonresident Alien Income Tax Return

Form 1040X
Amended U.S. Individual Income Tax Return

Form 1040-ES
Estimated Tax for Individuals

Form 1040-ES(NR)
U.S. Estimated Tax for Nonresident Alien Individuals

Form 1040 schedules

Schedule A
Itemized Deductions

Schedule B
Interest and Dividend Income

Schedule C
Profit or Loss From Business

Schedule C-EZ
Net Profit From Business

Schedule D
Capital Gains and Losses

Schedule E
Supplemental Income and Loss

Schedule EIC
Earned Income Credit

Schedule F
Profit or Loss From Farming

Schedule H
Household Employment Taxes

Schedule J
Income Averaging for Farmers

Schedule R
Credit for the Elderly or the Disabled

Schedule SE
Self-Employment Tax

Form 1040A schedules

Schedule 1
Interest and Dividend Income

Schedule 2
Child and Dependent Care Expenses

Schedule 3
Credit for the Elderly or the Disabled

Schedule EIC
Earned Income Credit

Other forms

Form TD F 90-22.1
Report of Foreign Bank and Financial Accounts

Form W-4
Employee's Withholding Allowance Certificate

Form W-4P
Withholding Certificate for Pension or Annuity Payments

Form W-5
Earned Income Credit Advance Payment Certificate

Form W-10
Dependent Care Provider's Identification and Certification

Form 709-A
United States Short Form Gift Tax Return

Form 843
Claim for Refund and Request for Abatement

Form 911
Application for Taxpayer Assistance Order

Form 940
Employer's Annual Federal Unemployment (FUTA) Tax Return

Form 940-EZ
Employer's Annual Federal Unemployment (FUTA) Tax Return

Form 1045
Application for Tentative Refund

Form 1116
Foreign Tax Credit

Form 1310
Statement of Person Claiming Refund Due a Deceased Taxpayer

Form 2106
Employee Business Expenses

Form 2106-EZ
Unreimbursed Employee Business Expenses

Form 2120
Multiple Support Declaration

Form 2210
Underpayment of Estimated Tax by Individuals, Estates, and Trusts

Form 2210F
Underpayment of Estimated Tax by Farmers and Fishermen

Form 2441
Child and Dependent Care Expenses

Form 2555
Foreign Earned Income

Form 2555-EZ
Foreign Earned Income Exclusion

Form 2688
Application for Additional Extension of Time to File U.S. Individual Income Tax Return

Form 3903
Moving Expenses

Form 3903-F
Foreign Moving Expenses

Form 3911
Taxpayer Statement Regarding Refund

Form 4070
Employee's Report of Tips to Employer

Form 4070A
Employee's Daily Record of Tips

Form 4136
Credit for Federal Tax Paid on Fuels

Form 4137
Social Security and Medicare Tax on Unreported Tip Income

Form 4255
Recapture of Investment Credit

Form 4506
Request for Copy or Transcript of Tax Form

Form 4562
Depreciation and Amortization

Form 4684
Casualties and Thefts

Form 4797
Sales of Business Property

Form 4835
Farm Rental Income and Expenses

Form 4868
Application for Automatic Extension of Time to File U.S. Individual Income Tax Return

Form 4952
Investment Interest Expense Deduction

Form 4970
Tax on Accumulation Distribution of Trusts

Form 4972
Tax on Lump-Sum Distributions

Form 5329
Additional Taxes Attributable to Qualified Retirement Plans (Including IRAs), Annuities, and Modified Endowment Contracts

Form 5884
Work Opportunity Credit

Form 6198
At-Risk Limitations

Form 6251
Alternative Minimum Tax — Individuals

Form 6252
Installment Sale Income

Form 6781
Gains and Losses From Section 1256 Contracts and Straddles

Form 8212
Additional Child Tax Credit

Form 8271
Investor Reporting of Tax Shelter Registration Number

Form 8275
Disclosure Statement

Form 8275-R
Regulation Disclosure Statement

Form 8283
Noncash Charitable Contributions

Form 8300
Report of Cash Payments Over $10,000 Received in a Trade or Business

Form 8332
Release of Claim to Exemption for Child of Divorced or Separated Parents

Form 8379
Injured Spouse Claim and Allocation

Form 8396
Mortgage Interest Credit

Form 8453
U.S. Individual Income Tax Declaration for Electronic Filing

Form 8582
Passive Activity Loss Limitations

Form 8582-CR
Passive Activity Credit Limitations

Form 8606
Nondeductible IRAs (Contributions, Distributions, and Basis)

Form 8611
Recapture of Low-Income Housing Credit

Form 8615
Tax for Children under Age 14 Who Have Investment Income of More Than $1,300

Form 8801
Credit for Prior Year Minimum Tax — Individuals, Estates, and Trusts

Form 8814
Parents' Election to Report Child's Interest and Dividends

Form 8815
Exclusion of Interest From Series EE U.S. Savings Bonds Issued after 1989

Form 8818
Optional Form To Record Redemption of Series EE U.S. Savings Bonds Issued after 1989

Form 8822
Change of Address

Form 8824
Like-Kind Exchanges

Form 8826
Disabled Access Credit

Form 8828
Recapture of Federal Mortgage Subsidy

Form 8829
Expenses for Business Use of Your Home

Form 8857
Request for Innocent Spouse Relief

Form 9465
Installment Agreement Request

IRS Tax Information Publications

If you want a more detailed explanation of the tax laws (you glutton), go for the gusto and request an IRS publication that suits your needs. Again, **800-TAX-FORM** is the magic (phone) number. IRS Publication 910 provides a complete list of the IRS's free publications by topic. Here's a shorter list that includes the most frequently used publications.

(SP) = available in Spanish

General publications

Publication 1(SP)
Your Rights as a Taxpayer

Publication 17
Your Federal Income Tax

Publication 225
Farmer's Tax Guide

Publication 334
Tax Guide for Small Business

Publication 579SP
Cómo Preparar la Declaración de Impuesto Federal (How to Prepare the Federal Income Tax Return)

Publication 910
Guide to Free Tax Services

Specialized publications

Publication 3
Armed Forces Tax Guide

Publication 4
Student's Guide to Federal Income Tax

Publication 15
Circular E, Employer's Tax Guide

Publication 54
Tax Guide for U.S. Citizens and Resident Aliens Abroad

Publication 378
Fuel Tax Credits and Refunds

Publication 463
Travel, Entertainment, Gift, and Car Expenses

Publication 501
Exemptions, Standard Deduction, and Filing Information

Publication 502
Medical and Dental Expenses

Publication 503
Child and Dependent Care Expenses

Publication 504
Divorced or Separated Individuals

Publication 505
Tax Withholding and Estimated Tax

Publication 508
Educational Expenses

Publication 513
Tax Information for
Visitors to the U.S.

Publication 514
Foreign Tax Credit for
Individuals

Publication 516
U.S. Government Civilian
Employees Stationed
Abroad

Publication 517
Social Security and Other
Information for Members
of the Clergy and
Religious Workers

Publication 519
U.S. Tax Guide for Aliens

Publication 520
Scholarships and
Fellowships

Publication 521
Moving Expenses

Publication 523
Selling Your Home

Publication 524
Credit for the Elderly or
the Disabled

Publication 525
Taxable and Nontaxable
Income

Publication 526
Charitable Contributions

Publication 527
Residential Rental
Property (Including
Rental of Vacation
Homes)

Publication 529
Miscellaneous Deductions

Publication 530
Tax Information for First-
Time Homeowners

Publication 531
Reporting Tip Income Tax

Publication 533
Self-Employment Tax

Publication 534
Depreciating Property
Placed in Service Before
1987

Publication 535
Business Expenses

Publication 536
Net Operating Losses

Publication 537
Installment Sales

Publication 538
Accounting Periods and
Methods

Publication 541
Partnerships

Publication 542
Corporations

Publication 544
Sales and Other
Dispositions of Assets

Publication 547
Casualties, Disasters, and
Thefts (Business and
Nonbusiness)

Publication 550
Investment Income and
Expenses Including
Capital Gains and Losses

Publication 551
Basis of Assets

Publication 552
Recordkeeping for
Individuals

Publication 554
Tax Information for Older
Americans

Publication 555
Community Property

Publication 556
Examination of Returns,
Appeal Rights, and Claims
for Refund

Publication 557
Tax-Exempt Status for
Your Organization

Publication 559
Survivors, Executors, and
Administrators

Publication 560
Retirement Plans for
Small Business

Publication 561
Determining the Value of
Donated Property

Publication 564
Mutual Fund Distributions

Publication 570
Tax Guide for Individuals
With Income From U.S.
Possessions

Publication 571
Tax-Sheltered Annuity
Programs for Employees
of Public Schools and
Certain Tax-Exempt
Organizations

Publication 575
Pension and Annuity
Income

Publication 583
Starting a Business and
Keeping Records

Publication 584(SP)
Nonbusiness Disaster,
Casualty, and Theft Loss
Workbook

Publication 587
Business Use of Your
Home (Including Use by
Day-Care Providers)

Publication 590
Individual Retirement
Arrangements (IRAs)
(Including SEP-IRAs and
SIMPLE IRAs)

Publication 593
Tax Highlights for U.S.
Citizens and Residents
Going Abroad

Publication 594 (SP)
Understanding the
Collection Process

Publication 595
Tax Highlights for
Commercial Fishermen

Publication 596 (SP)
Earned Income Credit

Publication 597
Information on the United
States-Canada Income Tax
Treaty

Publication 721
Tax Guide to U.S. Civil
Service Retirement
Benefits

Publication 850
English-Spanish Glossary
of Words and Phrases
Used in Publications
Issued by the Internal
Revenue Service

Publication 901
U.S. Tax Treaties

Publication 907
Tax Highlights for
Persons with Disabilities

Publication 908
Bankruptcy Tax Guide

Publication 911
Direct Sellers

Publication 915
Social Security and
Equivalent Railroad
Retirement Benefits

Publication 925
Passive Activity and
At-Risk Rules

Publication 926
Household Employer's
Tax Guide

Publication 929
Tax Rules for Children
and Dependents

Publication 936
Home Mortgage Interest
Deduction

Publication 939
General Rule for Pensions
and Annuities

Publication 945
Tax Information for Those
Affected by Operation
Desert Storm

Publication 946
How to Depreciate Your
Property

Publication 950
Introduction to Estate
and Gift Taxes

Publication 957
Reporting Back Pay and
Special Wage Payments to
the Social Security
Administration

Publication 967
The IRS Will Figure Your Tax

Publication 969
Medical Savings Accounts (MSA)

Publication 1212
List of Original Issue Discount Instruments

Publication 1244
Employee's Daily Record of Tips and Report to Employer

Publication 1542
Per Diem Rates

Publication 1544 *(SP)*
Reporting Cash Payments of over $10,000 (Received in a Trade or Business)

Publication 1546
How to Use the Problem Resolution Program of the IRS

Recorded Tax Information

Another free IRS service, paid for courtesy of your tax dollars, is TeleTax. TeleTax provides pre-recorded answers to commonly asked tax questions. It's often quicker and more accurate than trying to find an IRS employee who knows the answer. Admittedly, a question like, "I am a U.S. citizen and have my primary residence in Lizard Lick, North Carolina; I own a business in Brazil; I bought a coffee farm there; I patented a new coffee bean and made gads of money off it; how much money can I deduct on my taxes?" will be difficult to answer through TeleTax. However, a question like, "I am a U.S. citizen and have my primary residence in Lizard Lick, North Carolina; I own a business in Brazil; I bought a coffee farm there in 1994; I patented a new coffee bean and made gads of money off it; I filled out my tax forms; where do I send them?" can be answered quickly.

TeleTax

800-829-4477
(TTY/TDD) 800-829-4059

TeleTax provides recorded tax information for about 150 topics. You can listen to up to three topics on each call you make. TeleTax is available 24 hours a day, 7 days a week, 365 days a year. Call TeleTax at midnight on New Year's Eve just to test it!

When you call, you're asked if you want to listen to a TeleTax topic or if you're inquiring about a refund. You have to use a touch-tone phone after the main recording gives the basic instructions. TeleTax also explains the neat function of the (R)EPEAT and (C)ANCEL buttons on the touch-tone phone. The R button (#7) repeats your message as many times as you want — maybe until you understand! If you only have a rotary phone, you're out of luck. Your Form 1040 booklet has a complete listing of topics, or you can access the directory over the phone by listening to topic 123 when you call TeleTax. Some topics are also available in Spanish.

Automated refund information

800-829-4477 (same numbers as TeleTax)
(TTY/TDD) 800-829-4059

You haven't received your refund check, and you're getting antsy? Have you already spent your anticipated refund? Before you call the IRS to check on your refund, make sure that you have a copy of your tax return handy. For the IRS to check the status of your refund, you will need to know the first Social Security number shown on your return, your filing status, and the exact whole-dollar amount of your refund.

Simply place your call to 800-829-4477 and follow the cheerful recorded instructions. The IRS updates refund information every seven days. If you call about the status of your refund and do not receive a refund mailing date, wait a few days before calling back. This touch-tone service is available Monday through Friday from 7:00 a.m. to 11:30 p.m. (Eastern time).

Toll-free tax help

800-829-1040

The IRS prefers that you contact a local IRS office to rap about your tax questions. But a toll-free 800 number is also available. Remember to have the necessary information at your fingertips to help you get to the root of your question or problem.

If the IRS provides an incorrect answer to your question, you are still responsible for the payment of the correct tax. But if this situation occurs, you won't be charged any penalty. (Gee, thanks IRS!) Be sure that you obtain the name of the person to whom you spoke and record the date (as well as the time of the call) in order to abate for reasonable cause any penalty that may be imposed (see Chapter 19 for the lowdown on abating penalties). For example, when you call, you should always have in front of you the tax form, schedule, or notice to which your question relates. Don't be embarrassed if you don't understand the answer. If you don't, just say so, and ask the IRS representative to explain it again. Even better, call the IRS again and get a "second opinion" from another representative.

Where to File Your Federal Return

First things first. The address to which you send your completed form is listed in Table A-1.

Table A-1	Where the Checks (And Forms) Go
If an addressed envelope came with your return, please use it (unless you moved many miles away to a new residence). If you can't find that blasted envelope, mail your return to the Internal Revenue Service Center listed below for your home location. No street address is needed.	
If You Live in:	**Use This Address:**
Florida, Georgia, South Carolina	Atlanta, GA 39901-0002
New Jersey, New York (New York City and counties of Nassau, Rockland, Suffolk, and Westchester)	Holtsville, NY 00501-0002
New York (all other counties), Connecticut, Maine, Massachusetts, New Hampshire, Rhode Island, Vermont	Andover, MA 05501-0002
Illinois, Iowa, Minnesota, Missouri, Wisconsin	Kansas City, MO 64999-0002
Delaware, District of Columbia, Maryland, Pennsylvania, Virginia	Philadelphia, PA 19255-0002
Indiana, Kentucky, Michigan, Ohio, West Virginia	Cincinnati, OH 45999-0002
Kansas, New Mexico, Oklahoma, Texas	Austin, TX 73301-0002
Alaska, Arizona, California (counties of Alpine, Amador, Butte, Calaveras, Colusa, Contra Costa, Del Norte, El Dorado, Glenn, Humboldt, Lake, Lassen, Marin, Mendocino, Modoc, Napa, Nevada, Placer, Plumas, Sacramento, San Joaquin, Shasta, Sierra, Siskiyou, Solano, Sonoma, Sutter, Tehama, Trinity, Yolo, and Yuba), Colorado, Idaho, Montana, Nebraska, Nevada, North Dakota, Oregon, South Dakota, Utah, Washington, Wyoming	Ogden, UT 84201-0002
California (all other counties), Hawaii	Fresno, CA 93888-0002
Alabama, Arkansas, Louisiana, Mississippi, North Carolina, Tennessee	Memphis, TN 37501-0002
American Samoa	Philadelphia, PA 19255-0002

If You Live in:	Use This Address:
Guam: Permanent residents	Department of Revenue and Taxation, Government of Guam, Bldg. 13-1, Mariner Ave, Tiyjan Barrigada, GU 96913
Nonpermanent residents	Philadelphia, PA 19255-0002
Puerto Rico (or if excluding income under section 933)	Philadelphia, PA 19255-0002
Virgin Islands: Permanent residents	V.I. Bureau of Internal Revenue, 9601 Estate Thomas, Charlotte Amalie, St. Thomas VI 00802
Nonpermanent residents	Philadelphia, PA 19255-0002
Foreign country (or if dual-status alien): U.S. citizens and those filing Form 2555, Form 2555-EZ, or Form 4563	Philadelphia, PA 19255-0002
All A.P.O. and F.P.O. addresses	Philadelphia, PA 19255-0002

For state and local tax information check in the Blue Pages of your phone book for the phone numbers of your state and local tax agencies. If you have Internet access, a listing of state tax agencies with links to their Web sites is available online at www.taxsites.com. You can also link to state tax agencies through the IRS site at www.irs.ustreas.gov.

IRS Problem Resolution Program

Any problems that you cannot resolve through normal channels, as we discuss in Chapter 19, may qualify for the IRS Problem Resolution Program. (Don't worry; this has nothing to do with the Witness Relocation Program!)

Begin this journey by calling **800-829-1040.** Explain your problem to a specially trained representative who will try to fix it. If the representative can't fix it, he or she will evaluate your case to see whether it meets the necessary criteria for the Problem Resolution Program. The IRS representative will then assign you to a caseworker at your local district service center.

This may take some time on the phone, but it's generally better than corresponding by mail. The process could take months if you send your letter to the wrong address (or sometimes even if you send it to the correct address).

1998 Tax Forms in This Book

Many of the IRS forms that you need to complete your tax return are in the back of this book. We include the forms for your convenience. Feel free to tear them out, cut them out, or photocopy them (yes, you can use photocopied forms to complete your tax return). We suggest the following uses for the forms, but you're welcome to come up with your own:

✔ They are final, IRS-approved forms. You can file them with your tax return.

✔ Use the forms for your first draft tax return, when you sit down with *Taxe$ For Dummie$* and lay the foundation for preparing your return.

✔ Refer to the forms and follow along, line-by-line, as you read our tips and warnings in the rest of this book.

Appendix B
Glossary

•••

• A •

Accelerated Cost Recovery System (ACRS): A little tax history here. The ACRS method of depreciation lets you claim larger depreciation deductions for business property in the early years of ownership. It was replaced by the MACRS (Modified Accelerated Cost Recovery System) effective tax year 1987. (So, see *Modified ACRS.*)

accelerated depreciation: This depreciation method yields larger deduction amounts for you — as opposed to the straight-line depreciation method. Depreciation amounts are larger in the early years and lesser in the later years. (See *straight-line depreciation.*)

accrual method: This accounting method lets you report income in the year it is earned, even if not yet received, and expenses when incurred, even if not yet paid. (See *cash method.*)

active participation: This term is used to indicate whether you are eligible to participate in your employer's retirement savings or pension plan. If you are eligible, then your ability to deduct your IRA contribution is based on your income (actually, your adjusted gross income).

adjusted basis: The adjusted basis reflects your cost of property (see *basis*) plus the cost of improvements minus depreciation. You calculate your property's adjusted basis when you sell your property so that, for tax purposes, you can figure your profit or loss. If you acquire the property by inheritance, the property's adjusted basis is its fair market value on the deceased's date of death. If you acquire the property by gift, the property's adjusted basis is the donor's adjusted basis plus any gift tax paid by the donor on its transfer to the recipient.

adjusted gross income (AGI): AGI consists of all your income (including wages, salaries, tips, and taxable interest) minus allowable adjustments. You calculate your AGI *before* subtracting itemized deductions and personal exemptions. You arrive at this figure at the bottom of the front side of your Form 1040, also known as line 32.

after-tax contributions: Some retirement plans allow you to contribute money that has already been taxed. Such contributions are known as after-tax contributions.

alimony: Payments to a divorced or separated spouse that meet a number of requirements by the IRS and are then deductible by the payer and taxable to the recipient. Receiving alimony qualifies you to make an Individual Retirement Account (IRA) contribution.

alternative minimum tax (AMT): AMT is a second federal tax system designed to prevent higher income people from taking too many deductions and paying too little in taxes. Keep calculating!

amended return: Your chance to file another form — 1040X — within three years of the original return, correcting a mistake or making a change in your tax return for that year. Kind of like correcting an exam you've already turned in to the professor — neat, huh?

amortization: Similar to depreciation but relating to the deduction for using up intangible assets (such as goodwill). This is a way of writing off (depreciating) these assets over their projected lives.

annual gift tax exclusion: Each year, you may gift up to $10,000 per recipient to as many recipients as your heart desires. The gift is not taxable to the recipient (also not tax-deductible to the donor unless given to a qualifying charity).

annuity: Investment product that is essentially a contract backed by an insurance company, and is frequently purchased for retirement purposes. Its main benefit is that it allows your money to compound and grow until withdrawal without taxation. Selling annuities is a lucrative source of income for insurance agents and "financial planners" who work on commission, so don't buy one of these until you're sure that it makes sense for your situation.

assessment: An assessment of tax is a bill for additional tax made when a return is filed that shows a balance due or when the IRS determines, after reviewing your return, that you owe additional tax. Unless the collection of tax is in jeopardy (see *jeopardy assessment*) or a mathematical error has been made, the IRS cannot collect an assessment until you have exhausted all your administrative and legal avenues. When the IRS assesses additional tax beyond the amount shown on the original return, it must send you a Statutory Notice of Deficiency. If you choose not to challenge this determination, the IRS may collect the amount of the assessment after 90 days (150 days, if the notice is sent abroad).

asset: A property or investment, such as real estate, stocks, mutual funds, equipment, and so on, that has monetary value that could be realized if sold.

at-risk rules: Rules that limit your loss deductions to the cash amount you have invested.

attachment: A tactic whereby the government takes and holds your assets to settle your tax debt.

audit: IRS examination and inquisition, generally at the IRS offices, of your financial records that back up what you declare and claim on portions of or your entire tax return. One of life's ten worst experiences.

Automated Collection System (ACS): The IRS's "collection agency." If, after receiving three notices generated by an IRS Service Center, you have not paid what is owed, your delinquent account is sent to the ACS. The ACS has the authority to enter into an installment agreement, and its contact with you is exclusively by telephone (hence the automation portion of its name). If the ACS can't collect from you, a revenue officer at a district office takes over your account. (See *revenue officer.*)

away from home: Specific IRS guidelines that determine your ability to deduct business travel expenses.

● *B* ●

backup withholding: When you fail to give your Social Security or other Taxpayer Identification number to the person or organization that pays you interest, dividends, royalties, rents, or a consulting fee, or when you fail to furnish the payer with a statement that you are not subject to backup withholding, the payer must withhold federal income tax at the rate of 20 percent of the income received. The IRS, for example, notifies the payers of interest and dividends to begin backup withholding when you fail to report and pay tax on interest and dividend income on your tax return.

bad debt: Money that you're owed that you probably won't get. May be tax-deductible.

bankruptcy: Legal action that stops the IRS's and other creditors' collection actions against you.

basis: The tax basis of property (such as stock and real estate) used for determining the gain or loss on its sale or for claiming a depreciation, casualty loss, or other tax deduction. The tax basis is usually the property's cost to you. (See also *adjusted basis.*)

below-market-rate loan: A loan generally made between family members or friends at an interest rate lower than comparable loans available from financial institutions. The party making the loan, if audited, may be forced to pay income tax on the extra loan income they should have been receiving.

beneficiaries: The people to whom you desire to leave your assets. For each retirement account, for example, you denote beneficiaries.

boot: A term used to describe the receipt of cash, or its equivalent, in the tax-free exchange of investment real estate (known as a 1031 or Starker exchange). A tax-free exchange of real estate allows you, subject to IRS guidelines, to avoid paying tax on your profit when selling a rental property by rolling over that profit into another rental property. Boot is taxable when you're doing such a tax-free exchange, so if you don't want to owe any tax from a tax-free exchange of real estate, don't receive any boot!

business interest: The tax deduction that businesses may take for interest paid on business loans.

business meal: The closest thing to a free lunch you'll get from the IRS. Fifty percent of the cost of IRS-allowable business meals is deductible.

business use (of an automobile): If you use your car for noncommuting business purposes, you may deduct the actual costs of usage or claim a standard mileage rate. If you work for an employer, you take this deduction on Schedule A (Itemized Deductions).

bypass trust: Also known as *credit shelter* or *exemption equivalent* trust. A trust designed to provide benefits to a surviving spouse and increased shelter from estate taxes for more of your estate.

• C •

C Corporation: A business entity taxed according to the corporate, not individual, income tax rate schedule. Income, known as dividends, paid out to the corporation's shareholders is taxed on each shareholder's own tax return.

calendar year: A 12-month period ending on December 31. In contrast, some companies use a fiscal calendar that ends during another time of the year.

capital expenditures or expenses: Expenses that you may not immediately deduct but that you can depreciate over time by adding them to the basis of the property. For example, if you put a new roof on your investment real estate property, that expense is depreciated over time because the roof increases the usefulness/value of the property.

capital gain or loss: A taxable gain or loss realized through the sale of a property or financial asset, such as a stock, bond, or mutual fund held outside of a retirement account. The gain or loss is calculated by subtracting the adjusted basis from the sale price of the asset.

capital gains distribution: Taxable distribution by a mutual fund or a *real estate investment trust* (REIT) caused by securities that are sold at a profit.

capital loss carryover: If you sell stocks, bonds, or other securities with net losses totaling more than $3,000 in a year, for tax purposes you must "carry over" the losses in excess of $3,000 to the subsequent tax year(s). Only $3,000 may be taken as a tax loss on your tax return.

cash method: Business accounting method by which you report income when the income is actually received, and expenses when actually paid. This method gives you more control over when income and expenses are recognized for tax purposes than the accrual method. (See *accrual method*.)

casualty loss: A deductible loss resulting from an unexpected cause, such as an earthquake, fire, flood, and so on. These losses on your personal income tax return are deductible on Schedule A to the extent that they exceed 10 percent of your adjusted gross income (after a $100 deductible).

charitable contribution: Allowable deduction taken on Schedule A for donation of cash or property to IRS approved/qualified charities.

child and dependent care credit: Tax credit taken on Form 2441 for expenses you incur for the care of a dependent (child under the age of 13, or someone who is physically or mentally handicapped) in order to allow you to work.

child support: Payment specifically designated under a divorce decree. Child support payments are *not* tax deductible.

The Code: The Internal Revenue Code, or IRC; the verbiage that makes up the wonderfully complex tax laws.

Cohan Rule: Based on an actual case that George M. Cohan won against the IRS in the 1920s, the Cohan Rule allows deductions based on estimates rather than receipts for certain, primarily smaller, expenses such as taxi fares, tips, and cleaning and maintenance costs.

Collection Information Statement (CIS): A detailed financial and income statement (Form 433-A and Form 433-B) required by individuals and businesses applying for an installment agreement to pay delinquent taxes over a period of time.

The Commissioner: Not the *Batman* character, Commissioner Gordon, but rather the Commissioner of the Internal Revenue Service, currently Charles O. Rossotti.

community property: Property equally owned by husband and wife for which each spouse must, for state income tax purposes, report one-half of the joint income. Community property states include Arizona, California, Idaho, Louisiana, Nevada, New Mexico, Texas, Washington, and Wisconsin.

consumer interest: The interest incurred on personal and consumer debt (such as credit cards and auto loans). This interest is not tax-deductible.

correspondence audit: IRS audit conducted entirely by mail. (See *audit*.)

cost of goods sold: In businesses such as retailing and manufacturing, the term applies to the cost of products sold or manufactured. Cost of goods sold includes such items as raw materials, wholesale prices paid for finished goods, labor costs, and so on.

credit: A tax credit reduces your tax bill dollar-for-dollar.

credit for the elderly or the permanently and totally disabled: If you're 65 and over or if you're disabled, you may be able to claim this credit, but don't count on it. This credit has stringent requirements.

credit shelter trust: See *bypass trust*.

● **D** ●

declining-balance method: An aggressive depreciation method that allows faster writing off of business assets.

deduction: An expense you may subtract from your income so as to lower your taxable income. Examples include mortgage interest, property taxes (itemized deductions), and most retirement account contributions.

deficiency: The difference between the tax you originally reported as owing on your tax return and the amount of tax you actually owed as determined by the IRS. You may be notified by mail of additional tax that you owe, or this amount may be determined by an audit. (See *assessment*.)

defined-benefit plan: Company-based retirement plan that pays you a monthly income based on how long you worked (your years of service) for that company or nonprofit agency.

defined-contribution plan: Increasingly common type of company-based retirement plan, such as a 401(k) plan, whereby you contribute money to an individual account and the future value of that account depends on how well the investments you choose perform.

dependent: A person whom you support (such as a child) and whom you may claim as an exemption on your tax return, thus saving you tax dollars.

dependent care credit: See *child and dependent care credit*.

depletion: Deduction reflecting the decrease of a depletable natural resource, such as oil and gas, timber, minerals, and so on.

depreciation: Allowable tax deduction for writing off the cost of business assets, such as cars, computers, and cellular phones. Each type of property is depreciated over a certain, IRS-approved number of years. The term also applies to the allowable deduction for the wear and tear on investment real estate over time.

depreciation recapture: That portion of a capital gain attributable to depreciation taken during the years that the untaxed income sheltered by the depreciation deduction was taxed at ordinary income tax rates rather than the potentially more-favorable capital gains rates.

directly related meals and entertainment: Deductions you can take if you're entertaining clients immediately before, during, or after a business discussion.

District Director: In each of the 33 IRS districts throughout the country, this person is the chief delegate of the Commissioner of the IRS.

dividend: Income from your stock and/or mutual fund holdings. For assets held outside retirement accounts or in tax-free money market and tax-free bond funds, dividends are taxable.

dividend reinvestment plan: Plan by which you purchase additional shares of stock or mutual funds using dividends. Reinvestment does not impact whether or not these dividends are taxable.

double-declining-balance method: An aggressive depreciation method that allows for faster writing off of business assets.

● **E** ●

earned income: Money that you receive for doing work. Earned income is taxable and qualifies you to make a retirement account contribution that may be tax-deductible.

earned income credit: If your income is in the lower income brackets (for example, federal 15-percent tax bracket), you may qualify for this special and not-so-small tax credit.

effective marginal tax rate: See *marginal tax rate*.

enrolled agent: Licensed tax preparer who can represent you before the IRS.

equity: The difference between the market value of an asset and the loan amount owed on that asset. For example, if you own real estate worth $150,000 and have a $100,000 mortgage outstanding on it, your equity is $50,000 ($150,000 – $100,000).

estate: The value, at the time of your death, of your assets minus your loans and liabilities. Estates in excess of certain amounts are taxable at the federal and state level (see Chapter 26).

estimated tax: Tax payments you make to the IRS either through regular payroll withholding or on a quarterly basis if you're self-employed or retired. For most people, these estimated tax payments must total at least 90 percent of their actual tax bill; otherwise, penalties and interest are incurred.

executor: The person or organization named in a will who is responsible for administering the instructions in the will. It's best to choose someone responsible whom you trust to be careful and who will not rip you off; otherwise, increased estate taxes and other fees siphoned from your estate may result.

exemption: A personal deduction amount that you are allowed to deduct on your tax return for yourself and each of your dependents.

• *F* •

fair market value (FMV): The price at which an asset, such as stock or real estate, is being traded (that is, bought and sold) or is estimated to be worth by an independent, objective third party, such as an appraiser.

federal short-term rate: The interest rate that the IRS uses in computing interest owed on tax underpayments and overpayments. This rate is determined every calendar quarter by computing the average yield on U.S. Treasury bonds having a maturity of less than three years and adding 3 percent for tax underpayments and 2 percent for tax overpayments.

fiduciary: A person or organization (such as an executor, trustee, or administrator) responsible for managing assets for someone else.

field audit: An audit in which the IRS makes a house call, likely at your own business, to examine your records.

filing status: The applicable category, such as single, married filing jointly, married filing separately, head of household, and qualifying widow(er) with dependent child, that determines your tax rates.

fiscal year: Twelve-month accounting period for a business that may end on the last day of any month. Contrast with *calendar year,* which must end on December 31.

foreign tax credit: Put on your reading glasses to figure this credit. The instructions alone take the better part of a day to wade through. This credit applies to taxes paid to foreign countries. (This may apply to you — even if you didn't work overseas — if you own international mutual funds outside of a retirement account.)

401(k) plan: Type of retirement savings plan offered by many for-profit companies to their employees. Your contributions are exempt (yes!) from federal and state income taxes until you withdraw the funds, presumably in retirement.

403(b) plan: Similar to a 401(k) plan but for employees of nonprofit organizations.

• *G* •

GAO: General Accounting Office. Congress's auditing and investigation arm.

garnishment: Holding back a specified sum from wages to satisfy a debt.

goodwill: Purchase price paid for a business in excess of the business's assets minus its liabilities (net worth). Goodwill is depreciated or amortized over the years.

gross income: Your total taxable income before subtracting deductions.

gross receipts: The total revenue received by a business before subtracting cost of goods sold, returns, and so on.

• H •

half-year convention: A tax law that specifies claiming half a year's worth of depreciation for assets the first year that those assets are used or placed in service in the business.

head of household: Filing status under which you are unmarried — or considered to be unmarried — and are paying for more than 50 percent of the household costs in the place where you live with a relative whom you can claim as a dependent. (Whew!)

hobby loss: Losses arising from enjoyable activities that are not conducted for profit. These losses cannot be used to offset or reduce other taxable income.

holding period: The period of time for which you hold an asset (from date purchased until date sold).

home equity loan: Mortgage loan that allows you to borrow against the equity in your home. Generally, interest on the amount borrowed, up to $100,000, is tax-deductible.

home office: Tax deductions are allowed if your home is your principal place of business. These deductions lead to a fair number of audits, so make sure that you're entitled to the deduction.

• I •

IDRS: Integrated Data Retrieval System. Computer system that allows IRS employees instantaneous visual access to a taxpayer's tax account information.

imputed interest: Interest amount considered to have been earned on certain debts whose interest rates are below the applicable federal rate, that is, the rate set by the law. For example, if you get a loan at, say, 3 percent, the IRS says, not surprisingly, that this is a below market interest rate.

incentive stock option: Options allow for key company employees to exercise the right to buy stock in the company, typically at an attractive price. As a company grows and prospers, these options can end up being a significant portion of an employee's total compensation. Tax on the profit on this stock is not triggered until the stock is sold.

independent contractor: Status defined by (more!) IRS rules, allowing an employed person to be treated as self-employed. Among other criteria, self-employed people are expected to maintain their own work areas, work for multiple employers, and have control over their work and hours. People who qualify are responsible for paying their own estimated taxes.

Individual Retirement Account (IRA): A retirement account into which anyone with sufficient employment income or alimony may contribute up to $2,000 per year. Contributions may or may not be tax-deductible.

information release (IR): The IRS issues these releases to clarify a point of law or an IRS procedure.

information returns: IRS forms (such as 1099, W-2, 1065) that are required to be filed with the IRS by the payers of interest, dividends, pensions, and freelance income stating the amount of income that was paid to a taxpayer in a given year. The IRS uses this "information" to nail people who don't report all of their income.

installment agreement: An arrangement whereby an individual or business can pay delinquent taxes over a period of time. This agreement must be negotiated with the IRS.

installment sale: When property is sold and a portion of the sale price is paid in two different years, the profits from the sale may be taxable over a period of time as well.

intangible assets: Nonphysical property, such as patents and notes receivable. Compare to *tangible assets*.

Internal Revenue Service (IRS): A service or not, this is the U.S. Treasury agency that enforces the tax laws and collects taxes.

intestate: Means you die without a will. Dying intestate is generally not a good idea because state law determines what happens to your worldly possessions and assets as well as who cares for your minor children.

investment interest: Yes, investments pay in more ways than one; among them is your ability to borrow against your securities in a (nonretirement) margin account, and to claim the interest of that loan as a deduction. A margin account is simply a type of brokerage account in which you may borrow money from the brokerage firm against the value of your securities held in the brokerage account. These write-offs are limited to the amount of investment income you earn.

IRC: Internal Revenue Code of 1986.

IRM: Internal Revenue Manual. Procedural reference guide that IRS employees follow in administering the Internal Revenue Code.

IRS personnel: Revenue agents, that is, IRS employees assigned to the examination division of the IRS who are responsible for auditing tax returns. Revenue officers are responsible for collecting delinquent taxes.

itemized deductions: Expenditures such as mortgage interest, property taxes, state and local taxes, and so on that are deductible on Schedule A to the extent that they exceed your *standard deduction.*

• J •

jeopardy assessment: Has nothing to do with Alex Trebek or the game show. When the Commissioner of the Internal Revenue Service — or his or her delegate — believes that the collection of tax is in danger of not being collected at all, the IRS may bypass the normal assessment process as required by law and make an immediate assessment. A taxpayer may protest a jeopardy assessment administratively and by court action.

joint return: Filing status for legally married people. This is usually, but not always, cheaper than filing separate returns. In unusual cases where one spouse has high allowable deductions, filing as married filing separately may save the couple tax dollars. Filing individually may also make sense when marital problems cause a lack of trust in a spouse's keeping current with taxes.

joint tenants: A method of ownership of property. Each party is considered the co-owner of a one-half interest unless it is specifically stated otherwise. Creditors of one tenant may attach that tenant's interest. Either tenant or their creditors may petition a court to divide the property so it can be sold. (See also *tenants by the entirety.*)

• K •

Keogh plan: A retirement savings plan available to self-employed individuals. Allows for the maximum tax-deductible contributions.

kiddie tax: The relatively low rate of tax on the initial amounts of unearned income, such as interest and dividends from investments, for children under 14 years of age. Income over a certain limit for these children is taxed on the parent's income tax return (see Chapter 25 for the details).

• L •

levy (Notice of Levy): Means by which a delinquent taxpayer's employment income or property is seized in order to satisfy the amount of tax that is owed to the government. This is not how you want to pay your back taxes.

lien for taxes: A legal claim attaching to property (including bank and other accounts) of an individual who is delinquent in tax payments. The filing of a lien prohibits the sale or transfer of the property without satisfying the amount of the lien.

like-kind exchange: A tax-free exchange of real estate. Normally when you sell an asset, such as stock and mutual funds, that has appreciated in value, tax is owed on the profits realized. As long as you comply with the specific IRS rules, you may defer paying tax on the profits from investment real estate if you purchase another property. These exchanges are called 1031 or Starker exchanges.

long-term capital gain or loss: Gain or loss on the sale or exchange of an asset held for more than twelve months. For your pleasure, the IRS makes you complete Schedule D to report these gains or losses.

lump-sum distribution: The entire amount in your employer's retirement plan that is paid to you within one tax year. Among the qualifications are reaching age $59^1/_2$, having become disabled or passed away, having left the employer, and so on. Such distributions often may be rolled over into a retirement account so that tax owed on the distribution can be deferred.

• M •

marginal tax rate: Not all income is treated equally. In fact, the IRS tax laws treat your first dollars of taxable income differently than your last ones. Specifically, lower tax rates apply to lower income amounts. Your marginal tax rate is the combined federal and state tax rates that you paid on your highest or last dollar of earnings.

marital deduction: This deduction allows unlimited asset transfers from one spouse to another without having to pay any estate or gift taxes. If your spouse is a Scrooge or wants to leave someone else a lot of money, you're outta luck to take full advantage of this.

medical expense: Deduction you can take if you itemize your expenses on Schedule A, and your medical expenses exceed 7.5 percent of your adjusted gross income (AGI). You probably won't qualify, but it's worth checking out if you have a large amount of unreimbursed medical expenses.

miscellaneous itemized deduction: Expenses you can claim on Schedule A, such as job expenses, to the extent that they exceed 2 percent of your adjusted gross income.

Modified ACRS (MACRS): This term refers to the entire depreciation system, modified in 1986 by Congress. This depreciation is less favorable to businesses, and it stretches out the number of years during which business assets must be depreciated.

money-purchase plan: A type of Keogh plan where your annual contribution is a fixed percentage of your self-employment income.

mortgage interest: A tax cut for you unless the politicians in Congress take it away with a flat tax. Mortgage interest on your primary and secondary residence is deductible on the first $1,000,000 of mortgage debt and $100,000 of home equity debt.

mutual fund: A professionally managed, diversified fund that enables you to pool your money with that from many other investors. The three major types of funds are money markets (which are similar to savings accounts), bonds, and stock.

• N •

negligence: Negligence is a failure to make a reasonable attempt to comply with the tax laws. That portion of a tax underpayment attributable to negligence is subject to the negligence penalty.

net income: Business income left over after all deductions and expenses.

net operating loss (NOL): A loss from your business that exceeds your other income for the year. NOLs may be carried back three years to offset prior years' taxable income and then, if losses still remain, may be forwarded for the next 15 years until they are used up. A taxpayer may elect to forgo the carryback and elect to carry the NOL forward to future years.

nonresident alien: A person who is neither a U.S. citizen nor a permanent resident or green card holder. As far as the IRS is concerned, nonresident aliens usually must pay tax only on income from U.S. sources.

notice status: Reference to those taxpayers who are receiving tax notices demanding payment of unpaid taxes.

• O •

offer-in-compromise: A formal application you, or your tax advisor acting on your behalf, make to the IRS requesting that it accept less than full payment for what you owe for taxes, interest, and penalties. Offers may be made if there is doubt as to either collectibility of the tax or liability for the tax.

office audit: This examination of your tax records takes place at a local IRS office. The most common type of audit.

ordinary income: Income, such as from employment or investment interest and dividends, that is not derived from the sale or exchange of an asset. In other words, income other than that from capital gains.

original issue discount (OID): Debt instruments (that is, bonds) that don't pay interest but that should increase in value over time. The discounted price at which the bond is issued relative to its face value at maturity is considered taxable interest income to be reported on your tax return annually (if you hold the bond outside a retirement account).

• P •

partnership: An unincorporated business entity that is not itself taxable. Instead, tax obligations lie with the individual partners to whom the business's net profit (revenue minus expenses) is distributed annually.

passive activity: A business deal or venture in which you are a silent partner (that is, not actively involved in the management of the venture). Losses from these passive activities are limited in their deductibility to offset income from other passive activities.

passive-activity interest: This interest isn't considered investment-interest expense. The cost of this interest for tax purposes can be deducted only from passive-activity income.

payroll withholding: Withholding of taxes from your paycheck that your employer should perform.

pension: See *defined-benefit plan.*

personal exemption: It's great to be alive! Even the IRS acknowledges that and allows you a deduction on your tax return for you and your dependents.

personal interest: See *consumer interest.*

personal property: Includes your boat, plane, and car, but not real estate. Taxes on personal property may be deductible if the assets are used for business purposes. Auto registration fees based on the value of your car and paid to your state are deductible on your personal tax return.

points: The generally deductible prepaid interest that a borrower pays to obtain a mortgage.

probate: The legal process for administering and implementing the directions in your will. Makes probate attorneys wealthy. Minimize their income and maximize your estate by investigating living trusts, which keep your nonretirement assets out of probate.

profit-sharing plan: Type of an employer *Keogh plan* where the annual contribution made to the plan for employees may vary from year to year as a percentage of the employer's profits or each individual employee's salary.

• Q •

qualified plan: A government-approved retirement plan (such as a pension plan, Keogh plan, and employee stock ownership plan) that allows for the tax-deferred compounding of your investment dollars over the years until withdrawal.

qualifying widow(er): A special tax filing status that allows a surviving spouse with dependents to use the same tax rates applicable to joint filers.

• R •

Real Estate Investment Trust (REIT): An investment similar to a mutual fund but that invests in real estate properties. Provides the benefits of property ownership without the burden of landlording.

real property: Real estate, such as land and buildings.

refund: Great feeling to get money back, isn't it? In this case, though, the money was yours in the first place, and you gave the government too much of it and didn't figure it out until you filed your annual tax return! Take a look at adjusting your withholding (get a copy of Form W-4).

residential rental property: Investment real estate from which at least 80 percent of the total rental income comes from dwelling units. Such property that you own and purchased after May 12, 1993, is depreciated over 39 years.

revenue agents: IRS employees assigned to the Examination Division of the IRS who are responsible for auditing tax returns.

revenue officers: IRS collection agents in the IRS's Collection Division who are responsible for collecting delinquent taxes.

revocable trust: A trust you set up to keep your nonretirement assets out of probate. This trust can be changed or ended, if you so desire.

rollover: The term used to describe moving money from your employer's retirement plan, for example, into your own retirement account (IRA). Just make sure that you never take personal possession of the money. If you do take possession of the money, your employer is required to withhold 20 percent for federal income tax.

Roth IRA: A new type of IRA brought about by the 1997 tax bill. Subject to eligibility requirements, you may contribute up to $2,000 annually to a Roth IRA. Although contributions offer no up-front tax benefit, under current tax laws investment earnings are not taxed upon withdrawal (see Chapter 21 for the details).

royalty: You may not be a member of the nobility, but receiving income from the licensing or sale of intellectual and material property that you own, such as books, movies, patents, natural resources, and so on, is a nice way to make up for that. This income is taxable as ordinary income.

S Corporation: A business entity that enjoys the benefits, such as limited legal liability, of being incorporated, but the income from which is taxed on a person's individual income tax return.

salvage value: The estimated value of a depreciable asset at the end of its useful life.

Section 179 deduction: The IRS allows you, as a business owner, to write off or deduct up to a certain dollar limit for the cost of tangible business equipment (such as computers, office furniture) in the year it was placed in service. See Chapter 22 for details.

self-employment tax: The Social Security and Medicare taxes paid by self-employed people. If you work for an employer, your employer pays half of these taxes. If you're self-employed, you get to deduct half of the total self-employment taxes you pay.

separate returns: Individual tax returns filed by married people who are not filing jointly. Normally, filing separately when you're married does not make sense, because it leads to the payment of higher total taxes by the couple.

short-term capital gain or loss: The gain or loss that derives from selling or exchanging an asset, such as a stock, bond, mutual fund, or real estate, held for 12 months or less.

SIMPLE: A newer small business retirement plan (see Chapter 21).

Simplified Employee Pension (SEP-IRA): An easily established retirement plan for self-employed individuals in which you can put away up to $24,000 (for tax year 1997) on a tax-deductible basis.

single: Required tax filing status for a person not legally married.

standard deduction: Rather than spelling out (itemizing) each individual deduction, the IRS offers you the option of taking a flat deduction amount that depends on your filing status. If you don't own real estate or pay a lot in state income taxes, odds are you'll take the standard deduction.

statute of limitations: The period beyond which the government may not assess or collect a tax. Unless waived in writing, no tax may be assessed after three years from the date a return was filed nor may the tax be collected more than ten years after the assessment. From your perspective, no refund claims may be made after three years from the filing date or two years after the date the tax was paid, whichever is later.

straight-line depreciation: A method of depreciation in which the deduction is taken in equal amounts each year in the life of an asset.

surviving spouse: See *qualifying widow(er)*.

• T •

tangible assets: Physical property or equipment such as computers, cars, manufacturing assembly line equipment, and so on. Compare also to *intangible assets*.

tax account: Means by which the IRS records all tax information for a taxpayer. Every taxpayer is assigned a tax account under a Social Security or other Taxpayer Identification number.

tax deferral: The legally allowed delay in paying tax. For example, contributions to retirement accounts may grow and accumulate earnings, and the tax on these earnings is deferred until the money is withdrawn.

tax year: Usually a period of 12 months, beginning on January 1 and ending on December 31, for summarizing your income and expenses. Some businesses utilize tax years that start and end at some other time of the year, such as October 1 through September 30 or July 1 through June 30.

taxable income: The amount on which you actually pay tax. Not every dollar of your income is taxable. You are taxed on the amount left after having subtracted whatever deductions, exemptions, and credits apply from your adjusted gross income.

Taxpayer Identification number: For individuals, this number is their Social Security number; for businesses, it's the Employer Identification number.

tax-sheltered annuity (TSA): Annuities (offered by insurance companies) that are specific to nonprofit organizations. TSAs offer tax incentives to save and invest for retirement; however, TSAs do carry higher fees than no-load (commission-free) mutual funds, which are a better alternative for nonprofit 403(b) programs.

tenants by the entirety: A method of recording the ownership of property where each party is considered to have an interest in the entire property. Only a husband and wife may hold property in this manner. Without the consent of both parties, a creditor of one cannot attach or force the partitioning of the property so that a sale can be made. (See also *joint tenants.*)

tenants in common: Real estate ownership by two or more people; the share of property owned by one of the tenants goes into his or her estate upon his or her death.

Totten trust ("in trust for" account): Bank accounts you control during your lifetime, but which, upon your death, go to a named beneficiary without having to go through probate.

trust: Legal arrangement that passes ownership of your assets to someone else. There are many types of trusts.

200-percent-declining-balance method: An aggressive, fast method of depreciating business assets.

• U •

unified estate and gift tax credit: A huge tax credit that allows a person to pass — free of estate taxes — hundreds of thousands of dollars in their estate on to others. See Chapter 26.

useful life: The amount of time a depreciable asset is expected to be in business use.

• W •

waiver: A taxpayer's consent to give up a right possessed under the law. A taxpayer can waive or consent to extending the statute of limitations pertaining to when an assessment may be made and the time frame when a tax may be collected. A taxpayer can also waive the right that a Statutory Notice of Deficiency be issued so that an immediate assessment may be made.

will: A legal document stating your wishes regarding your assets and care of your minor children and requiring that your wishes be heeded when you die.

withholding: Amount withheld during the tax year from your income as a prepayment of your tax liability.

• Z •

zero-coupon bond: This bond doesn't pay annual interest but is purchased at a discount to its face value, which is paid at maturity. This increased value over time represents income on which taxes must be paid for nonretirement account holding of these bonds.

Form 1040

Department of the Treasury–Internal Revenue Service

U.S. Individual Income Tax Return 1998

(99) IRS Use Only–Do not write or staple in this space.

For the year Jan. 1±Dec. 31, 1998, or other tax year beginning _____ , 1998, ending _____ , 19 ___ | OMB No. 1545-0074

Label

(See instructions on page 18.)

Use the IRS label. Otherwise, please print or type.

L A B E L   H E R E

| Your first name and initial | Last name | Your social security number |
| If a joint return, spouse's first name and initial | Last name | Spouse's social security number |

Home address (number and street). If you have a P.O. box, see page 18. | Apt. no.

City, town or post office, state, and ZIP code. If you have a foreign address, see page 18.

▲ **IMPORTANT!** ▲
You **must** enter your SSN(s) above.

Presidential Election Campaign

(See page 18.)

▶ Do you want $3 to go to this fund? . . . .

If a joint return, does your spouse want $3 to go to this fund? . . . .

| | Yes | No | Note: Checking "Yes" will not change your tax or reduce your refund. |

Filing Status

Check only one box.

1 ☐ Single

2 ☐ Married filing joint return (even if only one had income)

3 ☐ Married filing separate return. Enter spouse's social security no. above and full name here. ▶ _____

4 ☐ Head of household (with qualifying person). (See page 18.) If the qualifying person is a child but not your dependent, enter this child's name here. ▶ _____

5 ☐ Qualifying widow(er) with dependent child (year spouse died ▶ 19 ___). (See page 18.)

Exemptions

6a ☐ **Yourself.** If your parent (or someone else) can claim you as a dependent on his or her tax return, **do not** check box 6a . . . .

b ☐ **Spouse** . . . .

c Dependents:

(1) First name Last name	(2) Dependent's social security number	(3) Dependent's relationship to you	(4) ✔ if qualifying child for child tax credit (see page 19)
			☐
			☐
			☐
			☐
			☐
			☐

If more than six dependents, see page 19.

No. of boxes checked on 6a and 6b }

No. of your children on 6c who:
• lived with you
• did not live with you due to divorce or separation (see page 19)

Dependents on 6c not entered above ____

Add numbers entered on lines above ▶ ☐

d Total number of exemptions claimed . . . .

Income

Attach Copy B of your Forms W-2, W-2G, and 1099-R here.

If you did not get a W-2, see page 20.

Enclose, but do not staple, any payment. Also, please use **Form 1040-V.**

7 Wages, salaries, tips, etc. Attach Form(s) W-2	7	
8a **Taxable** interest. Attach Schedule B if required	8a	
b **Tax-exempt** interest. DO NOT include on line 8a . . .	8b		
9 Ordinary dividends. Attach Schedule B if required	9	
10 Taxable refunds, credits, or offsets of state and local income taxes (see page 21) . .	10	
11 Alimony received	11	
12 Business income or (loss). Attach Schedule C or C-EZ	12	
13 Capital gain or (loss). Attach Schedule D	13	
14 Other gains or (losses). Attach Form 4797	14	
15a Total IRA distributions .	15a	b Taxable amount (see page 22)	15b	
16a Total pensions and annuities	16a	b Taxable amount (see page 22)	16b	
17 Rental real estate, royalties, partnerships, S corporations, trusts, etc. Attach Schedule E	17	
18 Farm income or (loss). Attach Schedule F	18	
19 Unemployment compensation	19	
20a Social security benefits .	20a	b Taxable amount (see page 24)	20b	
21 Other income. List type and amount–see page 24 _____	21	
22 Add the amounts in the far right column for lines 7 through 21. This is your **total income** ▶	22	

Adjusted Gross Income

If line 33 is under $30,095 (under $10,030 if a child did not live with you), see EIC inst. on page 36.

23 IRA deduction (see page 25)	23	
24 Student loan interest deduction (see page 27)	24	
25 Medical savings account deduction. Attach Form 8853 .	25	
26 Moving expenses. Attach Form 3903	26	
27 One-half of self-employment tax. Attach Schedule SE .	27	
28 Self-employed health insurance deduction (see page 28)	28	
29 Keogh and self-employed SEP and SIMPLE plans .	29	
30 Penalty on early withdrawal of savings	30	
31a Alimony paid b Recipient's SSN ▶ _____	31a	
32 Add lines 23 through 31a		32	
33 Subtract line 32 from line 22. This is your **adjusted gross income** . . . . . ▶		33	

For Disclosure, Privacy Act, and Paperwork Reduction Act Notice, see page 51. | Cat. No. 11320B | Form **1040** (1998)

Taxable income

19	Enter the amount from line 18.	19

20a Check if: ☐ **You** were 65 or older ☐ Blind ⎫ **Enter number of**
☐ **Spouse** was 65 or older ☐ Blind ⎭ **boxes checked ▶ 20a** ☐

b If you are married filing separately and your spouse itemizes deductions, see page 30 and check here . . . . ▶ **20b** ☐

21 Enter the **standard deduction** for your filing status. **But** see page 31 if you checked any box on line 20a or 20b **OR** if someone can claim you as a dependent.
• Single–$4,250   • Married filing jointly or Qualifying widow(er)–$7,100
• Head of household–$6,250   • Married filing separately–$3,550   **21**

22 Subtract line 21 from line 19. If line 21 is more than line 19, enter -0-.   22

23 Multiply $2,700 by the total number of exemptions claimed on line 6d.   23

24 Subtract line 23 from line 22. If line 23 is more than line 22, enter -0-. This is your **taxable income.**   ▶ 24

Tax, credits, and payments

25 Find the tax on the amount on line 24 (see page 31).   25

26 Credit for child and dependent care expenses. Attach Schedule 2.   26

27 Credit for the elderly or the disabled. Attach Schedule 3.   27

28 Child tax credit (see page 32).   28

29 Education credits. Attach Form 8863.   29

30 Adoption credit. Attach Form 8839.   30

31 Add lines 26 through 30. These are your **total credits.**   31

32 Subtract line 31 from line 25. If line 31 is more than line 25, enter -0-.   32

33 Advance earned income credit payments from Form(s) W-2.   33

34 Add lines 32 and 33. This is your **total tax.**   ▶ 34

35 Total Federal income tax withheld from Forms W-2 and 1099.   35

36 1998 estimated tax payments and amount applied from 1997 return.   36

37a **Earned income credit.** Attach Schedule EIC if you have a qualifying child.   37a

b Nontaxable earned income: amount ▶ | and type ▶

38 Additional child tax credit. Attach Form 8812.   38

39 Add lines 35, 36, 37a, and 38. These are your **total payments.**   ▶ 39

Refund

Have it directly deposited! See page 43 and fill in 41b, 41c, and 41d.

40 If line 39 is more than line 34, subtract line 34 from line 39. This is the amount you **overpaid.**   40

41a Amount of line 40 you want **refunded to you.**   41a

b Routing number [ ][ ][ ][ ][ ][ ][ ][ ][ ]   **c** Type: ☐ Checking ☐ Savings

d Account number [ ][ ][ ][ ][ ][ ][ ][ ][ ][ ][ ][ ][ ][ ][ ][ ][ ]

42 Amount of line 40 you want **applied to your 1999 estimated tax.**   42

Amount you owe

43 If line 34 is more than line 39, subtract line 39 from line 34. This is the **amount you owe.** For details on how to pay, see page 44.   43

44 Estimated tax penalty (see page 44).   44

Sign here

Joint return? See page 19.

Keep a copy for your records.

Under penalties of perjury, I declare that I have examined this return and accompanying schedules and statements, and to the best of my knowledge and belief, they are true, correct, and accurately list all amounts and sources of income I received during the tax year. Declaration of preparer (other than the taxpayer) is based on all information of which the preparer has any knowledge.

Your signature	Date	Your occupation	Daytime telephone number (optional)
Spouse's signature. If joint return, BOTH must sign.	Date	Spouse's occupation	( )

Paid preparer's use only

Preparer's signature ▶	Date	Check if self-employed ☐	Preparer's social security no.
Firm's name (or yours if self-employed) and address ▶		EIN	
		ZIP code	

Schedule 1 **(Form 1040A)**	Department of the Treasury–Internal Revenue Service **Interest and Ordinary Dividends** **for Form 1040A Filers**	**1998**	OMB No. 1545-0085

Name(s) shown on Form 1040A

Your social security number

Part I **Interest** (See pages 24 and 56.)	**Note:** *If you received a Form 1099±INT, Form 1099±OID, or substitute statement from a brokerage firm, enter the firm's name and the total interest shown on that form.*		
	1 List name of payer. If any interest is from a seller-financed mortgage and the buyer used the property as a personal residence, see page 56 and list this interest first. Also, show that buyer's social security number and address.		**Amount**
		1	
	2 Add the amounts on line 1.	**2**	
	3 Excludable interest on series EE U.S. savings bonds issued after 1989 from Form 8815, line 14. You **must** attach Form 8815 to Form 1040A.	**3**	
	4 Subtract line 3 from line 2. Enter the result here and on Form 1040A, line 8a.	**4**	

Part II **Ordinary dividends** (See pages 24 and 56.)	**Note:** *If you received a Form 1099±DIV or substitute statement from a brokerage firm, enter the firm's name and the ordinary dividends shown on that form.*		
	5 List name of payer		**Amount**
		5	
	6 Add the amounts on line 5. Enter the total here and on Form 1040A, line 9.	**6**	

For Paperwork Reduction Act Notice, see Form 1040A instructions.   Cat. No. 12075R   **1998 Schedule 1 (Form 1040A)**

Schedule 2 (Form 1040A)	Department of the Treasury–Internal Revenue Service **Child and Dependent Care** **Expenses for Form 1040A Filers** (99) **1998**		OMB No. 1545-0085

Name(s) shown on Form 1040A **Your social security number**

Before you begin, you need to understand the following terms. See **Definitions** on page 57.
- **Dependent Care Benefits** • **Qualifying Person(s)** • **Qualified Expenses** • **Earned Income**

Part I

Persons or organizations who provided the care

You MUST complete this part.

	(a) Care provider's name	(b) Address (number, street, apt. no., city, state, and ZIP code)	(c) Identifying number (SSN or EIN)	(d) Amount paid (see page 58)
1				

(If you need more space, use the bottom of page 2.)

Did you receive **dependent care benefits?**	— No ——→ Complete only Part II below.
	— Yes ——→ Complete Part III on the back next.

Caution: *If the care was provided in your home, you may owe employment taxes. If you do, you must use Form 1040. See* **Schedule H** *and its instructions for details.*

Part II

Credit for child and dependent care expenses

2 Information about your **qualifying person(s)**. If you have more than two qualifying persons, see page 58.

(a) Qualifying person's name		(b) Qualifying person's social security number	(c) Qualified expenses you incurred and paid in 1998 for the person listed in column (a)
First	Last		

3 Add the amounts in column (c) of line 2. DO NOT enter more than $2,400 for one qualifying person or $4,800 for two or more persons. If you completed Part III, enter the amount from line 24. **3**

4 Enter YOUR **earned income.** **4**

5 If married filing a joint return, enter YOUR SPOUSE'S earned income (if your spouse was a student or was disabled, see page 59); **all others,** enter the amount from line 4. **5**

6 Enter the **smallest** of line 3, 4, or 5. **6**

7 Enter the amount from Form 1040A, line 19. **7**

8 Enter on line 8 the decimal amount shown below that applies to the amount on line 7.

If line 7 is–		Decimal amount is	If line 7 is–		Decimal amount is
Over	But not over		Over	But not over	
$0–10,000		.30	$20,000–22,000		.24
10,000–12,000		.29	22,000–24,000		.23
12,000–14,000		.28	24,000–26,000		.22
14,000–16,000		.27	26,000–28,000		.21
16,000–18,000		.26	28,000–No limit		.20
18,000–20,000		.25			

8 × .

9 Multiply **line 6** by the decimal amount on line 8. Enter the result. Then, see page 59 for the amount of credit to enter on Form 1040A, line 26. **9**

Cat. No. 107491   **1998 Schedule 2 (Form 1040A)**

Part III

Dependent care benefits

10 Enter the total amount of **dependent care benefits** you received for 1998. This amount should be shown in box 10 of your W-2 form(s). DO NOT include amounts that were reported to you as wages in box 1 of Form(s) W-2.   **10**

11 Enter the amount forfeited, if any. See page 59.   **11**

12 Subtract line 11 from line 10.   **12**

13 Enter the total amount of **qualified expenses** incurred in 1998 for the care of the qualifying person(s).   **13**

14 Enter the **smaller** of line 12 or 13.   **14**

15 Enter YOUR **earned income.**   **15**

16 If married filing a joint return, enter YOUR SPOUSE'S earned income (if your spouse was a student or was disabled, see the instructions for line 5); if married filing a separate return, see the instructions for the amount to enter; **all others,** enter the amount from line 15.   **16**

17 Enter the **smallest** of line 14, 15, or 16.   **17**

18 **Excluded benefits.** Enter here the **smaller** of the following:
- The amount from line 17, or
- $5,000 ($2,500 if married filing a separate return **and** you were required to enter your spouse's earned income on line 16).   **18**

19 **Taxable benefits.** Subtract line 18 from line 12. Also, include this amount on Form 1040A, line 7. In the space to the left of line 7, enter ™DCB.∫   **19**

To claim the child and dependent care credit, complete lines 20–24 below.

20 Enter $2,400 ($4,800 if two or more qualifying persons).   **20**

21 Enter the amount from line 18.   **21**

22 Subtract line 21 from line 20. If zero or less, **STOP.** You cannot take the credit. **Exception.** If you paid 1997 expenses in 1998, see the instructions for line 9.   **22**

23 Complete line 2 on the front of this schedule. DO NOT include in column (c) any excluded benefits shown on line 18 above. Then, add the amounts in column (c) and enter the total here.   **23**

24 Enter the **smaller** of line 22 or 23 here. Also, enter this amount on line 3 on the front of this schedule and complete lines 4–9.   **24**

Schedule 3
(Form 1040A)

Department of the Treasury–Internal Revenue Service

Credit for the Elderly or the Disabled
for Form 1040A Filers

(99)   **1998**

OMB No. 1545-0085

Name(s) shown on Form 1040A

Your social security number

You may be able to take this credit and reduce your tax if by the end of 1998:

- You were age 65 or older,   **OR**   • You were under age 65, you retired on **permanent and total** disability, and you received taxable disability income.

But you must also meet other tests. See the separate instructions for Schedule 3.

TIP: In most cases, the IRS can figure the credit for you. See the instructions.

Part I	**If your filing status is:**	**And by the end of 1998:**	**Check only one box:**
Check the box for your filing status and age	Single, Head of household, or Qualifying widow(er) with dependent child	**1** You were 65 or older	1 ☐
		2 You were under 65 and you retired on permanent and total disability	2 ☐
	Married filing a joint return	**3** Both spouses were 65 or older	3 ☐
		4 Both spouses were under 65, but only one spouse retired on permanent and total disability	4 ☐
		5 Both spouses were under 65, and both retired on permanent and total disability	5 ☐
		6 One spouse was 65 or older, and the other spouse was under 65 and retired on permanent and total disability	6 ☐
		7 One spouse was 65 or older, and the other spouse was under 65 and **NOT** retired on permanent and total disability	7 ☐
	Married filing a separate return	**8** You were 65 or older and you lived apart from your spouse for all of 1998	8 ☐
		9 You were under 65, you retired on permanent and total disability, and you lived apart from your spouse for all of 1998	9 ☐

Did you check box 1, 3, 7, or 8?	**Yes** ⟶ Skip Part II and complete Part III on the back.
	No ⟶ Complete Parts II and III.

Part II

Statement of permanent and total disability

Complete this part **only** if you checked box 2, 4, 5, 6, or 9 above.

IF: 1 You filed a physician's statement for this disability for 1983 or an earlier year, or you filed a statement for tax years after 1983 and your physician signed line B on the statement, **AND**

2 Due to your continued disabled condition, you were unable to engage in any substantial gainful activity in 1998, check this box . . . . ▶ ☐

- If you checked this box, you do not have to get another statement for 1998.
- If you **did not** check this box, have your physician complete the statement on page 4 of the instructions. You **must** keep the statement for your records.

For Paperwork Reduction Act Notice, see Form 1040A instructions.   Cat. No. 12064K   **1998 Schedule 3 (Form 1040A)**

Part III

Figure your credit

10 If you checked (in Part I):   **Enter:**

Box 1, 2, 4, or 7. . . . . $5,000

Box 3, 5, or 6 . . . . $7,500

Box 8 or 9. . . . . $3,750   **10**

Did you check box 2, 4, 5, 6, or 9 in Part I? —— Yes ——▶ You **must** complete line 11.

—— No ——▶ Enter the amount from line 10 on line 12 and go to line 13.

---

11 • If you checked box 6 in Part I, add $5,000 to the taxable disability income of the spouse who was under age 65. Enter the total.

• If you checked box 2, 4, or 9 in Part I, enter your taxable disability income.

• If you checked box 5 in Part I, add your taxable disability income to your spouse's taxable disability income. Enter the total.

TIP: For more details on what to include on line 11, see the instructions.   **11**

12 If you completed line 11, enter the **smaller** of line 10 or line 11; **all others,** enter the amount from line 10.   **12**

13 Enter the following pensions, annuities, or disability income that you (and your spouse if filing a joint return) received in 1998.

a Nontaxable part of social security benefits, and

Nontaxable part of railroad retirement benefits treated as social security. See instructions.   **13a**

b Nontaxable veterans' pensions and any other pension, annuity, or disability benefit that is excluded from income under any other provision of law. See instructions.   **13b**

c Add lines 13a and 13b. (Even though these income items are not taxable, they **must** be included here to figure your credit.) If you did not receive any of the types of nontaxable income listed on line 13a or 13b, enter -0- on line 13c.   **13c**

14 Enter the amount from Form 1040A, line 19.   **14**

15 **If you checked (in Part I):**   **Enter:**

Box 1 or 2 . . . . $7,500

Box 3, 4, 5, 6, or 7 . . . . $10,000

Box 8 or 9 . . . . $5,000   **15**

16 Subtract line 15 from line 14. If zero or less, enter -0-.   **16**

17 Enter one-half of line 16.   **17**

18 Add lines 13c and 17.   **18**

19 Subtract line 18 from line 12. If zero or less, **stop;** you **cannot** take the credit. Otherwise, go to line 20.   **19**

20 Multiply line 19 by 15% (.15). Enter the result here and on Form 1040A, line 27.   **20**

✹

Form **1040**

Department of the Treasury—Internal Revenue Service

U.S. Individual Income Tax Return **1998** (99) IRS Use Only–Do not write or staple in this space.

For the year Jan. 1±Dec. 31, 1998, or other tax year beginning , 1998, ending , 19 | OMB No. 1545-0074

Label

(See instructions on page 18.)

Use the IRS label. Otherwise, please print or type.

L A B E L   H E R E

Your first name and initial	Last name	Your social security number
If a joint return, spouse's first name and initial	Last name	Spouse's social security number
Home address (number and street). If you have a P.O. box, see page 18.	Apt. no.	
City, town or post office, state, and ZIP code. If you have a foreign address, see page 18.		

▲ **IMPORTANT!** ▲
You **must** enter your SSN(s) above.

Presidential Election Campaign
(See page 18.)

▶ Do you want $3 to go to this fund? . . . .
If a joint return, does your spouse want $3 to go to this fund? . . . .

| | Yes | No | Note: Checking "Yes" will not change your tax or reduce your refund. |

Filing Status

Check only one box.

1 ☐ Single
2 ☐ Married filing joint return (even if only one had income)
3 ☐ Married filing separate return. Enter spouse's social security no. above and full name here. ▶ _____
4 ☐ Head of household (with qualifying person). (See page 18.) If the qualifying person is a child but not your dependent, enter this child's name here. ▶
5 ☐ Qualifying widow(er) with dependent child (year spouse died ▶ 19). (See page 18.)

Exemptions

If more than six dependents, see page 19.

6a ☐ **Yourself.** If your parent (or someone else) can claim you as a dependent on his or her tax return, **do not** check box 6a. . . . .
b ☐ **Spouse** . . . .

c Dependents:		(2) Dependent's social security number	(3) Dependent's relationship to you	(4)✓ if qualifying child for child tax credit (see page 19)
(1) First name	Last name			
				☐
				☐
				☐
				☐
				☐
				☐

No. of boxes checked on 6a and 6b
No. of your children on 6c who:
• lived with you
• did not live with you due to divorce or separation (see page 19)
Dependents on 6c not entered above
Add numbers entered on lines above ▶ ☐

d Total number of exemptions claimed . . . .

Income

Attach Copy B of your Forms W-2, W-2G, and 1099-R here.

If you did not get a W-2, see page 20.

Enclose, but do not staple, any payment. Also, please use **Form 1040-V.**

7	Wages, salaries, tips, etc. Attach Form(s) W-2	7	
8a	**Taxable** interest. Attach Schedule B if required	8a	
b	**Tax-exempt** interest. DO NOT include on line 8a . . . 8b		
9	Ordinary dividends. Attach Schedule B if required	9	
10	Taxable refunds, credits, or offsets of state and local income taxes (see page 21) . .	10	
11	Alimony received	11	
12	Business income or (loss). Attach Schedule C or C-EZ	12	
13	Capital gain or (loss). Attach Schedule D	13	
14	Other gains or (losses). Attach Form 4797	14	
15a	Total IRA distributions . 15a	b Taxable amount (see page 22)	15b	
16a	Total pensions and annuities 16a	b Taxable amount (see page 22)	16b	
17	Rental real estate, royalties, partnerships, S corporations, trusts, etc. Attach Schedule E	17	
18	Farm income or (loss). Attach Schedule F	18	
19	Unemployment compensation	19	
20a	Social security benefits . 20a	b Taxable amount (see page 24)	20b	
21	Other income. List type and amount–see page 24	21	
22	Add the amounts in the far right column for lines 7 through 21. This is your **total income** ▶	22	

Adjusted Gross Income

If line 33 is under $30,095 (under $10,030 if a child did not live with you), see EIC inst. on page 36.

23	IRA deduction (see page 25)	23	
24	Student loan interest deduction (see page 27) . . .	24	
25	Medical savings account deduction. Attach Form 8853 .	25	
26	Moving expenses. Attach Form 3903	26	
27	One-half of self-employment tax. Attach Schedule SE .	27	
28	Self-employed health insurance deduction (see page 28)	28	
29	Keogh and self-employed SEP and SIMPLE plans . .	29	
30	Penalty on early withdrawal of savings	30	
31a	Alimony paid b Recipient's SSN ▶ _____	31a	
32	Add lines 23 through 31a	32	
33	Subtract line 32 from line 22. This is your **adjusted gross income** . . . . . ▶	33	

For Disclosure, Privacy Act, and Paperwork Reduction Act Notice, see page 51. Cat. No. 11320B Form **1040** (1998)

Tax and Credits	34	Amount from line 33 (adjusted gross income)		34	
	35a	Check if: ☐ **You** were 65 or older, ☐ Blind; ☐ **Spouse** was 65 or older, ☐ Blind. Add the number of boxes checked above and enter the total here . . . . ▶ 35a			
	b	If you are married filing separately and your spouse itemizes deductions or you were a dual-status alien, see page 29 and check here . . . . . ▶ 35b ☐			
Standard Deduction for Most People	36	Enter the **larger** of your **itemized deductions** from Schedule A, line 28, **OR standard deduction** shown on the left. **But** see page 30 to find your standard deduction if you checked any box on line 35a or 35b **or** if someone can claim you as a dependent . . .		36	
Single: $4,250	37	Subtract line 36 from line 34		37	
Head of household: $6,250	38	If line 34 is $93,400 or less, multiply $2,700 by the total number of exemptions claimed on line 6d. If line 34 is over $93,400, see the worksheet on page 30 for the amount to enter .		38	
Married filing jointly or Qualifying widow(er): $7,100	39	**Taxable income.** Subtract line 38 from line 37. If line 38 is more than line 37, enter -0-		39	
	40	**Tax.** See page 30. Check if any tax from **a** ☐ Form(s) 8814 **b** ☐ Form 4972 . . ▶		40	
	41	Credit for child and dependent care expenses. Attach Form 2441	41		
	42	Credit for the elderly or the disabled. Attach Schedule R . .	42		
Married filing separately: $3,550	43	Child tax credit (see page 31)	43		
	44	Education credits. Attach Form 8863	44		
	45	Adoption credit. Attach Form 8839	45		
	46	Foreign tax credit. Attach Form 1116 if required	46		
	47	Other. Check if from **a** ☐ Form 3800 **b** ☐ Form 8396 **c** ☐ Form 8801 **d** ☐ Form (specify) _____	47		
	48	Add lines 41 through 47. These are your **total credits**		48	
	49	Subtract line 48 from line 40. If line 48 is more than line 40, enter -0- . . . . . . ▶		49	
Other Taxes	50	Self-employment tax. Attach Schedule SE		50	
	51	Alternative minimum tax. Attach Form 6251		51	
	52	Social security and Medicare tax on tip income not reported to employer. Attach Form 4137 .		52	
	53	Tax on IRAs, other retirement plans, and MSAs. Attach Form 5329 if required		53	
	54	Advance earned income credit payments from Form(s) W-2		54	
	55	Household employment taxes. Attach Schedule H		55	
	56	Add lines 49 through 55. This is your **total tax** . . . . ▶		56	
Payments	57	Federal income tax withheld from Forms W-2 and 1099 . .	57		
	58	1998 estimated tax payments and amount applied from 1997 return .	58		
Attach Forms W-2 and W-2G on the front. Also attach Form 1099-R if tax was withheld.	59a	**Earned income credit.** Attach Schedule EIC if you have a qualifying child **b** Nontaxable earned income: amount ▶ ▢ and type ▶ _____	59a		
	60	Additional child tax credit. Attach Form 8812	60		
	61	Amount paid with Form 4868 (request for extension) . . .	61		
	62	Excess social security and RRTA tax withheld (see page 43)	62		
	63	Other payments. Check if from **a** ☐ Form 2439 **b** ☐ Form 4136	63		
	64	Add lines 57, 58, 59a, and 60 through 63. These are your **total payments** . . . . ▶		64	
Refund	65	If line 64 is more than line 56, subtract line 56 from line 64. This is the amount you **OVERPAID**		65	
Have it directly deposited! See page 44 and fill in 66b, 66c, and 66d.	66a	Amount of line 65 you want **REFUNDED TO YOU** . . . . ▶		66a	
	▶ b	Routing number ▢▢▢▢▢▢▢▢▢ ▶ c Type: ☐ Checking ☐ Savings			
	▶ d	Account number ▢▢▢▢▢▢▢▢▢▢▢▢▢▢▢▢▢			
	67	Amount of line 65 you want **APPLIED TO YOUR 1999 ESTIMATED TAX** ▶	67		
Amount You Owe	68	If line 56 is more than line 64, subtract line 64 from line 56. This is the **AMOUNT YOU OWE.** For details on how to pay, see page 44 . . . . ▶		68	
	69	Estimated tax penalty. Also include on line 68	69		

Sign Here

Under penalties of perjury, I declare that I have examined this return and accompanying schedules and statements, and to the best of my knowledge and belief, they are true, correct, and complete. Declaration of preparer (other than taxpayer) is based on all information of which preparer has any knowledge.

Joint return? See page 18.

Keep a copy for your records.

Your signature	Date	Your occupation	Daytime telephone number (optional)
Spouse's signature. If a joint return, BOTH must sign.	Date	Spouse's occupation	( )

Paid Preparer's Use Only

Preparer's signature		Date	Check if self-employed ☐	Preparer's social security no.
Firm's name (or yours if self-employed) and address	▶			EIN
				ZIP code

SCHEDULES A&B (Form 1040)	Schedule A—Itemized Deductions	OMB No. 1545-0074
Department of the Treasury Internal Revenue Service (99)	(Schedule B is on back) ▶ Attach to Form 1040. ▶ See Instructions for Schedules A and B (Form 1040).	1998 Attachment Sequence No. 07

Name(s) shown on Form 1040 | Your social security number

Medical and Dental Expenses

Caution: *Do not include expenses reimbursed or paid by others.*

1 Medical and dental expenses (see page A-1) . . . . | 1 |
2 Enter amount from Form 1040, line 34. | 2 |
3 Multiply line 2 above by 7.5% (.075) . . . . . . | 3 |
4 Subtract line 3 from line 1. If line 3 is more than line 1, enter -0- . . . . . . | 4 |

Taxes You Paid
(See page A-2.)

5 State and local income taxes . . . . | 5 |
6 Real estate taxes (see page A-2) . . . . | 6 |
7 Personal property taxes . . . . | 7 |
8 Other taxes. List type and amount ▶ _____ | 8 |
9 Add lines 5 through 8 . . . . | 9 |

Interest You Paid
(See page A-3.)

Note: Personal interest is not deductible.

10 Home mortgage interest and points reported to you on Form 1098 | 10 |
11 Home mortgage interest not reported to you on Form 1098. If paid to the person from whom you bought the home, see page A-3 and show that person's name, identifying no., and address ▶ _____ | 11 |
12 Points not reported to you on Form 1098. See page A-3 for special rules . . . . | 12 |
13 Investment interest. Attach Form 4952 if required. (See page A-3.) . . . . | 13 |
14 Add lines 10 through 13 . . . . | 14 |

Gifts to Charity
If you made a gift and got a benefit for it, see page A-4.

15 Gifts by cash or check. If you made any gift of $250 or more, see page A-4 . . . . | 15 |
16 Other than by cash or check. If any gift of $250 or more, see page A-4. You **MUST** attach Form 8283 if over $500 | 16 |
17 Carryover from prior year . . . . | 17 |
18 Add lines 15 through 17 . . . . | 18 |

Casualty and Theft Losses

19 Casualty or theft loss(es). Attach Form 4684. (See page A-5.) . . . . | 19 |

Job Expenses and Most Other Miscellaneous Deductions
(See page A-6 for expenses to deduct here.)

20 Unreimbursed employee expenses–job travel, union dues, job education, etc. You **MUST** attach Form 2106 or 2106-EZ if required. (See page A-5.) ▶ _____ | 20 |
21 Tax preparation fees . . . . | 21 |
22 Other expenses–investment, safe deposit box, etc. List type and amount ▶ _____ | 22 |
23 Add lines 20 through 22 . . . . | 23 |
24 Enter amount from Form 1040, line 34. | 24 |
25 Multiply line 24 above by 2% (.02) . . . . . | 25 |
26 Subtract line 25 from line 23. If line 25 is more than line 23, enter -0- . . . . | 26 |

Other Miscellaneous Deductions

27 Other–from list on page A-6. List type and amount ▶ _____ | 27 |

Total Itemized Deductions

28 Is Form 1040, line 34, over $124,500 (over $62,250 if married filing separately)?

NO. Your deduction is not limited. Add the amounts in the far right column for lines 4 through 27. Also, enter on Form 1040, line 36, the **larger** of this amount or your standard deduction.

YES. Your deduction may be limited. See page A-6 for the amount to enter.

| 28 |

For Paperwork Reduction Act Notice, see Form 1040 instructions. | Cat. No. 11330X | Schedule A (Form 1040) 1998

Name(s) shown on Form 1040. Do not enter name and social security number if shown on other side.

Your social security number

Schedule B–Interest and Ordinary Dividends

Attachment
Sequence No. **08**

Note: *If you had over $400 in taxable interest income, you must also complete Part III.*

**Part I
Interest**

(See pages 20
and B-1.)

Note: If you
received a Form
1099-INT, Form
1099-OID, or
substitute
statement from
a brokerage firm,
list the firm's
name as the
payer and enter
the total interest
shown on that
form.

1 List name of payer. If any interest is from a seller-financed mortgage and the buyer used the property as a personal residence, see page B-1 and list this interest first. Also, show that buyer's social security number and address ▶

Amount

	1	

2 Add the amounts on line 1 . . . . | **2** |

3 Excludable interest on series EE U.S. savings bonds issued after 1989 from Form 8815, line 14. You MUST attach Form 8815 to Form 1040 . . . . . . | **3** |

4 Subtract line 3 from line 2. Enter the result here and on Form 1040, line 8a ▶ | **4** |

Note: *If you had over $400 in ordinary dividends, you must also complete Part III.*

**Part II
Ordinary
Dividends**

(See pages 21
and B-1.)

Note: If you
received a Form
1099-DIV or
substitute
statement from
a brokerage firm,
list the firm's
name as the
payer and enter
the ordinary
dividends shown
on that form.

5 List name of payer. Include only ordinary dividends. Report any capital gain distributions on Schedule D, line 13 ▶

Amount

	5	

6 Add the amounts on line 5. Enter the total here and on Form 1040, line 9 . ▶ | **6** |

**Part III
Foreign
Accounts
and Trusts**

(See
page B-2.)

You must complete this part if you **(a)** had over $400 of interest or ordinary dividends; **(b)** had a foreign account; or **(c)** received a distribution from, or were a grantor of, or a transferor to, a foreign trust.

	Yes	**No**
7a At any time during 1998, did you have an interest in or a signature or other authority over a financial account in a foreign country, such as a bank account, securities account, or other financial account? See page B-2 for exceptions and filing requirements for Form TD F 90-22.1		
b If ™Yes,∫ enter the name of the foreign country▶		
8 During 1998, did you receive a distribution from, or were you the grantor of, or transferor to, a foreign trust? If ™Yes,∫ you may have to file Form 3520. See page B-2		

SCHEDULE C (Form 1040)	Profit or Loss From Business	OMB No. 1545-0074

SCHEDULE C (Form 1040)

Department of the Treasury
Internal Revenue Service (99)

Profit or Loss From Business

(Sole Proprietorship)

► Partnerships, joint ventures, etc., must file Form 1065 or Form 1065-B.

► **Attach to Form 1040 or Form 1041.** ► See Instructions for Schedule C (Form 1040).

OMB No. 1545-0074

1998

Attachment Sequence No. **09**

Name of proprietor | Social security number (SSN)

A Principal business or profession, including product or service (see page C-1) | **B** Enter NEW code from pages C-8 & 9 ►

C Business name. If no separate business name, leave blank. | **D** Employer ID number (EIN), if any

E Business address (including suite or room no.) ► ....
City, town or post office, state, and ZIP code

F Accounting method: **(1)** ☐ Cash **(2)** ☐ Accrual **(3)** ☐ Other (specify) ► ....

G Did you "materially participate" in the operation of this business during 1998? If "No," see page C-2 for limit on losses . ☐ Yes ☐ No

H If you started or acquired this business during 1998, check here . . . . ► ☐

Part I   Income

1	Gross receipts or sales. **Caution:** *If this income was reported to you on Form W-2 and the "Statutory employee" box on that form was checked, see page C-3 and check here* . . . . . . ► ☐	**1**	
2	Returns and allowances	**2**	
3	Subtract line 2 from line 1	**3**	
4	Cost of goods sold (from line 42 on page 2)	**4**	
5	**Gross profit.** Subtract line 4 from line 3	**5**	
6	Other income, including Federal and state gasoline or fuel tax credit or refund (see page C-3) . .	**6**	
7	**Gross income.** Add lines 5 and 6 . . . . ►	**7**	

Part II   Expenses. Enter expenses for business use of your home **only** on line 30.

8	Advertising	**8**		19	Pension and profit-sharing plans	**19**	
9	Bad debts from sales or services (see page C-3) . .	**9**		20	Rent or lease (see page C-5):		
10	Car and truck expenses (see page C-3)	**10**		**a**	Vehicles, machinery, and equipment .	**20a**	
11	Commissions and fees . .	**11**		**b**	Other business property . .	**20b**	
12	Depletion	**12**		21	Repairs and maintenance . .	**21**	
13	Depreciation and section 179 expense deduction (not included in Part III) (see page C-4) . .	**13**		22	Supplies (not included in Part III)	**22**	
				23	Taxes and licenses	**23**	
14	Employee benefit programs (other than on line 19) . . .	**14**		24	Travel, meals, and entertainment:		
15	Insurance (other than health) .	**15**		**a**	Travel	**24a**	
16	Interest:			**b**	Meals and entertainment .		
a	Mortgage (paid to banks, etc.) .	**16a**		**c**	Enter 50% of line 24b subject to limitations (see page C-6) .		
b	Other	**16b**		**d**	Subtract line 24c from line 24b	**24d**	
17	Legal and professional services	**17**		25	Utilities	**25**	
18	Office expense	**18**		26	Wages (less employment credits) .	**26**	
				27	Other expenses (from line 48 on page 2)	**27**	

28	**Total expenses** before expenses for business use of home. Add lines 8 through 27 in columns ►	**28**	
29	Tentative profit (loss). Subtract line 28 from line 7	**29**	
30	Expenses for business use of your home. Attach **Form 8829**	**30**	
31	**Net profit or (loss).** Subtract line 30 from line 29.		
	If a profit, enter on **Form 1040, line 12,** and ALSO on **Schedule SE, line 2** (statutory employees, see page C-6). Estates and trusts, enter on Form 1041, line 3.	**31**	
	● If a loss, you MUST go on to line 32.		

32	If you have a loss, check the box that describes your investment in this activity (see page C-6).		
	● If you checked 32a, enter the loss on **Form 1040, line 12,** and ALSO on **Schedule SE, line 2** (statutory employees, see page C-6). Estates and trusts, enter on Form 1041, line 3.	**32a** ☐ All investment is at risk.	
	● If you checked 32b, you MUST attach **Form 6198.**	**32b** ☐ Some investment is not at risk.	

Part III   Cost of Goods Sold (see page C-7)

33 Method(s) used to value closing inventory: **a** ☐ Cost   **b** ☐ Lower of cost or market   **c** ☐ Other (attach explanation)

34 Was there any change in determining quantities, costs, or valuations between opening and closing inventory? If "Yes," attach explanation . . . .   ☐ **Yes**   ☐ **No**

35 Inventory at beginning of year. If different from last year's closing inventory, attach explanation . .	**35**	
36 Purchases less cost of items withdrawn for personal use	**36**	
37 Cost of labor. Do not include any amounts paid to yourself	**37**	
38 Materials and supplies	**38**	
39 Other costs	**39**	
40 Add lines 35 through 39	**40**	
41 Inventory at end of year	**41**	
42 **Cost of goods sold.** Subtract line 41 from line 40. Enter the result here and on page 1, line 4 . .	**42**	

Part IV   Information on Your Vehicle. Complete this part ONLY if you are claiming car or truck expenses on line 10 and are not required to file Form 4562 for this business. See the instructions for line 13 on page C-4 to find out if you must file.

43 When did you place your vehicle in service for business purposes? (month, day, year) ▶ ..../......../........ .

44 Of the total number of miles you drove your vehicle during 1998, enter the number of miles you used your vehicle for:

a Business .... **b** Commuting .... **c** Other ....

45 Do you (or your spouse) have another vehicle available for personal use? . . . .   ☐ **Yes**   ☐ **No**

46 Was your vehicle available for use during off-duty hours? . . . .   ☐ **Yes**   ☐ **No**

47a Do you have evidence to support your deduction? . . . .   ☐ **Yes**   ☐ **No**

b If "Yes," is the evidence written? . . . .   ☐ **Yes**   ☐ **No**

Part V   Other Expenses. List below business expenses not included on lines 8–26 or line 30.

....		
....		
....		
....		
....		
....		
....		
....		

48 **Total other expenses.** Enter here and on page 1, line 27	**48**	

SCHEDULE C-EZ (Form 1040)

Department of the Treasury
Internal Revenue Service   (99)

Net Profit From Business

(Sole Proprietorship)

▶ Partnerships, joint ventures, etc., must file Form 1065 or 1065-B.

▶ Attach to Form 1040 or Form 1041.   ▶ See instructions on back.

OMB No. 1545-0074

1998

Attachment
Sequence No. **09A**

Name of proprietor	Social security number (SSN)

Part I   General Information

You May Use Schedule C-EZ Instead of Schedule C Only If You:

- Had business expenses of $2,500 or less.
- Use the cash method of accounting.
- Did not have an inventory at any time during the year.
- Did not have a net loss from your business.
- Had only one business as a sole proprietor.

And You:

- Had no employees during the year.
- Are not required to file **Form 4562**, Depreciation and Amortization, for this business. See the instructions for Schedule C, line 13, on page C-4 to find out if you must file.
- Do not deduct expenses for business use of your home.
- Do not have prior year unallowed passive activity losses from this business.

A Principal business or profession, including product or service

B Enter NEW code from pages C-8 & 9
▶

C Business name. If no separate business name, leave blank.

D Employer ID number (EIN), if any

E Business address (including suite or room no.). Address not required if same as on Form 1040, page 1.

City, town or post office, state, and ZIP code

Part II   Figure Your Net Profit

1   **Gross receipts. Caution:** *If this income was reported to you on Form W-2 and the "Statutory employee" box on that form was checked, see **Statutory Employees** in the instructions for Schedule C, line 1, on page C-3 and check here* . . . . ▶ ☐   **1**

2   **Total expenses.** If more than $2,500, you **must** use Schedule C. See instructions **2**

3   **Net profit.** Subtract line 2 from line 1. If less than zero, you **must** use Schedule C. Enter on **Form 1040, line 12,** and ALSO on **Schedule SE, line 2.** (Statutory employees **do not** report this amount on Schedule SE, line 2. Estates and trusts, enter on Form 1041, line 3.) **3**

Part III   Information on Your Vehicle. Complete this part **ONLY** if you are claiming car or truck expenses on line 2.

4   When did you place your vehicle in service for business purposes? (month, day, year) ▶ .... / .... / ....

5   Of the total number of miles you drove your vehicle during 1998, enter the number of miles you used your vehicle for:

a Business .... **b** Commuting .... **c** Other ....

6   Do you (or your spouse) have another vehicle available for personal use? . . . .   ☐ Yes   ☐ No

7   Was your vehicle available for use during off-duty hours? . . . .   ☐ Yes   ☐ No

8a   Do you have evidence to support your deduction? . . . .   ☐ Yes   ☐ No

b   If "Yes," is the evidence written? . . . .   ☐ Yes   ☐ No

For Paperwork Reduction Act Notice, see Form 1040 instructions.   Cat. No. 14374D   Schedule C-EZ (Form 1040) 1998

Instructions

You may use Schedule C-EZ instead of Schedule C if you operated a business or practiced a profession as a sole proprietorship and you have met all the requirements listed in Part I of Schedule C-EZ.

Line A

Describe the business or professional activity that provided your principal source of income reported on line 1. Give the general field or activity and the type of product or service.

Line B

Enter the **new** six-digit code that identifies your principal business or professional activity. See pages C-8 and C-9 for the list of codes.

Line D

You need an employer identification number (EIN) only if you had a Keogh plan or were required to file an employment, excise, estate, trust, or alcohol, tobacco, and firearms tax return. If you need an EIN, file **Form SS-4,** Application for Employer Identification Number. If you do not have an EIN, leave line D blank. **Do not** enter your SSN.

Line E

Enter your business address. Show a street address instead of a box number. Include the suite or room number, if any.

Line 1

Enter gross receipts from your trade or business. Include amounts you received in your trade or business that were properly shown on **Forms 1099-MISC.** If the total amounts that were reported in box 7 of Forms 1099-MISC are more than the total you are reporting on line 1, attach a statement explaining the difference. You must show all items of taxable income actually or constructively received during the year (in cash, property, or services). Income is constructively received when it is credited to your account or set aside for you to use. Do not offset this amount by any losses.

Line 2

Enter the total amount of all deductible business expenses you actually paid during the year. Examples of these expenses include advertising, car and truck expenses, commissions and fees, insurance, interest, legal and professional services, office expense, rent or lease expenses, repairs and maintenance, supplies, taxes, travel, 50% of business meals and entertainment, and utilities (including telephone). For details, see the instructions for Schedule C, Parts II and V, on pages C-3 through C-7. If you wish, you may use the optional worksheet below to record your expenses.

If you claim car or truck expenses, be sure to complete Part III of Schedule C-EZ.

Optional Worksheet for Line 2 (keep a copy for your records)

a Business meals and entertainment	**a**			
b Less: 50% of business meals and entertainment subject to limitations (see the instructions for lines 24b and 24c on pages C-5 and C-6) .	**b**			
c Deductible business meals and entertainment. Subtract line **b** from line **a**			**c**	
d			**d**	
e			**e**	
f			**f**	
g			**g**	
h			**h**	
i			**i**	
j **Total.** Add lines **c** through **i.** Enter here and on line 2			**j**	

SCHEDULE D
(Form 1040)

Department of the Treasury
Internal Revenue Service   (99)

Capital Gains and Losses

▶ Attach to Form 1040.   ▶ See Instructions for Schedule D (Form 1040).

▶ Use Schedule D-1 for more space to list transactions for lines 1 and 8.

OMB No. 1545-0074

1998

Attachment
Sequence No. **12**

Name(s) shown on Form 1040

Your social security number

Part I — Short-Term Capital Gains and Losses–Assets Held One Year or Less

(a) Description of property (Example: 100 sh. XYZ Co.)	(b) Date acquired (Mo., day, yr.)	(c) Date sold (Mo., day, yr.)	(d) Sales price (see page D-6)	(e) Cost or other basis (see page D-6)	(f) GAIN or (LOSS) Subtract (e) from (d)	
1						

2 Enter your short-term totals, if any, from Schedule D-1, line 2	**2**				
3 **Total short-term sales price amounts.** Add column (d) of lines 1 and 2 . . .	**3**				
4 Short-term gain from Form 6252 and short-term gain or (loss) from Forms 4684, 6781, and 8824	**4**				
5 Net short-term gain or (loss) from partnerships, S corporations, estates, and trusts from Schedule(s) K-1	**5**				
6 Short-term capital loss carryover. Enter the amount, if any, from line 8 of your 1997 Capital Loss Carryover Worksheet	**6**	(	)		
7 **Net short-term capital gain or (loss).** Combine lines 1 through 6 in column (f) . . . . ▶	**7**				

Part II — Long-Term Capital Gains and Losses–Assets Held More Than One Year

(a) Description of property (Example: 100 sh. XYZ Co.)	(b) Date acquired (Mo., day, yr.)	(c) Date sold (Mo., day, yr.)	(d) Sales price (see page D-6)	(e) Cost or other basis (see page D-6)	(f) GAIN or (LOSS) Subtract (e) from (d)	(g) 28% RATE GAIN or (LOSS) * (see instr. below)
8						

9 Enter your long-term totals, if any, from Schedule D-1, line 9	**9**					
10 **Total long-term sales price amounts.** Add column (d) of lines 8 and 9 . . .	**10**					
11 Gain from Form 4797, Part I; long-term gain from Forms 2439 and 6252; and long-term gain or (loss) from Forms 4684, 6781, and 8824	**11**					
12 Net long-term gain or (loss) from partnerships, S corporations, estates, and trusts from Schedule(s) K-1	**12**					
13 Capital gain distributions. See page D-2	**13**					
14 Long-term capital loss carryover. Enter in both columns (f) and (g) the amount, if any, from line 13 of your 1997 Capital Loss Carryover Worksheet . . .	**14**	(	)	(	)	
15 Combine lines 8 through 14 in column (g)	**15**					
16 **Net long-term capital gain or (loss).** Combine lines 8 through 14 in column (f) . . . . ▶	**16**					

Next: Go to Part III on the back.

*28% Rate Gain or Loss includes **all** "collectibles gains and losses" (as defined on page D-6) and up to 50% of the eligible gain on qualified small business stock (see page D-5).

For Paperwork Reduction Act Notice, see Form 1040 instructions.   Cat. No. 11338H   **Schedule D (Form 1040) 1998**

Part III	Summary of Parts I and II		
17	Combine lines 7 and 16. If a loss, go to line 18. If a gain, enter the gain on Form 1040, line 13	**17**	

    Next: Complete Form 1040 through line 39. Then, go to **Part IV** to figure your tax if:
- Both lines 16 and 17 are gains, **and**
- Form 1040, line 39, is more than zero.

18	If line 17 is a loss, enter here and as a (loss) on Form 1040, line 13, the **smaller** of these losses:		
	• The loss on line 17; **or**		
	• ($3,000) or, if married filing separately, ($1,500)	**18**	( )

    Next: Complete Form 1040 through line 37. Then, complete the **Capital Loss Carryover Worksheet** on page D-6 if:
- The loss on line 17 exceeds the loss on line 18, **or**
- Form 1040, line 37, is a loss.

Part IV	Tax Computation Using Maximum Capital Gains Rates		
19	Enter your taxable income from Form 1040, line 39	**19**	
20	Enter the **smaller** of line 16 or line 17 of Schedule D	**20**	
21	If you are filing Form 4952, enter the amount from Form 4952, line 4e	**21**	
22	Subtract line 21 from line 20. If zero or less, enter -0-	**22**	
23	Combine lines 7 and 15. If zero or less, enter -0-	**23**	
24	Enter the **smaller** of line 15 or line 23, but not less than zero .	**24**	
25	Enter your unrecaptured section 1250 gain, if any (see page D-7) .	**25**	
26	Add lines 24 and 25	**26**	
27	Subtract line 26 from line 22. If zero or less, enter -0-	**27**	
28	Subtract line 27 from line 19. If zero or less, enter -0-	**28**	
29	Enter the **smaller** of:		
	• The amount on line 19, **or**		
	• $25,350 if single; $42,350 if married filing jointly or qualifying widow(er); $21,175 if married filing separately; or $33,950 if head of household	**29**	
30	Enter the **smaller** of line 28 or line 29	**30**	
31	Subtract line 22 from line 19. If zero or less, enter -0-	**31**	
32	Enter the **larger** of line 30 or line 31	**32**	
33	Figure the tax on the amount on line 32. Use the Tax Table or Tax Rate Schedules, whichever applies . . . . ▶	**33**	
34	Enter the amount from line 29	**34**	
35	Enter the amount from line 28	**35**	
36	Subtract line 35 from line 34. If zero or less, enter -0-	**36**	
37	Multiply line 36 by 10% (.10) . . . . ▶	**37**	
38	Enter the **smaller** of line 19 or line 27	**38**	
39	Enter the amount from line 36	**39**	
40	Subtract line 39 from line 38	**40**	
41	Multiply line 40 by 20% (.20) . . . . ▶	**41**	
42	Enter the **smaller** of line 22 or line 25	**42**	
43	Add lines 22 and 32	**43**	
44	Enter the amount from line 19	**44**	
45	Subtract line 44 from line 43. If zero or less, enter -0-	**45**	
46	Subtract line 45 from line 42. If zero or less, enter -0-	**46**	
47	Multiply line 46 by 25% (.25) . . . . ▶	**47**	
48	Enter the amount from line 19	**48**	
49	Add lines 32, 36, 40, and 46	**49**	
50	Subtract line 49 from line 48	**50**	
51	Multiply line 50 by 28% (.28) . . . . ▶	**51**	
52	Add lines 33, 37, 41, 47, and 51	**52**	
53	Figure the tax on the amount on line 19. Use the Tax Table or Tax Rate Schedules, whichever applies	**53**	
54	**Tax on taxable income (including capital gains).** Enter the **smaller** of line 52 or line 53 here and on Form 1040, line 40. . . . . ▶	**54**	

✿

SCHEDULE D-1
(Form 1040)

Department of the Treasury
Internal Revenue Service   (99)

Continuation Sheet for Schedule D
(Form 1040)

▶ See instructions for Schedule D (Form 1040).
▶ Attach to Schedule D if you need more space to list transactions for lines 1 and 8.

OMB No. 1545-0074

1998

Attachment
Sequence No. **12A**

Name(s) shown on Form 1040

Your social security number

Part I   Short-Term Capital Gains and Losses–Assets Held One Year or Less

(a) Description of property (Example: 100 sh. XYZ Co.)	(b) Date acquired (Mo., day, yr.)	(c) Date sold (Mo., day, yr.)	(d) Sales price (see page D-6)	(e) Cost or other basis (see page D-6)	(f) GAIN or (LOSS). Subtract (e) from (d)	
1						
2 Totals. Combine columns (d) and (f). Enter here and on Schedule D, line 2 . . . 2						

Name(s) shown on Form 1040. Do not enter name and social security number if shown on other side. | **Your social security number**

| Part II | Long-Term Capital Gains and Losses–Assets Held More Than One Year |

(a) Description of property (Example: 100 sh. XYZ Co.)	(b) Date acquired (Mo., day, yr.)	(c) Date sold (Mo., day, yr.)	(d) Sales price (see page D-6)	(e) Cost or other basis (see page D-6)	(f) GAIN or (LOSS). Subtract (e) from (d)	(g) 28% RATE GAIN or (LOSS) *(see instr. below)
8						
9 **Totals.** Combine columns (d), (f), and (g). Enter here and on Schedule D, line 9 ▶ **9**						

* 28% Rate Gain or Loss includes **all** ™collectibles gains and losses⌡ (as defined on page D-6) and up to 50% of the eligible gain on qualified small business stock (see page D-5).

✱

SCHEDULE E
(Form 1040)

Department of the Treasury
Internal Revenue Service   (99)

Supplemental Income and Loss
(From rental real estate, royalties, partnerships, S corporations, estates, trusts, REMICs, etc.)

► **Attach to Form 1040 or Form 1041.**   ► **See Instructions for Schedule E (Form 1040).**

OMB No. 1545-0074

1998

Attachment
Sequence No. **13**

Name(s) shown on return

Your social security number

Part I **Income or Loss From Rental Real Estate and Royalties** **Note:** *Report income and expenses from your business of renting personal property on **Schedule C** or **C-EZ** (see page E-1). Report farm rental income or loss from **Form 4835** on page 2, line 39.*

1	Show the kind and location of each **rental real estate property:**	2	For each rental real estate property listed on line 1, did you or your family use it during the tax year for personal purposes for more than the greater of:		Yes	No
A	....		● 14 days, **or**	A		
B	....		● 10% of the total days rented at fair rental value?	B		
C	....		(See page E-1.)	C		

Income:			**Properties**			**Totals** (Add columns A, B, and C.)	
			A	B	C		
3	Rents received	3		3		4	
4	Royalties received	4				4	
Expenses:							
5	Advertising	5					
6	Auto and travel (see page E-2) .	6					
7	Cleaning and maintenance . . .	7					
8	Commissions	8					
9	Insurance	9					
10	Legal and other professional fees	10					
11	Management fees	11					
12	Mortgage interest paid to banks, etc. (see page E-2)	12				12	
13	Other interest	13					
14	Repairs	14					
15	Supplies	15					
16	Taxes	16					
17	Utilities	17					
18	Other (list) ►............................	18					
19	Add lines 5 through 18	19				19	
20	Depreciation expense or depletion (see page E-3)	20				20	
21	Total expenses. Add lines 19 and 20	21					
22	Income or (loss) from rental real estate or royalty properties. Subtract line 21 from line 3 (rents) or line 4 (royalties). If the result is a (loss), see page E-3 to find out if you must file **Form 6198**. . .	22					
23	Deductible rental real estate loss. **Caution:** *Your rental real estate loss on line 22 may be limited. See page E-3 to find out if you must file **Form 8582**. Real estate professionals must complete line 42 on page 2*	23	( )	( )	( )		
24	**Income.** Add positive amounts shown on line 22. **Do not** include any losses					24	
25	**Losses.** Add royalty losses from line 22 and rental real estate losses from line 23. Enter total losses here					25	( )
26	Total rental real estate and royalty income or (loss). Combine lines 24 and 25. Enter the result here. If Parts II, III, IV, and line 39 on page 2 do not apply to you, also enter this amount on Form 1040, line 17. Otherwise, include this amount in the total on line 40 on page 2					26	

For Paperwork Reduction Act Notice, see Form 1040 instructions.   Cat. No. 11344L   **Schedule E (Form 1040) 1998**

Name(s) shown on return. Do not enter name and social security number if shown on other side. | **Your social security number**

Note: *If you report amounts from farming or fishing on Schedule E, you must enter your gross income from those activities on line 41 below. Real estate professionals must complete line 42 below.*

Part II   Income or Loss From Partnerships and S Corporations   Note: *If you report a loss from an at-risk activity, you MUST check either column (e) or (f) on line 27 to describe your investment in the activity. See page E-5. If you check column (f), you must attach Form 6198.*

27	(a) Name	(b) Enter P for partnership; S for S corporation	(c) Check if foreign partnership	(d) Employer identification number	Investment At Risk?	
					(e) All is at risk	**(f)** Some is not at risk
A						
B						
C						
D						
E						

	Passive Income and Loss		Nonpassive Income and Loss		
	(g) Passive loss allowed (attach **Form 8582** if required)	**(h)** Passive income from **Schedule K–1**	**(i)** Nonpassive loss from **Schedule K–1**	**(j)** Section 179 expense deduction from **Form 4562**	**(k)** Nonpassive income from **Schedule K–1**
A					
B					
C					
D					
E					
28a Totals					
b Totals					

29	Add columns (h) and (k) of line 28a	29	
30	Add columns (g), (i), and (j) of line 28b	30	( )
31	Total partnership and S corporation income or (loss). Combine lines 29 and 30. Enter the result here and include in the total on line 40 below	31	

Part III   Income or Loss From Estates and Trusts

32	(a) Name	(b) Employer identification number
A		
B		

	Passive Income and Loss		Nonpassive Income and Loss	
	(c) Passive deduction or loss allowed (attach **Form 8582** if required)	**(d)** Passive income from **Schedule K–1**	**(e)** Deduction or loss from **Schedule K–1**	**(f)** Other income from **Schedule K–1**
A				
B				
33a Totals				
b Totals				

34	Add columns (d) and (f) of line 33a	34	
35	Add columns (c) and (e) of line 33b	35	( )
36	Total estate and trust income or (loss). Combine lines 34 and 35. Enter the result here and include in the total on line 40 below	36	

Part IV   Income or Loss From Real Estate Mortgage Investment Conduits (REMICs)–Residual Holder

37	(a) Name	(b) Employer identification number	(c) Excess inclusion from Schedules Q, line 2c (see page E-6)	(d) Taxable income (net loss) from Schedules Q, line 1b	(e) Income from Schedules Q, line 3b

38	Combine columns (d) and (e) only. Enter the result here and include in the total on line 40 below	38	

Part V   Summary

39	Net farm rental income or (loss) from **Form 4835**. Also, complete line 41 below	39	
40	TOTAL income or (loss). Combine lines 26, 31, 36, 38, and 39. Enter the result here and on Form 1040, line 17 ▶	40	

41	**Reconciliation of Farming and Fishing Income.** Enter your **gross** farming and fishing income reported on Form 4835, line 7; Schedule K-1 (Form 1065), line 15b; Schedule K-1 (Form 1120S), line 23; and Schedule K-1 (Form 1041), line 14 (see page E-6)	41	
42	**Reconciliation for Real Estate Professionals.** If you were a real estate professional (see page E-4), enter the net income or (loss) you reported anywhere on Form 1040 from all rental real estate activities in which you materially participated under the passive activity loss rules . . .	42	

✱

SCHEDULE EIC (Form 1040A or 1040) Department of the Treasury Internal Revenue Service (99)	Earned Income Credit (Qualifying Child Information) ► Attach to Form 1040A or 1040. ► See instructions on back.	OMB No. 1545-0074 **1998** Attachment Sequence No. **43**

Name(s) shown on return	Your social security number

Before you begin . . .

- See the instructions for Form 1040A, lines 37a and 37b, or Form 1040, lines 59a and 59b, to find out if you can take this credit.
- If you can take the credit, fill in the Earned Income Credit Worksheet in the Form 1040A or Form 1040 instructions to figure your credit. **But if you want the IRS to figure it for you, see instructions on back.**

Then, you **must** complete and attach Schedule EIC only if you have a qualifying child (see boxes on back).

Information About Your Qualifying Child or Children

If you have more than two qualifying children, you only have to list two to get the maximum credit.

	Child 1		Child 2	
Caution: *If you do not attach Schedule EIC and fill in all the lines that apply, it will take us longer to process your return and issue your refund.*	First name	Last name	First name	Last name
1 Child's name				
2 Child's year of birth	19__ __		19__ __	
3 If the child was born **before 1980** AND–				
a was **under age 24** at the end of 1998 **and** a student, check "Yes," **OR**	☐ Yes		☐ Yes	
b was permanently and totally disabled (see back), check "Yes"	☐ Yes		☐ Yes	
4 Enter the child's social security number .				
5 Child's relationship to you (for example, son, grandchild, etc.)				
6 Number of months child lived with you in the United States in 1998	months		months	

TIP: Do you want the earned income credit added to your take-home pay in 1999? To see if you qualify, get **Form W-5** from your employer or by calling the IRS at 1-800-TAX-FORM (1-800-829-3676).

Instructions
Purpose of Schedule

If you can take the earned income credit and have a qualifying child, use Schedule EIC to give information about that child. To figure the amount of your credit, use the worksheet in the instructions for Form 1040A, lines 37a and 37b, or Form 1040, lines 59a and 59b.

If you want the IRS to figure the credit for you, enter"EIC⌡ directly to the right of line 37a of Form 1040A or line 59a of Form 1040. Also, enter the amount and type of any nontaxable earned income in the spaces provided on Form 1040A, line 37b, or Form 1040, line 59b, and attach Schedule EIC to your return.

Line 1

Enter each qualifying child's name.

Line 3a

If your child was born **before 1980** but was under age 24 at the end of 1998 and a student, check "Yes."

Your child was a **student** if, during any 5 months of 1998, he or she–

● Was enrolled as a full-time student at a school, or

● Took a full-time, on-farm training course. The course had to be given by a school or a state, county, or local government agency.

A **school** includes technical, trade, and mechanical schools. It does not include on-the-job training courses, correspondence schools, or night schools.

Line 3b

If your child was born **before 1980** and was permanently and totally disabled during any part of 1998, check "Yes."

A person is **permanently and totally disabled** if **both** of the following apply.

1. He or she cannot engage in any substantial gainful activity because of a physical or mental condition.

2. A doctor determines the condition has lasted or can be expected to last continuously for at least a year or can lead to death.

Line 4

You must enter your child's social security number (SSN) on line 4 unless he or she was born and died in 1998. If you do not enter the correct SSN, at the time we process your return, we may reduce or disallow your credit. If your child was born and died in 1998 and did not have an SSN, enter "Died" on line 4 **and** attach a copy of the child's birth certificate.

If your child does not have an SSN, apply for one by filing **Form SS-5** with your local Social Security Administration office. It usually takes about 2 weeks to get a number. If your child will not have an SSN by April 15, 1999, you can get an automatic 4-month extension by filing **Form 4868** with the IRS by that date.

Line 6

Enter the number of months your child lived with you in your home in the United States during 1998. (If you were in the military on extended active duty outside the United States, your home is considered to be in the United States during that duty period.) Do not enter more than 12. Count temporary absences, such as for school, vacation, or medical care, as time lived in your home. If the child lived with you for more than half of 1998 but less than 7 months, enter "7" on line 6.

Exception. If your child, including a foster child, was born or died in 1998 and your home was the child's home for the entire time he or she was alive during 1998, enter "12" on line 6.

Qualifying Child

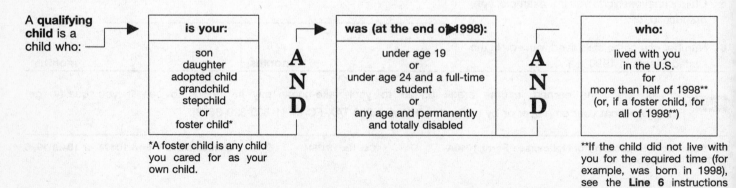

If the child was married or is also a qualifying child of another person (other than your spouse if filing a joint return), special rules apply. For details, see the instructions for Form 1040A, lines 37a and 37b, or Form 1040, lines 59a and 59b. Also, the child must have an SSN (as defined in those instructions) unless he or she was born and died in 1998.

SCHEDULE F
(Form 1040)

Department of the Treasury
Internal Revenue Service   (99)

Profit or Loss From Farming

▶ Attach to Form 1040, Form 1041, Form 1065, or Form 1065-B.

▶ See Instructions for Schedule F (Form 1040).

OMB No. 1545-0074

1998

Attachment
Sequence No. **14**

Name of proprietor

Social security number (SSN)

A Principal product. Describe in one or two words your principal crop or activity for the current tax year.

B Enter NEW code from Part IV
▶

C Accounting method: **(1)** ☐ Cash   **(2)** ☐ Accrual

D Employer ID number (EIN), if any

E Did you "materially participate" in the operation of this business during 1998? If "No," see page F-2 for limit on passive losses.   ☐ Yes   ☐ No

Part I   Farm Income—Cash Method. Complete Parts I and II (Accrual method taxpayers complete Parts II and III, and line 11 of Part I.)
Do not include sales of livestock held for draft, breeding, sport, or dairy purposes; report these sales on Form 4797.

1	Sales of livestock and other items you bought for resale	**1**	
2	Cost or other basis of livestock and other items reported on line 1	**2**	
3	Subtract line 2 from line 1	**3**	
4	Sales of livestock, produce, grains, and other products you raised	**4**	
5a	Total cooperative distributions (Form(s) 1099-PATR) **5a**	**5b** Taxable amount	**5b**
6a	Agricultural program payments (see page F-3) **6a**	**6b** Taxable amount	**6b**
7	Commodity Credit Corporation (CCC) loans (see page F-3):		
a	CCC loans reported under election	**7a**	
b	CCC loans forfeited **7b**	**7c** Taxable amount	**7c**
8	Crop insurance proceeds and certain disaster payments (see page F-3):		
a	Amount received in 1998 **8a**	**8b** Taxable amount	**8b**
c	If election to defer to 1999 is attached, check here ▶ ☐	**8d** Amount deferred from 1997	**8d**
9	Custom hire (machine work) income	**9**	
10	Other income, including Federal and state gasoline or fuel tax credit or refund (see page F-3)	**10**	
11	**Gross income.** Add amounts in the right column for lines 3 through 10. If accrual method taxpayer, enter the amount from page 2, line 51 ▶	**11**	

Part II   Farm Expenses—Cash and Accrual Method. Do not include personal or living expenses such as taxes, insurance, repairs, etc., on your home.

12	Car and truck expenses (see page F-4–also attach **Form 4562**)	**12**		25	Pension and profit-sharing plans	**25**	
13	Chemicals	**13**		26	Rent or lease (see page F-6):		
14	Conservation expenses (see page F-4)	**14**		a	Vehicles, machinery, and equipment	**26a**	
15	Custom hire (machine work)	**15**		b	Other (land, animals, etc.)	**26b**	
16	Depreciation and section 179 expense deduction not claimed elsewhere (see page F-5)	**16**		27	Repairs and maintenance	**27**	
				28	Seeds and plants purchased	**28**	
				29	Storage and warehousing	**29**	
17	Employee benefit programs other than on line 25	**17**		30	Supplies purchased	**30**	
18	Feed purchased	**18**		31	Taxes	**31**	
19	Fertilizers and lime	**19**		32	Utilities	**32**	
20	Freight and trucking	**20**		33	Veterinary, breeding, and medicine	**33**	
21	Gasoline, fuel, and oil	**21**		34	Other expenses (specify):		
22	Insurance (other than health)	**22**		a		**34a**	
23	Interest:			b		**34b**	
a	Mortgage (paid to banks, etc.)	**23a**		c		**34c**	
b	Other	**23b**		d		**34d**	
24	Labor hired (less employment credits)	**24**		e		**34e**	
				f		**34f**	

35	**Total expenses.** Add lines 12 through 34f ▶	**35**	
36	**Net farm profit or (loss).** Subtract line 35 from line 11. If a profit, enter on **Form 1040, line 18,** and ALSO on **Schedule SE, line 1.** If a loss, you MUST go on to line 37 (estates, trusts, and partnerships, see page F-6).	**36**	
37	If you have a loss, you MUST check the box that describes your investment in this activity (see page F-6). • If you checked 37a, enter the loss on **Form 1040, line 18,** and ALSO on **Schedule SE, line 1.** • If you checked 37b, you MUST attach **Form 6198.**	**37a** ☐ All investment is at risk. **37b** ☐ Some investment is not at risk.	

For Paperwork Reduction Act Notice, see Form 1040 instructions.   Cat. No. 11346H   **Schedule F (Form 1040) 1998**

Part III **Farm Income—Accrual Method** (see page F-7)

Do not include sales of livestock held for draft, breeding, sport, or dairy purposes; report these sales on Form 4797 and do not include this livestock on line 46 below.

38	Sales of livestock, produce, grains, and other products during the year	**38**	
39a	Total cooperative distributions (Form(s) 1099-PATR) **39a**	**39b** Taxable amount	**39b**	
40a	Agricultural program payments **40a**	**40b** Taxable amount	**40b**	
41	Commodity Credit Corporation (CCC) loans:		
a	CCC loans reported under election	**41a**	
b	CCC loans forfeited **41b**	**41c** Taxable amount	**41c**	
42	Crop insurance proceeds	**42**	
43	Custom hire (machine work) income	**43**	
44	Other income, including Federal and state gasoline or fuel tax credit or refund	**44**	
45	Add amounts in the right column for lines 38 through 44	**45**	
46	Inventory of livestock, produce, grains, and other products at beginning of the year	**46**	
47	Cost of livestock, produce, grains, and other products purchased during the year	**47**	
48	Add lines 46 and 47	**48**	
49	Inventory of livestock, produce, grains, and other products at end of year	**49**	
50	Cost of livestock, produce, grains, and other products sold. Subtract line 49 from line 48*	**50**	
51	**Gross income.** Subtract line 50 from line 45. Enter the result here and on page 1, line 11 . . . . . ▶	**51**	

*If you use the unit-livestock-price method or the farm-price method of valuing inventory and the amount on line 49 is larger than the amount on line 48, subtract line 48 from line 49. Enter the result on line 50. Add lines 45 and 50. Enter the total on line 51.

Part IV **Principal Agricultural Activity Codes**

Caution: *File Schedule C (Form 1040), Profit or Loss From Business, or Schedule C-EZ (Form 1040), Net Profit From Business, instead of Schedule F if:*

• *Your principal source of income is from providing agricultural services such as soil preparation, veterinary, farm labor, horticultural, or management for a fee or on a contract basis, or*

• *You are engaged in the business of breeding, raising, and caring for dogs, cats, or other pet animals.*

These **new** codes for the Principal Agricultural Activity classify farms by the type of activity they are engaged in to facilitate the administration of the Internal Revenue Code. These six-digit codes are based on the new North American Industry Classification System (NAICS) and do not resemble prior year codes.

Select one of the following new codes and enter the six-digit number on page 1, line B:

Crop Production

111100	Oilseed and grain farming
111210	Vegetable and melon farming
111300	Fruit and tree nut farming
111400	Greenhouse, nursery, and floriculture production
111900	Other crop farming

Animal Production

112111	Beef cattle ranching and farming
112112	Cattle feedlots
112120	Dairy cattle and milk production
112210	Hog and pig farming
112300	Poultry and egg production
112400	Sheep and goat farming
112510	Animal aquaculture
112900	Other animal production

Forestry and Logging

113000	Forestry and logging (including forest nurseries and timber tracts)

SCHEDULE SE	Self-Employment Tax	OMB No. 1545-0074
(Form 1040)	▶ See Instructions for Schedule SE (Form 1040).	**1998**
Department of the Treasury Internal Revenue Service	▶ Attach to Form 1040.	Attachment Sequence No. **17**

Name of person with **self-employment** income (as shown on Form 1040)	Social security number of person with **self-employment** income ▶

Who Must File Schedule SE

You must file Schedule SE if:

c You had net earnings from self-employment from **other than** church employee income (line 4 of Short Schedule SE or line 4c of Long Schedule SE) of $400 or more, **OR**

c You had church employee income of $108.28 or more. Income from services you performed as a minister or a member of a religious order **is not** church employee income. See page SE-1.

Note: *Even if you had a loss or a small amount of income from self-employment, it may be to your benefit to file Schedule SE and use either "optional method" in Part II of Long Schedule SE. See page SE-3.*

Exception. If your only self-employment income was from earnings as a minister, member of a religious order, or Christian Science practitioner **and** you filed Form 4361 and received IRS approval not to be taxed on those earnings, **do not** file Schedule SE. Instead, write "Exempt–Form 4361" on Form 1040, line 50.

May I Use Short Schedule SE or MUST I Use Long Schedule SE?

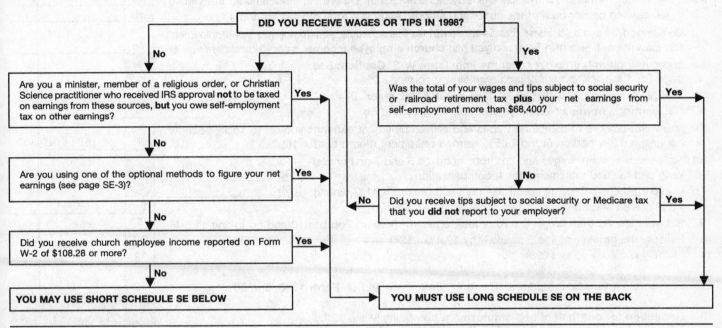

Section A—Short Schedule SE. Caution: *Read above to see if you can use Short Schedule SE.*

1	Net farm profit or (loss) from Schedule F, line 36, and farm partnerships, Schedule K-1 (Form 1065), line 15a	**1**	
2	Net profit or (loss) from Schedule C, line 31; Schedule C-EZ, line 3; Schedule K-1 (Form 1065), line 15a (other than farming); and Schedule K-1 (Form 1065-B), box 9. Ministers and members of religious orders, see page SE-1 for amounts to report on this line. See page SE-2 for other income to report	**2**	
3	Combine lines 1 and 2	**3**	
4	**Net earnings from self-employment.** Multiply line 3 by 92.35% (.9235). If less than $400, **do not** file this schedule; you do not owe self-employment tax . . . . ▶	**4**	
5	**Self-employment tax.** If the amount on line 4 is: ● $68,400 or less, multiply line 4 by 15.3% (.153). Enter the result here and on **Form 1040, line 50.** ● More than $68,400, multiply line 4 by 2.9% (.029). Then, add $8,481.60 to the result. Enter the total here and on **Form 1040, line 50.**	**5**	
6	**Deduction for one-half of self-employment tax.** Multiply line 5 by 50% (.5). Enter the result here and on **Form 1040, line 27**	**6**		

For Paperwork Reduction Act Notice, see Form 1040 instructions.	Cat. No. 11358Z	Schedule SE (Form 1040) 1998

Name of person with **self-employment** income (as shown on Form 1040)	Social security number of person with **self-employment** income ▶		

Section B–Long Schedule SE

Part I Self-Employment Tax

Note: *If your only income subject to self-employment tax is **church employee income,** skip lines 1 through 4b. Enter -0- on line 4c and go to line 5a. Income from services you performed as a minister or a member of a religious order **is not** church employee income. See page SE-1.*

A If you are a minister, member of a religious order, or Christian Science practitioner **and** you filed Form 4361, but you had $400 or more of **other** net earnings from self-employment, check here and continue with Part I . . . . . ▶ ☐

1	Net farm profit or (loss) from Schedule F, line 36, and farm partnerships, Schedule K-1 (Form 1065), line 15a. **Note:** *Skip this line if you use the farm optional method. See page SE-4* . .	**1**		
2	Net profit or (loss) from Schedule C, line 31; Schedule C-EZ, line 3; Schedule K-1 (Form 1065), line 15a (other than farming); and Schedule K-1 (Form 1065-B), box 9. Ministers and members of religious orders, see page SE-1 for amounts to report on this line. See page SE-2 for other income to report. **Note:** *Skip this line if you use the nonfarm optional method. See page SE-4* .	**2**		
3	Combine lines 1 and 2	**3**		
4a	If line 3 is more than zero, multiply line 3 by 92.35% (.9235). Otherwise, enter amount from line 3	**4a**		
b	If you elected one or both of the optional methods, enter the total of lines 15 and 17 here . .	**4b**		
c	Combine lines 4a and 4b. If less than $400, **do not** file this schedule; you do not owe self-employment tax. **Exception.** If less than $400 and you had **church employee income,** enter -0- and continue ▶	**4c**		
5a	Enter your **church employee income** from Form W-2. **Caution:** *See page SE-1 for definition of church employee income* . . . . **5a** ⬚			
b	Multiply line 5a by 92.35% (.9235). If less than $100, enter -0-	**5b**		
6	**Net earnings from self-employment.** Add lines 4c and 5b	**6**		
7	Maximum amount of combined wages and self-employment earnings subject to social security tax or the 6.2% portion of the 7.65% railroad retirement (tier 1) tax for 1998	**7**	68,400	00
8a	Total social security wages and tips (total of boxes 3 and 7 on Form(s) W-2) and railroad retirement (tier 1) compensation **8a**			
b	Unreported tips subject to social security tax (from Form 4137, line 9) **8b**			
c	Add lines 8a and 8b	**8c**		
9	Subtract line 8c from line 7. If zero or less, enter -0- here and on line 10 and go to line 11 . ▶	**9**		
10	Multiply the **smaller** of line 6 or line 9 by 12.4% (.124)	**10**		
11	Multiply line 6 by 2.9% (.029)	**11**		
12	**Self-employment tax.** Add lines 10 and 11. Enter here and on **Form 1040, line 50**	**12**		
13	**Deduction for one-half of self-employment tax.** Multiply line 12 by 50% (.5). Enter the result here and on **Form 1040, line 27** . . . . **13** ⬚			

Part II Optional Methods To Figure Net Earnings (See page SE-3.)

Farm Optional Method. You may use this method **only** if:

● Your gross farm income[1] was not more than $2,400, **or**

● Your gross farm income[1] was more than $2,400 and your net farm profits[2] were less than $1,733.

14	Maximum income for optional methods	**14**	1,600	00
15	Enter the **smaller** of: two-thirds (⅔) of gross farm income[1] (not less than zero) **or** $1,600. Also, include this amount on line 4b above	**15**		

Nonfarm Optional Method. You may use this method **only** if:

● Your net nonfarm profits[3] were less than $1,733 and also less than 72.189% of your gross nonfarm income,[4] **and**

● You had net earnings from self-employment of at least $400 in 2 of the prior 3 years.

Caution: *You may use this method no more than five times.*

16	Subtract line 15 from line 14	**16**	
17	Enter the **smaller** of: two-thirds (⅔) of gross nonfarm income[4] (not less than zero) **or** the amount on line 16. Also, include this amount on line 4b above	**17**	

[1]From Sch. F, line 11, and Sch. K-1 (Form 1065), line 15b.
[2]From Sch. F, line 36, and Sch. K-1 (Form 1065), line 15a.
[3]From Sch. C, line 31; Sch. C-EZ, line 3; Sch. K-1 (Form 1065), line 15a; and Sch. K-1 (Form 1065-B), box 9.
[4]From Sch. C, line 7; Sch. C-EZ, line 1; Sch. K-1 (Form 1065), line 15c; and Sch. K-1 (Form 1065-B), box 9.

✴

Form 1040X

(Rev. November 1997)

Department of the Treasury–Internal Revenue Service

Amended U.S. Individual Income Tax Return

► See separate instructions.

OMB No. 1545-0091

This return is for calendar year ► 19 **, OR fiscal year ended ►** , 19 .

Please print or type

Your first name and initial	Last name	Your social security number

If a joint return, spouse's first name and initial	Last name	Spouse's social security number

Home address (no. and street) or P.O. box if mail is not delivered to your home	Apt. no.	Telephone number (optional) ( )

City, town or post office, state, and ZIP code. If you have a foreign address, see instructions.	For Paperwork Reduction Act Notice, see page 4.

A If the name or address shown above is different from that shown on the original return, check here . . . . ► ☐

B Has the original return been changed or audited by the IRS or have you been notified that it will be? . . ☐ **Yes** ☐ **No**

C Filing status. Be sure to complete this line. **Note:** *You cannot change from joint to separate returns after the due date.*

On original return ► ☐ Single ☐ Married filing joint return ☐ Married filing separate return ☐ Head of household ☐ Qualifying widow(er)

On this return ► ☐ Single ☐ Married filing joint return ☐ Married filing separate return ☐ Head of household* ☐ Qualifying widow(er)

* If the qualifying person is a child but not your dependent, see instructions.

USE PART II ON BACK TO EXPLAIN ANY CHANGES

	Income and Deductions (see instructions)		A. Original amount or as previously adjusted (see instructions)	B. Net change– Increase or (Decrease)– explain in Part II	C. Correct amount
1	Adjusted gross income (see instructions)	1			
2	Itemized deductions or standard deduction	2			
3	Subtract line 2 from line 1	3			
4	Exemptions. If changing, fill in Parts I and II on back . . .	4			
5	Taxable income. Subtract line 4 from line 3	5			

Tax Liability

6	Tax (see instructions). Method used in col. C _____	6			
7	Credits (see instructions)	7			
8	Subtract line 7 from line 6. Enter the result but not less than zero .	8			
9	Other taxes (see instructions)	9			
10	Total tax. Add lines 8 and 9	10			

Payments

11	Federal income tax withheld and excess social security and RRTA tax withheld. If changing, see instructions	11			
12	Estimated tax payments, including amount applied from prior year's return	12			
13	Earned income credit	13			
14	Credits from Form 4136 or Form 2439	14			
15	Amount paid with Form 4868, 2688, or 2350 (applications for extension of time to file)	15		
16	Amount of tax paid with original return plus additional tax paid after it was filed	16		
17	Total payments. Add lines 11 through 16 in column C	17		

Refund or Amount You Owe

18	Overpayment, if any, as shown on original return or as previously adjusted by the IRS	18	
19	Subtract line 18 from line 17 (see instructions)	19	
20	**AMOUNT YOU OWE.** If line 10, column C, is more than line 19, enter the difference and see instructions	20	
21	If line 10, column C, is less than line 19, enter the difference	21	
22	Amount of line 21 you want **REFUNDED TO YOU**	22	
23	Amount of line 21 you want **APPLIED TO YOUR 19** **ESTIMATED TAX** 23		

Sign Here

Keep a copy of this return for your records.

Under penalties of perjury, I declare that I have filed an original return and that I have examined this amended return, including accompanying schedules and statements, and to the best of my knowledge and belief, this amended return is true, correct, and complete. Declaration of preparer (other than taxpayer) is based on all information of which the preparer has any knowledge.

► Your signature	Date	► Spouse's signature. If a joint return, BOTH must sign.	Date

Paid Preparer's Use Only

Preparer's signature ►	Date	Check if self-employed ☐	Preparer's social security no.
Firm's name (or yours if self-employed) and address ►		EIN	
		ZIP code	

Cat. No. 11360L

Form **1040X** (Rev. 11-97)

Part I — Exemptions. See Form 1040, Form 1040A, or Form 1040-T instructions.

If you are **not changing your exemptions,** do not complete this part.
If claiming **more exemptions,** complete lines 24–30 and, if applicable, line 31.
If claiming **fewer exemptions,** complete lines 24–29.

		A. Original number of exemptions reported or as previously adjusted	B. Net change	C. Correct number of exemptions
24	Yourself and spouse			
	Caution: If your parents (or someone else) can claim you as a dependent (even if they chose not to), you cannot claim an exemption for yourself.			
25	Your dependent children who lived with you			
26	Your dependent children who did not live with you due to divorce or separation			
27	Other dependents			
28	Total number of exemptions. Add lines 24 through 27			
29	Multiply the number of exemptions claimed on line 28 by the amount listed below for the tax year you are amending. Enter the result here and on line 4.			

Tax year	Exemption amount	But see the instructions if the amount on line 1 is over:
1997	$2,650	$90,900
1996	2,550	88,475
1995	2,500	86,025
1994	2,450	83,850

30 Dependents (children and other) not claimed on original (or adjusted) return:

(a) First name Last name	(b) Dependent's social security number. If born in the tax year you are amending, see instructions.	(c) Dependent's relationship to you	(d) No. of months lived in your home

No. of your children on line 30 who:
- lived with you ▶ ☐
- **did not** live with you due to divorce or separation (see instructions) ▶ ☐

Dependents on line 30 not entered above ▶ ☐

31 For tax years before 1996, if your child listed on line 30 did not live with you but is claimed as your dependent under a pre-1985 agreement, check here ▶ ☐

Part II — Explanation of Changes to Income, Deductions, and Credits

Enter the line number from the front of the form for each item you are changing and give the reason for each change. Attach only the supporting forms and schedules for the items changed. If you do not attach the required information, your Form 1040X may be returned. Be sure to include your name and social security number on any attachments.

If the change relates to a net operating loss carryback or a general business credit carryback, attach the schedule or form that shows the year in which the loss or credit occurred. See instructions. Also, check here ▶ ☐

Part III — Presidential Election Campaign Fund. Checking below will not increase your tax or reduce your refund.

If you did not previously want to have $3 go to the fund but now want to, check here ▶ ☐
If a joint return and your spouse did not previously want to have $3 go to the fund but now wants to, check here ▶ ☐

Form **2106**	**Employee Business Expenses**	OMB No. 1545-0139
Department of the Treasury Internal Revenue Service (99)	▶ See separate instructions. ▶ Attach to Form 1040.	**1998** Attachment Sequence No. **54**

Your name	Social security number	Occupation in which you incurred expenses

Part I **Employee Business Expenses and Reimbursements**

STEP 1 Enter Your Expenses

		Column A Other Than Meals and Entertainment		Column B Meals and Entertainment	
1	Vehicle expense from line 22 or line 29. (Rural mail carriers: See instructions.)	**1**			
2	Parking fees, tolls, and transportation, including train, bus, etc., that **did not** involve overnight travel or commuting to and from work	**2**			
3	Travel expense while away from home overnight, including lodging, airplane, car rental, etc. **Do not** include meals and entertainment	**3**			
4	Business expenses not included on lines 1 through 3. **Do not** include meals and entertainment	**4**			
5	Meals and entertainment expenses (see instructions)	**5**			
6	**Total expenses.** In Column A, add lines 1 through 4 and enter the result. In Column B, enter the amount from line 5	**6**			

Note: *If you were not reimbursed for any expenses in Step 1, skip line 7 and enter the amount from line 6 on line 8.*

STEP 2 Enter Reimbursements Received From Your Employer for Expenses Listed in STEP 1

7	Enter reimbursements received from your employer that were **not** reported to you in box 1 of Form W-2. Include any reimbursements reported under code "L" in box 13 of your Form W-2 (see instructions)	**7**			

STEP 3 Figure Expenses To Deduct on Schedule A (Form 1040)

8	Subtract line 7 from line 6	**8**			
	Note: *If **both columns** of line 8 are zero, **stop here.** If Column A is less than zero, report the amount as income on Form 1040, line 7.*				
9	In Column A, enter the amount from line 8. In Column B, multiply the amount on line 8 by 50% (.50). If either column is zero or less, enter -0- in that column. (Employees subject to Department of Transportation (DOT) hours of service limits: Multiply meal expenses by 55% (.55) instead of 50%. For more details, see instructions.)	**9**			
10	Add the amounts on line 9 of both columns and enter the total here. **Also, enter the total on Schedule A (Form 1040), line 20.** (Fee-basis state or local government officials, qualified performing artists, and individuals with disabilities: See the instructions for special rules on where to enter the total.) ▶	**10**			

For Paperwork Reduction Act Notice, see instructions.   Cat. No. 11700N   Form **2106** (1998)

Part II   Vehicle Expenses (See instructions to find out which sections to complete.)

Section A–General Information

			(a) Vehicle 1	(b) Vehicle 2
11	Enter the date vehicle was placed in service	11	/ /	/ /
12	Total miles vehicle was driven during 1998	12	miles	miles
13	Business miles included on line 12	13	miles	miles
14	Percent of business use. Divide line 13 by line 12	14	%	%
15	Average daily round trip commuting distance	15	miles	miles
16	Commuting miles included on line 12	16	miles	miles
17	Other miles. Add lines 13 and 16 and subtract the total from line 12 . .	17	miles	miles

18	Do you (or your spouse) have another vehicle available for personal purposes? . . . . ☐ Yes ☐ No
19	If your employer provided you with a vehicle, is personal use during off-duty hours permitted? ☐ Yes ☐ No ☐ Not applicable
20	Do you have evidence to support your deduction? . . . . ☐ Yes ☐ No
21	If "Yes," is the evidence written? . . . . ☐ Yes ☐ No

Section B–Standard Mileage Rate

22	Multiply line 13 by 32½¢ (.325). Enter the result here and on line 1	22		

Section C–Actual Expenses

			(a) Vehicle 1		(b) Vehicle 2	
23	Gasoline, oil, repairs, vehicle insurance, etc.	23				
24a	Vehicle rentals	24a				
b	Inclusion amount (see instructions)	24b				
c	Subtract line 24b from line 24a	24c				
25	Value of employer-provided vehicle (applies only if 100% of annual lease value was included on Form W-2—see instructions)	25				
26	Add lines 23, 24c, and 25 . .	26				
27	Multiply line 26 by the percentage on line 14 . . .	27				
28	Depreciation. Enter amount from line 38 below	28				
29	Add lines 27 and 28. Enter total here and on line 1	29				

Section D–Depreciation of Vehicles (Use this section only if you own the vehicle.)

			(a) Vehicle 1		(b) Vehicle 2	
30	Enter cost or other basis (see instructions)	30				
31	Enter amount of section 179 deduction (see instructions) .	31				
32	Multiply line 30 by line 14 (see instructions if you elected the section 179 deduction) . . .	32				
33	Enter depreciation method and percentage (see instructions) .	33				
34	Multiply line 32 by the percentage on line 33 (see instructions) . .	34				
35	Add lines 31 and 34	35				
36	Enter the limit from the table in the line 36 instructions . . .	36				
37	Multiply line 36 by the percentage on line 14 . . .	37				
38	Enter the **smaller** of line 35 or line 37. Also, enter this amount on line 28 above	38				

Form **2106-EZ**

Department of the Treasury
Internal Revenue Service (99)

Unreimbursed Employee Business Expenses

▶ **Attach to Form 1040.**

OMB No. 1545-1441

1998

Attachment
Sequence No. **54A**

Your name	Social security number	Occupation in which you incurred expenses

---

Part I — General Information

You May Use This Form ONLY if All of the Following Apply:

- You are an employee deducting expenses attributable to your job.
- You **do not** get reimbursed by your employer for any expenses (amounts your employer included in box 1 of your Form W-2 are not considered reimbursements).
- If you are claiming vehicle expense,
  - a You are using the standard mileage rate for 1998, **and**
  - b If you owned the vehicle, you also used the standard mileage rate for the year you first placed your vehicle in service.

Part II — Figure Your Expenses

1 Vehicle expense using the standard mileage rate. Complete Part III and multiply line 8a by 32½¢ (.325)	**1**	
2 Parking fees, tolls, and transportation, including train, bus, etc., that **did not** involve overnight travel or commuting to and from work	**2**	
3 Travel expense while away from home overnight, including lodging, airplane, car rental, etc. **Do not** include meals and entertainment	**3**	
4 Business expenses not included on lines 1 through 3. **Do not** include meals and entertainment .	**4**	
5 Meals and entertainment expenses: $ _____ x 50% (.50) (Employees subject to Department of Transportation (DOT) hours of service limits: Multiply meal expenses by 55% (.55) instead of 50%. For more details, see instructions.)	**5**	
6 **Total expenses.** Add lines 1 through 5. Enter here and **on line 20 of Schedule A (Form 1040).** (Fee-basis state or local government officials, qualified performing artists, and individuals with disabilities: See the instructions for special rules on where to enter this amount.)	**6**	

Part III — Information on Your Vehicle. Complete this part ONLY if you are claiming vehicle expense on line 1.

7 When did you place your vehicle in service for business purposes? (month, day, year) ▶ .... / .... / ....

8 Of the total number of miles you drove your vehicle during 1998, enter the number of miles you used your vehicle for:

a Business .... b Commuting .... c Other ....

9 Do you (or your spouse) have another vehicle available for personal use? . . . . ☐ Yes ☐ No

10 Was your vehicle available for use during off-duty hours? . . . . ☐ Yes ☐ No

11a Do you have evidence to support your deduction? . . . . ☐ Yes ☐ No

b If "Yes," is the evidence written? . . . . ☐ Yes ☐ No

General Instructions

Section references are to the Internal Revenue Code.

Changes To Note

- The standard mileage rate has been increased to 32½ cents for each mile of business use in 1998.
- Beginning in 1998, you may use the standard mileage rate instead of actual expenses for leased vehicles, but you must use the rate for the entire lease period (except for the period, if any, that began before January 1, 1998).

- For tax years beginning in 1998, employees subject to Department of Transportation (DOT) hours of service limits are allowed to deduct 55% of their allowable business meal expenses. For more details, see the line 5 instructions.

Purpose of Form

You may use Form 2106-EZ instead of Form 2106 if you meet all the requirements listed in Part I of this form.

Recordkeeping

You cannot deduct expenses for travel (including meals unless you used the standard meal allowance), entertainment, gifts, or use of a car or other listed property, unless you keep records to prove the time, place, business purpose, business relationship (for entertainment and gifts), and amounts of these expenses. Generally, you must also have receipts for all lodging expenses (regardless of the amount) and any other expense of $75 or more.

Additional Information

If you need more information about employee business expenses, you will find the following publications helpful:

Pub. 463, Travel, Entertainment, Gift, and Car Expenses

Pub. 529, Miscellaneous Deductions

For Paperwork Reduction Act Notice, see back of form.   Cat. No. 20604Q   Form **2106-EZ** (1998)

Pub. 587, Business Use of Your Home (Including Use by Day-Care Providers)
Pub. 946, How To Depreciate Property

Specific Instructions

Part II–Figure Your Expenses

Line 2. See the line 8b instructions for the definition of commuting.

Line 3. Enter lodging and transportation expenses connected with overnight travel away from your tax home (defined below). You cannot deduct expenses for travel away from your tax home for any period of temporary employment of more than 1 year. **Do not** include expenses for meals and entertainment. For more details, including limits, see Pub. 463.

Generally, your **tax home** is your main place of business or post of duty regardless of where you maintain your family home. If you do not have a regular or main place of business because of the nature of your work, then your tax home is the place where you regularly live. If you do not fit in either of these categories, you are considered an itinerant and your tax home is wherever you work. As an itinerant, you are not away from home and cannot claim a travel expense deduction. For more details on your tax home, see Pub. 463.

Line 4. Enter other job-related expenses not listed on any other line of this form. Include expenses for business gifts, education (tuition and books), home office, trade publications, etc. For details, including limits, see Pub. 463 and Pub. 529. If you are deducting home office expenses, see Pub. 587 for special instructions on how to report these expenses. If you are deducting depreciation or claiming a section 179 deduction on a cellular telephone or other similar telecommunications equipment, a home computer, etc., see **Form 4562,** Depreciation and Amortization, to figure the depreciation and section 179 deduction to enter on line 4.

Do not include expenses for meals and entertainment, taxes, or interest on line 4. Deductible taxes are entered on lines 5 through 9 of Schedule A (Form 1040). Employees cannot deduct car loan interest.

Note: *If line 4 is your only entry, do not complete Form 2106-EZ unless you are claiming:*

- *Expenses for performing your job as a fee-basis state or local government official,*
- *Performing-arts-related business expenses as a qualified performing artist, or*
- *Impairment-related work expenses as an individual with a disability.*

See the line 6 instructions for definitions. If you are not required to file Form 2106-EZ, enter your expenses directly on Schedule A (Form 1040), line 20.

Line 5. Enter your allowable meals and entertainment expense and multiply the total by 50%. Include meals while away from your tax home overnight and other business meals and entertainment.

If you were an employee subject to Department of Transportation (DOT) hours of service limits, multiply the amount of your allowable business meals by 55%. To be eligible for the 55% deduction, the meals must have been consumed during, or incident to, a period of duty subject to these limits. Employees subject to the DOT hours of service limits include certain air transportation employees, such as pilots, crew, dispatchers, mechanics, and control tower operators; interstate truck operators and interstate bus drivers; certain railroad employees, such as engineers, conductors, train crews, dispatchers, and control operations personnel; and certain merchant mariners.

Instead of actual cost, you may be able to claim the **standard meal allowance** for your daily meals and incidental expenses while away from your tax home overnight. Under this method, you deduct a specified amount, depending on where you travel, instead of keeping records of your actual meal expenses. However, you must still keep records to prove the time, place, and business purpose of your travel. See Pub. 463 to figure your deduction using the standard meal allowance.

Line 6. If you were a **fee-basis state or local government official** (defined below), include the expenses you incurred for services performed in that job in the total on Form 1040, line 32. Write "FBO" and the amount in the space to the left of line 32. Your employee business expenses are deductible whether or not you itemize deductions. A fee-basis state or local government official is an official who is an employee of a state or political subdivision of a state and is compensated, in whole or in part, on a fee basis.

If you were a **qualified performing artist** (defined below), include your performing-arts-related expenses in the total on Form 1040, line 32. Write "QPA" and the amount in the space to the left of line 32. Your performing-arts-related business expenses are deductible whether or not you itemize deductions. The expenses are not subject to the 2% limit that applies to most other employee business expenses.

A qualified performing artist is an individual who:

1. Performed services in the performing arts as an employee for at least two employers during the tax year,

2. Received from at least two of those employers wages of $200 or more per employer,

3. Had allowable business expenses attributable to the performing arts of more than 10% of gross income from the performing arts, and

4. Had adjusted gross income of $16,000 or less before deducting expenses as a performing artist.

To be treated as a qualified performing artist, a married individual must also file a joint return, unless the individual and his or her spouse lived apart for all of 1998. On a joint return, requirements **1, 2,** and **3** must be figured separately for each spouse. However, requirement **4** applies to the combined adjusted gross income of both spouses.

If you were an **individual with a disability** and are claiming impairment-related work expenses (defined below), enter the part of the line 6 amount attributable to those expenses on Schedule A (Form 1040), line 27, instead of on Schedule A (Form 1040), line 20. Your impairment-related work expenses are not subject to the 2% limit that applies to most other employee business expenses.

Impairment-related work expenses are the allowable expenses of an individual with physical or mental disabilities for attendant care at his or her place of employment. They also include other expenses in connection with the place of employment that enable the employee to work. See Pub. 463 for more details.

Part III–Information on Your Vehicle

If you claim vehicle expense, you must provide certain information on the use of your vehicle by completing Part III. Include an attachment listing the information requested in Part III for any additional vehicles you used for business during the year.

Line 7. Date placed in service is generally the date you first start using your vehicle. However, if you first start using your vehicle for personal use and later convert it to business use, the vehicle is treated as placed in service on the date you started using it for business.

Line 8a. Do not include commuting miles on this line; commuting miles are not considered business miles. See the line 8b instructions for the definition of commuting.

Line 8b. If you do not know the total actual miles you used your vehicle for commuting during the year, figure the amount to enter on line 8b by multiplying the number of days during the year that you used your vehicle for commuting by the average daily round trip commuting distance in miles.

Generally, **commuting** is travel between your home and a work location. However, such travel is not commuting if you meet **any** of the following conditions:

1. You have at least one regular work location away from your home and you travel to a temporary work location in the same trade or business, regardless of the distance. A temporary work location is one where you perform services on an irregular or short-term basis (generally a matter of days or weeks).

2. You travel to a temporary work location outside the metropolitan area where you live and normally work.

3. Your home is your principal place of business under section 280A(c)(1)(A) (for purposes of deducting expenses for business use of your home) and you travel to another work location in the same trade or business, regardless of whether that location is regular or temporary and regardless of distance.

Form **2441**	**Child and Dependent Care Expenses**	OMB No. 1545-0068
Department of the Treasury Internal Revenue Service (99)	▶ **Attach to Form 1040.** ▶ **See separate instructions.**	**1998** Attachment Sequence No. **21**

Name(s) shown on Form 1040	Your social security number

Before you begin, you need to understand the following terms. See **Definitions** on page 1 of the instructions.

- **Dependent Care Benefits**
- **Qualifying Person(s)**
- **Qualified Expenses**
- **Earned Income**

Part I — Persons or Organizations Who Provided the Care— You **must** complete this part.
(If you need more space, use the bottom of page 2.)

1	(a) Care provider's name	(b) Address (number, street, apt. no., city, state, and ZIP code)	(c) Identifying number (SSN or EIN)	(d) Amount paid (see instructions)

Did you receive **dependent care benefits?**	No ──▶ Complete only Part II below.
	Yes ──▶ Complete Part III on the back next.

Caution: *If the care was provided in your home, you may owe employment taxes. See the instructions for Form 1040, line 55.*

Part II — Credit for Child and Dependent Care Expenses

2 Information about your **qualifying person(s).** If you have more than two qualifying persons, see the instructions.

(a) Qualifying person's name		(b) Qualifying person's social security number	(c) Qualified expenses you incurred and paid in 1998 for the person listed in column (a)
First	Last		

3 Add the amounts in column (c) of line 2. DO NOT enter more than $2,400 for one qualifying person or $4,800 for two or more persons. If you completed Part III, enter the amount from line 24	**3**	
4 Enter YOUR **earned income**	**4**	
5 If married filing a joint return, enter YOUR SPOUSE'S earned income (if your spouse was a student or was disabled, see the instructions); **all others,** enter the amount from line 4	**5**	
6 Enter the **smallest** of line 3, 4, or 5	**6**	

7 Enter the amount from Form 1040, line 34 . . . . . | **7** | |

8 Enter on line 8 the decimal amount shown below that applies to the amount on line 7

If line 7 is—		Decimal amount is	If line 7 is—		Decimal amount is
Over	But not over		Over	But not over	
$0	10,000	.30	$20,000	22,000	.24
10,000	12,000	.29	22,000	24,000	.23
12,000	14,000	.28	24,000	26,000	.22
14,000	16,000	.27	26,000	28,000	.21
16,000	18,000	.26	28,000	No limit	.20
18,000	20,000	.25			

8	✕ .

9 Multiply **line 6** by the decimal amount on line 8. Enter the result. Then, see the instructions for the amount of credit to enter on Form 1040, line 41 . . . . | **9** | |

For Paperwork Reduction Act Notice, see page 3 of the instructions.   Cat. No. 11862M   Form **2441** (1998)

Part III Dependent Care Benefits

10 Enter the total amount of **dependent care benefits** you received for 1998. This amount should be shown in box 10 of your W-2 form(s). DO NOT include amounts that were reported to you as wages in box 1 of Form(s) W-2 . . . . | **10** |

11 Enter the amount forfeited, if any. See the instructions . . . . | **11** |

12 Subtract line 11 from line 10 . . . . | **12** |

13 Enter the total amount of **qualified expenses** incurred in 1998 for the care of the **qualifying person(s)** . . . | **13** |

14 Enter the **smaller** of line 12 or 13 . . . . | **14** |

15 Enter YOUR **earned income** . . . . | **15** |

16 If married filing a joint return, enter YOUR SPOUSE'S earned income (if your spouse was a student or was disabled, see the instructions for line 5); if married filing a separate return, see the instructions for the amount to enter; **all others,** enter the amount from line 15 . . . | **16** |

17 Enter the **smallest** of line 14, 15, or 16 . . . . . . | **17** |

18 **Excluded benefits.** Enter here the **smaller** of the following:

  • The amount from line 17, or
  • $5,000 ($2,500 if married filing a separate return **and** you were required to enter your spouse's earned income on line 16). . . . . | **18** |

19 **Taxable benefits.** Subtract line 18 from line 12. Also, include this amount on Form 1040, line 7. On the dotted line next to line 7, enter "DCB" . . . . | **19** |

To claim the child and dependent care
credit, complete lines 20–24 below.

20 Enter $2,400 ($4,800 if two or more qualifying persons) . . . . | **20** |

21 Enter the amount from line 18 . . . . | **21** |

22 Subtract line 21 from line 20. If zero or less, **STOP.** You cannot take the credit. **Exception.** If you paid 1997 expenses in 1998, see the instructions for line 9 . . . . | **22** |

23 Complete line 2 on the front of this form. DO NOT include in column (c) any excluded benefits shown on line 18 above. Then, add the amounts in column (c) and enter the total here . . . . | **23** |

24 Enter the **smaller** of line 22 or 23. Also, enter this amount on line 3 on the front of this form and complete lines 4–9 . . . . | **24** |

Form **8814**

Department of the Treasury
Internal Revenue Service (99)

Parents' Election To Report Child's Interest and Dividends
▶ See instructions below and on back.
▶ Attach to parents' Form 1040 or Form 1040NR.

OMB No. 1545-1128

1998

Attachment
Sequence No. **40**

Name(s) shown on your return	Your social security number

Caution: *The Federal income tax on your child's income, including capital gain distributions, may be less if you file a separate tax return for the child instead of making this election. This is because you cannot take certain tax benefits that your child would be entitled to on his or her own return. For details, see* **Tax Benefits You May Not Take** *on the back.*

A	Child's name (first, initial, and last)	B Child's social security number

C If more than one Form 8814 is attached, check here . . . . ▶ ☐

Part I — Child's Interest and Dividends To Report on Your Return

1a	Enter your child's **taxable** interest. If this amount is different from the amounts shown on the child's Forms 1099-INT and 1099-OID, see the instructions	**1a**	
b	Enter your child's **tax-exempt** interest. **DO NOT** include this amount on line 1a . . . . [**1b**]		
2	Enter your child's ordinary dividends, including any Alaska Permanent Fund dividends. If your child received any ordinary dividends as a nominee, see the instructions	**2**	
3	Enter your child's capital gain distributions. If your child received any capital gain distributions as a nominee, see the instructions	**3**	
4	Add lines 1a, 2, and 3. If the total is $1,400 or less, skip lines 5 and 6 and go to line 7. If the total is $7,000 or more, **do not** file this form. Your child **must** file his or her own return to report the income	**4**	
5	Base amount	**5**	1,400 00
6	Subtract line 5 from line 4. If you checked the box on line C above or if you entered an amount on line 3, see the instructions. Also, include this amount in the total on Form 1040, line 21, or Form 1040NR, line 21. In the space next to line 21, enter "Form 8814" and show the amount. Go to line 7 below. . . . . ▶	**6**	

Part II — Tax on the First $1,400 of Child's Interest and Dividends

7	Amount not taxed	**7**	700 00
8	Subtract line 7 from line 4. If the result is zero or less, enter -0-	**8**	
9	**Tax.** Is the amount on line 8 less than $700? **No.** Enter $105 here and see the **Note** below. **Yes.** Multiply line 8 by 15% (.15). Enter the result here and see the **Note** below.	**9**	

Note: *If you checked the box on line C above, see the instructions. Otherwise, include the amount from line 9 in the tax you enter on Form 1040, line 40, or Form 1040NR, line 39. Be sure to check box **a** on Form 1040, line 40, or Form 1040NR, line 39.*

General Instructions

Purpose of Form. Use this form if you elect to report your child's income on your return. If you do, your child will not have to file a return. You can make this election if your child meets **all** of the following conditions:

- Was under age 14 on January 1, 1999.
- Is required to file a 1998 return.
- Had income only from interest and dividends, including Alaska Permanent Fund dividends.
- Had gross income for 1998 that was less than $7,000.
- Had no estimated tax payments for 1998 (including any overpayment of tax from his or her 1997 return applied to 1998 estimated tax).

c Had no Federal income tax withheld from his or her income.

You must also qualify. See **Parents Who Qualify To Make the Election** below.

How To Make the Election. To make the election, complete and attach Form(s) 8814 to your tax return and file your return by the due date (including extensions). A separate Form 8814 must be filed for **each** child whose income you choose to report.

Parents Who Qualify To Make the Election. You qualify to make this election if you file Form 1040 or Form 1040NR and any of the following apply:

- You are filing a joint return for 1998 with the child's other parent.
- You and the child's other parent were married to each other but file separate

returns for 1998 AND you had the **higher** taxable income. If you do not know if you had the higher taxable income, see **Pub. 929**, Tax Rules for Children and Dependents.

c You were unmarried, treated as unmarried for Federal income tax purposes, or separated from the child's other parent by a divorce or separate maintenance decree. You must have had custody of your child for most of the year (you were the custodial parent). If you were the custodial parent and you remarried, you may make the election on a joint return with your new spouse. But if you and your new spouse do not file a joint return, you qualify to make the election only if you had **higher** taxable income than your new spouse.

(continued)

For Paperwork Reduction Act Notice, see back of form.　　　Cat. No. 10750J　　　Form **8814** (1998)

Note: *If you and the child's other parent were not married but lived together during the year with the child, you qualify to make the election only if you are the parent with the **higher** taxable income.*

Tax Benefits You May Not Take. If you elect to report your child's income on your return, you may not take any of the following deductions that your child would be entitled to on his or her own return.

• Standard deduction of $1,750 for a blind child.

• Penalty on early withdrawal of child's savings.

• Itemized deductions such as child's investment expenses or charitable contributions.

If your child received **capital gain distributions,** you may pay up to $35 more tax on those distributions if you make this election instead of filing a separate tax return for the child. This is because the tax rate on the child's income between $700 and $1,400 is 15% if you make the election. However, if you file a separate return for the child, the tax rate on those distributions may be 10% because of the preferential capital gains tax rates.

If any of the above apply to your child, first figure the tax on your child's income as if he or she is filing a return. Next, figure the tax as if you are electing to report your child's income on **your** return. Then, compare the methods to determine which results in the lower tax.

Alternative Minimum Tax. If your child received tax-exempt interest (or exempt-interest dividends paid by a regulated investment company) from certain private activity bonds, you must take this into account in determining if you owe the alternative minimum tax. See **Form 6251,** Alternative Minimum Tax–Individuals, and its instructions for details.

Investment Interest Expense. Your child's income (excluding Alaska Permanent Fund dividends and capital gain distributions) that you report on your return is considered to be **your** investment income for purposes of figuring your investment interest expense deduction. If your child received Alaska Permanent Fund dividends or capital gain distributions, see **Pub. 550,** Investment Income and Expenses, to figure the amount you may treat as your investment income.

Foreign Accounts and Trusts. Complete Part III of **Schedule B** (Form 1040) for your child if he or she **(1)** had a foreign financial account, or **(2)** received a distribution from, or was the grantor of, or transferor to, a foreign trust. If you answer "Yes" to either question, you must file this Schedule B with **your** return. Enter "Form 8814" next to line 7a or line 8, whichever applies. Also, complete line 7b if applicable.

Change of Address. If your child filed a return for a year before 1998 and the address shown on the last return filed is not your child's current address, be sure to notify the IRS, in writing, of the new address. To do this, you may:

• Use **Form 8822,** Change of Address, or

• Write to the Internal Revenue Service Center where your child's last return was filed, or

• Write to the Chief, Customer Service Division, in your local IRS district office.

Additional Information. See Pub. 929 for more details.

Line Instructions

Name and Social Security Number. If filing a joint return, include your spouse's name but enter the social security number of the person whose name is shown first on the return.

Line 1a. Enter **ALL** taxable interest income received by your child in 1998. If your child received a **Form 1099-INT** for tax-exempt interest, such as from municipal bonds, enter the amount and "Tax-exempt interest" on the dotted line next to line 1a. **Do not** include this interest in the total for line 1a but be sure to include it on line 1b.

If your child received, as a **nominee,** interest that actually belongs to another person, enter the amount and "ND" (for nominee distribution) on the dotted line next to line 1a. **Do not** include amounts received as a nominee in the total for line 1a.

If your child had accrued interest that was paid to the seller of a bond, amortizable bond premium (ABP) allowed as a reduction to interest income, or if any original issue discount (OID) included on line 1a is less than the amount shown on your child's **Form 1099-OID,** follow the instructions above for nominee interest to see how to report the nontaxable amounts. But on the dotted line next to line 1a, enter the nontaxable amount and "Accrued interest," "ABP adjustment," or "OID adjustment," whichever applies. **Do not** include any nontaxable amounts in the total for line 1a.

Line 1b. If your child received any tax-exempt interest income, such as from certain state and municipal bonds, report it on line 1b. Also, include any exempt-interest dividends your child received as a shareholder in a mutual fund or other regulated investment company.

Note: *If line 1b includes tax-exempt interest or exempt-interest dividends paid by a regulated investment company from private activity bonds, see **Alternative Minimum Tax** on this page.*

Line 2. Enter the ordinary dividends received by your child in 1998. Ordinary dividends should be shown in box 1 of **Form 1099-DIV.** Also, include ordinary dividends your child received through a partnership, an S corporation, or an estate or trust.

If your child received, as a **nominee,** ordinary dividends that actually belong to another person, enter the amount and "ND" on the dotted line next to line 2. **Do not** include amounts received as a nominee in the total for line 2.

Line 3. Enter the capital gain distributions received by your child in 1998. Capital gain distributions should be shown in box 2a of Form 1099-DIV. Also, see the instructions for line 6.

If your child received, as a **nominee,** capital gain distributions that actually belong to another person, enter the amount and "ND" on the dotted line next to line 3. **Do not** include amounts received as a nominee in the total for line 3.

Line 6. If you checked the box on line C, add the amounts from line 6 of **all** your Forms 8814. Include the total on line 21 of Form 1040 or Form 1040NR, whichever applies. Be sure to enter "Form 8814" and the total of the line 6 amounts in the space next to line 21.

If you entered an amount on line 3, you must file **Schedule D** (Form 1040). Part or all of those capital gain distributions must be reported on your Schedule D instead of on Form 8814, line 6. See Pub. 929 for details.

Line 9. If you checked the box on line C, add the amounts from line 9 of **all** your Forms 8814. Include the total on Form 1040, line 40, or Form 1040NR, line 39. Be sure to check box **a** on that line.

Paperwork Reduction Act Notice. We ask for the information on this form to carry out the Internal Revenue laws of the United States. You are required to give us the information. We need it to ensure that you are complying with these laws and to allow us to figure and collect the right amount of tax.

You are not required to provide the information requested on a form that is subject to the Paperwork Reduction Act unless the form displays a valid OMB control number. Books or records relating to a form or its instructions must be retained as long as their contents may become material in the administration of any Internal Revenue law. Generally, tax returns and return information are confidential, as required by Internal Revenue Code section 6103.

The time needed to complete and file this form will vary depending on individual circumstances. The estimated average time is: **Recordkeeping,** 26 min.; **Learning about the law or the form,** 10 min.; **Preparing the form,** 14 min.; and **Copying, assembling, and sending the form to the IRS,** 17 min.

If you have comments concerning the accuracy of these time estimates or suggestions for making this form simpler, we would be happy to hear from you. See the instructions for the tax return with which this form is filed.

Form **9465**
(Rev. January 1996)

Department of the Treasury
Internal Revenue Service

Installment Agreement Request

► See instructions below and on back.

OMB No. 1545-1350

Note: *Do not file this form if you are currently making payments on an installment agreement. You must pay your other Federal tax liabilities in full or you will be in default on your agreement.*

If you can't pay the full amount you owe, you can ask to make monthly installment payments. If we approve your request, you will be charged a $43 fee. **Do not include the fee with this form.** We will deduct the fee from your first payment after we approve your request, unless you choose **Direct Debit** (see the line 13 instructions). We will usually let you know within 30 days after we receive your request whether it is approved or denied. But if this request is for tax due on a return you filed after March 31, it may take us longer than 30 days to reply.

To ask for an installment agreement, complete this form. Attach it to the front of your return when you file. If you have already filed your return or you are filing this form in response to a notice, see **How Do I File Form 9465?** on page 2. If you have any questions about this request, call 1-800-829-1040.

Caution: *A Notice of Federal Tax Lien may be filed to protect the government's interest until you pay in full.*

1	Your first name and initial	Last name	Your social security number
	If a joint return, spouse's first name and initial	Last name	Spouse's social security number

Your current address (number and street). If you have a P.O. box and no home delivery, show box number. | Apt. number

City, town or post office, state, and ZIP code. If a foreign address, show city, state or province, postal code, and full name of country.

2   If this address is new since you filed your last tax return, check here . . . . ► ☐

3   (   )
     Your home phone number   Best time for us to call

4   (   )
     Your work phone number   Ext.   Best time for us to call

5   Name of your bank or other financial institution:

Address

City, state, and ZIP code

6   Your employer's name:

Address

City, state, and ZIP code

7   Enter the tax return for which you are making this request (for example, Form 1040). But if you are filing this form in response to a notice, don't complete lines 7 through 9. Instead, attach the bottom section of the notice to this form and go to line 10 . . . . ► _____

8   Enter the tax year for which you are making this request (for example, 1995) . . . . ► _____

9   Enter the total amount you owe as shown on your tax return . . . . ► $ _____

10   Enter the amount of any payment you are making with your tax return (or notice). See instructions . ► $ _____

11   Enter the amount you can paym each month. **Make your payments as large as possible to limit interest and penalty charges.** The charges will continue until you pay in full . . . . ► $ _____

12   Enter the date you want to make your payment each month. Do not enter a date later than the 28th ► _____

13   If you would like to make your monthly payments using **Direct Debit** (automatic withdrawals from your bank account), check here. ► ☐

Your signature	Date	Spouse's signature. If a joint return, BOTH must sign.	Date

Privacy Act and Paperwork Reduction Act Notice.– Our legal right to ask for the information on this form is Internal Revenue Code sections 6001, 6011, 6012(a), 6109, and 6159 and their regulations. We will use the information to process your request for an installment agreement. The reason we need your name and social security number is to secure proper identification. We require this information to gain access to the tax information in our files and properly respond to your request. If you do not enter the information, we may not be able to process your request. We may give this information to the Department of Justice as provided by law. We may also give it to cities, states, and the District of Columbia to carry out their tax laws.

Cat. No. 14842Y

Form **9465** (Rev. 1-96)

The time needed to complete and file this form will vary depending on individual circumstances. The estimated average time is: **Learning about the law or the form,** 2 min.; **Preparing the form,** 24 min.; and **Copying, assembling, and sending the form to the IRS,** 20 min.

If you have comments concerning the accuracy of this time estimate or suggestions for making this form simpler, we would be happy to hear from you. You can write to the Tax Forms Committee, Western Area Distribution Center, Rancho Cordova, CA 95743-0001. **DO NOT** send the form to this address. Instead, see **How Do I File Form 9465?** on this page.

General Instructions

If you cannot pay the full amount you owe shown on your tax return (or on a notice we sent you), you can ask to make monthly installment payments. But before requesting an installment agreement, you should consider other less costly alternatives, such as a bank loan.

You will be charged interest and may be charged a late payment penalty on any tax not paid by its due date, even if your request to pay in installments is granted. To limit interest and penalty charges, file your return on time and pay as much of the tax as possible with your return (or notice).

You will be charged a $43 fee if your request is approved. **Do not include the fee with this form.** We will send you a letter telling you your request has been approved, how to pay the fee, and how to make your first installment payment. After we receive each payment, we will send you a letter showing the remaining amount you owe, and the due date and amount of your next payment.

By approving your request, we agree to let you pay the tax you owe in monthly installments instead of immediately paying the amount in full. In return, you agree to make your monthly payments on time. **You also agree to meet all your future tax liabilities.** This means that you must have adequate withholding or estimated tax payments so that your tax liability for future years is paid in full when you timely file your return. If you do not make your payments on time or have an outstanding past-due amount in a future year, you will be in default on your agreement and we may take enforcement actions to collect the entire amount you owe.

Bankruptcy–Offer-in-Compromise.– If you are in bankruptcy or we have accepted your offer-in-compromise, **do not** file this form. Instead, call your local IRS District Office Special Procedures function. You can get the number by calling 1-800-829-1040.

Specific Instructions

Line 1

If you are making this request for a joint tax return, show the names and SSNs in the same order as on your tax return.

Line 10

Even if you can't pay the full amount you owe now, you should pay as much of it as possible to limit penalty and interest charges. If you are filing this form with your tax return, make the payment with your return. If you are filing this form by itself, for example, in response to a notice, include a check or money order payable to the Internal Revenue Service with this form. **Do not** send cash. On your payment, write your name, address, social security number, daytime phone number, and the tax year and tax return for which you are making this request (for example, "1995 Form 1040").

Line 11

You should try to make your payments large enough so that your balance due will be paid off by the due date of your next tax return.

Line 12

You can choose the date your monthly payment is due. For example, if your rent or mortgage payment is due on the first of the month, you may want to make your installment payments on the 15th. When we approve your request, we will tell you the month and date that your first payment is due. If we have not replied by the date you choose for your first payment, you may send the first payment to the Internal Revenue Service Center at the address shown on this page for the place where you live. Make your check or money order payable to the Internal Revenue Service. See the instructions for line 10 for what to write on your payment.

Line 13

Check the box on line 13 if you want your monthly payments automatically deducted **(Direct Debit)** from your bank account. If your installment agreement request is approved, we will send you the required Direct Debit enrollment form and you must include the $43 fee when you return it.

How Do I File Form 9465?

● If you haven't filed your return, attach Form 9465 to the front of your return.

● If you have already filed your return, you are filing your return electronically, or you are filing this form in response to a notice, mail it to the **Internal Revenue Service Center** at the address shown below for the place where you live. No street address is needed.

If you live in:	Use this address:
Florida, Georgia, South Carolina	Atlanta, GA 39901
New Jersey, New York (New York City and counties of Nassau, Rockland, Suffolk, and Westchester)	Holtsville, NY 00501
New York (all other counties), Connecticut, Maine, Massachusetts, New Hampshire, Rhode Island, Vermont	Andover, MA 05501
Illinois, Iowa, Minnesota, Missouri, Wisconsin	Kansas City, MO 64999
Delaware, District of Columbia, Maryland, Pennsylvania, Virginia	Philadelphia, PA 19255
Indiana, Kentucky, Michigan, Ohio, West Virginia	Cincinnati, OH 45999
Kansas, New Mexico, Oklahoma, Texas	Austin, TX 73301
Alaska, Arizona, California (counties of Alpine, Amador, Butte, Calaveras, Colusa, Contra Costa, Del Norte, El Dorado, Glenn, Humboldt, Lake, Lassen, Marin, Mendocino, Modoc, Napa, Nevada, Placer, Plumas, Sacramento, San Joaquin, Shasta, Sierra, Siskiyou, Solano, Sonoma, Sutter, Tehama, Trinity, Yolo, and Yuba), Colorado, Idaho, Montana, Nebraska, Nevada, North Dakota, Oregon, South Dakota, Utah, Washington, Wyoming	Ogden, UT 84201
California (all other counties), Hawaii	Fresno, CA 93888
Alabama, Arkansas, Louisiana, Mississippi, North Carolina, Tennessee	Memphis, TN 37501
American Samoa Guam: Nonpermanent residents only* Puerto Rico (or if excluding income under section 933) Virgin Islands: Nonpermanent residents only* Foreign country (or if a dual-status alien): U.S. citizens and those filing Form 2555, 2555-EZ, or 4563 All APO and FPO addresses	Philadelphia, PA 19255

*Permanent residents of Guam and the Virgin Islands cannot use Form 9465.

Child Tax Credit Worksheet—Line 28

▶ Keep for your records.

1. $400.00 × _____ . Multiply and enter the result . . . . 1. _____

   ▲ Enter number of qualifying children (see page 32)

2. Enter the amount from Form 1040A, line 19 . . . . 2. _____

3. Is line 2 above more than $55,000?

   ☐ **No.** Skip lines 3 through 5, enter -0- on line 6, and go to line 7.

   ☐ **Yes.** Enter: $75,000 if single, head of household, or qualifying widow(er); $110,000 if married filing jointly; $55,000 if married filing separately . . . . 3. _____

4. Subtract line 3 from line 2. If zero or less, enter -0- here and on line 6, and go to line 7 . . . . 4. _____

5. Divide line 4 by $1,000. If the result is not a whole number, round it up to the next higher whole number (for example, round 0.01 to 1) . . . . 5. _____

6. Multiply $50 by the number on line 5 . . . . . . 6. _____

7. Subtract line 6 from line 1. If zero or less, **stop here;** you **cannot** take this credit . 7. _____

8. Enter the amount from Form 1040A, line 25 . . . . 8. _____

9. Is line 1 above more than $800?

   ☐ **No.** Add the amounts from Form 1040A, lines 26, 27, and 29. Enter the total.

   ☐ **Yes.** Enter the amount from the worksheet on page 34. 9. _____

10. Subtract line 9 above from line 8 . . . . 10. _____

11. **Child tax credit.** Enter the **smaller** of line 7 or line 10 here and on Form 1040A, line 28 ▶ 11. _____

TIP *If line 1 above is more than $800, you may be able to take the* **Additional Child Tax Credit.** *See page 32.*

Use this worksheet **only** if you checked "Yes" on line 9 of the worksheet on page 33.

1. Add the amounts from Form 1040A, lines 26, 27, and 29. Enter the total . . . . .   1. _____

2. Are you claiming the adoption credit **(Form 8839)?**

   ☐ **No. Stop here;** enter the amount from line 1 above on line 9 of the worksheet on page 33.

   ☐ **Yes.** Enter the amount from line 7 of the worksheet on page 33 . . . .   2. _____

   Next, complete Form 1040A, lines 37a and 37b if they apply to you, and figure any amount to enter to the left of line 39 (see page 43). Then, go to line 3 below.

3. Enter the total social security and Medicare taxes withheld from your pay (and your spouse's if filing a joint return). These taxes should be shown in boxes 4 and 6 of your W-2 form(s). If you worked for a railroad, see below . . . .   3. _____

4. Enter the total of the amount from Form 1040A, line 37a, plus any amount entered to the left of line 39 for excess social security and railroad retirement (RRTA) taxes withheld .   4. _____

5. Subtract line 4 from line 3. If zero, **stop here;** enter the amount from line 1 above on line 9 of the worksheet on page 33 .   5. _____

6. Subtract line 5 from line 2. If line 5 is more than line 2, enter -0-. This is your child tax credit for purposes of figuring the adoption credit . . . .   6. _____

   Next, figure your adoption credit on Form 8839. Use the amount from line 6 above in place of the amount from Form 1040A, line 28. Enter the credit on Form 1040A, line 30. Then, go to line 7 below.

7. Enter the amount from Form 1040A, line 30 . . . .   7. _____

8. Add lines 1 and 7. Enter the total here and on line 9 of the worksheet on page 33   8. _____

Railroad Employees. Include the following taxes in the total on line 3 above.

- Tier 1 tax withheld from your pay. This tax should be shown in box 14 of your W-2 form(s) and identified as "Tier 1 tax."

- If you were an employee representative, 50% of the total Tier 1 tax and Tier 1 Medicare tax you paid for 1998.

Line 29

Education Credits

If you (or your dependent) paid expenses in 1998 for yourself, your spouse, or your dependent to enroll in or attend the first 2 years of post-secondary education, you may be able to take the Hope credit. For qualified expenses paid after June 30, 1998, you may be able to take the lifetime learning credit. See **Form 8863** for details. However, if you are married filing a separate return, you **cannot** take either credit.

Line 30

Adoption Credit

You may be able to take this credit if you paid expenses in 1997 or 1998 to adopt a child. See **Form 8839** for details.

Line 33

Advance Earned Income Credit Payments

If you received advance earned income credit (EIC) payments, enter them on line 33. These payments should be shown in box 9 of your W-2 form(s).

Child Tax Credit Worksheet—Line 43

▶ Keep for your records.

1. $400.00 3 _____ . Multiply and enter the result . . . . **1.**

   ▲ Enter number of qualifying
   children (see page 31)

2. Are you filing **Form 2555, 2555-EZ,** or **4563,** or are you excluding income from Puerto Rico?

   ☐ **No.** Enter the amount from Form 1040, line 34.

   ☐ **Yes.** Enter your **modified adjusted gross income**
   (see page 31). } . . . **2.**

3. Enter the amount shown below for your filing status:

   ● Married filing jointly, enter $110,000

   ● Single, head of household, or qualifying widow(er),
   enter $75,000 } . . . **3.**

   ● Married filing separately, enter $55,000

4. Is line 2 more than line 3?

   ☐ **No.** Skip lines 4 and 5, enter -0- on line 6, and go to line 7.

   ☐ **Yes.** Subtract line 3 from line 2 . . . . **4.**

5. Divide line 4 by $1,000. If the result is not a whole number, round
   it up to the next higher whole number (for example, round 0.01
   to 1) . . . . **5.**

6. Multiply $50 by the number on line 5. . . . . **6.**

7. Subtract line 6 from line 1. If zero or less, **stop here;** you **cannot** take this credit . . **7.**

8. Enter the amount from Form 1040, line 40 . . . . **8.**

9. Is line 1 above more than $800?

   ☐ **No.** Add the amounts from Form 1040, lines 41,
   42, and 44. Enter the total. } . . . **9.**

   ☐ **Yes.** Enter the amount from the worksheet on
   page 33.

10. Subtract line 9 above from line 8 . . . . **10.**

11. **Child tax credit.** Enter the **smaller** of line 7 or line 10 here and on Form 1040, line 43 **11.**

TIP *If line 1 above is more than $800, you may be able to take the **Additional Child Tax Credit.** See page 31.*

Line 9 of Child Tax Credit Worksheet on Page 32 (keep for your records)

Use this worksheet **only** if you checked "Yes" on line 9 of the worksheet on page 32.

1. Add the amounts from Form 1040, lines 41, 42, and 44. Enter the total . . . . **1.**

2. Are you claiming any of the following credits: the adoption credit **(Form 8839)**, the mortgage interest credit **(Form 8396)**, or the District of Columbia first-time homebuyer credit **(Form 8859)?**

   ☐ **No.** **Stop here;** enter the amount from line 1 above on line 9 of the worksheet on page 32.

   ☐ **Yes.** Enter the amount from line 7 of the worksheet on page 32 . **2.**

   Next, complete Form 1040, lines 52, 59a, 59b, and 62 if they apply to you. Then, go to line 3 below.

3. Enter the total social security and Medicare taxes withheld from your pay (and your spouse's if filing a joint return). These taxes should be shown in boxes 4 and 6 of your W-2 form(s). If you worked for a railroad, see below . . . . **3.**

4. Enter the total of the amounts from Form 1040, line 27 and line 52, plus any uncollected social security and Medicare or RRTA tax on tips or group-term life insurance. This tax should be shown in box 13 of your W-2 form(s) with codes **A** and **B** or **M** and **N.** **4.**

5. Add lines 3 and 4 . . . . **5.**

6. Add the amounts from Form 1040, lines 59a and 62. Enter the total . . . . . . **6.**

7. Subtract line 6 from line 5. If zero, **stop here;** enter the amount from line 1 above on line 9 of the worksheet on page 32 . . . . **7.**

8. Subtract line 7 from line 2. If line 7 is more than line 2, enter -0-. This is your child tax credit for purposes of figuring the credits listed on line 2 **8.**

   Next, complete the applicable credit form(s) listed on line 2. Use the amount from line 8 above in place of the amount from Form 1040, line 43. Then, go to line 9 below.

9. Enter the total of any adoption credit from Form 8839, line 14, mortgage interest credit from Form 8396, line 11, and District of Columbia first-time homebuyer credit from Form 8859, line 11 . . **9.**

10. Add lines 1 and 9. Enter the total here and on line 9 of the worksheet on page 32 . . . . . **10.**

Railroad Employees. Include the following taxes in the total on line 3 above.

- Tier 1 tax withheld from your pay. This tax should be shown in box 14 of your W-2 form(s) and identified as "Tier 1 tax."
- If you were an employee representative, 50% of the total Tier 1 tax and Tier 1 Medicare tax you paid for 1998.

Line 44
Education Credits

If you (or your dependent) paid expenses in 1998 for yourself, your spouse, or your dependent to enroll in or attend the first 2 years of post-secondary education, you may be able to take the Hope credit. For qualified expenses paid after June 30, 1998, you may be able to take the lifetime learning credit. See **Form 8863** for details. However, if you are married filing separately, you **cannot** take either credit.

Line 45
Adoption Credit

You may be able to take this credit if you paid expenses in 1997 or 1998 to adopt a child. See **Form 8839** for details.

Line 46
Foreign Tax Credit

If you paid income tax to a foreign country, you may be able to take this credit. But you must complete and attach **Form 1116** to do so.

Exception. You do not have to file Form 1116 to take this credit if **all five** of the following apply.

1. All of your gross foreign-source income is from interest and dividends and all of that income and the foreign tax paid on it is reported to you on **Form

1998 Tax Table

Use if your taxable income is less than $100,000. If $100,000 or more, use the Tax Rate Schedules.

Example. Mr. and Mrs. Brown are filing a joint return. Their taxable income on line 39 of Form 1040 is $25,300. First, they find the $25,300–25,350 income line. Next, they find the column for married filing jointly and read down the column. The amount shown where the income line and filing status column meet is $3,799. This is the tax amount they should enter on line 40 of their Form 1040.

Sample Table

At least	But less than	Single	Married filing jointly *	Married filing separately	Head of a house-hold
			Your tax is—		
25,200	25,250	3,784	3,784	4,310	3,784
25,250	25,300	3,791	3,791	4,324	3,791
25,300	25,350	3,799	(3,799)	4,338	3,799
25,350	25,400	3,810	3,806	4,352	3,806

If line 39 (taxable income) is— At least	But less than	Single	Married filing jointly *	Married filing sepa-rately	Head of a house-hold
			Your tax is—		
0	5	0	0	0	0
5	15	2	2	2	2
15	25	3	3	3	3
25	50	6	6	6	6
50	75	9	9	9	9
75	100	13	13	13	13
100	125	17	17	17	17
125	150	21	21	21	21
150	175	24	24	24	24
175	200	28	28	28	28
200	225	32	32	32	32
225	250	36	36	36	36
250	275	39	39	39	39
275	300	43	43	43	43
300	325	47	47	47	47
325	350	51	51	51	51
350	375	54	54	54	54
375	400	58	58	58	58
400	425	62	62	62	62
425	450	66	66	66	66
450	475	69	69	69	69
475	500	73	73	73	73
500	525	77	77	77	77
525	550	81	81	81	81
550	575	84	84	84	84
575	600	88	88	88	88
600	625	92	92	92	92
625	650	96	96	96	96
650	675	99	99	99	99
675	700	103	103	103	103
700	725	107	107	107	107
725	750	111	111	111	111
750	775	114	114	114	114
775	800	118	118	118	118
800	825	122	122	122	122
825	850	126	126	126	126
850	875	129	129	129	129
875	900	133	133	133	133
900	925	137	137	137	137
925	950	141	141	141	141
950	975	144	144	144	144
975	1,000	148	148	148	148

1,000

At least	But less than	Single	Married filing jointly *	Married filing sepa-rately	Head of a house-hold
1,000	1,025	152	152	152	152
1,025	1,050	156	156	156	156
1,050	1,075	159	159	159	159
1,075	1,100	163	163	163	163
1,100	1,125	167	167	167	167
1,125	1,150	171	171	171	171
1,150	1,175	174	174	174	174
1,175	1,200	178	178	178	178
1,200	1,225	182	182	182	182
1,225	1,250	186	186	186	186
1,250	1,275	189	189	189	189
1,275	1,300	193	193	193	193

At least	But less than	Single	Married filing jointly *	Married filing sepa-rately	Head of a house-hold
			Your tax is—		
1,300	1,325	197	197	197	197
1,325	1,350	201	201	201	201
1,350	1,375	204	204	204	204
1,375	1,400	208	208	208	208
1,400	1,425	212	212	212	212
1,425	1,450	216	216	216	216
1,450	1,475	219	219	219	219
1,475	1,500	223	223	223	223
1,500	1,525	227	227	227	227
1,525	1,550	231	231	231	231
1,550	1,575	234	234	234	234
1,575	1,600	238	238	238	238
1,600	1,625	242	242	242	242
1,625	1,650	246	246	246	246
1,650	1,675	249	249	249	249
1,675	1,700	253	253	253	253
1,700	1,725	257	257	257	257
1,725	1,750	261	261	261	261
1,750	1,775	264	264	264	264
1,775	1,800	268	268	268	268
1,800	1,825	272	272	272	272
1,825	1,850	276	276	276	276
1,850	1,875	279	279	279	279
1,875	1,900	283	283	283	283
1,900	1,925	287	287	287	287
1,925	1,950	291	291	291	291
1,950	1,975	294	294	294	294
1,975	2,000	298	298	298	298

2,000

At least	But less than	Single	Married filing jointly *	Married filing sepa-rately	Head of a house-hold
2,000	2,025	302	302	302	302
2,025	2,050	306	306	306	306
2,050	2,075	309	309	309	309
2,075	2,100	313	313	313	313
2,100	2,125	317	317	317	317
2,125	2,150	321	321	321	321
2,150	2,175	324	324	324	324
2,175	2,200	328	328	328	328
2,200	2,225	332	332	332	332
2,225	2,250	336	336	336	336
2,250	2,275	339	339	339	339
2,275	2,300	343	343	343	343
2,300	2,325	347	347	347	347
2,325	2,350	351	351	351	351
2,350	2,375	354	354	354	354
2,375	2,400	358	358	358	358
2,400	2,425	362	362	362	362
2,425	2,450	366	366	366	366
2,450	2,475	369	369	369	369
2,475	2,500	373	373	373	373
2,500	2,525	377	377	377	377
2,525	2,550	381	381	381	381
2,550	2,575	384	384	384	384
2,575	2,600	388	388	388	388
2,600	2,625	392	392	392	392
2,625	2,650	396	396	396	396
2,650	2,675	399	399	399	399
2,675	2,700	403	403	403	403

At least	But less than	Single	Married filing jointly *	Married filing sepa-rately	Head of a house-hold
			Your tax is—		
2,700	2,725	407	407	407	407
2,725	2,750	411	411	411	411
2,750	2,775	414	414	414	414
2,775	2,800	418	418	418	418
2,800	2,825	422	422	422	422
2,825	2,850	426	426	426	426
2,850	2,875	429	429	429	429
2,875	2,900	433	433	433	433
2,900	2,925	437	437	437	437
2,925	2,950	441	441	441	441
2,950	2,975	444	444	444	444
2,975	3,000	448	448	448	448

3,000

At least	But less than	Single	Married filing jointly *	Married filing sepa-rately	Head of a house-hold
3,000	3,050	454	454	454	454
3,050	3,100	461	461	461	461
3,100	3,150	469	469	469	469
3,150	3,200	476	476	476	476
3,200	3,250	484	484	484	484
3,250	3,300	491	491	491	491
3,300	3,350	499	499	499	499
3,350	3,400	506	506	506	506
3,400	3,450	514	514	514	514
3,450	3,500	521	521	521	521
3,500	3,550	529	529	529	529
3,550	3,600	536	536	536	536
3,600	3,650	544	544	544	544
3,650	3,700	551	551	551	551
3,700	3,750	559	559	559	559
3,750	3,800	566	566	566	566
3,800	3,850	574	574	574	574
3,850	3,900	581	581	581	581
3,900	3,950	589	589	589	589
3,950	4,000	596	596	596	596

4,000

At least	But less than	Single	Married filing jointly *	Married filing sepa-rately	Head of a house-hold
4,000	4,050	604	604	604	604
4,050	4,100	611	611	611	611
4,100	4,150	619	619	619	619
4,150	4,200	626	626	626	626
4,200	4,250	634	634	634	634
4,250	4,300	641	641	641	641
4,300	4,350	649	649	649	649
4,350	4,400	656	656	656	656
4,400	4,450	664	664	664	664
4,450	4,500	671	671	671	671
4,500	4,550	679	679	679	679
4,550	4,600	686	686	686	686
4,600	4,650	694	694	694	694
4,650	4,700	701	701	701	701
4,700	4,750	709	709	709	709
4,750	4,800	716	716	716	716
4,800	4,850	724	724	724	724
4,850	4,900	731	731	731	731
4,900	4,950	739	739	739	739
4,950	5,000	746	746	746	746

Continued on next page

* This column must also be used by a qualifying widow(er).

Column headers for all sections:

If line 39 (taxable income) is– At least	But less than	And you are– Single	Married filing jointly *	Married filing separately	Head of a household
		Your tax is–			

5,000

At least	But less than	Single	Married filing jointly *	Married filing separately	Head of a household
5,000	5,050	754	754	754	754
5,050	5,100	761	761	761	761
5,100	5,150	769	769	769	769
5,150	5,200	776	776	776	776
5,200	5,250	784	784	784	784
5,250	5,300	791	791	791	791
5,300	5,350	799	799	799	799
5,350	5,400	806	806	806	806
5,400	5,450	814	814	814	814
5,450	5,500	821	821	821	821
5,500	5,550	829	829	829	829
5,550	5,600	836	836	836	836
5,600	5,650	844	844	844	844
5,650	5,700	851	851	851	851
5,700	5,750	859	859	859	859
5,750	5,800	866	866	866	866
5,800	5,850	874	874	874	874
5,850	5,900	881	881	881	881
5,900	5,950	889	889	889	889
5,950	6,000	896	896	896	896

6,000

At least	But less than	Single	Married filing jointly *	Married filing separately	Head of a household
6,000	6,050	904	904	904	904
6,050	6,100	911	911	911	911
6,100	6,150	919	919	919	919
6,150	6,200	926	926	926	926
6,200	6,250	934	934	934	934
6,250	6,300	941	941	941	941
6,300	6,350	949	949	949	949
6,350	6,400	956	956	956	956
6,400	6,450	964	964	964	964
6,450	6,500	971	971	971	971
6,500	6,550	979	979	979	979
6,550	6,600	986	986	986	986
6,600	6,650	994	994	994	994
6,650	6,700	1,001	1,001	1,001	1,001
6,700	6,750	1,009	1,009	1,009	1,009
6,750	6,800	1,016	1,016	1,016	1,016
6,800	6,850	1,024	1,024	1,024	1,024
6,850	6,900	1,031	1,031	1,031	1,031
6,900	6,950	1,039	1,039	1,039	1,039
6,950	7,000	1,046	1,046	1,046	1,046

7,000

At least	But less than	Single	Married filing jointly *	Married filing separately	Head of a household
7,000	7,050	1,054	1,054	1,054	1,054
7,050	7,100	1,061	1,061	1,061	1,061
7,100	7,150	1,069	1,069	1,069	1,069
7,150	7,200	1,076	1,076	1,076	1,076
7,200	7,250	1,084	1,084	1,084	1,084
7,250	7,300	1,091	1,091	1,091	1,091
7,300	7,350	1,099	1,099	1,099	1,099
7,350	7,400	1,106	1,106	1,106	1,106
7,400	7,450	1,114	1,114	1,114	1,114
7,450	7,500	1,121	1,121	1,121	1,121
7,500	7,550	1,129	1,129	1,129	1,129
7,550	7,600	1,136	1,136	1,136	1,136
7,600	7,650	1,144	1,144	1,144	1,144
7,650	7,700	1,151	1,151	1,151	1,151
7,700	7,750	1,159	1,159	1,159	1,159
7,750	7,800	1,166	1,166	1,166	1,166
7,800	7,850	1,174	1,174	1,174	1,174
7,850	7,900	1,181	1,181	1,181	1,181
7,900	7,950	1,189	1,189	1,189	1,189
7,950	8,000	1,196	1,196	1,196	1,196

8,000

At least	But less than	Single	Married filing jointly *	Married filing separately	Head of a household
8,000	8,050	1,204	1,204	1,204	1,204
8,050	8,100	1,211	1,211	1,211	1,211
8,100	8,150	1,219	1,219	1,219	1,219
8,150	8,200	1,226	1,226	1,226	1,226
8,200	8,250	1,234	1,234	1,234	1,234
8,250	8,300	1,241	1,241	1,241	1,241
8,300	8,350	1,249	1,249	1,249	1,249
8,350	8,400	1,256	1,256	1,256	1,256
8,400	8,450	1,264	1,264	1,264	1,264
8,450	8,500	1,271	1,271	1,271	1,271
8,500	8,550	1,279	1,279	1,279	1,279
8,550	8,600	1,286	1,286	1,286	1,286
8,600	8,650	1,294	1,294	1,294	1,294
8,650	8,700	1,301	1,301	1,301	1,301
8,700	8,750	1,309	1,309	1,309	1,309
8,750	8,800	1,316	1,316	1,316	1,316
8,800	8,850	1,324	1,324	1,324	1,324
8,850	8,900	1,331	1,331	1,331	1,331
8,900	8,950	1,339	1,339	1,339	1,339
8,950	9,000	1,346	1,346	1,346	1,346

9,000

At least	But less than	Single	Married filing jointly *	Married filing separately	Head of a household
9,000	9,050	1,354	1,354	1,354	1,354
9,050	9,100	1,361	1,361	1,361	1,361
9,100	9,150	1,369	1,369	1,369	1,369
9,150	9,200	1,376	1,376	1,376	1,376
9,200	9,250	1,384	1,384	1,384	1,384
9,250	9,300	1,391	1,391	1,391	1,391
9,300	9,350	1,399	1,399	1,399	1,399
9,350	9,400	1,406	1,406	1,406	1,406
9,400	9,450	1,414	1,414	1,414	1,414
9,450	9,500	1,421	1,421	1,421	1,421
9,500	9,550	1,429	1,429	1,429	1,429
9,550	9,600	1,436	1,436	1,436	1,436
9,600	9,650	1,444	1,444	1,444	1,444
9,650	9,700	1,451	1,451	1,451	1,451
9,700	9,750	1,459	1,459	1,459	1,459
9,750	9,800	1,466	1,466	1,466	1,466
9,800	9,850	1,474	1,474	1,474	1,474
9,850	9,900	1,481	1,481	1,481	1,481
9,900	9,950	1,489	1,489	1,489	1,489
9,950	10,000	1,496	1,496	1,496	1,496

10,000

At least	But less than	Single	Married filing jointly *	Married filing separately	Head of a household
10,000	10,050	1,504	1,504	1,504	1,504
10,050	10,100	1,511	1,511	1,511	1,511
10,100	10,150	1,519	1,519	1,519	1,519
10,150	10,200	1,526	1,526	1,526	1,526
10,200	10,250	1,534	1,534	1,534	1,534
10,250	10,300	1,541	1,541	1,541	1,541
10,300	10,350	1,549	1,549	1,549	1,549
10,350	10,400	1,556	1,556	1,556	1,556
10,400	10,450	1,564	1,564	1,564	1,564
10,450	10,500	1,571	1,571	1,571	1,571
10,500	10,550	1,579	1,579	1,579	1,579
10,550	10,600	1,586	1,586	1,586	1,586
10,600	10,650	1,594	1,594	1,594	1,594
10,650	10,700	1,601	1,601	1,601	1,601
10,700	10,750	1,609	1,609	1,609	1,609
10,750	10,800	1,616	1,616	1,616	1,616
10,800	10,850	1,624	1,624	1,624	1,624
10,850	10,900	1,631	1,631	1,631	1,631
10,900	10,950	1,639	1,639	1,639	1,639
10,950	11,000	1,646	1,646	1,646	1,646

11,000

At least	But less than	Single	Married filing jointly *	Married filing separately	Head of a household
11,000	11,050	1,654	1,654	1,654	1,654
11,050	11,100	1,661	1,661	1,661	1,661
11,100	11,150	1,669	1,669	1,669	1,669
11,150	11,200	1,676	1,676	1,676	1,676
11,200	11,250	1,684	1,684	1,684	1,684
11,250	11,300	1,691	1,691	1,691	1,691
11,300	11,350	1,699	1,699	1,699	1,699
11,350	11,400	1,706	1,706	1,706	1,706
11,400	11,450	1,714	1,714	1,714	1,714
11,450	11,500	1,721	1,721	1,721	1,721
11,500	11,550	1,729	1,729	1,729	1,729
11,550	11,600	1,736	1,736	1,736	1,736
11,600	11,650	1,744	1,744	1,744	1,744
11,650	11,700	1,751	1,751	1,751	1,751
11,700	11,750	1,759	1,759	1,759	1,759
11,750	11,800	1,766	1,766	1,766	1,766
11,800	11,850	1,774	1,774	1,774	1,774
11,850	11,900	1,781	1,781	1,781	1,781
11,900	11,950	1,789	1,789	1,789	1,789
11,950	12,000	1,796	1,796	1,796	1,796

12,000

At least	But less than	Single	Married filing jointly *	Married filing separately	Head of a household
12,000	12,050	1,804	1,804	1,804	1,804
12,050	12,100	1,811	1,811	1,811	1,811
12,100	12,150	1,819	1,819	1,819	1,819
12,150	12,200	1,826	1,826	1,826	1,826
12,200	12,250	1,834	1,834	1,834	1,834
12,250	12,300	1,841	1,841	1,841	1,841
12,300	12,350	1,849	1,849	1,849	1,849
12,350	12,400	1,856	1,856	1,856	1,856
12,400	12,450	1,864	1,864	1,864	1,864
12,450	12,500	1,871	1,871	1,871	1,871
12,500	12,550	1,879	1,879	1,879	1,879
12,550	12,600	1,886	1,886	1,886	1,886
12,600	12,650	1,894	1,894	1,894	1,894
12,650	12,700	1,901	1,901	1,901	1,901
12,700	12,750	1,909	1,909	1,909	1,909
12,750	12,800	1,916	1,916	1,916	1,916
12,800	12,850	1,924	1,924	1,924	1,924
12,850	12,900	1,931	1,931	1,931	1,931
12,900	12,950	1,939	1,939	1,939	1,939
12,950	13,000	1,946	1,946	1,946	1,946

13,000

At least	But less than	Single	Married filing jointly *	Married filing separately	Head of a household
13,000	13,050	1,954	1,954	1,954	1,954
13,050	13,100	1,961	1,961	1,961	1,961
13,100	13,150	1,969	1,969	1,969	1,969
13,150	13,200	1,976	1,976	1,976	1,976
13,200	13,250	1,984	1,984	1,984	1,984
13,250	13,300	1,991	1,991	1,991	1,991
13,300	13,350	1,999	1,999	1,999	1,999
13,350	13,400	2,006	2,006	2,006	2,006
13,400	13,450	2,014	2,014	2,014	2,014
13,450	13,500	2,021	2,021	2,021	2,021
13,500	13,550	2,029	2,029	2,029	2,029
13,550	13,600	2,036	2,036	2,036	2,036
13,600	13,650	2,044	2,044	2,044	2,044
13,650	13,700	2,051	2,051	2,051	2,051
13,700	13,750	2,059	2,059	2,059	2,059
13,750	13,800	2,066	2,066	2,066	2,066
13,800	13,850	2,074	2,074	2,074	2,074
13,850	13,900	2,081	2,081	2,081	2,081
13,900	13,950	2,089	2,089	2,089	2,089
13,950	14,000	2,096	2,096	2,096	2,096

* This column must also be used by a qualifying widow(er).

Continued on next page

If line 39 (taxable income) is–		And you are–				If line 39 (taxable income) is–		And you are–				If line 39 (taxable income) is–		And you are–			
At least	But less than	Single	Married filing jointly *	Married filing separately	Head of a household	At least	But less than	Single	Married filing jointly *	Married filing separately	Head of a household	At least	But less than	Single	Married filing jointly *	Married filing separately	Head of a household
		Your tax is–						Your tax is–						Your tax is–			

14,000 / 17,000 / 20,000

At least	But less than	Single	MFJ	MFS	HoH	At least	But less than	Single	MFJ	MFS	HoH	At least	But less than	Single	MFJ	MFS	HoH
14,000	14,050	2,104	2,104	2,104	2,104	17,000	17,050	2,554	2,554	2,554	2,554	20,000	20,050	3,004	3,004	3,004	3,004
14,050	14,100	2,111	2,111	2,111	2,111	17,050	17,100	2,561	2,561	2,561	2,561	20,050	20,100	3,011	3,011	3,011	3,011
14,100	14,150	2,119	2,119	2,119	2,119	17,100	17,150	2,569	2,569	2,569	2,569	20,100	20,150	3,019	3,019	3,019	3,019
14,150	14,200	2,126	2,126	2,126	2,126	17,150	17,200	2,576	2,576	2,576	2,576	20,150	20,200	3,026	3,026	3,026	3,026
14,200	14,250	2,134	2,134	2,134	2,134	17,200	17,250	2,584	2,584	2,584	2,584	20,200	20,250	3,034	3,034	3,034	3,034
14,250	14,300	2,141	2,141	2,141	2,141	17,250	17,300	2,591	2,591	2,591	2,591	20,250	20,300	3,041	3,041	3,041	3,041
14,300	14,350	2,149	2,149	2,149	2,149	17,300	17,350	2,599	2,599	2,599	2,599	20,300	20,350	3,049	3,049	3,049	3,049
14,350	14,400	2,156	2,156	2,156	2,156	17,350	17,400	2,606	2,606	2,606	2,606	20,350	20,400	3,056	3,056	3,056	3,056
14,400	14,450	2,164	2,164	2,164	2,164	17,400	17,450	2,614	2,614	2,614	2,614	20,400	20,450	3,064	3,064	3,064	3,064
14,450	14,500	2,171	2,171	2,171	2,171	17,450	17,500	2,621	2,621	2,621	2,621	20,450	20,500	3,071	3,071	3,071	3,071
14,500	14,550	2,179	2,179	2,179	2,179	17,500	17,550	2,629	2,629	2,629	2,629	20,500	20,550	3,079	3,079	3,079	3,079
14,550	14,600	2,186	2,186	2,186	2,186	17,550	17,600	2,636	2,636	2,636	2,636	20,550	20,600	3,086	3,086	3,086	3,086
14,600	14,650	2,194	2,194	2,194	2,194	17,600	17,650	2,644	2,644	2,644	2,644	20,600	20,650	3,094	3,094	3,094	3,094
14,650	14,700	2,201	2,201	2,201	2,201	17,650	17,700	2,651	2,651	2,651	2,651	20,650	20,700	3,101	3,101	3,101	3,101
14,700	14,750	2,209	2,209	2,209	2,209	17,700	17,750	2,659	2,659	2,659	2,659	20,700	20,750	3,109	3,109	3,109	3,109
14,750	14,800	2,216	2,216	2,216	2,216	17,750	17,800	2,666	2,666	2,666	2,666	20,750	20,800	3,116	3,116	3,116	3,116
14,800	14,850	2,224	2,224	2,224	2,224	17,800	17,850	2,674	2,674	2,674	2,674	20,800	20,850	3,124	3,124	3,124	3,124
14,850	14,900	2,231	2,231	2,231	2,231	17,850	17,900	2,681	2,681	2,681	2,681	20,850	20,900	3,131	3,131	3,131	3,131
14,900	14,950	2,239	2,239	2,239	2,239	17,900	17,950	2,689	2,689	2,689	2,689	20,900	20,950	3,139	3,139	3,139	3,139
14,950	15,000	2,246	2,246	2,246	2,246	17,950	18,000	2,696	2,696	2,696	2,696	20,950	21,000	3,146	3,146	3,146	3,146

15,000 / 18,000 / 21,000

At least	But less than	Single	MFJ	MFS	HoH	At least	But less than	Single	MFJ	MFS	HoH	At least	But less than	Single	MFJ	MFS	HoH
15,000	15,050	2,254	2,254	2,254	2,254	18,000	18,050	2,704	2,704	2,704	2,704	21,000	21,050	3,154	3,154	3,154	3,154
15,050	15,100	2,261	2,261	2,261	2,261	18,050	18,100	2,711	2,711	2,711	2,711	21,050	21,100	3,161	3,161	3,161	3,161
15,100	15,150	2,269	2,269	2,269	2,269	18,100	18,150	2,719	2,719	2,719	2,719	21,100	21,150	3,169	3,169	3,169	3,169
15,150	15,200	2,276	2,276	2,276	2,276	18,150	18,200	2,726	2,726	2,726	2,726	21,150	21,200	3,176	3,176	3,176	3,176
15,200	15,250	2,284	2,284	2,284	2,284	18,200	18,250	2,734	2,734	2,734	2,734	21,200	21,250	3,184	3,184	3,190	3,184
15,250	15,300	2,291	2,291	2,291	2,291	18,250	18,300	2,741	2,741	2,741	2,741	21,250	21,300	3,191	3,191	3,204	3,191
15,300	15,350	2,299	2,299	2,299	2,299	18,300	18,350	2,749	2,749	2,749	2,749	21,300	21,350	3,199	3,199	3,218	3,199
15,350	15,400	2,306	2,306	2,306	2,306	18,350	18,400	2,756	2,756	2,756	2,756	21,350	21,400	3,206	3,206	3,232	3,206
15,400	15,450	2,314	2,314	2,314	2,314	18,400	18,450	2,764	2,764	2,764	2,764	21,400	21,450	3,214	3,214	3,246	3,214
15,450	15,500	2,321	2,321	2,321	2,321	18,450	18,500	2,771	2,771	2,771	2,771	21,450	21,500	3,221	3,221	3,260	3,221
15,500	15,550	2,329	2,329	2,329	2,329	18,500	18,550	2,779	2,779	2,779	2,779	21,500	21,550	3,229	3,229	3,274	3,229
15,550	15,600	2,336	2,336	2,336	2,336	18,550	18,600	2,786	2,786	2,786	2,786	21,550	21,600	3,236	3,236	3,288	3,236
15,600	15,650	2,344	2,344	2,344	2,344	18,600	18,650	2,794	2,794	2,794	2,794	21,600	21,650	3,244	3,244	3,302	3,244
15,650	15,700	2,351	2,351	2,351	2,351	18,650	18,700	2,801	2,801	2,801	2,801	21,650	21,700	3,251	3,251	3,316	3,251
15,700	15,750	2,359	2,359	2,359	2,359	18,700	18,750	2,809	2,809	2,809	2,809	21,700	21,750	3,259	3,259	3,330	3,259
15,750	15,800	2,366	2,366	2,366	2,366	18,750	18,800	2,816	2,816	2,816	2,816	21,750	21,800	3,266	3,266	3,344	3,266
15,800	15,850	2,374	2,374	2,374	2,374	18,800	18,850	2,824	2,824	2,824	2,824	21,800	21,850	3,274	3,274	3,358	3,274
15,850	15,900	2,381	2,381	2,381	2,381	18,850	18,900	2,831	2,831	2,831	2,831	21,850	21,900	3,281	3,281	3,372	3,281
15,900	15,950	2,389	2,389	2,389	2,389	18,900	18,950	2,839	2,839	2,839	2,839	21,900	21,950	3,289	3,289	3,386	3,289
15,950	16,000	2,396	2,396	2,396	2,396	18,950	19,000	2,846	2,846	2,846	2,846	21,950	22,000	3,296	3,296	3,400	3,296

16,000 / 19,000 / 22,000

At least	But less than	Single	MFJ	MFS	HoH	At least	But less than	Single	MFJ	MFS	HoH	At least	But less than	Single	MFJ	MFS	HoH
16,000	16,050	2,404	2,404	2,404	2,404	19,000	19,050	2,854	2,854	2,854	2,854	22,000	22,050	3,304	3,304	3,414	3,304
16,050	16,100	2,411	2,411	2,411	2,411	19,050	19,100	2,861	2,861	2,861	2,861	22,050	22,100	3,311	3,311	3,428	3,311
16,100	16,150	2,419	2,419	2,419	2,419	19,100	19,150	2,869	2,869	2,869	2,869	22,100	22,150	3,319	3,319	3,442	3,319
16,150	16,200	2,426	2,426	2,426	2,426	19,150	19,200	2,876	2,876	2,876	2,876	22,150	22,200	3,326	3,326	3,456	3,326
16,200	16,250	2,434	2,434	2,434	2,434	19,200	19,250	2,884	2,884	2,884	2,884	22,200	22,250	3,334	3,334	3,470	3,334
16,250	16,300	2,441	2,441	2,441	2,441	19,250	19,300	2,891	2,891	2,891	2,891	22,250	22,300	3,341	3,341	3,484	3,341
16,300	16,350	2,449	2,449	2,449	2,449	19,300	19,350	2,899	2,899	2,899	2,899	22,300	22,350	3,349	3,349	3,498	3,349
16,350	16,400	2,456	2,456	2,456	2,456	19,350	19,400	2,906	2,906	2,906	2,906	22,350	22,400	3,356	3,356	3,512	3,356
16,400	16,450	2,464	2,464	2,464	2,464	19,400	19,450	2,914	2,914	2,914	2,914	22,400	22,450	3,364	3,364	3,526	3,364
16,450	16,500	2,471	2,471	2,471	2,471	19,450	19,500	2,921	2,921	2,921	2,921	22,450	22,500	3,371	3,371	3,540	3,371
16,500	16,550	2,479	2,479	2,479	2,479	19,500	19,550	2,929	2,929	2,929	2,929	22,500	22,550	3,379	3,379	3,554	3,379
16,550	16,600	2,486	2,486	2,486	2,486	19,550	19,600	2,936	2,936	2,936	2,936	22,550	22,600	3,386	3,386	3,568	3,386
16,600	16,650	2,494	2,494	2,494	2,494	19,600	19,650	2,944	2,944	2,944	2,944	22,600	22,650	3,394	3,394	3,582	3,394
16,650	16,700	2,501	2,501	2,501	2,501	19,650	19,700	2,951	2,951	2,951	2,951	22,650	22,700	3,401	3,401	3,596	3,401
16,700	16,750	2,509	2,509	2,509	2,509	19,700	19,750	2,959	2,959	2,959	2,959	22,700	22,750	3,409	3,409	3,610	3,409
16,750	16,800	2,516	2,516	2,516	2,516	19,750	19,800	2,966	2,966	2,966	2,966	22,750	22,800	3,416	3,416	3,624	3,416
16,800	16,850	2,524	2,524	2,524	2,524	19,800	19,850	2,974	2,974	2,974	2,974	22,800	22,850	3,424	3,424	3,638	3,424
16,850	16,900	2,531	2,531	2,531	2,531	19,850	19,900	2,981	2,981	2,981	2,981	22,850	22,900	3,431	3,431	3,652	3,431
16,900	16,950	2,539	2,539	2,539	2,539	19,900	19,950	2,989	2,989	2,989	2,989	22,900	22,950	3,439	3,439	3,666	3,439
16,950	17,000	2,546	2,546	2,546	2,546	19,950	20,000	2,996	2,996	2,996	2,996	22,950	23,000	3,446	3,446	3,680	3,446

* This column must also be used by a qualifying widow(er).

Continued on next page

1998 Tax Table– *Continued*

If line 39 (taxable income) is–		And you are–				If line 39 (taxable income) is–		And you are–				If line 39 (taxable income) is–		And you are–			
At least	But less than	Single	Married filing jointly *	Married filing separately	Head of a household	At least	But less than	Single	Married filing jointly *	Married filing separately	Head of a household	At least	But less than	Single	Married filing jointly *	Married filing separately	Head of a household
		Your tax is–						Your tax is–						Your tax is–			
23,000						**26,000**						**29,000**					
23,000	23,050	3,454	3,454	3,694	3,454	26,000	26,050	3,992	3,904	4,534	3,904	29,000	29,050	4,832	4,354	5,374	4,354
23,050	23,100	3,461	3,461	3,708	3,461	26,050	26,100	4,006	3,911	4,548	3,911	29,050	29,100	4,846	4,361	5,388	4,361
23,100	23,150	3,469	3,469	3,722	3,469	26,100	26,150	4,020	3,919	4,562	3,919	29,100	29,150	4,860	4,369	5,402	4,369
23,150	23,200	3,476	3,476	3,736	3,476	26,150	26,200	4,034	3,926	4,576	3,926	29,150	29,200	4,874	4,376	5,416	4,376
23,200	23,250	3,484	3,484	3,750	3,484	26,200	26,250	4,048	3,934	4,590	3,934	29,200	29,250	4,888	4,384	5,430	4,384
23,250	23,300	3,491	3,491	3,764	3,491	26,250	26,300	4,062	3,941	4,604	3,941	29,250	29,300	4,902	4,391	5,444	4,391
23,300	23,350	3,499	3,499	3,778	3,499	26,300	26,350	4,076	3,949	4,618	3,949	29,300	29,350	4,916	4,399	5,458	4,399
23,350	23,400	3,506	3,506	3,792	3,506	26,350	26,400	4,090	3,956	4,632	3,956	29,350	29,400	4,930	4,406	5,472	4,406
23,400	23,450	3,514	3,514	3,806	3,514	26,400	26,450	4,104	3,964	4,646	3,964	29,400	29,450	4,944	4,414	5,486	4,414
23,450	23,500	3,521	3,521	3,820	3,521	26,450	26,500	4,118	3,971	4,660	3,971	29,450	29,500	4,958	4,421	5,500	4,421
23,500	23,550	3,529	3,529	3,834	3,529	26,500	26,550	4,132	3,979	4,674	3,979	29,500	29,550	4,972	4,429	5,514	4,429
23,550	23,600	3,536	3,536	3,848	3,536	26,550	26,600	4,146	3,986	4,688	3,986	29,550	29,600	4,986	4,436	5,528	4,436
23,600	23,650	3,544	3,544	3,862	3,544	26,600	26,650	4,160	3,994	4,702	3,994	29,600	29,650	5,000	4,444	5,542	4,444
23,650	23,700	3,551	3,551	3,876	3,551	26,650	26,700	4,174	4,001	4,716	4,001	29,650	29,700	5,014	4,451	5,556	4,451
23,700	23,750	3,559	3,559	3,890	3,559	26,700	26,750	4,188	4,009	4,730	4,009	29,700	29,750	5,028	4,459	5,570	4,459
23,750	23,800	3,566	3,566	3,904	3,566	26,750	26,800	4,202	4,016	4,744	4,016	29,750	29,800	5,042	4,466	5,584	4,466
23,800	23,850	3,574	3,574	3,918	3,574	26,800	26,850	4,216	4,024	4,758	4,024	29,800	29,850	5,056	4,474	5,598	4,474
23,850	23,900	3,581	3,581	3,932	3,581	26,850	26,900	4,230	4,031	4,772	4,031	29,850	29,900	5,070	4,481	5,612	4,481
23,900	23,950	3,589	3,589	3,946	3,589	26,900	26,950	4,244	4,039	4,786	4,039	29,900	29,950	5,084	4,489	5,626	4,489
23,950	24,000	3,596	3,596	3,960	3,596	26,950	27,000	4,258	4,046	4,800	4,046	29,950	30,000	5,098	4,496	5,640	4,496
24,000						**27,000**						**30,000**					
24,000	24,050	3,604	3,604	3,974	3,604	27,000	27,050	4,272	4,054	4,814	4,054	30,000	30,050	5,112	4,504	5,654	4,504
24,050	24,100	3,611	3,611	3,988	3,611	27,050	27,100	4,286	4,061	4,828	4,061	30,050	30,100	5,126	4,511	5,668	4,511
24,100	24,150	3,619	3,619	4,002	3,619	27,100	27,150	4,300	4,069	4,842	4,069	30,100	30,150	5,140	4,519	5,682	4,519
24,150	24,200	3,626	3,626	4,016	3,626	27,150	27,200	4,314	4,076	4,856	4,076	30,150	30,200	5,154	4,526	5,696	4,526
24,200	24,250	3,634	3,634	4,030	3,634	27,200	27,250	4,328	4,084	4,870	4,084	30,200	30,250	5,168	4,534	5,710	4,534
24,250	24,300	3,641	3,641	4,044	3,641	27,250	27,300	4,342	4,091	4,884	4,091	30,250	30,300	5,182	4,541	5,724	4,541
24,300	24,350	3,649	3,649	4,058	3,649	27,300	27,350	4,356	4,099	4,898	4,099	30,300	30,350	5,196	4,549	5,738	4,549
24,350	24,400	3,656	3,656	4,072	3,656	27,350	27,400	4,370	4,106	4,912	4,106	30,350	30,400	5,210	4,556	5,752	4,556
24,400	24,450	3,664	3,664	4,086	3,664	27,400	27,450	4,384	4,114	4,926	4,114	30,400	30,450	5,224	4,564	5,766	4,564
24,450	24,500	3,671	3,671	4,100	3,671	27,450	27,500	4,398	4,121	4,940	4,121	30,450	30,500	5,238	4,571	5,780	4,571
24,500	24,550	3,679	3,679	4,114	3,679	27,500	27,550	4,412	4,129	4,954	4,129	30,500	30,550	5,252	4,579	5,794	4,579
24,550	24,600	3,686	3,686	4,128	3,686	27,550	27,600	4,426	4,136	4,968	4,136	30,550	30,600	5,266	4,586	5,808	4,586
24,600	24,650	3,694	3,694	4,142	3,694	27,600	27,650	4,440	4,144	4,982	4,144	30,600	30,650	5,280	4,594	5,822	4,594
24,650	24,700	3,701	3,701	4,156	3,701	27,650	27,700	4,454	4,151	4,996	4,151	30,650	30,700	5,294	4,601	5,836	4,601
24,700	24,750	3,709	3,709	4,170	3,709	27,700	27,750	4,468	4,159	5,010	4,159	30,700	30,750	5,308	4,609	5,850	4,609
24,750	24,800	3,716	3,716	4,184	3,716	27,750	27,800	4,482	4,166	5,024	4,166	30,750	30,800	5,322	4,616	5,864	4,616
24,800	24,850	3,724	3,724	4,198	3,724	27,800	27,850	4,496	4,174	5,038	4,174	30,800	30,850	5,336	4,624	5,878	4,624
24,850	24,900	3,731	3,731	4,212	3,731	27,850	27,900	4,510	4,181	5,052	4,181	30,850	30,900	5,350	4,631	5,892	4,631
24,900	24,950	3,739	3,739	4,226	3,739	27,900	27,950	4,524	4,189	5,066	4,189	30,900	30,950	5,364	4,639	5,906	4,639
24,950	25,000	3,746	3,746	4,240	3,746	27,950	28,000	4,538	4,196	5,080	4,196	30,950	31,000	5,378	4,646	5,920	4,646
25,000						**28,000**						**31,000**					
25,000	25,050	3,754	3,754	4,254	3,754	28,000	28,050	4,552	4,204	5,094	4,204	31,000	31,050	5,392	4,654	5,934	4,654
25,050	25,100	3,761	3,761	4,268	3,761	28,050	28,100	4,566	4,211	5,108	4,211	31,050	31,100	5,406	4,661	5,948	4,661
25,100	25,150	3,769	3,769	4,282	3,769	28,100	28,150	4,580	4,219	5,122	4,219	31,100	31,150	5,420	4,669	5,962	4,669
25,150	25,200	3,776	3,776	4,296	3,776	28,150	28,200	4,594	4,226	5,136	4,226	31,150	31,200	5,434	4,676	5,976	4,676
25,200	25,250	3,784	3,784	4,310	3,784	28,200	28,250	4,608	4,234	5,150	4,234	31,200	31,250	5,448	4,684	5,990	4,684
25,250	25,300	3,791	3,791	4,324	3,791	28,250	28,300	4,622	4,241	5,164	4,241	31,250	31,300	5,462	4,691	6,004	4,691
25,300	25,350	3,799	3,799	4,338	3,799	28,300	28,350	4,636	4,249	5,178	4,249	31,300	31,350	5,476	4,699	6,018	4,699
25,350	25,400	3,810	3,806	4,352	3,806	28,350	28,400	4,650	4,256	5,192	4,256	31,350	31,400	5,490	4,706	6,032	4,706
25,400	25,450	3,824	3,814	4,366	3,814	28,400	28,450	4,664	4,264	5,206	4,264	31,400	31,450	5,504	4,714	6,046	4,714
25,450	25,500	3,838	3,821	4,380	3,821	28,450	28,500	4,678	4,271	5,220	4,271	31,450	31,500	5,518	4,721	6,060	4,721
25,500	25,550	3,852	3,829	4,394	3,829	28,500	28,550	4,692	4,279	5,234	4,279	31,500	31,550	5,532	4,729	6,074	4,729
25,550	25,600	3,866	3,836	4,408	3,836	28,550	28,600	4,706	4,286	5,248	4,286	31,550	31,600	5,546	4,736	6,088	4,736
25,600	25,650	3,880	3,844	4,422	3,844	28,600	28,650	4,720	4,294	5,262	4,294	31,600	31,650	5,560	4,744	6,102	4,744
25,650	25,700	3,894	3,851	4,436	3,851	28,650	28,700	4,734	4,301	5,276	4,301	31,650	31,700	5,574	4,751	6,116	4,751
25,700	25,750	3,908	3,859	4,450	3,859	28,700	28,750	4,748	4,309	5,290	4,309	31,700	31,750	5,588	4,759	6,130	4,759
25,750	25,800	3,922	3,866	4,464	3,866	28,750	28,800	4,762	4,316	5,304	4,316	31,750	31,800	5,602	4,766	6,144	4,766
25,800	25,850	3,936	3,874	4,478	3,874	28,800	28,850	4,776	4,324	5,318	4,324	31,800	31,850	5,616	4,774	6,158	4,774
25,850	25,900	3,950	3,881	4,492	3,881	28,850	28,900	4,790	4,331	5,332	4,331	31,850	31,900	5,630	4,781	6,172	4,781
25,900	25,950	3,964	3,889	4,506	3,889	28,900	28,950	4,804	4,339	5,346	4,339	31,900	31,950	5,644	4,789	6,186	4,789
25,950	26,000	3,978	3,896	4,520	3,896	28,950	29,000	4,818	4,346	5,360	4,346	31,950	32,000	5,658	4,796	6,200	4,796

* This column must also be used by a qualifying widow(er).

Continued on next page

32,000 – 34,950

If line 39 (taxable income) is— At least	But less than	Single	Married filing jointly *	Married filing separately	Head of a household
32,000	32,050	5,672	4,804	6,214	4,804
32,050	32,100	5,686	4,811	6,228	4,811
32,100	32,150	5,700	4,819	6,242	4,819
32,150	32,200	5,714	4,826	6,256	4,826
32,200	32,250	5,728	4,834	6,270	4,834
32,250	32,300	5,742	4,841	6,284	4,841
32,300	32,350	5,756	4,849	6,298	4,849
32,350	32,400	5,770	4,856	6,312	4,856
32,400	32,450	5,784	4,864	6,326	4,864
32,450	32,500	5,798	4,871	6,340	4,871
32,500	32,550	5,812	4,879	6,354	4,879
32,550	32,600	5,826	4,886	6,368	4,886
32,600	32,650	5,840	4,894	6,382	4,894
32,650	32,700	5,854	4,901	6,396	4,901
32,700	32,750	5,868	4,909	6,410	4,909
32,750	32,800	5,882	4,916	6,424	4,916
32,800	32,850	5,896	4,924	6,438	4,924
32,850	32,900	5,910	4,931	6,452	4,931
32,900	32,950	5,924	4,939	6,466	4,939
32,950	33,000	5,938	4,946	6,480	4,946
33,000	33,050	5,952	4,954	6,494	4,954
33,050	33,100	5,966	4,961	6,508	4,961
33,100	33,150	5,980	4,969	6,522	4,969
33,150	33,200	5,994	4,976	6,536	4,976
33,200	33,250	6,008	4,984	6,550	4,984
33,250	33,300	6,022	4,991	6,564	4,991
33,300	33,350	6,036	4,999	6,578	4,999
33,350	33,400	6,050	5,006	6,592	5,006
33,400	33,450	6,064	5,014	6,606	5,014
33,450	33,500	6,078	5,021	6,620	5,021
33,500	33,550	6,092	5,029	6,634	5,029
33,550	33,600	6,106	5,036	6,648	5,036
33,600	33,650	6,120	5,044	6,662	5,044
33,650	33,700	6,134	5,051	6,676	5,051
33,700	33,750	6,148	5,059	6,690	5,059
33,750	33,800	6,162	5,066	6,704	5,066
33,800	33,850	6,176	5,074	6,718	5,074
33,850	33,900	6,190	5,081	6,732	5,081
33,900	33,950	6,204	5,089	6,746	5,089
33,950	34,000	6,218	5,096	6,760	5,100
34,000	34,050	6,232	5,104	6,774	5,114
34,050	34,100	6,246	5,111	6,788	5,128
34,100	34,150	6,260	5,119	6,802	5,142
34,150	34,200	6,274	5,126	6,816	5,156
34,200	34,250	6,288	5,134	6,830	5,170
34,250	34,300	6,302	5,141	6,844	5,184
34,300	34,350	6,316	5,149	6,858	5,198
34,350	34,400	6,330	5,156	6,872	5,212
34,400	34,450	6,344	5,164	6,886	5,226
34,450	34,500	6,358	5,171	6,900	5,240
34,500	34,550	6,372	5,179	6,914	5,254
34,550	34,600	6,386	5,186	6,928	5,268
34,600	34,650	6,400	5,194	6,942	5,282
34,650	34,700	6,414	5,201	6,956	5,296
34,700	34,750	6,428	5,209	6,970	5,310
34,750	34,800	6,442	5,216	6,984	5,324
34,800	34,850	6,456	5,224	6,998	5,338
34,850	34,900	6,470	5,231	7,012	5,352
34,900	34,950	6,484	5,239	7,026	5,366
34,950	35,000	6,498	5,246	7,040	5,380

35,000 – 37,950

If line 39 (taxable income) is— At least	But less than	Single	Married filing jointly *	Married filing separately	Head of a household
35,000	35,050	6,512	5,254	7,054	5,394
35,050	35,100	6,526	5,261	7,068	5,408
35,100	35,150	6,540	5,269	7,082	5,422
35,150	35,200	6,554	5,276	7,096	5,436
35,200	35,250	6,568	5,284	7,110	5,450
35,250	35,300	6,582	5,291	7,124	5,464
35,300	35,350	6,596	5,299	7,138	5,478
35,350	35,400	6,610	5,306	7,152	5,492
35,400	35,450	6,624	5,314	7,166	5,506
35,450	35,500	6,638	5,321	7,180	5,520
35,500	35,550	6,652	5,329	7,194	5,534
35,550	35,600	6,666	5,336	7,208	5,548
35,600	35,650	6,680	5,344	7,222	5,562
35,650	35,700	6,694	5,351	7,236	5,576
35,700	35,750	6,708	5,359	7,250	5,590
35,750	35,800	6,722	5,366	7,264	5,604
35,800	35,850	6,736	5,374	7,278	5,618
35,850	35,900	6,750	5,381	7,292	5,632
35,900	35,950	6,764	5,389	7,306	5,646
35,950	36,000	6,778	5,396	7,320	5,660
36,000	36,050	6,792	5,404	7,334	5,674
36,050	36,100	6,806	5,411	7,348	5,688
36,100	36,150	6,820	5,419	7,362	5,702
36,150	36,200	6,834	5,426	7,376	5,716
36,200	36,250	6,848	5,434	7,390	5,730
36,250	36,300	6,862	5,441	7,404	5,744
36,300	36,350	6,876	5,449	7,418	5,758
36,350	36,400	6,890	5,456	7,432	5,772
36,400	36,450	6,904	5,464	7,446	5,786
36,450	36,500	6,918	5,471	7,460	5,800
36,500	36,550	6,932	5,479	7,474	5,814
36,550	36,600	6,946	5,486	7,488	5,828
36,600	36,650	6,960	5,494	7,502	5,842
36,650	36,700	6,974	5,501	7,516	5,856
36,700	36,750	6,988	5,509	7,530	5,870
36,750	36,800	7,002	5,516	7,544	5,884
36,800	36,850	7,016	5,524	7,558	5,898
36,850	36,900	7,030	5,531	7,572	5,912
36,900	36,950	7,044	5,539	7,586	5,926
36,950	37,000	7,058	5,546	7,600	5,940
37,000	37,050	7,072	5,554	7,614	5,954
37,050	37,100	7,086	5,561	7,628	5,968
37,100	37,150	7,100	5,569	7,642	5,982
37,150	37,200	7,114	5,576	7,656	5,996
37,200	37,250	7,128	5,584	7,670	6,010
37,250	37,300	7,142	5,591	7,684	6,024
37,300	37,350	7,156	5,599	7,698	6,038
37,350	37,400	7,170	5,606	7,712	6,052
37,400	37,450	7,184	5,614	7,726	6,066
37,450	37,500	7,198	5,621	7,740	6,080
37,500	37,550	7,212	5,629	7,754	6,094
37,550	37,600	7,226	5,636	7,768	6,108
37,600	37,650	7,240	5,644	7,782	6,122
37,650	37,700	7,254	5,651	7,796	6,136
37,700	37,750	7,268	5,659	7,810	6,150
37,750	37,800	7,282	5,666	7,824	6,164
37,800	37,850	7,296	5,674	7,838	6,178
37,850	37,900	7,310	5,681	7,852	6,192
37,900	37,950	7,324	5,689	7,866	6,206
37,950	38,000	7,338	5,696	7,880	6,220

38,000 – 40,950

If line 39 (taxable income) is— At least	But less than	Single	Married filing jointly *	Married filing separately	Head of a household
38,000	38,050	7,352	5,704	7,894	6,234
38,050	38,100	7,366	5,711	7,908	6,248
38,100	38,150	7,380	5,719	7,922	6,262
38,150	38,200	7,394	5,726	7,936	6,276
38,200	38,250	7,408	5,734	7,950	6,290
38,250	38,300	7,422	5,741	7,964	6,304
38,300	38,350	7,436	5,749	7,978	6,318
38,350	38,400	7,450	5,756	7,992	6,332
38,400	38,450	7,464	5,764	8,006	6,346
38,450	38,500	7,478	5,771	8,020	6,360
38,500	38,550	7,492	5,779	8,034	6,374
38,550	38,600	7,506	5,786	8,048	6,388
38,600	38,650	7,520	5,794	8,062	6,402
38,650	38,700	7,534	5,801	8,076	6,416
38,700	38,750	7,548	5,809	8,090	6,430
38,750	38,800	7,562	5,816	8,104	6,444
38,800	38,850	7,576	5,824	8,118	6,458
38,850	38,900	7,590	5,831	8,132	6,472
38,900	38,950	7,604	5,839	8,146	6,486
38,950	39,000	7,618	5,846	8,160	6,500
39,000	39,050	7,632	5,854	8,174	6,514
39,050	39,100	7,646	5,861	8,188	6,528
39,100	39,150	7,660	5,869	8,202	6,542
39,150	39,200	7,674	5,876	8,216	6,556
39,200	39,250	7,688	5,884	8,230	6,570
39,250	39,300	7,702	5,891	8,244	6,584
39,300	39,350	7,716	5,899	8,258	6,598
39,350	39,400	7,730	5,906	8,272	6,612
39,400	39,450	7,744	5,914	8,286	6,626
39,450	39,500	7,758	5,921	8,300	6,640
39,500	39,550	7,772	5,929	8,314	6,654
39,550	39,600	7,786	5,936	8,328	6,668
39,600	39,650	7,800	5,944	8,342	6,682
39,650	39,700	7,814	5,951	8,356	6,696
39,700	39,750	7,828	5,959	8,370	6,710
39,750	39,800	7,842	5,966	8,384	6,724
39,800	39,850	7,856	5,974	8,398	6,738
39,850	39,900	7,870	5,981	8,412	6,752
39,900	39,950	7,884	5,989	8,426	6,766
39,950	40,000	7,898	5,996	8,440	6,780
40,000	40,050	7,912	6,004	8,454	6,794
40,050	40,100	7,926	6,011	8,468	6,808
40,100	40,150	7,940	6,019	8,482	6,822
40,150	40,200	7,954	6,026	8,496	6,836
40,200	40,250	7,968	6,034	8,510	6,850
40,250	40,300	7,982	6,041	8,524	6,864
40,300	40,350	7,996	6,049	8,538	6,878
40,350	40,400	8,010	6,056	8,552	6,892
40,400	40,450	8,024	6,064	8,566	6,906
40,450	40,500	8,038	6,071	8,580	6,920
40,500	40,550	8,052	6,079	8,594	6,934
40,550	40,600	8,066	6,086	8,608	6,948
40,600	40,650	8,080	6,094	8,622	6,962
40,650	40,700	8,094	6,101	8,636	6,976
40,700	40,750	8,108	6,109	8,650	6,990
40,750	40,800	8,122	6,116	8,664	7,004
40,800	40,850	8,136	6,124	8,678	7,018
40,850	40,900	8,150	6,131	8,692	7,032
40,900	40,950	8,164	6,139	8,706	7,046
40,950	41,000	8,178	6,146	8,720	7,060

* This column must also be used by a qualifying widow(er).

Continued on next page

Column headings for each panel:

If line 39 (taxable income) is— At least	But less than	Single	Married filing jointly *	Married filing separately	Head of a household
			Your tax is—		

41,000

At least	But less than	Single	Married filing jointly *	Married filing separately	Head of a household
41,000	41,050	8,192	6,154	8,734	7,074
41,050	41,100	8,206	6,161	8,748	7,088
41,100	41,150	8,220	6,169	8,762	7,102
41,150	41,200	8,234	6,176	8,776	7,116
41,200	41,250	8,248	6,184	8,790	7,130
41,250	41,300	8,262	6,191	8,804	7,144
41,300	41,350	8,276	6,199	8,818	7,158
41,350	41,400	8,290	6,206	8,832	7,172
41,400	41,450	8,304	6,214	8,846	7,186
41,450	41,500	8,318	6,221	8,860	7,200
41,500	41,550	8,332	6,229	8,874	7,214
41,550	41,600	8,346	6,236	8,888	7,228
41,600	41,650	8,360	6,244	8,902	7,242
41,650	41,700	8,374	6,251	8,916	7,256
41,700	41,750	8,388	6,259	8,930	7,270
41,750	41,800	8,402	6,266	8,944	7,284
41,800	41,850	8,416	6,274	8,958	7,298
41,850	41,900	8,430	6,281	8,972	7,312
41,900	41,950	8,444	6,289	8,986	7,326
41,950	42,000	8,458	6,296	9,000	7,340

42,000

At least	But less than	Single	Married filing jointly *	Married filing separately	Head of a household
42,000	42,050	8,472	6,304	9,014	7,354
42,050	42,100	8,486	6,311	9,028	7,368
42,100	42,150	8,500	6,319	9,042	7,382
42,150	42,200	8,514	6,326	9,056	7,396
42,200	42,250	8,528	6,334	9,070	7,410
42,250	42,300	8,542	6,341	9,084	7,424
42,300	42,350	8,556	6,349	9,098	7,438
42,350	42,400	8,570	6,360	9,112	7,452
42,400	42,450	8,584	6,374	9,126	7,466
42,450	42,500	8,598	6,388	9,140	7,480
42,500	42,550	8,612	6,402	9,154	7,494
42,550	42,600	8,626	6,416	9,168	7,508
42,600	42,650	8,640	6,430	9,182	7,522
42,650	42,700	8,654	6,444	9,196	7,536
42,700	42,750	8,668	6,458	9,210	7,550
42,750	42,800	8,682	6,472	9,224	7,564
42,800	42,850	8,696	6,486	9,238	7,578
42,850	42,900	8,710	6,500	9,252	7,592
42,900	42,950	8,724	6,514	9,266	7,606
42,950	43,000	8,738	6,528	9,280	7,620

43,000

At least	But less than	Single	Married filing jointly *	Married filing separately	Head of a household
43,000	43,050	8,752	6,542	9,294	7,634
43,050	43,100	8,766	6,556	9,308	7,648
43,100	43,150	8,780	6,570	9,322	7,662
43,150	43,200	8,794	6,584	9,336	7,676
43,200	43,250	8,808	6,598	9,350	7,690
43,250	43,300	8,822	6,612	9,364	7,704
43,300	43,350	8,836	6,626	9,378	7,718
43,350	43,400	8,850	6,640	9,392	7,732
43,400	43,450	8,864	6,654	9,406	7,746
43,450	43,500	8,878	6,668	9,420	7,760
43,500	43,550	8,892	6,682	9,434	7,774
43,550	43,600	8,906	6,696	9,448	7,788
43,600	43,650	8,920	6,710	9,462	7,802
43,650	43,700	8,934	6,724	9,476	7,816
43,700	43,750	8,948	6,738	9,490	7,830
43,750	43,800	8,962	6,752	9,504	7,844
43,800	43,850	8,976	6,766	9,518	7,858
43,850	43,900	8,990	6,780	9,532	7,872
43,900	43,950	9,004	6,794	9,546	7,886
43,950	44,000	9,018	6,808	9,560	7,900

44,000

At least	But less than	Single	Married filing jointly *	Married filing separately	Head of a household
44,000	44,050	9,032	6,822	9,574	7,914
44,050	44,100	9,046	6,836	9,588	7,928
44,100	44,150	9,060	6,850	9,602	7,942
44,150	44,200	9,074	6,864	9,616	7,956
44,200	44,250	9,088	6,878	9,630	7,970
44,250	44,300	9,102	6,892	9,644	7,984
44,300	44,350	9,116	6,906	9,658	7,998
44,350	44,400	9,130	6,920	9,672	8,012
44,400	44,450	9,144	6,934	9,686	8,026
44,450	44,500	9,158	6,948	9,700	8,040
44,500	44,550	9,172	6,962	9,714	8,054
44,550	44,600	9,186	6,976	9,728	8,068
44,600	44,650	9,200	6,990	9,742	8,082
44,650	44,700	9,214	7,004	9,756	8,096
44,700	44,750	9,228	7,018	9,770	8,110
44,750	44,800	9,242	7,032	9,784	8,124
44,800	44,850	9,256	7,046	9,798	8,138
44,850	44,900	9,270	7,060	9,812	8,152
44,900	44,950	9,284	7,074	9,826	8,166
44,950	45,000	9,298	7,088	9,840	8,180

45,000

At least	But less than	Single	Married filing jointly *	Married filing separately	Head of a household
45,000	45,050	9,312	7,102	9,854	8,194
45,050	45,100	9,326	7,116	9,868	8,208
45,100	45,150	9,340	7,130	9,882	8,222
45,150	45,200	9,354	7,144	9,896	8,236
45,200	45,250	9,368	7,158	9,910	8,250
45,250	45,300	9,382	7,172	9,924	8,264
45,300	45,350	9,396	7,186	9,938	8,278
45,350	45,400	9,410	7,200	9,952	8,292
45,400	45,450	9,424	7,214	9,966	8,306
45,450	45,500	9,438	7,228	9,980	8,320
45,500	45,550	9,452	7,242	9,994	8,334
45,550	45,600	9,466	7,256	10,008	8,348
45,600	45,650	9,480	7,270	10,022	8,362
45,650	45,700	9,494	7,284	10,036	8,376
45,700	45,750	9,508	7,298	10,050	8,390
45,750	45,800	9,522	7,312	10,064	8,404
45,800	45,850	9,536	7,326	10,078	8,418
45,850	45,900	9,550	7,340	10,092	8,432
45,900	45,950	9,564	7,354	10,106	8,446
45,950	46,000	9,578	7,368	10,120	8,460

46,000

At least	But less than	Single	Married filing jointly *	Married filing separately	Head of a household
46,000	46,050	9,592	7,382	10,134	8,474
46,050	46,100	9,606	7,396	10,148	8,488
46,100	46,150	9,620	7,410	10,162	8,502
46,150	46,200	9,634	7,424	10,176	8,516
46,200	46,250	9,648	7,438	10,190	8,530
46,250	46,300	9,662	7,452	10,204	8,544
46,300	46,350	9,676	7,466	10,218	8,558
46,350	46,400	9,690	7,480	10,232	8,572
46,400	46,450	9,704	7,494	10,246	8,586
46,450	46,500	9,718	7,508	10,260	8,600
46,500	46,550	9,732	7,522	10,274	8,614
46,550	46,600	9,746	7,536	10,288	8,628
46,600	46,650	9,760	7,550	10,302	8,642
46,650	46,700	9,774	7,564	10,316	8,656
46,700	46,750	9,788	7,578	10,330	8,670
46,750	46,800	9,802	7,592	10,344	8,684
46,800	46,850	9,816	7,606	10,358	8,698
46,850	46,900	9,830	7,620	10,372	8,712
46,900	46,950	9,844	7,634	10,386	8,726
46,950	47,000	9,858	7,648	10,400	8,740

47,000

At least	But less than	Single	Married filing jointly *	Married filing separately	Head of a household
47,000	47,050	9,872	7,662	10,414	8,754
47,050	47,100	9,886	7,676	10,428	8,768
47,100	47,150	9,900	7,690	10,442	8,782
47,150	47,200	9,914	7,704	10,456	8,796
47,200	47,250	9,928	7,718	10,470	8,810
47,250	47,300	9,942	7,732	10,484	8,824
47,300	47,350	9,956	7,746	10,498	8,838
47,350	47,400	9,970	7,760	10,512	8,852
47,400	47,450	9,984	7,774	10,526	8,866
47,450	47,500	9,998	7,788	10,540	8,880
47,500	47,550	10,012	7,802	10,554	8,894
47,550	47,600	10,026	7,816	10,568	8,908
47,600	47,650	10,040	7,830	10,582	8,922
47,650	47,700	10,054	7,844	10,596	8,936
47,700	47,750	10,068	7,858	10,610	8,950
47,750	47,800	10,082	7,872	10,624	8,964
47,800	47,850	10,096	7,886	10,638	8,978
47,850	47,900	10,110	7,900	10,652	8,992
47,900	47,950	10,124	7,914	10,666	9,006
47,950	48,000	10,138	7,928	10,680	9,020

48,000

At least	But less than	Single	Married filing jointly *	Married filing separately	Head of a household
48,000	48,050	10,152	7,942	10,694	9,034
48,050	48,100	10,166	7,956	10,708	9,048
48,100	48,150	10,180	7,970	10,722	9,062
48,150	48,200	10,194	7,984	10,736	9,076
48,200	48,250	10,208	7,998	10,750	9,090
48,250	48,300	10,222	8,012	10,764	9,104
48,300	48,350	10,236	8,026	10,778	9,118
48,350	48,400	10,250	8,040	10,792	9,132
48,400	48,450	10,264	8,054	10,806	9,146
48,450	48,500	10,278	8,068	10,820	9,160
48,500	48,550	10,292	8,082	10,834	9,174
48,550	48,600	10,306	8,096	10,848	9,188
48,600	48,650	10,320	8,110	10,862	9,202
48,650	48,700	10,334	8,124	10,876	9,216
48,700	48,750	10,348	8,138	10,890	9,230
48,750	48,800	10,362	8,152	10,904	9,244
48,800	48,850	10,376	8,166	10,918	9,258
48,850	48,900	10,390	8,180	10,932	9,272
48,900	48,950	10,404	8,194	10,946	9,286
48,950	49,000	10,418	8,208	10,960	9,300

49,000

At least	But less than	Single	Married filing jointly *	Married filing separately	Head of a household
49,000	49,050	10,432	8,222	10,974	9,314
49,050	49,100	10,446	8,236	10,988	9,328
49,100	49,150	10,460	8,250	11,002	9,342
49,150	49,200	10,474	8,264	11,016	9,356
49,200	49,250	10,488	8,278	11,030	9,370
49,250	49,300	10,502	8,292	11,044	9,384
49,300	49,350	10,516	8,306	11,058	9,398
49,350	49,400	10,530	8,320	11,072	9,412
49,400	49,450	10,544	8,334	11,086	9,426
49,450	49,500	10,558	8,348	11,100	9,440
49,500	49,550	10,572	8,362	11,114	9,454
49,550	49,600	10,586	8,376	11,128	9,468
49,600	49,650	10,600	8,390	11,142	9,482
49,650	49,700	10,614	8,404	11,156	9,496
49,700	49,750	10,628	8,418	11,170	9,510
49,750	49,800	10,642	8,432	11,184	9,524
49,800	49,850	10,656	8,446	11,198	9,538
49,850	49,900	10,670	8,460	11,212	9,552
49,900	49,950	10,684	8,474	11,226	9,566
49,950	50,000	10,698	8,488	11,240	9,580

* This column must also be used by a qualifying widow(er).

Continued on next page

If line 39 (taxable income) is— / And you are—

Columns: At least | But less than | Single | Married filing jointly * | Married filing separately | Head of a household — **Your tax is—**

50,000

At least	But less than	Single	Married filing jointly *	Married filing separately	Head of a household
50,000	50,050	10,712	8,502	11,254	9,594
50,050	50,100	10,726	8,516	11,268	9,608
50,100	50,150	10,740	8,530	11,282	9,622
50,150	50,200	10,754	8,544	11,296	9,636
50,200	50,250	10,768	8,558	11,310	9,650
50,250	50,300	10,782	8,572	11,324	9,664
50,300	50,350	10,796	8,586	11,338	9,678
50,350	50,400	10,810	8,600	11,352	9,692
50,400	50,450	10,824	8,614	11,366	9,706
50,450	50,500	10,838	8,628	11,380	9,720
50,500	50,550	10,852	8,642	11,394	9,734
50,550	50,600	10,866	8,656	11,408	9,748
50,600	50,650	10,880	8,670	11,422	9,762
50,650	50,700	10,894	8,684	11,436	9,776
50,700	50,750	10,908	8,698	11,450	9,790
50,750	50,800	10,922	8,712	11,464	9,804
50,800	50,850	10,936	8,726	11,478	9,818
50,850	50,900	10,950	8,740	11,492	9,832
50,900	50,950	10,964	8,754	11,506	9,846
50,950	51,000	10,978	8,768	11,520	9,860

51,000

At least	But less than	Single	Married filing jointly *	Married filing separately	Head of a household
51,000	51,050	10,992	8,782	11,534	9,874
51,050	51,100	11,006	8,796	11,548	9,888
51,100	51,150	11,020	8,810	11,562	9,902
51,150	51,200	11,034	8,824	11,577	9,916
51,200	51,250	11,048	8,838	11,593	9,930
51,250	51,300	11,062	8,852	11,608	9,944
51,300	51,350	11,076	8,866	11,624	9,958
51,350	51,400	11,090	8,880	11,639	9,972
51,400	51,450	11,104	8,894	11,655	9,986
51,450	51,500	11,118	8,908	11,670	10,000
51,500	51,550	11,132	8,922	11,686	10,014
51,550	51,600	11,146	8,936	11,701	10,028
51,600	51,650	11,160	8,950	11,717	10,042
51,650	51,700	11,174	8,964	11,732	10,056
51,700	51,750	11,188	8,978	11,748	10,070
51,750	51,800	11,202	8,992	11,763	10,084
51,800	51,850	11,216	9,006	11,779	10,098
51,850	51,900	11,230	9,020	11,794	10,112
51,900	51,950	11,244	9,034	11,810	10,126
51,950	52,000	11,258	9,048	11,825	10,140

52,000

At least	But less than	Single	Married filing jointly *	Married filing separately	Head of a household
52,000	52,050	11,272	9,062	11,841	10,154
52,050	52,100	11,286	9,076	11,856	10,168
52,100	52,150	11,300	9,090	11,872	10,182
52,150	52,200	11,314	9,104	11,887	10,196
52,200	52,250	11,328	9,118	11,903	10,210
52,250	52,300	11,342	9,132	11,918	10,224
52,300	52,350	11,356	9,146	11,934	10,238
52,350	52,400	11,370	9,160	11,949	10,252
52,400	52,450	11,384	9,174	11,965	10,266
52,450	52,500	11,398	9,188	11,980	10,280
52,500	52,550	11,412	9,202	11,996	10,294
52,550	52,600	11,426	9,216	12,011	10,308
52,600	52,650	11,440	9,230	12,027	10,322
52,650	52,700	11,454	9,244	12,042	10,336
52,700	52,750	11,468	9,258	12,058	10,350
52,750	52,800	11,482	9,272	12,073	10,364
52,800	52,850	11,496	9,286	12,089	10,378
52,850	52,900	11,510	9,300	12,104	10,392
52,900	52,950	11,524	9,314	12,120	10,406
52,950	53,000	11,538	9,328	12,135	10,420

53,000

At least	But less than	Single	Married filing jointly *	Married filing separately	Head of a household
53,000	53,050	11,552	9,342	12,151	10,434
53,050	53,100	11,566	9,356	12,166	10,448
53,100	53,150	11,580	9,370	12,182	10,462
53,150	53,200	11,594	9,384	12,197	10,476
53,200	53,250	11,608	9,398	12,213	10,490
53,250	53,300	11,622	9,412	12,228	10,504
53,300	53,350	11,636	9,426	12,244	10,518
53,350	53,400	11,650	9,440	12,259	10,532
53,400	53,450	11,664	9,454	12,275	10,546
53,450	53,500	11,678	9,468	12,290	10,560
53,500	53,550	11,692	9,482	12,306	10,574
53,550	53,600	11,706	9,496	12,321	10,588
53,600	53,650	11,720	9,510	12,337	10,602
53,650	53,700	11,734	9,524	12,352	10,616
53,700	53,750	11,748	9,538	12,368	10,630
53,750	53,800	11,762	9,552	12,383	10,644
53,800	53,850	11,776	9,566	12,399	10,658
53,850	53,900	11,790	9,580	12,414	10,672
53,900	53,950	11,804	9,594	12,430	10,686
53,950	54,000	11,818	9,608	12,445	10,700

54,000

At least	But less than	Single	Married filing jointly *	Married filing separately	Head of a household
54,000	54,050	11,832	9,622	12,461	10,714
54,050	54,100	11,846	9,636	12,476	10,728
54,100	54,150	11,860	9,650	12,492	10,742
54,150	54,200	11,874	9,664	12,507	10,756
54,200	54,250	11,888	9,678	12,523	10,770
54,250	54,300	11,902	9,692	12,538	10,784
54,300	54,350	11,916	9,706	12,554	10,798
54,350	54,400	11,930	9,720	12,569	10,812
54,400	54,450	11,944	9,734	12,585	10,826
54,450	54,500	11,958	9,748	12,600	10,840
54,500	54,550	11,972	9,762	12,616	10,854
54,550	54,600	11,986	9,776	12,631	10,868
54,600	54,650	12,000	9,790	12,647	10,882
54,650	54,700	12,014	9,804	12,662	10,896
54,700	54,750	12,028	9,818	12,678	10,910
54,750	54,800	12,042	9,832	12,693	10,924
54,800	54,850	12,056	9,846	12,709	10,938
54,850	54,900	12,070	9,860	12,724	10,952
54,900	54,950	12,084	9,874	12,740	10,966
54,950	55,000	12,098	9,888	12,755	10,980

55,000

At least	But less than	Single	Married filing jointly *	Married filing separately	Head of a household
55,000	55,050	12,112	9,902	12,771	10,994
55,050	55,100	12,126	9,916	12,786	11,008
55,100	55,150	12,140	9,930	12,802	11,022
55,150	55,200	12,154	9,944	12,817	11,036
55,200	55,250	12,168	9,958	12,833	11,050
55,250	55,300	12,182	9,972	12,848	11,064
55,300	55,350	12,196	9,986	12,864	11,078
55,350	55,400	12,210	10,000	12,879	11,092
55,400	55,450	12,224	10,014	12,895	11,106
55,450	55,500	12,238	10,028	12,910	11,120
55,500	55,550	12,252	10,042	12,926	11,134
55,550	55,600	12,266	10,056	12,941	11,148
55,600	55,650	12,280	10,070	12,957	11,162
55,650	55,700	12,294	10,084	12,972	11,176
55,700	55,750	12,308	10,098	12,988	11,190
55,750	55,800	12,322	10,112	13,003	11,204
55,800	55,850	12,336	10,126	13,019	11,218
55,850	55,900	12,350	10,140	13,034	11,232
55,900	55,950	12,364	10,154	13,050	11,246
55,950	56,000	12,378	10,168	13,065	11,260

56,000

At least	But less than	Single	Married filing jointly *	Married filing separately	Head of a household
56,000	56,050	12,392	10,182	13,081	11,274
56,050	56,100	12,406	10,196	13,096	11,288
56,100	56,150	12,420	10,210	13,112	11,302
56,150	56,200	12,434	10,224	13,127	11,316
56,200	56,250	12,448	10,238	13,143	11,330
56,250	56,300	12,462	10,252	13,158	11,344
56,300	56,350	12,476	10,266	13,174	11,358
56,350	56,400	12,490	10,280	13,189	11,372
56,400	56,450	12,504	10,294	13,205	11,386
56,450	56,500	12,518	10,308	13,220	11,400
56,500	56,550	12,532	10,322	13,236	11,414
56,550	56,600	12,546	10,336	13,251	11,428
56,600	56,650	12,560	10,350	13,267	11,442
56,650	56,700	12,574	10,364	13,282	11,456
56,700	56,750	12,588	10,378	13,298	11,470
56,750	56,800	12,602	10,392	13,313	11,484
56,800	56,850	12,616	10,406	13,329	11,498
56,850	56,900	12,630	10,420	13,344	11,512
56,900	56,950	12,644	10,434	13,360	11,526
56,950	57,000	12,658	10,448	13,375	11,540

57,000

At least	But less than	Single	Married filing jointly *	Married filing separately	Head of a household
57,000	57,050	12,672	10,462	13,391	11,554
57,050	57,100	12,686	10,476	13,406	11,568
57,100	57,150	12,700	10,490	13,422	11,582
57,150	57,200	12,714	10,504	13,437	11,596
57,200	57,250	12,728	10,518	13,453	11,610
57,250	57,300	12,742	10,532	13,468	11,624
57,300	57,350	12,756	10,546	13,484	11,638
57,350	57,400	12,770	10,560	13,499	11,652
57,400	57,450	12,784	10,574	13,515	11,666
57,450	57,500	12,798	10,588	13,530	11,680
57,500	57,550	12,812	10,602	13,546	11,694
57,550	57,600	12,826	10,616	13,561	11,708
57,600	57,650	12,840	10,630	13,577	11,722
57,650	57,700	12,854	10,644	13,592	11,736
57,700	57,750	12,868	10,658	13,608	11,750
57,750	57,800	12,882	10,672	13,623	11,764
57,800	57,850	12,896	10,686	13,639	11,778
57,850	57,900	12,910	10,700	13,654	11,792
57,900	57,950	12,924	10,714	13,670	11,806
57,950	58,000	12,938	10,728	13,685	11,820

58,000

At least	But less than	Single	Married filing jointly *	Married filing separately	Head of a household
58,000	58,050	12,952	10,742	13,701	11,834
58,050	58,100	12,966	10,756	13,716	11,848
58,100	58,150	12,980	10,770	13,732	11,862
58,150	58,200	12,994	10,784	13,747	11,876
58,200	58,250	13,008	10,798	13,763	11,890
58,250	58,300	13,022	10,812	13,778	11,904
58,300	58,350	13,036	10,826	13,794	11,918
58,350	58,400	13,050	10,840	13,809	11,932
58,400	58,450	13,064	10,854	13,825	11,946
58,450	58,500	13,078	10,868	13,840	11,960
58,500	58,550	13,092	10,882	13,856	11,974
58,550	58,600	13,106	10,896	13,871	11,988
58,600	58,650	13,120	10,910	13,887	12,002
58,650	58,700	13,134	10,924	13,902	12,016
58,700	58,750	13,148	10,938	13,918	12,030
58,750	58,800	13,162	10,952	13,933	12,044
58,800	58,850	13,176	10,966	13,949	12,058
58,850	58,900	13,190	10,980	13,964	12,072
58,900	58,950	13,204	10,994	13,980	12,086
58,950	59,000	13,218	11,008	13,995	12,100

* This column must also be used by a qualifying widow(er).

Continued on next page

| If line 39 (taxable income) is– | | And you are– | | | |
At least	But less than	Single	Married filing jointly *	Married filing separately	Head of a household
			Your tax is–		
59,000					
59,000	59,050	13,232	11,022	14,011	12,114
59,050	59,100	13,246	11,036	14,026	12,128
59,100	59,150	13,260	11,050	14,042	12,142
59,150	59,200	13,274	11,064	14,057	12,156
59,200	59,250	13,288	11,078	14,073	12,170
59,250	59,300	13,302	11,092	14,088	12,184
59,300	59,350	13,316	11,106	14,104	12,198
59,350	59,400	13,330	11,120	14,119	12,212
59,400	59,450	13,344	11,134	14,135	12,226
59,450	59,500	13,358	11,148	14,150	12,240
59,500	59,550	13,372	11,162	14,166	12,254
59,550	59,600	13,386	11,176	14,181	12,268
59,600	59,650	13,400	11,190	14,197	12,282
59,650	59,700	13,414	11,204	14,212	12,296
59,700	59,750	13,428	11,218	14,228	12,310
59,750	59,800	13,442	11,232	14,243	12,324
59,800	59,850	13,456	11,246	14,259	12,338
59,850	59,900	13,470	11,260	14,274	12,352
59,900	59,950	13,484	11,274	14,290	12,366
59,950	60,000	13,498	11,288	14,305	12,380
60,000					
60,000	60,050	13,512	11,302	14,321	12,394
60,050	60,100	13,526	11,316	14,336	12,408
60,100	60,150	13,540	11,330	14,352	12,422
60,150	60,200	13,554	11,344	14,367	12,436
60,200	60,250	13,568	11,358	14,383	12,450
60,250	60,300	13,582	11,372	14,398	12,464
60,300	60,350	13,596	11,386	14,414	12,478
60,350	60,400	13,610	11,400	14,429	12,492
60,400	60,450	13,624	11,414	14,445	12,506
60,450	60,500	13,638	11,428	14,460	12,520
60,500	60,550	13,652	11,442	14,476	12,534
60,550	60,600	13,666	11,456	14,491	12,548
60,600	60,650	13,680	11,470	14,507	12,562
60,650	60,700	13,694	11,484	14,522	12,576
60,700	60,750	13,708	11,498	14,538	12,590
60,750	60,800	13,722	11,512	14,553	12,604
60,800	60,850	13,736	11,526	14,569	12,618
60,850	60,900	13,750	11,540	14,584	12,632
60,900	60,950	13,764	11,554	14,600	12,646
60,950	61,000	13,778	11,568	14,615	12,660
61,000					
61,000	61,050	13,792	11,582	14,631	12,674
61,050	61,100	13,806	11,596	14,646	12,688
61,100	61,150	13,820	11,610	14,662	12,702
61,150	61,200	13,834	11,624	14,677	12,716
61,200	61,250	13,848	11,638	14,693	12,730
61,250	61,300	13,862	11,652	14,708	12,744
61,300	61,350	13,876	11,666	14,724	12,758
61,350	61,400	13,890	11,680	14,739	12,772
61,400	61,450	13,904	11,694	14,755	12,786
61,450	61,500	13,920	11,708	14,770	12,800
61,500	61,550	13,935	11,722	14,786	12,814
61,550	61,600	13,951	11,736	14,801	12,828
61,600	61,650	13,966	11,750	14,817	12,842
61,650	61,700	13,982	11,764	14,832	12,856
61,700	61,750	13,997	11,778	14,848	12,870
61,750	61,800	14,013	11,792	14,863	12,884
61,800	61,850	14,028	11,806	14,879	12,898
61,850	61,900	14,044	11,820	14,894	12,912
61,900	61,950	14,059	11,834	14,910	12,926
61,950	62,000	14,075	11,848	14,925	12,940

| If line 39 (taxable income) is– | | And you are– | | | |
At least	But less than	Single	Married filing jointly *	Married filing separately	Head of a household
			Your tax is–		
62,000					
62,000	62,050	14,090	11,862	14,941	12,954
62,050	62,100	14,106	11,876	14,956	12,968
62,100	62,150	14,121	11,890	14,972	12,982
62,150	62,200	14,137	11,904	14,987	12,996
62,200	62,250	14,152	11,918	15,003	13,010
62,250	62,300	14,168	11,932	15,018	13,024
62,300	62,350	14,183	11,946	15,034	13,038
62,350	62,400	14,199	11,960	15,049	13,052
62,400	62,450	14,214	11,974	15,065	13,066
62,450	62,500	14,230	11,988	15,080	13,080
62,500	62,550	14,245	12,002	15,096	13,094
62,550	62,600	14,261	12,016	15,111	13,108
62,600	62,650	14,276	12,030	15,127	13,122
62,650	62,700	14,292	12,044	15,142	13,136
62,700	62,750	14,307	12,058	15,158	13,150
62,750	62,800	14,323	12,072	15,173	13,164
62,800	62,850	14,338	12,086	15,189	13,178
62,850	62,900	14,354	12,100	15,204	13,192
62,900	62,950	14,369	12,114	15,220	13,206
62,950	63,000	14,385	12,128	15,235	13,220
63,000					
63,000	63,050	14,400	12,142	15,251	13,234
63,050	63,100	14,416	12,156	15,266	13,248
63,100	63,150	14,431	12,170	15,282	13,262
63,150	63,200	14,447	12,184	15,297	13,276
63,200	63,250	14,462	12,198	15,313	13,290
63,250	63,300	14,478	12,212	15,328	13,304
63,300	63,350	14,493	12,226	15,344	13,318
63,350	63,400	14,509	12,240	15,359	13,332
63,400	63,450	14,524	12,254	15,375	13,346
63,450	63,500	14,540	12,268	15,390	13,360
63,500	63,550	14,555	12,282	15,406	13,374
63,550	63,600	14,571	12,296	15,421	13,388
63,600	63,650	14,586	12,310	15,437	13,402
63,650	63,700	14,602	12,324	15,452	13,416
63,700	63,750	14,617	12,338	15,468	13,430
63,750	63,800	14,633	12,352	15,483	13,444
63,800	63,850	14,648	12,366	15,499	13,458
63,850	63,900	14,664	12,380	15,514	13,472
63,900	63,950	14,679	12,394	15,530	13,486
63,950	64,000	14,695	12,408	15,545	13,500
64,000					
64,000	64,050	14,710	12,422	15,561	13,514
64,050	64,100	14,726	12,436	15,576	13,528
64,100	64,150	14,741	12,450	15,592	13,542
64,150	64,200	14,757	12,464	15,607	13,556
64,200	64,250	14,772	12,478	15,623	13,570
64,250	64,300	14,788	12,492	15,638	13,584
64,300	64,350	14,803	12,506	15,654	13,598
64,350	64,400	14,819	12,520	15,669	13,612
64,400	64,450	14,834	12,534	15,685	13,626
64,450	64,500	14,850	12,548	15,700	13,640
64,500	64,550	14,865	12,562	15,716	13,654
64,550	64,600	14,881	12,576	15,731	13,668
64,600	64,650	14,896	12,590	15,747	13,682
64,650	64,700	14,912	12,604	15,762	13,696
64,700	64,750	14,927	12,618	15,778	13,710
64,750	64,800	14,943	12,632	15,793	13,724
64,800	64,850	14,958	12,646	15,809	13,738
64,850	64,900	14,974	12,660	15,824	13,752
64,900	64,950	14,989	12,674	15,840	13,766
64,950	65,000	15,005	12,688	15,855	13,780

| If line 39 (taxable income) is– | | And you are– | | | |
At least	But less than	Single	Married filing jointly *	Married filing separately	Head of a household
			Your tax is–		
65,000					
65,000	65,050	15,020	12,702	15,871	13,794
65,050	65,100	15,036	12,716	15,886	13,808
65,100	65,150	15,051	12,730	15,902	13,822
65,150	65,200	15,067	12,744	15,917	13,836
65,200	65,250	15,082	12,758	15,933	13,850
65,250	65,300	15,098	12,772	15,948	13,864
65,300	65,350	15,113	12,786	15,964	13,878
65,350	65,400	15,129	12,800	15,979	13,892
65,400	65,450	15,144	12,814	15,995	13,906
65,450	65,500	15,160	12,828	16,010	13,920
65,500	65,550	15,175	12,842	16,026	13,934
65,550	65,600	15,191	12,856	16,041	13,948
65,600	65,650	15,206	12,870	16,057	13,962
65,650	65,700	15,222	12,884	16,072	13,976
65,700	65,750	15,237	12,898	16,088	13,990
65,750	65,800	15,253	12,912	16,103	14,004
65,800	65,850	15,268	12,926	16,119	14,018
65,850	65,900	15,284	12,940	16,134	14,032
65,900	65,950	15,299	12,954	16,150	14,046
65,950	66,000	15,315	12,968	16,165	14,060
66,000					
66,000	66,050	15,330	12,982	16,181	14,074
66,050	66,100	15,346	12,996	16,196	14,088
66,100	66,150	15,361	13,010	16,212	14,102
66,150	66,200	15,377	13,024	16,227	14,116
66,200	66,250	15,392	13,038	16,243	14,130
66,250	66,300	15,408	13,052	16,258	14,144
66,300	66,350	15,423	13,066	16,274	14,158
66,350	66,400	15,439	13,080	16,289	14,172
66,400	66,450	15,454	13,094	16,305	14,186
66,450	66,500	15,470	13,108	16,320	14,200
66,500	66,550	15,485	13,122	16,336	14,214
66,550	66,600	15,501	13,136	16,351	14,228
66,600	66,650	15,516	13,150	16,367	14,242
66,650	66,700	15,532	13,164	16,382	14,256
66,700	66,750	15,547	13,178	16,398	14,270
66,750	66,800	15,563	13,192	16,413	14,284
66,800	66,850	15,578	13,206	16,429	14,298
66,850	66,900	15,594	13,220	16,444	14,312
66,900	66,950	15,609	13,234	16,460	14,326
66,950	67,000	15,625	13,248	16,475	14,340
67,000					
67,000	67,050	15,640	13,262	16,491	14,354
67,050	67,100	15,656	13,276	16,506	14,368
67,100	67,150	15,671	13,290	16,522	14,382
67,150	67,200	15,687	13,304	16,537	14,396
67,200	67,250	15,702	13,318	16,553	14,410
67,250	67,300	15,718	13,332	16,568	14,424
67,300	67,350	15,733	13,346	16,584	14,438
67,350	67,400	15,749	13,360	16,599	14,452
67,400	67,450	15,764	13,374	16,615	14,466
67,450	67,500	15,780	13,388	16,630	14,480
67,500	67,550	15,795	13,402	16,646	14,494
67,550	67,600	15,811	13,416	16,661	14,508
67,600	67,650	15,826	13,430	16,677	14,522
67,650	67,700	15,842	13,444	16,692	14,536
67,700	67,750	15,857	13,458	16,708	14,550
67,750	67,800	15,873	13,472	16,723	14,564
67,800	67,850	15,888	13,486	16,739	14,578
67,850	67,900	15,904	13,500	16,754	14,592
67,900	67,950	15,919	13,514	16,770	14,606
67,950	68,000	15,935	13,528	16,785	14,620

* This column must also be used by a qualifying widow(er).

Continued on next page

1998 Tax Table– *Continued*

If line 39 (taxable income) is— At least	But less than	Single	Married filing jointly *	Married filing separately	Head of a household
			Your tax is—		

68,000

At least	But less than	Single	Married filing jointly *	Married filing separately	Head of a household
68,000	68,050	15,950	13,542	16,801	14,634
68,050	68,100	15,966	13,556	16,816	14,648
68,100	68,150	15,981	13,570	16,832	14,662
68,150	68,200	15,997	13,584	16,847	14,676
68,200	68,250	16,012	13,598	16,863	14,690
68,250	68,300	16,028	13,612	16,878	14,704
68,300	68,350	16,043	13,626	16,894	14,718
68,350	68,400	16,059	13,640	16,909	14,732
68,400	68,450	16,074	13,654	16,925	14,746
68,450	68,500	16,090	13,668	16,940	14,760
68,500	68,550	16,105	13,682	16,956	14,774
68,550	68,600	16,121	13,696	16,971	14,788
68,600	68,650	16,136	13,710	16,987	14,802
68,650	68,700	16,152	13,724	17,002	14,816
68,700	68,750	16,167	13,738	17,018	14,830
68,750	68,800	16,183	13,752	17,033	14,844
68,800	68,850	16,198	13,766	17,049	14,858
68,850	68,900	16,214	13,780	17,064	14,872
68,900	68,950	16,229	13,794	17,080	14,886
68,950	69,000	16,245	13,808	17,095	14,900

69,000

At least	But less than	Single	Married filing jointly *	Married filing separately	Head of a household
69,000	69,050	16,260	13,822	17,111	14,914
69,050	69,100	16,276	13,836	17,126	14,928
69,100	69,150	16,291	13,850	17,142	14,942
69,150	69,200	16,307	13,864	17,157	14,956
69,200	69,250	16,322	13,878	17,173	14,970
69,250	69,300	16,338	13,892	17,188	14,984
69,300	69,350	16,353	13,906	17,204	14,998
69,350	69,400	16,369	13,920	17,219	15,012
69,400	69,450	16,384	13,934	17,235	15,026
69,450	69,500	16,400	13,948	17,250	15,040
69,500	69,550	16,415	13,962	17,266	15,054
69,550	69,600	16,431	13,976	17,281	15,068
69,600	69,650	16,446	13,990	17,297	15,082
69,650	69,700	16,462	14,004	17,312	15,096
69,700	69,750	16,477	14,018	17,328	15,110
69,750	69,800	16,493	14,032	17,343	15,124
69,800	69,850	16,508	14,046	17,359	15,138
69,850	69,900	16,524	14,060	17,374	15,152
69,900	69,950	16,539	14,074	17,390	15,166
69,950	70,000	16,555	14,088	17,405	15,180

70,000

At least	But less than	Single	Married filing jointly *	Married filing separately	Head of a household
70,000	70,050	16,570	14,102	17,421	15,194
70,050	70,100	16,586	14,116	17,436	15,208
70,100	70,150	16,601	14,130	17,452	15,222
70,150	70,200	16,617	14,144	17,467	15,236
70,200	70,250	16,632	14,158	17,483	15,250
70,250	70,300	16,648	14,172	17,498	15,264
70,300	70,350	16,663	14,186	17,514	15,278
70,350	70,400	16,679	14,200	17,529	15,292
70,400	70,450	16,694	14,214	17,545	15,306
70,450	70,500	16,710	14,228	17,560	15,320
70,500	70,550	16,725	14,242	17,576	15,334
70,550	70,600	16,741	14,256	17,591	15,348
70,600	70,650	16,756	14,270	17,607	15,362
70,650	70,700	16,772	14,284	17,622	15,376
70,700	70,750	16,787	14,298	17,638	15,390
70,750	70,800	16,803	14,312	17,653	15,404
70,800	70,850	16,818	14,326	17,669	15,418
70,850	70,900	16,834	14,340	17,684	15,432
70,900	70,950	16,849	14,354	17,700	15,446
70,950	71,000	16,865	14,368	17,715	15,460

71,000

At least	But less than	Single	Married filing jointly *	Married filing separately	Head of a household
71,000	71,050	16,880	14,382	17,731	15,474
71,050	71,100	16,896	14,396	17,746	15,488
71,100	71,150	16,911	14,410	17,762	15,502
71,150	71,200	16,927	14,424	17,777	15,516
71,200	71,250	16,942	14,438	17,793	15,530
71,250	71,300	16,958	14,452	17,808	15,544
71,300	71,350	16,973	14,466	17,824	15,558
71,350	71,400	16,989	14,480	17,839	15,572
71,400	71,450	17,004	14,494	17,855	15,586
71,450	71,500	17,020	14,508	17,870	15,600
71,500	71,550	17,035	14,522	17,886	15,614
71,550	71,600	17,051	14,536	17,901	15,628
71,600	71,650	17,066	14,550	17,917	15,642
71,650	71,700	17,082	14,564	17,932	15,656
71,700	71,750	17,097	14,578	17,948	15,670
71,750	71,800	17,113	14,592	17,963	15,684
71,800	71,850	17,128	14,606	17,979	15,698
71,850	71,900	17,144	14,620	17,994	15,712
71,900	71,950	17,159	14,634	18,010	15,726
71,950	72,000	17,175	14,648	18,025	15,740

72,000

At least	But less than	Single	Married filing jointly *	Married filing separately	Head of a household
72,000	72,050	17,190	14,662	18,041	15,754
72,050	72,100	17,206	14,676	18,056	15,768
72,100	72,150	17,221	14,690	18,072	15,782
72,150	72,200	17,237	14,704	18,087	15,796
72,200	72,250	17,252	14,718	18,103	15,810
72,250	72,300	17,268	14,732	18,118	15,824
72,300	72,350	17,283	14,746	18,134	15,838
72,350	72,400	17,299	14,760	18,149	15,852
72,400	72,450	17,314	14,774	18,165	15,866
72,450	72,500	17,330	14,788	18,180	15,880
72,500	72,550	17,345	14,802	18,196	15,894
72,550	72,600	17,361	14,816	18,211	15,908
72,600	72,650	17,376	14,830	18,227	15,922
72,650	72,700	17,392	14,844	18,242	15,936
72,700	72,750	17,407	14,858	18,258	15,950
72,750	72,800	17,423	14,872	18,273	15,964
72,800	72,850	17,438	14,886	18,289	15,978
72,850	72,900	17,454	14,900	18,304	15,992
72,900	72,950	17,469	14,914	18,320	16,006
72,950	73,000	17,485	14,928	18,335	16,020

73,000

At least	But less than	Single	Married filing jointly *	Married filing separately	Head of a household
73,000	73,050	17,500	14,942	18,351	16,034
73,050	73,100	17,516	14,956	18,366	16,048
73,100	73,150	17,531	14,970	18,382	16,062
73,150	73,200	17,547	14,984	18,397	16,076
73,200	73,250	17,562	14,998	18,413	16,090
73,250	73,300	17,578	15,012	18,428	16,104
73,300	73,350	17,593	15,026	18,444	16,118
73,350	73,400	17,609	15,040	18,459	16,132
73,400	73,450	17,624	15,054	18,475	16,146
73,450	73,500	17,640	15,068	18,490	16,160
73,500	73,550	17,655	15,082	18,506	16,174
73,550	73,600	17,671	15,096	18,521	16,188
73,600	73,650	17,686	15,110	18,537	16,202
73,650	73,700	17,702	15,124	18,552	16,216
73,700	73,750	17,717	15,138	18,568	16,230
73,750	73,800	17,733	15,152	18,583	16,244
73,800	73,850	17,748	15,166	18,599	16,258
73,850	73,900	17,764	15,180	18,614	16,272
73,900	73,950	17,779	15,194	18,630	16,286
73,950	74,000	17,795	15,208	18,645	16,300

74,000

At least	But less than	Single	Married filing jointly *	Married filing separately	Head of a household
74,000	74,050	17,810	15,222	18,661	16,314
74,050	74,100	17,826	15,236	18,676	16,328
74,100	74,150	17,841	15,250	18,692	16,342
74,150	74,200	17,857	15,264	18,707	16,356
74,200	74,250	17,872	15,278	18,723	16,370
74,250	74,300	17,888	15,292	18,738	16,384
74,300	74,350	17,903	15,306	18,754	16,398
74,350	74,400	17,919	15,320	18,769	16,412
74,400	74,450	17,934	15,334	18,785	16,426
74,450	74,500	17,950	15,348	18,800	16,440
74,500	74,550	17,965	15,362	18,816	16,454
74,550	74,600	17,981	15,376	18,831	16,468
74,600	74,650	17,996	15,390	18,847	16,482
74,650	74,700	18,012	15,404	18,862	16,496
74,700	74,750	18,027	15,418	18,878	16,510
74,750	74,800	18,043	15,432	18,893	16,524
74,800	74,850	18,058	15,446	18,909	16,538
74,850	74,900	18,074	15,460	18,924	16,552
74,900	74,950	18,089	15,474	18,940	16,566
74,950	75,000	18,105	15,488	18,955	16,580

75,000

At least	But less than	Single	Married filing jointly *	Married filing separately	Head of a household
75,000	75,050	18,120	15,502	18,971	16,594
75,050	75,100	18,136	15,516	18,986	16,608
75,100	75,150	18,151	15,530	19,002	16,622
75,150	75,200	18,167	15,544	19,017	16,636
75,200	75,250	18,182	15,558	19,033	16,650
75,250	75,300	18,198	15,572	19,048	16,664
75,300	75,350	18,213	15,586	19,064	16,678
75,350	75,400	18,229	15,600	19,079	16,692
75,400	75,450	18,244	15,614	19,095	16,706
75,450	75,500	18,260	15,628	19,110	16,720
75,500	75,550	18,275	15,642	19,126	16,734
75,550	75,600	18,291	15,656	19,141	16,748
75,600	75,650	18,306	15,670	19,157	16,762
75,650	75,700	18,322	15,684	19,172	16,776
75,700	75,750	18,337	15,698	19,188	16,790
75,750	75,800	18,353	15,712	19,203	16,804
75,800	75,850	18,368	15,726	19,219	16,818
75,850	75,900	18,384	15,740	19,234	16,832
75,900	75,950	18,399	15,754	19,250	16,846
75,950	76,000	18,415	15,768	19,265	16,860

76,000

At least	But less than	Single	Married filing jointly *	Married filing separately	Head of a household
76,000	76,050	18,430	15,782	19,281	16,874
76,050	76,100	18,446	15,796	19,296	16,888
76,100	76,150	18,461	15,810	19,312	16,902
76,150	76,200	18,477	15,824	19,327	16,916
76,200	76,250	18,492	15,838	19,343	16,930
76,250	76,300	18,508	15,852	19,358	16,944
76,300	76,350	18,523	15,866	19,374	16,958
76,350	76,400	18,539	15,880	19,389	16,972
76,400	76,450	18,554	15,894	19,405	16,986
76,450	76,500	18,570	15,908	19,420	17,000
76,500	76,550	18,585	15,922	19,436	17,014
76,550	76,600	18,601	15,936	19,451	17,028
76,600	76,650	18,616	15,950	19,467	17,042
76,650	76,700	18,632	15,964	19,482	17,056
76,700	76,750	18,647	15,978	19,498	17,070
76,750	76,800	18,663	15,992	19,513	17,084
76,800	76,850	18,678	16,006	19,529	17,098
76,850	76,900	18,694	16,020	19,544	17,112
76,900	76,950	18,709	16,034	19,560	17,126
76,950	77,000	18,725	16,048	19,575	17,140

* This column must also be used by a qualifying widow(er).

Continued on next page

77,000

At least	But less than	Single	Married filing jointly*	Married filing separately	Head of a household
77,000	77,050	18,740	16,062	19,591	17,154
77,050	77,100	18,756	16,076	19,606	17,168
77,100	77,150	18,771	16,090	19,622	17,182
77,150	77,200	18,787	16,104	19,637	17,196
77,200	77,250	18,802	16,118	19,653	17,210
77,250	77,300	18,818	16,132	19,668	17,224
77,300	77,350	18,833	16,146	19,684	17,238
77,350	77,400	18,849	16,160	19,699	17,252
77,400	77,450	18,864	16,174	19,715	17,266
77,450	77,500	18,880	16,188	19,730	17,280
77,500	77,550	18,895	16,202	19,746	17,294
77,550	77,600	18,911	16,216	19,761	17,308
77,600	77,650	18,926	16,230	19,777	17,322
77,650	77,700	18,942	16,244	19,792	17,336
77,700	77,750	18,957	16,258	19,808	17,350
77,750	77,800	18,973	16,272	19,823	17,364
77,800	77,850	18,988	16,286	19,839	17,378
77,850	77,900	19,004	16,300	19,854	17,392
77,900	77,950	19,019	16,314	19,870	17,406
77,950	78,000	19,035	16,328	19,885	17,420

78,000

At least	But less than	Single	Married filing jointly*	Married filing separately	Head of a household
78,000	78,050	19,050	16,342	19,903	17,434
78,050	78,100	19,066	16,356	19,921	17,448
78,100	78,150	19,081	16,370	19,939	17,462
78,150	78,200	19,097	16,384	19,957	17,476
78,200	78,250	19,112	16,398	19,975	17,490
78,250	78,300	19,128	16,412	19,993	17,504
78,300	78,350	19,143	16,426	20,011	17,518
78,350	78,400	19,159	16,440	20,029	17,532
78,400	78,450	19,174	16,454	20,047	17,546
78,450	78,500	19,190	16,468	20,065	17,560
78,500	78,550	19,205	16,482	20,083	17,574
78,550	78,600	19,221	16,496	20,101	17,588
78,600	78,650	19,236	16,510	20,119	17,602
78,650	78,700	19,252	16,524	20,137	17,616
78,700	78,750	19,267	16,538	20,155	17,630
78,750	78,800	19,283	16,552	20,173	17,644
78,800	78,850	19,298	16,566	20,191	17,658
78,850	78,900	19,314	16,580	20,209	17,672
78,900	78,950	19,329	16,594	20,227	17,686
78,950	79,000	19,345	16,608	20,245	17,700

79,000

At least	But less than	Single	Married filing jointly*	Married filing separately	Head of a household
79,000	79,050	19,360	16,622	20,263	17,714
79,050	79,100	19,376	16,636	20,281	17,728
79,100	79,150	19,391	16,650	20,299	17,742
79,150	79,200	19,407	16,664	20,317	17,756
79,200	79,250	19,422	16,678	20,335	17,770
79,250	79,300	19,438	16,692	20,353	17,784
79,300	79,350	19,453	16,706	20,371	17,798
79,350	79,400	19,469	16,720	20,389	17,812
79,400	79,450	19,484	16,734	20,407	17,826
79,450	79,500	19,500	16,748	20,425	17,840
79,500	79,550	19,515	16,762	20,443	17,854
79,550	79,600	19,531	16,776	20,461	17,868
79,600	79,650	19,546	16,790	20,479	17,882
79,650	79,700	19,562	16,804	20,497	17,896
79,700	79,750	19,577	16,818	20,515	17,910
79,750	79,800	19,593	16,832	20,533	17,924
79,800	79,850	19,608	16,846	20,551	17,938
79,850	79,900	19,624	16,860	20,569	17,952
79,900	79,950	19,639	16,874	20,587	17,966
79,950	80,000	19,655	16,888	20,605	17,980

80,000

At least	But less than	Single	Married filing jointly*	Married filing separately	Head of a household
80,000	80,050	19,670	16,902	20,623	17,994
80,050	80,100	19,686	16,916	20,641	18,008
80,100	80,150	19,701	16,930	20,659	18,022
80,150	80,200	19,717	16,944	20,677	18,036
80,200	80,250	19,732	16,958	20,695	18,050
80,250	80,300	19,748	16,972	20,713	18,064
80,300	80,350	19,763	16,986	20,731	18,078
80,350	80,400	19,779	17,000	20,749	18,092
80,400	80,450	19,794	17,014	20,767	18,106
80,450	80,500	19,810	17,028	20,785	18,120
80,500	80,550	19,825	17,042	20,803	18,134
80,550	80,600	19,841	17,056	20,821	18,148
80,600	80,650	19,856	17,070	20,839	18,162
80,650	80,700	19,872	17,084	20,857	18,176
80,700	80,750	19,887	17,098	20,875	18,190
80,750	80,800	19,903	17,112	20,893	18,204
80,800	80,850	19,918	17,126	20,911	18,218
80,850	80,900	19,934	17,140	20,929	18,232
80,900	80,950	19,949	17,154	20,947	18,246
80,950	81,000	19,965	17,168	20,965	18,260

81,000

At least	But less than	Single	Married filing jointly*	Married filing separately	Head of a household
81,000	81,050	19,980	17,182	20,983	18,274
81,050	81,100	19,996	17,196	21,001	18,288
81,100	81,150	20,011	17,210	21,019	18,302
81,150	81,200	20,027	17,224	21,037	18,316
81,200	81,250	20,042	17,238	21,055	18,330
81,250	81,300	20,058	17,252	21,073	18,344
81,300	81,350	20,073	17,266	21,091	18,358
81,350	81,400	20,089	17,280	21,109	18,372
81,400	81,450	20,104	17,294	21,127	18,386
81,450	81,500	20,120	17,308	21,145	18,400
81,500	81,550	20,135	17,322	21,163	18,414
81,550	81,600	20,151	17,336	21,181	18,428
81,600	81,650	20,166	17,350	21,199	18,442
81,650	81,700	20,182	17,364	21,217	18,456
81,700	81,750	20,197	17,378	21,235	18,470
81,750	81,800	20,213	17,392	21,253	18,484
81,800	81,850	20,228	17,406	21,271	18,498
81,850	81,900	20,244	17,420	21,289	18,512
81,900	81,950	20,259	17,434	21,307	18,526
81,950	82,000	20,275	17,448	21,325	18,540

82,000

At least	But less than	Single	Married filing jointly*	Married filing separately	Head of a household
82,000	82,050	20,290	17,462	21,343	18,554
82,050	82,100	20,306	17,476	21,361	18,568
82,100	82,150	20,321	17,490	21,379	18,582
82,150	82,200	20,337	17,504	21,397	18,596
82,200	82,250	20,352	17,518	21,415	18,610
82,250	82,300	20,368	17,532	21,433	18,624
82,300	82,350	20,383	17,546	21,451	18,638
82,350	82,400	20,399	17,560	21,469	18,652
82,400	82,450	20,414	17,574	21,487	18,666
82,450	82,500	20,430	17,588	21,505	18,680
82,500	82,550	20,445	17,602	21,523	18,694
82,550	82,600	20,461	17,616	21,541	18,708
82,600	82,650	20,476	17,630	21,559	18,722
82,650	82,700	20,492	17,644	21,577	18,736
82,700	82,750	20,507	17,658	21,595	18,750
82,750	82,800	20,523	17,672	21,613	18,764
82,800	82,850	20,538	17,686	21,631	18,778
82,850	82,900	20,554	17,700	21,649	18,792
82,900	82,950	20,569	17,714	21,667	18,806
82,950	83,000	20,585	17,728	21,685	18,820

83,000

At least	But less than	Single	Married filing jointly*	Married filing separately	Head of a household
83,000	83,050	20,600	17,742	21,703	18,834
83,050	83,100	20,616	17,756	21,721	18,848
83,100	83,150	20,631	17,770	21,739	18,862
83,150	83,200	20,647	17,784	21,757	18,876
83,200	83,250	20,662	17,798	21,775	18,890
83,250	83,300	20,678	17,812	21,793	18,904
83,300	83,350	20,693	17,826	21,811	18,918
83,350	83,400	20,709	17,840	21,829	18,932
83,400	83,450	20,724	17,854	21,847	18,946
83,450	83,500	20,740	17,868	21,865	18,960
83,500	83,550	20,755	17,882	21,883	18,974
83,550	83,600	20,771	17,896	21,901	18,988
83,600	83,650	20,786	17,910	21,919	19,002
83,650	83,700	20,802	17,924	21,937	19,016
83,700	83,750	20,817	17,938	21,955	19,030
83,750	83,800	20,833	17,952	21,973	19,044
83,800	83,850	20,848	17,966	21,991	19,058
83,850	83,900	20,864	17,980	22,009	19,072
83,900	83,950	20,879	17,994	22,027	19,086
83,950	84,000	20,895	18,008	22,045	19,100

84,000

At least	But less than	Single	Married filing jointly*	Married filing separately	Head of a household
84,000	84,050	20,910	18,022	22,063	19,114
84,050	84,100	20,926	18,036	22,081	19,128
84,100	84,150	20,941	18,050	22,099	19,142
84,150	84,200	20,957	18,064	22,117	19,156
84,200	84,250	20,972	18,078	22,135	19,170
84,250	84,300	20,988	18,092	22,153	19,184
84,300	84,350	21,003	18,106	22,171	19,198
84,350	84,400	21,019	18,120	22,189	19,212
84,400	84,450	21,034	18,134	22,207	19,226
84,450	84,500	21,050	18,148	22,225	19,240
84,500	84,550	21,065	18,162	22,243	19,254
84,550	84,600	21,081	18,176	22,261	19,268
84,600	84,650	21,096	18,190	22,279	19,282
84,650	84,700	21,112	18,204	22,297	19,296
84,700	84,750	21,127	18,218	22,315	19,310
84,750	84,800	21,143	18,232	22,333	19,324
84,800	84,850	21,158	18,246	22,351	19,338
84,850	84,900	21,174	18,260	22,369	19,352
84,900	84,950	21,189	18,274	22,387	19,366
84,950	85,000	21,205	18,288	22,405	19,380

85,000

At least	But less than	Single	Married filing jointly*	Married filing separately	Head of a household
85,000	85,050	21,220	18,302	22,423	19,394
85,050	85,100	21,236	18,316	22,441	19,408
85,100	85,150	21,251	18,330	22,459	19,422
85,150	85,200	21,267	18,344	22,477	19,436
85,200	85,250	21,282	18,358	22,495	19,450
85,250	85,300	21,298	18,372	22,513	19,464
85,300	85,350	21,313	18,386	22,531	19,478
85,350	85,400	21,329	18,400	22,549	19,492
85,400	85,450	21,344	18,414	22,567	19,506
85,450	85,500	21,360	18,428	22,585	19,520
85,500	85,550	21,375	18,442	22,603	19,534
85,550	85,600	21,391	18,456	22,621	19,548
85,600	85,650	21,406	18,470	22,639	19,562
85,650	85,700	21,422	18,484	22,657	19,576
85,700	85,750	21,437	18,498	22,675	19,590
85,750	85,800	21,453	18,512	22,693	19,604
85,800	85,850	21,468	18,526	22,711	19,618
85,850	85,900	21,484	18,540	22,729	19,632
85,900	85,950	21,499	18,554	22,747	19,646
85,950	86,000	21,515	18,568	22,765	19,660

* This column must also be used by a qualifying widow(er).

Continued on next page

If line 39 (taxable income) is–		And you are–			
At least	But less than	Single	Married filing jointly *	Married filing separately	Head of a household
		Your tax is–			

86,000

At least	But less than	Single	Married filing jointly *	Married filing separately	Head of a household
86,000	86,050	21,530	18,582	22,783	19,674
86,050	86,100	21,546	18,596	22,801	19,688
86,100	86,150	21,561	18,610	22,819	19,702
86,150	86,200	21,577	18,624	22,837	19,716
86,200	86,250	21,592	18,638	22,855	19,730
86,250	86,300	21,608	18,652	22,873	19,744
86,300	86,350	21,623	18,666	22,891	19,758
86,350	86,400	21,639	18,680	22,909	19,772
86,400	86,450	21,654	18,694	22,927	19,786
86,450	86,500	21,670	18,708	22,945	19,800
86,500	86,550	21,685	18,722	22,963	19,814
86,550	86,600	21,701	18,736	22,981	19,828
86,600	86,650	21,716	18,750	22,999	19,842
86,650	86,700	21,732	18,764	23,017	19,856
86,700	86,750	21,747	18,778	23,035	19,870
86,750	86,800	21,763	18,792	23,053	19,884
86,800	86,850	21,778	18,806	23,071	19,898
86,850	86,900	21,794	18,820	23,089	19,912
86,900	86,950	21,809	18,834	23,107	19,926
86,950	87,000	21,825	18,848	23,125	19,940

87,000

At least	But less than	Single	Married filing jointly *	Married filing separately	Head of a household
87,000	87,050	21,840	18,862	23,143	19,954
87,050	87,100	21,856	18,876	23,161	19,968
87,100	87,150	21,871	18,890	23,179	19,982
87,150	87,200	21,887	18,904	23,197	19,996
87,200	87,250	21,902	18,918	23,215	20,010
87,250	87,300	21,918	18,932	23,233	20,024
87,300	87,350	21,933	18,946	23,251	20,038
87,350	87,400	21,949	18,960	23,269	20,052
87,400	87,450	21,964	18,974	23,287	20,066
87,450	87,500	21,980	18,988	23,305	20,080
87,500	87,550	21,995	19,002	23,323	20,094
87,550	87,600	22,011	19,016	23,341	20,108
87,600	87,650	22,026	19,030	23,359	20,122
87,650	87,700	22,042	19,044	23,377	20,136
87,700	87,750	22,057	19,058	23,395	20,150
87,750	87,800	22,073	19,072	23,413	20,166
87,800	87,850	22,088	19,086	23,431	20,181
87,850	87,900	22,104	19,100	23,449	20,197
87,900	87,950	22,119	19,114	23,467	20,212
87,950	88,000	22,135	19,128	23,485	20,228

88,000

At least	But less than	Single	Married filing jointly *	Married filing separately	Head of a household
88,000	88,050	22,150	19,142	23,503	20,243
88,050	88,100	22,166	19,156	23,521	20,259
88,100	88,150	22,181	19,170	23,539	20,274
88,150	88,200	22,197	19,184	23,557	20,290
88,200	88,250	22,212	19,198	23,575	20,305
88,250	88,300	22,228	19,212	23,593	20,321
88,300	88,350	22,243	19,226	23,611	20,336
88,350	88,400	22,259	19,240	23,629	20,352
88,400	88,450	22,274	19,254	23,647	20,367
88,450	88,500	22,290	19,268	23,665	20,383
88,500	88,550	22,305	19,282	23,683	20,398
88,550	88,600	22,321	19,296	23,701	20,414
88,600	88,650	22,336	19,310	23,719	20,429
88,650	88,700	22,352	19,324	23,737	20,445
88,700	88,750	22,367	19,338	23,755	20,460
88,750	88,800	22,383	19,352	23,773	20,476
88,800	88,850	22,398	19,366	23,791	20,491
88,850	88,900	22,414	19,380	23,809	20,507
88,900	88,950	22,429	19,394	23,827	20,522
88,950	89,000	22,445	19,408	23,845	20,538

89,000

At least	But less than	Single	Married filing jointly *	Married filing separately	Head of a household
89,000	89,050	22,460	19,422	23,863	20,553
89,050	89,100	22,476	19,436	23,881	20,569
89,100	89,150	22,491	19,450	23,899	20,584
89,150	89,200	22,507	19,464	23,917	20,600
89,200	89,250	22,522	19,478	23,935	20,615
89,250	89,300	22,538	19,492	23,953	20,631
89,300	89,350	22,553	19,506	23,971	20,646
89,350	89,400	22,569	19,520	23,989	20,662
89,400	89,450	22,584	19,534	24,007	20,677
89,450	89,500	22,600	19,548	24,025	20,693
89,500	89,550	22,615	19,562	24,043	20,708
89,550	89,600	22,631	19,576	24,061	20,724
89,600	89,650	22,646	19,590	24,079	20,739
89,650	89,700	22,662	19,604	24,097	20,755
89,700	89,750	22,677	19,618	24,115	20,770
89,750	89,800	22,693	19,632	24,133	20,786
89,800	89,850	22,708	19,646	24,151	20,801
89,850	89,900	22,724	19,660	24,169	20,817
89,900	89,950	22,739	19,674	24,187	20,832
89,950	90,000	22,755	19,688	24,205	20,848

90,000

At least	But less than	Single	Married filing jointly *	Married filing separately	Head of a household
90,000	90,050	22,770	19,702	24,223	20,863
90,050	90,100	22,786	19,716	24,241	20,879
90,100	90,150	22,801	19,730	24,259	20,894
90,150	90,200	22,817	19,744	24,277	20,910
90,200	90,250	22,832	19,758	24,295	20,925
90,250	90,300	22,848	19,772	24,313	20,941
90,300	90,350	22,863	19,786	24,331	20,956
90,350	90,400	22,879	19,800	24,349	20,972
90,400	90,450	22,894	19,814	24,367	20,987
90,450	90,500	22,910	19,828	24,385	21,003
90,500	90,550	22,925	19,842	24,403	21,018
90,550	90,600	22,941	19,856	24,421	21,034
90,600	90,650	22,956	19,870	24,439	21,049
90,650	90,700	22,972	19,884	24,457	21,065
90,700	90,750	22,987	19,898	24,475	21,080
90,750	90,800	23,003	19,912	24,493	21,096
90,800	90,850	23,018	19,926	24,511	21,111
90,850	90,900	23,034	19,940	24,529	21,127
90,900	90,950	23,049	19,954	24,547	21,142
90,950	91,000	23,065	19,968	24,565	21,158

91,000

At least	But less than	Single	Married filing jointly *	Married filing separately	Head of a household
91,000	91,050	23,080	19,982	24,583	21,173
91,050	91,100	23,096	19,996	24,601	21,189
91,100	91,150	23,111	20,010	24,619	21,204
91,150	91,200	23,127	20,024	24,637	21,220
91,200	91,250	23,142	20,038	24,655	21,235
91,250	91,300	23,158	20,052	24,673	21,251
91,300	91,350	23,173	20,066	24,691	21,266
91,350	91,400	23,189	20,080	24,709	21,282
91,400	91,450	23,204	20,094	24,727	21,297
91,450	91,500	23,220	20,108	24,745	21,313
91,500	91,550	23,235	20,122	24,763	21,328
91,550	91,600	23,251	20,136	24,781	21,344
91,600	91,650	23,266	20,150	24,799	21,359
91,650	91,700	23,282	20,164	24,817	21,375
91,700	91,750	23,297	20,178	24,835	21,390
91,750	91,800	23,313	20,192	24,853	21,406
91,800	91,850	23,328	20,206	24,871	21,421
91,850	91,900	23,344	20,220	24,889	21,437
91,900	91,950	23,359	20,234	24,907	21,452
91,950	92,000	23,375	20,248	24,925	21,468

92,000

At least	But less than	Single	Married filing jointly *	Married filing separately	Head of a household
92,000	92,050	23,390	20,262	24,943	21,483
92,050	92,100	23,406	20,276	24,961	21,499
92,100	92,150	23,421	20,290	24,979	21,514
92,150	92,200	23,437	20,304	24,997	21,530
92,200	92,250	23,452	20,318	25,015	21,545
92,250	92,300	23,468	20,332	25,033	21,561
92,300	92,350	23,483	20,346	25,051	21,576
92,350	92,400	23,499	20,360	25,069	21,592
92,400	92,450	23,514	20,374	25,087	21,607
92,450	92,500	23,530	20,388	25,105	21,623
92,500	92,550	23,545	20,402	25,123	21,638
92,550	92,600	23,561	20,416	25,141	21,654
92,600	92,650	23,576	20,430	25,159	21,669
92,650	92,700	23,592	20,444	25,177	21,685
92,700	92,750	23,607	20,458	25,195	21,700
92,750	92,800	23,623	20,472	25,213	21,716
92,800	92,850	23,638	20,486	25,231	21,731
92,850	92,900	23,654	20,500	25,249	21,747
92,900	92,950	23,669	20,514	25,267	21,762
92,950	93,000	23,685	20,528	25,285	21,778

93,000

At least	But less than	Single	Married filing jointly *	Married filing separately	Head of a household
93,000	93,050	23,700	20,542	25,303	21,793
93,050	93,100	23,716	20,556	25,321	21,809
93,100	93,150	23,731	20,570	25,339	21,824
93,150	93,200	23,747	20,584	25,357	21,840
93,200	93,250	23,762	20,598	25,375	21,855
93,250	93,300	23,778	20,612	25,393	21,871
93,300	93,350	23,793	20,626	25,411	21,886
93,350	93,400	23,809	20,640	25,429	21,902
93,400	93,450	23,824	20,654	25,447	21,917
93,450	93,500	23,840	20,668	25,465	21,933
93,500	93,550	23,855	20,682	25,483	21,948
93,550	93,600	23,871	20,696	25,501	21,964
93,600	93,650	23,886	20,710	25,519	21,979
93,650	93,700	23,902	20,724	25,537	21,995
93,700	93,750	23,917	20,738	25,555	22,010
93,750	93,800	23,933	20,752	25,573	22,026
93,800	93,850	23,948	20,766	25,591	22,041
93,850	93,900	23,964	20,780	25,609	22,057
93,900	93,950	23,979	20,794	25,627	22,072
93,950	94,000	23,995	20,808	25,645	22,088

94,000

At least	But less than	Single	Married filing jointly *	Married filing separately	Head of a household
94,000	94,050	24,010	20,822	25,663	22,103
94,050	94,100	24,026	20,836	25,681	22,119
94,100	94,150	24,041	20,850	25,699	22,134
94,150	94,200	24,057	20,864	25,717	22,150
94,200	94,250	24,072	20,878	25,735	22,165
94,250	94,300	24,088	20,892	25,753	22,181
94,300	94,350	24,103	20,906	25,771	22,196
94,350	94,400	24,119	20,920	25,789	22,212
94,400	94,450	24,134	20,934	25,807	22,227
94,450	94,500	24,150	20,948	25,825	22,243
94,500	94,550	24,165	20,962	25,843	22,258
94,550	94,600	24,181	20,976	25,861	22,274
94,600	94,650	24,196	20,990	25,879	22,289
94,650	94,700	24,212	21,004	25,897	22,305
94,700	94,750	24,227	21,018	25,915	22,320
94,750	94,800	24,243	21,032	25,933	22,336
94,800	94,850	24,258	21,046	25,951	22,351
94,850	94,900	24,274	21,060	25,969	22,367
94,900	94,950	24,289	21,074	25,987	22,382
94,950	95,000	24,305	21,088	26,005	22,398

* This column must also be used by a qualifying widow(er).

Continued on next page

If line 39 (taxable income) is–		And you are–				If line 39 (taxable income) is–		And you are–			
At least	But less than	Single	Married filing jointly *	Married filing separately	Head of a household	At least	But less than	Single	Married filing jointly *	Married filing separately	Head of a household
		Your tax is–						Your tax is–			
95,000						**98,000**					
95,000	95,050	24,320	21,102	26,023	22,413	98,000	98,050	25,250	21,942	27,103	23,343
95,050	95,100	24,336	21,116	26,041	22,429	98,050	98,100	25,266	21,956	27,121	23,359
95,100	95,150	24,351	21,130	26,059	22,444	98,100	98,150	25,281	21,970	27,139	23,374
95,150	95,200	24,367	21,144	26,077	22,460	98,150	98,200	25,297	21,984	27,157	23,390
95,200	95,250	24,382	21,158	26,095	22,475	98,200	98,250	25,312	21,998	27,175	23,405
95,250	95,300	24,398	21,172	26,113	22,491	98,250	98,300	25,328	22,012	27,193	23,421
95,300	95,350	24,413	21,186	26,131	22,506	98,300	98,350	25,343	22,026	27,211	23,436
95,350	95,400	24,429	21,200	26,149	22,522	98,350	98,400	25,359	22,040	27,229	23,452
95,400	95,450	24,444	21,214	26,167	22,537	98,400	98,450	25,374	22,054	27,247	23,467
95,450	95,500	24,460	21,228	26,185	22,553	98,450	98,500	25,390	22,068	27,265	23,483
95,500	95,550	24,475	21,242	26,203	22,568	98,500	98,550	25,405	22,082	27,283	23,498
95,550	95,600	24,491	21,256	26,221	22,584	98,550	98,600	25,421	22,096	27,301	23,514
95,600	95,650	24,506	21,270	26,239	22,599	98,600	98,650	25,436	22,110	27,319	23,529
95,650	95,700	24,522	21,284	26,257	22,615	98,650	98,700	25,452	22,124	27,337	23,545
95,700	95,750	24,537	21,298	26,275	22,630	98,700	98,750	25,467	22,138	27,355	23,560
95,750	95,800	24,553	21,312	26,293	22,646	98,750	98,800	25,483	22,152	27,373	23,576
95,800	95,850	24,568	21,326	26,311	22,661	98,800	98,850	25,498	22,166	27,391	23,591
95,850	95,900	24,584	21,340	26,329	22,677	98,850	98,900	25,514	22,180	27,409	23,607
95,900	95,950	24,599	21,354	26,347	22,692	98,900	98,950	25,529	22,194	27,427	23,622
95,950	96,000	24,615	21,368	26,365	22,708	98,950	99,000	25,545	22,208	27,445	23,638
96,000						**99,000**					
96,000	96,050	24,630	21,382	26,383	22,723	99,000	99,050	25,560	22,222	27,463	23,653
96,050	96,100	24,646	21,396	26,401	22,739	99,050	99,100	25,576	22,236	27,481	23,669
96,100	96,150	24,661	21,410	26,419	22,754	99,100	99,150	25,591	22,250	27,499	23,684
96,150	96,200	24,677	21,424	26,437	22,770	99,150	99,200	25,607	22,264	27,517	23,700
96,200	96,250	24,692	21,438	26,455	22,785	99,200	99,250	25,622	22,278	27,535	23,715
96,250	96,300	24,708	21,452	26,473	22,801	99,250	99,300	25,638	22,292	27,553	23,731
96,300	96,350	24,723	21,466	26,491	22,816	99,300	99,350	25,653	22,306	27,571	23,746
96,350	96,400	24,739	21,480	26,509	22,832	99,350	99,400	25,669	22,320	27,589	23,762
96,400	96,450	24,754	21,494	26,527	22,847	99,400	99,450	25,684	22,334	27,607	23,777
96,450	96,500	24,770	21,508	26,545	22,863	99,450	99,500	25,700	22,348	27,625	23,793
96,500	96,550	24,785	21,522	26,563	22,878	99,500	99,550	25,715	22,362	27,643	23,808
96,550	96,600	24,801	21,536	26,581	22,894	99,550	99,600	25,731	22,376	27,661	23,824
96,600	96,650	24,816	21,550	26,599	22,909	99,600	99,650	25,746	22,390	27,679	23,839
96,650	96,700	24,832	21,564	26,617	22,925	99,650	99,700	25,762	22,404	27,697	23,855
96,700	96,750	24,847	21,578	26,635	22,940	99,700	99,750	25,777	22,418	27,715	23,870
96,750	96,800	24,863	21,592	26,653	22,956	99,750	99,800	25,793	22,432	27,733	23,886
96,800	96,850	24,878	21,606	26,671	22,971	99,800	99,850	25,808	22,446	27,751	23,901
96,850	96,900	24,894	21,620	26,689	22,987	99,850	99,900	25,824	22,460	27,769	23,917
96,900	96,950	24,909	21,634	26,707	23,002	99,900	99,950	25,839	22,474	27,787	23,932
96,950	97,000	24,925	21,648	26,725	23,018	99,950	100,000	25,855	22,488	27,805	23,948
97,000											
97,000	97,050	24,940	21,662	26,743	23,033						
97,050	97,100	24,956	21,676	26,761	23,049						
97,100	97,150	24,971	21,690	26,779	23,064						
97,150	97,200	24,987	21,704	26,797	23,080						
97,200	97,250	25,002	21,718	26,815	23,095						
97,250	97,300	25,018	21,732	26,833	23,111						
97,300	97,350	25,033	21,746	26,851	23,126						
97,350	97,400	25,049	21,760	26,869	23,142						
97,400	97,450	25,064	21,774	26,887	23,157						
97,450	97,500	25,080	21,788	26,905	23,173						
97,500	97,550	25,095	21,802	26,923	23,188						
97,550	97,600	25,111	21,816	26,941	23,204						
97,600	97,650	25,126	21,830	26,959	23,219						
97,650	97,700	25,142	21,844	26,977	23,235						
97,700	97,750	25,157	21,858	26,995	23,250						
97,750	97,800	25,173	21,872	27,013	23,266						
97,800	97,850	25,188	21,886	27,031	23,281						
97,850	97,900	25,204	21,900	27,049	23,297						
97,900	97,950	25,219	21,914	27,067	23,312						
97,950	98,000	25,235	21,928	27,085	23,328						

$100,000 or over – use the Tax Rate Schedules on page 64

* This column must also be used by a qualifying widow(er).

1998 Tax Rate Schedules

Caution: *Use **only** if your taxable income (Form 1040, line 39) is $100,000 or more. If less, use the **Tax Table**. Even though you cannot use the Tax Rate Schedules below if your taxable income is less than $100,000, all levels of taxable income are shown so taxpayers can see the tax rate that applies to each level.*

Schedule X– Use if your filing status is **Single**

If the amount on Form 1040, line 39, is: Over–	But not over–	Enter on Form 1040, line 40	of the amount over–
$0	$25,350	15%	$0
25,350	61,400	$3,802.50 + 28%	25,350
61,400	128,100	13,896.50 + 31%	61,400
128,100	278,450	34,573.50 + 36%	128,100
278,450	....	88,699.50 + 39.6%	278,450

Schedule Y-1– Use if your filing status is **Married filing jointly** or **Qualifying widow(er)**

If the amount on Form 1040, line 39, is: Over–	But not over–	Enter on Form 1040, line 40	of the amount over–
$0	$42,350	15%	$0
42,350	102,300	$6,352.50 + 28%	42,350
102,300	155,950	23,138.50 + 31%	102,300
155,950	278,450	39,770.00 + 36%	155,950
278,450	....	83,870.00 + 39.6%	278,450

Schedule Y-2– Use if your filing status is **Married filing separately**

If the amount on Form 1040, line 39, is: Over–	But not over–	Enter on Form 1040, line 40	of the amount over–
$0	$21,175	15%	$0
21,175	51,150	$3,176.25 + 28%	21,175
51,150	77,975	11,569.25 + 31%	51,150
77,975	139,225	19,885.00 + 36%	77,975
139,225	....	41,935.00 + 39.6%	139,225

Schedule Z– Use if your filing status is **Head of household**

If the amount on Form 1040, line 39, is: Over–	But not over–	Enter on Form 1040, line 40	of the amount over–
$0	$33,950	15%	$0
33,950	87,700	$5,092.50 + 28%	33,950
87,700	142,000	20,142.50 + 31%	87,700
142,000	278,450	36,975.50 + 36%	142,000
278,450	....	86,097.50 + 39.6%	278,450

Index

prior notices not received, 312
Problem Resolution Program, 453
refund not received, 314–316
tax assessed after statute of
limitations, 310
Taxpayer Advocate, 312–314
Taxpayer Bill of Rights, 331–332
wrong income, 304, 308
wrong year, 312
mistakes, personal. *See also*
audits; IRS notices; letters to
IRS; penalties
abating interest, 328–331
abating penalties, 323–328
amending a return, 152, 163,
317–319, 436
costs of, 10
Problem Resolution Program, 453
tax planning mistakes, 337–340
Taxpayer Bill of Rights, 331–332
unable to pay, 319–322
Modified Accelerated Cost
Recovery System (MACRS)
for business equipment and real
estate, 204–206
for cars and trucks, 200, 252–253
defined, 462
for farm equipment, 253, 254–255
modified adjusted gross income,
109, 110, 237–238
money market mutual funds,
379–380
money-purchase pension plans,
348–349, 462. *See also* Keogh
plans
moonlighting car expenses, 198
mortgage interest
credit, 136
deductions, 161–163, 392
defined, 462
home equity loans, 162, 400,
415, 460
refinanced loans, 162–163, 401, 445
rental real estate, 235
mortgage payments
as alimony, 123
maximum affordable house price,
396–397
types of mortgages, 398–399
moving expenses, 118, 267–268
MSA. *See* medical savings account
(MSA)
mutual funds. *See also*
investments; stocks
average cost method and, 219, 390
bond mutual funds, 379–380
closed-end funds, 385
costs of shares sold, 218–219
defined, 381, 462
distributions, 381–382
as educational funds, 417
figuring profit or loss, 218–219
index funds, 382
load mutual funds, 385–386
money market, 379–380
records, 384
Schedule D, 218–219, 224
stock mutual funds, 380–382
unit investment trust, 385
when to purchase, 382
Mutual Funds For Dummies, 381

• N •

nanny tax, 140, 276–277, 410
National Association of Enrolled
Agents, 23
National Taxpayer Advocate,
312–313
National Viatical Association, 105
negligence, 462
negligent spouses (Innocent
Spouse Rule), 42, 48–50, 434
net income, 462
net operating loss (NOL)
amended returns for, 318–319
casualty loss as, 168
deduction, 104
defined, 462
Schedule C, 211
New In '98 icon, 4
New Law icon, 4
new tax law
1998 changes, 1
amending returns, 318
audits, 434
bankruptcy, 322
bills from IRS, 330
business equipment
deduction, 207
canceled debts, 103
capital gains, 431–432
casualty losses, 170
Child Tax Credit, 68, 74–75,
78, 133
credit card tax payments, 66
credit for minor children, 432
education credits, 76, 134–135,
173, 432
educational assistance by
employer, 86, 172
estates, 434
estimated tax payments, 141
farming, 243, 245
foreign earned income, 104
foreign gifts and inheritances, 191
foreign taxes, 136, 161
innocent spouse relief, 49, 434
installment agreements, 321
IRAs, 89, 90, 109, 110, 116, 350,
352, 354, 431, 433
IRS notices, 330–331
legal fees, 208
medical savings account
(MSA), 433
nanny tax, 276–277
NOL carry back, 104, 211,
318–319
nontaxable earned income, 143
notice of additional tax due, 292
retirement account options, 92,
93, 95
Roth IRAs, 431
sale of home, 225–226, 432
self-employed health insurance
deduction, 119, 433
small business tax breaks, 433
standard meal and hotel
allowance, 177
statute of limitations, 302
Student Loan Interest Deduction,
116–117, 164
taxpayer rights, 434

wage levies, 290
Washington, D.C. home
purchase, 136–137
newsgroups for tax information, 22
newspaper ads, property values
from, 33–34
NOL. *See* net operating loss (NOL)
Nolo Press
Living Trust software, 428
WillMaker, 428
nonassessment notices, 291–294.
See also IRS notices
nonbusiness bad debts, 232
noncustodial parents, dependent
exemptions and, 54
nonfilers, 10, 56–57, 326, 441
Nonqualified plans box of Form
W-2, 86
nonresident alien spouses
alimony paid to, 125
filing status and, 43
nonresident aliens, 462
nonstatutory stock options, 230,
231, 390
nontaxable earned income
Form 1040, line 59b, 143
Form 1040A, 78
Form 1040EZ, 65
Notice of Allocation, 246
notice status, 462
notices. *See* IRS notices
Novus Services, 66
nursing homes, 52, 157

• O •

offer-in-compromise, 321, 332, 462
office audits, 296–297, 462
office expenses, 208. *See also*
home office
Office of Appeals, 293, 294
OID (original issue discount), 462
online tax information, 21–22, 437
operating loss. *See* net operating
loss (NOL)
ordinary income, 462
original issue discount (OID), 462
origination fee. *See* points
(mortgage)
overspending, 336, 341–342

• P •

paired plans, 349. *See also* Keogh
plans
partial payment of taxes, 321
partially corrected error by IRS,
304, 310–311
partnerships. *See also* Schedule E
defined, 463
failure to file, 326
limited partnerships, 376, 384
Schedule D, 220, 223
Schedule E, 240–241
self-employed health insurance
deduction, 119
short-term gain or loss, 220
passive activities
defined, 237, 463
estates and trusts, 241

IDG BOOKS WORLDWIDE
BOOK REGISTRATION

Register This Book and Win!

We want to hear from you!

Visit **http://my2cents.dummies.com** to register this book and tell us how you liked it!

✔ Get entered in our monthly prize giveaway.

✔ Give us feedback about this book — tell us what you like best, what you like least, or maybe what you'd like to ask the author and us to change!

✔ Let us know any other ...*For Dummies®* topics that interest you.

Your feedback helps us determine what books to publish, tells us what coverage to add as we revise our books, and lets us know whether we're meeting your needs as a ...*For Dummies* reader. You're our most valuable resource, and what you have to say is important to us!

Not on the Web yet? It's easy to get started with *Dummies 101®: The Internet For Windows® 98* or *The Internet For Dummies®, 5th Edition*, at local retailers everywhere.

Or let us know what you think by sending us a letter at the following address:

...*For Dummies* Book Registration
Dummies Press
7260 Shadeland Station, Suite 100
Indianapolis, IN 46256-3945
Fax 317-596-5498

...FOR DUMMIES™

BESTSELLING BOOK SERIES FROM IDG